MASTERWORKS
OF
CHILDREN'S
LITERATURE

MASTERWORKS OF CHILDREN'S LITERATURE

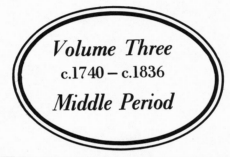

Volume Three
c.1740 – c.1836
Middle Period

EDITED BY **Robert Bator**

GENERAL EDITOR: *Jonathan Cott*

THE STONEHILL PUBLISHING COMPANY
IN ASSOCIATION WITH
CHELSEA HOUSE PUBLISHERS
NEW YORK

GENERAL EDITOR: Jonathan Cott
ADVISORY EDITOR: Robert G. Miner, Jr.
VOLUME EDITOR: Robert Bator
PROJECT DIRECTOR: Esther Mitgang
DESIGNER: Paul Bacon
EDITORIAL STAFF: Joy Johannessen, Philip Minges III, Claire Bottler
PRODUCTION: Coco Dupuy, Heather White, Sandra Su, Susan Lusk,
   Christopher Newton

First Printing
Printed and Bound in the United States of America
ISBN: 0-87754-377-1
LC: 79-89986

Chelsea House Publishers
   Harold Steinberg, Chairman and Publisher
   Andrew E. Norman, President
   Susan Lusk, Vice President
A Division of Chelsea House Educational Communications, Inc.,
133 Christopher Street, New York, NY 10014.

ACKNOWLEDGMENTS

For assistance in the preparation of these two volumes, we would like to thank: Dana Tenny of Boys and Girls House, Toronto Public Library, and Judith St. John, former Head of its Osborne Collection, for suggesting corrections and improvements in the headnotes and the introduction and for concern and answers to queries during the vagaries of this often-delayed publication; Sidney Huttner, Assistant Head of Special Collections, Regenstein Library of the University of Chicago, for permission to reprint several important books; Carey Bliss, Curator of the Henry E. Huntington Library, San Marino, California, for making available copies of the extremely rare Boreman volumes; Miranda and Aaron Bator and Nicole Niblack for reading page proofs like dutiful Georgian children; and the following institutions for their cooperation and permission to duplicate rare juvenile works: The British Library; The Guildhall Library, London; and the University of Illinois Library, Urbana, Illinois.

*Dedicated to the Memory of
Jeffrey Joshua Steinberg
Founder and President of
Stonehill Communications, Inc.*

To Sheila,
who has always known and shown
that children are persons no less in need
of liberation than the rest of us.
R.B.

Contents

Robert Bator is a professor of English at Olive-Harvey College of the City Colleges of Chicago, where he has taught children's literature. He compiled and edited the recent anthology *Signposts to Criticism of Children's Literature* (Chicago: American Library Association, 1983). Children's literature of eighteenth-century England was the subject of his doctoral dissertation (Loyola University, Chicago, 1969). It remains his chief research interest, the focus for several scholarly articles on Georgian juvenile fiction and for extensive postdoctoral research in special collections of early children's books in the United States, Canada and England.

"Neatly Bound and Gilt": Children's Literature in England, 1740–1836

By Robert Bator

Isaac watts, in his preface to *Divine and Moral Songs* (1715), expressed a hope to "provoke some fitter pen" to write for children a book "flowing with chearfulness" and lacking the "solemnities of religion." In about a generation, in the 1740s in England, Watts's hopes were realized when secular, deliberately cheerful children's books were first published.

At a London bookstall Thomas Boreman was peddling his *Gigantick Histories* (1740–1743) for children.[1] Earlier, Boreman, with two other publishers, had presented a survey of natural history in *A Description of Three Hundred Animals* (1730), which was followed by a supplement in 1736 and a sequel about 1739. But it was the *Gigantick Histories* that marked Boreman's true innovations for the youth of England. There were ten volumes in all, five separate titles in one, two or three volumes, each volume at least one hundred pages and of a size no more than two and one-half by one and seven-eighths inches:

> *The Gigantick History of the Two Famous Giants and Other Curiosities in Guildhall* (2 vols., 1740)
> *Curiosities in the Tower of London* (2 vols., 1741)
> *The History and Description of the Famous Cathedral of St. Paul's* (2 vols., 1741)
> *Westminster Abbey* (3 vols., 1742, 1743)
> *The History of Cajanus the Swedish Giant from His Birth to the Present Time* (1 vol., 1742)

Before Boreman—and aside from the Puritan works—there was little beyond what John Locke in 1693 labelled the "ordinary road" of children's books: psalms, old romances, Aesop. About a half century later, Boreman likewise lamented that books used to teach children to read "tend rather to cloy than entertain them."

The *Gigantick Histories* do not cloy. Guided urban tours, they are arranged with some attempt at amusement:

> Too rigid precepts often fail,
> Where short amusing tales prevail.
> That author, doubtless, aims aright,
> Who joins instruction with delight.
> Tom Thumb shall now be thrown away,
> And Jack, who did the giants slay;
> Such ill concerted, artless lyes,
> Our British Youth shall now despise.

While harshly castigating the chapbook characters, Boreman sprinkles a light tone on his rambles. But if the content of Boreman's works seems pedestrian today (". . . On the right, the wall which encompasseth the Tower; over which is a delightful prospect of the River Thames, with the Ships, Boats &c, passing up and down . . ."—*Curiosities in the Tower of London*, II) , still the Boreman books not only represent the first commercial success in publishing for children in England but also present some physical innovations later to be associated with John Newbery. With Boreman we encounter what children actually purchased themselves and read voluntarily. The four-pence-per-volume price was somewhat competitive with the rival chapbook, but each Boreman book was several times the length of the longest chapbook. And in design and binding Boreman provided another substantial improvement over the chapbook. Covered with Dutch[2] flowered paper, his books shone with bright colors, sometimes with silver or gold foil. Designed for children's pockets, Boreman's physically attractive product was no small factor in the evolution of the children's book.

Boreman was also the first to solicit child subscribers from England, America, and even Portugal. While some adult books had subscriber lists, Boreman was the first to permit children to buy books in advance of publication, allowing them the added thrill of seeing their own names in print. It worked then—just as it does today when, through the magic of computers, you can add a child's own name to the print in some modern juvenile storybooks.

Another pioneer was Mary Cooper, who, after her husband died, published from 1743 to 1761. In 1743 she brought out *The Child's New Play-Thing* (2nd edition), and in 1744, *Tommy Thumb's Pretty Song Book* (2 vols.), one of the first compilations of nursery rhymes. *The Child's New Play-Thing*, a miscellany of spelling lessons, medieval tales, and an alphabet, also included chapbook favorites: St. George, Fortunatus, Guy of Warwick, and Reynard the Fox—just the sort of stuff that Richard Steele's eight-year-old godson loved to read in 1709 (see *The Tatler*, No. 95). An advertisement for the book claims: "The Child's Plaything / I recommend for Cheating / Children into learning / Without any Beating."

It looks as if Mary Cooper had read John Locke, whose *Some Thoughts Concerning Education* (1693) suggested ways to encourage a child to read: "Cheat him into it if you can, but make it not a Business for him." While the similarity of language may be coincidental, Locke's book forms a rationale for what Mary Cooper, Thomas Boreman, and John Newbery produced. Forbidding the rod, which he felt was a most unfit instrument for teaching, Locke vowed that children would "play themselves into what others are whipp'd for." And, so that children could be "cozen'd into a Knowledge of the Letters," Locke asked for alphabetic dice. His request is seconded in Cooper's "Preface Shewing the Use of the Alphabets."

The work of the most important figure of the century, John Newbery, was also informed by the writings of John Locke (1632–1704). Known to English parents and publishers mostly through the private letters eventually published as *Some Thoughts Concerning Education*, Locke was as concerned about children as any Puritan. To Locke, however, the child was not wicked. Granted that premise, Locke condemned rote learning, urging a rational education which gave a child a "Liking and Inclination" to what he should learn. By championing the picture book, by suggesting that children be subverted into learning, i.e., that learning be made a pleasure, not a task, Locke influenced the quality and quantity of children's books for at least a century.

Locke is used almost as imprimatur for John Newbery's first original book for children. The preface to *A Little Pretty Pocket-Book* (1744) cites "the great Mr. Locke" in a long paraphrase from the philosopher. Son of a Berkshire farmer, Newbery was born in 1713, a generation after *Some Thoughts Concerning Education*. Apprenticed to a printer, he eventually married his master's widow and moved from Reading to London. Newbery's own Horatio Alger–type success story reads like many of his children's books. From 1744 until his death in 1767, John Newbery sold not only books and gingerbread for children but Cephalic Snuff and Dr. Hooper's Female Pills for adults. He was gently portrayed as Dr. Primrose in Goldsmith's *The Vicar of Wakefield* and mildly satirized as Jack Whirler in Johnson's *The Idler* (No. 19).

In a typically clever advertisement Newbery the entrepreneur heralded his first original book for youth as "neatly bound and gilt." Entitled *A Little Pretty Pocket-Book, Intended for the Instruction and Amusement of Little Master Tommy and Pretty Miss Polly*,[3] this sixpenny publication (a "tuppence" additional if a child wanted a real ball or pincushion as well) was published anonymously. Newbery himself may have written this early original recreational children's book.

Boreman ceased publishing in 1744, the year *A Little Pretty Pocket-Book* first appeared. By coincidence or design, Boreman declined while Newbery, using his predecessor's innovations, rose. In size *A Little Pretty Pocket-Book* was more generous than Boreman's volumes, but not by much, measuring three and three-fourths by two and one-half inches. Also covered with Dutch floral paper, Newbery's book abounds in woodcuts, a major improvement over Boreman. Where Newbery used fifty-eight pictures in a text of ninety pages, Boreman had about that many in all ten of his *Gigantick Histories* taken together.

A Little Pretty Pocket-Book is an amalgamation of Boreman in form, Cooper in content. After the Lockean preface about diet and exercise mentioned above, Newbery gives the child a miscellany. The text includes a letter from Jack the Giant Killer, an advertisement, an alphabet, poetry, and proverbs. The theme, if there is one, is that learning pays. The giant-killer urges the reader to learn songs to earn the favor of gentlemen and ladies, with the stock reward being the "coach and six" which Newbery promises the boy who learns to read well. The way Horatio Alger, Jr., passed out bank positions, Newbery earlier passed out mayoralties to Billies and Tommies. Kept from political power, the Arabellas and Fannys were rewarded by marrying into wealth.

Besides the "coach and six" hallmark, other indications attest to a pervasive middle-classness. In the alphabet section the child is warned: "*Chuck-farthing*, like Trade,/ Requires great Care;/The more you observe,/The better you'll fare."[4] Interest in trade later blossomed into the Newbery slogan "Trade and Plumbcake for ever. Huzza!" (*Nurse Truelove's New Years Gift*, ca. 1753). For those on the way up socially and mate-rially, such mercantile obsession was calculated to appeal in books which, although only six or eight pence, were intended not for the poor but for the middle- or upper-class child.

Enough amusement was scattered throughout *A Little Pretty Pocket-Book* that it became one of the most influential and important books in the evolution of juvenile literature. Newbery's first commercial success in books of amusements for youth had gone through ten editions by 1760. This alone would merit Newbery a place in the history of children's literature.

Newbery produced much more. From 1744 to 1802 his firm and its successors published about four hundred separate titles for children, many of them original. And in his own lifetime Newbery was responsible for at least sixteen original books to amuse children. A sentimental ethic that equated hard work with instant financial and social success was the virtue-pays theme of the Newbery books. Self-taught, John Newbery was writing for the young who might rise, just as he did, so long as their parents could come up with the sixpence for each volume.

The Lilliputian Magazine (John Newbery, 1751), possibly the first children's magazine,[5] centers on the Lilliputian Society, a group of young scholars. Surviving today only as a single volume in book form, the magazine was a miscellany with a list of juvenile subscribers. One of its selections, "The History of Miss Sally Spellwell," presents the daughter of a country curate rising through marriage to possession of her own coach. The motto of her tale promises: "If Virtue, Learning, Goodness are your Aim, / Each pretty Miss may hope to do the same."

The Lilliputian Society met again in another Newbery work, *The Newtonian System of Philosophy . . . by Tom Telescope, A.M.* (1761). The amusing pseudonym was Newbery's stock in trade. (Abraham Aesop, Tommy Trapwit, and Giles Gingerbread are some of the other alliterative names under which many early Newbery books were published.) In *Newtonian System,* Newbery uses Tom, the child genius, to comment on the frivolity of adults, while aiming directly at a child's experience with copious references to marbles, swimming, and similar childhood pursuits. The eighteenth-century child was seldom ex-posed to science in such a pleasant, palatable form. Through Newbery the child got science laced with wit and amusement; later he would learn to take science in a more pedestrian fashion or not at all.

Newbery's break from the miscellany format to the child's novel was hailed this way:

The Philosophers, Politicians, Necromancers, and the Learned in every Faculty are desired to observe that on the 1st of January, being New Year's Day (Oh, that we may all lead new lives!), Mr. Newbery intends to publish the following important Volumes, bound and gilt, and hereby invites all his little Friends who are good to call for them at the Bible and Sun, in St. Paul's Churchyard: but those who are naughty are to have none. [He then lists *The History of Giles Gingerbread* and other titles.] There is in the Press and speedily will be published either by Subscription or otherwise, as the Public shall please to determine, The History of Little Goody Two-Shoes, otherwise called Margery Two-Shoes.

Though not the first novel for children, *The History of Little Goody Two-Shoes* (1765) was the most influential of stories for eighteenth-century children. Wilbur Macey Stone located 174 English and American editions up to the nineteenth century. Still in print or reprint today, *Goody Two-Shoes* shows how the Newbery book and, therefore, children's literature improved in the twenty or so years Newbery published for youth.

Margery Meanwell, like many a Newbery hero, is the poor child who makes good. Her story is told for those

> Who from a State of Rags and Care
> And having Shoes but half a Pair,
> Their Fortune and Their Fame would fix,
> And Gallop in a Coach and Six.

The plot is well known. Mr. Meanwell, who can no longer afford the price of justice against Farmer Graspall and Sir Timothy Gripe, dies of a fever aggravated by want of Dr. James's Fever Powder (sold by John Newbery!). Soon, orphaned Margery and brother Tommy are taken in by a clergyman and his wife. Given her first shoes, she cries proudly, "See two shoes" to the townspeople. Tommy is soon off to sea, but, natural rustic genius that she is, Goody tails the children coming home from school and thus learns to read. A quick study, she is soon principal of a "country college." Her dame school is remarkably Lockean, with alphabet letters scattered around the classroom. Rote learning is abolished. (If Goody had not read Locke, her author had.) At long last, of course, Goody marries. And, as Lady Jones, she fares as well as brother Tom, who returns, at book's end, splendid, handsome, and rich.

Even in brief summary it can be seen that *Goody Two-Shoes* shows sustained effort far beyond what the chapbook offered. To know *Goody Two-Shoes* is to know the best of Newbery; to know Newbery is to know children's literature in the eighteenth century; to know that literature is to know the range and potential of juvenile prose.

Imitations of Newbery's first children's novel abounded, like Toby Teachem's *The Orphan; or, The Entertaining History of Little Goody Goosecap* (ca. 1780). In a generation, the book Newbery printed—if not wrote[6]—changed drastically. In the 1780 imitation the hero is now an adult, Mrs. Bountiful. Goosecap falls into a ditch while pursuing flowers and therefore receives a moral lecture. In Newbery's original, Goody does all the lecturing, even to adults. But in less than thirty years the child heroine has now fallen victim to the cult of sensibility, that fashionable Georgian disease. Given a diamond necklace, Goody (Fanny Fairchild) leaves the room to have to a good cry. Presented by Mrs. Bountiful to her son (who has ten thousand pounds), Fanny is "drowned in tears." The Cinderella story became cautionary; the moral tale became moralistic.

The only predecessor to *Goody Two-Shoes* in the ranks of the juvenile novel was Sarah Fielding's *The Governess; or, Little Female Academy* (1749), which relates fiction-

xxvi MASTERWORKS OF CHILDREN'S LITERATURE

alized confessions of nine girls at Mrs. Teachum's boarding school. Two fairy tales and a fable are interspersed among the biographies, but Mrs. Teachum is quick to point out that "the common Course of Things would produce the same Incidents, without the Help of Fairies."[7]

Appearing slightly before her brother Henry's *The History of Tom Jones*, Sarah Fielding's *The Governess* is credited as the first novel for children. A generation later the juvenile novel was a fixture in the nursery, with many of the works directly influenced by Sarah Fielding. Among these were Jeanne Marie Le Prince de Beaumont's *The Young Misses Magazine*[8] (1756), Dorothy Kilner's *The Village School* (ca. 1783), Mary and Charles Lamb's *Mrs. Leicester's School* (1809), and Martha Butt Sherwood's *The Governess* (1820). Replacing the fairy tales with moral tales, Mrs. Sherwood overhauled the original book.

Even before Mrs. Sherwood, fairy tales were in trouble in England. *Histoires ou Contes du Temps passé, avec des Moralités* (1697 in French; 1729 in English) by Charles Perrault (or his son) suffered the same fate as many other purely imaginative works. The Perrault Mother Goose tales, which included Bluebeard, Sleeping Beauty, and Cinderella, were not at first available in texts for children, nor were the moral warnings directed at them. Red Riding Hood, in Perrault, for example, ends with a warning to coquettes. What militated against Perrault's fairy tales (or those of anyone else) was a climate of opinion which held works of magic and the supernatural to be reprehensible for children. Branded the ridiculous stories of illiterate servants, fairy tales were largely ignored. An eighteenth-century review of a children's book states proudly:

> The notion that seemed formerly to have prevailed that the minds of children could only be amused with the idle tales of giants, fairies, &c. is happily exploded. It is the peculiar praise of the present generation to have substituted rational information in the place of all that nonsensical trifling. (*The Monthly Review*, 1784)

Samuel Johnson was of another opinion: "Babies do not want . . . to hear about babies; they like to be told of giants and castles, and of somewhat which can stretch and stimulate their little minds," he told Mrs. Piozzi. But, by the century's end, "rational information" prevailed. Maria Edgeworth, Oliver Goldsmith, and Sarah Trimmer all attacked fairy tales. Johnson, the public defender of the fairy tale, lost to the prosecution.

The more specifically English fairy characters like Tom Thumb, when they appear at all, are hardly discernible from their chapbook counterparts. Donning a teacher's gown, Tom Thumb meets his pupils on Education Road in *Tom Thumb's Exhibition* (1780). As the fairy moved from pixie to pedant, so too the fairy tale was subsumed under the moral and educational tales that ironically appeared after Rousseau's attempt to banish books for children.

Some fairy tales survived. Comtesse d'Aulnoy's *Contes des Fées* (4 vols., 1698) was translated into English as *Tales of the Fairys* in 1699. Her work was as well or perhaps better known in England than that of Perrault, which preceded hers in France. For example, Swift wrote to Stella in 1712 that he was reading a couple of volumes of fairy tales (probably d'Aulnoy's *Diverting Works* of 1707).

It was Jean-Jacques Rousseau, especially in *Émile* (1762 in English), who most deftly jettisoned the fairy tale and every book for the young child except *Robinson Crusoe*. To cross the border into the nursery, those fairy tales that survived often surrendered their identity and became moralized tracts. *Mother Goose's Melodies* (1780) presented nursery rhymes but only with morals attached. ("The more you think of dying, the better you will live" was added to "Jack and Gill.")

Rousseau wrote not for, but about, children. Unwittingly, he influenced much of the children's literature of the last third of the eighteenth century and beyond. A year or two after *Émile* came out in England, real life Émiles were being reared like the child of nature in Rousseau's fictional tract. Through the persona of a tutor, Rousseau guided an imaginary child from birth to manhood. Kept in a state of nature, Émile, while no hermit, is removed from corrupting influences such as books and is constantly conditioned by contrivance to be punished or rewarded by nature. One is reminded of the automatic feelings of guilt experienced by young William Wordsworth on the occasion when he stole a rowboat ride, as described in *The Prelude* (Bk. I, 357–400). Soon Émile fears no thunder, no vermin, no privation. Given an occasional sampling of society, he "naturally" takes to the woods.

It took a generation for Rousseau's philosophy to infiltrate juvenile literature. In the 1770s he was still ignored. In 1772 a typical book from the press of Francis Newbery (John Newbery's nephew) was *The Prettiest Book for Children Being the History of the Enchanted Castle* under the pseudonym of Don Stephano Bunyano. Hints of the fairy tale vanish when it is discovered that the giant's name is Instruction, virtuous governor of the Enchanted Castle. Virtuous governors of enchanted castles! At story's end the giant converts his castle to a picture gallery, museum, and library.

Eventually, however, the English child's book began to pay court to Rousseau. The first clear reaction came in Ellenor Fenn's *Fables in Monosyllables* (ca. 1783). The title page quotes the French philosopher on the utility of childhood impressions, and the preface pays him his first compliment and criticism in a book for children. Labelling his remarks on fables "just," Lady Fenn appends this comment: "However mistaken, however detestable many notions of Rousseau's may be; there are useful maxims to be gleaned from his work respecting children. I wish the wheat were separated from the chaff."

Thomas Day's *The History of Sandford and Merton* (3 vols., 1783–1789) marks the most conscious imitation of *Émile* in English children's literature. Day, an eccentric philanthropist, was so fanatic about Rousseau's methods that he, a bachelor, adopted two foundling girls and raised them on an Émilian plan. Whether or not the girls got used to the shotguns fired at their skirts or the spiders thrust before them, they eventually went off and married elsewhere. Day later found a wife who was reared more conventionally. He died in an experiment with nature—from the kick of a horse he was trying to train.

Day's beliefs suffuse *Sandford and Merton*. A rich Jamaican planter's son, Tommy Merton, is placed under the tutelage of rustic Mr. Barlow and his nature-boy pupil, Harry Sandford. Spoiled Tommy resists, but three volumes later the powder is gone from his hair and the buckles are off his shoes. Though looking like a plowboy to his mother, Tom bids adieu to finery and thanks poor Harry: "You have made me sensible, how much better it is to be useful than to be rich or fine, and that it is more amiable to be good than great."

Dreary as it may seem today, *Sandford and Merton* (or *"l'Émile anglais,"* as it was aptly termed) was immensely popular; forty-three editions appeared during the hundred years after the publication of its first volume.

After Thomas Day, books of improving conversations, such as Richard Johnson's *Juvenile Rambles Through the Paths of Nature* (1786), began to flourish. Influenced somewhat by *An Easy Introduction to the Knowledge of Nature* (1780) by Sarah Trimmer, Johnson, a hack writer, argues that children should be taught only what is natural and necessary and learn no artificial manners. To achieve this he takes his fictional children on country walks where they encounter peacocks and porcupines. The tour guide is knowledgeable and the children super-attentive.

The improving conversation book was soon everywhere. Absolutely omniscient parents or their surrogates guide eager pupils through the woods. It is hard to distinguish these books marked by rapid-fire questions fielded in an unbelievably encyclopedic manner. In *Rudiments of Reason* (1793) by Stephen Jones, Lady Caroline asks: "Tell me, Kitty, how can water be made to ascend?" From the child comes a thirteen-line, technically perfect answer.

One distinctive work, though undoubtedly influenced by Rousseau, was *Hymns in Prose* (1781) by Anna Aikin Barbauld (1743–1825). She wrote both it and *Lessons for Children* (1778) for her adopted child because of the want of books on *"good paper, a clear* and *large* type, and large spaces" between the lines. Considering the cramped type in the miniature volumes, this was no small innovation. In content, *Hymns in Prose* is permeated by a Rousseauistic reverence for nature. However, in her admitted aim of impressing ideas of God on everyday objects, Barbauld differs from Rousseau, who kept the young from religion as well as from fables. The Émilian child of reason, whom she finds wanting, she would convert to the child of immortality. While F. J. Harvey Darton labelled *Hymns in Prose* "like no other in our language," Mrs. Barbauld had her critics. Samuel Johnson (in Boswell's *Life*) struck out at her smugness: "She tells the children, 'This is a cat, and that is a dog, with four legs and a tail; see there! you are much better than a cat or a dog, for you can speak.'" The passage which incurred Johnson's wrath was probably from Barbauld's *Lessons for Children:* "But can Puss talk? No. Can Puss read? No. Then that is the reason why you are better than Puss because you can talk and read." (It should be noted that this book was intended for the child of three.)

While Barbauld's religious aim precludes Rousseau's secular methods, direct punishment and reward by nature permeates *Lessons for Children*. Disobedient lambs, for example, are devoured by wolves. In the Barbauld guided tour all good is rewarded, all evil punished. Even the harsh criticism of Lamb and Coleridge did not prevail against her popularity. Though few in number, her books had much influence on writers like Sarah Trimmer and Maria Edgeworth.

A more typical book for children is Lady Fenn's *Rational Sports in Dialogues* (ca. 1783), which consists of dialogues on such subjects as insects and timber merchants. Rousseau would not have approved the method, however much he might have sanctioned the contents. Significantly, *Rational Sports* provides an important point of comparison by which the development or regression of books for children after John Newbery can be observed. Newbery's *Twelfth-Day Gift* (1767) tells of a Lord of the Manor's son who will not share cake with the son of a mere merchant. Once shown that it is merchants who procure ingredients for the cake, he swiftly changes his mind. In Fenn's book a man sends his grandchildren a cake; only if they can explain the nature and origin of each ingredient can they eat it. About a generation later in a Maria Edgeworth story, "Frank Divides the Cake" (*Early Lessons*, 1801), the cake again assumes the role of teacher. Asked by his mother to cut a plum cake into six pieces, Frank comes up with only five. After lengthy Socratic discussion about how to equalize the portions, and after much experimentation, the cake, a lump of sugar, and even the smallest of crumbs, weighed on ivory scales, are divided equally. Thus in all three stories the cake is used as an object lesson: in Newbery, to teach tolerance and cooperation; in the post-Émilian Fenn and Edgeworth, to teach geography and science.

Science is ever-present in Lady Fenn's books. In *The Rational Dame*, a work of nonfiction (ca. 1785), she urges that "there is no need of invention. . . . banishing all fabulous narratives, let us introduce our little people to the wonders of the insect world." When children are not rattling off geographical details, they are inspecting flies under a microscope. And in Fenn's *Cobwebs to Catch Flies or Dialogues in Short Sentences Adapted to Children from the Age of Three to Eight Years* (2 vols., ca. 1783) the nature lore continues as Mama puts a wood louse in William's hand. (Émile would have found his own wood louse, or his tutor would have made it look as if he had.)

In Lady Fenn's books kindness to animals becomes fastidious. William won't finish his breakfast because there is a fly at the edge of his basin. Mama asks if he is hungry:

> Yes, mamma; but I would not hinder this little fly
> from getting his breakfast.
>
> Good child! said his mamma, rising from her tea; we
> will look at him as he eats. See how he sucks
> through his long tube. How pleased he is!
> (*Cobwebs to Catch Flies*, II, 28)

Fenn felt it was a mother's duty to "seize every occasion for giving a lesson to her children" (*The Female Guardian*, 1784).

Eagerness to impose the object lesson is also demonstrated in *The Fairy Spectator* (1789). The child who requests a fairy tale is promised: "I will write you a dialogue, in which the Fairy shall converse; and I will give you a moral for your dream." Lady Fenn's many books for children (at least seventeen) show that Day's lead in anglicizing Rousseau was no false trail.

The substitution of the moral for the dream was thoroughly implanted by the increasing number of women who produced more and more children's books in the latter part of the eighteenth century. John Marshall, a publisher, claimed he alone had seventy different books for children in 1786, many by Fenn and by Dorothy (1755–1836) and Mary Ann Kilner (1753–1831). The Kilners were responsible for at least twenty of Marshall's books in the 1780s and '90s. Mary Kilner's *The Adventures of a Pincushion Designed Chiefly for the Use of Young Ladies* (2 vols., ca. 1780) is among the early children's books intended for a single gender, along with Sarah Fielding's *The Governess* (1749).

Lady Fenn's *School Dialogues for Boys*, appearing about the same time as Kilner's

book, also was directed at a single-sex audience. It is difficult to isolate the first book for
children deliberately limited in this way. Popularly associated with Victorian tastes are
domestic tales for girls, such as *Little Women* by Louisa May Alcott (1868), and tales of
adventure for boys: R. M. Ballantyne's *The Coral Island* (1857) or Robert Louis
Stevenson's *Treasure Island* (1883). Although the later nineteenth century bifurcated
children's books into separate series for boys and girls, the appeal to boys and girls,
latent in John Newbery's separate toys and rewards, became bolder with Mary Kilner's
book "designed chiefly for the use of Young Ladies." Calculated sexism in audience
appeal is not entirely the product of the nineteenth century.

Mary Kilner's *Memoirs of a Peg-Top* (ca. 1783) was the boy's companion to the
pincushion book. Both were among the early children's stories centered on an inanimate
object, an idea borrowed from adult literature of the 1760s. The pincushion's adventures are
related in an ingenious but somewhat prosaic manner; when the book comes out strongly
against nail biting, any perceptive child can see it as a parental mouthpiece. Children are
punished by nature for their transgressions, but with a vengeance. Betsey, who lies about a
horse chasing her, is later run over by a horse and crippled for life. Similarly, in Dorothy
Kilner's *Short Conversations* (ca. 1785) a little girl falls out of a forbidden window and knocks
out three teeth, while little Jack who mistreats a cat is tied to a rolling stone and
horsewhipped. Disobedience is graphically and chillingly punished in both Mary and
Dorothy Kilner's stories.

But Dorothy Kilner, Mary Ann's sister-in-law, seems somewhat more imaginative.
While moral sermons abound in *The Life and Perambulation of a Mouse* (2 vols., 1783–
1784), there are also descriptions of lively scurrying mice who outwit servants and steal
cakes. And Dorothy is as graphic as Mary Ann. What child could forget John's grinding
the mouse Softdown under his foot while the brother mouse Nimble narrates the
painful event?

In fierceness the Kilners resemble the Puritans of the previous century. A child has his
arm amputated in Dorothy's *The Rotchfords* (1786). In a preface to this book, Dorothy
admits that her principal design is to inculcate Christianity and to teach the young to
reflect on each word and action. If petrifying the young makes them reflective, Dorothy
Kilner succeeded. Despite, or even because of, their excesses, the Kilners were popular.
Their picaresque fiction is loosely structured, but it avoids the swollen rhetoric of Thomas
Day.

A friend of the Kilners, Sarah Kirby Trimmer, came up with the most popular imaginative tale of the century. *Fabulous Histories, Designed for the Instruction of Children,
Respecting their Treatment of Animals* (1786) is its cold, tractlike title. More popularly
known as *The History of the Robins*, it reached thirteen editions by 1821. Sarah Trimmer (1741–1810), the mother of twelve children, also wrote *An Easy Introduction to the
Knowledge of Nature* (1780). Influenced by Barbauld, Trimmer presents the Rousseauistic walk again, with a mother lecturing on gooseberries and Christianity. It was a
popular and rare piece of nonfiction for the young child.

Her better-known *Fabulous Histories* is long, but sustained in interest by narrative
shifts from the Benson family to a family of robins. Told from the point of view of
the birds, the story is often lively. Contemporaneous reviews praised her for curbing the
pathetic fallacy which might easily have overrun the plot. The child reader is warned

not to overindulge in feelings for animals: "All we have to do is avoid barbarity." Mrs. Addis, to whom pets are more important than people, is satirized. Action is stopped to announce, "The Mock-Bird is properly a native of America, but it is introduced here for the sake of the moral." Speculation as to what the book might have been had imagination been given freer rein ought not to blind us to what the book was attempting. If the Kilner books seem more spirited today, it was Trimmer's work that was loved and reprinted by the Victorians. (*The History of the Robins* remained in print until the early twentieth century.)

Naturally there were French writers who also spread the gospel of Rousseau in their books for children. Arnaud Berquin (1749–1791) wrote *L'Ami des Enfans* in serial form (1782–1783); in England it was known as *The Children's Friend* (1783–1784). This Rousseauistic miscellany of closet drama, tales, and letters was not entirely original with Berquin. Maria Edgeworth's father praised its "universal popularity" and claimed that it could be found in every home where there were children. Berquin was popular in abridged form as well: his *Looking-Glass for the Mind* (1787) alone sold 50,000 copies.

An artificiality pervades many Berquin stories. The children are hard to believe. Matilda in *The Children's Friend* kneels during thunderstorms to pray for all the other children who are afraid of thunder and lightning. The young talk in stilted fashion: "I have sufficiently felt the wearisomeness of doing nothing." This did not seem to dampen the popularity of Berquin, whose *Looking-Glass for the Mind* had ten editions by 1871. Many of the stories read like directives from *Émile*. Rousseau urged that the spoiled child be dressed in the most uncomfortable, cramped, and constrained clothes: "If he wanted to take part in the games of children more simply dressed, they would cease their play and run away." Berquin complies with this directive in the story of Caroline, who gives up her finery because it keeps her from playing games. Perhaps Berquin's most bizarre story is that of Nancy, whose canary dies when she neglects it. Addressing the dead bird, her father laments "so merciless a guardian" as his daughter. The bird is stuffed and hung from the ceiling as a memorial to Nancy's carelessness.

Another prolific French writer was Stéphanie Félicité du Crest de St.-Aubin, Comtesse de Genlis (1746–1830). Her popular books for juveniles in English translation were *Adele and Theodore* (1783), *Theatre of Education* (1781), and *Tales of the Castle* (1785). The last, a five-volume title, was especially popular, reaching nine editions in its first twenty-five years. Among its imitators were Mary Ellen Pilkington's *Tales of the Hermitage* (1798) and *Tales of the Cottage* (1798) and Charlotte Sanders' *The Little Family* (1797).

In *Tales of the Castle* Madame Clémire tries her educational theories on her captive audience of three children while her husband is away. Rousseau, whom Genlis knew as a friend, influenced the lessons. In one story the sickly, overdelicate child who shrieks at the sight of a spider is sent to a dairy farm and cured by a Swiss doctor. When Rousseau, in *Émile*, said, "Men may be taught by fables; children require the naked truth," his disciples, like Madame de Genlis, took him literally and banished all imagination. After forbidding fairy tales, Madame de Clémire vows to rival them with tales of volcanos and meteorites. Genlis admitted that Rousseau's practical influence lasted all her life. At seventy she prided herself on knowing twenty trades, any one of which could have earned her a living.

Rousseau's influence continued for many years and was reflected in the themes of the reliance on nature as a father figure, the glorification of primitivism and the noble savage, and the emphasis on a sentimentality that stressed feeling over intellect, coupled, paradoxically, with the positive impression of facts or natural lore on children. In books for juveniles this is often manifested in the contrast between the inquisitive child of sensibility eager for books and the spoiled, selfish truant who lives unhappily.

Against this background, *The Comical Adventures of a Little White Mouse; or, A Bad Boy Happily Changed into a Good Boy* (ca. 1786) appears as a rarity—a post-Émilian children's book that endorses fairy tales. Fairy Fidget brings up Whitelocks, who, straying from fairyland, is turned into a white mouse and has lots of adventure hiding in mince pies and cheeses. He even converts Mr. Noddy, who professes that fairy stories are "Fibs." When Whitelocks causes a ruckus in the kitchen, Noddy is the first to run off scared. Alas, Whitelocks is somewhat enlisted to enforce morality, biting the toe of a boy who lies, for example. Eventually restored to his human state, Whitelocks is made King of Fairyland. This open advocation of a fairy tale is clearly an exception to the mass of totally moral tales of the latter part of the eighteenth century.

Direct disciples of Rousseau and those who received his theories secondhand created a literature for children which Rousseau would have disapproved of. Whereas he forbade his model child to read before maturity (because books were artificial), dozens of writers exempted their own books from Rousseau's condemnations. To encourage a child to develop by using the external world as the best and almost exclusive textbook was Rousseau's aim. The books of Thomas Day and those after him took little pupils on long walks where they received short stories with long, long morals. Rousseau's methods, gentle by contrast, calcified in the hands of his followers.

Rousseau's nature worship is also present in Mary Wollstonecraft's *Original Stories from Real Life* (1788). In its second edition (1791) it was sold in both two-shilling and five-shilling editions—the first without and the second with the six engravings by William Blake. There is a familiar framework: Mary and Caroline are left with a widowed relative, Mrs. Mason, while papa is conveniently away. Drilling the girls in morality and kindness to animals, Mrs. Mason shows she is not soft-headed as she squeamishly but deliberately steps on a wounded lark. The direct experience of reward and punishment and the reverence for nature indicate that Wollstonecraft was influenced by *Émile,* which she had read. Though she faulted his attitudes toward women, she confessed she was always "half in love" with the French philosopher. Despite the rigid Mrs. Mason, or maybe because of her, *Original Stories* had six London editions by 1835. There were also two Dublin editions by 1803 and a German translation.

Considerably less known than Mary Wollstonecraft was Elizabeth Pinchard, the wife of an attorney. In addition to *Dramatic Dialogues* (2 vols., 1792), she wrote *The Blind Child* (1791) and *The Two Cousins, A Moral Story* (1794). The last title features a long French passage from Rousseau with her own English translation. Pinchard agreed with Rousseau that nature purposely made the child helpless and dependent, and that it was unnatural for a child to order adults around. Her *Dramatic Dialogues,* a collection of closet dramas (that is, plays not meant to be performed), attempt to provide variety by using a form popularized by Hannah More's *Sacred Dramas* (1782).

The longest book of the century for children followed Berquin's example. John

Aikin (1747–1822) and his sister Anna Aikin Barbauld together wrote *Evenings at Home* (6 vols., 1792–1796). Mrs. Barbauld wrote only fourteen of the ninety-nine original pieces in this potpourri of allegory, drama, and stories. The moral lessons overextend Rousseau. By eating delicate foods, even a cat gets asthma; in the woods, he would have thrived. "Eyes and No Eyes," written by John Aikin and much praised by Charles Kingsley, puts two boys on an identical nature walk. William reports a plethora of phenomena; Robert sadly relates that he saw nothing.

Having lived through the French Revolution, Aikin and Barbauld were more conservative than the radical Mr. Day. Still ready to assist the deserving poor, they were less interested in seeing them rise from poverty. When Charles pities a poor weaver in one of the stories, Mr. Everard says such work would be difficult for the well-born Charles, but that the poor are used to it and therefore content. The Aikin-Barbauld compilation was reprinted until 1899.

Most gifted of the children's writers of the century was Maria Edgeworth (1767–1849), the second of Richard Lovell Edgeworth's twenty-two children. Maria often tested her children's stories on her own numerous siblings. In 1796 the three-volume *The Parent's Assistant* was published. While Edgeworth, like her family friend Day, used the moral foil in many stories, she had a more dramatic gift. "Best in the little touches," as Scott said, she wrote about believable children. Who can forget seven-year-old Rosamond, who forfeits new shoes because she spends her money on the inviting purple jar? Some thirty years after *Émile*, the child is still punished by her own mistakes.

Criticism of *The Parent's Assistant* reveals the emergence of new criteria for judging juvenile books. A 1797 review, for example, found the book sensible, the stories well written and calculated to develop the best affections of the heart. Tears, the badge of sensibility, were in. Scott himself confessed that when he first read how the lamb was returned to "Simple Susan," he had to put the book down to cry.

One is tempted to compare Maria Edgeworth with John Newbery. Both produced fresh, inventive, and suspenseful plots in narrative scaled for a child. Both created lovable, believable child characters who get rewarded for their virtues. Neither deals in fairy tales; both provide instead everyday success stories. One important difference is that Newbery promised monetary rewards would accrue to the diligent child. In *Practical Education* (1798), which Maria co-authored with her father, the idea of "enticing a child to learn his letters by a promise of a gilt coach" is condemned. For Maria Edgeworth, the education of a child's feelings was reward enough.

Other post–French Revolution books in the 1790s, while numerous, are deservedly less famous and less studied. Following Trimmer's success with robins, there was a whole menagerie of books about talking animals in the 1790s and 1800s. Titles alone often tell what this humane-society fiction was about: Daniel Jackson Pratt's *Pity's Gift: A Collection of Interesting Tales, to Excite the Compassion of Youth for the Animal Creation* (1798); *The Hare; or, Hunting Incompatible with Humanity* (1799); Elizabeth Sandham's *The Adventures of Poor Puss* (1809); and her *The Perambulations of a Bee and a Butterfly* (1812). In the last title the story ends with the bees setting up their hive far from man's meddling. And there is much indictment of mankind. In Dorothy Kilner's *The Rational Brutes* (1799) a fish complains: "Surely, of all created beings, the *human-race* is the most inconsiderate and cruel!" The fiction of Edward Augustus Kendall (1776–1842) follows the same plan. *The Canary Bird* (1799), *The Crested Wren* (1799), and *Keeper's Travels* (1798) are all humanitarian tales told by or about suffering animals.

Perhaps it is Kendall's realism that makes his animal stories more readable than similar tracts. In an introduction to *The Sparrow* (1798) he noted that children torture animals out of no malice but "love of action." To call a child wicked was "a ridiculous charge," according to Kendall. *Keeper's Travels* is the best of his books. Though preachy, it is full of action, all of it stemming from Keeper's sole indiscretion of spying some birds in a basket. *The Lady's Monthly Museum* (1798) praised the book because it "affords many occasions for the exertion of sensibility." Five editions by 1809 attest to the popularity of this moral tale.

The period's prize for moralizing must go to Priscilla Bell Wakefield's *Domestic Recreation* (1805). Children beg to see a Punch and Judy show; mama instead projects on a screen a mass of reticulated rootlets. When Emily craves more novelty, mother whips out another slide and beams: "Behold the wing of an earwig!" Charles Lamb blamed such lecturing on Mrs. Barbauld:

> *Goody Two-Shoes* is almost out of print. Mrs. Barbauld's stuff has banished all the old classics of the nursery. The shopman at Newbery's hardly deigned to reach them off an exploded corner of a shelf when Mary asked for them. Mrs. Barbauld's and Mrs. Trimmer's nonsense lay in piles about. Knowledge must come to a child *in the shape of knowledge*, and his empty noddle must be turned with conceit of his own powers when he has learnt that a horse is an animal, and Billy is better than a horse, and such like; instead of that beautiful interest in wild tales, which made the child a man, while all the while he suspected himself to be no bigger than a child. Science has succeeded to poetry no less in the little walks of children than with men. Is there no possibility of averting this sore evil? Think what you would have been now, if, instead of being fed with tales and old-wives' fables in childhood, you had been crammed with geography and natural history.
>
> (Letter to Coleridge, Oct. 23, 1802)

Ironically, Lamb's lament that science had superseded poetry is borne out even in his and Mary Lamb's *Mrs. Leicester's School* (1809), in which they carry on the school story tradition inaugurated by Sarah Fielding without much change except for a heightening of sentimentality. *The King and Queen of Hearts* (1805) and *Prince Dorus* (1811) in Lamb's versions do show a light comic genius. Lamb would have fared better earlier in the age of his beloved Newbery books or later in the heyday of fantasy. When Henry Crabb Robinson urged Lamb to do *Reynard the Fox* in verse, Lamb replied testily that the world was not ready for humor.

There was little poetry for children in the eighteenth century. Occasionally a poem like "To a Dormouse" is slipped into a moral tale like *Goody Two-Shoes*, but original poetry for children had to await Jane Taylor (1783–1824), Ann Taylor (1782–1866), and others in *Original Poems, for Infant Minds* (2 vols., 1804–1805). (William Blake's magnificent poetry was meant for an adult audience.) The poetry for children by Isaac Watts still was in vogue, and Ann and Jane Taylor in *Hymns for Infant Minds* (1810) admitted that his *Divine Songs* "lead the way where it appears temerity to follow." There were one hundred editions of *Divine and Moral Songs* by 1750, but later in the century cold water had to be sprinkled on his fire and brimstone. "Lest I be struck to Death and Hell" became—in 1785—"And keep my Tongue from Ill." By 1865 Watts was still popular enough to be parodied by Lewis Carroll.

The Taylors need not have been so reticent about following in the Watts tradition. Their *Original Poems*, written when Ann was twenty-two and Jane twenty-one, were in seven editions by 1808 and thirty editions by 1834; they are still in print. Adelaide O'Keeffe and others had a hand in the poems assembled as *Original Poems*. The first book published by the Taylor sisters alone was *Rhymes for the Nursery* (1806), best known today for "Twinkle, twinkle little star" but once known as well for its "awful warning" school of poetry. It had twenty-seven editions by 1835. These poems may now seem prosaic, but it should be noted that the Taylors admitted that they deliberately chose "the plainness of prose" over "the decoration of poetry." Their cautionary tone frightens the modern reader. A boy whose only wrong was fishing ("And one most cruel trick of his / Was that of catching fishes") is caught on the chin by a meat hook. But it is the quiet simplicity, even of moral warnings, that charms and endures: "Now little girls should never climb / And Sophy won't another time." Somehow even poems titled "Climbing on Backs of Chairs" come off fresh. And there is the plaintive expression of sibling jealousy:

> 'O dear Mama,' said little Fred,
> Put baby down—take me instead;
> Upon the carpet let her be
> Put baby down, and take up me.

The Taylors, along with Adelaide O'Keeffe, set a vogue for cautionary verse. For example, Elizabeth Turner's *The Daisy; or, Cautionary Stories in Verse* (1807) was written for children up to eight years old. It had twenty-one editions by 1840, and Turner's *The Cowslip; or, More Cautionary Stories in Verse* (1811) had twenty editions by the mid-nineteenth century.

In their own vein Charles and Mary Lamb imitated the Taylor sisters' verse in *Poetry for Children Entirely Original* (2 vols., 1809), but the results of what Lamb himself saw as task work make the Lambs' poetry less satisfying than the Taylors'. Occasionally in the Lambs there is some nice doggerel: ". . . but appetite o'er indecision/Prevails, and Philip makes incision" ("The Orange"). But the great mass of the poems for children by the bachelor and the spinster are largely forgettable. There was no second edition, although twenty-two of the poems were anthologized in William Frederick Mylius' *The First Book of Poetry* (1811).

In order to be saleable, the Lambs, like many others throughout the century, felt they had to maintain a balance whereby amusement and imagination, if allowed at all, had to be matched with some more worthy purpose. Thus the titles betray the forced union: *Rational Sports, Entertaining Histories, Domestic Recreation, Fabulous Histories,* etc.

The careful balance represented in the rational treatment of children espoused by Locke and unwittingly furthered by Rousseau was first abandoned by William Roscoe, both a member of Parliament and, interestingly enough, a scientist. (Maybe it is not too surprising; it took a mathematician to write *Alice*.) Roscoe's short verses of *The Butter-fly's Ball* with illustrations—and without added morals—originally intended for his own son, were tremendously successful in print. In their initial year of publication (1807) forty thousand copies were sold of *The Butterfly's Ball* and Catherine Ann Turner Dor-set's *The Peacock at Home*. Besides Dorset's verses, many other imitations of Roscoe ap-peared, such as *The Elephant's Ball, The Lion's Masquerade*, and Ann Taylor Gilbert's *The Wedding among the Flowers* (1808).

Despite the vogue for children's nonsense verse as revealed in the Butterfly's Ball craze, with the prose of the early nineteenth century it was business as usual. A neo-evangelical thrust combined with Rousseauism produced such works as Martha Butt Sherwood's *The History of Little Henry and His Bearer* (1814). This short, simple tale aims at the pathetic in its depiction of a little child trying mightily to convert his pagan servant Boosy before his own death at the age of eight. The setting in India, where Mrs. Sher-wood lived with her Army Captain husband, gave the story a believable context. Sherwood's *The History of the Fairchild Family* (3 vols., 1818–1847) is crammed with religious and scientific object lessons—even a visit to a hanging corpse, for the edification of children.

Ironic humor flashes occasionally in *The Juvenile Spectator* (2 vols., 1810–1812). Arabella Argus, a pseudonym for a persona not unlike Mr. Spectator, enlivens this basic-ally reformatory book (". . . there is scarcely a moment in the lives of children which might not be converted to their profit or their reformation, if they require it"). Still there is some self-conscious irony as the grandmother narrator comments on various styles in walking or is unmasked by her own grandchildren.

Mary Halsey Budden's *Claudine* (1822) is more in the Sherwood tradition that por-trayed the religiously simple and dutiful child in the face of adversity. The wife of Major Budden[9] and the mother of six children, Budden was most popular with *Always Happy!!! or, Anecdotes of Felix and His Sister Serena* (1814). It had five editions by 1823 and was published by J. Harris, successor to Elizabeth Newbery. Her *Claudine, A Swiss Tale* also had five early editions. A sentimental tale of Claudine and her brother Valence, it was composed near and set in Switzerland, whose atmosphere permeates the book. In *Claudine*, unlike the Newbery books, poverty is not overcome; it is enshrined: "It offers opportunities for displaying many a splendid virtue."

In *Always Happy!!!* a brother-sister team star as well. The mother's calm dismissal of nightmares as "only a name for an oppression on the chest, produced by indigestion, an awkward position of the head and neck, or some such cause" is hard to accept. And the encyclopedic lore expected of the post-Émilian tale is there, too, as a parent explains how sound travels slower than light.

Serena is very tractable, and the peevish Felix gets most of the moral lessons. But even Serena learns one. Upon obtaining the coach ride she eagerly wanted, Serena, alas, finds she can't see nature all "boxed up in the coach." The mother jumps in to note: "You find, Serena, walking has some pleasures which a coach cannot indulge." Thus, we have come full circle. In the 1740s the supreme reward for reading was the cherished coach ride. Several generations later, even that fondly awaited treat is dismissed. Children are left without reward save being good, which, Budden promises, will make them "always happy."

The Monthly Review in 1788 complained that children's books were almost as numerous as novels. By the latter part of the eighteenth century, a child could not ride without being given the history of travel, could not snack without dissecting the ingredients, could not even ask the time of day without receiving a lecture on the history of clockmaking. But sparks of imagination do flicker through. "Twinkle, twinkle little star" gleams in a mass of cautionary poems, and clever animals poke through moral novels. How eagerly must children have come across *The Butterfly's Ball*, which is unfettered by a moral—the way later children would find Catherine Sinclair's *Holiday House* (1839), which portrayed "that species of noisy, frolicsome, mischievous children, which is now almost extinct, wishing to preserve a sort of fabulous remembrance of days long past, when young people were like wild horses on the prairies, rather than like well-broken hacks on the road." If Georgian children may not have roamed free and wild on the prairies of imagination, even in a circumscribed green paddock they could find much on which to graze.

Footnotes

[1] Details of the Boreman books from Wilbur Macey Stone, *The Gigantick Histories of Thomas Boreman* (Portland, Maine: Southworth Press, 1933).

[2] The multicolored Dutch floral paper was imported mostly through Holland, although it was manufactured in Germany and Italy.

[3] Before *A Little Pretty Pocket-Book*, in 1742, John Newbery did publish a third edition of John Merrick's *Festival Hymns for the Use of Charity-Schools*, according to S. Roscoe, *John Newbery and His Successors: A Bibliography* (Wormley, England: Five Owls Press, 1973), p. 184. A school text, it was not meant for children's amusement.

[4] "The Great A Play," in M. F. Thwaite, ed., *John Newbery: A Little Pretty Pocket-Book, A Facsimile* (New York: Harcourt Brace and World, 1967), p. 71.

[5] See Jill E. Grey, "The Lilliputian Magazine—A Pioneering Periodical?" *Journal of Librarianship* 2 (April 1970): 107–115.

[6] Credit for authorship is assigned to one or more of the following: Giles Jones, Griffith Jones, Oliver Goldsmith, and John Newbery.

[7] Jill E. Grey, ed., *Sarah Fielding: The Governess or, Little Female Academy, A Facsimile Reproduction of the First Edition of 1749* (London: Oxford University Press, 1968), p. 277.

[8] *Young Misses Magazine* was the English title of Jeanne Marie Le Prince de Beaumont's *Magasin des Enfans*. The French title suggests the publication was aimed at children of both sexes.

[9] Details of Budden's life from Judith St. John, comp., *The Osborne Collection of Early Children's Books, 1566–1910: A Catalogue* (Toronto: University of Toronto Press, 1966), p. 234. This catalogue is invaluable for dates and biographies in the period. A second volume was published in 1975. [Because of space limitations, *Claudine* and some later selections do not appear in this collection—Gen. Ed.]

The History and Description of the Famous Cathedral of St. Paul's, London

ANONYMOUS

Published by Thomas Boreman

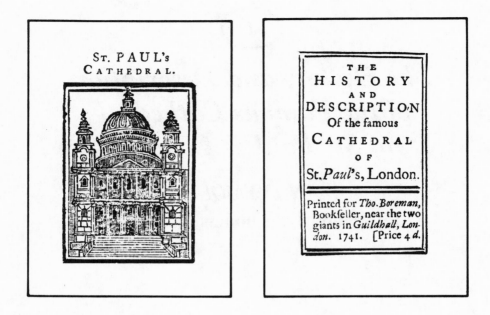

St. PAUL's
CATHEDRAL.

THE
HISTORY
AND
DESCRIPTION
Of the famous
CATHEDRAL
OF
St. *Paul*'s, London.

Printed for *Tho. Boreman*,
Bookseller, near the two
giants in *Guildhall*, Lon-
don. 1741. [Price 4 *d*.

EARLY HISTORIES *of children's literature unconsciously ignored the accomplishments of* Thomas Boreman. *Largely due to Wilbur Macey Stone's monograph,* The Gigantick Histories of Thomas Boreman *(Portland, Maine: Southworth Press, 1933), Boreman is now recognized as an early producer of what are perhaps the first secular juvenile recreational books and certainly the first topographical books for youth in England.*

In 1730, with two other publishers, Boreman put out A Description of Three Hundred Animals. *Alone, he published in 1736* A Description of a Great Variety of Animals *and (in 1739)* A Description of Some Curious and Uncommon Creatures, *omitted in the* Description of Three Hundred Animals. *Natural history profusely illustrated and scaled for an older child reader is found in Boreman's first books for children. Witness this capsule comment: "The Tumbler is a small Sort of Pigeon. Tumblers are of divers Colours; they have strange Motions, turning themselves backward over their Heads, and shew like Footballs in the Air." There is a modern facsimile edition of* A Description of Three Hundred Animals *(New York: Johnson Reprint Corporation, 1968).*

Not animals but buildings are the focus of the Gigantick Histories *(1740–1743), Boreman's collective title for nine miniscule volumes which tour famous London structures, plus an additional single-volume biography. The contents of the* Gigantick Histories *are detailed in the introduction to this volume. Guided tours for the most part, they nonetheless fascinate today as social history. Like the child for whom the books were originally intended, the modern reader learns about the zoo in the Tower of London and discovers how large a tip was required if one wanted to see the Crown Jewels. The tours are sometimes tedious, but they are enlivened with poetry, biblical stories and a genuine solicitude for the child reader. The child is told not only what he must see but also what he must avoid (for example, the gloomy vaults of St. Paul's Cathedral).*

The topographical tour Boreman began had a limited success—several editions and several hundred copies sold per volume in each edition. Others followed suit. In 1770 Francis Newbery, John's nephew, sold a four-volume set of The Curiosities of London and Westminster, *and in 1806 the Taylor sisters revised* City Scenes, or a Peep into London for Children, *an 1801 work by William Darton.*

Essentially, Boreman is of historical importance. He was first to sell books to children on a subscription basis and the first in England to use Dutch flowery paper to cover his approximately two-inch-square books. He did not publish exclusively for children, nor did he found a publishing house, but his innovations were utilized and expanded by John Newbery and others.

The History and Description of the Famous Cathedral of St. Paul's *is reprinted from the first edition (1741) from the Huntington Library, San Marino, California, supplemented by eight pages—missing from the Huntington Library copy—from the Guildhall Library, London. (N.B. The three lists of child subscribers included in the original edition have been omitted here.)*

To Master Tommy Boreman, Near the Two Giants in Guildhall, London.

I Send this greeting,
Master *Tommy*,
Tho', I believe, you
    may not know me;
To shew how greatly
    I am smitten
With what so lately
    you have written.
Whether your age, your
    parts and stature
Agree with mine, it
    is no matter;
Or whether, like old
    Dad of Jason,
Yo've drank Medea's
    magick bason;
And after sixty
    years compleated,
Begin to find your
    youth repeated;
As once, I now
    remember well,
I've heard papa
    from Ovid tell.
Howe'er it be,
    the Books you write
Give me much pastime
    and delight.
My sister Betsy,
    (set her down,
And one of your
    Subscribers own)

Has some degree of
    wit and spirit,
And loves, she says,
    t'encourage merit.
Bobby and Jemmy,
    tho' as yet
They have not learn'd
    to read a bit,
Take much delight
    to hear your wit;
Add them to your Sub-
    scribers number,
If't won't too much
    your page incumber.
For my part, I ne'er
    yet did see
What you describe
    so prettily;
And long to have it
    in my power
To see the Giants
    and the Tower.
I' th' mean time what
    you publish more
Mark me six books,
    I'll pay the score:
And whate'er profit
    I can make ye
Believe me heartily

Yours,   JACKY
    HEATHERLY.

Feb. 28. 1741.

Volume One
Book I

CHAPTER I
Of old St. Paul's.

IT WILL BE PROPER first to inform my young Readers, that upon the same spot of ground on which St. Paul's now stands, there was formerly a fine old church, built by Ethelbert king of Kent in the year of our Lord six hundred and ten, and dedicated to the same Apostle. This church suffered many times by lightning, fire, and other accidents; which was as often repaired: and such parts of it as fell to decay thro' age, were rebuilt; till at last it was destroy'd in the great fire of London in 1666, and one thousand and fifty-six years from its first building.

CHAPTER II
Of the foundation, building, and situation of the present Church.

THE OLD CHURCH of St. Paul's having been destroy'd, as mention'd in the first chapter, and the ruins and rubbish of it cleared in about eight or nine years after; the first foundation stone of this present church was laid by Mr. Strong, a mason, and the second by Mr. Longland, on the twenty first of June, 1675. at the north-east corner, facing Cheapside: From which time it was not completely finish'd till the year 1724. being about forty-nine years in building. It was begun and finish'd by the same architect, Sir Christopher Wren, and by the same mason, Mr. Strong abovementioned: The charge of which is said to amount to one million of money, or upwards. The whole building is encompassed with strong iron palisades, all curiously turn'd, about five and twenty hundred in number; which cost fifteen thousand pounds.

This magnificent structure, which stands upon the highest ground in the city, near to the west gate, called Ludgate, is the first Cathedral in England built according to the rules of architecture. Its walls are of fine Portland stone, rustic work. Two ranges of pilasters adorn the outside, one above the other; the lower consists of about an hundred and twenty, with their entablatures of the Corinthian order, and the upper of as many of the Composite, or Roman order: besides twenty columns at the west and four at the east end, and those of the portico's, &c.

The spaces between the arches of the windows and the architrave of the lower order, are filled with great variety of curious enrichments, such as cherubims, festoons of flowers, &c. and at the east end is the cipher of W. R. within a garter, on which are the words HONI SOIT QUI MAL Y PENSE; in English, *Evil be to him that evil thinks:* and this within a fine compartment of palm-branches, and placed under an imperial crown, &c. all finely cut in stone.

All the parts of this grand church, both within and without, are built with such proportion and art, that the eye is charmed with the exact order of its pillars, which support the portico's dome, &c. the beauty of their capitals; the rich cornish wherewith they are embellished; the number of spacious windows, &c. In short, the whole fabrick is full of beauty and harmony; and in bigness, strength of building, figure, and other enrichments in wood, stone, iron, &c. equal, if not superior, to any church in Europe.

CHAPTER III
Of the length, breadth, heighth, and other dimensions of St. Paul's Church.

ITS LENGTH within the wall, from east to west is five hundred feet.

The breadth of the west end is a hundred and sixty two feet.

The breadth between the north and south portico's, or doors, within the walls, is two hundred and forty nine feet.

The breadth of the rest is about a hundred and seventeen feet.

The circuit of the walls outwardly is two thousand two hundred and ninety two feet.

The ground plot that this great church stands upon, is two acres, sixteen perches, twenty three yards and one foot.

Its height within, over the middle isle, is eighty-eight feet.

To the top of the west pediment, under the figure of St. Paul, a hundred and twenty feet.

The height of the two Towers at the west front, two hundred and eight feet.

To the gallery of the cupolo, two hundred and eight feet.

To the upper gallery two hundred and seventy six feet; and from thence to the top of the cross, sixty four feet.

The height of the cross from the ball, is ten feet; the diameter of the ball is six feet; its circumference eighteen feet; and it will contain ninety bushels; and I have been told, that since it has been up, sixteen men have been drinking in it at one time; I suppose, to the good health of all their friends round about St. Paul's.

CHAPTER IV
Of the strange conceptions four Indian Kings had of this great building; and how they imagin'd it at first to be one great rock that grew in that place.

SA GA YEAN QUA RASH TOW, one of the four Indian Kings who were in this country about thirty-two years ago, amongst other curious remarks which he made whilst he was in England, left behind him the following concerning St. Paul's church.

There stands, says he, on the most rising part of the town a huge house, big enough to contain the whole nation of which I am king.

Our good brother, *E Tow O Koam*, king of the Rivers, is of opinion it was made by the hands of the great God to whom it is consecrated (*meaning* St. Paul.)

The kings of Granajah and of the Six Nations, believe that it was created with the earth, and produced on the same day with the sun and moon.

But, says he, for my own part, and from the best information that I can get of this matter, I am apt to think that this vast temple was fashioned into the shape it now bears by
several tools and instruments, of which they have a wonderful variety in this country.

I imagine it was at first only an huge mis-shapen rock that grew upon the top of the hill;
which the natives of the country, after having cut it into a kind of regular figure, bored
and hollowed with incredible pains and industry, till they had wrought in it all those
beautiful vaults and caverns into which it is divided at this day.

As soon as this rock was thus curiously scooped to their liking, then a prodigious number of hands must have been employ'd in chipping the outside of it, and smoothing the
surface; which is in several places hewn out into pillars, that stand like the trunks of so
many trees, bound about the top with garlands of leaves.

It is probable, says this Indian monarch, that when this great work was begun, which
must have been many hundred years ago, there was some religion among this people; for
they give it the name of a Temple, and have a tradition that it was designed for men to
pay their devotions in.

And indeed, there are several reasons which make us think that the natives of this country had formerly among them some sort of worship; for they set apart every seventh day
as sacred. But upon my going into one of those holy houses on that day, I could not
observe any circumstance of devotion in their behaviour: There was indeed a man in
black who, mounted above the rest, seemed to utter something with great vehemence; but
as for those underneath him, instead of paying their worship to the Deity of the place,
they were most of them bowing and curtesying to one another; and a great number of
them fast asleep.

Whether these were the real thoughts of those royal strangers, I will not take upon me
to answer. But what wonder is it that such savage kings, whose dwellings are in huts and
thickets, should form such wild notions of this prodigious structure, when we ourselves,
who see it daily, are filled with astonishment at the magnitude and grandeur of this glorious building; and how such a work could be performed by mortal hands!

We shall now proceed to examine the particular curiosities of this church.

CHAPTER V
Of the fine statue of the late Queen Anne.

BEFORE THE WEST front of this grand Cathedral, is a spacious yard; in which, upon a
lofty pedestal, stands the effigy of the late queen Anne; with four supporters, representing
those dominions in her title.

She has her crown upon her head; the scepter in her right hand, and the globe in her
left: her dress is very rich, and the workmanship of it exceeding curious.

On her right hand is Britannia; who appears with a very lovely and chearful countenance: she has a crown of laurel upon her head; a spear in her right hand, and her left
reaching to the royal arms in the front of the pedestal.

On her left hand is France: she seems much dejected, very thoughtful, and in a
languishing state. Her right hand rests upon a truncheon, and her left holds a crown,

which lies down in her lap. She is clothed with a very rich robe, adorned with flower de lis; and upon her head she has a warrior's cap, or helmet.

Behind the queen is Ireland, with her harp in her lap: her looks are amiable and pleasant.

The fourth is America, in the habit of her country; her body being almost naked: she has upon her head a crown of curious feathers, a bow in her left hand, and a quiver of arrows on her back: she has the head of an European under her foot, with an arrow sticking in it; supposed to have been just shot from her bow. There is likewise an allegator creeping from beneath her feet; being an animal very common in some parts of America, and which lives both on the land and in the water.

The queen's, and all the other figures, are of fine Italian, statuary marble; the pedestal of veined marble.

The former were all cut out of one solid, rough block of marble, which was taken by one of our English ships, during the late war, in its passage from Leghorn to France; and was designed for the effigy of Lewis the fourteenth, on horseback.

The carver was the late ingenious Mr. Francis Bird.

The foot of the pedestal is encircled with three marble steps; and the whole encompassed with beautiful, strong, iron palisades.

This royal statue, on account of its grand supporters, fine pedestal, and curious workmanship, is esteemed superior to all others in Europe.

CHAPTER VI
Of the west front of St. Paul's.

M Y YOUNG READERS having satisfy'd their curiosities in examining the queen's statue, &c. from thence they have a full view of this grand church, where they may behold the beauty and majesty of the whole, and the just symmetry of all its parts.

Observe first, the twelve large pillars which support the portico, each four feet thick, and eight and forty in height, of the Corinthian order.

Second, the eight above, which support the pediment, of the Composite, or Roman order; each three feet and a half thick, and about thirty four feet in height.

See in the large triangular pediment a lively representation of St. Paul's conversion in his journey to Damascus, carved in relievo, by the ingenious hand of the late Mr. Bird; the history of which, my young readers will see hereafter.

Over the pitch or top of this pediment, is the figure of St. Paul with a sword in his hand. On his right hand is St. Peter with a cock; and on his left, St. James.

In the front of the two lofty and beautiful towers, are the four Evangelists: In the north, St. Matthew with an angel, and St. Mark with a lion. In the south, St. Luke with an ox, and St. John with an eagle.

These two towers are each adorn'd with circular ranges of columns, of the Corinthian order, with domes on the upper part, and on the top of each a gilded pine-apple.

In the south tower is the famous large clock, the bell of which weighs four ton and four hundred and four pounds; and its sound may be heard at five or six miles distance. The work of this clock is large and curious: it is kept in excellent good order, and generally carries the hour of the day very exactly; a skilful person being appointed to look after it for that purpose.

Observe likewise the fine carvings, and other rich embellishments, over the whole front of this noble structure.

And lastly, you ascend to the great door by twenty four spacious stone steps; the first ten of which extend in width above forty yards each, and the other fourteen full thirty six yards.

The door-case is white marble: and over the entrance is cut in relievo the history of St. Paul preaching to the Bereans. It consists of a group of nine figures besides that of St. Paul, with books, &c. These Bereans were a sort of people ingenuous and mild, and who spent great part of their time in reading the Scriptures, observing whether what Paul taught was agreeable with what the Scriptures say of the Messias: and many of whom, from his preaching, chearfully embraced the faith. *Acts* xvii. 11.

Under the arch on the right hand, in a pannel, is St. Paul's imprisonment; and on the left hand in the pannel, his preaching to the Athenians, with some other scripture stories, all neatly carved in stone, by the same hand as the conversion.

My young readers will find the history of St. Paul's imprisonment in the sixteenth chapter of the *Acts*, and his preaching to the Athenians in the seventeenth chapter, both beautifully related.

CHAPTER VII
Of the north portico of St. Paul's.

THE ASCENT to the north portico is by twelve circular steps of black marble: The dome of the portico is supported and adorn'd with six very spacious columns of the Corinthian order. Above the door-case is a large urn, with festoons, &c. over this is a large pediment, where are the royal arms with the regalia, supported by two angels, with each a palm-branch in their hands; under whose feet appear the figures of the lion and unicorn; and over the pediment, on the top of this north front, are the effigies of five Apostles, carved in stone.

CHAPTER VIII
Of the south portico of St. Paul's.

YOU ASCEND to the south portico by twenty five steps, the ground on this side of the church being lower than that on the north: The portico is supported with six grand lofty columns, like those of the west and north fronts; and is in most other respects like the latter.

In the pediment over it is the figure of a phœnix, with her wings expanded, arising out of the flames; which emblem signifies, a new church arising out of the old one; under which is the word RESURGAM; that is, *I shall rise again.*

On the top of the pediment is the effigy of St. Andrew, and those of two other saints on each hand of him.

These five figures, with those on the north and west fronts, represent the four Evangelists, and the rest of the Apostles. They bear in their hands the several instruments whereby they suffer'd death; or such remarkable ensigns as allude to some important incident of their lives.

These images are each about eleven feet high, and their pedestals about four feet: they were all carv'd by the late Mr. Bird, before mention'd, and are reckon'd to be well done.

CHAPTER IX
Of what is remarkable in going up the cupola, or top of St. Paul's.

HAVING EXAMIN'D what is most curious on the outside of St. Paul's, I shall next endeavour to ascend the cupola; and in my journey to the top of it, take notice of what I meet with most worthy of my young readers attention.

To go up St. Paul's, you must enter a door at the south side, which stands open all the day long for that purpose.

After you have ascended a few steps, you come to a door which will not open till *each person pays Two-pence.*

The whole number of steps to the upper gallery is five hundred and thirty four; of which the first two hundred and sixty are so exceeding easy, that a child might go up them; they being but about four or five inches deep.

The other two hundred and seventy four steps are pretty steep, and in many places, from the large stone gallery to the upper gallery, very dark; so that one person can scarce discern another.

In this place we have a glimmering sight of such prodigious works in iron, stone, and timber, which hold together the dome, cupola, &c. that it is impossible to convey an idea of it to my readers: And though these amasing works are very curious to see, yet my young masters and misses must not by any means venture themselves here without a guide.

The iron gallery on the top of the cupola, is the highest any one is suffer'd to go; above that are the lantern, ball and cross; to the top of which, from the gallery just mention'd, is sixty four feet; and the passage thither by ladders, very difficult and dangerous to ascend.

From this gallery, in fine clear weather, we may agreeably observe the vast extent of this great city and suburbs; the great number of churches, steeples, publick buildings and houses that present themselves, which way soever we turn our eyes; as also the ships in the river, that look like a huge forest, and the vessels, boats, &c. spread all over the Thames. Here likewise we have a delightful prospect of the country, for many miles round about.

CHAPTER X
Of the whispering-gallery, and fine paintings within the cupola.

IN YOUR RETURN from the top of St. Paul's, you will be ask'd to see the whispering-gallery, which will cost *Two-pence each person.*

This gallery is a very great curiosity: 'Tis a large circle, which runs round the bottom of the inside of the dome, of about an hundred and forty three feet in diameter, or cross the widest part: 'tis rail'd in with iron of very fine workmanship, gilt with gold. The walls all around are painted and gilded with great beauty: but the greatest curiosity of all is the whispering-place; where, leaning your head against the wall, you may easily hear all that is said, though it be ever so low, and at the most distant place from you in the gallery: which affords great matter of surprize and innocent diversion to all young persons who come to amuse themselves with this curiosity.

Here you have the best view of the eight pieces of history on the inside of the dome, painted by the late Sir James Thornhill, with inimitable art and beauty.

The first represents the conversion of St. Paul. *Acts* ix. 4.

The second, Elymas the sorcerer struck with blindness. *Acts* xiii. 2.

Third, the priest of Jupiter, offering sacrifice to Paul and Barnabas. *Acts* xiv. 15.

Fourth, the jaylor converted. *Acts* xvi. 30.

Fifth, Paul preaching at Athens. *Acts* xvii. 15.

Sixth, the conjuring books burnt. *Acts* xix. 19.

Seventh, King Agrippa almost persuaded to be a Christian. *Acts* xxvi. 28.

Eighth, St. Paul's ship-wreck on the island of Melita. *Acts* xxviii. 6.

CHAPTER XI
Of the conversion of St. Paul.

S T. PAUL, before his conversion, having been principally concern'd in the death of St. Stephen, and his bloody mind not satisfied with this cruelty, threatens nothing less than prisons and death to the Christians wherever he found them. And to qualify himself the better for the execution of this bloody purpose, he goes to the high priest to enlarge his commission: and having obtain'd power to seise all Christians, and send them bound to Jerusalem to be try'd, he immediately sets out for Damascus to put it in practice: but whilst he was on the road, entertaining himself with the bloody prospect, God, in mercy to him, and those he went to persecute, takes him off from his wicked design: a bright shining cloud incompassed him, which struck him with great terror, as at the presence of God, and threw him prostrate on the ground, where as he lay, he heard a voice out of it, saying unto him, *Saul, Saul, why persecutest thou me?* This increas'd his amazement: and being desirous to know the meaning of this vision, he asks, *Who art thou, Lord!* The voice reply'd, *I am* JESUS, *whom thou persecutest:* It is in vain for thee to resist the decrees of providence, therefore be no longer disobedient, but hearken to the commands that shall be given thee. At this Saul, full of fear and trembling, cried out, 'Lord, instruct me what thou wouldst have me to do:' The voice returned, 'Go to Damascus, and there thou shalt know my will.

Those who attended Paul on this journey, were struck dumb with fear and amazement, wondring that they should hear a voice, but see no man speaking: therefore taking up Saul, they led him to the city; and by this miraculous vision he was converted to the Christian faith.

This history is the subject of the first piece of painting.

CHAPTER XII
Elymas the Sorcerer struck blind.

PAUL AND MARK, as they travelled through the isle of Cyprus, came to the city of Paphos, where the temple of Venus was; at which place they met with Elymas a noted sorcerer; who being intimate with Sergius Paulus the proconsul, a prudent virtuous man, and inclinable to receive the faith, did all he could to divert him from the conversation of these two Apostles. But Paul, in an holy rage, casting his eyes on Elymas, thus expressed his abhorrence; 'O thou vile Sorcerer, like the Devil, by whom thou workest, thou art an enemy to all goodness; wilt thou persist in sorcery, in defiance of the faith of Christ, which comes armed with a much greater power of miracles, than those to which thou falsly pretendest? Thou shalt soon see the vengeance of heaven upon thee; for thou that perversly holdest out against the light of the gospel, shalt lose thy sight, which by the immediate power of God shall be taken from thee for some time. And immediately he was struck blind, begging the aid of some kind hand to lead him: and the proconsul, convinced by this miracle, was converted to the Christian faith.

This is the subject of the second piece of painting.

CHAPTER XIII
The priest of Jupiter offering sacrifice to Paul and Barnabas.

WHILST THOSE APOSTLES were preaching at Lystra, a poor cripple, lame from the hour of his birth, being one of their hearers, was observed by St. Paul, who said to him, *Stand upright on thy feet*; and by the bare speaking of the word, his feet were made so strong that he leaped and walked.

When they saw it, they concluded this miracle could not be done but by the immediate presence of the Deity; and therefore running about in great confusion, they cried out, that the gods had put on human shape, and were come down among them.

They look'd on Barnabas as Jupiter, the supreme God; and Paul, as Mercury, the interpreter of the will of the gods, because he spoke more than Barnabas.

But as soon as this miracle came to the ear of the priest of Jupiter, he came to Paul and Barnabas, bringing oxen with garlands of flowers; being such victims as they offered to the gods they worshiped, intending to offer sacrifice to the Apostles: but they abhorring such idolatry, rent their garments; endeavouring by arguments drawn from some of the plainest instances of nature, such as day, night, summer, winter, &c. to convince them, that worship was due only to that God who was the author of all those blessings; yet this discourse, so pressingly urg'd by the Apostles, could scarce restrain those poor idolaters from sacrificing to them.

This is the history of the third piece of painting in the cupola.

CHAPTER XIV
The jaylor converted.

IT HAPPEN'D ONE DAY, as St. Paul was going to the house of prayer, there met him a young maid possess'd with an evil spirit, which spake from her, by which means, telling strange things, whether past or to come, she had gain'd her masters much money: this maid Paul cures by casting out the evil spirit. When her masters saw that all hope of future gain from her divination was gone, they apprehended Paul and his companion, and brought them before the magistrates, complaining that these men occasioned great disturbance in the city. Upon which a tumult arising, the magistrates order'd them to be scourg'd, and committed to prison; strictly charging the jailor to put them in irons, and secure them in the strongest part of the prison; where they spent their midnight hours in prayers and praises to God; and whilst they thus enjoy'd themselves, the earth began to tremble, the very foundation of the prison shook, the prison doors flew open, and every prisoner's chains dropt from him. The jailor waking with the fright, and seeing the prison-doors open, concluded that all the prisoners had made their escape; and thinking with himself that this would be imputed to his neglect, in despair drew his sword with design to kill himself: which Paul happily prevents, telling him his prisoners were all secure. Then calling for a light, he came into the presence of the two saints, trembling; and prostrating himself before them, beseeches them to instruct him in the way of salvation.

This is the history of the fourth piece of painting in the cupola of St. Paul's.

> The other paintings
>   in the cupolo,
> And num'rous beauties
>   in the church below,
> Must all into my
>   SECOND VOLUME go.
> For tho' my Books
>   folk do *Gigantick* call,
> ONE will not hold the
>   great church of St. Paul.
> Kind reader, in my next
>   you'll see a wonder,
> The Monument so tall,
> Shall come close to S. Paul,
>   Tho' now so far asunder.

The SECOND Volume of this History, with an *Account of the Monument* added to it, will be ready to deliver to the Subscribers punctually on Saturday the 20th of June 1741. and all those who intend to have their names inserted, are desired to send them speedily to *T. Boreman* in Guildhall, London.

The reader is desired to excuse the delay in publishing this Volume, as it was occasion'd by the author's illness; who takes this opportunity to inform his young readers, that the *History of Westminster Abbey* is now in hand, and will be got ready for the press with all convenient speed: Subscribers are desired to bring or send their names as above, and to pay down *Six-pence* a Set in part at subscribing, it being a large undertaking.

Volume Two
Book I

To which is added, An Account of the Monument of the Fire of London

CHAPTER I
Paul preaching at Athens.

WHILST PAUL was at Athens, he saw the city wholly given to idolatry: for which reason he not only preached in the synagogue to the Jews and proselytes; but in other places of concourse he took occasion to make known the Christian doctrine to all the heathens he met.

Some learned men of Athens seeing Paul so ready to engage in dispute with every one, undertook him: but not understanding him, some cried, he was a prating, babbling fellow; others, that he came to discover some strange God to them, because he frequently mentioned Jesus and the resurrection.

After this they brought him before the magistrates, to be examined what new religion it was he taught: for all that they had hitherto heard was new and strange, and therefore they desired to have a full account of all. Paul being at full liberty to speak, said,—'I perceive, O Athenians, that ye have a great number of idols; for as I passed by and saw your superstitious devotions, I found an altar with this inscription, TO THE UN-KNOWN GOD. This GOD therefore, whom you acknowledge not to know, yet profess to worship, is he whom I preach, the invisible God of heaven and earth, who cannot be contained in temples of man's making; nor can any image made by man be a proper object of his worship; he being so far from wanting our help, that it is he that gives to all their life and all that they have: And from one man he hath made a whole world of men, appointing times and places in great order. And the end of all this is, that they should seek after their Creator and worship him, who is indeed near every one of us, even as the Soul that animates us.

For our life, motion, and subsistance are wholly thro' him, according to that which one of your own poets hath said.

God therefore being our Creator, we cannot in reason suppose him to be the work of our hands, such as a piece of gold, silver, or a stone graved. This time of ignorance hath lasted long; but now God calls you all to repentance, having determined the way by which all the world shall be judged; that is, by receiving or refusing the faith of Christ; who being rais'd from the dead, is offered to all men to believe in.'

When they heard him mention the resurrection, the Epicureans especially, who denied a future state, fell a laughing at him; others said, we will hear thee about this another time: and so Paul left them.

This is the representation of the fifth piece of painting in the cupola.

CHAPTER II
The conjuring books burnt.

Some of the vagabond Jewish exorcists seeing the many extraordinary miracles which were wrought by the hand of Paul, insomuch that he did not only cure them who came to him, but by his touching linen clothes, and sending them to such as were sick, or possessed with devils, they were immediately healed: The exorcists, I say, seeing this, they also attempted to cast out devils by using the name of Jesus; among whom were the seven sons of one Scæva a Jew, one of the chief of the families of the priests, who adjuring the evil spirit in the name of Jesus, were thus answered by the possessed, *'Jesus I know, and Paul I know*; but you come not with any authority from Jesus, who hath given it to Paul.'

And the man who was possessed fell furiously upon them, and was too hard for them; tearing off their clothes, and wounding them, so that they were glad to fly from him.

This being soon rumoured among the Jews and natives of Ephesus, prevailed so with them, that they were convinced, and converted to the faith.

And they that were so happy came to Paul and his company, confessing their former course of life, to know what they should do: And many that had studied and practised magick, brought their books out, and burnt them publickly, tho' they were of a very high price. Of so great authority was the word of God, as it was preached by Paul among the Ephesians and those of Asia.

This latter part, of the burning of the books, is the subject of the sixth piece of painting.

CHAPTER III
King Agrippa almost persuaded to be a Christian.

Paul having been brought before king Agrippa to answer to divers complaints made against him by the Jews in general, as a most notorious malefactor; and after Festus, a noble orator, had open'd his case in an elegant speech before the court; Agrippa told Paul he had liberty to speak: who desiring silence of the audience, began with this apology for himself:

'I cannot but think my self happy, O king Agrippa, in that I am permitted to make my defence against the accusation laid by the Jews before your Majesty, whom I know to be a perfect master of the Jewish laws and customs; for which reason I beg your patience.

He then acquaints the king with the manner of his life from his youth; of his being bred a Pharisee, of his being accused for asserting the resurrection of the dead; appeals to him why it should be thought a thing incredible, that God, who is omnipotent, should raise the dead. Confesses his own former unbelief; the havock that he made amongst the church; his extraordinary conversion; and many other things, relating both to himself and to the gospel of Jesus Christ. And at last asked king Agrippa this question; *'Believest thou the prophets, O king?* I am satisfied thou dost; and knowest their predictions to be fulfilled.

This was so home a challenge to Agrippa, that in the publick presence he declared, that Paul had almost persuaded him to be a Christian.

Upon this the assembly broke up: And when Agrippa and Festus had consulted together about Paul's case, they freely owned that the accusation laid against him was not punishable by death or imprisonment.

This history is the subject of the seventh piece of painting.

CHAPTER IV
Paul's voyage, and shipwreck on the island of Melita, or Malta.

PAUL HAVING APPEALED unto Cæsar, and an opportunity offering, Festus sends him to Rome, under a guard commanded by one Julius, in a ship belonging to a sea port of Mysia; in which they set sail, and coasted along Asia till they arrived at Sidon; where Julius, who treated Paul very respectfully, gave him leave to go ashore and refresh himself.

Sailing from thence, they came in sight of the island of Cyprus, where they were to lie by a while; but the winds presenting, they passed the seas of Cilicia and Pamphylia, and came to Mira, a maritime city of Lycia. Here Julius finding a large ship bound for Italy, took his prisoners on board her, and with much ado made Salome, a city of Crete: from whence, after they had been long beating at sea with contrary winds, and very stormy weather, they arrived at Fair-havens, near Lasca; where Paul would have persuaded captain Julius to wait for more seasonable weather: but he preferring the master of the ship's judgment, they put to sea, intending to reach Phœnice, a harbour of Crete, where there was safe riding, and there to winter; and they having a light gale at south, they questioned not in the least of gaining their point.

But they soon found themselves mistaken; for the wind suddenly tacking about, blew so very hard at north-east, that they were forced to hand all their sails, and let her drive before the wind. And coming under a little island called Clauda, they had like to have lost their boat; but with much ado recovering it, they hoisted it into the ship.

The next day, the storm continuing, they were forced to cut away their masts, and throw all their tackle overboard, and lighten their ship. The storm still increasing, and neither sun nor stars for many days appearing, they gave themselves over for lost.

Which Paul perceiving, he told them that he had seen a vision, which assured him that not a soul of them should be lost, tho' the ship should.

The ship thus driving for fourteen days at the mercy of the winds and waves, about midnight the sailors fansied they were near land; and throwing the lead, they sounded, and found it twenty fathoms, then fifteen, and it still shaling, and being night, they apprehended they might strike upon some shelves in the dark, so they let go four anchors astern, and waited for day.

And now the seamen resolving to shift for themselves, had hoisted the boat overboard, under pretence of mooring the ship ahead as they had done astern: but Paul perceiving their design, told captain Julius, that if the sailors were suffered to quit the ship, they should be in danger of being all lost. Upon this the soldiers, to prevent their design, cut the ropes, and let the boat go adrift.

Now Paul persuades them on board to take some refreshment. The number of all that were in the ship was two hundred seventy six, including soldiers and passengers.

In the space between that and day-break, they all eat and drank, and were refreshed; having had no leisure or thought of eating for a considerable time before. After this refreshment they fell chearfully to work, unloading the ship not only of goods but of the provisions, and throwing them into the sea.

When it was day, they discovered a creek and a haven, into which they endeavoured to put; and when they had weighed the anchors, they made to the shore, and run the ship aground, where she soon bulg'd. The captain then ordered the prisoners that could swim to throw themselves into the sea first; and the rest on broken pieces got safe to land: where when they were all arrived, they knew the place to be the island Melita, or Malta.

The islanders seeing them in distress, treated them with great humanity; making fires to warm their wet and weary limbs. But whilst they were drying and warming themselves, a viper, driven from her hole by the heat of the fire, leaped out and fastened upon Paul's hand: which when the natives saw, they concluded him guilty of murder, and that divine vengeance had pursued him to that place, to die by the bite of this venomous creature: but he shook it off into the fire, and felt no harm. On seeing this, they presently alter'd their opinion, and concluded him a God.

The latter part of this history, is the subject of the eighth and last piece of painting.

CHAPTER V
Of the Library, the Model of St. Peter's at Rome, the great Bell, and geometrical Staircase.

Having quitted the whispering gallery, you are next invited to see the above curiosities; for which favour *each person pays Two-pence.*

The Library room is large and beautiful; the wainscoting, carvings, shelves, &c. are of nice workmanship; but notwithstanding there is a large collection of books in it the shelves appear very thin, and those lock'd up in a profound silence; some lolling fast asleep one way, and some another.

These books were designed for the use of the clergy belonging to the cathedral: but what from the height of its situation, which is half way up the cupola; and the dulness of its company, consisting mostly of a parcel of antiquated, musty, crabbed old authors; makes it very seldom visited by them. Their chief use now is to be made a publick shew of (like so many monsters) to strangers, country people, and little masters and misses; who, whenever they come to see this fine Library, must always take care to go into the room on tiptoe, for fear of disturbing any of these drousy old gentlemen.

The floor of this room is very curious, being inlaid, without peg or nail, with so much art and ingenuity, that it really looks very beautiful.

There is also a fine picture in it, of the right reverend Henry Compton, late lord bishop of London.

The Model of St. Peter's at Rome.

This was taken by Sir Christopher Wren from the church of St. Peter at Rome, whilst he resided there; and from this, with some alterations, our cathedral of St. Paul was built: he having took care to correct in the latter, what he saw a blemish in the former. This model stands in a large room, where those who are curious may examine it. 'Tis a fine piece, though now fallen somewhat to decay.

As to the great Bell and Clock, I have spoke of them before in the first Volume, pag. 8 to which I must refer my young readers; and shall only add, that the way to them is both dark and somewhat difficult to ascend, and therefore not advisable for my young readers to venture up, without a proper guide. Besides, should the clock happen to strike whilst they are in the bell loft, the sound is so surprisingly loud and shocking to those who are unaccustomed to it, that they would imagine it would rend the very tower all to pieces.

There is one thing more which is observable, that this clock is wound up once a day, which generally takes up an hour's time: and as 'tis then set, it is looked upon to be very exact.

Lastly, You are shewn the grand Geometrical Staircase; which is a curious and wonderful piece of workmanship, and so artfully contrived, that the support of the whole principally depends on the foot-stone only. This, and the stone staircase at Hampton-court, are the only two of the kind that are to be met with in any of our publick buildings.

To give a more particular account of its beauties, would require the judgment of one who is conversant in the science, to which I must ingenuously acknowledge my self a stranger.

Next we shall proceed to the inside of the church.

Book II

CHAPTER I
Of the inside of St. Paul's.

THE PILLARS of the church that support the roof, are two ranges, with their entablature and beautiful arches, whereby the body of the church and choir are divided into three isles. The roof of each is adorn'd with arches, and spacious peripheries of enrichments; as shields, leaves, chaplets, &c. admirably carved in stone.

At the west end of the church there are three doors which lead to the above isles; from each of which you have a beautiful prospect the whole length of the church, without any interception from the pillars, &c.

Just within the door of the north isle, on the left hand, is the morning prayer chapel, where divine service is performed every day in the week, excepting Sundays: from Lady-day to Michaelmas, at six in the morning; and from Michaelmas to Lady-day, at seven. In the north tower is the bell for calling people to prayers.

The front of this chapel has a very beautiful skreen of curious wainscot, and adorn'd with twelve columns; their entablatures, arched pediments, and the royal arms, enriched with cherubims, and each pediment between four vases, all curiously carved; and the skreen is fenced with ironwork.

Next to the morning prayer chapel is the Lord Mayor's vestry; to which he generally repairs with his attendants, before he takes his seat in the choir: and then divine service immediately begins.

At the entrance of the south isle, on the right hand, is the door that leads to the geometrical staircase: Next to that is the bishop of London's spiritual court; which has a beautiful skreen of curious wainscot; with columns, carvings, and other enrichments, like those of the morning prayer chapel. A little beyond this court, on the left hand, is a beautiful marble font; which for largeness, the fineness of its marble, and curious workmanship, excels all others; for which reason, I thought the picture of it would not be unacceptable to my young readers. You go up two circular steps to it.

Farther on the right hand is the door which leads up to the cupola.

CHAPTER III
Of the fine organ-case, &c.

THE ORGAN-CASE is magnificent, finely ornamented, and enrich'd with the carved figures of several cupids, and eight fames with their trumpets standing on the top of the case, four looking eastward and four westward; each appearing near six feet high.

It is also enriched with cherubims, fruit, leaves, &c. represented in a very lively manner. The organ-pipes are very spacious, gilt with gold, and preserved from dust with fine sashes: all which are raised on eight beautiful fluted columns of the Corinthian order, of polished marble, white vein'd with blue.

CHAPTER III *
Of the altar-piece, &c.

T HE ALTAR-PIECE is adorned with four noble fluted pilasters, finely painted, and veined with gold, in imitation of lapis lazuli, with their entablature; where the enrichments, and also the capitals of the pilasters are double gilt with gold; the inter-columns are twenty one pannels of figured crimson velvet: above all is a glory finely done.

The openings north and south into the choir are ascending up three steps of black marble, by two iron folding doors, like those under the organ gallery, and facing the choir; exquisitely wrought into divers figures, spiral branches, and other flourishes: and there are two others of these fine iron doors, the one opening into the south isle, the other into the north: they were all done by that celebrated artist in his way, Monsieur Tijan.

CHAPTER IV
Of the choir, the officers of the church, their seats, &c.

T HIS CATHEDRAL hath a Bishop, a Dean, a Precentor, Chancellor, Treasurer, and five Arch-deacons; to wit, London, Middlesex, Essex, Colchester, and St. Albans. It hath thirty Prebendaries, twelve Canons, and six Vicars choral.

The north and south sides of the choir have each thirty stalls, besides the Bishop's throne and seat on the south side, and the Lord Mayor's on the north: all which compose one vast body of curious carved work of the finest wainscot, done by that excellent artist the late Mr. Gribeline Gibbon; as was likewise all the other carved work, both of the choir and church.

On the south side of the entrance into the choir is the dean's vestry; and near that the singing boys vestry; and on the north side the residentiarys and singing mens vestry, where they all robe and unrobe.

There are four Vergers belonging to this church; so called from *virga*, a rod, which each bears in his hand. The dean's has the cross daggers at top; the others have no ensign at all.

The floor of the choir and church is pav'd with marble; but within the rail of the altar with fine porphyry, polish'd, and laid in several geometrical figures: the arabathrum whereon the communion table is placed, is five steps higher than that of the choirs isles.

We shall next descend into the vaults under St. Paul's.

CHAPTER V
Of the vaults, tombs, and St. Faith's church under St. Paul's.

T HE PASSAGE DOWN to these vaults, is by a door in the body of the church.

These vaults are indeed very spacious, but at the same time dark and gloomy, and strike a kind of horror in those who descend, in order to survey the numerous and massy

---

* The duplication of the chapter number (III) follows the original edition.—R.B.

pillars and arches which support this prodigious pile of buildings; of which they may be able to form some idea, from the glimmering light that is introduced into it from the small windows that open into the church-yard.

However, this place is too solemn, melancholy and unpleasant, for our young readers to roam about in; neither indeed are they invited to see it, as they are the other curiosities belonging to the church: and therefore would advise them to be contented with this account of it, rather than to gratify their curiosity by taking so gloomy a prospect.

Under the choir there was formerly the parish church of St. Faith, commonly called, *St. Faith's under St. Paul's*; of which there is now no remains. There is indeed a spot of ground railed in, and set apart for the burial of the dead of that parish, which is still subsisting, and united to that of St. Austin's. So that the notion which is entertain'd by several persons, and by others confidently asserted, that there is a parish church now beneath the choir; and that there are prayers and preaching still performed therein on some particular days, is a vulgar error, and altogether groundless.

There are under the choir, in this dark repository, the monuments of several eminent persons; but as it would be too tedious to give a description of them all, and no ways entertaining to the young reader, we shall pass them over in silence, and take notice only of that of the Architect of this grand building, who lies interr'd in a little corner close to the foundation wall, on the south-east side, next Watling-street. There is a plain stone fix'd against the wall at his head, with the following inscription in capitals:

SUBTUS CONDITOR

HUIUS ECCLESIÆ ET

VRBIS CONDITOR

CRISTOPHORUS WREN

QUI VIXIT ANNOS

ULTRA NONAGINTA

NON SIBI SED BONO

PUBLICO

LECTOR SI MONUMEN-

TUM REQUIRIS

CIRCUMSPICE

OBIIT XXV FEB. ANNO

MDCCXXIII ET. XCI.

The purport of which is this: *Here lies the body of Christopher Wren, the Architect of this cathedral church, &c. who lived above ninety years, and studied the good of the publick, and not his own private interest and advantage. Reader, If thou art curious to know where his monument is, cast thy eyes all around thee. He died 25 Feb. 1723. aged 91.*

This inscription is much admired for the justness and simplicity of the thought.

Over his body is a plain stone, with the following inscription:

HERE LIETH CHRISTOPHER WREN KNIGHT THE BUILDER OF THIS CATHEDRAL CHURCH OF ST. PAUL &C. WHO DIED IN THE YEAR OF OUR LORD MDCCXXIII AND OF HIS AGE XCI.

The End of the History of St. Paul's.

An Account of the Monument
Of the Fire of London

CHAPTER I
Its situation, description, and building.

On THE EAST SIDE of Fish-street-hill, near to the foot of London-bridge, stands the Monument, in a square open to the street.

It was set up by order of parliament, in perpetual memory of the dreadful fire that hapned [sic] the second day of *September*, 1666. within one hundred and thirty feet of the house where the fire first broke out; and upon the spot where the church of St. Margaret's New-fish-street stood.

This Monument stands upon an ascent from the street of three or four steps, upon a large vault of stone, arched.

The column is of the Dorick order, built all of excellent Portland stone. 'Tis erected upon a pedestal, or square of about twenty seven feet high: The body, or shaft of it is fluted; and is in height, from the pedestal to the balcony, a hundred and thirty three feet; and from the balcony to the top of the flame, is thirty eight feet: And the height of the whole Monument from the ground, besides the vault and foundation, to the top of the flame, is two hundred and two feet; the circumference of the shaft forty seven feet and a half; its diameter from without the wall, fifteen feet; within side, nine feet diameter; the thickness of the stone wall of the shaft is three feet.

It hath three hundred and forty five steps, or stairs, from the ground up to the balcony; and niches in the wall with seats to rest in, as people go up: and from the balcony upwards is a ladder of iron steps to go into the urn; out of which the flame, all gilt with gold, issueth; and to the stairs, having an open newel, there is a rail of iron to rest the hand upon all the way up.

This Monument is not unlike those two antient white marble pillars at Rome, erected in honour of the emperors Trajan and Antoninus, which were built above fifteen hundred years since; and are still standing entire.

The whole of this Monument taken together is a curious piece of workmanship: The charge of erecting it is said to amount to thirteen thousand seven hundred pounds and upwards.

This building loftily shews itself above the houses, and gives a gallant prospect for many miles round, to those that are in the balcony; so that many people have the curiosity to go up, and look about them from thence. The person appointed to keep it is allowed a salary for his attendance, besides the money people give him: The price demanded is *Twopence each person.*

It was begun in the mayoralty of Sir Richard Ford, 1671. and finish'd in that of Sir Joseph Sheldon, 1676.

CHAPTER II
Of the carved figures in the west front.

THE SIDE TOWARDS the street hath a representation of the destruction of the city by the fire, and the rebuilding of it again, by several curiously engraven figures made in full proportion.

First is the figure of a woman representing London, sitting on ruins, in a most disconsolate posture, her head hanging down, and her hair all loose about her, the sword lying by her, and her left hand carelessly laid upon it. A second figure is Time with his wings and bald head, coming behind her, and gently lifting her up. Another female figure on the side of her, laying her hand upon her, and with a scepter winged in her other hand, directing her to look upwards; for it points up to two beautiful goddesses sitting in the clouds; one leaning on a cornucopia, denoting Plenty: the other having a palm-branch in her hand, signifying Victory or Triumph. Underneath this figure of London in the midst of the ruins is a dragon with his paw upon the shield of a red cross, the arms of London: Over her head are represented houses burning, and flames breaking out thro' the windows; behind her citizens looking on, and some of them lifting up their hands.

Opposite to these figures is a pavement of stone, rais'd with three or four steps; on which appears king Charles the second in a Roman habit, with a truncheon in his right hand, and a laurel about his head, coming towards the woman in the despairing posture aforesaid; and giving orders to two or three others to descend the steps towards her. The first hath wings on her head, and a crown of naked boys dancing; and in her hand something resembling an harp. Then another figure of one going down the steps, following her, representing Architect; shewing a scheme, or model for rebuilding the city, held in the right hand; and the left holding a square and compasses. Behind these two stands another figure holding up an hat, denoting Liberty. Next behind the king is the duke of York, holding a garland ready to crown the rising city, and a sword lifted up in the other hand to defend her. Behind this a third figure, with an earl's coronet on his head. A fourth, behind all, holding a lion with a bridle in his mouth. Over these figures is represented an house in building, and a labourer going up a ladder with an hodd upon his back. Lastly, underneath the stone pavement whereon the king stands, is a good figure of envy, peeping forth, gnawing an heart.

An Explanation of some of the hard Words made use of in the two Volumes of the History of St. Paul's.

A.

ADjuring, to charge in the name of God to declare a matter.

Adrift, loose; to drive with the tide.

Animates, to stir up, enliven, or give life to.

Arch, is a hollow building, in the form of a rainbow.

Architecture, the art of building.

Architrave, that part of a column, or order of columns that is above, lying next the capital.

Ascent, a rising, going, or getting up.

Astern, the hinder part of a ship.

B.

Bulg'd, a ship is said to be so, when struck against any thing and broke, so as to let in much water.

C.

Capital, the uppermost part, or head of a column.

Cathedral, a church wherein is a bishop's see, or seat.

Cherubims, Angels of the second order; there are in all nine orders.

Choir, that part of a church where the singers perform their parts.

Circular, round, like a ball.

Circumference, the compass round about any body.

Column, a round pillar, to bear up or adorn a building.

Compartment, a particular square, or devise, in the ornamental part of a building.

Conception, ideas, thoughts.

Consecrated, set apart for religious uses.

Corinthian order of architecture, so called because first used at Corinth.

Cornice, the flourishing work at the upper part of a pillar.

Cupola, an arched tower of a church, or building, in form of a bowl turned bottom upwards.

D.

Dedicated, devoted, or set apart for some religious purpose.

Diameter, the width of any round body.

Dome, an arched roof, tower, or cupola of a church, &c.

Dorick order of architecture, the second of the five orders, said to be invented by the *Dorians*, a people of Greece.

E.

East, that quarter of the earth where the sun rises.

Effigy, image, shape, or form of a person.

Embellishment, ornament, finery.

Encircled, girt round about.

Encompassed, compassed, or girt round about.

Enrichments, beautiful ornaments.

Entablature, the architrave, freeze, and cornice of a column, together.

Exorcists, pretenders to miracles, conjurers.

F.

Festoons, ornaments of carved work, in wreathes or garlands of flowers.

Flower de luce, or *Fleurs de lys*; the flower of light, supposed to be the lilly. The lys, on account of its three branches, is the emblem of wisdom, faith and courage.

Fluted, the channels, hollows, or gutters, cut in a column, to render them still more beautiful.

Font, wherein water is put to baptize, or christen.

Freeze, that part of a pilaster between the architrave and cornice.

G.

Geometrical, done according to the rules of the science of geometry.

Glory, it has several meanings; over the altar, 'tis a representation of the beatifick vision, or joys of heaven.

Group, a crowd or cluster of figures in any painting, or carved work.

I.

Interception, stop'd by any thing between the eye and the object view'd.

Invisible, not to be seen.

M.

Maritime, a sea port.

Messiah, that is Anointed, a title of our Saviour.

Mooring, the fastening of a ship with anchors, &c.

N.

Newel, that part of a staircase that supports the steps.

Niches, hollows made in a wall.

O.

Omnipotent, all-powerful, strong, or mighty.

P.

Pedestal, the square bottom or foot of a column.

Pediment, an ornament in the fronts of large buildings, chiefly over gates.

Peripheries, the outlines of geometrick figures, as of a circle, &c.

Phœnix, an Arabian bird, of which it is said, there is never but one in being at a time.

Pilasters, square pillars.

Porphyry, a brownish red marble, exceeding hard, found in Egypt.

Portico, a porch, or covered place before the door of some great building.

R.

Relievo, any raised work, that swells or stands out above the surface.

Rustick, a method of building in imitation of nature rather than art.

V.

Vases, ornamental pots, on the tops of cornices, pedestals, &c.

The END.

The Newtonian System of Philosophy

By "TOM TELESCOPE"

Published by John Newbery

THE
NEWTONIAN SYSTE?
OF
PHILOSOPHY

Adapted to the Capacities of young
GENTLEMEN and LADIES, and familiarized and made entertaining by Objects with which they are intimately
acquainted:

BEING

The Substance of SIX LECTURES read to the
LILLIPUTIAN SOCIETY,

By TOM TELESCOPE, A.M.

And collected and methodized for the Benefit
of the Youth of these Kingdoms,

By their old Friend Mr. NEWBERY, in *St.
Paul's Church Yard;*

Who has also added Variety of Copper-Plate Cuts, to
illustrate and confirm the Doctrines advanced.

*O Lord, how manifold are thy Works! In Wisdom
hast thou made them all, the Earth is full of thy
Riches.*
*Young Men and Maidens, Old Men and Children,
praise the Lord.* PSALMS.

LONDON,
Printed for J. NEWBERY, at the BIBLE and SUN,
in *St. Paul's Church Yard.* 1761.

THE NEWTONIAN SYSTEM OF PHILOSOPHY Adapted to the Capacities of Young Gentlemen and Ladies . . . by Tom Telescope, A.M. *(1761) represents John Newbery's nonfiction for the older child. There were three editions in Newbery's lifetime and seven editions by 1787. Only Newbery's* The Circle of the Sciences: Or, the Compendious Library *(1745–1748; ten volumes on chronology, geography, etc.) rivals it as first-class science for children.*

The Newtonian System *considers the capacities of the young. References to kites and tops are studded throughout the sober lectures delivered by the well-informed, boyish Tom Telescope. The Marchioness of Setstar mildly reprimands Tom when, child that he is, he loses his temper in the middle of his lectures to his peers and elders. Some adult-type references invade the volume: the jokes about a poet's not being familiar with expensive food, the Ambassador of Bantam's reaction to whipping pigs to death, etc.*

The copperplate engravings elevated the price of the original book to a shilling, which was still cheaper than the three-shilling Pocket Dictionary *Newbery recommends in one of his typical advertising plugs for his own products. Fourteen original illustrations show the care Newbery took to amuse and instruct. They also reflect a simpler age of science when only six planets were known. An 1806 edition of the book added a seventh or Georgian planet and an appendix of optical and philosophical instruments which children could buy directly from the publishers. John Newbery would have sanctioned such entrepreneurship had he still been alive.*

Perhaps because so many books of amusement included science in some form, there were not many notable books of pure science for children. Besides Thomas Boreman's A Description of Three Hundred Animals *(1730) and* A Description of a Great Variety of Animals and Vegetables *(1736), there was Lady Fenn's* The Rational Dame *(ca. 1785). Fenn's book, like Boreman's, had many illustrations, but the language was judged too technical by an eighteenth-century reviewer. Priscilla Bell Wakefield (1751–1832) wrote at least a dozen books for children, some of which dealt with natural science, e.g.,* An Introduction to Botany in a Series of Familiar Letters *(1796), which had eleven British editions by mid-nineteenth century. Other popular science books in the period were Jane Marcet's* Conversations on Chemistry *(1806) and John Aikin's* The Calendar of Nature *(1784). For a discussion of books of science for children, see Mary Thwaite,* From Primer to Pleasure *(Boston: The Horn Book, Inc., 1972), pp. 200–212.*

The Newtonian System *is reprinted from the first edition (1761) in the Special Collections Department of the Regenstein Library of the University of Chicago.*

To The
Young Gentlemen and Ladies
of *Great Britain* and *Ireland,*
This Philosophy of *Tops* and *Balls*
Is humbly inscribed, By their most obedient Servant,
J. NEWBERY.

INTRODUCTION
Being the Substance of a Letter to the Hon. ****

D EAR SIR, I am desired by the Marchioness of *Setstar* to give you some account of those young Gentlemen and Ladies whom you saw enter the saloon the morning you left us, and who came to his Lordship's seat on an adventure the most extraordinary and the most to be admired of any I ever knew. You may remember it was holiday time, and these little gentry being come from school met first at the Countess of *Twilight's* to divert themselves; where they were so divided in their taste for amusements, that warm debates ensued. One proposed *Threading the Needle,* another *Hot-cockles,* a third *Shuttlecock,* a fourth *Blind-Man's-Buff;* and at last *Cards* were mentioned. Master *Telescope,* a young Gentleman of distinguished abilities, sat silent, and heard all with complacency and temper till this diversion was proposed; but then he started from his seat, and begged they would think of some more innocent amusement. Playing at cards for money, says he, is so nearly allied to covetousness and cheating, that I abhor it; and have often wondered, when I was at *Bath* with my papa, how people, seemingly of years of discretion, could so far mistake themselves, and abandon common sense, as to lead a young *urchin* just breeched, or a little *doddle-my-lady* in hanging sleeves, up to a gaming-table, to play and bet for shillings, crowns, and perhaps guineas, among a circle of sharpers. Parents, continued he, might almost as well teach their children to thieve as to game; for they are kindred employments, and generally terminate in the ruin of both fortune and character. Lady *Twilight,* who is no friend to the modern modes of education, smiled at this young gentleman's remark, and desired him to point out some diversion himself. 'Tis impossible for me, Madam, says he, to find out an amusement suitable to the taste of the company, unless I was perfectly acquainted with their dispositions; but were I to chuse, I should prefer those which not only divert the mind, but improve the understanding: and such are many of the diversions at the school where I am placed. We often play at *sham Orations, comical Disputes, measuring of Land and Houses, taking the Heights and Distances of Mountains and Steeples, solving Problems and Paradoxes on Globes and Maps,* and sometimes at *Natural Philosophy,* which I think is very entertaining, and at the same time extremely useful; for whether our knowledge is acquired by these amusements, and reading little books, or by serious and elaborate study, what is obtained will be equally serviceable: nay, perhaps that which is acquired in the entertaining manner may have the advantage; for, as it is conveyed to the mind with a train of pleasing ideas, it will be the more permanent and lasting, and the easier called up by the memory to our assistance.

The Countess was very desirous of knowing what sort of diversion could be made of Natural Philosophy; and finding her young visitors in the same disposition, she conducted them to the Marquiss of *Setstar*'s, that they might have the use of proper instruments. As my Lord Marquiss was engaged in company, Lady *Twilight,* though nearly related to his Lordship, would not disturb him, but led them through the saloon into a private parlour, where our little Philosopher, at the request of her Ladyship, immediately opened the Lecture, without making idle excuses, or waiting for farther solicitations, which he knew would be ill manners.

LECTURE I
Of Matter and Motion.

BY MATTER, my dear friends, *we mean the substance of all things,* or *that* of which all bodies are composed, in whatever form or manner they may present themselves to our senses: for this top, *Tom Wilson*'s ivory ball, the hill before us, that orange on the table, and all things you see, are made of matter differently formed.

As to *Motion,* I may save myself and you the trouble of explaining that; for every boy who can whip his top knows what motion is as well as his master.

Matter, or *Body, is indifferent to motion or rest.* As for example, now I whip my top, and it runs round, or is in motion; but when I no longer whip it, the top falls down, as you see, and is at rest.

When a body is in motion, as much force is required to make it rest, as was required, while it was at rest, to put it in motion. Thus, suppose a boy strikes a trap-ball with one hand, and another stands close by to catch it with one of his hands, it will require as much strength or force to stop that ball, or put it in a state of rest, as the other gave to put it in motion; allowing for the distance the two boys stand apart.

No body or part of matter can give itself either motion or rest: and therefore a body at rest will remain so for ever, unless it be put in motion by some external cause; and a body in motion will move for ever, unless some external cause stops it.

This seemed so absurd to Master *Wilson,* that he burst into a loud laugh. What, says he, shall any body tell me that my hoop or my top will run for ever, when I know by daily experience that they drop of themselves, without being touched by any body? At which our little Philosopher was angry, and having commanded silence, Don't expose your ignorance, *Tom Wilson,* for the sake of a laugh, says he: if you intend to go through my Course of Philosophy, and to make yourself acquainted with the nature of things, you must prepare to hear what is more extarordinary than this. When you say that nothing touched the top or the hoop, you forget their friction or rubbing against the ground they run upon, and the resistance they meet with from the air in their course, which is very considerable though it has escaped your notice. Somewhat too might be said on the gravity and attraction between the top or the hoop, and the earth; but *that* you are not yet able to comprehend, and therefore we shall proceed in our Lecture.

A body in motion will always move on in a strait line, unless it be turned out of it by some external cause. Thus we see that a marble shot upon the ice, if the surface be very smooth, will continue its motion in a strait line, till it is put to rest by the friction of the ice and air, and the force of attraction and gravitation.

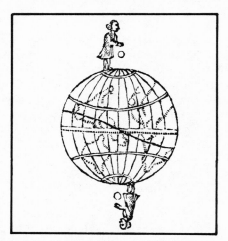

The swiftness of motion is measured by distance of place, and the length of time in which it is performed. Thus if a cricket-ball and a fives-ball move each of them twenty yards in the same time, their motions are equally swift; but if the fives-ball moves two yards while the cricket-ball is moving one, then is the motion of the fives-ball twice as swift as the other.

But the quantity of motion is measured by the swiftness of motion, as above described, and the quantity of matter moved considered together. For instance, if the cricket-ball be equal in bulk and weight to the fives-ball, and move as swift, then it hath an equal quantity of motion. But if the cricket ball be twice as big and as heavy as the fives-ball, and yet moves equally swift, it hath double the quantity of motion; and so in proportion.

All bodies have a natural tendency, attraction, or gravitation towards each other. Here *Tom Wilson*, again laughing, told the company that Philosophy was made up of nothing but hard words. That is because you have not sense enough to enquire into, and retain the signification of words, says our Philosopher. All words, continued he, are difficult till they are explained; and when that is done, we shall find that gravity or gravitation will be as easily understood as praise or commendation, and attraction as easily as correction; which you deserve, *Tom Wilson*, for your impertinence.

Gravity, my dear friends, *is that universal disposition of matter which inclines or carries the lesser part towards the centre of the greater part; which is called* weight *or gravitation in the lesser body, but* attraction *in the greater, because it draws, as it were, the lesser body to it.* Thus all bodies on or near the earth's surface have a tendency, or seeming inclination, to descend towards its middle part or centre; and but for this principle in nature, the earth (considering its form and situation in the universe) could not subsist as it is: for we all suppose the earth to be nearly round, (nay, we are sure it is so, for my Lord *Anson* and many other gentlemen, you know, have sailed round it) and as it is suspended in such a mighty void or space and always in motion, what should hinder the stones, water, and other parts of matter falling from the surface, but the almighty arm of God, or this principle or universal law in nature, of attraction and gravitation, which he has established to keep the universe in order. To illustrate and explain what I have said, let us suppose the following figure to be the earth and seas. Let *Tom Wilson* stand at this point of the globe or earth where we are, and *Hal Thompson* at the opposite part of the earth, with his feet (as they must be) towards us: if *Tom* drop an orange out of his hand, it will fall down towards *Hal*; and if *Hal* drop an orange, it will fall seemingly upwards (if I may so express myself) towards *Tom:* and if these oranges had weight and power sufficient to displace the other particles of matter of which the earth is composed, so as to make way to the centre, they would there unite together and remain fixed; and they would then lose their power of gravitation, as being at the center of gravity and unable to fall, and only retain in themselves the power of attraction.

This occasioned a general laugh; and *Tom Wilson* starting up, asked how Master *Thompson* was to stand with his feet upwards, as here represented, without having any thing to support his head? Have patience, says the little Philosopher, and I will tell you; but pray behave with good manners, Master *Wilson,* and don't laugh at every thing you cannot comprehend. This difficulty is solved, and all the seeming confusion which you apprehend of bodies flying off from each other is removed, by means of this attraction and gravitation. Ask any of the sailors who have been round the world, and they will tell you that the people on the part of the globe over-against us do not walk upon their heads, though the earth is round; and though their heels are opposite ours, they are in no more danger of falling into the mighty space beneath them, than we are of falling (or rather rising I must call it here) up to the moon or the stars.

But besides this general law of attraction and gravitation, which affects all bodies equally and universally, there are particular bodies that attract and repel each other, as may be seen by the *Magnet* or *Loadstone,* which has not only the property of directing the needle of the mariner's compass when touched with it to the north, but also of attracting or bringing iron to it with one end, and repelling or forcing it away with the other end: and *Sam Jones*'s knife, which was whet on a Loadstone some years ago, still retains the power you see of picking up needles and small pieces of iron.

Glass, Sealing-Wax, Amber, and *Precious Stones,* when chafed or rubbed till they are warm, will likewise both attract and repel feathers, hairs, straw, &c. which is sufficient to prove that each of these bodies has a sphere of attraction assigned it, beyond which it will repel the same body it would otherwise attract.

When bodies are so attracted by each other as to be united or brought into close contact, they then adhere or cohere together so as not to be easily separated, and this is called in Philosophy the *Power of Cohesion,* and is undoubtedly that principle which binds large bodies together; for all large bodies are made up of atoms or particles inconceiveab'y small. And this cohesion will be always proportioned to the number of particles or quantity of the surface of bodies that come into contact or touch each other; for those bodies that are of a spherical form will not adhere so strongly as those that are flat or square; because they can only touch each other at a certain point; and this is the reason why the particles of water and quicksilver, which are globular or round, are so easily separated with a touch, while those of metals and some other bodies are not to be parted but with great force. To give us a familiar instance of this cohesion of matter, our Philosopher took two leaden balls, and filing a part off each so that the two flat parts might come into close contact, he gently pressed them together and they united so firmly that it required considerable force to get them asunder.

One thing I must tell you of magnetism, which seems pretty extraordinary. Master *Brown* took his uncle's sword, and supported it with the point downwards, by resting the shell of the hilt on the top of his two forefingers; and Master *Smith* was placed with his father's amber-headed cane at about three or four feet distance, where he kept rubbing the amber head round on his waistcoat. After some little time the sword began to move, tho' at that distance; and some time after that it turned quite round; but was soon turned back again by master *Smith's* rubbing the amber head backwards, or in a contrary direction.

But what seems most worthy of our admiration is the Electrical Fire, which so plentifully abounds in the universe, and which is excited, or made visible, by the friction or rubbing of a glass globe. This fire, by a very simple machine, may be conveyed into the human body, every part of which it pervades in an instant, and is said to have been very serviceable in the cure of some disorders. It may be drawn from the ladies eyes, yet leaves them no less brilliant than they were before. It may be drawn from thunder-clouds, and is probably the same species of fire with the lightning; for Professor *Richmann* of *Hamburgh*, who fixed a machine to bring it down from the clouds in large quantities, was killed by the stroke it gave him.

The same force applied to two different bodies will always produce the same quantity of motion in each of them. To prove this, we put Master *Jones* into a boat, which (including his own weight) weighed ten hundred, on the *Thames* by the *Mill-bank*; and on the *Lambeth* side, just opposite, we placed another boat (of one hundred weight) with a string tied to it. This string Master *Jones* pulled in the other boat; and we observed that as the boats approached each other, the small boat moved ten feet for every foot the other moved; which proves what we have before observed as to the quantity of motion.

Attraction is the stronger, the nearer the attracting bodies are to each other; and in different distances of the same bodies it decreases as the squares of the distances between the centres of those bodies increase. For if two bodies at a given distance attract each other with a certain force, at half the distance they will attract each other with four times that force. But this I shall farther explain in my next course of Lectures.

Two bodies at a distance will put each other into motion by the force of Attraction or Gravitation. This we know to be true by experience, though we cannot account for it; and therefore it is to be received as a principle in Natural Philosophy.

Here Master *Wilson*, again interrupting him, said that could not be true; for if two bodies at any distance could put one another in motion by their power of attraction, the earth and the moon would move towards each other in a strait line, and unite; and then, says he, laughing, all Dr. *Wilkins's* machines for flying thither would be useless.

But you should consider, says the Philosopher, if a body, that by the attraction of another would move in a strait line towards it, receives a new-motion any ways oblique to the first, it will no longer move in a straight line, according to either of these directions, but in a curve that will partake of both. And this curve will differ according to the nature and quantity of the forces that concurred to produce it: as for instance, in many cases it will be such a curve as ends where it begun, or recurs into itself; that is, makes up a circle, like this ball; or an ellipsis or oval, like this egg, which shall be farther explained in our next course of Lectures.

LECTURE II
Of the Universe, and particularly of the Solar System.

T HE LAST LECTURE was read at the Marquiss of *Setstar*'s, who was so well pleased at these young gentlemen's meeting thus to improve themselves, that he ordered them to be elegantly treated with tarts, sweatmeats, syllabubs, and such other dainties as his Lordship thought were most proper for youth: and I must observe, that the Marchioness did them the honour of her company, and was particularly pleased with the conversation of Master *Telescope*. As it was a moonlight night, her Ladyship, after supper, led them to the top of a tower, where his Lordship has an observatory furnished with all the instruments necessary for astronomical and philosophical observations; and the place itself is the best that can be conceived for enquiries of this kind, and for meditation. To see an extensive horizon thus shaded by the brow of night, and at intervals brightened up by the borrowed light of the moon dancing among the clouds, was to me inexpressibly pleasing. Nothing was heard but a gentle breeze whispering the top of the battlements; the dying murmurs of a distant cascade; the melancholy hootings of the bird of night, who kept watch in an ivy tower near us; the mansion clock, that recorded the time; and old Echo, who repeated the hours from the side of a rock, where she has secluded herself ever since the deluge. Night, the nurse of Nature, had hushed all things else to silence.—But silence was soon broke by our Philosopher, who thus began his Lecture.

Look round, my dear friends, says he, you see the earth seems to be bounded at an equal distance from us every way, where it appears to meet the sky, that forms this beautiful arch or concave over our heads. Now that distance round, where we lose sight of the earth, is called the horizon; and when the sun, moon, and stars emerge from beneath and come into our sight, we say they are risen, or got above the horizon. For all this glorious canopy bespangled with lights, that bedeck the sky and illuminate the earth, as the *Sun*, the *Fixed Stars*, the *Comets* and *Planets*, (to which last our *Earth* and the *Moon* belong) have all apparent motions, as may be perceived by the naked eye; tho' in fact none move but the planets and comets, as will be proved hereafter.

But besides the stars which we see, there are others not discernible by the naked eye, some of which are fixed stars, and some are bodies moving about the most distant planets, which were invisible and unknown to us before the discovery of prospective glasses.—Pray hand me the reflecting telescope—Here it is.

And the refracting telescope, if you please.—Oh, here it is also.

If you use the reflecting telescope, you must turn this screw on the side of it till you can see the object you want to examine in the most perfect manner: and if you use the refracting telescope, you must move backwards or forwards this small part, till you have adjusted it to your sight. Then look at that part of the heavens where I have pointed them, or indeed any other part, and you will perceive more stars than you saw before with your eye alone. These are fixed stars, and are called fixed because they always keep the same distance one from another, and the same distance from the sun, which is supposed to be also fixed; and was he placed at the immense distance they are at, would probably appear no bigger than one of them. Hence some Philosophers have concluded, and I think not without reason, that every fixed star is a sun, that has a system of planets revolving round it, like our solar system. And if so, how immensely great, how wonderfully glorious, is the structure of this universe, which contains many thousand worlds, large as ours, suspended in æther, rolling like the earth round their several suns, and filled with animals, plants, and minerals, all perhaps different from ours, but all intended to magnify the Almighty Architect; *who weighed the mountains in his golden scales, who measured the ocean in the hollow of his hand, who drew out the heavens as a curtain, who maketh the clouds his chariot, and walketh upon the wings of the wind.*

The fervour and air of piety with which he delivered this, silenced all his companions, and gave infinite satisfaction to the Marchioness. Master *Wilson,* who had before been very impertinent, began now to consider himself as a fool in comparison of our Philosopher; and as Master *Telescope* had mentioned the solar system, he begged that he would explain it to him.

That I will with pleasure, replied the Philosopher; but first let me observe to you, that of these heavenly bodies some are *luminous,* and lend us their own light, as doth the *Sun* and *Fixed Stars;* while others are *opaque,* and have no light of their own to give us; but reflect to us a part of the light they receive from the sun. This is particularly the case with respect to the planets and comets of our solar system, which all give us a portion of the light they have received, and we in return reflect to them a portion of ours: for I make no doubt, but those who inhabit the moon have as much of the sun's light reflected to them from the earth, as we have reflected to us from the moon.

The inhabitants of the moon! says Master *Lovelace,* with some emotion, Whither will you lead me? What, are the stories that have been told of the Man in the Moon then true?

I don't know what stories you have heard, replied the Philosopher; but it is no extravagant conjecture to suppose that the moon is inhabited, as well as the earth; though what sort of inhabitants they are, we on the earth are unable to discover. As to my part, I am lost in this boundless abyss. It appears to me that the sun, which gives life to the world, is only a beam of the glory of God; and the air, which supports that life, is, as it were the breath of his nostrils.

Do thou, O God, support me while I gaze with astonishment at thy wonderful productions; since it is not idle impertinent curiosity that leads me to this enquiry, but a fervent desire to see only the skirts of thy glory, that I may magnify thy power and thy mercy to mankind.

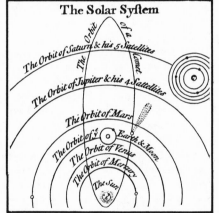

Of the Solar System.

Our Solar System contains the sun in the centre, and the planets and comets moving about it.—Pray look at the figure on the other side, where I have drawn the sun, and the planets in their several orbits or circles, with their respective distances from the sun, and from each other; together with the orbit of a comet.

The planets, as I have already observed, are bodies that appear like stars, but are not luminous; that is, they have no light in themselves, tho' they give us light; for they shine by reflecting the light of the sun. Of these there are two kinds, the one called *primary,* and the other *secondary* planets.

There are six *primary* planets, and these are *Mercury, Venus,* the *Earth, Mars, Jupiter,* and *Saturn;* all which move round the Sun, as you may see in the figure before you;

whereas the *secondary* planets move round other planets. The *Moon,* you know, (which is one of the secondary planets) moves round the *Earth*; four moons, or *Satellites,* as they are frequently called, move round *Jupiter*; and five round *Saturn.* And thus has the Almighty provided light for those regions that lie at such an immense distance from the Sun.

The amazing distance which each planet is at from the Sun, may be seen by the time which it takes in its periodical revolution.

Mercury		88 days.
Venus	revolves	225 days.
The *Earth*	about the	365 d. 5h. 49 m.
Mars	Sun in the	one year 322 days
Jupiter	space of	11 years 319 days
Saturn		29 years 138 days

These move round about the Sun from west to east in the time above mentioned. They are always to be found among the stars of those constellations that compose the twelve signs of the Zodiac; and in their progress do not describe a perfect circle, but an orbit a little inclining to an oval: the reason whereof I shall give you in a future Lecture.

The comets move about the sun in a long slender oval of an amazing extent; one of the focus's being near the centre of the sun, and the shortest of the other far beyond the sphere of *Saturn;* so that the periodical revolutions of any are not performed in less than 70 or 80 years. See the *Plate.*

But let us quit these bodies, of which we know so little, and speak of our old companion the moon, with whom we ought to be better acquainted; since she not only lights us home in the night, but lends her aid to get our ships out of the docks, and to bring in and carry out our merchandize; for without the assistance of Lady *Luna* you would have no tides: but more of this hereafter.—A little more now, if you please, says *Tom Wilson.* What then, does the moon pour down water to occasion the tide? I am at a loss to understand you. No, replied our Philosopher, the moon does not pour down water to occasion the tides; that were impossible: but she by attracting the waters of the sea raises them higher, and that is the reason why the tides are always governed by the moon.

The moon moves round the earth in the same manner as the earth does round the sun, and performs her synodical motion, as it is called, in 29 days, 12 hours, and 44 minutes, though the periodical is 27d. 7h. 43m. By this motion of the moon are occasioned the eclipses of the sun and moon, and the different appearances, aspects, or phases she at different times puts on: for when the earth is so situated between the sun and the moon, that we see all her enlightened parts it is *full Moon*; when the moon is so situated between the sun and the earth, that her enlightened parts are hid or turned from us, it is *new Moon*; and when her situation is such that only a portion of her enlightened part is hid from us, we see a *horned Moon,* a *half Moon,* or a *gibbous Moon,* according to the quantity of the enlightened part we can perceive.

The total or longest *Eclipse of the Moon* happens when the earth is directly between the sun and the moon, and prevents the light of the sun from falling upon and being reflected by the moon; as I'll shew you. You will suppose this orange to be the sun, this cricket-ball the earth, and this top the moon; now if you place them in a strait line, with

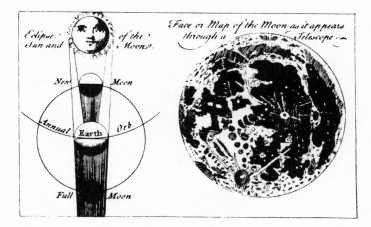

the ball in the middle, and then put your eye to the top; you'll find that the ball will entirely hide the orange from your view, and would prevent the rays of light (which always proceed in right lines) from falling upon it, whence would ensue a *total* eclipse. But move the top, which represents the moon, a little on either side, and with your eye placed as before you will perceive a part of the orange, which will be now in such a position that a strait line máy be drawn from a part of the orange or sun, to a part of the top or moon, without touching the ball that represents the earth; and in this position the moon would be partly illuminated, and the eclipse be only *partial*.

An *Eclipse of the Sun* is occasioned by the moon's being betwixt the sun and the earth, and preventing the light of the sun from coming to that part of the earth which we inhabit.—If the moon hides from us the whole body of the sun, it is a *total* eclipse; but if the whole be not hid, it is a *partial* one. An *Eclipse* of the *Sun* never happens but at a *new* moon; nor one of the *Moon* but when she is at *full*.

The moon, as to matter and form, appears not much unlike our earth, as you may perceive by this Map. The bright parts are supposed to be the high illumined tracts of land, as *mountains, islands*, &c. and the dark parts it is imagined are the *seas, lakes*, and *vales*, which reflect but little light. But of this there is no certainty.

The *Earth*, by its revolution about the sun in 365 days, 5 hours, and 49 minutes, measures out that space of time which we call a *Year*; and the line described by the earth in this annual revolution about the sun is called the *Ecliptic*. To give you a perfect idea of this and other circles necessary to be known, I have on the opposite side presented you with the figure of a Sphere.

The annual motion of the earth round the sun is from west to east, or to speak more philosophically, it is according to the order of the signs of the *Zodiac*; which we shall hereafter explain.

But besides this annual motion or revolution about the sun in the line of the *Ecliptic*, the earth turns round upon its own axis in about 24 hours; so that it hath two motions at one and the same time.

The Marchioness, whose curiosity had kept her during the Lecture, desired to have this explained. That shall be done, Madam, in a minute, says the little Philosopher,

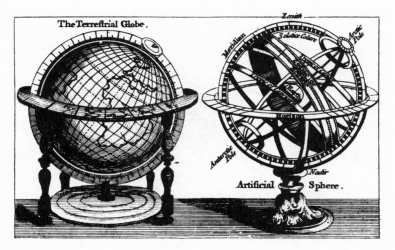

and I can never have a better opportunity; for I see the Duke of *Galaxy* is coming to make your Ladyship a visit. His coach is just entering the iron gates, and will presently wheel round the circle, or rather oval, before the portico. Pray, Madam, fix your eye on one of the wheels, which you may do as it is moon-light, and you will perceive it turn round upon its own axis, at the same time that it runs round the circle before the house. This double motion of the wheel very fitly represents the two motions of the earth, which have heretofore been explained by the motion of a bowl on a bowling-green; but I believe your Ladyship will think the instance or example before us is better. It is hard to reason from similitudes, because they generally fail in some part: all the members of a simile seldom correspond with the subject it is intended to illustrate; and, if I mistake not, that is the case with the bowl upon the green; which, though it aptly represents the earth's motion on its own axis, is far from representing its revolution about the sun, because the bias in the bowl will never induce it to form either a circle or an oval; for the figure it describes is rather a parabola, or that sort of figure which a long fishing-rod forms when it is bent by drawing a fish out of the water.

Your Ladyship knóws perfectly that the earth turning on its own axis makes the difference of day and night: you will therefore give me leave, Madam, to address my discourse to these young gentlemen and ladies, who may be ignorant of this branch of Philosophy.

That the turning of the earth on its own axis makes the difference of *day* and *night* is most certain; for in those parts of the earth which are turned towards the sun it will be *day*, and of consequence it must be *night* in those which are turned from it.

But the length of *days* and *nights*, and the variation of the *seasons*, are occasioned by the annual revolution of the earth about the sun in the *Ecliptic*; for as the earth in this course keeps its axis equally inclined every where to the plane of the Ecliptic and parallel to itself, and as the plane of the Ecliptic inclines 23 degrees and a half towards the Equator, the earth in this direction has sometimes one of its poles nearest the sun, and sometimes the other. Hence heat and cold, summer and winter, and length of days and nights. Yet notwithstanding these effects of the sun, which gives us light and heat, his distance from us is so great, that a cannon-ball would be 25 years coming thence to the earth, even if it flew with the same velocity as it does when it is first discharged from the mouth of a cannon.

Here they were all amazed, and Lady *Caroline* said this doctrine could not be true; for if the sun was at that immense distance, his light could not reach us every morning, in the manner it does.—I beg your pardon, Madam, replied the Philosopher; your Ladyship's mistake arises from your not knowing, or at least not considering, the amazing velocity of light; which flies after the rate of 200,000 miles in a *second* of time; so that notwithstanding a cannon-ball would be 25 years in coming from the sun, the light finds its way to us in about eight minutes. But if you are so surprized at the sun's distance, Madam, what think you of that of the fixed stars, which are so far remote from us, that a cannon-ball, flying with the same velocity as when first discharged, would be 700,000 years in coming to the earth? Yet many of these stars are seen, and even without the use of telescopes.

There are other things observable in our Solar System, which if attended to will excite our admiration: such are the dark spots which are seen on the *Sun's* surface, and which often change their *place, number,* and *magnitude.* Such also is the amazing Ring which encompasses the body of the planet *Saturn* at the distance of 21,000 miles; and such are the Belts that gird the body of *Jupiter:* concerning all which there are various conjectures, but conjectures in Philosophy are rarely to be admitted.

LECTURE III
Of the Air, Atmosphere, and Meteors.

WHAT WAS SAID by the Marchioness and Lady *Caroline* in favour of Master *Telescope* excited the Duke of *Galaxy's* curiosity to see him, and the next morning he came into the Observatory just as the Lecture began. The presence of so great a personage as the Duke put our young gentlemen into some confusion, and several of them offered to go away; which the Duke observing stepped into the next room, and Master *Telescope* took this opportunity to correct their folly.

Gentlemen, says he, I am amazed at your meanness and ill-manners. What, because the Duke does you the honour of a visit, will you run away from him? There is nothing betrays a mean spirit and low education so much as this ridiculous awe and dread which some people shew in the company of their superiors; and besides, it is troublesome; for the uneasiness that one person is in communicates itself to the rest of the company, and abridges them of a portion of their pleasure. The easier you appear in the company of the Great, the more polite you will be esteemed. None but a clown hangs down his head, and hides his face; for a gentleman always looks in the face of his superior when he talks to him, and behaves with openness and freedom. As to my part, I venerate his Grace; but then it is for his great worthiness of character, which has engaged my affection, and inclines me to wish for his company, not to avoid it. *Civility we owe to every one,* and *Respect* is due to the Great: it is claimed, and it is given, in consequence of their superior birth and fortune; but that is all; for our affection is only to be obtained by worthiness of character. Birth and fortune are merely accidental, and may happen to be the portion of a man without merit; but the man of genius and virtue is enobled, as it were by himself, and is honoured not so much for his grandfather's greatness as his own. This reproof had its proper effect; for they all sat down, and his Grace being returned, with Lady *Caroline,* our Philosopher began his Lecture on the nature and properties of the *Air, Atmosphere,* and *Meteors* contained therein.

We have already considered the earth as a planet, says he, and observed its diurnal and annual motion; we are now to speak of the materials of which it is composed, and of the Atmosphere, and the Meteors that surround and attend it.

In order to explain these effectually, says the Duke, you should, I think, Sir, begin with an account of the first principles or four Elements, which are *Fire, Air, Earth,* and *Water,* and then shew how they affect each other, and by their mutual aid give motion, life and spirit to all things; for without fire the water would assume a different form, and become solid ice; without water the fire would scorch up the earth, and destroy both animals and plants. Without air, the fire perhaps would be unable to execute its office, nor without air could the water, tho' exhaled by the sun into clouds, be distributed over the earth for the nourishment of plants and animals. Nor is the earth inactive but lends her aid to the other elements. She filtres, or strains and purifies the salt water which runs from the sea, and makes it fresh and fit for the use of animals and plants; and by reflecting the sun's beams occasions that warmth which nourishes all things on her surface; but which would be very inconsiderable and scarcely felt if a man was placed on the highest mountain, above the common level of the earth, and in such a situation as to be deprived of her reflection.

All this, my Lord Duke, I have considered, replied the Philosopher, and had thoughts of carrying it farther, and shewing how those elements pervade and are become indeed constituent parts of the same body; for *Fire, Air, Earth,* and *Water* are to be drawn even from a dry stick of wood. That two sticks rubbed violently together will produce fire is very well known; for coach or waggon wheels frequently take fire when not properly clouted with iron, and supplied with grease: And if pieces of wood, seemingly dry, be put into a glass retort over a furnace, you'll obtain both air and water, and then if you burn the wood to ashes, and wash out the salts with water, as the good women do when they make lye, the remaining part will be pure earth: And thus we can at any time draw the four elements out of a stick of wood. But as these speculations are above the comprehension of some of the young gentlemen whom I have the honour to instruct, I shall defer the consideration of such minute and abstruse matters till another opportunity. Science is to be taught as we teach children the use of their legs, they are at first shewn how to stand alone, after this they are taught to walk with safety, and then suffered to run as fast as they please; and I beg your Grace will permit me to pursue this method in the course of my Lectures. The Duke gave his assent with a nod, and our Philosopher thus proceeded.

The air is a light, thin, elastic or springy body, which may be felt but not seen; it is fluid and runs in a current like water, (as you may perceive by opening the window) but it cannot, like water, be congealed into ice; and the Atmosphere is that great body or shell of air, which surrounds the earth, and which reaches many miles above its surface, as is known by considering the elasticity, or springiness of the air and its weight together; for a column of air is of equal weight to a column of quicksilver of between 29 and 30 inches high; now quicksilver being near fourteen times heavier than water, if the air was as heavy as water, the Atmosphere would be about fourteen times higher than the column of quicksilver, or about 34 feet; but the air is near 1000 times lighter than water, therefore the Atmosphere must be many miles high, even at this rate of computing: And when with this you consider the elasticity of the air, which when the pressure of the incumbent Atmosphere is taken off, will dilate itself so as to fill more than 150 times the space it occupied before, you will perceive that the height of the Atmosphere must be very great. For as the air is a springy body, that part next the earth must be more dense than the upper part, as being pressed down by the air above it. Look at that hay-stack yonder, which the groom is cutting, and you'll perceive that the hay at bottom is much closer and harder to cut than that at the top, because it has been pressed into less space than it otherwise would have occupied, by the other hay above it; and had not the whole stack been trodden and pressed down by the man who made it, the difference would have been still more considerable.

The air, however, even near the earth, is not always in the same state. It is sometimes rarified, and becomes lighter than at other times, as appears by the quicksilver's falling in the Barometer, and the rain's descending on the earth; for it is the dense state or weight of the air which raises the quicksilver in the Barometer, the water in the pump, and prevents the clouds from falling down in rain.

This elastic principle in the air, which renders it so capable of being rarified and condensed, has been productive of the most wonderful effects. But before you proceed farther, says Lady *Caroline*, pray do me the favour, Sir, to convince me, by some experiment that the air is endowed with this wonderful quality. That he cannot do, replied the Duke, without the use of proper instruments. Almost any thing will do, an't please your Grace, says the Philosopher.—Little Master's *Pop-gun*, that lies in the window, is sufficient for my purpose.—Do me the honour to step this way, Lady *Caroline*. You see here is a pellet in the top of this tube, made of hemp or brown paper. With this piece of paper we will make another pellet, and put into the other end. Now with the gun-stick drive it forward. There, you have forced the pellet some part of the way with ease, but it will be more difficult to get it farther, because the air, being compressed, and made more dense or compact will make more resistance; and when you have pressed it so close that its force overpowers the resistance which the pellet makes at the other end, that pellet will fly off with a bounce, and be thrown by the spring of the air to a considerable distance.—There, see with what force it is thrown.

This you have taken little notice of, because it is a school boy's action, and is seen every day; for indeed, we seldom trouble ourselves to reason about things that are so familiar; yet on this principle, my Lady, depends the force of a cannon; for it is not the gunpowder and fire that drives out the ball with such prodigious velocity; no, that force is occasioned by the fire's suddenly rarifying the air, which was contained in the chamber or breach of the cannon, and that generated by the powder itself. As a proof of this, place the same ball, in the same quantity of powder in an open vessel, and when fired you will scarce see it move. But there have been guns lately invented, called wind-guns, which abundantly prove what I have advanced; for they are charged only with concentrated or condensed air and with ball, yet so contrived, that six or seven balls may be let off, one after the other, each of which would kill a buck or a doe at a very considerable distance.

You seem all amazed, and I don't wonder at it, since you have never yet considered the extraordinary properties of this element; and it must seem strange to you that the air, which is so necessary for life, that without it we cannot breathe, should be tortured into an instrument of destruction. You will however be more surprized when I tell you, that this is the cause of earthquakes; and that the noble city of *Lisbon* was lately destroyed by a sudden rarifation of the air contained in some of the caverns of the earth, and perhaps under the sea. *Tom Wilson* gave a leer of impertinence, but was ashamed to shew his folly before such good company. All the rest stared at each other without speaking a word, except Lady *Caroline*, who protested she could not believe what he had said about earthquakes; for, says she, I remember to have read in the News Papers, that the flames burst out of the ground. That might be, my Lady, says the little Philosopher, for there could be no such sudden rarifation of the air without fire. Fire, therefore, did contribute towards the earthquake, and fire might burn down a mountain composed of combustibles; but fire could never blow one up. No, my Lady, that effect is the sole property of the air. This dispute would, in all probability, have taken up much time; but his Grace put an end to the controversy, by declaring it was true Philosophy.

In this property of being rarified and condensed, the air differs amazingly from water, which tho' composed of such small particles as not to be distinguished or seen separately with a microscope, and its readiness to rise or be evaporated with heat, and to be separated with a touch, cannot when confined, be at all concentrated or brought into a less compass. This experiment was once tried, by filling a golden globe full of water, then closing it up, and placing it in a screw press, which was pulled down with great force. In this situation it remained till the water sweated thro' the pores of the gold, and till that happened it would never give way.

Air is the medium which diffuses light to the world; for if there was no Atmosphere to refract the sun's rays round the globe, it would be almost as dark in the day time as in the night, and the *Sun, Moon,* and *Stars,* would only be visible. It is also the medium of sounds, which are conveyed by the tremulous motion of the air when agitated by any noise. Let me throw this peach stone into the moat, and you will perceive circles of small waves diffuse themselves by degrees to a great distance round it. Now as the air is fluid as well as the water, we may conclude that sound is conveyed somewhat in this manner, tho' as that is nearly a thousand times lighter than water, sounds are propagated at an amazing rate, some say after the rate of 1142 feet in a second of time; but, however that be, we may rest assured, that sound is conveyed in this manner. Only throw up the sash, and halloo, and the echo, which I spoke of in the beginning of the second Lecture, will return you the sound; that is, the waves or pulses of air, which are put in motion by the noise you make, will strike against the rocks, and return to you again; for echo is nothing but the *reverberation* of sound: and that there can be no sound conveyed without air, is proved by experiment; for a bell struck in an exhausted receiver in an air pump, cannot be heard, that is, it has little or no sound.

Without air there would be no merchandize, for your ships could not sail to foreign climates; and without air the birds could not fly, since they would have nothing to support them, and their wings would be useless; for we know, that a feather falls with as much velocity as a guinea in an exhausted receiver. But above all, air is the principle which preserves life, both in plants and animals; there is no breathing without air, and you know, when our breath is stopt we die. This is one of those truths that are called

self-evident, because it is universally known, and needs no confirmation; but if demonstration be thought necessary you may have it in a minute, by putting some living creature into the air pump; but it is cruel to torture a poor animal: So said Lady *Caroline*, and violently opposed this experiment's being tried; but as all the rest were for it, the Duke was willing to gratify their curiosity; and therefore told our Philosopher, that he might try the experiment with a rat, which they had caught in a trap, and if he survived it, give him his life for the pain they had put him to. This creature was accordingly put in the receiver, and when the air was partly exhausted, he appeared in great agony, and convulsed; and more air being pumped out, he fell on his side for dead; but fresh air being immediately admitted, it rushed into his lungs, which put them in motion again, and he recovered. The manner of the animal's recovery puts me in mind, says the Philosopher, of an accident which I once saw, and which I would have you all remember, for it may be of service to mankind.

Some time ago I was bathing, with several of my school-fellows, in a river by the road-side. Master *Curtis*, who was an obstinate silly boy, would dastard the rest, as he called it; that is, he would foolishly exceed them in running into dangers and difficulties, and with this view, tho' he could swim no more than a stone, he plunged into a part of the river, which we told him was greatly above his depth, where he rose, and struggled to get out, but could not. We were all, you must imagine, in the utmost distress, and unable to assist him; for none of us could swim. At this instant came by some Gentlemen on horseback, who immediately dismounted, and got him out, but not till after he had sunk the third time. He was brought to shore without signs of life, and blooded without any effect; when one of the Gentlemen, who I have since heard was a great Philosopher, advised them to blow some air down his throat; this was done, and the elasticity of the air put his lungs in motion, as I imagine, for a pulsation immediately ensued, and he recovered almost as soon as this animal. Now, from what I heard that Gentleman say, and from the instance before us, there is reason to believe, that the lives of many might be saved, who are supposed drowned, if this method was put in practice of conveying air to the lungs; for you are to consider, that unless the lungs are in motion, there can be no circulation, and it was for want of air, that their motion ceased in the water. Pray, Gentlemen, let this be remembered, for it is a matter of great importance.

We are to observe, Gentlemen, that air which has past thro' fire, or is become foul, or stagnated, and has lost its spring, is unfit for respiration. It was the want of fresh air, or, in other words, the being obliged to breathe air that was foul, and had lost its spring, or elastic force, that killed so many of our poor country-men in the black hole at *Calcutta*, in the *East Indies,* as you have seen by the News Papers; and this breathing of foul air in inflammatory, putrid, and eruptive disorders, such, for instance, as the small-pox, and some fevers, has destroyed more than can be imagined. If therefore you should be seized with any of these disorders, advise the people about you to make use of their common sense, and not, because a man is ill, deprive him of that vital principle the air, without which he could not live, even in a state of health. Never suffer your curtains to be drawn close, or exclude the fresh air, even when you sleep.

I am greatly mistaken, says Lady *Caroline,* if the air we are now in has not lost its spring; for I breathe with difficulty. Was that the case, Madam, replied the little Philosopher, you would not be able to breathe at all; but if your Ladyship finds the air so disposed, you should make use of the instrument that lies by you, which, by putting the air in motion, will in part recover its spring. What instrument, Sir? says the Lady. Your fan, Madam, returned the Philosopher. Every fan is a philosophical instrument, and was originally contrived, we may suppose, for the purpose above-mentioned.

A bird dying in an Air-pump will be in some measure recovered by the convulsive fluttering of its own wings, because that motion alters the state of the air remaining in the receiver, and for a time renders it fit for respiration.

Motion is the only preservative for air and water; both of which become unwholsome if kept long in a state of rest; and both may be recovered and made salutary by being again put into motion.

If foul and stagnated air has such dire effects, how much are we obliged to the learned and ingenious Dr. *Hales* for discovering the *Ventilator,* an instrument which, in a little time, discharges the foul air from ships, prisons, and other close places, and supplies them with that which is fresh?

The air, by some Philosophers, has been esteemed an universal *menstruum,* because, say they, it dissolves all bodies in time, and reduces their substances to a new form; as iron into rust, copper into verdigrease, *&c.* but this, I am inclined to think, is not so much owing to the air as to certain saline or acid particles, which the air extracts from some bodies, and which afterwards cleave to other bodies, with which they have a closer affinity than with the air itself. But this I shall endeavour to explain in a future work.

We are now to speak of the Wind, which is only a stream or current of air, as a river is of water, and is occasioned by heat, eruptions of vapours, condensations, rarifications, the pressure of clouds, the fall of rains, or some other accident that disturbs the equilibrium of the air; for Nature abhors a vacuum, and for that reason, when the air is extremely rarified in one part, that which is more dense will immediately rush in to supply the vacant places, and preserve the equilibrium; as is the case with water and other fluid substances. Only raise a vessel of water suddenly out of a cistern, and see with what speed the other water will rush in, to fill up the space and preserve its level. And these rarefactions in the air may happen near the earth, or much above it, and is the reason why clouds fly in contrary directions. This occasioned the loss of the great *Kite*, which we were a whole fortnight in making; for, tho' there was scarcely wind in the Park sufficient to raise it, yet when lifted extremely high by the air, it was seized by a current of wind and torn in pieces.

Winds are violent, or gentle, in proportion to the rarifaction or disturbance there has been in the atmosphere. A violent wind in a great storm, flies after the rate of 50 or 60 miles in an hour, and is often so dense, or strong, as to bear down trees, houses, and even churches before it. What the sailors call a brisk wind flies after the rate of about 15 miles an hour, and is of great use in cooling the air, and cleaning it from poisonous and pestilentious exhalations.

The winds have various qualities, they are generally hot or cold, according to the quarter from whence they blow. I remember, some years ago, we had a South-West wind in *February,* which blew so long from that quarter, that it brought us the very air of *Lisbon,* and it was as hot as in summer. Winds from the North and North-East, which come off large tracts of land, are generally cold. Some winds moisten and dissolve, others dry and thicken; some raise rain, and others disperse it: Some winds blow constantly from one quarter, and are therefore called the *general Trade Winds.* These are met with on each side of the *Equator,* in the *Atlantic, Ethiopic,* and *Pacific Oceans,* between the Tropicks, and to near 24 degrees of latitude; and are occasioned by the Sun in his rotation round his axis, agitating the æther, or by the rarifaction of the air by the solar rays, and the denser air continually pouring in from the distant parts of each hemisphere to maintain the equilibrium. Some winds, again, blow constantly one way for one half, or one quarter of the year, and then blow the contrary way. These are met with in the *East-Indian Seas,* and are called *Monsoons,* or periodical Trade Winds. But as these subjects are abstruse and difficult, and afford little entertainment, we shall defer an explanation of them till our next course of Lectures, and endeavour to give you some account of the Meteors that attend the air.

We have already observed, that besides pure air, the atmosphere contains minute particles of different sorts, which are continually arising in steams from the earth and waters, and are suspended and kept floating in the air.

The most considerable of these are the small particles of water, which are so separated as to be lighter than air, and are raised by the Sun's heat, or lifted up by the wind from the sea, rivers, lakes, and marshy or moist parts of the earth, and which descend again in *Dews, Rain, Hail,* and *Snow.*

When these small particles are by a rarified state of the air suffered to unite many of them together, and descend so as to render the hemisphere more opaque, and by its humidity to moisten bodies on the Earth, it is called a *Mist.* And on the contrary, those particles of water that arise after a hot day from rivers, lakes, and marshy places, and by filling the air moisten objects, and render them less visible, are called *Fogs.*

Clouds are the greatest and most beneficial of all the *meteors,* for they are borne about on the wings of the wind, and, as the Psalmist observes, *distribute fatness to the Earth.* Clouds contain very small particles of water, which are raised a considerable distance above the surface of the earth; for a cloud is nothing but a mist flying high in the air, as a mist is nothing but a cloud here below.

That these vapours are raised in the air, in the manner abovementioned, may be readily conceived; for it is an action that is seen every day in common distillations; but how these invisible particles, which float in the air, are collected into clouds in order to bring the water back again, is not so easy to determine. Perhaps, says the Marchioness, who had just before entered the room, it may be occasioned by the winds driving the clouds together and uniting the particles, which may by that means become specifically heavier than the air, and therefore fall down. There is reason, my Lady, in what you say, replied the Philosopher, but I would wish to know how these clouds are sometimes all of a sudden collected. It frequently happens, Madam, that you go abroad when the sky is so serene and clear, that not a cloud is to be seen, and before your Ladyship has taken a turn round the *Park*, you shall see clouds gather round, and all the hemisphere overcast, and the drops begin to fall. How happens this? There were no clouds for the winds to drive against each other, nor could the aqueous vapours arise from the Earth, and descend at the same instant of time. Whence then could they come? I am afraid, Madam, says the Duke, this young Gentleman has shaken your Ladyship's Philosophy; for the question he has put is not to be answered without some knowledge of Chemistry, which is, I think, too little studied in this kingdom. I am not uneasy about it, my Lord Duke, says the Marchioness, he is the Lecturer, and let him account for it if he can.—I shall get little honour by solving this question, says the Philosopher, since his Grace has pointed out the only method, by which it can be done, that is to say, by Chemistry; for that action of bodies which the Chemists call *precipitation*, will answer it in all respects; but the explanation of it is a task so difficult, that I must defer it till another opportunity. Some idea, however, I will endeavour to give these young Gentlemen of precipitation, if your Ladyship will favour me with the tincture of bark which I saw in your hand this morning. The bark, Gentlemen, at least the resinous part of the bark, is here suspended in spirits of wine; and so suspended that you see it is perfectly bright. Now in order to precipitate this bark, I must find out a body which has a closer affinity or relation with the spirits of wine, than the bark has (for things inanimate have all their relations when chemically considered;) that body is water, which when I add to the tincture, you will perceive it grow foul; for the spirits of wine will immediately let go the bark to lay hold of the water, which will occupy the space the bark before filled, and that will fall to the bottom. This perhaps may be the case in the atmosphere; some substance may be brought into the air, to which it is nearer allied than to the water, that it suspended before in such a pellucid manner, as not to be seen, but which water becomes obvious, when the air lets it go to embrace its nearer ally, and by uniting first into small drops, then into larger, becomes too heavy to be suspended by the air, and falls down in *rain*.

But all clouds are not composed of watery vapours only; they are sometimes impregnated with sulphureous and even saline particles, which are exhaled from the earth; for the Chemists will tell you by experience, that volatile bodies will volatilize some fixed bodies, and carry them off: And this happens to be the case here, as may be particularly seen in *Thunder* and *Lightning*, which is occasioned, we may suppose, by the sulphureous and nitrous particles taking fire, and bursting the cloud with a tremendous noise, which is preceded by a flash of fire, much resembling that of lighted *gunpowder*, only more penetrating, which is owing, perhaps, to its extreme volatility.—But look, there is a cloud rising before us, which seems replete with that electrical matter, and may by and by discover, in a more sensible manner, those effects to you which I have been endeavouring to describe.

That there are some sort of nitrous particles, or a substance very much like it raised in the air, is, I think, evident, from that nourishment which rain (and particularly that rain which is attended with thunder) gives to vegetables, above common water; and from the quantities of nitre which have been found in heaps of earth that were exposed to the air, at the same time that it was kept from the rain.

Snow seems to be the small particles of water frozen in the air before they had united into drops, and *hail* seems to be drops of rain frozen in their fall. From the regular figures which *snow* and *hail* put on in their descent, some have been inclined to think, that they contain particles of salt mixed with the water, and which occasioned them to shoot and unite in certain angles; but an experiment should, I think, be tried before this is admitted as true Philosophy, and it might be done by boiling the snow and hail over the fire, till it put on a pellicle or scum at the top, and then setting it in a cold place, for the salts to crystallize, or shoot to the bottom.

"I know nothing of Crystallizations, says Lady *Caroline*, nor shall I ever turn Chemist; therefore, good Sir, give us something more entertaining. Pray can you tell me what occasioned those terrible lights in the air which we had last week."

The *Aurora Borealis*, or northern lights, says he, are occasioned, Madam, by certain *nitrous and sulphureous vapours*, which are thinly spread through the atmosphere above the clouds, where they ferment, and taking fire, the *explosion* of one portion kindles the next, and the flashes succeed one another, till all the vapour is set on fire, the streams whereof seem to converge towards the zenith of the spectator, or that point of the heavens which is immediately over his head.

At this instant up started Master *Long,* and told her Ladyship, if she had done, he would be glad to ask a question: Sir, says she, with a smile, it was you made the compliment, I should be glad to hear your question, for, I dare say, it will be a sensible one. I wish you may find it so, replied he; but what I want to have an account of, is this same *Jack with a Lanthorn*, which so haunts my Lord Marquis's park, and t'other day led my friend *Tom Wilson* into a large pond. Master *Wilson*, you are to understand, had been at his uncle's, where he staid rather too late, and therefore his uncle ordered the Footman to light him home; but *Tom* being a very courageous fellow, and a little obstinate, would walk home alone, and in the dark; but just as he came into the marshy meadow, who should he almost overtake but this same Gentleman, this *Jack with the Lanthorn*, who he mistook for Goody *Curtis*, the chare-woman, and thought she was lighting herself home from work. *Tom* ran to overtake Dame *Curtis*, but Mr. *Jack with his Lanthorn* still kept out of reach, and led my friend *Tom* out of the path, which he did not perceive till he had lost himself; on which *Tom* ran, and *Jack* ran; *Tom* halloo'd, and *Jack* would not answer; at last souse came *Tom* into *Duckweed Pond,* where he might have lain till this time, if Mr. *Goodall* had not heard him call out as he was riding by, and ran to his assistance. This put all the company in good humour, and *Tom* had good nature and good sense enough to join them in the laugh, which being subsided, our Philosopher thus proceeded in his Lecture.

The *Ignis Fatuus, Jack with a Lanthorn,* or *Will with the Wisp,* as it is frequently called, says he, is supposed to be only a *fat, unctuous,* and *sulphureous vapour,* which in the night appears lucid, and being driven about by the air near the earth's surface, is often mistaken for a light in a lanthorn, as my friend Master *Wilson* can testify. Vapours of this kind are in the night frequently kindled in the air, and some of them appear like falling stars, and are by ignorant people so called.

It may be here necessary to mention that beautiful phenomenon the Rainbow, since it has the appearance of a meteor, though, in reality, it is none; for the Rainbow is occasioned by the refraction or reflection of the sun's beams from the very small drops of a cloud or mist seen in a certain angle made by two lines, the one drawn from the sun, and the other from the eye of the spectator, to those small drops in the cloud which reflect the sun's beams: so that two persons looking on a Rainbow at the same time, do not, in reality, see the same Rainbow.

There are other appearances in the atmosphere which ought to be taken notice of, and these are the halo's, or circles, which sometimes seem to encompass the sun and moon, and are often of different colours. These always appear in a *rimy* or *frosty* season, and are therefore, we may suppose, occasioned by the refraction of light, in the frozen particles in the air.

Here the Lecture would have ended, but a sudden clap of thunder brought on fresh matter for meditation; some of the company, and particularly the Ladies, endeavoured to avoid the lightning; but Master *Telescope*, after the second clap, threw up the sash, and assured the Ladies and Gentlemen there was no danger, for that the clouds were very high in the air. The danger, in a thunder-storm, says he, is in proportion to the violence of the tempest, and the distance of the clouds; but this tempest is not violent, and that the cloud is at a great distance, or high in the air, you may know by the length of time there is between your seeing the flash of lightning, and hearing the clap of thunder. Look, see how the sky opens, to emit the fire, presently you will hear the thunder; for you know we see the fire from a gun at a distance long before we hear the report! There it is! and how tremendous! These tempests always put me in mind of that beautiful passage in *Shakespear's King Lear*; where when the good old King is out in a storm, and obliged to fly from his unnatural children, he says,

———Let the great gods,
That keep this dreadful thund'ring o'er our heads,
Find out their enemies now. Tremble, thou wretch,
That hast within thee undivulged crimes
Unwhipt of justice! Hide thee, thou bloody hand;
Thou perjur'd, and thou simular of virtue,
That art incestuous! Caitiff, shake to pieces,
That under covert and convenient seeming
Has practis'd on man's life! Close pent-up guilt,
Rive your concealing continents, and ask
These dreadful summoners grace!—
This tempest will not give me leave to ponder
On things would hurt me more——

Poor naked wretches, wheresoe'er you are,
That bide the pelting of this pitiless storm!

How shall your houseless heads, and unfed sides,
Your loop'd and window'd raggedness, defend you
From seasons such as these?—O, I have ta'en
Too little care of this: Take physic, pomp!
Expose thyself to feel what wretches feel,
That thou may'st shake the superflux to them,
And shew the Heav'ns more just.

LECTURE IV
Of Mountains, Springs, Rivers, and the Sea.

Wᴇ ᴄᴏᴍᴇ ɴᴏᴡ, says the Philosopher, to the consideration of things with which we are more intimately acquainted, but which are not, on that account, the less wonderful. How was that Mountain lifted up to the sky? How came this crystal Spring to bubble on its lofty brow, or that large River to flow from its massy side? But above all, how came this mighty body of water, the Sea, so collected together; and why and how was it impregnated with salt, seeing the fish and other animals taken out of it are perfectly fresh? These are questions not to be answered even by the Sages in science. Here the Philosopher, at the end of his judgment, and lost in admiration, can only say with the Psalmist, *They that go down into the Sea, and occupy their business in the great waters, these men see the greatness of God, and his wonders in the deep.* Wonderful are thy works, O Lord, in judgment hast thou made them all!—The earth is full of thy greatness!

It is the business of philosophy, however, to enquire into these things, tho' our enquiries are sometimes vain; we shall, therefore, in this Lecture give the best account we can of the *Mountains, Springs, Rivers,* and the *Sea.*

The ancients supposed that Mountains were originally occasioned by the Deluge, before which time they imagined that the earth was a perfect level; and a certain Abbot was taken into custody and punished, for asserting that the earth was round; tho' there is so great a necessity for its being so, that according to the properties with which the Almighty has endowed the substances that compose the world, it could not conveniently subsist in any other form; for, not to mention the formation of rivers, which are generally occasioned by the mists that fall on the mountains, if the earth was not round it would be for ever covered with water; for it is, I think, supposed, that there is full as much water as earth, and as the water is specifically lighter than earth, that would be always uppermost, and we should have no dry land.

I protest, says Lady *Caroline*, I think you carry this argument too far, and seem to question the power of the Creator. How can you tell that the earth and water thus disposed would have that effect? From daily experience, Madam, says the Philosopher. Throw this stone into the moat and you will see it sink, or this clot of dirt, and it will fall to the bottom. But, says she, this is not always the case, for when I water my flowers the water sinks into the ground and disappears. That is because there is abundantly more earth than water, Madam, says he; and the earth being porous, or hollow, the water runs into the cavities and fills them; but was you to keep on pouring out of the water-pot till all these crevices were full, you would find the water flow at top, and the garden-mould, or earth, would remain at the bottom; for if you take a pint pot of earth, and another of water, and mix them ever so well together, the earth will in a little time subside or fall to the bottom, and the water will be seen at the top. This is to me a demonstration, Madam; and it is so far from calling in question the wisdom of God, that it is vindicating his wisdom in the works of Creation. So that you may perceive from hence, as well as from the motion of the heavenly bodies, that the earth is round, and that the ancients were in an error.

And with regard to Mountains, tho' the Deluge might throw up many, and much alter the face of the earth, yet from the great use mountains are of in collecting the waters of the atmosphere into springs and rivers, it is reasonable to suppose there were mountains even in the first age of the world.

If I am not mistaken, says Lady *Twilight*, it has been supposed, even by men of learning, that this irregularity of the earth's surface was occasioned by some Comets striking against it; and this opinion, I know, put Lady *Lucy* and many others in great pain when the late Comet was expected. What say you to this, young Gentleman?

I am unable to answer for all the extravagant conceits and ridiculous follies of the human race, Madam, says he, and your Ladyship might as well expect me to give a reason for the poor Soldier's prophesying an earthquake some time ago, and of the terrors of the people on that occasion, as to account for this. That the Earth has undergone amazing changes since its first formation, is, I think, evident from the contents of some mountains even in our own country, in which we find not only petrefactions in abundance, but the shells of sea fish, and even the bones of animals that were never inhabitants of this climate. At *Reading* in *Berkshire*, which is above forty miles from the sea, there is a stratum of oyster-shells which appear like real oysters, and are spread through a hill of considerable extent; they lie upon a chalky rock in a bed of sand, much resembling that of the sea, and the upper part of the hill, which is a loamy soil, is thirty or forty feet perpendicular above them; and at *Burton*, near *Petworth* in *Sussex*, was dug out of a pit, the bones or skeleton of an elephant. Numberless curiosities of this kind have been discovered here, (some of which I shall take particular notice of in my next course of Lectures) but I think there are few but what may be accounted for from the effects of the deluge, earthquakes, and subterraneous fires. Earthquakes at the bottom of the sea, for instance, have sometimes thrown up mountains or little islands, with the fish upon them, which have been covered by the sandy or loose earth giving way and falling over them. It is not long since an island was raised in this manner, in the *Archipelago*, of ten miles circumference, the hills of which abound with oysters not yet petrified, and which are much larger than those taken on the coast, whence we may conclude, that they were thrown up from the deepest part of the sea. Sea-fish have been also found in other mountains, some of which have been petrified, while others have been found with the flesh only browned or mummied.

And from the amazing quantity of fire contained in the earth, and of the subterranean air rarified thereby, great alterations must have been made in its surface, in the course of so many years.

Very well, says Lady *Caroline*, and so you are going to turn the earth into a hot-bed, and I suppose we, who are its inhabitants, are by and by to be complimented with the title of mushrooms and cucumbers, or perhaps pumpkins. This is fine philosophy, indeed. Have patience, my dear, says the Marchioness. Patience, Ma'am, returned Lady *Caroline*, why I hope your Ladyship would not have me believe, that we have a furnace of fire under us? I don't know, Madam, whether it be immediately under us or not, replied the little Philosopher; but that there are a number of those furnaces in the earth is beyond dispute, and is evidently proved by the great number of burning mountains, which are continually sending up flames, attended with large stones and metallic substances. I am sorry his Grace of *Galaxy* is gone, Madam, for he would have set you right in this particular, which, pardon me, I shall not attempt, since I find my veracity is so much questioned. The company all laughed at the Philosopher in a *pet*; but the Marchioness took up the matter, and soon put an end to the dispute. She blamed Lady *Caroline* for offering to decide upon a point which she did not understand; and then turning to the young Gentleman, told him, that patience ought to be a principal ingredient in the character of a Philosopher: upon which Lady *Caroline* and he composed their difference with a mutual smile, and after asking the Marchioness pardon for betraying too much warmth, even in the cause of truth, he told Lady *Caroline*, she should have some account of these mountains from the best authority, when taking a book out of his pocket, he read as follows:

"The most famous of these mountains is *Ætna* in *Sicily*, whose eruptions of flame and smoke are discovered at a great distance, by those that sail on the *Mediterranean*, even as far as the harbour of *Malta*, which is forty *German* miles from the shore of *Sicily*. Tho' fire and smoke are continually vomiting up by it, yet at some particular times it rages with greater violence. In the year 1536 it shook all *Sicily*, from the first to the twelfth of *May*; after that, there was heard a most horrible bellowing and cracking, as if great guns had been fired: there were a great many houses overthrown throughout the whole island. When this storm had continued about eleven days, the ground opened in several places, and dreadful gapings appeared here and there, from which issued forth fire and flame with great violence, which in four days consumed and burnt up all that were within five leagues of *Ætna*. A little after the funnel, which is on the top of the mountain, disgorged a great quantity of hot embers and ashes, for three whole days together, which were not only dispersed throughout the whole island, but also carried beyond sea to *Italy*; and several ships that were sailing to *Venice*, at two hundred leagues distance, suffered damage. *Facellus* hath given us an historical account of the eruptions of this mountain, and says, that the bottom of it is one hundred leagues in circuit.

Hecla, a mountain in *Iceland*, rages sometimes with as great violence as *Ætna*, and casts out great stones. The imprisoned fire often, by want of vent, causes horrible sounds, like lamentations and howlings, which make some credulous people think it the place of Hell, where the souls of the wicked are tormented.

Vesuvius in *Campania*, not far from the town of *Naples*, tho' it be planted with most fruitful vines, and at other times yieldeth the best *Muscadel* wine; yet it is very often annoyed with violent eruptions. *Dion Cassius* relates, that in the reign of *Vespasian*, there was such a dreadful eruption of impetuous flames, that great quantities of ashes and sulphureous smoke were not only carried to *Rome* by the wind, but also beyond the *Mediterranean*, into *Africa*, and even into *Egypt*. Moreover, birds were suffocated in the air, and fell down dead upon the ground, and fishes perished in the neighbouring

waters, which were made hot and infected by it. There happened another eruption in *Martial*'s time, which he elegantly describes in one of his *Epigrams*, and laments the sad change of the mountain, which he saw first in its verdure, and immediately after black with ashes and embers. When the burning ceased, the rain and dew watered the surface of the mountain, and made these sulphureous ashes and embers fruitful, so that they produced a large increase of excellent wine; but when the mountain began to burn again, and to disgorge fire and smoke afresh, (which sometimes happened within a few years) then were the neighbouring fields burnt up, and the highways made dangerous to travellers.

A mountain in *Java*, not far from the town of *Panacura*, in the year 1586, was shattered to pieces by a violent eruption of glowing sulphur (tho' it had never burnt before) whereby (as it was reported) 10,000 people perished in the under-land fields: It threw up large stones and cast them as far as *Pancras*, and continued for three days to throw out so much black smoke, mixed with flame and hot embers, that it darkened the face of the Sun, and made the day appear as dark as the night."

There are a great number of other mountains, or (as your Ladyship is pleased to call them) furnaces in the known world, which I shall take some notice of in my next course of Lectures.

We come now to the consideration of Springs, which are occasioned principally, we may suppose, by the water exhaled from the sea, rivers, lakes, and marshy places, and, forming clouds, are dispersed by the winds. These clouds, when they are so collected together as to become too heavy to be supported by the air, fall down in rain to water the herbs and plants, but those that are lighter, being driven aloft in the air, dash against the mountains, and to them give up their contents in small particles; whence entering the crevices, they descend till they meet together, and form Springs; and this is the reason why we have such plenty of Springs in mountainous countries, and few or none in those that are flat. And you may observe, that it frequently rains in hilly countries, when it is clear and fine in the valleys beneath; for the air in the valleys is dense enough to support the clouds and keep them suspended; but being driven up among the mountains, where, in consequence of their height, the air is so much lighter, they descend in mists or such small drops of rain that will not run off, as is the case in a heavy rain, but sink into the crevices of the earth in the manner already mentioned. Now that a great part of this water is exhaled from the sea, may be known by the extraordinary rains and great dews which fall upon islands that are surrounded by the sea: But some Springs, it is reasonable to suppose, have their source from the ocean, since those which we meet with near the sea, are generally somewhat salt or brackish.

These springs thus formed by the mists on mountains, and the rain meeting together, form little rivulets or brooks, and those again uniting, compose large rivers, which empty themselves into the sea, and in this manner the water, exhaled from the sea by the sun, is returned to it again; for Providence has established such wise laws or regulations for the world, that no part of the elements can be annihilated. But the very large rivers must have some other source besides the springs formed by the mists, dews, and rains, since these seem insufficient to support their prodigious discharge; it is therefore no improbable conjecture to suppose that they have some communication with the sea, and that the salt water is purified and rendered sweet by passing through the sand, gravel, and crevices of the earth. And this I shall endeavour to prove in my next Course of Lectures.

Lakes are collections of water contained in the cavities of the surface of the earth, some of which are said to be stagnant, and made up of the waste water that flows, after rain or snow, from the adjacent countries, and these must be unwholsome. Other Lakes are supplied by rivers, the contents of which they receive and convey under ground, to form other springs and rivers; others, again, are fed by springs which arise in the Lake itself, and some (as that of *Haerlem*, and other salt Lakes) have a communication, it is supposed, with the sea, whence they receive their waters, and afterwards discharge them by subterranean streams.

The Sea is a great collection of waters in the deep valleys of the earth; I say, in the deep valleys; for if there were not prodigious cavities in the earth to contain this amazing quantity of water, thus collected together, the whole surface of the globe would be over-flowed; for the water being lighter than the earth, would be above the earth, as the air is above the water.

Now you speak of the Sea, says the Marchioness, I wish you would tell me, why the Sea water is always salt. Madam, replied he, I wish I could, but it is beyond the reach of my Philosophy; and, indeed, I believe, of any Philosophy whatever. You might as well ask me, why there is water, as why there is salt in the water, which indeed seems almost as much an element as that: And I have often thought, from the prodigious quantity of salt distributed in the earth and water, that it must have qualities that we know not of, and answer purposes in the scale of Being with which we are unacquainted.

The most remarkable quality in the Sea, next to its saltness, is that motion or rising and falling of the water, which we call *tides*, and which is occasioned by the attraction of the Moon; for that part of the water in the great ocean, which is nearest the Moon, being strongly attracted, is raised higher than the rest; and the part opposite to it, on the contrary side, being least attracted, is also higher than the rest: and these two opposite sides of the surface of the water, in the great ocean, following the motion of the Moon from East to West, and striking against the large coasts of the Continent, from thence rebound back again, and so make *floods* and *ebbs*, in narrow seas and rivers, at a distance from the great ocean. This also accounts for the periodical times of the *tides*, and for their constantly following the course of the Moon.

LECTURE V
Of Minerals, Vegetables, and Animals.

COULD A PHILOSOPHER condescend to envy the Great, it would not be for their sumptuous palaces and numerous attendants, but for the means and opportunities they have of enquiring into the secrets of Nature, and contemplating the wonderful works of God. There is no subject so worthy of a rational creature, except that of promoting the happiness of Mankind; and none, except that, can give a man of refined taste, and good understanding, so much real satisfaction. But 'tis our misfortune, that few engage in those enquiries, but men of small estate, whose circumstances will not permit them to spare the time, nor support the expence of travelling, which is often necessary to obtain the knowledge they seek after, and for the want of which they are obliged to depend on the relations of those, who have not, perhaps, been so accurate or so faithful as they ought. Considering the quantity of foreign drugs that are used in *Britain*, it is amazing how little even those who deal in them know of the matter; so little, indeed, that they cannot tell where they grow, or how they are found or manufactured; are unable to distinguish the genuine from the factitious, and may therefore, through mistake, often substitute the one for the other. Health and Life are of too much consequence to be trifled with; yet these are neglected, while Fashion, Dress, and Diversions, are sought after throughout the world. This is a melancholy consideration; but this, you'll say, is no part of our Lecture, therefore we shall drop a subject which has thrust itself, as it were, into our way, and speak of the contents of the earth and its products, and inhabitants: for this globe, besides the earth and water which are necessary for the production and support of Plants and Animals, contains other materials which have been found useful to Man. That Reflecting Telescope, this Gold Watch, and Lady *Caroline's* Diamond Earrings, were all dug out of the Earth; at least, the materials were there found of which these things are composed.

Those sorts of earth which, with the assistance of rain, produce Vegetables or Plants in such abundance, are *common mould*, *loam*, *clay*, and *sandy soils*. There are earths, also, that are different from these, and which are used in medicine, as the *Japan Earth, Armenian Bole*, &c.

The barren parts of the earth are, for the most part, *sand*, *gravel*, *chalk*, and *rocks*; for these produce nothing, unless they have earth mixed with them.—Of barren sands there are various kinds, though their chief difference is in their colour; for the sand which we throw on paper, to prevent blotting, and that the maid throws on the floor, are both composed of little irregular stones, without any earth, and of such there are large deserts in some parts of the world, and one in particular, where *Cambyses*, an Eastern Monarch, lost an army of 50,000 men. Sure, says Lady *Caroline*, you must mistake, Sir. How was it possible for a whole army to be lost in that manner? Why, Madam, returned the Philosopher, the wind, as it frequently does in those parts, raised the sands in clouds for many days together, and the whole army was smothered. And if you read the Life of *Alexander the Great*, you'll find, Madam, that his army was in great danger, when he crossed the same desert, in his frantick expedition to visit the temple of his pretended Father *Jupiter Ammon*—But we return to our subject.

Besides these materials which compose the surface of the earth, if we dig deeper, we frequently find bodies very different from those we discover near the surface; and these, because they are discovered by digging into the bowels of the earth, are called by the common name of *Fossils*; though under this head are included all *metals*, and *metallic ores, minerals,* or half *metals*, stones of various sorts, *petrifactions*, or *animal* substances turned into stone; and many other bodies which have a texture between stone and earth, as, *oker* of several sorts, with one of which the Farmers colour their sheep; *black lead*, with which are made those pencils that we use for drawing; and some kinds of *chalk*, *sea coal*, and other bodies that are harder than earth, and yet not of the consistency of perfect stone.

Of *stones*, there are an amazing variety. They are classed by Naturalists under two heads, that is to say, *spars* and *crystals*; and by others into *vulgar* and *precious stones*. Some of the most considerable, both for beauty and use, are *marble, alabaster, porphyry, granite, free-stone,* &c. *Flints, agats, carnelians,* and *pebbles,* under which kind are placed the *precious stones,* otherwise called *gems* or *jewels;* which are only *stones* of an excessive hardness, and which, when cut and polished, have an extraordinary lustre. The most valuable of these are *diamonds, rubies, saphires, amethysts, emeralds, topazes* and *opals*.

But there are other stones, which, tho' void of beauty, may, perhaps, have more virtue than many of those already mentioned; such as the *loadstone*, which has the property of directing the needle in the mariners compass always to or near the North Pole; by which means we are enabled to sail even in the darkest night[.] Such also are *whetstones*, with which we sharpen our knives and other edge tools; *limestones, talc, calamine,* or *lapis calaminaris,* and many others.

Beside the bodies already mentioned, there are also found in the earth a variety of salts, such as *rock salt,* or *sal gem, vitriol, nitre,* and many others.

The *minerals, marcasites,* or *semi-metals,* as they are called by the Chemists, are *antimony, zink, bismuth,* &c. These are not inflammable, ductile, or malleable, but are hard and brittle, and may be reduced to powder, and the first after melting, may be calcined by fire.

Mercury or *quicksilver*, has generally been classed with *semi-metals*, and, indeed, sometimes among the metals; but I think it ought not to be classed under either of these heads, but considered separately; as also should *brimstone*, though it be a part of the composition of *crude antimony*.

Ores are those kinds of earth which are dug out of mines, and that contain in them metallic particles from whence metals are extracted.

Metals are distinguished from other bodies by their weight, fusibility or melting in the fire, and their malleability, or giving way, and extending under the stroke of the hammer without breaking in pieces. These are six, viz. *gold, silver, copper, tin, lead,* and *iron*, which last is the most valuable of them all. They are seldom or never found in any part of the earth but what is mountainous, which, by the way, in some measure proves what we ventured to assert in a former Lecture, *viz*. that there were mountains before the Deluge; for that there were metals before the Deluge appears by what is said in Holy Writ concerning *Tubal Cain,* who wrought in brass, &c. and was the inventor of organs.

All *stones, minerals,* and *metals,* are supposed to grow organically in the earth from their proper seeds, as vegetables do on the earth's surface. And what sort of bodies are to be found deeper in the earth, I mean towards its centre, is unknown to us; for we can only make ourselves acquainted with the fossils contained in its shell, and the vegetables and animals on its surface, whose nature and properties alone are, indeed, too many to be discovered by human sagacity.

Of Vegetables or Plants.

The Vegetables or Plants growing on the earth may be divided into three classes, I mean those of *herbs, shrubs,* and *trees.*

Herbs are those sort of vegetables whose stalks are soft, and have no wood in them, as *parsley, lettuce, violets, pinks, grass nettles, thistles,* and an infinite number of others.

Shrubs are those plants which, tho' woody, never grow into trees, but bow down their branches near the earth's surface; such are those plants that produce *roses, honeysuckles, gooseberries, currants,* and the like.

But trees shoot up in one great stem or body, and rise to a considerable distance from the ground before they spread their branches, as may be seen by the *oak,* the *beech,* the *elm,* the *ash,* the *fir,* the *walnut-tree, cherry-tree,* and others. From the bodies of trees we have our timber for building, and of the oak-tree in particular for ship-building, no timber being so tough, strong, and durable, as old *English* oak; nor does any tree, perhaps, yield more timber; for there was one lately sold for forty pounds, from *Langley* woods, belonging to the Bishop of *Salisbury,* which measured six feet two inches in diameter, contained ten tons of timber, and was supposed to be a thousand years old.

> From a small acorn see the oak arise
> Supremely tall, and tow'ring in the skies!
> Queen of the groves, her stately head she rears,
> Her bulk increasing with the length of years;
> Now ploughs the sea, a warlike gallant ship!
> Whilst in her womb destructive thunders sleep!
> Hence *Britain* boasts her wide extensive reign,
> And by th' expanded acorn rules the Main.

The most considerable parts of plants are the *root,* the *stalk,* the *leaves,* the *flowers,* and the *seed;* most of them have these several parts, tho' there are some, indeed, that have no stalk, as the *aloe;* others that have no leaves, as *savine;* and others that have no flowers, as *fern.* But I think there are none without *root* or *seed,* though some say that *fern* is an exception as to the last.

What most excites our wonder with respect to plants (and what, indeed, has been the subject of much dispute among the learned) is their *nourishment* and *propagation.*—This, says Master *Blossom,* I have often heard my father discourse upon when I have been in the garden with him; but as what he said has escaped my memory, I should be glad, Sir, if you would tell me how they receive their nourishment, and how their species are propagated. A disquisition of this nature, says the little Philosopher, would take up too much of your time, and could not be understood without reciting many experiments and observations that have been made by the learned; I shall, therefore, defer the consideration of these till my next course of Lectures. I see no reason for that, says Master *Wilson*, nor to me does there appear any difficulty in the affair. Why, they receive their nourishment from the earth, don't they? And you sow the seeds of the old plants and they produce new ones.

You are too apt, Master *Wilson*, says the Philosopher, to talk about things you don't understand. The earth has not, perhaps, so much to do with the nourishment of plants as is generally imagined; for, without water, and particularly rain water and dew, there would be but little increase in vegetables of any kind; and this you may know by the languid state of plants in a dry season, tho' watered ever so often from the river or well. This is known also by the small quantity of earth which is taken up in the growth of plants; for both Mr. *Boyle* and Dr. *Woodward* raised several plants in earth watered with rain or spring-water, and even distilled water, and upon weighing the dry earth, both before and after the production of the plants, they have found that very little of it was diminished or taken up by the plant. Taken up by the plant, says Lady *Caroline*, in some surprize, why you don't imagine there is earth in herbs and trees? Indeed I do, Madam, replied the little Philosopher, and have already hinted as much in what was said on the four elements, and at the same time told your Ladyship, if I mistake not, how it might be extracted from the plant; which was, by burning the plant to ashes, and washing off the salts, as your laundry maid does when she makes lye; for when these salts are washed away the remainder will be earth.

If the earth contributes so little towards the production of plants, says Master *Blyth*, the water, I apprehend, must be a good deal concerned, and that is evident from the quantity of water which most plants require to keep them in a state of health and vigour. Your observation, says the Philosopher, deserves some notice; but how will you account for the growth of plants in sandy deserts where it seldom rains, and of plants, too, that contain juices in great abundance; for God Almighty, for the preservation of his creatures, has caused those wonderful plants to grow in such barren deserts to supply, in some measure, the want of water; and some are so constructed as to hold great quantities of water for the use of animals. This is the case of the ground Pine*, which, tho' it seems to grow like a fungus or excrescence on the branch of a tree, often contains a pint or quart of sweet water for the birds, beasts, and even men, to refresh themselves with in the sultry climates where they abound. But a plant may hold much water for the subsistance of animals, and yet not subsist on water itself; and that this is the case experience testifies. Dr. *Woodward* put a plant of *spearmint*, which weighed 27 grains, into a phial of water, where it stood 77 days, and in that time drank up 2558 grains of spring water; and then being taken out weighed 42 grains, so that the increase was only 15 grains, which is not a hundredth part of the water expended—We are therefore to look for other principles of vegetation than what are generally known; but this I shall consider in my next course of Lectures.

What the plant can obtain by the earth, water, and otherwise for its nourishment, is

---

* For a more particular account of this plant, we must refer our readers to the *Christian's Magazine*, Numb. II. where it is introduced with suitable reflections to demonstrate the wonders of God in the works of creation.

generally supposed to be received by the fibres of the roots, and conveyed by the stalk or body of the plant up into the branches and leaves thro' small tubes, and then returned by the bark to the root again; so that there is a constant circulation of vital fluids in plants as well as in animals. But I am inclined to think, that a great part of the nourishment of plants is received by the pores of the leaves and skin or bark, as well as from the root, else how happens it that plants are so much refreshed by the dew?

Plants also require air for their nourishment, as well as a circulation of these alimentary juices; for they respire as well as animals, and for that respiration require fresh air, and even exercise; since we know that plants, that are always confined in a close room, will never rise to perfection. And that they perspire as well as animals is evident from the instance of the *mint* growing in spring water above-mentioned; for if not a hundredth part of the water taken up by that plant became a part of the plant itself, all the rest must be perspired thro' the pores, or little imperceptible holes in the skin and leaves. This calls to my mind, says Lady *Caroline,* a charge my Lord Marquis gave me, which was, never to sit in the *yew arbor*; for the matter perspired by the yew-tree, says he, is noxious, and will make you ill; and I believe that was the reason of his Lordship's ordering that old arbor to be demolished.

But pray, Sir, why and in what manner can plants perspire? For the same reason, Madam, and in the same manner, perhaps, that animals do, returned the Philosopher. It is occasioned, probably, by heat; for we know that they perspire abundantly more in summer than in winter; nay, when this vegetative principle has been long checked by cold, it breaks out with such force, when warm weather comes on, that it is no uncommon thing, in the cold northern countries, to see the trees covered with snow one week, and with blossoms the next.

Plants are propagated different ways, but the most general method is by seed. Some plants, however, are raised by a part of the root of the old plant set in the ground, as potatoes; others, by new roots propagated from the old ones, as *hyacinths* and *tulips*; others, by cutting off branches and putting them into the ground, which will there take root and grow, as *vines*; and others are propagated by grafting and budding, or inoculation. But what I represented as most mysterious, and intend for the subject of a Lecture in my next Course, is the Sexes of Plants; for many sorts have both male and female organs, and the one will not flourish and increase without the aid of the other.

Of Animals.

We are now to speak of the Animals that inhabit the earth, which are naturally divided into *Men* and *Brutes.*

Of Men, there seem to be four different sorts—Nay, don't be frightned, Lady *Caroline!* —Sir, says she, I should have made no objection, had you said four hundred, provided you had distinguished them according to their different dispositions.—True, Madam, says the Philosopher, or according to their different features, and then you might have said four hundred thousand; for it is very true, Madam, tho' very wonderful, that out of four hundred thousand faces you will not find two exactly alike; and but for this miraculous and gracious providence in God, the world would have been all in confusion. But the division I would willingly make of men, Lady *Caroline,* is that of *white, tawney, black,* and *red;* and these you will allow are, with respect to colour, essentially different. Most of the *Europeans,* and some of the *Asiatics,* are *white;* the *Africans* on the coast of the *Mediterranean* sea are *tawney;* those on the coast of *Guinea black;* and the original *Americans, red,* or of a red copper colour: How they came so is only known to their Maker; and therefore I beg you would spare yourselves the trouble of asking me any questions on that head.

Brutes may be divided into four classes; that is to say, 1. *Aerial,* or such as have wings and fly in the air, as *birds, wasps, flies,* &c. 2. *Terrestrial,* or those who are confined to the earth, as *quadrupeds,* or four-footed beasts; *reptiles,* which have many feet; and *serpents,* which have no feet at all. 3. *Aquatick,* or those who live in the water, as *fish* of all kinds, whether they are covered with scales or shells, or are like the *eel,* without either. 4. *Amphibious,* or those that can live for a long time either upon the earth, or in the water; as *otters, alligators, turtles,* &c. I say for a long time, because I apprehend that the use of both these elements are necessary for the subsistance of those animals; and that tho' they can live for a considerable time upon land in the open air, or as long in the water, excluded in a manner from air, yet they would languish and die, if confined entirely either to the one or the other of these elements.

In this division of animals we are to observe, however, that there are some which cannot be considered under either class, as being, as it were, of a middle nature and partaking of two kinds; thus *bats* seem to be part beasts and part birds. Some *reptiles,* likewise, and some of the water animals, want one or more of the five senses with which other animals are endowed, as *worms, cockles, oysters,* &c. If I mistake not, says Lady *Caroline,* I have seen the animals divided into different classes in books of Natural History, and described under the heads of *beasts, birds, fishes,* and *insects.* Very true, Madam, says the Philosopher; but the present method suits my present purpose the best, and can make no alteration in the nature of things; however, as I have not yet mentioned the word *insects,* tho' they are included in my division of animals, it may be necessary for me to observe, that they are so called from a separation in their bodies, by which they are seemingly divided into two parts, those parts being only joined together by a small ligament, as in *flies, wasps,* &c. And as some of these *insects* undergo different changes, and in time become quite different animals, I shall consider them more particularly in my next course of Lectures, not having time for it at present; for it is a field that is full of wonders, and ought to be examined with great attention. There is something so amazing and miraculous in the transformation of insects, that I am lost in reflection whenever the subject strikes my mind, and sometimes inclined to think that other animals may undergo some such change. Who, that had not made the observation, would think, Madam, that this *grub* crawling, or rather sleeping here, would by and by become a fine *butterfly,* decked out in all the gaudy colours of the rainbow; or that this *silk-worm* should be capable of assuming so many different forms. And is it not altogether as miraculous, that if some animals are cut in pieces, every separate piece or part of the original animal will become one entire animal of itself? Yet that the *polype* or *polypus* is endowed with this property has been demonstrated; and I have here one that was divided into several parts some time ago, which parts are now become distinct and perfect polypes and alive, as you may see by viewing them thro' this microscope.

But the sagacity and acute senses of some of the animals (in which they seem to exceed

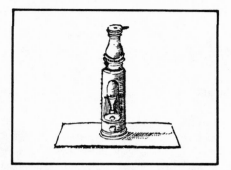

man) are altogether as surprizing, as I shall demonstrate in my next course. In your next course, says Master *Wilson,* why don't you do it now? Peace, prythee, *Tom,* says the Philosopher, learn this first, and then I'll talk to you about *beavers* building of houses; *bees* forming themselves into a society and choosing a Queen to govern them; *birds* knowing the latitude and longitude, and sailing over sea thro' vast tracks of air, from one country to another, without the use of any compass; and of other things, which are sufficient, I think, to lower the pride of man, and make even Philosophers blush at their own ignorance.—And now, Lady *Caroline,* prepare to hear a few hard words and I will finish this Lecture. But why must it be finished in an unintelligible manner? says the Lady. Because I cannot deliver what I am going to say, Madam, without making use of the terms of art, says he, and those I must desire your Ladyship, and the rest of the good company, to learn from Mr. *Newbery's* pocket dictionary, or some other book of that kind.

All animals receive their food at the mouth, and most animals, but especially those of the human kind, chew it there till it is intimately mixed with the saliva or spittle, and thereby prepared for the easier and better digestion in the stomach. When the stomach has digested the food it is thence conveyed into the *guts* (pardon the expression, Ladies, for I cannot avoid it) through which it is moved gently, by what is called the *peristaltick motion;* as it passes there, the *chyle,* which is the nutritive part, is separated by the *lacteal veins,* from the excrementitious part, and by them conveyed into the blood, with which it circulates, and is concocted into blood also; and this circulation is thus performed: The blood being, by the *vena cava,* brought into the right ventricle of the heart, by the contraction of that muscle, is forced into the *pulmonary artery* of the lungs; where the air, which is continually inspired or drawn in by the lungs, mixes with and enlivens it; and from thence the blood, being conveyed by the *pulmonary vein* into the left ventricle of the heart, the contraction of the heart forces it out, and by the arteries distributes it into all parts of the body, from whence it returns by the veins to the right ventricle of the heart, to pursue the same course again, in order to communicate life and heat to every part of this wonderful machine, the body. But this is not all; for, according to Anatomists, some part of the blood, in the course of its circulation, goes to the head; where a portion of it is separated by the brain, and concocted into *animal spirits,* which are distributed by the nerves, and impart sense and motion throughout the body. The instruments of motion, however, are the muscles; the fibres, or small threads, whereof contracting themselves, move the different parts of the body; which in some of them is done by the direction of the mind, and called *voluntary motion;* but, in others, the mind seems not to be concerned, and therefore these motions are called *involuntary.*

This is the progress of animal life; by which you will perceive, that a man may, even at home, and within himself, see the Wonders of God in the Works of Creation.

We have now finished our survey of the Universe, and considered these great masses of matter, the Stars and Planets; but particularly our earth and its inhabitants; all which large bodies are made up of inconceivably small *bodies,* or *atoms:* And by the figure, texture, bulk, and motion of these insensible *corpuscles,* or infinitely small bodies, all the phænomena of larger bodies may be explained.

LECTURE VI
Of the Five Senses of Man, and of his Understanding.

AT OUR NEXT meeting there was a great deal of good company, who came to hear the *Boys Philosophy,* as they called it; on which account I could observe that Master *Telescope* took less pains to be understood by the young Gentlemen and Ladies, and addressed himself more particularly to those of greater abilities.

As the company came in laughing, and affected to talk, and behaved in a supercilious manner, which even some great personages do in these our days of refinement, he stood silent, till my Lord Marquis desired him to open the Lecture; upon which he bowed, to his Lordship and the rest of the company and began; but had scarcely spoke three words before he was interrupted by Sir *Harry;* he therefore stopt for some time, and then began again; but the tongue of the young Baronet soon silenced him, and he stood, without speaking, a considerable time. On this, the company looked at each other, and the Marquis bad him go on. My Dear, says the Marchioness, how can you expect this young Gentleman to read a long Lecture, when you know that Sir *Harry,* who loves to hear himself talk of all things, has not patience to support so much taciturnity! Why, Madam, says the Ambassador of *Bantam* (who came in with the Marquis) I thought we had all been assembled to hear this Lecture. That was indeed the intention of our meeting, says the Marchioness; but I hope your Excellency knows the polite world better, than to expect people should be so old fashioned as to behave, on these occasions, with any sort of good-manners or decorum. In my country, says the Ambassador, all the company keep a profound silence at these meetings. It may be so, replied the Marchioness; but, I assure your Excellency, it is not the custom here. Why, Sir, I have been often interrupted in the middle of a fine air, at an Oratorio, by a Gentleman's whistling an Hornpipe; and at the Rehearsal at St. *Paul's,* it is no uncommon thing to hear both Gentlemen and Ladies laugh louder than the organ. Hush, Madam, says the Marquis, if your friends and neighbours are fools, you ought not to expose them, and especially to foreigners. Take care, while you condemn this unpolite behaviour in others, that you don't run into it yourself. *Politeness* is the art of being always agreeable in company; it can therefore seldom deal in *sarcasm* or *irony;* because it should never do any thing to abridge the happiness of others; and you see, my Dear, you have made Sir *Harry* uneasy, for he blushes. The company laughed at Sir *Harry,* who joined them, and being determined to hold his tongue, our Philosopher thus proceeded.

After the cursory view of Nature, which was concluded in my last Lecture, it may not be amiss to examine our own faculties, and see by what means we acquire and treasure up a knowledge of these things; and this is done, I apprehend, by means of the *senses,* the

operations of the *mind,* and the *memory,* which last may be called the Storehouse of the *understanding.* The first time little Master is brought to a looking-glass, he thinks he has found a new play-mate, and calls out *Little boy! little boy!* for having never seen his own face before, it is no wonder that he should not know it. Here is the idea, therefore, of something new acquired by *sight.*—Presently the father, and mother, and nurse come forward to partake of the child's diversion. Upon seeing these figures in the glass with whom he is so well acquainted, he immediately calls out, *There, Papa! there, Mamma! there, Nurse!* And now the *mind* begins to operate; for feeling his father's hand on his own head, and seeing it on the little boy's head in the glass, he cries, *There me!*—Now this transaction is lodged in the *memory,* which, whenever a looking-glass is mentioned, will give back to the mind this idea of its reflecting objects.

The whole company were pleased with this familiar demonstration; but Sir *Harry* asked how he came, of all things, to make use of a looking-glass? Because, Sir, says he, it is an object with which some people are the most intimately acquainted.—As Sir *Harry* is an egregious fop, this reply produced a loud laugh, and Master *Telescope* was looked upon to be a *Wit* as well as a *Philosopher;* however, I am inclined to think the expression was accidental, and not intended to hit Sir *Harry,* because I know his good sense would not permit him to treat an elder and superior in that manner—The laugh being a little subsided, our Philosopher thus proceeded on his Lecture.

All our ideas, therefore, are obtained either by *sensation* or *reflection,* that is to say, by means of our five senses, as *seeing, hearing, smelling, tasting,* and *touching,* or by the *operations of the mind.*

Before you proceed further, says the Countess of *Twylight,* you should, I think, explain to the company what is meant by the term *idea.* That, I apprehend, is sufficiently explained by what was said about the looking glass, says the Philosopher; but if your Ladyship requires another definition you shall have it. By an *idea,* then, I mean that *image* or *picture,* Madam, which is formed in the *mind,* of any thing which we have *seen,* or even *heard talk of;* for the mind is so adroit and ready at this kind of *painting,* that a town, for instance, is no sooner mentioned, but the *imagination* shapes it into form and presents it to the *memory.* None of this company, I presume, have ever seen *Dresden,* yet there is not one, perhaps, but has formed, or conceived in his mind, some *idea* or *picture* of that unhappy place. Not one of us ever saw the *Nabob*'s prodigious army and elephants, yet we have all formed to ourselves a *picture* of their running away from a small party of our brave countrymen, led against them by the gallant and courageous Colonel *Clive.* When we read in the news-papers a description of a *sea-engagement,* or of the taking of *Louis-bourg, Quebec,* or any other important fortress, the mind immediately gives us a *picture* of the *transaction,* and we see our valiant officers issuing their orders, and their intrepid men furling their sails, firing their guns, scaling the walls, and driving their foes before them. To pursue this subject a little farther—No man has ever seen a *dragon,* a *griffin,* or a *fairy*; yet every one has formed in his mind a *picture, image,* or, in other words, an *idea,* of these imaginary beings—Now when this *idea* or *image* is formed in the mind from a view of the object itself, it may be called an *adequate* or *real idea;* but when it is conceived in the mind without seeing the object, it is an *inadequate* or *imaginary idea.*

I shall begin my discourse of the Senses with that of the SIGHT, says he, because, as Mr. *Addison* observes, the *sight* is the most perfect and pleasing of them all. The organ of *seeing* is the *eye,* which is made up of a number of parts, and so wonderfully contrived for admitting and refracting the rays of light, that those which come from the same point of the object, and fall upon different parts of the pupil, are again brought together at the bottom of the eye, and by that means the whole object is painted on a membrane called the *retina,* which is spread there.

But how is it possible, says Sir *Harry,* for you to know that the object is thus painted on the *retina?* In some measure from the structure of the eye, replied the Philosopher; but, I think, it is manifest from that disorder of the eye which Surgeons call the *gutta serena,* the very complaint which my Lord's Butler has in one of his eyes. If you examine it you will find that he has no sight with that eye, tho' it looks as perfect as the other with which he sees well; this is, therefore, occasioned by some paralytic, or other disorder in that membrane, or expansion of the optic nerve, which we call the *retina,* and proves that all vision arises from thence.

That which produces in us the sensation which we call Seeing, is *light,* for without *light* nothing is visible. Now light may be considered either as it radiates from luminous bodies directly to our eyes, and thus we see those luminous bodies themselves; as the *Sun,* a lighted *torch,* &c. or as it is reflected from other bodies, and thus we see a *flower,* a *man,* &c. or a picture reflected from them to our eyes by the rays of light.

It is to be observed that the bodies which respect the light are of three sorts, 1. Those that emit the rays of light, as the sun and fix'd stars. 2. Those that transmit the rays of light, as the air; and, 3. Those that reflect them, as the Moon, the Earth, Iron, &c. The first we call *luminous,* the second, *pellucid,* and the third, *opaque* bodies. It is also to be observed, that the rays of light themselves are never seen; but by their means we see the luminous bodies from which they originally came, and the opaque bodies from which they are reflected; thus, for instance, when the Moon shines, we cannot see the rays which pass from the Sun to the Moon; but, by their means, we see the Moon from whence they are reflected.

If the eye be placed directly in the Medium through which the rays pass to it, the Medium is not seen; for we never see the air through which the rays come to our eyes. But if a *pellucid* body, thro' which the rays are to pass, be placed at a distance from our eye, that body will be seen, as well as those bodies from whence the rays came that pass through it to our eyes; for instance, he who looks through a pair of spectacles, not only sees bodies through them, but also sees the glass itself; because the glass, being a solid body, reflects some rays of light from its surface; and being placed at a convenient distance from the eye, may be seen by those reflected rays, at the same time that bodies, at a greater distance, are seen by the transmitted rays; and this is the reason, perhaps, why objects are seen more distinctly through a reflecting, than through a refracting telescope.

There are two kinds of opaque bodies, namely, those that are not *specular,* as the *moon,* the *earth,* a *horse,* a *man,* &c. and others that are *specular* or *mirrors,* like those in reflecting telescopes, whose surfaces being polished, reflect the rays in the same order as they came from other bodies, and shew us their images. And rays that are thus reflected from opaque bodies, always bring with them to the eye the idea of colour, tho' this colour in bodies is nothing more than a disposition to reflect to the eye one sort of rays more copiously or in greater plenty than another; for particular rays impress upon the eye particular colours; some are *red,* others *blue, yellow, green,* &c. Now it is to be observed, that every body of light which comes from the *Sun* seems to be compounded of these various sorts of rays; and as some of them are more *refrangible* than others, that is to say, are more turned out of their course in passing from one medium to another, it necessarily follows that they will be separated after such refraction, and their colours appear distinct. The most *refrangible* of these are the *violet,* and the least the *red;* the intermediate ones, in order, are *indigo, blue, green, yellow,* and *orange.*

How do you know, Mr. Philosopher, that colours are separated in this manner? says Sir *Harry.* I have no notion of these doctrines without demonstration. That you may have, if you please, replied the Philosopher. Pray, Master *Lovelace,* hand me that *prism.*

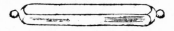

Now, Sir *Harry,* if you will please to hold this *prism* in the beams of the *Sun,* you will see the colours separated in the manner I have mentioned. Please to look, Lady *Caroline,* the separation is very pleasing, and you will find what I said of the *rainbow* in my third Lecture confirmed by this experiment.

All these rays differ not only in *refrangibility* but in *reflexibility;* I mean in the property of being reflected some more easily than others. And hence arise all the various colours of bodies.

The *whiteness* of the Sun's light is owing, it is supposed, to a mixture of all the original colours in a due proportion; and *whiteness* in other bodies, is a disposition to reflect all the colours of light, nearly in the same proportion as they are mixed in the original rays of the Sun; as *blackness,* on the contrary, is only a disposition to absorb or stifle, without reflection, most of the rays of every sort that fall on those bodies; and it is for that reason, we may suppose, that *black* cloaths are warmer than those of any other colour; and are therefore rejected by the inhabitants of hot countries, who choose such colours for their raiment as will reflect the *Sun's* rays, and not absorb them.

Light, as we have already observed, is successively propagated with most amazing swiftness; for it comes from the Sun to the Earth in about seven or eight minutes, tho' at the distance of seventy millions of miles.

HEARING is the next most extensive of our senses, the organ of which is the *Ear,* whose structure is extremely curious, as may be seen in the books of Anatomy.

That which the ear conveys to the brain is called sound, tho' till it reaches and affects the perceptive part, it is in reality nothing but motion; and this motion, which produces in us the perception of sound, is a vibration of the air, occasioned by a very short and quick tremulous motion of the body from whence it is propagated. That sound is conveyed in this manner, may be known by what is observed and felt in the strings of musical instruments, and of bells, which tremble or vibrate as long as we perceive any sound come from them; and from this effect which they produce in us they are called Sounding Bodies.

Sound is propagated at a great rate, but not near so fast as light. I don't know that, says Lady *Caroline*. Then your Ladyship has forgot what passed in our Lecture upon *Air,* replied the Philosopher; and to confirm by experiment what I advanced, I must beg his Lordship to order one of the servants to go a distance into the park, and discharge a *gun*. The Gentlemen were averse to this, it being an observation they had made an hundred times; but to gratify the young people, my Lord ordered his Game-keeper out, and when the piece was discharged, they had the satisfaction of seeing the fire long before they heard the report.

SMELLING is another sense which seems to be excited in us by external bodies, and sometimes by bodies at a great distance; but that which immediately affects the nose, the organ of smelling, and produces in us the sensation of any smell, are effluvia or invisible particles that fly from those bodies to our *olfactory* nerves. How do you prove this, young Gentleman? says Sir *Harry*. Sir, replied the Philosopher, had you been here yesterday, you would not have asked this question, for, as the wind was North-East, the *effluvia* from my Lord's brick kilns were ready to suffocate us; but now the wind is turned to the South-West you observe no such thing, because those *effluvia* are driven a contrary way.

The power which some bodies have of emitting these *effluvia* or steams without being visibly diminished, is to me most amazing; yet that it is true we know by abundant experience. A single grain of *musk* will scent a thousand rooms, and send forth these odoriferous particles for a great number of years without being spent. Surely these particles must be extremely small; yet their minuteness is nothing when compared with the particles of light, which pervade and find their way thro' glass, or to the magnetic *effluvia* which pass freely through metallic bodies; whereas those effluvia that produce the sensation of smelling, notwithstanding their wonderful property of scenting all places into which they are brought, and without any sensible diminution, are yet too gross to pass the membranes of a bladder, and many of them will scarce find their way through a common white paper.

There are but few names to express the infinite number of scents that we meet with. I know of none but those of *sweet, stinking, rank, musty,* and *sour;* for so barren is our language in this respect, that the rest are expressed either by degrees of comparison, or by epithets borrowed from bodies that produce scent, which must, in many cases, be very inexpressive; for the smell of a *rose,* of a *violet,* and of *musk,* tho' all sweet, are as distinct as any scents whatever.

The next sense under our consideration is TASTE, the organ of which is the *tongue* and the *palate,* but principally the tongue. Ay, and a pretty organ it is, says Lady *Caroline*. When used with your Ladyship's discretion, Madam, replied the Philosopher. But I must observe to your Ladyship, and the rest of the good company, that though bodies which emit *light, sounds,* and *scents,* are seen, heard, and smelt at a distance; yet no bodies can produce taste, without being immediately applied to the organ; for tho' the meat be placed at your mouth, you know not what taste it will produce till you have touched it with your tongue or palate.

Though there are an amazing variety of tastes, yet here, as in scents, we have but a few general names to express the whole; *sweet, sour, bitter, harsh, smooth,* and *rank,* are all that I can recollect; and our other ideas of taste are generally conveyed by borrowed similitudes and expressions like those of *scents.* It is surprizing, says the Ambassador, that in this age of gluttony, your language should be so barren as not to afford you words to express those ideas which are excited by exquisite flavours. Sir, says the Marquis, this may be easily accounted for. I must inform your Excellency, that we are indebted for our most expressive terms to the Poets, who were never much acquainted with good eating, and are less so since literature has lost its zest. Very true, my Lord, says Sir *Harry,* their dishes, poor creatures, have lately been of the mental kind; but had you a few rich Poets that could afford to live like people of taste, instead of your sweets and your sours, and such old fashion terms, you would have the *calapash* and *calape* flavour, the *live-lobster* flavour, the *whipt-pig* flavour, and a list of others, as long—as my arm. Fye, Sir *Harry,* says the Marchioness, no more of that, I beg; you know Lady *Caroline* can't bear the name of Barbarity. Nor I neither, says the Ambassador, but pray what barbarity is there in this, Madam? Oh! none at all, replied Sir *Harry,* I only meant to insinuate that some of our great people are not content with having food brought from the *East* and *West Indies,* and every other part of the world, to gratify their palates, but they must roast lobsters alive, and whip young pigs to death to make them tender. Good God! says the Ambassador, are there people in *England* capable of such acts of inhumanity? A man that will do that would murder me, if the law did not stand between us; and the law is but a poor screen where humanity is lost and conscience is lulled asleep. I'll apply to the King my master for my dismission, and no longer live with a people who have adopted such diabolical customs. The Ambassador was so much in a passion, that it was with difficulty my Lord Marquis pacified him; and poor Lady *Caroline,* whose kind soul sympathizes with every creature in distress, was in tears at the bare rehearsal of these acts of cruelty. Upon which the Baronet was blamed by all the company, except myself, and, I think, he never shewed so much good sense in his life; for there was one in the room who deserved the reproof.

When the Ambassador had sat down with a sigh, and Lady *Caroline* had wiped the precious pearly drops from her cheeks, our Philosopher arose and thus pursued his Lecture.

I have already taken notice of four of our senses, and am now come to the fifth and last, I mean that of the TOUCH, which is a sense spread over the whole body, tho' it is more particularly the business of the hands and fingers; for by them the tangible qualities of bodies are known, since we discover by the *touch* of the fingers, and sometimes, indeed, by the *touch* of other parts of the body, whether things are *hard, soft, rough, smooth, wet, dry,* &c. But the qualities which most affect this sense are *heat* and *cold,* and which, indeed, are the great engines of Nature; for by a due temperament of those two opposite qualities most of her productions are formed.

What we call *heat* is occasioned by the agitation of the insensible parts of the body that produces in us that sensation; and when the parts of a body are violently agitated, we say, and indeed we feel, that body is *hot*; so that that which to our sensation is *heat*, in the object is nothing but *motion.* Hey-day, says Lady *Caroline*, what sort of Philosophy is this? Why, Madam, says Sir *Harry,* this is a position which has been laid down by these airy Gentlemen for a long time, but which never has been proved by experiment. Take care,

Baronet, says the Marquis, or you'll forfeit all pretensions to Philosophy. The forfeiture, my Lord, is made already, says the Philosopher; Sir *Harry* has been bold enough to deny that which experience every day confirms for truth. If what we call Heat is not motion, or occasioned by the motion of bodies, how came my Lord's mill to take fire the other day, when it was running round without a proper supply of corn? And how came your post-chariot to fire while running down *Breakneck-hill,* Sir *Harry?* Consider, there was nobody with a torch under the axle-tree; but this is a part of Philosophy known even to the poor ignorant *Indians,* who, when hunting at a great distance from home, and wanting fire to dress their meat, take a bow and a string and rub two pieces of wood together till they produce flame. But you may see, Sir *Harry,* that heat is occasioned by the motion of bodies, by only rubbing this piece of smooth *brass* on the table—stay, I'll rub it.—It must be done briskly. There, now you'll feel it hot; but cease this motion for a time, and the brass will become cold again; whence we may infer, that as heat is nothing but the insensible particles of bodies put into motion, so cold, on the contrary, is occasioned by the cessation of the motion of those particles, or their being placed in a state of rest.

But bodies appear *hot* or *cold* in proportion to the temperament of that part of the human body to which they are applied; so that what seems hot to one, may not seem so to another: This is so true, that the same body felt by the two hands of the same man, may at the same instant of time appear warm to the one hand, and cold to the other, if with the one hand he has been rubbing any thing, while the other was kept in a state of rest; and for no other reason but because the motion of the insensible particles of that hand with which he has been rubbing, will be more brisk than the particles of the other which was at rest.

I have mentioned those objects which are peculiar to each of our senses, as *light* and *colour* to the *sight; sound* to the *hearing; odors* to the *smell,* &c. but there are two others common to all the senses, which deserve our notice, and these are *pleasure* and *pain,* which the senses may receive by their own peculiar objects; for we know that a proper portion of light is pleasing, but that too much offends the eye; some sounds delight, while others are disagreeable, and grate the ear; so heat, in a moderate degree, is very pleasant; yet that heat may be so increased as to give the most intolerable pain. But these things are too well known to be longer insisted on.

Now from the *ideas* or *conceptions* formed in the mind, by means of our senses, and the operations of the mind itself, are laid the foundation of the human understanding, the lowest degree of which is *perception;* and to conceive a right notion of this, we must distinguish the first objects of it, which are *simple ideas,* such as are represented by the words, *red, blue, bitter, sweet,* &c. from the other objects of our senses; to which we may add the internal operations of our own minds, or the objects of reflection, such as are *thinking, willing,* &c. for all our ideas are first obtained by *sensation* and *reflection.* The mind having gained variety of *simple ideas,* by putting them together, forms what are called *compounded* or *complex ideas,* as those signified by the words, *man, horse, marygold, windmill,* &c.

The next operation of the mind (or of the understanding) in its progress to knowledge, is that of abstracting its ideas; for by abstraction they are made general; and a *general idea* is to be considered as separated from time and place, and lodged in the mind to represent any particular thing that is conformable to it.

Knowledge, which is the highest degree of the speculative faculties, consists in the perception of the truth of affirmative or negative propositions; and this perception is either immediate or mediate. When, by comparing two ideas together in the mind, we perceive their agreement or disagreement, as that black is not white; that the whole is bigger than a part; that two and two are equal to four, &c. it is called immediate perception, or *intuitive* knowledge; and as the truth of these and the like propositions is so evident as to be known by a simple intuition of the ideas themselves, they are also called *self-evident propositions.*

Mediate perception, is when the agreement or disagreement of two ideas is made known by the intervention of some other ideas: Thus if it be affirmed that my Lord's bay horse is as high as my father's, the agreement or disagreement may be seen by applying the same measure to both; and this is called *demonstration,* or *rational knowledge.* The dimensions of any two bodies which cannot be brought together, may be thus known, by the same measure being applied to them both.

But the understanding is not confined to certain truth; it also judges of *probability,* which consists in the *likely* agreement or disagreement of ideas; and the assenting to any proposition as probable, is called *opinion,* or *belief.*—We have now finished this Course of Lectures. I hope not, says Lady *Caroline,* with some emotion!—Why, Madam, returned the Philosopher, we have taken a cursory view of natural bodies, and their causes and effects; which I have endeavoured to explain in such a manner as to be intelligible, at least, if not entertaining; and pray what more did your Ladyship expect? Sir, replied the Lady, I am greatly pleased with the account you have given us, and I thank you, Sir, for the pains you have taken to answer the many questions I have troubled you with. What I had farther to hope, was, that you would have given us, when you was on the subject of Animals, some strictures on the cruelty with which they are too often treated; and have thrown in reflections and observations tending to inforce in mankind a different conduct. This I wished for, and should have been glad to have had Sir *Thomas* and his Lady here at the same time; who are both extremely fond of their little domestic creatures, and I admire them for their tenderness and compassion. These feelings and sentiments of the human heart, Madam, says the Philosopher, add much to the dignity of our nature, and I am greatly delighted with such behaviour; but I am afraid, Lady *Caroline,* that we often mistake characters of this kind, and [take] that for humanity and tenderness, which is only the effect of fancy or self love. That Sir *Thomas* has compassion, I grant you; but I am afraid it is only for himself. He loves his dogs and horses, because his dogs and horses give him pleasure; but to other creatures that afford him none, he is absolutely insensible. I have seen him, even at *Christmas,* feed his pretty *pupps,* as he calls them, with delicacies; but rave, at the same time, in a merciless manner, at poor children who were shivering at his gate, and send them away empty handed. Our neighbour Sir *William* is also of the same disposition; he will not sell a horse, that is declining, for fear he should fall into the hands of a master who might treat him with cruelty; but he is largely concerned in the slave trade (which, I think, is carried on by none but *we good Christians,* to the dishonour of our *cælestial Master)* and makes no difficulty of separating the husband from the wife, the parents from the children, and all of them (as well as our own people, who are procured by his *crimps,)* from their native country, to be sold in a foreign market, like so many horses, and often to the most merciless of the human race. I remember him in great distress for his pointer *Phillis,* who had lost her *puppies;* but the same afternoon I saw him, without the least compunction of mind, press a poor man into the sea service, and tear him from his wife and children; for no other *crime,* but because he had fought bravely for his King and country in the last war, and being now settled in business, and having a family, did not chuse to enter the service again. Is this humanity, Madam? Is this morality? But above all, is this Christianity? And are these the blessed effects of the liberty we boast of?—I don't expect a reply, Lady *Caroline,* for I shall have occasion to say much more on these subjects in my next course of Lectures, and then, perhaps, you will honour me with your observations. But in the mean time don't let us be misled by specious pretences. We cannot judge of any man, Madam, by one single action, but by the tenour and result of all his actions, and this requires deep penetration and an intimate knowledge of human life.

Benevolence, Lady *Caroline,* should be universal, for it is an emanation of the Supreme Being, whose mercy and goodness are extended to all his creatures; as ours also should be, for they are fellow tenants with us of the globe we inhabit.

I have often thought, Madam, that most of the mischiefs which embarrass society, and render one man contemptible to another, are owing to inordinate *ambition* or extreme love of *power,* and of *wealth,* the means by which it is procured; for all the gold a man possesses beyond that portion which is requisite for himself and family, only serves to inflame his ambition; as all the wine we drink more than is necessary to recruit the drooping spirits, answers no other purpose but to intoxicate the mind.

I have seen a book, Lady *Caroline,* in my Pappa's library, which gives some account of one *Lycurgus,* an old *Grecian* Lawgiver, with whose character you ought to be acquainted.—This man, Madam, was of opinion, that religion, virtue, and good manners, were the only natural cements and preservatives of liberty, peace, and friendship; which he found had been destroyed and extirpated by means of wealth and self-interest; he therefore prohibited the use of gold and silver, and of all kinds of luxury in the state, and established such a plan for the education of youth of every denomination, as was most likely to confirm and habituate them in the practice of religion and virtue, and secure to the *Spartans* and their posterity the blessings of liberty and peace.

The event proved that his institutions were founded on sound policy, and a perfect knowledge of human nature; for in the space of five hundred years, that is to say, from the time of *Lycurgus* to the introduction of wealth in the state by *Lysander*, in the reign of the first *Agis*, there was no mutiny among the people; every man submitted chearfully to the laws of *Lycurgus*, and all were so united and powerful in consequence of their virtue, sobriety, and the martial discipline he had established (which was that of a national militia) that *Sparta*, a very small inconsiderable State, not only gave laws to the rest of *Greece*, but made even the *Persian* Monarchs tremble, though masters of the richest and most extensive empire in the world. But when these great and virtuous people of *Sparta* had conquered *Athens*, and from thence introduced wealth and luxury into their own country, they lost their virtue, dwindled to nothing, and were themselves enslaved. Nor is this a matter of wonder; for where Religion and Virtue are set at a distance, and Wealth leads the way to posts of honour and trust, some people will stick at nothing to obtain gold; but were dignities of this kind conferred on the most deserving, and none but men of virtue and superior abilities promoted to places of trust and power, there would be no frauds in the State, or violence among the People, and we might then hope to enjoy the felicities of the *Golden Age*.

> Man in that Age no rule but Reason knew,
> And with a native bent did good pursue;
> Unaw'd by punishment, and void of fear,
> His words were simple and his soul sincere.
> By no *forc'd laws* his passions were confin'd,
> For *conscience* kept his heart, and calm'd his mind;
> *Peace* o'er the world, her blessed sway maintain'd,
> And e'en in Desarts smiling *Plenty* reign'd.

F I N I S.

The History of
Little Goody Two-Shoes

ANONYMOUS

Published by John Newbery

THE
HISTORY
OF
Little Goody Two-Shoes;

Otherwise called,

Mrs. Margery Two-Shoes.

WITH

The Means by which she acquired her
Learning and Wisdom, and in consequence thereof her Estate; set forth
at large for the Benefit of those,

Who from a State of Rags and Care,
And having Shoes but half a Pair;
Their Fortune and their Fame would fix,
And gallop in a Coach and Six.

See the Original Manuscript in the *Vatican*
at *Rome,* and the Cuts by *Michael Angelo.*
Illustrated with the Comments of our
great modern Critics.

The THIRD EDITION.

LONDON:

Printed for J. NEWBERY, at the *Bible* and
Sun in St. *Paul's-Church-Yard,* 1766.

[Price Six-pence.]

N O ANTHOLOGY *of Georgian children's literature could do without* The History of Little Goody Two-Shoes *(1765), the most popular and imitated juvenile book of its day. Fifteen editions were put out by John Newbery and his successors up to 1784. In 1802 Charles Lamb feared that* Goody Two-Shoes *would be supplanted by Barbauld's "stuff," but it weathered innumerable changes in fashion. Hundreds of editions later, it is still in print in the twentieth century.*

Goody Two-Shoes, the orphan who rises to Lady of the Manor, is the central character, whose name is now a household word. Far from being simplistic, she, like many child characters in books John Newbery published, is resourceful and beguiling. Goody Two-Shoes, *moreover, has an unusually finished quality for so early a child novel. In 1749 Sarah Fielding penned the first juvenile novel,* The Governess, *which, unlike* Goody Two-Shoes, *is not centered around one dominant and intriguing character.*

Scarcity of early copies of Goody Two-Shoes *suggests the book was so popular that it was read to pieces. All copies of the first edition were long presumed to be lost, but two hundred years after the first edition, Julian Roberts described a new acquisition of the British Library in "The 1765 Edition of Goody Two Shoes,"* British Museum Quarterly *29 (Summer 1965): 67–70.*

It would be intriguing to know whom we should credit for writing the book that founded the moral tale for children. Was it Giles or Griffith Jones? Oliver Goldsmith and/or John Newbery? Scholars seem duty-bound to discover whom to credit for such a plucky, precocious heroine who was never a prig like many a later child character.

The text reproduced here is reprinted from a facsimile edition (London: Griffith and Farran, 1881) of the 1766 edition of The History of Little Goody Two-Shoes.

To All Young Gentlemen and Ladies, Who are good, or intend to be good, This Book is inscribed by Their old Friend in St. Paul's Church-yard.

Part I

INTRODUCTION
By the Editor.

ALL THE WORLD must allow, that *Two Shoes* was not her real Name. No; her Father's Name was *Meanwell*; and he was for many Years a considerable Farmer in the Parish where *Margery* was born; but by the Misfortunes which he met with in Business, and the wicked Persecutions of Sir *Timothy Gripe*, and an over-grown Farmer called *Graspall*, he was effectually ruined.

The Case was thus. The Parish of *Mouldwell* where they lived, had for many Ages been let by the Lord of the Manor into twelve different Farms, in which the Tenants lived comfortably, brought up large Families, and carefully supported the poor People who laboured for them; until the Estate by Marriage and by Death came into the Hands of Sir *Timothy.*

This Gentleman, who loved himself better than all his Neighbours, thought it less Trouble to write one Receipt for his Rent than twelve, and Farmer *Graspall* offering to take all the Farms as the Leases expired, Sir *Timothy* agreed with him, and in Process of Time he was possessed of every Farm, but that occupied by little *Margery's* Father; which he also wanted; for as Mr. *Meanwell* was a charitable good Man, he stood up for the Poor at the Parish Meetings, and was unwilling to have them oppressed by Sir *Timothy,* and this avaricious Farmer.—Judge, oh kind, humane and courteous Reader, what a terrible Situation the Poor must be in, when this covetous Man was perpetual Overseer, and every Thing for their Maintenance was drawn from his hard Heart and cruel Hand. But he was not only perpetual Overseer, but perpetual Church-warden; and judge, oh ye Christians, what State the Church must be in, when supported by a Man without Religion or Virtue. He was also perpetual Surveyor of the Highways, and what Sort of Roads he kept up for the Convenience of Travellers, those best know who have had the Misfortune to be obliged to pass thro' that Parish.—Complaints indeed were made, but to what Purpose are Complaints, when brought against a Man, who can hunt, drink, and smoak with the Lord of the Manor, who is also the Justice of Peace?

The Opposition which little *Margery*'s Father made to this Man's Tyranny, gave Offence to Sir *Timothy*, who endeavoured to force him out of his Farm; and to oblige him to throw up the Lease, ordered both a BrickKiln and a Dog-kennel to be erected in the Farmer's Orchard. This was contrary to Law, and a Suit was commenced, in which *Margery*'s Father got the better. The same Offence was again committed three different Times, and as many Actions brought, in all of which the Farmer had a Verdict and Costs paid him; but notwithstanding these Advantages, the Law was so expensive, that he was ruined in the Contest, and obliged to give up all he had to his Creditors; which effectually answered the Purpose of Sir *Timothy*, who erected those Nuisances in the Farmer's Orchard with that Intention only. Ah, my dear Reader, we brag of Liberty, and boast of our Laws: but the Blessings of the one, and the Protection of the other, seldom fall to the Lot of the Poor; and especially when a rich Man is their Adversary. How, in the Name of Goodness, can a poor Wretch obtain Redress, when thirty Pounds are insufficient to try his Cause? Where is he to find Money to see Council, or how can he plead his Cause himself (even if he was permitted) when our Laws are so obscure, and so multiplied, that an Abridgment of them cannot be contained in fifty Volumes in Folio?

As soon as Mr. *Meanwell* had called together his Creditors, Sir *Timothy* seized for a Year's Rent, and turned the Farmer, his Wife, little *Margery*, and her Brother out of Doors, without any of the Necessaries of Life to support them.

This elated the Heart of Mr. *Graspall*, this crowned his Hopes, and filled the Measure of his Iniquity; for besides gratifying his Revenge, this Man's Overthrow gave him the sole Dominion of the Poor, whom he depressed and abused in a Manner too horrible to mention.

Margery's Father flew into another Parish for Succour, and all those who were able to move left their Dwellings and sought Employment elsewhere, as they found it would be impossible to live under the Tyranny of two such People. The very old, the very lame and the blind were obliged to stay behind, and whether they were starved, or what became of them, History does not say; but the Character of the great Sir *Timothy*, and his avaricious Tenant, were so infamous, that nobody would work for them by the Day, and Servants were afraid to engage themselves by the Year, lest any unforeseen Accident should leave them Parishioners in a Place, where they knew they must perish miserably; so that great Part of the Land lay untilled for some Years, which was deemed a just Reward for such diabolical Proceedings.

But what, says the Reader, can occasion all this? Do you intend this for Children, Mr. NEWBERY? Why, do you suppose this is written by Mr. NEWBERY, Sir? This may come from another Hand. This is not the Book, Sir, mentioned in the Title, but the Introduction to that Book; and it is intended, Sir, not for those Sort of Children, but for Children of six Feet high, of which, as my Friend has justly observed, there are many Millions in the Kingdom; and these Reflections, Sir, have been rendered necessary, by the unaccountable and diabolical Scheme which many Gentlemen now give into, of laying a Number of Farms into one, and very often of a whole Parish into one Farm; which in the End must reduce the common People to a State of Vassalage, worse than that under the Barons of old, or of the Clans in *Scotland*; and will in Time depopulate the Kingdom. But as you are tired of the Subject, I shall take myself away, and you may visit *Little Margery*. So, Sir, your Servant, THE EDITOR.

CHAPTER I
How and about Little Margery *and her* Brother.

Care and discontent shortened the Days of Little *Margery*'s Father.—He was forced from his Family, and seized with a violent Fever in a Place where Dr. *James*'s Powder was not to be had, and where he died miserably. *Margery*'s poor Mother survived the Loss of her Husband but a few Days, and died of a broken Heart, leaving *Margery* and her little Brother to the wide World; but, poor Woman, it would have melted your Heart to have seen how frequently she heaved up her Head, while she lay speechless, to survey with languishing Looks her little Orphans, as much as to say, *Do Tommy, do Margery, come with me.* They cried, poor Things, and she sighed away her Soul; and I hope is happy.

It would both have excited your Pity, and have done your Heart good, to have seen how fond these two little ones were of each other, and how, Hand in Hand, they trotted about. Pray see them.

They were both very ragged, and *Tommy* had two Shoes, but *Margery* had but one. They had nothing, poor Things, to support them (not being in their own Parish) but what they picked from the Hedges, or got from the poor People, and they lay every Night in a Barn. Their Relations took no Notice of them; no, they were rich, and ashamed to own such a poor little ragged Girl as *Margery*, and such a dirty little curl-pated Boy as *Tommy*. Our Relations and Friends seldom take Notice of us when we are poor; but as we grow rich they grow fond. And this will always be the Case, while People love Money better than Virtue, or better than they do God Almighty. But such wicked Folks, who love nothing but Money, and are proud and despise the Poor, never come to any good in the End, as we shall see by and by.

CHAPTER II
How and about Mr. Smith.

Mr. smith was a very worthy Clergyman, who lived in the Parish where Little *Margery* and *Tommy* were born; and having a Relation come to see him, who was a charitable good Man, he sent for these Children to him. The Gentleman ordered Little *Margery* a new Pair of Shoes, gave Mr. *Smith* some Money to buy her Cloathes; and said, he would take *Tommy* and make him a little Sailor; and accordingly had a Jacket and Trowsers made for him, in which he now appears. Pray look at him.

After some Days the Gentleman intended to go to *London*, and take little *Tommy* with him, of whom you will know more by and by, for we shall at a proper Time present you with some Part of his History, his Travels and Adventures.

The Parting between these two little Children was very affecting. *Tommy* cried, and *Margery* cried, and they kissed each other an hundred Times. At last *Tommy* thus wiped off her Tears with the End of his Jacket, and bid her cry no more, for that he would come to her again, when he returned from Sea. However, as they were so very fond, the Gentleman would not suffer them to take Leave of each other; but told *Tommy* he should ride out with him, and come back at Night. When night came, Little *Margery* grew very uneasy about her Brother, and after sitting up as late as Mr. *Smith* would let her, she went crying to Bed.

CHAPTER III
How Little Margery *obtained the Name of* Goody Two-Shoes, *and what happened in the Parish.*

As soon as Little *Margery* got up in the Morning, which was very early, she ran all round the Village, crying for her Brother; and after some Time returned greatly distressed. However, at this Instant, the Shoemaker very opportunely came in with the new Shoes, for which she had been measured by the Gentleman's Order.

Nothing could have supported Little *Margery* under the Affliction she was in for the Loss of her Brother, but the Pleasure she took in her *two Shoes*. She ran out to Mrs. *Smith* as soon as they were put on, and stroking down her ragged Apron thus, cried out, *Two Shoes, Mame, see two Shoes.* And so she behaved to all the People she met, and by that Means obtained the Name of *Goody Two-Shoes*, though her Playmates called her *Old Goody Two-Shoes.*

Little *Margery* was very happy in being with Mr. and Mrs. *Smith*, who were very charitable and good to her, and had agreed to breed her up with their Family; but as soon as that Tyrant of the Parish, that *Graspall*, heard of her being there, he applied first to Mr. *Smith*, and threatened to reduce his Tythes if he kept her; and after that he spoke to Sir *Timothy*, who sent Mr. *Smith* a peremptory Message by his Servant, that *he should send back* Meanwell's *Girl to be kept by her Relations, and not harbour her in the Parish.* This so distressed Mr. *Smith* that he shed Tears, and cried, *Lord have Mercy on the Poor!*

The Prayers of the Righteous fly upwards, and reach unto the Throne of Heaven, as will be seen in the Sequel.

Mrs. *Smith* was also greatly concerned at being thus obliged to discard poor Little *Margery*. She kissed her and cried; as also did Mr. *Smith*, but they were obliged to send her away; for the People who had ruined her Father could at any Time have ruined them.

CHAPTER IV
How Little Margery *learned to read, and by Degrees taught others.*

Little margery saw how good, and how wise Mr. *Smith* was, and concluded, that this was owing to his great Learning, therefore she wanted of all Things to learn to read. For this Purpose she used to meet the little Boys and Girls as they came from School, borrow their Books, and sit down and read till they returned;

By this Means she soon got more Learning than any of her Playmates, and laid the following Scheme for instructing those who were more ignorant than herself. She found, that only the following Letters were required to spell all the Words in the World; but as some of these Letters are large and some small, she with her Knife cut out of several Pieces of Wood ten Setts of each of these:

a b c d e f g h i j k l m n o
p q r s t u v w x y z.

And six Setts of these:

A B C D E F G H I J K L M N O
P Q R S T U V W X Y Z.

And having got an old Spelling-Book, she made her Companions set up all the Words they wanted to spell, and after that she taught them to compose Sentences. You know what a Sentence is, my Dear, *I will be good*, is a Sentence; and is made up, as you see, of several Words.

The usual Manner of Spelling, or carrying on the Game, as they called it, was this: Suppose the Word to be spelt was Plumb Pudding (and who can suppose a better) the Children were placed in a Circle, and the first brought the Letter *P*, the next *l*, the next *u*, the next *m*, and so on till the Whole was spelt; and if any one brought a wrong Letter, he was to pay a Fine, or play no more. This was at their Play; and every Morning she used to go round to teach the Children with these Rattle-traps in a Basket, as you see in the Print.

I once went her Rounds with her, and was highly diverted, as you may be, if you please to look into the next Chapter.

CHAPTER V
How Little Two-Shoes *became a trotting Tutoress, and how she taught her young Pupils.*

IT WAS ABOUT seven o'Clock in the Morning when we set out on this important Business, and the first House we came to was Farmer *Wilson*'s. See here it is.

Here *Margery* stopped, and ran up to the Door, *Tap, tap, tap.* Who's there? Only little goody *Two-Shoes*, answered *Margery*, come to teach *Billy*. Oh Little *Goody*, says Mrs. *Wilson*, with Pleasure in her Face, I am glad to see you, *Billy* wants you sadly, for he has learned all his Lesson. Then out came the little Boy. *How do doody Two-Shoes*, says he, not able to speak plain. Yet this little Boy had learned all his Letters; for she threw down this Alphabet mixed together thus:

b d f h k m o q s u w y z
a c e g i l n p r t v x j

and he picked them up, called them by their right Names, and put them all in order thus:

a b c d e f g h i j k l m n o
p q r s t u v w x y z.

She then threw down the Alphabet of Capital Letters in the Manner you here see them.

B D F H K M O Q S U W Y Z
A C E G I L N P R T V X J.

and he picked them all up, and having told their Names, placed them thus:

A B C D E F G H I J K L M
N O P Q R S T U V W X Y Z.

Now, pray little Reader, take this Bodkin, and see if you can point out the Letters from these mixed Alphabets, and tell how they should be placed as well as little Boy *Billy*.

The next Place we came to was Farmer *Simpson*'s, and here it is.

Bow wow, wow, says the Dog at the Door. Sirrah, says his Mistress, what do you bark at Little *Two-Shoes*. Come in *Madge*; here, *Sally* wants you sadly, she has learned all her Lesson. Then out came the little one: So *Madge!* says she; so *Sally!* answered the other, have you learned your Lesson? Yes, that's what I have, replied the little one in the Country Manner; and immediately taking the Letters she set up these Syllables:

ba be bi bo bu, ca ce ci co cu
da de di do du, fa fe fi fo fu.

and gave them their exact Sounds as she composed them; after which she set up the following:

ac ec ic oc uc, ad ed id od ud
af ef if of uf, ag eg ig og ug.

And pronounced them likewise. She then sung the Cuzz's Chorus (which may be found in the *Little Pretty Play Thing*, published by Mr. NEWBERY) and to the same Tune to which it is there set.

After this, Little *Two-Shoes* taught her to spell Words of one Syllable, and she soon set up Pear, Plumb, Top, Ball, Pin, Puss, Dog, Hog, Fawn, Buck, Doe, Lamb, Sheep, Ram, Cow, Bull, Cock, Hen, and many more.

The next Place we came to was *Gaffer Cook*'s Cottage; there you see it before you.

Here a number of poor Children were met to learn; who all came round Little *Margery* at once; and, having pulled out her Letters, she asked the little Boy next her, what he had for Dinner? Who answered, *Bread.* (the poor Children in many Places live very hard) Well then, says she, set the first Letter. He put up the Letter B, to which the next added r, and the next e, the next a, the next d, and it stood thus, *Bread.*

And what had you *Polly Comb* for your Dinner? *Apple-pye,* answered the little Girl: Upon which the next in Turn set up a great A, the two next a p each, and so on till the two Words Apple and Pye were united and stood thus, *Apple-pye.*

The next had *Potatoes,* the next *Beef and Turnip* which were spelt with many others, till the Game of Spelling was finished. She then set them another Task, and we proceeded.

The next Place we came to was Farmer *Thompson's,* where there were a great many little ones waiting for her.

So little Mrs. *Goody Two-Shoes,* says one of them, where have you been so long? I have been teaching, says she, longer than I intended, and am afraid I am come too soon for you now. No, but indeed you are not, replied the other; for I have got my Lesson, and so has *Sally Dawson,* and so has *Harry Wilson,* and so we have all; and they capered about as if they were overjoyed to see her. Why then, says she, you are all very good, and GOD Almighty will love you; so let us begin our Lessons. They all huddled round her, and though at the other Place they were employed about Words and Syllables, here we had People of much greater Understanding who dealt only in Sentences.

The Letters being brought upon the Table, one of the little ones set up the following Sentence.

The Lord have Mercy upon me, and grant that I may be always good, and say my Prayers, and love the Lord my God with all my Heart, with all my Soul, and with all my Strength; and honour the King, and all good Men in Authority under him.

Then the next took the Letters, and composed this Sentence.

Lord have Mercy upon me, and grant that I may love my Neighbour as myself, and do unto all Men as I would have them do unto me, and tell no Lies; but be honest and just in all my Dealings.

The third composed the following Sentence.

The Lord have Mercy upon me, and grant that I may honour my Father and Mother, and love my Brothers and Sisters, Relations and Friends, and all my Playmates, and every Body, and endeavour to make them happy.

The fourth composed the following.

I pray GOD to bless this whole Company, and all our Friends, and all our Enemies.

To this last *Polly Sullen* objected, and said, truly, she did not know why she should pray for her Enemies? Not pray for your Enemies, says Little *Margery*; yes, you must, you are no Christian, if you don't forgive your Enemies, and do Good for Evil. *Polly* still pouted; upon which Little *Margery* said, though she was poor, and obliged to lie in a Barn, she would not keep Company with such a naughty, proud, perverse Girl as *Polly*; and was going away; however the Difference was made up, and she set them to compose the following

LESSONS
For the Conduct of LIFE.

LESSON I.

He that will thrive,
Must rise by Five.
He that hath thriv'n,
May lie till Seven.
Truth may be blam'd,
But cannot be sham'd.
Tell me with whom you go;
And I'll tell what you do.
A Friend in your Need,
Is a Friend indeed.
They ne'er can be wise,
Who good Counsel despise.

LESSON II.

A wise Head makes a close Mouth.
Don't burn your Lips with another Man's Broth.
Wit is Folly, unless a wise Man hath the keeping of it.
Use soft Words and hard Arguments.
Honey catches more Flies than Vinegar.
To forget a Wrong is the best Revenge.
Patience is a Plaister for all Sores.
Where Pride goes, Shame will follow.
When Vice enters the Room, Vengeance is near the Door.
Industry is Fortune's right Hand, and Frugality her left.
Make much of Three-pence, or you ne'er will be worth a Groat.

LESSON III.

A Lie stands upon one Leg, but Truth upon two.
When a Man talks much, believe but half what he says.
Fair Words butter no Parsnips.

Bad Company poisons the Mind.
A covetous Man is never satisfied.
Abundance, like Want, ruins many.
Contentment is the best Fortune.
A contented Mind is a continual Feast.

A LESSON IN RELIGION.

Love GOD, for he is good.
Fear GOD, for he is just.
Pray to GOD, for all good Things come from him.
Praise GOD, for great is his Mercy towards us, and wonderful are all his Works.
Those who strive to be good, have GOD on their Side.
Those who have GOD for their Friend, shall want nothing.
Confess your Sins to GOD, and if you repent he will forgive you.
Remember that all you do, is done in the Presence of GOD.
The Time will come, my Friends, when we must give
Account to GOD, how we on Earth did live.

A MORAL LESSON.

A good Boy will make a good Man.
Honour your Parents, and the World will honour you.
Love your Friends, and your Friends will love you.
He that swims in Sin, will sink in Sorrow.
Learn to live, as you would wish to die.
   As you expect all Men should deal by you:
   So deal by them, and give each Man his Due.

As we were returning Home, we saw a Gentleman, who was very ill, sitting under a shady Tree at the Corner of his Rookery. Though ill, he began to joke with Little *Margery*, and said, laughingly, so, *Goody Two-Shoes*, they tell me you are a cunning little Baggage; pray, can you tell what I shall do to get well? Yes, Sir, says she, go to Bed when your Rooks do. You see they are going to Rest already: Do you so likewise, and get up with them in the morning; earn, as they do, every Day what you eat, and eat and drink no more than you earn; and you'll get Health and keep it. What should induce the Rooks to frequent Gentlemens Houses only, but to tell them how to lead a prudent Life? They never build over Cottages or Farm-houses, because they see, that these People know how to live without their Admonition.

> *Thus Health and Wit you may improve,*
> *Taught by the Tenants of the Grove.*

The Gentleman laughing gave *Margery* Sixpence; and told her she was a sensible Hussey.

CHAPTER VI

How the whole Parish was frighted.

WHO DOES NOT KNOW Lady *Ducklington*, or who does not know that she was buried at this Parish Church? Well, I never saw so grand a Funeral in all my Life; but the Money they squandered away, would have been better laid out in little Books for Children, or in Meat, Drink, and Cloaths for the Poor.

This is a fine Hearse indeed, and the nodding Plumes on the Horses look very grand; but what End does that answer, otherwise than to display the Pride of the Living, or the

Vanity of the Dead. Fie upon such Folly, say I, and Heaven grant that those who want more Sense may have it.

But all the Country round came to see the Burying, and it was late before the Corpse was interred. After which, in the Night, or rather about Four o'Clock in the Morning, the Bells were heard to jingle in the Steeple, which frightened the People prodigiously, who all thought it was Lady *Ducklington*'s Ghost dancing among the Bell-ropes. The People flocked to *Will Dobbins* the Clerk, and wanted him to go and see what it was; but *William* said, he was sure it was a Ghost, and that he would not offer to open the Door. At length Mr. *Long* the Rector, hearing such an Uproar in the Village, went to the Clerk, to know why he did not go into the Church, and see who was there. I go, Sir, says *William*, why the Ghost would frighten me out of my Wits.—Mrs. *Dobbins* too cried, and laying hold of her Husband said, he should not be eat up by the Ghost. A Ghost, you Blockheads, says Mr. *Long* in a Pet, did either of you ever see a Ghost, or know any Body that did? Yes, says the Clerk, my Father did once in the Shape of a Windmill, and it walked all round the Church in a white Sheet, with Jack Boots on, and had a Gun by its Side instead of a Sword. A fine Picture of a Ghost, truly, says Mr. *Long*, give me the Key of the Church, you Monkey; for I tell you there is no such Thing now, whatever may have been formerly.—Then taking the Key, he went to the Church, all the people following him. As soon as he had opened the Door, what Sort of Ghost do ye think appeared? Why Little *Two-Shoes*, who being weary, had fallen asleep in one of the Pews during the Funeral Service, and was shut in all Night. She immediately asked Mr. *Long*'s Pardon for the Trouble she had given him, told him, she had been locked into the Church, and said, she should not have rung the Bells, but that she was very cold, and hearing Farmer *Boult*'s Man go whistling by with his Horses, she was in Hopes he would have went to the Clerk for the Key to let her out.

CHAPTER VII
Containing an Account of all the Spirits, or Ghosts, she saw in the Church.

T HE PEOPLE were ashamed to ask Little *Madge* any Questions before Mr. *Long*, but as soon as he was gone, they all got round her to satisfy their Curiosity, and desired she would give them a particular Account of all that she had heard and seen.

Her Tale.

I went to the Church, said she, as most of you did last Night, to see the Burying, and being very weary, I sate me down in Mr. *Jones*'s Pew, and fell fast asleep. At Eleven of the Clock I awoke; which I believe was in some measure occasioned by the Clock's striking, for I heard it. I started up, and could not at first tell where I was; but after some Time I recollected the Funeral, and soon found that I was shut in the Church. It was dismal dark, and I could see nothing; but while I was standing in the Pew, something jumped up upon me behind, and laid, as I thought, its Hands over my Shoulders. —I own, I was a little afraid at first; however, I considered that I had always been constant at Prayers and at Church, and that I had done nobody any Harm, but had endeavoured to do what Good I could; and then, thought I, what have I to fear? Yet I kneeled down to say my Prayers. As soon as I was on my Knees something very cold, as cold as Marble, ay, as cold as Ice, touched my Neck, which made me start; however, I continued my Prayers, and having begged Protection from Almighty GOD, I found my Spirits come, and I was sensible that I had nothing to fear; for GOD Almighty protects not only all those who are good, but also all those who endeavour to be good.—Nothing can withstand the Power, and exceed the Goodness of GOD Almighty. Armed with the Confidence of his Protection, I walked down the Church Isle, when I heard something, pit pat, pit pat, pit pat, come after me, and something touched my Hand, which seemed as cold as a Marble Monument. I could not think what this was, yet I knew it could not hurt me, and therefore I made myself easy, but being very cold, and the Church being paved with Stone, which was very damp, I felt my Way as well as I could to the Pulpit, in doing which something brushed by me, and almost threw me down. However I was not frightened, for I knew, that GOD Almighty would suffer nothing to hurt me.

At last, I found out the Pulpit, and having shut too the Door, I laid me down on the Mat and Cushion to sleep; when something thrust and pulled the Door, as I thought for Admittance, which prevented my going to sleep. At last it cries, *Bow, wow, wow*; and I concluded it must be Mr. *Saunderson*'s Dog, which had followed me from their House to Church, so I opened the Door, and called *Snip, Snip*, and the Dog jumped up upon me immediately. After this *Snip* and I lay down together, and had a most comfortable Nap; for when I awoke again it was almost light. I then walked up and down all the Isles of the Church to keep myself warm; and though I went into the Vault, and trod on Lady *Ducklington*'s Coffin, I saw no Ghost, and I believe it was owing to the Reason Mr. *Long* has given you, namely, that there is no such Thing to be seen. As to my Part, I would as soon lie all Night in the Church as in any other Place; and I am sure that any little Boy or Girl, who is good, and loves GOD Almighty, and keeps his Commandments, may as safely lie in the Church, or the Church-yard, as any where else, if they take Care not to get Cold; for I am sure there are no Ghosts, either to hurt, or to frighten them; though any one possessed of Fear might have taken Neighbour *Saunderson*'s Dog with his cold Nose for a Ghost; and if they had not been undeceived, as I was, would never have thought otherwise. All the Company acknowledged the Justness of the Observation, and thanked Little *Two-Shoes* for her Advice.

Reflection.

After this, my dear Children, I hope you will not believe any foolish Stories that ignorant, weak, or designing People may tell you about *Ghosts*; for the Tales of *Ghosts*, *Witches*, and *Fairies*, are the Frolicks of a distempered Brain. No wise Man ever saw either of them. Little *Margery* you see was not afraid; no, she had *good Sense*, and a *good Conscience*, which is a Cure for all these imaginary Evils.

CHAPTER VIII

Of something which happened to Little Two-Shoes *in a Barn,
more dreadful than the Ghost in the Church; and how she
returned Good for Evil to her Enemy Sir* Timothy.

SOME DAYS after this a more dreadful Accident befel Little *Madge*. She happened to be
coming late from teaching, when it rained, thundered, and lightened, and therefore she
took Shelter in a Farmer's Barn at a Distance from the Village. Soon after, the Tempest
drove in four Thieves, who, not seeing such a little creep-mouse Girl as *Two-Shoes*, lay
down on the Hay next to her, and began to talk over their Exploits, and to settle Plans
for future Robberies. Little *Margery* on hearing them, covered herself with Straw. To be
sure she was sadly frighted, but her good Sense taught her, that the only Security she had
was in keeping herself concealed; therefore she laid very still, and breathed very softly.
About Four o'Clock these wicked People came to a Resolution to break both Sir *William
Dove's* House, and Sir *Timothy Gripe's*, and by Force of Arms to carry off all their
Money, Plate and Jewels; but as it was thought then too late, they agreed to defer it till
the next Night. After laying this Scheme they all set out upon their Pranks, which greatly
rejoiced *Margery*, as it would any other little Girl in her Situation. Early in the Morning
she went to Sir *William*, and told him the whole of their Conversation. Upon which, he
asked her Name, gave her Something, and bid her call at his House the Day following.
She also went to Sir *Timothy*, notwithstanding he had used her so ill; for she knew it was
her Duty to *do Good for Evil*. As soon as he was informed who she was, he took no
Notice of her; upon which she desired to speak to Lady *Gripe*; and having informed her
Ladyship of the Affair, she went her Way. This Lady had more Sense than her Husband,
which indeed is not a singular Case; for instead of despising Little *Margery* and her
Information, she privately set People to guard the House. The Robbers divided them-
selves, and went about the Time mentioned to both Houses, and were surprized by the
Guards, and taken. Upon examining these Wretches, one of which turned Evidence, both
Sir *William* and Sir *Timothy* found that they owed their Lives to the Discovery made by
Little *Margery*; and the first took great Notice of her, and would no longer let her lie
in a Barn; but Sir *Timothy* only said, that he was ashamed to owe his Life to the
Daughter of one who was his Enemy; so true it is, *that a proud Man seldom forgives
those he has injured.*

CHAPTER IX
How Little Margery *was made Principal of a Country College.*

Mrs. WILLIAMS, of whom I have given a particular Account in my *New Year's Gift*, and who kept a College for instructing little Gentlemen and Ladies in the Science of A, B, C, was at this Time very old and infirm, and wanted to decline that important Trust. This being told to Sir *William Dove*, who lived in the Parish, he sent for Mrs. *Williams*, and desired she would examine Little *Two-Shoes*, and see whether she was qualified for the Office.—This was done, and Mrs. *Williams* made the following Report in her Favour, namely, *that Little* Margery *was the best Scholar, and had the best Head, and the best Heart of any one she had examined.* All the Country had a great Opinion of Mrs. *Williams*, and this Character gave them also a great Opinion of Mrs. *Margery*; for so we must now call her.

This Mrs. *Margery* thought the happiest Period of her Life; but more Happiness was in Store for her. God Almighty heaps up Blessings for all those who love him, and though for a Time he may suffer them to be poor and distressed, and hide his good Purposes from human Sight, yet in the End they are generally crowned with Happiness here, and no one can doubt of their being so hereafter.

On this Occasion the following Hymn, or rather a Translation of the twenty-third Psalm, is said to have been written, and was soon after published in the *Spectator*.

I.

The Lord my Pasture shall prepare,
And feed me with a Shepherd's Care:
His Presence shall my Wants supply,
And guard me with a watchful Eye;
My Noon-day Walks he shall attend,
And all my Midnight Hours defend.

II.

When in the sultry Glebe I faint,
Or on the thirsty Mountain pant;
To fertile Vales and dewy Meads,
My weary wand'ring Steps he leads;
Where peaceful Rivers, soft and slow,
Amid the verdant Landskip flow.

III.

Tho' in the Paths of Death I tread,
With gloomy Horrors overspread,
My stedfast Heart shall fear no Ill,
For thou, O Lord, art with me still;
Thy friendly Crook shall give me Aid,
And guide me thro' the dreadful Shade.

IV.

Tho' in a bare and rugged Way,
Thro' devious lonely Wilds I stray,

Thy Bounty shall my Pains beguile:
The barren Wilderness shall smile,
With sudden Greens & herbage crown'd,
And Streams shall murmur all around.

Here ends the History of Little *Two-Shoes*. Those who would know how she behaved after she came to be Mrs. *Margery Two-Shoes* must read the Second Part of this Work, in which an Account of the Remainder of her Life, her Marriage, and Death are set forth at large, according to Act of Parliament.

Part II

INTRODUCTION

IN THE FIRST PART of this Work, the young Student has read, and I hope with Pleasure and Improvement, the History of this Lady, while she was known and distinguished by the Name of *Little Two-Shoes*; we are now come to a Period of her Life when that Name was discarded, and a more eminent one bestowed upon her, I mean that of Mrs. *Margery Two-Shoes:* For as she was now President of the A, B, C College, it became necessary to exalt her in Title as well as in Place.

No sooner was she settled in this Office, but she laid every possible Scheme to promote the Welfare and Happiness of all her Neighbours, and especially of the Little Ones, in whom she took great Delight, and all those whose Parents could not afford to pay for their Education, she taught for nothing, but the Pleasure she had in their Company, for you are to observe, that they were very good, or were soon made so by her good Management.

CHAPTER I
Of her School, her Ushers, or Assistants, and her Manner of Teaching.

WE HAVE already informed the Reader, that the School where she taught, was that which was before kept by Mrs. *Williams*, whose Character you may find in my *New Year's Gift*. The Room was large, and as she knew, that Nature intended Children should be always in Action, she placed her different Letters, or Alphabets, all round the School, so that every one was obliged to get up to fetch a Letter, or to spell a Word, when it came to their Turn; which not only kept them in Health, but fixed the Letters and Points firmly in their Minds.

She had the following Assistants or Ushers to help her, and I will tell you how she came by them. Mrs. *Margery*, you must know, was very humane and compassionate; and her Tenderness extended not only to all Mankind, but even to all Animals that were not noxious; as your's ought to do, if you would be happy here, and go to Heaven hereafter. These are GOD Almighty's Creatures as well as we. He made both them and us; and for wise Purposes, best known to himself, placed them in this World to live among us; so that they are our fellow Tenants of the Globe. How then can People dare

to torture and wantonly destroy GOD Almighty's Creatures? They as well as you are capable of feeling Pain, and of receiving Pleasure, and how can you, who want to be made happy yourself, delight in making your fellow Creatures miserable? Do you think the poor Birds, whose Nest and young ones that wicked Boy *Dick Wilson* ran away with Yesterday, do not feel as much Pain, as your Father and Mother would have felt, had any one pulled down their House and ran away with you? To be sure they do. Mrs. *Two-Shoes* used to speak of those Things, and of naughty Boys throwing at Cocks, torturing Flies, and whipping Horses and Dogs, with Tears in her Eyes, and would never suffer any one to come to her School who did so.

One Day, as she was going through the next Village, she met with some wicked Boys who had got a young Raven, which they were going to throw at, she wanted to get the poor Creature out of their cruel Hands, and therefore gave them a Penny for him, and brought him home. She called his Name *Ralph*, and a fine Bird he is. Do look at him. [A]nd remember what *Solomon* says, *The Eye that despiseth his Father, and regardeth not the Distress of his Mother, the Ravens of the Valley shall peck it out, and the young Eagles eat it.* Now this Bird she taught to speak, to spell and to read; and as he was particularly fond of playing with the large Letters, the Children used to call this *Ralph*'s Alphabet.

A B C D E F G H I J K L M
N O P Q R S T U V W X Y Z.

He always sat at her Elbow, as you see in the first Picture, and when any of the Children were wrong, she used to call out, *Put them right Ralph.*

Some Days after she had met with the Raven, as she was walking in the Fields, she saw some naughty Boys, who had taken a Pidgeon, and tied a String to its Leg, in order to let it fly, and draw it back again when they pleased; and by this Means they tortured the poor Animal with the Hopes of Liberty and repeated Disappointment. This Pidgeon she also bought, and taught him how to spell and read, though not to talk, and he performed all those extraordinary Things which are recorded of the famous Bird, that was some Time since advertised in the *Haymarket*, and visited by most of the great People in the Kingdom. This Pidgeon was a very pretty Fellow, and [s]he called him *Tom*. See here he is. And as the Raven *Ralph* was fond of the large Letters, *Tom* the Pidgeon took Care of the small ones, of which he composed this Alphabet.

a b c d e f g h i j k l m
n o p q r s t u v w x y z.

The Neighbours knowing that Mrs. *Two-Shoes* was very good, as to be sure nobody was better, made her a Present of a little Sky-lark, and a fine Bird he is.

Now as many People, even at that Time had learned to lie in Bed long in the Morning, she thought the Lark might be of Use to her and her Pupils, and tell them when to get up.

For he that is fond of his Bed, and lays'till Noon, lives but half his Days, the rest being lost in Sleep, which is a Kind of Death.

Some Time after this a poor Lamb had lost its Dam, and the Farmer being about to kill it, she bought it of him, and brought it home with her to play with the Children, and teach them when to go to Bed; for it was a Rule with the wise Men of that Age (and a very good one, let me tell you) to

Rise with the Lark, and lie down with the Lamb.

This Lamb she called *Will,* and a pretty Fellow he is; do, look at him.

No sooner was *Tippy* the Lark and *Will* the Ba-lamb brought into the School, but that sensible Rogue *Ralph,* the Raven, composed the following Verse, which every little good Boy and Girl should get by Heart.

Early to Bed, and early to rise;
Is the Way to be healthy, and wealthy, and wise.

A sly Rogue; but it is true enough; for those who do not go to Bed early cannot rise early; and those who do not rise early cannot do much Business. Pray, let this be told at the Court, and to People who have Routs and Rackets.

Soon after this, a Present was made to Mrs. *Margery* of little Dog *Jumper,* and a pretty Dog he is. Pray, look at him.

Jumper, Jumper, Jumper! He is always in a good Humour, and playing and jumping about, and therefore he was called *Jumper.* The Place assigned for *Jumper* was that of keeping the Door, so that he may be called the Porter of the College, for he would let nobody go out, or any one come in, without the Leave of his Mistress. See how he sits, a saucy Rogue.

Billy the Ba-lamb was a chearful Fellow, and all the Children were fond of him, wherefore Mrs. *Two-Shoes* made it a Rule, that those who behaved best should have *Will* home with them at Night to carry their Satchel or Basket at his Back, and bring it in the Morning. See what a fine Fellow he is, and how he trudges along.

CHAPTER II
A Scene of Distress in the School.

IT HAPPENED one Day, when Mrs. *Two-Shoes* was diverting the Children after Dinner, as she usually did with some innocent Games, or entertaining and instructive Stories, that a Man arrived with the melancholy News of *Sally Jones*'s Father being thrown from his Horse, and thought past all Recovery; nay, the Messenger said, that he was seemingly dying, when he came away. Poor *Sally* was greatly distressed, as indeed were all the School, for she dearly loved her Father, and Mrs. *Two-Shoes,* and all the Children dearly loved her. It is generally said, that we never know the real Value of our Parents or Friends till we have lost them; but poor *Sally* felt this by Affection, and her Mistress knew it by Experience. All the School were in Tears, and the Messenger was obliged to return; but before he went, Mrs. *Two-Shoes,* unknown to the Children, ordered *Tom* Pidgeon to go home with the Man, and bring a Letter to inform her how Mr. *Jones* did. They set out together, and the Pidgeon rode on the Man's Head, (as you see here) for the Man was able to carry the Pidgeon, though the Pidgeon was not able to carry the Man, if he had, they would have been there much sooner, for *Tom* Pidgeon was *very good,* and never staid on an Errand.

Soon after the Man was gone the Pidgeon was lost, and the Concern the Children were under for Mr. *Jones* and little *Sally* was in some Measure diverted, and Part of their Attention turned after *Tom,* who was a great Favourite, and consequently much bewailed. Mrs. *Margery,* who knew the great Use and Necessity of teaching Children to submit chearfully to the Will of Providence, bid them wipe away their Tears, and then kissing *Sally,* you must be a good Girl, says she, and depend upon GOD Almighty for his Blessing and Protection; for *he is a Father to the Fatherless, and defendeth all those who put their Trust in him.* She then told them a Story, which I shall relate in as few Words as possible.

The History of Mr. Lovewell, *Father to Lady* Lucy.

MR. LOVEWELL was born at *Bath,* and apprenticed to a laborious Trade in *London,* which being too hard for him, he parted with his Master by Consent, and hired himself as a common Servant to a Merchant in the City. Here he spent his leisure Hours not as Servants too frequently do, in Drinking and Schemes of Pleasure, but in improving his Mind; and among other Acquirements, he made himself a complete Master of Accompts.

His Sobriety, Honesty, and the Regard he paid to his Master's Interest, greatly recommended him in the whole Family, and he had several Offices of Trust committed to his Charge, in which he acquitted himself so well, that the Merchant removed him from the Stable into the Counting-house.

Here he soon made himself Master of the Business, and became so useful to the Merchant, that in regard to his faithful Services, and the Affection he had for him, he married him to his own Niece, a prudent agreeable young Lady; and gave him a Share in the Business. See what Honesty and Industry will do for us. Half the great Men in *London,* I am told, have made themselves by this Means, and who would but be honest and industrious, when it is so much our Interest and our Duty.

After some Years the Merchant died, and left Mr. *Lovewell* possessed of many fine Ships at Sea, and much Money, and he was happy in a Wife, who had brought him a Son and two Daughters, all dutiful and obedient. The Treasures and good Things, however, of this Life are so uncertain, that a Man can never be happy, unless he lays the Foundation for it in his own Mind. So true is that Copy in our Writing Books, which tells us, that *a contented Mind is a continual Feast.*

After some Years successful Trade, he thought his Circumstances sufficient to insure his own Ships, or, in other Words, to send his Ships and Goods to Sea without being insured by others, as is customary among Merchants; when, unfortunately for him, four of them richly laden were lost at Sea. This he supported with becoming Resolution; but the next Mail brought him Advice, that nine others were taken by the *French,* with whom we were then at War; and this, together with the Failure of three foreign Merchants whom he had trusted, compleated his Ruin. He was then obliged to call his Creditors together, who took his Effects, and being angry with him for the imprudent Step of not insuring his Ships, left him destitute of all Subsistence. Nor did the Flatterers of his Fortune, those who had lived by his Bounty when in his Prosperity, pay the least Regard either to him or his Family. So true is another Copy, that you will find in your Writing Book, which says, *Misfortune tries our Friends.* All these Slights of his pretended Friends, and the ill Usage of his Creditors, both he and his Family bore with Christian Fortitude; but other Calamities fell upon him, which he felt more sensibly.

In this Distress, one of his Relations, who lived at *Florence,* offered to take his Son; and another, who lived at *Barbadoes,* sent for one of his Daughters. The Ship which his Son sailed in was cast away, and all the Crew supposed to be lost; and the Ship, in which his Daughter went a Passenger, was taken by Pyrates, and one Post brought the miserable Father an Account of the Loss of his two Children. This was the severest Stroke of all: It made him compleatly wretched, and he knew it must have a dreadful Effect on his Wife and Daughter; he therefore endeavoured to conceal it from them. But the perpetual Anxiety he was in, together with the Loss of his Appetite and Want of Rest, soon alarmed his Wife. She found something was labouring in his Breast, which was concealed from her; and one Night being disturbed in a Dream, with what was ever in his Thoughts, and calling out upon his dear Children; she awoke him, and insisted upon knowing the Cause of his Inquietude. *Nothing, my Dear, nothing,* says he, *The Lord gave, and the Lord hath taken away, blessed be the Name of the Lord.* This was sufficient to alarm the poor Woman; she lay till his Spirits were composed, and as she thought asleep, then stealing out of Bed, got the Keys and opened his Bureau, where she found the fatal Account. In the Height of her Distractions, she flew to her Daughter's Room, and waking her with her

Shrieks, put the Letters into her Hands. The young Lady, unable to support this Load of Misery, fell into a Fit, from which it was thought she never could have been recovered. However, at last she revived; but the Shock was so great, that it entirely deprived her of her Speech.

Thus loaded with Misery, and unable to bear the Slights and Disdain of those who had formerly professed themselves Friends, this unhappy Family retired into a Country, where they were unknown, in order to hide themselves from the World; when, to support their Independency, the Father laboured as well as he could at Husbandry, and the Mother and Daughter sometimes got spinning and knitting Work, to help to furnish the Means of Subsistence; which however was so precarious and uncertain, that they often, for many Weeks together, lived on nothing but Cabbage and Bread boiled in Water. But God never forsaketh the Righteous, nor suffereth those to perish who put their Trust in him. At this Time a Lady, who was just come to England, sent to take a pleasant Seat ready furnished in that Neighbourhood, and the Person who was employed for the Purpose, was ordered to deliver a Bank Note of an hundred Pounds to Mr. *Lovewell,* another hundred to his Wife, and fifty to the Daughter, desiring them to take Possession of the House, and get it well aired against she came down, which would be in two or three Days at most. This, to People who were almost starving, was a sweet and seasonable Relief, and they were all sollicitous to know their Benefactress, but of that the Messenger himself was too ignorant to inform them. However, she came down sooner than was expected, and with Tears embraced them again and again: After which she told the Father and Mother she had heard from their Daughter, who was her Acquaintance, and that she was well and on her Return to England. This was the agreeable Subject of their Conversation till after Dinner, when drinking their Healths, she again with Tears saluted them, and falling upon her Knees asked their Blessings.

Tis impossible to express the mutual Joy which this occasioned. Their Conversation was made up of the most endearing Expressions, intermingled with Tears and Caresses. Their Torrent of Joy, however, was for a Moment interrupted, by a Chariot which stopped at the Gate, and which brought as they thought a very unseasonable Visitor, and therefore she sent to be excused from seeing Company.

But this had no Effect, for a Gentleman richly dressed jumped out of the Chariot, and pursuing the Servant into the Parlour saluted them round, who were all astonished at his Behaviour. But when the Tears trickled from his Cheeks, the Daughter, who had been some Years dumb, immediately cried out, *my Brother! my Brother! my Brother!* and from that Instant recovered her Speech. The mutual Joy which this occasioned, is better felt than expressed. Those who have proper Sentiments of Humanity, Gratitude, and filial

Piety will rejoice at the Event, and those who have a proper Idea of the Goodness of God, and his gracious Providence, will from this, as well as other Instances of his Goodness and Mercy, glorify his holy Name, and magnify his Wisdom and Power, who is a Shield to the Righteous, and defendeth all those who put their Trust in him.

As you, my dear Children, may be sollicitous to know how this happy Event was brought about, I must inform you, that Mr. *Lovewell's* Son, when the Ship foundered, had with some others got into the long Boat, and was taken up by a Ship at Sea, and carried to the East Indies, where in a little Time he made a large Fortune; and the Pirates who took his Daughter, attempted to rob her of her Chastity; but finding her Inflexible, and determined to die rather than to submit, some of them behaved to her in a very cruel Manner; but others, who had more Honour and Generosity, became her Defenders; upon which a Quarrel arose between them, and the Captain, who was the worst of the Gang, being killed, the rest of the Crew carried the Ship into a Port of the *Manilla* Islands, belonging to the *Spaniards;* where, when her Story was known, she was treated with great Respect, and courted by a young Gentlemen, who was taken ill of a Fever, and died before the Marriage was agreed on, but left her his whole Fortune.

You see, my dear *Sally,* how wonderfully these People were preserved, and made happy after such extreme Distress; we are therefore never to despair, even under the greatest Misfortunes, for GOD Almighty is All-powerful and can deliver us at any Time. Remember *Job,* but I think you have not read so far, take the Bible, *Billy Jones,* and read the History of that good and patient Man. At this Instant something was heard to flap at the Window, *Wow, wow, wow,* says Jumper, and attempted to leap up and open the Door, at which the Children were surprized; but Mrs. *Margery* knowing what it was, opened the Casement, as *Noah* did the Window of the Ark, and drew in *Tom* Pidgeon with a Letter, and see here he is.

As soon as he was placed on the Table, he walked up to little *Sally,* and dropping the Letter, cried, *Co, Co, Coo,* as much as to say, *there read it.* Now this poor Pidgeon had travelled fifty Miles in about an Hour, to bring *Sally* this Letter, and who would destroy such pretty Creatures.—But let us read the Letter.

My dear Sally,

GOD Almighty has been very merciful, and restored your Pappa to us again, who is now so well as to be able to sit up. I hear you are a good Girl, my Dear, and I hope you will never forget to praise the Lord for this his great Goodness and Mercy to us—What a sad Thing it would have been if your Father had died, and left both you and me, and little *Tommy* in Distress, and without a Friend: Your Father sends his Blessing with mine—Be good, my dear Child, and God Almighty will also bless you, whose Blessing is above all Things.

I am, my Dear Sally,
Your ever affectionate Mother,
Martha Jones.

CHAPTER III
Of the amazing Sagacity and Instinct of a little Dog.

Soon after this, a dreadful Accident happened in the School. It was on a *Thursday* Morning, I very well remember, when the Children having learned their Lessons soon, she had given them Leave to play, and they were all running about the School, and diverting themselves with the Birds and the Lamb; at this Time the Dog, all of a sudden, laid hold of his Mistress's Apron, and endeavoured to pull her out of the School. She was at first surprized, however, she followed him to see what he intended. No sooner had he led her into the Garden, but he ran back, and pulled out one of the Children in the same manner; upon which she ordered them all to leave the School immediately, and they had not been out five Minutes, before the Top of the House fell in. What a miraculous Deliverance was here! How gracious! How good was God Almighty, to save all these Children from Destruction, and to make Use of such an Instrument, as a little sagacious Animal to accomplish his Divine Will. I should have observed, that as soon as they were all in the Garden, the Dog came leaping round them to express his Joy, and when the House was fallen, laid himself down quietly by his Mistress.

Some of the Neighbours, who saw the School fall, and who were in great Pain for *Margery* and the little ones, soon spread the News through the Village, and all the Parents, terrified for their Children, came crowding in Abundance; they had, however, the Satisfaction to find them all safe, and upon their Knees, with their Mistress, giving God thanks for their happy Deliverance.

Advice *from the* Man *in the* Moon.

Jumper, Jumper, Jumper, what a pretty Dog he is, and how sensible? Had Mankind half the Sagacity of *Jumper,* they would guard against Accidents of this Sort, by having a public Survey, occasionally made of all the Houses in every Parish (especially of those, which are old and decayed) and not suffer them to remain in a crazy State, 'till they fall down on the Heads of the poor Inhabitants, and crush them to Death. Why, it was but Yesterday, that a whole House fell down in *Grace-church-street,* and another in *Queen's-street,* and an hundred more are to tumble, before this Time twelve Months; so Friends, take Care of yourselves, and tell the Legislature, they ought to take Care for you. How can you be so careless? Most of your Evils arise from Carelessness and Extravagance, and yet you excuse yourselves, and lay the Fault upon Fortune. Fortune is a Fool, and you are a Blockhead, if you put it in her Power to play Tricks with you.

Yours,
The Man in the Moon.

You are not to wonder, my dear Reader, that this little Dog should have more Sense than you, or your Father, or your Grandfather.

Though God Almighty has made Man the Lord of the Creation, and endowed him with Reason, yet in many Respects, he has been altogether as bountiful to other Creatures of his forming. Some of the senses of other Animals are more acute than ours, as we find by

daily Experience. You know this little Bird, *sweet Jug, Jug, Jug,* 'tis a Nightingale. This little Creature, after she has entertained us with her Songs all the Spring, and bred up her little ones, flies into a foreign Country, and finds her Way over the Great Sea, without any of the Instruments and Helps which Men are obliged to make Use of for that Purpose. Was you as wise as the Nightingale, you might make all the Sailors happy, and have twenty thousand Pounds for teaching them the Longitude.

You would not think *Ralph* the Raven half so wise and so good as he is, though you see him here reading his book. Yet when the Prophet *Elijah,* was obliged to fly from *Ahab* King of *Israel,* and hide himself in a Cave, the Ravens, at the Command of God Almighty, fed him every Day, and preserved his Life.

And the Word of the Lord came unto Elijah, *saying, Hide thyself by the Brook* Cherith, *that is before* Jordan, *and I have commanded the Ravens to feed thee there. And the Ravens brought him Bread and Flesh in the Morning, and Bread and Flesh in the Evening, and he drank of the Brook,* Kings, B. 1. C. 17.

And the pretty Pidgeon when the World was drowned, and he was confined with *Noah* in the Ark, was sent forth by him to see whether the Waters were abated. *And he sent forth a Dove from him, to see if the Waters were abated from off the Face of the Ground. And the Dove came in to him in the Evening, and lo, in her Mouth was an Olive Leaf plucked off: So* Noah *knew that the Waters were abated from off the Earth.* Gen. viii. 8. 11.

As these, and other Animals, are so sensible and kind to us, we ought to be tender and good to them, and not beat them about, and kill them, and take away their young ones, as many wicked Boys do. Does not the Horse and the Ass carry you and your burthens; don't the Ox plough your Ground, the Cow give you Milk, the Sheep cloath your Back, the Dog watch your House, the Goose find you in Quills to write with, the Hen bring Eggs for your Custards and Puddings, and the Cock call you up in the Morning, when you are lazy, and like to hurt yourselves by laying too long in Bed? If so, how can you be so cruel to them, and abuse God Almighty's good Creatures? Go, naughty Boy, go; be sorry for what you have done, and do so no more, that God Almighty may forgive you. *Amen,* say I, again and again. God will bless you, but not unless you are merciful and good.

The downfal of the School, was a great Misfortune to Mrs. *Margery*; for she not only lost all her Books, but was destitute of a Place to teach in; but Sir William *Dove,* being informed of this, ordered the House to be built at his own Expence, and 'till that could be done, Farmer *Grove* was so kind, as to let her have his large Hall to teach in.

The House built by Sir *William,* had a Statue erected over the Door of a Boy sliding on the Ice, and under it were these Lines, written by Mrs. *Two-Shoes,* and engraved at her Expence.

ON SIN. A SIMILE.

As a poor Urchin on the Ice,
When he has tumbl'd once or twice,
With cautious Step, and trembling
  goes,
The drop-stile Pendant on his Nose,
And trudges on to seek the Shore,
Resolv'd to trust the Ice no more;
But meeting with a daring Mate,
Who often us'd to slide and scate,
Again is into Danger led,
And falls again, and breaks his head.
  So Youth when first they're drawn
    to sin,
And see the Danger they are in,
  Would gladly quit the thorney Way,
And think it is unsafe to stay;
But meeting with their wicked Train,
Return with them to sin again:
With them the Paths of Vice explore;
With them are ruin'd ever more.

CHAPTER IV
*What happened at Farmer Grove's; and how she gratified
him for the Use of his Room.*

WHILE AT Mr. *Grove's*, which was in the Heart of the Village, she not only taught the
Children in the Day Time, but the Farmer's Servants, and all the Neighbours, to read and
write in the Evening; and it was a constant Practice before they went away, to make them
all go to Prayers, and sing Psalms. By this Means, the People grew extremely regular, his
Servants were always at Home, instead of being at the Ale-house, and he had more Work
done than ever. This gave not only Mr. *Grove*, but all the Neighbours, an high Opinion
of her good Sense and prudent Behaviour: And she was so much esteemed, that most of
the Differences in the Parish were left to her Decision; and if a Man and Wife quarrelled
(which sometimes happened in that Part of the Kingdom) both Parties certainly came to
her for Advice. Every Body knows, that *Martha Wilson* was a passionate scolding Jade, and
that *John* her husband, was a surly ill-tempered Fellow. These were one Day brought by
the Neighbours for *Margery* to talk to them, when they fairly quarrelled before her, and
were going to Blows; but she stepping between them, thus addressed the Husband; *John,*
says she, you are a Man, and ought to have more Sense than to fly in a Passion, at every
Word that is said amiss by your Wife; and *Martha,* says she, you ought to know your Duty
better, than to say any Thing to aggravate your Husband's Resentment. These frequent
Quarrels, arise from the Indulgence of your violent Passions; for I know, you both love
one another, notwithstanding what has passed between you. Now, pray tell me *John,* and

tell me *Martha,* when you have had a Quarrel the over Night, are you not both sorry for it the next Day? They both declared that they were; Why then, says she, I'll tell you how to prevent this for the future, if you will both promise to take my Advice. They both promised her. You know, says she, that a small Spark will set Fire to Tinder, and that Tinder properly placed will fire a House; an angry Word is with you as that Spark, for you are both as touchy as Tinder, and very often make your own House too hot to hold you. To prevent this, therefore, and to live happily for the future, you must solemnly agree, that if one speaks an angry Word, the other will not answer, 'till he or she has distinctly called over all the Letters in the Alphabet, and the other not reply, 'till he has told twenty; by this Means your Passions will be stifled, and Reason will have Time to take the Rule.

This is the best Recipe that was ever given for a married Couple to live in Peace: Though *John* and his Wife frequently attempted to quarrel afterwards, they never could get their Passions to any considerable Height, for there was something so droll in thus carrying on the Dispute, that before they got to the End of the Argument, they saw the Absurdity of it, laughed, kissed, and were Friends.

Just as Mrs. *Margery* had settled this Difference between *John* and his Wife, the Children (who had been sent out to play, while that Business was transacting) returned some in Tears, and others very disconsolate, for the Loss of a little Dormouse they were very fond of, and which was just dead. Mrs. *Margery,* who had the Art of moralizing and drawing Instructions from every Accident, took this Opportunity of reading them a Lecture on the Uncertainty of Life, and the Necessity of being always prepared for Death. You should get up in the Morning, says she, and so conduct yourselves, as if that Day was to be your last, and lie down at Night, as if you never expected to see this World any more. This may be done, says she, without abating of your Chearfulness, for you are not to consider Death as an Evil, but as a Convenience, as an useful Pilot, who is to convey you to a Place of greater Happiness: Therefore, play my dear Children, and be merry; but be innocent and good. The good Man sets Death at Defiance, for his Darts are only dreadful to the Wicked.

After this, she permitted the Children to bury the little Dormouse, and desired one of them to write his Epitaph, and here it is.

Epitaph on a Dormouse, *really written by a little* Boy.

I.

In Paper Case,
Hard by this Place,
Dead a poor Dormouse lies;
And soon or late,
Summon'd by Fate,
Each Prince, each Monarch dies.

II.

Ye Sons of Verse,
While I rehearse,
Attend instructive Rhyme;
No Sins had *Dor,*
To answer for,
Repent of yours in Time.

CHAPTER V

The whole History of the Considering Cap, set forth at large for the Benefit of all whom it may concern.

THE GREAT Reputation Mrs. *Margery* acquired by composing Differences in Families, and especially, between Man and Wife, induced her to cultivate that Part of her System of Morality and Œconomy, in order to render it more extensively useful. For this Purpose, she contrived what she called a Charm for the Passions; which was a considering Cap, almost as large as a Grenadier's, but of three equal Sides; on the first of which was written, I MAY BE WRONG; on the second, IT IS FIFTY TO ONE BUT YOU ARE; and on the third, I'LL CONSIDER OF IT. The other Parts on the out-side, were filled with odd Characters, as unintelligible as the Writings of the old *Egyptians;* but within Side there was a Direction for its Use, of the utmost Consequence; for it strictly enjoined the Possessor to put on the Cap, whenever he found his Passions begin to grow turbulent, and not to deliver a Word whilst it was on, but with great Coolness and Moderation. As this Cap was an universal Cure for Wrong-headedness, and prevented numberless Disputes and Quarrels, it greatly hurt the Trade of the poor Lawyers, but was of the utmost Service to the rest of the Community. They were bought by Husbands and Wives, who had themselves frequent Occasion for them, and sometimes lent them to their Children: They were also purchased in large Quantities by Masters and Servants; by young Folks, who were intent on Matrimony, by Judges, Jurymen, and even Physicians and Divines; nay, if we may believe History, the Legislators of the Land did not disdain the Use of them; and we are told, that when any important Debate arose, *Cap, was the Word,* and each House looked like a grand Synod of *Egyptian* Priests. Nor was this Cap of less Use to Partners in Trade, for with these, as well as with Husband and Wife, if one was out of Humour, the other threw him the Cap, and he was obliged to put it on, and keep it till all was quiet. I myself saw thirteen Caps worn at a Time in one Family, which could not have subsisted an Hour without them; and I was particularly pleased at Sir *Humphry Huffum*'s, to hear a little Girl, when her Father was out of Humour, ask her Mamma, *if she should reach down the Cap?* These Caps, indeed, were of such Utility, that People of Sense never went without them; and it was common in the Country, when a Booby made his Appearance, and talked Nonsense, to say, *he had no Cap in his Pocket.*

Advice from Friar Bacon.

What was *Fortunatus's* Wishing Cap, when compared to this? That Cap, is said to have conveyed People instantly from one Place to another; but, as the Change of Place does not change the Temper and Disposition of the Mind, little Benefit can be expected from it; nor indeed is much to be hoped from his famous Purse: That Purse, it is said, was never empty, and such a Purse, may be sometimes convenient; but as Money will not purchase Peace, it is not necessary for a Man to encumber himself with a great deal of it. Peace and Happiness depend so much upon the State of a Man's own Mind, and upon the Use of the considering Cap, that it is generally his own Fault, if he is miserable. One of these Caps will last a Man his whole Life, and is a Discovery of much greater Importance to the Public than the Philosopher's Stone. Remember what was said by my Brazen Head, *Time is, Time was, Time is past:* Now the *Time is,* therefore buy the Cap immediately, and make a proper Use of it, and be happy before the *Time is past.*

Yours, ROGER BACON.

CHAPTER VI

How Mrs. Margery *was taken up for a Witch, and what happened on that Occasion.*

AND so it is true? And they have taken up Mrs. *Margery* then, and accused her of being a Witch, only because she was wiser than some of her Neighbours! Mercy upon me! People stuff Children's Heads with Stories of Ghosts, Faries, Witches, and such Nonsense when they are young, and so they continue Fools all their Days. The whole World ought to be made acquainted with her Case, and here it is at their Service.

The Case of Mrs. Margery.

Mrs. *Margery,* as we have frequently observed, was always doing Good, and thought she could never sufficiently gratify those who had done any Thing to serve her. These generous Sentiments, naturally led her to consult the Interest of Mr. *Grove,* and the rest of her Neighbours; and as most of their Lands were Meadow, and they depended much on their

Hay, which had been for many Years greatly damaged by wet Weather, she contrived an Instrument to direct them when to mow their Grass with Safety, and prevent their Hay being spoiled. They all came to her for Advice, and by that Means got in their Hay without Damage, while most of that in the neighbouring Villages was spoiled.

This made a great Noise in the Country, and so provoked were the People in the other Parishes, that they accused her of being a Witch, and sent *Gaffer Goosecap*, a busy Fellow in other People's Concerns, to find out Evidence against her. This Wise-acre happened to come to her School, when she was walking about with the Raven on one Shoulder, the Pidgeon on the other, the Lark on her Hand, and the Lamb and the Dog by her Side; which indeed made a droll Figure, and so surprized the Man, that he cried out, a Witch! a Witch! upon this she laughing, answered, a Conjurer! a Conjurer! and so they parted; but it did not end thus, for a Warrant was issued out against Mrs. *Margery,* and she was carried to a Meeting of the Justices, whither all the Neighbours followed her.

At the Meeting, one of the Justices, who knew little of Life, and less of the Law, behaved very idly; and though no Body was able to prove any Thing against her, asked, who she could bring to her Character? *Who* can you bring against my Character, Sir, says she, there are People enough who would appear in my Defence, were it necessary; but I never supposed that any one here could be so weak, as to believe there was any such Thing as a Witch. If I am a Witch, this is my Charm, and (laying a Barometer or Weather Glass on the Table) it is with this, says she, that I have taught my Neighbours to know the State of the Weather. All the Company laughed, and Sir *William Dove,* who was on the Bench, asked her Accusers, how they could be such Fools, as to think there was any such Thing as a Witch. It is true, continued he, many innocent and worthy People have been abused and even murdered on this absurd and foolish Supposition; which is a Scandal to our Religion, to our Laws, to our Nation, and to common Sense; but I will tell you a Story.

There was in the West of *England* a poor industrious Woman, who laboured under the same evil Report, which this good Woman is accused of. Every Hog that died with the Murrain, every Cow that slipt her Calf, she was accountable for: If a Horse had the Staggers, she was supposed to be in his Head; and whenever the Wind blew a little harder than ordinary, *Goody Giles* was playing her Tricks, and riding upon a Broomstick in the Air. These, and a thousand other Phantasies, too ridiculous to recite, possessed the Pates of the common People: Horse-shoes were nailed with the Heels upwards, and many Tricks made use of, to mortify the poor Creature; and such was their Rage against her, that they petitioned Mr. *Williams,* the Parson of the Parish, not to let her come to Church; and at last, even insisted upon it: But this he over-ruled, and allowed the poor old Woman a Nook in one of the Isles to herself, where she muttered over her Prayers in the best Manner she could. The Parish, thus disconcerted and enraged, withdrew the small Pittance they allowed for her Support, and would have reduced her to the Necessity of starving, had she not been still assisted by the benevolent Mr. *Williams.*

But I hasten to the Sequel of my Story, in which you will find, that the true Source from whence Witchcraft springs is *Poverty, Age,* and *Ignorance*; and that it is impossible for a Woman to pass for a Witch, unless she is *very poor, very old,* and lives in a Neighbourhood where the People are *void of common Sense.*

Some Time after, a Brother of her's died in *London,* who, though he would not part with a Farthing while he lived, at his Death was obliged to leave her five thousand

Pounds, that he could not carry with him—This altered the Face of *Jane's* Affairs prodigiously: She was no longer *Jane*, alias *Joan Giles*, the ugly old Witch, but Madam *Giles*; her old ragged Garb was exchanged for one that was new and genteel; her greatest Enemies made their Court to her, even the Justice himself came to wish her Joy; and though several Hogs and Horses died, and the Wind frequently blew afterwards, yet Madam *Giles* was never supposed to have a Hand in it; and from hence it is plain, as I observed before, that a Woman must be *very poor, very old*, and live in a Neighbour-hood, where the People are *very stupid*, before she can possibly pass for a Witch.

'Twas a Saying of Mr. *Williams*, who would sometimes be jocose, and had the Art of making even Satire agreeable; that if ever *Jane* deserved the Character of a Witch, it was after this Money was left her; for that with her five thousand Pounds, she did more Acts of Charity and friendly Offices, than all the People of Fortune within fifty Miles of the Place.

After this, Sir *William* inveighed against the absurd and foolish Notions, which the Country People had imbibed concerning Witches, and Witchcraft, and having proved that there was no such Thing, but that all were the Effects of Folly and Ignorance, he gave the Court such an Account of Mrs. *Margery*, and her Virtue, good Sense, and prudent Behaviour, that the Gentlemen present were enamoured with her, and returned her public Thanks for the great Service she had done the Country. One Gentleman in particular, I mean Sir *Charles Jones*, had conceived such an high Opinion of her, that he offered her a considerable Sum to take the Care of his Family, and the Education of his Daughter, which, however, she refused; but this Gentleman, sending for her after-wards when he had a dangerous Fit of Illness, she went, and behaved so prudently in the Family, and so tenderly to him and his Daughter, that he would not permit her to leave his House, but soon after made her Proposals of Marriage. She was truly sensible of the Honour he intended her, but, though poor, she would not consent to be made a Lady, till he had effectually provided for his Daughter; for she told him, that Power was a dangerous Thing to be trusted with, and that a good Man or Woman would never throw themselves into the Road of Temptation.

All Things being settled, and the Day fixed, the Neighbours came in Crouds to see the Wedding; for they were all glad, that one who had been such a good little Girl, and was become such a virtuous and good Woman, was going to be made a Lady; but just as the Clergyman had opened his Book, a Gentleman richly dressed ran into the Church, and cry'd, Stop! stop! This greatly alarmed the Congregation, particularly the intended Bride and Bridegroom, whom he first accosted, and desired to speak with them apart. After they had been talking some little Time, the People were greatly surprized to see Sir *Charles* stand Motionless, and his Bride cry, and faint away in the Stranger's Arms. This seeming Grief, however, was only a Prelude to a Flood of Joy, which immediately succeeded; for you must know, gentle Reader, that this Gentleman, so richly dressed and bedizened with Lace, was that identical little Boy, whom you before saw in the Sailor's Habit; in short, it was little *Tom Two-Shoes*, Mrs. *Margery's* Brother, who was just come from beyond Sea, where he had made a large Fortune, and hearing, as soon as he landed, of his Sister's intended Wedding, had rode Post, to see that a proper Settlement was made on her; which he thought she was now intitled to, as he himself was both able and willing to give her an ample Fortune. They soon returned to the Communion-Table, and were married in Tears, but they were Tears of Joy.

There is something wonderful in this young Gentleman's Preservation and Success in Life; which we shall acquaint the Reader of, in the History of his Life and Adventures, which will soon be published.

CHAPTER VII and Last.
The true Use of Riches.

THE HARMONY and Affection that subsisted between this happy Couple, is inexpressible; but Time, which dissolves the closest Union, after six Years, severed Sir *Charles* from his Lady; for being seized with a violent Fever he died, and left her full of Grief, tho possessed of a large Fortune.

We forgot to remark, that after her Marriage, *Lady Jones* (for so we must now call her) ordered the Chapel to be fitted up, and allowed the Chaplain a considerable Sum out of her own private Purse, to visit the Sick, and say Prayers every Day to all the People that could attend. She also gave Mr. *Johnson* ten Guineas a Year, to preach a Sermon annually, on the Necessity and Duties of the marriage State, and on the Decease of Sir *Charles*; she gave him ten more, to preach yearly on the Subject of Death; she had put all the Parish into Mourning for the Loss of her Husband; and to those Men who attended this yearly Service, she gave Harvest Gloves, to their Wives Shoes and Stockings, and to all the Children little Books and Plumb-cakes: We must also observe, that she herself wove a Chaplet of Flowers, and before the Service, placed it on his Grave-stone; and a suitable Psalm was always sung by the Congregation.

About this Time, she heard that Mr. *Smith* was oppressed by Sir *Timothy Gripe*, the Justice, and his Friend *Graspall*, who endeavoured to deprive him of Part of his Tythes; upon which she, in Conjunction with her Brother, defended him, and the Cause was tried in *Westminster-hall*, where Mr. *Smith* gained a Verdict; and it appearing that Sir *Timothy* had behaved most scandalously, as a Justice of the Peace, he was struck off the List, and no longer permitted to act in that Capacity. This was a Cut to a Man of his imperious Disposition, and this was followed by one yet more severe; for a Relation of his, who had an undoubted Right to the *Mouldwell* Estate, finding that it was possible to get the better at Law of a rich Man, laid Claim to it, brought his Action, and recovered the whole Manor of *Mouldwell*; and being afterwards inclined to sell it, he, in Consideration of the Aid Lady *Margery* had lent him during his Distress, made her the first Offer, and she purchased the Whole, and threw it into different Farms, that the Poor might be no longer under the Dominion of two over-grown Men.

This was a great Mortification to Sir *Timothy*, as well as to his Friend *Graspall*, who from this Time experienced nothing but Misfortunes, and was in a few Years so dispossessed of his Ill-gotten Wealth, that his Family were reduced to seek Subsistance from the Parish, at which those who had felt the Weight of his Iron Hand rejoiced; but Lady *Margery* desired, that his Children might be treated with Care and Tenderness; *for they*, says she, *are no Ways accountable for the Actions of their Father.*

At her first coming into Power, she took Care to gratify her old Friends, especially Mr. and Mrs. *Smith*, whose Family she made happy.—She paid great Regard to the Poor, made their Interest her own, and to induce them to come regularly to Church, she ordered a Loaf, or the Price of a Loaf, to be given to every one who would accept of it. This brought many of them to Church, who by degrees learned their Duty, and then came on a more noble Principle. She also took Care to encourage Matrimony; and in order to induce her Tenants and Neighbours to enter into that happy State, she always gave the young Couple something towards House-keeping; and stood Godmother to all their Children, whom she had in Parties, every *Sunday* Evening, to teach them their Catechism, and lecture them in Religion and Morality; after which she treated them with a Supper, gave them such Books as they wanted, and then dispatched them with her Blessing. Nor did she forget them at her Death, but left each a Legacy, as will be seen among other charitable Donations when we publish her Will, which we may do in some future Volume. There is one Request however so singular, that we cannot help taking some Notice of it in this Place; which is, that of her giving so many Acres of Land to be planted yearly with Potatoes, for all the Poor of any Parish who would come and fetch them for the Use of their Families; but if any took them to sell they were deprived of that Privilege ever after. And these Roots were planted and raised from the Rent arising from a Farm which she had assigned over for that purpose. In short, she was a Mother to the Poor, a Physician to the Sick, and a Friend to all who were in Distress. Her Life was the greatest Blessing, and her Death the greatest Calamity that ever was felt in the Neighbourhood. A Monument, but without Inscription, was erected to her Memory in the Church-yard, over which the Poor as they pass weep continually, so that the Stone is ever bathed in Tears.

On this Occasion the following Lines were spoken extempore by a young Gentleman.

> *How vain the Tears that fall from you,*
> *And here supply the Place of Dew?*
> *How vain to weep the happy Dead,*
> *Who now to heavenly Realms are fled?*
> *Repine no more, your Plaints forbear,*
> *And all prepare to meet them there.*

The E N D.

A P P E N D I X
The Golden Dream; *or, the* Ingenuous Confession.

T o SHEW the Depravity of human Nature, and how apt the Mind is to be misled by Trinkets and false Appearances, Mrs. *Two-Shoes* does acknowledge, that after she became rich, she had like to have been too fond of Money; for on seeing her Husband receive a very large Sum, her Heart went pit pat, pit pat, all the Evening, and she began to think that Guineas were pretty Things. To suppress this Turbulence of Mind, which was a Symptom of approaching Avarice, she said her Prayers earlier than usual, and at Night had the following Dream; which I shall relate in her own Words.

"Methought, as I slept, a Genii stept up to me with a *French* Commode, which having placed on my Head, he said, now go and be happy; for from henceforth every Thing you touch shall turn to Gold. Willing to try the Experiment, I gently touched the Bed-post and Furniture, which immediately became massy Gold burnished, and of surprizing Brightness. I then touched the Walls of the House which assumed the same Appearance, and looked amazingly magnificent. Elated with this wonderful Gift, I rang hastily for my Maid to carry the joyful News to her Master, who, as I thought, was then walking in the Garden. *Sukey* came, but in the Extacy I was in, happening to touch her Hand, she became instantly an immoveable Statue. Go, said I, and call your Master; but she made no reply, nor could she stir. Upon this I shrieked, and in came my dear Husband, whom I ran to embrace; when no sooner had I touched him, but he became good for nothing; that is, good for nothing but his Weight in Gold; and that you know could be nothing, where Gold was so plenty. At this instant up came another Servant with a Glass of Water, thinking me ill; this I attempted to swallow, but no sooner did it touch my Mouth, than it became a hard solid Body, and unfit for drinking. My Distress now grew insupportable! I had destroyed, as I thought, my dear Husband, and my favourite Servant; and I plainly perceived, that I should die for want in the midst of so much Wealth. Ah, said I, why did I long for Riches! Having enough already, why did I covet more? Thus terrified, I began to rave, and beat my Breast, which awaked Sir *Charles*, who kindly called me from this State of Inquietude, and composed my Mind."

This Scene I have often considered as a Lesson, instructing me, that a Load of Riches bring, instead of Felicity, a Load of Troubles; and that the only Source of Happiness is *Contentment*. Go, therefore, you who have too much, and give it to those who are in want; so shall you be happy yourselves, by making others happy. This is a Precept from the Almighty, a Precept which must be regarded; for *The Lord is about your Paths, and about your Bed, and spieth out all your Ways.*

An Anecdote, respecting Tom Two-Shoes, communicated by a Gentleman, who is now writing the History of his Life.

IT IS GENERALLY known, that *Tom Two-Shoes* went to Sea when he was a very little Boy, and very poor; and that he returned a very great Man, and very rich; but no one knows how he acquired so much Wealth but myself, and a few Friends, who have perrused the Papers from which I am compiling the History of his Life.

After *Tom* had been at Sea some Years, he was unfortunately cast away, on that Part of the Coast of *Africa* inhabited by the *Hottentots*. Here he met with a strange Book, which the *Hottentots* did not understand, and which gave him some Account of *Prester John's* Country; and being a Lad of great Curiosity and Resolution he determined to see it; accordingly he set out on the Pursuit, attended by a young Lion, which he had

tamed and made so fond of him, that he followed him like a Dog, and obeyed all his Commands; and indeed it was happy for him that he had such a Companion; for as his Road lay through large Woods and Forests, that were full of wild Beasts and without Inhabitants, he must have been soon starved or torn in Pieces, had he not been both fed and protected by this noble Animal.

Tom had provided himself with two Guns, a Sword, and as much Powder and Ball as he could carry; with these Arms, and such a Companion, it was mighty easy for him to get Food; for the Animals in these wild and extensive Forests, having never seen the Effects of a Gun, readily ran from the Lion, who hunted on one Side, to *Tom*, who hunted on the other, so that they were either caught by the Lion, or shot by his Master; and it was pleasant enough, after a hunting Match, and the Meat was dressed, to see how Cheek by Joul they sat down to Dinner.

When they came into the Land of *Utopia*, he discovered the Statue of a Man erected on an open Plain, which had this Inscription on the Pedestal: *On* May-day *in the Morning, when the Sun rises, I shall have a Head of Gold.* As it was now the latter End of *April*, he stayed to see this wonderful Change; and in the mean time, enquiring of a poor Shepherd what was the Reason of the Statue being erected there, and with that Inscription, he was informed, that it was set up many Years ago by an *Arabian* Philosopher, who travelled all the World over in Search of a real Friend; that he lived with, and was extremely fond of a great Man who inhabited the next Mountain; but that on some Occasion they quarrelled, and the Philosopher, leaving the Mountain, retired into the Plain, where he erected this Statue with his own Hands, and soon after died. To this he added, that all the People for many Leagues round came there every *May* Morning, expecting to see the Stone-head turned to Gold.

Tom got up very early on the first of *May* to behold this amazing Change, and when he came near the Statue he saw a Number of People, who all ran away from him in the utmost Consternation, having never before seen a Lion follow a Man like a Lap-dog. Being thus left alone, he fixed his Eyes on the Sun, then rising with resplendent Majesty, and afterwards turned to the Statue, but could see no Change in the Stone.—Surely, says he to himself, there is some mystical Meaning in this! This Inscription must be an Ænigma, the hidden Meaning of which I will endeavour to find; for a Philosopher would never expect a Stone to be turned to Gold; accordingly he measured the Length of the Shadow, which the Statue gave on the Ground by the Sun shining on it, and marked that particular Part where the Head fell, then getting a *Chopness* (a Thing like a Spade) and digging, he discovered a Copper-chest, full of Gold, with this Inscription engraved on the Lid of it.

THY WIT,

Oh Man! whoever thou art,
Hath disclos'd the Ænigma,
And discover'd the GOLDEN HEAD,
Take it and use it,
But use it with WISDOM;
For know,
That GOLD, properly employ'd,
May dispense Blessings,
And promote the Happiness of Mortals;
But when hoarded up,
Or misapply'd,
Is but Trash, that makes Mankind mise-
rable.
Remember
The unprofitable Servant,
Who hid his *Talent* in a Napkin;
And
The profligate Son,
Who squander'd away his Substance and
fed with the Swine.
As thou hast got the GOLDEN HEAD,
Observe the *Golden Mean*,
Be *Good* and be happy.

This Lesson, coming as it were from the Dead, struck him with such Awe, and Reverence for Piety and Virtue, that, before he removed the Treasure, he kneeled down, and earnestly and fervently prayed that he might make a prudent, just and proper Use of it. He then conveyed the Chest away; but how he got it to *England*, the Reader will be informed in the History of his Life. It may not be improper, however, in this Place, to give the Reader some Account of the Philosopher who hid this Treasure, and took so much Pains to find a true and real Friend to enjoy it. As *Tom* had Reason to venerate his Memory, he was very particular in his Enquiry, and had this Character of him;— that he was a Man well acquainted with Nature and with Trade; that he was pious, friendly, and of a sweet and affable Disposition. That he had acquired a Fortune by Commerce, and having no Relations to leave it to, he travelled through *Arabia*, *Persia*, *India*, *Libia* and *Utopia* in search of a real Friend. In this Pursuit he found several with whom he exchanged good Offices, and that were polite and obliging, but they often flew off for Trifles; or as soon as he pretended to be in Distress, and requested their Assistance, left him to struggle with his own Difficulties. So true is that Copy in our Books, which says, *Adversity is the Touchstone of Friendship*. At last, however, he met with the *Utopian* Philosopher, or the wise Man of the Mountain, as he is called, and thought in him he had found the Friend he wanted; for though he often pretended to be in Distress, and abandoned to the Frowns of Fortune, this Man always relieved him, and with such Chearfulness and Sincerity, that concluding he had found out the only Man to whom he ought to open both his Purse and his Heart, he let him so far into his Secrets, as to desire his Assistance in hiding a large Sum of Money, which he wanted to conceal, lest the Prince of the Country, who was absolute, should, by the Advice of his wicked Minister, put him to Death for his Gold. The two Philosophers met and hid the Money, which the Stranger, after some Days, went to see, but found it gone. How was he struck to the Heart, when he found that his Friend, whom he had often tried, and who had relieved him in his Distress, could not withstand this Temptation, but broke through the sacred Bonds of Friendship, and turned even a Thief for Gold which he did not want, as he was already very rich. Oh! said he, what is the Heart of Man made of? Why am I condemned to live among People who have no Sincerity, and who barter the most sacred Ties of Friendship and Humanity for the Dirt that we tread on? Had I lost my Gold and found a real Friend, I should have been happy with the Exchange, but now I am most miserable. After some Time he wiped off his Tears, and being determined not to be so imposed on, he had Recourse to Cunning and the Arts of Life. He went to his pretended Friend with a chearful Countenance, told him he had more Gold to hide, and desired him to appoint a Time when they might go together, and open the Earth to put it into the same Pot; the other, in Hopes of getting more Wealth, appointed the next Evening. They went together, opened the Ground, and found the Money they had first placed there, for the artful Wretch, he so much confided in, had conveyed it again into the Pot, in order to obtain more. Our Philosopher immediately took the Gold, and putting it into his Pocket, told the other he had now altered his Mind, and should bury it no more, till he found a Man more worthy of his Confidence. See what People lose by being dishonest. This calls to my Mind the Words of the Poet:

A Wit's a Feather, and a Chief's a Rod,
An honest Man's the noblest Work of God.

Remember this Story, and take Care whom you trust; but don't be covetous, sordid and miserable; for the Gold we have is but lent us to do Good with. We received all from the Hand of God, and every Person in Distress hath a just Title to a Portion of it.

4

Hymns in Prose

By ANNA LAETITIA AIKIN BARBAULD

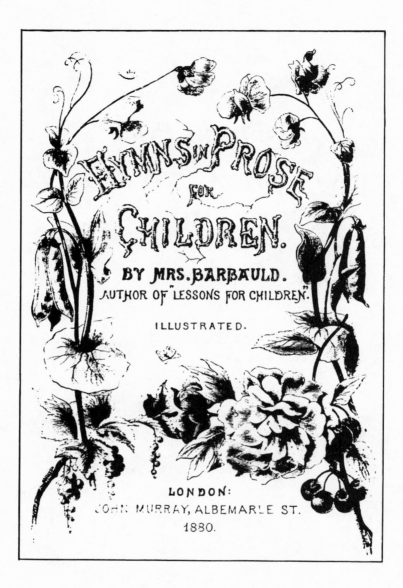

HYMNS in PROSE

FOR

CHILDREN.

BY MRS. BARBAULD.

AUTHOR OF "LESSONS FOR CHILDREN."

ILLUSTRATED.

LONDON:

JOHN MURRAY, ALBEMARLE ST.

1880.

Aɴɴᴀ ʟᴀᴇᴛɪᴛɪᴀ ᴀɪᴋɪɴ ʙᴀʀʙᴀᴜʟᴅ *(1743–1825) was surrounded by religion. Her father was a Unitarian minister, her mother the daughter of a minister. In 1774 she married the Reverend Rochemont Barbauld and established a boarding school for boys at Palgrave, Suffolk. For a nephew she had adopted, she wrote* Lessons for Children *(1778–1789), in four parts, for children from two to four years of age; the Edgeworths regarded these books as "the best . . . of the kind that have ever appeared."* The Juvenile Review *(1817) had to reassure those parents whose children at three could not get beyond the alphabet. Barbauld was probably using her own precociousness as a guide. Reading at three, she soon mastered Latin and Greek and, as a child, impressed Samuel Johnson. As he confessed to Dr. Burney, however, Johnson was not pleased with Barbauld's later life:*

> *Miss Aikin was an instance of early cultivation, but in what did it terminate? In marrying a little Presbyterian parson, who keeps an infant boarding-school, so that all her employment now is "To suckle fools, and chronicle small beer."*

Hymns in Prose *(1781) is proof enough that Barbauld's life was not wasted. A unique work, without verse or meter, it ". . . everywhere bursts forth in poetry"* (The Works of Anna Laetitia Barbauld with a Memoir by Lucy Aikin. *Boston, 1826, I, xx). There were two dozen editions by 1824, and the book, much reprinted by the Victorians, was translated into five languages, including Italian.*

Coleridge blasted Barbauld as "that pleonasm of nakedness, as if it were not enough to be bare, she was also bald." Parts of Lessons for Children *were rather severe. The Edgeworths objected to a passage in which a boy who mistreats a robin is deserted by his parents and finally eaten by bears.* Hymns in Prose *is a less threatening, more pastoral book. While we may not want it committed to memory as Mrs. Barbauld intended, it remains a memorable and unique work.*

The text used is a Victorian one which testifies to Barbauld's continuing popularity: Hymns in Prose for Children by Mrs. Barbauld, Author of "Lessons for Children" *(London: John Murray, 1880). It contains three hymns (X, XI, and XII) not in the original edition of 1781. Except for capitalization and an occasional change in word form, it is virtually the same as a twenty-seventh edition of 1832.*

PREFACE

AMONG THE NUMBER of books composed for the use of children, though there are many, and some on a very rational plan, which unfold the system, and give a summary of the doctrines of religion, it would be difficult to find one calculated to assist them in the devotional part of it, except indeed Dr. Watts's Hymns for Children. These are in pretty general use; and the Author is deservedly honoured for the condescension of his Muse, which was very able to take a loftier flight. But it may well be doubted whether poetry ought to be lowered to the capacities of children, or whether they should not rather be kept from reading verse till they are able to relish good verse; for the very essence of poetry is an elevation in thought and style above the common standard; and if it wants this character, it wants all that renders it valuable.

The Author of these Hymns has therefore chosen to give them in prose. They are intended to be committed to memory, and recited. And it will probably be found that the measured prose in which such pieces are generally written, is nearly as agreeable to the ear as a more regular rythmus. Many of these Hymns are composed in alternate parts, which will give them something of the spirit of social worship.

The peculiar design of this publication is to impress devotional feelings as early as possible on the infant mind; fully convinced, as the Author is, that they cannot be impressed too soon, and that a child, to feel the full force of the idea of God, ought never to remember the time when he had no such idea—to impress them, by connecting religion with a variety of sensible objects, with all that he sees, all he hears, all that affects his young mind with wonder or delight; and thus, by deep, strong, and permanent associations, to lay the best foundation for practical devotion in future life. For he who has early been accustomed to see the Creator in the visible appearances of all around him, to feel His continual presence, and lean upon His daily protection—though his religious ideas may be mixed with many improprieties, which his correcter reason will refine away—has made large advances towards that habitual piety, without which religion can scarcely regulate the conduct, and will never warm the heart.

A. L. B.

HYMN I

COME, let us praise God, for He is exceeding great; let us bless God, for He is very good.

He made all things; the sun to rule the day, the moon to shine by night.

He made the great whale, and the elephant; and the little worm that crawleth on the ground.

The little birds sing praises to God, when they warble sweetly in the green shade.

The brooks and rivers praise God, when they murmur melodiously amongst the smooth pebbles.

I will praise God with my voice; for I may praise Him, though I am but a little child.

A few years ago, and I was a little infant, and my tongue was dumb within my mouth: And I did not know the great name of God, for my reason was not come unto me.

But now I can speak, and my tongue shall praise Him:

I can think of all His kindness, and my heart shall love Him.

Let Him call me, and I will come unto Him: let Him command, and I will obey Him.

When I am older, I will praise Him better; and I will never forget God, so long as my life remaineth in me.

HYMN II

COME, let us go forth into the fields, let us see how the flowers spring, let us listen to the warbling of the birds, and sport ourselves upon the new grass.

The winter is over and gone, the buds come out upon the trees, the crimson blossoms of the peach and the nectarine are seen, and the green leaves sprout.

The hedges are bordered with tufts of primroses, and yellow cowslips, that hang down their heads; and the blue violet lies hid beneath the shade.

The young goslings are running upon the green, they are just hatched, their bodies are covered with yellow down; the old ones hiss with anger if any one comes near.

The hen sits on her nest of straw, she watches patiently the full time, then she carefully breaks the shell, and the young chickens come out.

The lambs just dropped are in the field, they totter by the side of their dams, their young limbs can hardly support their weight. If you fall, little lambs, you will not be hurt; there is spread under you a carpet of soft grass; it is spread on purpose to receive you.

The butterflies flutter from bush to bush and open their wings to the warm sun.

The young animals of every kind are sporting about, they feel themselves happy, they are glad to be alive,—they thank Him that hath made them alive.

They may thank Him in their hearts, but we can thank Him with our tongues; we are better than they, and can praise Him better.

The birds can warble and the young lambs can bleat, but we can open our lips in His praise, we can speak of all His goodness.

Therefore we will thank Him for ourselves, and we will thank Him for those that cannot speak.

Trees that blossom and little lambs that skip about, if you could, you would say how good He is; but you are dumb, we will say it for you.

We will not offer you in sacrifice, but we will offer sacrifice for you; on every hill and in every green field, we will offer the sacrifice of thanksgiving, and the incense of praise.

HYMN III

BEHOLD THE SHEPHERD of the flock, he taketh care for his sheep, he leadeth them among clear brooks, he guideth them to fresh pasture: if the young lambs are weary, he carrieth them in his arms; if they wander, he bringeth them back.

But who is the shepherd's Shepherd? who taketh care for him? who guideth him in the path he should go? and, if he wander, who shall bring him back? God is the shepherd's Shepherd. He is the Shepherd over all; He taketh care for all; the whole earth is His fold; we are all His flock; and every herb, and every green field, is the pasture which He hath prepared for us.

The mother loveth her little child; she bringeth it up on her knees; she nourisheth its body with food; she feedeth its mind with knowledge; if it is sick, she nurseth it with tender love; she watcheth over it when asleep; she forgetteth it not for a moment; she teacheth it how to be good; she rejoiceth daily in its growth.

But who is the Parent of the mother? who nourisheth her with good things, and watcheth over her with tender love, and remembereth her every moment? Whose arms are about her to guard her from harm? and if she is sick, who shall heal her?

God is the Parent of the mother; He is the Parent of all, for He created all. All the men and all the women, who are alive in the wide world, are His children; He loveth all, He is good to all.

The king governeth his people; he hath a golden crown upon his head, and the royal sceptre is in his hand; he sitteth upon a throne, and sendeth forth his demands; his subjects fear before him: if they do well, he protecteth them from danger; and if they do evil, he punisheth them.

But who is the Sovereign of the king? who commandeth him what he must do? whose hand is reached out to protect him from danger? and if he doeth evil, who shall punish him?

God is the Sovereign of the king; His crown is of rays of light, and His throne is amongst the stars. He is King of kings, and Lord of lords: if He biddeth us live, we live; and if He biddeth us die, we die; His dominion is over all worlds, and the light of His countenance is upon all His works.

God is our Shepherd, therefore we will follow Him; God is our Father, therefore we will love Him; God is our King, therefore we will obey Him.

HYMN IV

COME, and I will show you what is beautiful. It is a rose fully blown. See how she sits upon her mossy stem, like the queen of all the flowers! her leaves glow like fire: the air is filled with her sweet odour; she is the delight of every eye.

She is beautiful, but there is a fairer than she. He that made the rose is more beautiful than the rose; He is all lovely; He is the delight of every heart.

I will show you what is strong. The lion is strong; when he raiseth up himself from his lair, when he shaketh his mane, when the voice of his roaring is heard, the cattle of the field fly, and the wild beasts of the desert hide themselves, for he is very terrible.

The lion is strong, but He that made the lion is stronger than he: His anger is terrible: He could make us die in a moment, and no one could save us out of His hand.

I will show you what is glorious. The sun is glorious. When he shineth in the clear sky, when he sitteth on the bright throne in the heavens, and looketh abroad over all the earth, he is the most excellent and glorious creature the eye can behold.

The sun is glorious, but He that made the sun is more glorious than he. The eye beholdeth Him not, for His brightness is more dazzling than we could bear.

He seeth in all dark places; by night as well as by day; and the light of His countenance is over all His works.

Who is this great Name, and what is He called, that my lips may praise Him?

This great Name is GOD. He made all things, but He is himself more excellent than all which He hath made: they are beautiful, but He is beauty; they are strong, but He is strength; they are perfect, but He is perfection.

HYMN V

THE GLORIOUS SUN is set in the west; the night dews fall; and the air, which was sultry, becomes cool.

The flowers fold up their coloured leaves; they fold themselves up, and hang their heads on the slender stalk.

The chickens are gathered under the wing of the hen, and are at rest; the hen herself is at rest also.

The little birds have ceased their warbling, they are asleep on the boughs, each one has his head behind his wing.

There is no murmur of bees around the hive, or among the honeyed woodbines; they have done their work, and lie close in their waxen cells.

The sheep rest upon their soft fleeces, and their loud bleating is no more heard amongst the hills.

There is no sound of a number of voices, or of children at play, or the trampling of busy feet, and of people hurrying to and fro.

The smith's hammer is not heard upon the anvil; nor the harsh saw of the carpenter.

All men are stretched on their quiet beds; and the child sleeps upon the breast of its mother.

Darkness is spread over the skies, and darkness is upon the ground; every eye is shut and every hand is still.

Who taketh care of all people when they are sunk in sleep; when they cannot defend themselves, nor see if danger approacheth?

There is an eye that never sleepeth; there is an eye that seeth in dark night as well as in the bright sunshine.

When there is no light of the sun, nor of the moon; when there is no lamp in the house, nor any little star twinkling through the thick clouds; that eye seeth everywhere, in all places, and watcheth continually over all the families of the earth.

The eye that sleepeth not is God's; His hand is always stretched out over us.

He made sleep to refresh us when we are weary: He made night that we might sleep in quiet.

As the mother moveth about the house with her finger on her lips, and stilleth every little noise that her infant be not disturbed,—as she draweth the curtains around its bed, and shutteth out the light from its tender eyes, so God draweth the curtains of darkness around us; so He maketh all things to be hushed and still, that His large family may sleep in peace.

Labourers, spent with toil, and young children, and every little humming insect, sleep quietly, for God watcheth over you.

You may sleep, for He never sleeps; you may close your eyes in safety, for His eye is always open to protect you.

When the darkness is passed away, and the beams of the morning sun strike through your eyelids, begin the day with praising God, who hath taken care of you through the night.

Flowers, when you open again, spread your leaves, and smell sweet to His praise.

Birds, when you awake, warble your thanks amongst the green boughs; sing to Him before you sing to your mates.

Let His praise be in our hearts, when we lie down; let His praise be on our lips, when we awake.

HYMN VI

CHILD OF REASON, whence comest thou? What has thine eye observed, and whither has thy foot been wandering?

I have been wandering along the meadows in the thick grass; the cattle were feeding around me or reposing in the cool shade; the corn sprung up in the furrows; the poppy and the harebell grew among the wheat; the fields were bright with summer, and glowing with beauty.

Didst thou see nothing more? Didst thou observe nothing besides? Return again, child of reason, for there are greater things than these.—God was among the fields; and didst thou not perceive Him? His beauty was upon the meadows: His smiles enlivened the sunshine.

I have walked through the thick forest; the wind whispered among the trees; the brook fell from the rocks with a pleasant murmur; the squirrel leapt from bough to bough; and the birds sung to each other amongst the branches.

Didst thou hear nothing but the murmur of the brook? no whispers but the whispers of the wind? Return again, child of reason, for there are greater things than these.—God was amongst the trees; His voice sounded in the murmur of the water; His music warbled in the shade; and didst thou not attend?

I saw the moon rising behind the trees; it was like a lamp of gold. The stars one after another appeared in the clear firmament.

Presently I saw black clouds arise, and roll towards the south; the lightning streamed in thick flashes over the sky; the thunder growled at a distance; it came nearer, and I felt afraid, for it was loud and terrible.

Did thy heart feel no terror, but of the thunderbolt? Was there nothing bright and terrible but the lightning? Return, O child of reason, for there are greater things than these.—God was in the storm, and didst thou not perceive Him? His terrors were abroad, and did not thine heart acknowledge Him?

God is in every place; He speaks in every sound we hear; He is seen in all that our eyes behold; nothing, O child of reason, is without God;—let God therefore be in all thy thoughts.

HYMN VII

Come, let us go into the thick shade, for it is the noon of day, and the summer sun beats hot upon our heads.

The shade is pleasant and cool; the branches meet above our heads, and shut out the sun as with a green curtain; the grass is soft to our feet, and a clear brook washes the roots of the trees.

The sloping bank is covered with flowers; let us lie down upon it; let us throw our limbs on the fresh grass and sleep; for all things are still, and we are quite alone.

The cattle can lie down to sleep in the cool shade, but we can do what is better; we can raise our voices to heaven; we can praise the great God who made us.

He made the warm sun and the cool shade; the trees that grow upwards, and the brooks that run murmuring along. All the things that we see are His work.

Can we raise our voices up to the high heaven? Can we make Him hear who is above the stars? We need not raise our voices to the stars: for He heareth us when we only whisper: when we breathe out words softly with a low voice. He that filleth the heavens is here also.

May we that are so young speak to Him that always was? May we, that can hardly speak plain, speak to God?

We that are so young are but lately made alive; therefore we should not forget His forming hand who hath made us alive. We that cannot speak plain, should lisp out praises to Him who teacheth us how to speak, and hath opened our dumb lips.

When we could not think of Him, He thought of us; before we could ask Him to bless us, He had already given us many blessings.

He fashioneth our tender limbs, and causeth them to grow; He maketh us strong, and tall, and nimble.

Every day we are more active than the former day, therefore every day we ought to praise Him better than the former day.

The buds spread into leaves, and the blossoms swell to fruit; but they know not how they grow, nor who caused them to spring up from the bosom of the earth.

Ask them if they will tell thee; bid them to break forth into singing, and fill the air with pleasant sounds.

They smell sweet; they look beautiful; but they are quite silent: no sound is in the still air; no murmur of voices amongst the green leaves.

The plants and the trees are made to give fruit to man; but man is made to praise God who made him.

We love to praise Him, because He loveth to bless us; we thank Him for life, because it is a pleasant thing to be alive.

We love God, who hath created all beings; we love all beings, because they are the creatures of God.

We cannot be good, as God is good, to all persons everywhere; but we can rejoice that everywhere there is a God to do them good.

We will think of God when we play, and when we work; when we walk out, and when we come in; when we sleep, and when we wake; His praise shall dwell continually upon our lips.

HYMN VIII

SEE WHERE stands the cottage of the labourer covered with warm thatch! The mother is spinning at the door; the young children sport before her on the grass; the elder ones learn to labour, and are obedient; the father worketh to provide them food: either he tilleth the ground, or he gathereth in the corn, or shaketh his ripe apples from the tree. His children run to meet him when he cometh home, and his wife prepareth the wholesome meal.

The father, the mother, and the children make a family; the father is the master thereof. If the family be numerous, and the grounds large, there are servants to help to do the work: all these dwell in one house; they sleep beneath the same roof; they eat the same bread; they kneel down together and praise God every night and every morning with one voice; they are very closely united, and are dearer to each other than any strangers. If one is sick they mourn together; and if one is happy they rejoice together.

Many houses are built together; many families live near one another; they meet together on the green, and in pleasant walks, and to buy and sell, and in the house of justice: and the sound of the bell calleth them to the house of God in company. If one is poor, his neighbour helpeth him; if he is sad, he comforteth him. This is a village; see where it stands enclosed in a green shade, and the tall spire peeps above the trees.

If there be very many houses, it is a town, it is governed by a magistrate.

Many towns, and a large extent of country, make a kingdom; it is enclosed by mountains; it is divided by rivers; it is washed by seas; the inhabitants thereof are countrymen; they speak the same language; they make war and peace together; a king is the ruler thereof. Many kingdoms and countries full of people, and islands, and large continents, and different climates, make up this whole world—God governeth it. The people swarm upon the face of it like ants upon a hillock; some are black with the hot sun; some cover themselves with furs against the sharp cold; some drink of the fruit of the vine; some the pleasant milk of the cocoa-nut, and others quench their thirst with the running stream. All are God's family; He knoweth every one of them, as a shepherd knoweth his flock; they pray to Him in different languages, but He understandeth them all; He heareth them all; He taketh care of all: none are so great that He cannot punish them; none are so mean that He will not protect them.

Negro woman, who sittest pining in captivity, and weepest over thy sick child: though no one seeth thee, God seeth thee; though no one pitieth thee, God pitieth thee; raise thy voice, forlorn and abandoned one; call upon Him from amidst thy bonds, for assuredly He will hear thee.

Monarch, that rulest over a hundred states; whose frown is terrible as death, and whose armies cover the land, boast not thyself as though there were none above thee:—God is above thee; His powerful arm is always over thee; and if thou doest ill, assuredly He will punish thee.

Nations of the earth, fear the Lord; families of men, call upon the name of your God.

Is there any one whom God hath not made? let him not worship Him: is there any one whom He hath not blessed? let him not praise Him.

HYMN IX

COME, let us walk abroad; let us talk of the works of God. Take up a handful of sand; number the grains of it; tell them one by one into your lap. Try if you can count the blades of grass in the field, or the leaves on the trees. You cannot count them, they are innumerable; much more the things which God has made.

The fir groweth on the high mountain, and the grey willow bends above the stream.

The thistle is armed with sharp prickles, the mallow is soft and woolly.

The hop layeth hold with her tendrils, and claspeth the tall pole; the oak hath firm root in the ground, and resisteth the winter storm.

The daisy enamelleth the meadows, and groweth beneath the foot of the passenger.

The tulip asketh a rich soil, and the careful hand of the gardener.

The iris and the reed spring up in the marsh; the rich grass covereth the meadows; and the purple heath-flower enliveneth the waste ground.

The water-lilies grow beneath the stream; their broad leaves float on the surface of the water; the wall-flower takes root in the hard stone, and spreads its fragrance amongst broken ruins.

Every leaf is of a different form; every plant hath a separate inhabitant.

Look at the thorns that are white with blossoms, and the flowers that cover the fields, and the plants that are trodden in the green path. The hand of man hath not planted them; the sower hath not scattered the seeds from his hand, nor the gardener digged a place for them with his spade.

Some grow on steep rocks, where no man can climb; in shaking bogs, and deep forests, and desert islands: they spring up everywhere, and cover the bosom of the whole earth.

Who causeth them to grow everywhere, and bloweth the seeds about in winds, and mixeth them with the mould, and watereth them with soft rains, and cherisheth them with dews? Who fanneth them with the pure breath of heaven; and giveth them colours and smells, and spreadeth out their thin transparent leaves?

How doth the rose draw its crimson from the dark brown earth, or the lily its shining white? How can a small seed contain a plant? How doth every plant know its season to put forth? They are marshalled in order: each one knoweth his place, and standeth up in his own rank.

The snow-drop and the primrose make haste to lift their heads above the ground. When the spring cometh they say, Here we are. The carnation waiteth for the full strength of the year; and the hardy laurustinus cheereth the winter months.

Every plant produceth its like. An ear of corn will not grow from an acorn; nor will a grapestone produce cherries; but every one springeth from its proper seed.

Who preserveth them alive through the cold winter, when the snow is on the ground, and the sharp frost bites on the plain? Who soweth a small seed, and a little warmth in the bosom of the earth, and causeth them to spring up afresh, and sap to rise through the hard fibres?

The trees are withered, naked and bare; they are like dry bones.

Who breathed on them with the breath of spring, and they are covered with verdure, and green leaves sprout from the dead wood?

Lo, these are a part of His works; and a little portion of His wonders.

There is little need that I should tell you of God, for everything speaks of Him.

Every field is like an open book; every painted flower hath a lesson written on its leaves.

Every murmuring brook hath a tongue; a voice is in every whispering wind.

They all speak of Him who made them; they all tell us, He is very good.

We cannot see God, for He is invisible; but we can see His works, and worship His footsteps in the green sod. They that know the most will praise God the best; but which of us can number half His works?

HYMN X

Look at that spreading oak, the pride of the village green: its trunk is massy, its branches are strong. Its roots, like crooked fangs, strike deep into the soil, and support its huge bulk. The birds build among the boughs: the cattle repose beneath its shade: the neighbours form groups beneath the shelter of its green canopy. The old men point it out to their children, but they themselves remember not its growth: generations of men one after another have been born and died, and this son of the forest has remained the same, defying the storms of two hundred winters.

Yet this large tree was once a little acorn; small in size, insignificant in appearance; such as you are now picking up upon the grass beneath it. Such an acorn, whose cup can only contain a drop or two of dew, contained the whole oak. All its massy trunk, all its knotted branches, all its multitude of leaves, were in that acorn; it grew, it spread, it unfolded itself by degrees, it received nourishment from the rain, and the dews, and the well-adapted soil, but it was all there. Rain and dews, and soil, could not raise an oak without the acorn; nor could they make the acorn anything but an oak.

The mind of a child is like the acorn; its powers are folded up, they do not yet appear, but they are all there. The memory, the judgment, the invention, the feeling of right and wrong, are all in the mind of a child; of a little infant just born; but they are not expanded, you cannot perceive them.

Think of the wisest man you ever knew or heard of; think of the greatest man; think of the most learned man, who speaks a number of languages and can find out hidden things; think of a man who stands like that tree, sheltering and protecting a number of his fellow men, and then say to yourself, the mind of that man was once like mine, his thoughts were childish like my thoughts, nay, he was like the babe just born, which knows nothing, remembers nothing, which cannot distinguish good from evil, nor truth from falsehood.

If you had only seen an acorn, you could never guess at the form and size of an oak; if you had never conversed with a wise man, you could form no idea of him from the mute and helpless infant.

Instruction is the food of the mind; it is like the dew and the rain and the rich soil.

As the soil and the rain and the dew cause the tree to swell and put forth its tender shoots, so do books and study and discourse feed the mind, and make it unfold its hidden powers.

Reverence therefore your own mind; receive the nurture of instruction, that the man within you may grow and flourish. You cannot guess how excellent he may become.

It was long before this oak showed its greatness; year after year passed away, and it had only shot a little way above the ground, a child might have plucked it up with his little hands; it was long before any one called it a tree; it is long before the child becomes a man.

The acorn might have perished in the ground, the young tree might have been shorn of its graceful boughs, the twig might have bent, and the tree would have been crooked; but if it grew at all, it could have been nothing but an oak, it would not have been grass or flowers, which live their season and then perish from the face of the earth.

The child may be a foolish man, he may be a wicked man, but he must be a man; his nature is not that of any inferior creature, his soul is not akin to the beasts that perish.

O cherish then this precious mind, feed it with truth, nourish it with knowledge; it comes from God, it is made in His image: the oak will last for centuries, but the mind of man is made for immortality.

Respect in the infant the future man. Destroy not in man the rudiments of an angel.

HYMN XI

T HE GOLDEN ORB of the sun is sunk behind the hills, the colours fade away from the western sky, and the shades of evening fall fast around me.

Deeper and deeper they stretch over the plain; I look at the grass, it is no longer green; the flowers are no more tinted with various hues; the houses, the trees, the cattle, are all lost in the distance. The dark curtain of night is let down over the works of God; they are blotted out from the view as if they were no longer there.

Child of little observation, canst thou see nothing because thou canst not see grass and flowers, trees and cattle? Lift up thine eyes from the ground shaded with darkness, to the heavens that are stretched over thy head; see how the stars one by one appear and light up the vast concave. There is the moon bending her bright horns like a silver bow, and shedding her mild light, like liquid silver, over the blue firmament. There is Venus, the evening and morning star; and the Pleiades, and the Bear that never sets, and the Pole-star that guides the mariner over the deep.

Now the mantle of darkness is over the earth; the last little gleam of twilight is faded away; the lights are extinguished in the cottage windows, but the firmament burns with innumerable fires; every little star twinkles in its place. If you begin to count them they are more than you can number; they are like the sands on the sea shore. The telescope shows you far more, and there are thousands and ten thousands of stars which no telescope has ever reached.

Now Orion heaves his bright shoulder above the horizon, and Sirius, the Dog-star, follows him the brightest of the train.

Look at the milky way, it is a field of brightness; its pale light is composed of myriads of burning suns.

All these are God's families. He gave the sun to shine with a ray of His own glory; He marks the path of the planets, He guides their wanderings through the sky, and traces out their orbit with the finger of His power.

If you were to travel as swift as an arrow from a bow, and to travel on further and further still for millions of years, you would not be out of the creation of God. New suns in the depth of space would still be burning round you, and other planets fulfilling their appointed course.

Lift up thine eyes, child of earth, for God has given thee a glimpse of heaven. The light of one sun is withdrawn that thou mayest see ten thousand. Darkness is spread over the earth that thou mayest behold, at a distance, the regions of eternal day.

This earth has a variety of inhabitants; the sea, the air, the surface of the ground, swarm with creatures of different natures, sizes, and powers; to know a very little of them is to be wise among the sons of men. What then, thinkest thou, are the various forms and natures and senses and occupations of the peopled universe?

Who can tell the birth and generations of so many worlds? who can relate their histories? who can describe their inhabitants?

Canst thou measure infinity with a line? canst thou grasp the circle of infinite space?

Yet all these depend upon God, they hang upon Him as a child upon the breast of its mother; He tempereth the heat to the inhabitant of Mercury; He provideth resources against the cold in the frozen orb of Saturn. Doubt not that He provideth for all beings that He has made.

Look at the moon when it walketh in brightness; gaze at the stars when they are marshalled in the firmament, and adore the Maker of so many worlds.

HYMN XII

It is now winter, dead Winter. Desolation and silence reign in the fields, no singing of birds is heard, no humming of insects. The streams murmur no longer; they are locked up in frost.

The trees lift their naked boughs like withered arms into the bleak sky, the green sap no longer rises in their veins; the flowers and the sweet-smelling shrubs are decayed to their roots.

The sun himself looks cold and cheerless; he gives light only enough to show the universal desolation.

Nature, child of God, mourns for her children. A little while ago and she rejoiced in her offspring: the rose spread its perfume upon the gale; the vine gave its fruit; her children were springing and blooming around her, on every lawn and every green bank.

O Nature, beautiful Nature, beloved child of God, why dost thou sit mourning and desolate? Has thy Father forsaken thee? has He left thee to perish? Art thou no longer the object of His care?

He has not forsaken thee, O Nature? thou art His beloved child, the eternal image of His perfections: His own beauty is spread over thee, the light of His countenance is shed upon thee.

Thy children shall live again, they shall spring up and bloom around thee; the rose shall again breathe its sweetness on the soft air, and from the bosom of the ground verdure shall spring forth.

And dost thou not mourn, O Nature, for thy human births; for thy sons and thy daughters that sleep under the sod; and shall not they also revive? Shall the rose and the myrtle bloom anew, and shall man perish? Shall goodness sleep in the ground, and the light of wisdom be quenched in the dust, and shall tears be shed over them in vain?

They also shall live; their winter shall pass away; they shall bloom again. The tears of thy children shall be dried up when the eternal year proceeds. O come that eternal year!

HYMN XIII

CHILD OF MORTALITY, whence comest thou? why is thy countenance sad, and why are thine eyes red with weeping?

I have seen the rose in its beauty; it spread its leaves to the morning sun—I returned, it was dying upon its stalk; the grace of the form of it was gone; its loveliness was vanished away; the leaves thereof were scattered on the ground, and no one gathered them again.

A stately tree grew on the plain; its branches were covered with verdure; its boughs spread wide and made a goodly shadow; the trunk was like a strong pillar; the roots were like crooked fangs—I returned, the verdure was nipped by the east wind; the branches were lopped away by the axe; the worm had made its way into the trunk, and the heart thereof was decayed; it mouldered away, and fell to the ground.

I have seen insects sporting in the sunshine, and darting along the streams; their wings glittered with gold and purple; their bodies shone like the green emerald: they were more numerous than I could count; their motions were quicker than my eye could glance—I returned, they were brushed into the pool; they were perishing with the evening breeze; the swallow had devoured them; the pike had seized them; there were none found of so great a multitude.

I have seen a man in the pride of his strength; his cheeks glowed with beauty; his limbs were full of activity; he leaped; he walked; he ran; he rejoiced in that he was more excellent than those—I returned, he lay stiff and cold on the bare ground; his feet could no longer move, nor his hands stretch themselves out; his life was departed from him; and therefore do I weep because Death is in the world; the spoiler is among the works of God: all that is made must be destroyed; all that is born must die: let me alone, for I will weep yet longer.

HYMN XIV

I HAVE SEEN the flower withering on the stalk, and its bright leaves spread on the ground—I looked again, and it sprung forth afresh; the stem was crowned with new buds, and the sweetness thereof filled the air.

I have seen the sun set in the west, and the shades of night shut in the wide horizon; there was no colour, nor shape, nor beauty, nor music; gloom and darkness brooded around—I looked, the sun broke forth again from the east, he gilded the mountain tops; the lark rose to meet him from her low nest, and the shades of darkness fled away.

I have seen the insect, being come to its full size, languish and refuse to eat: it spun itself a tomb, and was shrouded in the silken cone; it lay without feet, or shape, or power to move. I looked again, it had burst its tomb: it was full of life, and sailed on coloured wings through the soft air; it rejoiced in its new being.

Thus shall it be with thee, O man! and so shall thy life be renewed.

Beauty shall spring up out of ashes; and life out of the dust.

A little while thou shalt lie in the ground, as the seed lieth in the bosom of the earth; but thou shalt be raised again; and if thou art good thou shalt never die any more.

Who is He that cometh to burst open the prison doors of the tomb, to bid the dead awake and to gather His redeemed from the four winds of heaven?

He descendeth on a fiery cloud; the sound of a trumpet goeth before Him; thousands of angels are on His right hand.

It is JESUS, the Son of God; the Saviour of men; the friend of the good.

He cometh in the glory of His Father; He hath received power from on high.

Mourn not, therefore, child of mortality;—for the spoiler, the cruel spoiler, that laid waste the works of God is subdued; JESUS hath conquered death: child of immortality! mourn no longer.

HYMN XV

THE ROSE is sweet, but it is surrounded with thorns; the lily of the valley is fragrant, but it springeth up amongst the brambles. The spring is pleasant, but it is soon past: the summer is bright, but the winter destroyeth the beauty thereof.

The rainbow is very glorious, but it soon vanisheth away: life is good, but it is quickly swallowed up in death.

There is a land where the roses are without thorns, where the flowers are not mixed with brambles.

In that land there is eternal spring, and light without any cloud.

The tree of life groweth in the midst thereof; rivers of pleasures are there, and flowers that never fade.

Myriads of happy spirits are there, and surround the throne of God with a perpetual hymn.

The angels with their golden harps sing praises continually, and the cherubim fly on wings of fire.

This country is Heaven: it is the country of those that are good; and nothing that is wicked must enter there.

The toad must not spit its venom amongst turtle doves; nor the poisonous henbane grow amongst sweet flowers. Neither must any one that doeth ill enter into that good land.

This earth is pleasant, for it is God's earth, and it is filled with many delightful things.

But that country is far better; there we shall not grieve any more, nor be sick any more, nor do wrong any more; there the cold of winter shall not wither us, nor the heats of summer scorch us.

In that country there are no wars nor quarrels, but all love one another with dear love.

When our parents and friends die, and are laid in the cold ground, we see them here no more; but there we shall embrace them again, and live with them and be separated no more.

There we shall meet all good men, whom we read of in holy books. There we shall see Abraham, the called of God, the father of the faithful; and Moses, after his long wanderings in the Arabian desert; and Elijah, the prophet of God; and Daniel, who escaped from the lions' den; and there the son of Jesse, the shepherd king, the sweet singer of Israel. They loved God on earth; they praised Him on earth; but in that country they will praise Him better and love Him more.

There we shall see JESUS, who is gone before us to that happy place; and there we shall behold the glory of the High God. We cannot see Him here, but we will love Him here; we must be now on earth, but we will often think on Heaven.

That happy land is our home; we are to be here but for a little while and there for ever, even for ages of eternal years.

The History of Sandford and Merton

By THOMAS DAY

ABRIDGED FROM THE ORIGINAL

THE

HISTORY

OF

SANDFORD & MERTON.

ABRIDGED

From the Original.

FOR

THE AMUSEMENT AND INSTRUCTION

OF

JUVENILE MINDS.

Embellished with elegant Plates.

LONDON:

Thomas Day *(1748–1789) wrote to his friend Richard Lovell Edgeworth that if all books were being destroyed, the one book he would save, after the Bible, would be Rousseau's Émile. Day's own lifelong experimentation with nature and his "History of Little Jack" (in* The Children's Miscellany, *1788) reflect his zeal for Rousseau's ideas. The fifty-eight-page story of Jack the orphan, suckled by a goat and raised in the woods by a hermit, is more straightforward than* The History of Sandford and Merton *(3 vols., 1783–1789). It owes something to Henry Brooke's* The Fool of Quality *(1765–1770), but the debt was ultimately to Rousseau.*

Sandford and Merton *was begun as a short story intended to be part of* Harry and Lucy, *which Richard and Honora Sneyd Edgeworth began. When Honora died in 1778, the work was temporarily abandoned, and Day, on his own, produced a three-volume novel that was to reach nine editions by 1812 and forty-three by 1883.*

Leigh Hunt in his autobiography (1860) saw Sandford and Merton *as a counterreaction to the Newbery books:*

> *The pool of mercenary and time-serving ethics was first blown over by the fresh country breeze of Mr. Day's* Sandford and Merton—*a production that I well remember, and shall ever be grateful to. It came in aid of my mother's perplexities between delicacy and hardihood, between courage and conscientiousness.*

To the Victorians the book must have been widely known. The New History of Sandford and Merton *(1872), a parody by F. C. Burnand, warns children to beware of Mr. Barlow, "an immortal humbug." Harry, in the parody, comes off an insufferable prig. Destroying eggs from bird nests, he rationalizes that "by this means he had saved many a poor bird from a life of suffering and misery, from the pains of hunger and thirst, the necessities of daily labour, the cruel gun of the unskillful sportsman, or the voracious maw of the domesticated cat." Welcome as the parody from an editor of* Punch *is today, the original reviews of Day were more respectful.* The English Review *(November 1783) praised* Sandford and Merton *for its plan and execution, "which is much the best we have seen, and is adapted to the capacities of very young children." Ironically, it was Day's friend Maria Edgeworth, whose writing for the public he disapproved of, who outstripped Day in adapting books to the capacities of children.*

Sandford and Merton *was popularized in abridged form as early as 1792 as well as in full editions. The present text is reprinted from an abridgement of 1818 (London: Darton, Harvey, and Darton) in the Regenstein Library of the University of Chicago. It is approximately one-third the size of Day's original, which is too long to reproduce in its entirety.*

CHAPTER I

THE PRINCIPAL SUBJECT of this history is Tommy Merton, the only son of a gentleman of great fortune, who had large possessions in the island of Jamaica, but who had come to reside for some time in the western part of England. As Tommy was his only child, it was no wonder if he were spoiled by too much indulgence. His mother was so very fond of him, that, however unreasonable his requests at any time were, he need only cry for them, and he was generally sure to have them complied with: though it sometimes happened, that it was totally impossible to procure him what he wanted; and then the house, from top to bottom, was one complete scene of confusion.

When any company came to visit at their house, he was sure to behave in such a manner as disgusted every one present. He must have the first out of every thing at dinner; and at tea, the cups and saucers were frequently overset, by his eagerness to reach at a bit of toast, or any other favourite object he had in view. He was so delicately brought up, that he was hardly ever well; for a little wind gave him cold, and the heat of the sun brought on a fever. When Tommy arrived in England he was six years of age. He had not learned so much as to read, and had been so much indulged, that he hardly knew the proper use of his limbs.

At no great distance from Mr. Merton's seat, lived a plain and honest farmer, who, like him, had an only son, but a few months older than Tommy Merton. His name was Harry Sandford. This youth was strong, active, hardy, and fresh-coloured, being accustomed to run about in the fields, and engage in those rural employments his age would admit of. His affable temper made him beloved by every one; and so tender were his feelings, that he would never rob the innocent birds of their eggs, but has frequently given half his bread and butter to feed the poor robins in the winter. He would destroy no animal whatever, saying, that God had made nothing in vain, and we had no right to put an end to the existence of any creature he had been pleased to make.

Such accomplishments as these drew on him the attention of the clergyman of the parish, who was so much pleased with him, that he taught him to read and write. Little Harry was an obliging creature, and cheerfully submitted to do whatever he was bidden, and was so much attached to truth, that he abhorred telling a lie on any occasion. The gratification of his appetite had no share in his mind, and he frequently preferred his homely fare to the delicacies he met with at other tables.

Accident happened to bring him and Tommy Merton together. The latter was one morning walking in the fields with his female attendant, amusing themselves with hunting butterflies, and collecting a nosegay from the wild beauties of the fields. In the course of this amusement, a large snake rushed from its concealed abode, and entwined himself round one of the legs of poor Tommy. His female attendant fled as fast as she could to procure assistance, while the little enervated youth stood motionless with the fright.

Harry, who happened to be at a little distance, and saw all that had passed, instantly ran to his assistance: he seized hold of the snake, and soon relieved Tommy from his terror.

By this time, Mrs. Merton, who had heard the shrieks of the maid, ran to the assistance of her darling son. In her emotions of tenderness, she caught him in her arms and caressed him. At last, however, she was happy to find he had received no injury, and then enquired of him in what manner he had got rid of the cruel animal. "Indeed, mamma," said Tommy, "had not that little boy come to my assistance, I fear the nasty creature would have bitten me."

"Pray, my dear," said the lady, "whose good boy are you, to whom I am so much obliged?" "My name," said he, "is Harry Sandford." Mrs. Merton then insisted that he should go home and dine with them; but Harry endeavoured to excuse himself, saying his father would want him. The lady asked him who his father was, when he replied, "Farmer Sandford, madam, who lives at the bottom of yonder hill." The lady said, that she should in future consider him as her child; but Harry did not seem much to like the idea of giving up his own father and mother.

The matter, however, was soon settled. Mrs. Merton sent a servant to the farmer, and, taking Harry by the hand, led him to her house, where every thing appeared new to him. He had never before seen such large apartments, and yet did not seem to show many marks of wonder or surprise. When seated at table, Harry, to the astonishment of every one, appeared neither pleased nor surprised at the novelty of the scene, nor at the delicacy of the provisions. He could find no differnce between the silver cup, out of which he drank at Mr. Merton's, and the horn one, which he made use of for the same purpose at home. He could not see the superior utility of gold and silver, when horn would answer the same purposes.

Dinner being over, the lady presented Harry with a large glass of wine, which he thanked her for, but begged to be excused drinking it, saying, that his master, Mr. Barlow, told him, that he should never eat but when he was hungry, nor drink but when he was dry; that he should accustom himself to eat and drink those things only which are easily to be procured, or otherwise he might grow peevish and fretful when he could not get them. The more they conversed with this little youth, the more they were surprised to find so much good sense in a farmer's son.

Mr. Merton observed to his lady, that he wished Mr. Barlow would take their Tommy under his care, as it was time he should learn something. Mr. Merton then asked his son if he should like to be a philosopher: to which he replied, that he did not know what a philosopher was, but he should like to be a king; because kings having many persons to wait upon them, have no occasion to do any thing themselves, and live in so much grandeur.

Mrs. Merton caught Tommy in her arms, and gave him many kisses for so witty an answer, and asked Harry how he should like to be a king. The little fellow replied, that he did not know what a king was; but he should be very happy when he was grown big enough to work at the plough, and get his own bread; for he wanted nobody to wait upon him.

The lady observed, in a whisper to her husband, what a difference there was between the children of gentlefolks and those of poor people. Mr. Merton, however, was a very sensible man, and chose rather to be silent than offend his lady, though he was far from being of her opinion.

Mrs. Merton then asked Harry if he should like to be rich; and on the honest little fellow's answering in the negative, she requested of him to know, with a smile of contempt, why he preferred poverty to riches.

"For this reason, madam," replied Harry, "because I know but one rich man, and that is 'Squire Chase, who lives just by us. He rides over fields of ripe corn, demolishes hedges, destroys other people's dogs, and does many injuries to the poor, and all this merely because he says he is rich. He is, however, universally hated, though it would be dangerous for any one to tell him so."

Mrs. Merton then asked Harry if he should not like to be dressed in fine laced clothes, to have a coach to carry him wherever he pleased, and a number of servants to attend his orders.

"As to clothes, madam," replied Harry, "one coat is as good as another, so as it does but keep one warm; and so long as I can walk where I choose, I shall have no occasion for a coach to carry me. Had I a hundred servants, I should find it more trouble to tell them what to do, than to do it myself." The lady viewed Harry with a countenance mixed with astonishment and contempt, but forebore asking him any further questions.

When Harry returned home in the evening to his parents, they asked him how he liked what he had seen at the great house. Harry replied, that they had all been very civil to him, but that he would much rather have been at home. "I never in my life," said he, "had so much trouble to eat my dinner. One would have thought that I was either lame or blind, as a servant stood behind me all the time I was at dinner, to help me to beer and bread, and take away my plate; and so many dishes followed one another, that I thought there would never have been an end to it. What was still worse, after dinner was over, I was obliged to sit two hours on my seat, as if I had been nailed to it, while the lady asked me how I should like to be a king, to be rich, and, like 'Squire Chase, to be hated by every one."

After Harry was gone, a long conversation took place between Mr. Merton and his lady. The lady preferred what she called the polite notions of Tommy, to the honest rusticity of Harry; but the gentleman was of a different opinion, and preferred sincerity and honesty to the empty parade of greatness.

This conversation concluded with an agreement, that their son Tommy should be put under the care of the same master as Harry. Mr. Barlow was accordingly invited the next Sunday to dinner, when Mr. Merton introduced the subject, made the proposal to him, and Tommy was delivered into the hands of this good man, to treat him in such a manner as should appear to him best.

CHAPTER II

W E HAVE NOW brought Tommy to the vicarage, which was about two miles from his father's house, to undergo a very material change in his temper and dispositions. The next morning, after breakfast, Mr. Barlow conducted him and Harry into the garden. He then took a spade himself, gave a hoe to Harry, and they both began their work. Tommy was invited to join them in their labour, and Mr. Barlow promised to give him a piece of ground to himself, if he would undertake the cultivation of it; but he rejected with contempt an offer, which he thought was more proper to be made to a plough-boy, than to a young gentleman.

Mr. Barlow told Tommy he might do as he liked; and, after he and Harry had worked

about two hours, they left off, and went into a pleasant summer-house, where they sat down. Here Mr. Barlow, taking a plateful of fine cherries out of a cupboard, divided them between himself and Harry: they eat them up, without offering a single one to Tommy, who undoubtedly expected to have his share of them.

This put the little youth into a sullen state, which at last found vent in tears; but his indulgent mother was not at hand to sooth and caress him, and he wandered about the garden, equally surprised and vexed, on finding himself in a place where no one concerned themselves whether he was pleased or not.

As soon as the cherries were demolished, Harry proposed to read a lesson, which was the story of the Flies and the Ants. To this Mr. Barlow agreed, and told Harry to take care that he read slowly and distinctly, and to pronounce his words properly. He then read the following lesson:

"In one corner of a farmer's garden, a nest of ants was discovered. These animals, during all the warm and pleasant months of the year, were fully occupied in dragging to their cells all the little seeds and grains of corn they were capable of collecting. A bed of flowers happened to be near the habitation of these ants, and was frequented by number-less flies, who diverted themselves in sporting from flower to flower. The farmer's little son, having frequently observed the different employments of these animals, and being young and ignorant, he one day broke out into these expressions: 'Surely these ants are the most simple of all creatures! How they toil and labour all the day, instead of revelling in the warmth of the sun, and wandering from flower to flower, like these flies, who seem to know how to enjoy themselves!'—It was not long after he had made this idle remark, when the weather began to grow very cold, the sun seldom made its appearance, and the evenings were sharp and frosty. This same little boy, walking with his father in the gar-den at this period of the year, did not perceive a single ant, but observed that all the flies were lying about, either dead or dying. As he was a good-natured youth, he could not help regretting the fate of the unfortunate flies, and asked his father what was become of the ants he had so often seen on the same spot. His father replied, 'The flies are all dead, because they made no provision against the approach of severe weather. The ants, on the contrary, in laying by a store against the winter, are now snug in their cells, alive and well.' "

This story being finished, Mr. Barlow and Harry took a walk into the fields; and the latter was very inquisitive, in asking the names of all the shrubs and plants they met with. In the midst of their conversation, Harry espied a large bird, called a kite, which seemed to be very busy with something in its claws. He instantly ran to the spot, and by making a loud noise and shouting as he approached, frightened the bird away, leaving a chicken behind him. Harry picked it up, and, though he found it much hurt, it was still alive. The humane little fellow told Mr. Barlow he would put it into his bosom, in order to recover it; that he would carry it home, and give it part of his dinner every day, till it should be able to do without his assistance. This promise he afterwards punctually performed, and his endeavours were crowned with success.

On their arrival at home to dinner, Tommy, who had been all this time rambling in the garden in a solitary manner, made his appearance, and being very hungry, was going to sit down at the table with the rest; but Mr. Barlow observed to him, that as he was too much of a gentleman to think of working, he must go without victuals, as it was not reasonable that the industrious should work for the idle.

Tommy now withdrew into a corner, crying most bitterly; but these were rather tears of grief than of obstinacy, as he found nobody seemed inclined to humour his bad temper. Harry, however, was very unhappy to see his friend in so humiliating a situation, and begged Mr. Barlow, with tears in his eyes, that he might give him a part of his dinner. Having obtained permission to do so, he got up, went to Tommy, and gave him the whole of it; when the young gentleman took it, thanked him for it, and eat it all up. Here Mr. Barlow observed, though gentlemen are above working for themselves, they will eat the bread that others earn by the sweat of their brow. This threw Tommy again into tears.

Mr. Barlow and Harry went the next morning to work as usual, when Tommy came to them, and desired that he also might have a hoe. Mr. Barlow instantly gave him one, and instructed him how to use it, so that in a short time he became a good workman, and pursued his labour with pleasure.

Their work being finished for that day, they all withdrew to the summer-house; and the joy of Tommy was inexpressible, when he found he was to have his share of the fruit. When the fruit was demolished, Mr. Barlow took up a book, and asked Tommy to read them a story; but he said, he had not yet learned to read. Mr. Barlow, after expressing his sorrow for the young gentleman's ignorance, desired Harry to read the following story of the Gentleman and the Basket–maker.

"In a distant part of the world lived a rich man, who spent all his time in the luxurious enjoyments of eating, drinking, gaming, and every kind of pleasure. Such were the errors of his education, that he thought the poor were only made for his use.

"At no great distance from this rich person's house, lived a poor man, who made shift to maintain himself by making baskets out of dried rushes, which grew in a swamp near his habitation. So small was his income, that his food was very coarse, and his bed was nothing better than spare rushes. Notwithstanding this, he was contented, and bore a very respectable and amiable character. The rich man was of a contrary character; he was a stranger to a good state of health, and never sat down to any meal with an appetite. He was universally hated for his tyranny and oppression, and even his own servants detested him.

"Whenever this tyrant went abroad, it was on a kind of bed borne on the shoulders of men. As he frequently passed by the habitation of the poor basket-maker, he constantly observed that he was always merry at his work. What, said he to himself, shall such a gentleman as I be always melancholy and gloomy, while such a reptile as this is gay and cheerful.

"This invidious and wicked reflection was strengthened by the repetition of the poor man's happiness: he therefore determined to make him as miserable as himself, and with that view ordered his servant one night to set fire to the rushes that surrounded the poor man's house. The whole marsh was soon in a flame, which extended nearly to the cottage of the basket-maker.

"Sorrowful indeed was the situation of this poor creature, who found himself totally deprived of the means of procuring subsistence, by the wicked cruelty of a rich man, whom he had never offended. Naked and miserable as he was, he set out bare-footed to tell his melancholy tale to the governor of the province, who was a good and just man. He instantly sent for the rich tyrant, who was unable to make any defence, the crime being clearly proved against him.

"Since this rich tyrant," said the governor, "is so much puffed up with his own consequence, I will convince him of what little value he is to the public, and what a wicked and contemptible mortal he is. As to you, (addressing himself to the poor man,) it must be a matter of indifference as to what part you go, since your honesty and industry will procure you a livelihood any where.

"The governor then gave orders to put them both on board a ship, and to carry them to a remote country, inhabited by a rude and savage kind of men, who principally got their living by fishing, and lived in huts. The sailors having put them on shore, left them, when they were presently surrounded by the inhabitants. The situation of the rich man was now terrible, and he began to cry and wring his hands in the most abject manner; while the poor man seemed perfectly at ease, well knowing his labour would procure him his bread.

"The natives made them understand by signs, that they would not hurt them, but would employ them in fishing and carrying wood. They were then both conducted to a distant wood, and shown several logs, which they were ordered to carry to the cabins of the natives. They instantly set about their business, when the strength and activity of the poor man soon enabled him to complete his business, before the rich man had finished half his.

"The natives, seeing the difference between the abilities of these two men, were very much prepossessed in favour of the basket-maker, who they supposed would be very useful to them. They therefore fed him with what they call their dainties, while they gave the rich man a very scanty allowance of their ordinary fare. However, labour had created him an appetite, and he swallowed that meagre fare more heartily, than he would at home have eat the most luxurious food.

"Experience soon taught the rich man on what false pretensions he had before valued himself, and how much superior to him was a plain, honest, labouring man.

"The basket-maker, on the other hand, bound twigs together in so pretty a manner, as ornaments for the heads of the natives, that they became enraptured with him. They relieved him from his former drudgery, brought him their choicest provisions, and built him a hut to dwell in. As to the gentleman, who had neither abilities to do any thing pleasing, nor strength to labour, they made him the basket-maker's servant, and employed him in cutting reeds for his use.

"Several months had elapsed in this manner, when the governor of their native country sent for them home, and ordered them to be brought before him. As soon as they appeared, he cast a stern and severe look upon the gentleman, and thus addressed him:

"I have now taught you, what a feeble, helpless, and contemptible creature you are, and how inferior you are to the person you insulted. I shall take care that you make him reparation for the injury you have done him. Were I to punish you as you deserve, I should strip you of all your riches, as you wantonly deprived this man of the little all he possessed in this world; but I will act more humanely than you did; and therefore sentence you to give one half of your possessions to this poor injured man.

"The basket-maker instantly thanked the governor for his goodness, but begged leave to remind him, that having lived all his life in poverty, and laboured for his daily bread, he had no inclination for those possessions, of which he should not know the use. All he required, therefore, was to be put in the same condition he formerly enjoyed, and thereby be enabled to get his bread.

"The noble generosity of the basket-maker astonished the rich man, of whom misfortunes had made a different creature. He ever after treated the poor man as his friend, and was a benefactor to the distressed all the rest of his life."

As soon as the story was ended, Tommy allowed it was very entertaining; but said, had he been in the basket-maker's place, he would have accepted of the governor's decree, and have taken one half of the gentleman's fortune. But Harry said he would have done no such thing, lest it should make him as proud, as idle, and as wicked, as the other. Mr. Barlow and the two young folks then went in to dinner.

CHAPTER III

F ROM THIS TIME, Mr. Barlow and his two pupils worked every morning in the garden, and retired after their labour to the summer-house, where they refreshed themselves before dinner. By degrees, Tommy began to grow angry with himself that he could not read, and at last spoke privately to Harry on the occasion, who very generously proposed to teach him. He accordingly began with teaching him the alphabet, which he learned in the course of a day. He then proceeded to spelling, and in a little time read tolerably well. All this was to be done without Mr. Barlow knowing any thing of the matter, as Tommy wished to surprise him by reading him a lesson unexpectedly.

He pursued his study with very great attention, and Harry was by no means backward in giving him assistance. At last, being all three assembled in the summer-house, and the book being given to Harry, Tommy said, that, if Mr. Barlow would give him permission, he would try to read. Mr. Barlow replied, that he should have no objection, but he should as soon expect to see him fly as to read. Tommy, however, with a smile of confidence and self-approbation, took up the book, and, with great fluency, read the following history of the two dogs.

"In one particular part of the world, which abounds with strong and fierce wild beasts, a poor man happened to rear two puppies, of that sort which is most esteemed for size and courage. From the very promising appearance the puppies made, he thought one of them would be a very acceptable present to his landlord. Accordingly he gave him one, which he called Jowler, and kept the other, which he named Keeper, to look after his own flocks. Jowler was sent into a plentiful kitchen, where he soon became the favourite of the servants, whom he diverted by his little tricks and gambols: hence it is no wonder that he lived in a dainty manner, and increased in size and comeliness. This pampered way of living, however, made him cowardly; he became a great glutton, and though he had plenty, yet he could not help thieving.

"With respect to Keeper, his mode of living was very different; for his master was a poor man, who lived hard and was exposed to all weathers. Keeper grew active, diligent, and hardy; and being exposed to perpetual danger from the wolves with whom he had frequent combats, he grew bold and courageous. His honesty was unconquerable; for though left alone with meat on the table, he never touched any thing but what was given to him. The poor man's landlord happening to come into the country to examine his estates, brought Jowler with him to the place of his birth. On his arrival there, he was much suprised to find Keeper so much unlike his brother Jowler, who received a pat or two on the back from his master, as a mark of his superiority. An accident, however, brought Jowler into disgrace.

"As the gentleman was one day walking in a thick wood, attended only by the two dogs, an hungry wolf, whose eyes sparkled like fire, with his bristles standing erect, and an horrid snarl that filled the gentleman with terror, rushed out of a thicket, and seemed determined to devour him. The unfortunate man gave himself over for lost; especially when he saw that his dog Jowler, instead of flying to his assistance, sneaked away, howling with fear, and hanging his tail between his legs.

"Happily for the gentleman, the courageous Keeper, who had followed him at a distance, humble and unobserved, rushed to his assistance, and so courageously attacked the furious animal, that he at last laid him dead on the spot, though poor Keeper received some terrible wounds in the conflict.—So pleased was the gentleman with the courageous behaviour of the dog, that he desired his tenant would make an exchange with him, giving him permission, at the same time, to hang Jowler, as a cowardly, worthless cur.

"The gentleman was no sooner gone, than the poor man was proceeding to hang Jowler, and was actually putting the cord about his neck; but the unfortunate animal, who had been spoiled by his master, licked his hand, and looked so pitifully, that his tender heart relented, and he determined to try if he could not work a reformation in him.

"He was accordingly fed very sparingly, and exposed to all the inclemencies of the weather; so that in a little time he became as vigorous and active, as he had before been lazy and indolent.

"Jowler being one day in the woods, and still fearful of engaging with a wild beast, was suddenly attacked by a furious wolf, from whom he wished to make his escape, but found it impossible. They say, necessity makes cowards brave; at least it proved so with Jowler, who then faced about, engaged the wolf, and killed him.

"The applauses and caresses Jowler received on this first proof of his courage, animated him to greater exploits, and he soon became a terror to all the beasts of prey in that neighbourhood.

"Keeper, in the mean time, leading a life of luxury and ease, soon degenerated, and acquired all the evil qualities that Jowler was possessed of while in his place. Idleness and gluttony soon destroy all the qualities of the mind and body, and in the end lead to ruin.

"The gentleman being desirous of making another excursion into the country, took his dog Keeper with him, in order to give him an opportunity of exercising his skill against his old enemies, the wolves. The country people soon turned out one from a neighbouring wood: but great indeed was the astonishment of the gentleman, when he saw his dog run away on the first onset. While the wolf was pursuing Keeper, another dog sprang forward, attacked the enraged animal, and soon killed him.

"It was natural for the gentleman to lament the cowardice of his favourite dog, and praise the noble spirit of the other: but judge what must be his surprise, when he found it was his discarded dog Jowler. "I now plainly see," said the gentleman, "that courage is not to be expected from those who live a life of indolence and repose. Unremitted exercise, and proper discipline only, are capable of forcing the faculties to exert themselves."

The story being finished, "I clearly see," said Mr. Barlow, "that if young gentlemen will but take pains, that they may do as well as others." He rejoiced to find that Tommy had made so useful an acquisition as that of learning to read. "I have no doubt," continued he, "that Tommy will one day become a sensible man, and will hereafter be able to teach others."

Tommy seemed highly pleased with these praises, and seemed determined to make himself as clever as other people. Indeed, he was naturally of a good disposition, though the talents he possessed had been prevented from appearing, by the habits of a wrong education. He was very passionate, and thought every one obliged to obey him who was not so finely dressed as himself. This opinion often led him into errors, attended with disagreeable consequences, of which the following [is] an instance:

Tommy one day happened to strike a ball with his bat into an adjoining field, in which a little ragged boy was walking. Tommy called to the boy, in a very commanding tone, to throw the ball over, but he took no notice of what was said to him. Tommy then called out in a more angry tone than before, and asked the boy if he was deaf. "No," replied the boy, "for the matter of that, I am not deaf." This enraged the young gentleman still more, and he threatened the boy, that, if he did not immediately throw the ball over, he would come into the field, and thrash him within an inch of his life. The boy then set up a loud laugh, which so provoked Tommy, that he clambered over the hedge with an intent to leap into the field; but his foot happening to slip, down he went into a ditch full of mud and water. There Tommy lay tumbling about for some time, in vain attempting to get out. His fine waistcoat was totally spoiled, his white stockings had assumed another colour, and his breeches were filled with muddy water. In struggling to get out, he first lost one shoe and buckle, and then the other; and his hat fell in and sunk to the bottom.

At last, the little ragged boy took pity on him, and helped him out, and Tommy was so vexed and ashamed, that he was not able to say a word, but set off for home. Mr. Barlow seeing him in such a plight, was afraid he might have received some injury; but, on hearing the whole of the business, he could not help smiling, advising Tommy to be more careful in future how he threatened others with punishment.

The next day, being all three in the arbour together, Mr. Barlow desired Harry to read the following story of Androcles and the Lion.

"A slave, named Androcles, was so ill treated by his master, that his life became an insupportable burden. Seeing no probability of an end to his misery, he determined within himself, that it would be better to die, than to endure the severities and hardships to which he was exposed. He accordingly took an opportunity of quitting his master's house, and went and hid himself in the recesses of a gloomy forest, at some distance from the town. In endeavouring to shun one misery, we often run into another: thus poor Androcles, though he had escaped from the cruelty of his master, had fresh difficulties to encounter. He found himself in a vast and trackless wood, where he could find no food, and where his flesh was torn by thorns and brambles every step he took. At last, coming by accident to a large cavern, he there lay down, overcome with hunger, fatigue, and despair.

"Androcles had not been long reposing in the cavern, when he heard a dreadful noise, resembling the roar of a wild beast, which terrified him exceedingly. He started up, in order to make his escape, and ran to the mouth of the cave, when he saw an enormous lion coming towards him, and from whom there seemed no possibility of escaping. He now gave himself up as devoted to destruction; but great indeed was his astonishment, when he saw the animal advancing towards him in a grave and gentle pace, without showing the least mark of rage or fury, but uttering a kind of mournful sound, as if he himself wanted assistance.

"This unexpected event gave fresh courage to Androcles, who was naturally bold and resolute. He attentively surveyed every part of his new savage acquaintance, who stood still to give him leisure for that purpose. He observed that the lion did not put all his feet to the ground, and that one of them seemed wounded. He boldly advanced, took hold of it, and attentively surveyed it, when he perceived in it a large thorn, which must have occasioned great pain to the animal, as the leg was in consequence very much swelled. However, he carefully pulled out the thorn, and then squeezed the foot, to force out the matter that had gathered there.

"The operation was no sooner completed, than the grateful animal jumped round him, and put himself into many attitudes of joy.

Androcles became the lion's surgeon, and completely cured his patient, who, in return, never went out in pursuit of prey, without bringing something for the support of his kind physician, and such as was more adapted to the nature of man, than to that of a lion.

"Our fugitive and his savage friend lived in this strange kind of hospitality for some months, when Androcles, happening one day to wander too far from his retreat, was taken by a party of soldiers, and conducted back to his master. Being tried and convicted, by the severe laws of his country, he was condemned to be devoured by a lion, kept for some time without food, to make him more fierce and ravenous.

"The fatal moment arrived, and the wretched Androcles was exposed unarmed, in a spacious place properly enclosed, round which were assembled an innumerable crowd, to be witnesses to this inhuman scene. A den was opened, and out of it rushed a furious lion, uttering so dreadful a yell as filled all the spectators with horror. He sprang towards the helpless victim, with an erected mane, flaming eyes, and jaws gaping with destruction.

"Pity commanded a mournful silence, and every eye was turned on the devoted victim, whose miseries seemed to be hastening to a period. Pity and horror, however, were soon changed into wonder and astonishment, when they beheld the furious animal, instead of tearing the victim in pieces, stop suddenly in his career, and submissively crouch at the feet of Androcles, as a faithful dog does at those of his master.

"Androcles was then loudly called upon by the governor of the town, to explain to him and the spectators, the cause of so unintelligible a mystery, how such a fierce and savage wild beast should, in a moment, be converted into a quiet and peaceful animal. Androcles then related every thing that had passed between him and the lion in the wood, and in what manner he had there entertained him.

"Every one present was equally delighted and astonished at the honest narrative, and were happy to find that even the most savage beast may be softened by gratitude, and moved by humanity. They unanimously exerted their interests to gain pardon for Androcles, and they succeeded in their endeavours. He was pardoned, and presented with the lion, to whom Androcles twice owed his life."

The story being now finished, Tommy seemed vastly pleased with it; but could not comprehend how the wild beasts of the forest could thus be tamed. To this Mr. Barlow observed, that wild beasts never do any mischief but when they are hungry; whereas many human beings, and some children in particular, tease and torment animals frequently out of mere wantonness and cruelty, and in that respect are worse than the beasts of the forest.

This just observation of Mr. Barlow struck Harry very forcibly. "I remember, Sir," said he, "in going along the road, I met with a wicked boy, who was treating a poor ass very cruelly. The animal was lame, and the boy beat him unmercifully, because he could not go faster than he was able. I asked him how he would like to be treated in that manner himself. He replied, it was his father's ass, and he had a right to do with it as he pleased. He added, if I were saucy, he would serve me in the same manner. I do not like to be quarrelsome, or offend any one; but, as I thought he was very much in the wrong, I told him he was a cruel creature, and that I was not afraid of him, though he was almost twice my size. Upon this he attacked me with his stick; but I soon made him sick of the contest. You have often told me, that those who bluster most, are generally the greatest cowards. He no sooner found I had mastered him, than he earnestly begged, while he lay upon the ground, that I would not hurt him. I told him I would not, if he would promise not to use his ass ill any more. Upon his solemnly assuring me that he would never again treat the poor animal with inhumanity, I forgave him, and we both went on our own way."

Mr. Barlow applauded the conduct of Harry, and observed, that he supposed the boy looked as foolish as Tommy did, when the ragged boy helped him out of the ditch. A conversation then took place between Mr. Barlow and Tommy, which so much convinced the little gentleman of his imprudent behaviour, that he could hardly refrain from tears;

and, as he was naturally of a generous temper, he determined to make the poor boy amends, the first time he should meet with him.

CHAPTER IV

IT WAS NOT LONG before he had an opportunity of displaying his promised generosity; for as he was that afternoon walking over the fields, he saw the poor boy gathering blackberries. Tommy instantly ran up to him, and asked him if he had not better clothes than those on his back, which hung all in rags. "No, Sir," said the poor boy, "these are my best: I have brothers and sisters who are as ragged as myself; but what is worse, we are all half starved."

On Tommy's asking him what could be the cause of that, the poor boy replied, "that his father was very ill of a fever, and was unable to work; and that his mammy told him, they must all starve, unless God Almighty took pity on them." Tommy, without making any reply, ran home as fast as he could, and presently returned with a loaf of bread, and a suit of his plainest clothes, "Here, poor boy," said he, "you behaved very kindly to me, and therefore I give you these. I am a gentleman, and shall not miss them." The boy received this present with every mark of gratitude, and Tommy turned from him without saying a word, but highly delighted with his own feelings on this his first act of humanity.

The next morning early, Tommy desired Harry to accompany him to an old-clothes shop in a neighbouring village. On their arrival there, Tommy laid out all his money, which amounted to fifteen shillings and sixpence, in buying clothes for the poor ragged family. As they were tied up in a bundle, Tommy gave them to Harry to carry, to which he readily consented; but at the same time asked him, in a friendly manner, why he could not carry it himself. Tommy replied, gentlemen never carry bundles, but that common people always carry them for them. Harry hereupon very justly observed, that gentlefolks should have neither hands, nor feet, nor eyes, nor ears, nor mouths, because common people have them.

They walked on, conversing in this manner, till they arrived at the cottage of the poor man, whom they found much better, owing to some medicines Mr. Barlow had given to him the preceding night. Tommy then asked for the little boy, and, as soon as he appeared, told him, that he had brought some clothes for him and the rest of the little family. The manner in which they were received, showed how much they were wanted. The sincere blessings of the poor woman and her husband were so affecting, that Tommy and his companion could not help shedding tears of joy. As they were returning home, the young gentleman observed, that he had never spent money with so much satisfaction as on this occasion; and that, for the time to come, he would save all the money that was given him, and apply it to these charitable purposes, instead of spending it in the purchase of baubles.

On their return home, Tommy acquainted Mr. Barlow with what he had done, which met with the applauses of that worthy man. In the evening Mr. Barlow, in return for Tommy's goodness, read him the following story of the Two Brothers.

"Among the numerous adventurers, who went to South America, in pursuit of gold and silver, was a Spaniard whose name was Pizarro, and who, like others, was anxious to try his fortune. As he had a great affection for his elder brother, he communicated to him his design, and earnestly entreated him to go along with him, promising to give him an equal share of whatever the expedition should produce.

"His brother, whose name was Alonzo, was a man of good understanding and easy temper. He did not much like the proposed expedition, and endeavoured to persuade Pizarro to abandon it, representing to him the certain dangers he would have to encounter, and the great uncertainty of success. However, perceiving that all arguments were in vain, he consented to accompany him, declaring at the same time, that he wanted no part of the riches he might procure, and only asked to have a few servants and his baggage taken on board the ship with him. Pizzaro then disposed of all his effects, purchased a vessel, and embarked with several other adventurers, who had no doubt of making immense fortunes. Alonzo, on the other hand, took with him only a few ploughs, harrows, and other implements of husbandry; together with some corn, and seeds of different sorts of vegetables. Though this conduct appeared very strange to Pizzaro, yet he took no notice of it to his brother, wishing to avoid the least appearance of altercation.

"A prosperous gale wafted them across the Atlantic, when they put into the last port they intended to stop at till they should reach the land of gold and silver. Here Pizarro purchased several more implements used in digging for, melting, and refining the gold he doubted not of finding, and also procured more labourers to assist him in the work; but Alonzo purchased only a few sheep, and four stout oxen properly harnessed for ploughing.

"From hence they set sail, and arrived safe at the destined port. Alonzo then acquainted his brother that as his intentions were only to accompany and assist him in the voyage, he should stay near the borders of the sea with his servants and cattle, while he traversed the country in search of gold; and, as soon as he had procured as much as he wanted, he should be ready to accompany him back to Spain, whenever he should return to the coast.

"When Pizarro set out, though he said nothing to his brother, he could not help expressing his contempt of him to his companions. 'I have always been accustomed,' said he, to his followers, 'to consider my brother as a man of sense; but I now perceive my mistake. He intends to amuse himself with his sheep and oxen, as if he were actually on his own farm in Spain. We, however, know better than to waste our time in that manner. We, in a short time, shall enrich ourselves for the rest of our lives.' His speech was universally applauded, excepting by one Spaniard, who, as he marched on, shook his head, and told Pizarro, that he probably might not find his brother so great a fool as he imagined.

"They continued their journey for several days, and met with many obstacles, such as being obliged to cross rivers, to ascend craggy mountains, and penetrate almost impervious forests; sometimes scorched with the intense heat of the sun, and then soaked by the violent rains that fell. In spite of all difficulties, they pursued their search for gold, and at last came to a place where they found it in tolerable quantities. Success inspired them with courage, and they continued their labours till their provisions were all expended.

Though they gained gold, they suffered much from hunger, but contented themselves with living on such roots and berries as the earth spontaneously produced. Even this supply at last failed them, and, after losing several of their company by famine and hardships, the rest with difficulty crawled back to the place where they had left Alonzo, carrying with them that pernicious gold, for which they had exposed themselves to the dangers of death in so many miserable shapes.

"In the mean time Alonzo, who foresaw all these disasters, was employing himself in a far more useful manner. His knowledge in husbandry pointed out to him a spot of considerable extent and fruitful soil, which he ploughed up by the assistance of his servants and the oxen he had brought with him. He then committed the different seeds, with which he had furnished himself, to the bosom of the earth; they prospered beyond expectation, and a plentiful harvest rewarded his toils. His sheep also proved prolific. In the intervals of time, Alonzo and his servants employed themselves in fishing; and the fish they caught they dried and salted, having found salt upon the sea-shore: so that by this time they had formed a tolerable magazine of provisions.

"Alonzo received his brother Pizarro, on his return, with the utmost respect, and enquired what success he had met with. Pizarro then informed him of the vast quantity of gold they had found, but that several of his comrades had perished, and that those who remained were in a starving condition. He immediately requested his brother to give him something to eat, as he had tasted no other food for two days than the roots and barks of trees.

"To this request, Alonzo very coolly replied, that his brother should remember, on their departure from Europe, they had agreed not to interfere with each other; and that, as he had relinquished all pretensions to the gold they might discover, they could have no right to any part of the produce of his labour. 'If you think proper,' added Alonzo, 'to exchange some of your gold for provisions, I shall then be ready to accommodate you.'

"However unkind Pizarro thought this behaviour of his brother, he and his companions, being in a starving condition, were obliged to submit to his demands. Alonzo placed so high a value on his provisions, that he soon became master of all the gold they had collected, merely to procure them articles of subsistence. Alonzo then proposed to his brother to embark for Europe.

"Pizarro, with a stern, haughty, and disdainful look replied, that since he had stripped him of all the wealth he had acquired with such danger and fatigue, and treated him so unbrotherly, he might return without him. As to himself, he said he would remain upon that desert shore, and there end his life. Alonzo, instead of resenting this language, caught his brother in his arms, and thus addressed him:—'Is it possible that my dear brother could believe that I meant to deprive him of the gold he had so dearly bought? May all the gold in the universe perish, rather than that I should treat you in such a manner! I perceived your impetuous desire for riches, and I have taken this method to draw you from your attachment to them. My conduct appeared to you as chimerical, since you imagined that nothing can be wanting to him who possesses riches; but you have now learned, that all the gold you had found would not have prevented you and your followers from starving, had not my industry and foresight prevented it. I am willing to flatter myself that you will be wiser for the future; and, therefore, take back your gold, and make a proper use of it for the time to come.'

"This unexpected generosity of Alonzo, filled Pizarro with astonishment and gratitude, and he was, for the first time, obliged to confess that industry and prudence were preferable to gold. They then embarked for Europe, and, after an easy passage, arrived safe in Spain. Pizarro, during the voyage, often entreated his brother to accept of one half of the gold, which Alonzo invincibly refused, saying, that he who can raise what is sufficient for the supply of his natural wants, stands in no need of the assistance of gold."

When Mr. Barlow had finished this story, Tommy observed, "It must be a bad thing to be in a country where one can get nothing to eat." Mr. Barlow replied, that the sufferings of Pizarro and his men were not to be compared to those of some Russians, who were left upon the coast of Spitzbergen.

On Tommy's asking where Spitzbergen was, Mr. Barlow replied, "It is a far northern country, which is perpetually covered with ice and snow. The soil is hardly capable of producing any vegetable, and only a few animals are found in the country. The island is, a great part of the year, in perpetual darkness, and is at that time inaccessible to ships. Though it is impossible to form to the mind a more dreary country, and where human life must be supported with the greatest difficulty; yet, in spite of all these obstacles, four men struggled with them six years, and three of them returned safe to their own country."

Tommy observed, that this must be a very curious story, and that he should be very glad to hear it. Mr. Barlow replied, that he would take the first opportunity to gratify his curiosity.

CHAPTER V

T HE NEXT DAY, Mr. Barlow entertained Tommy with the following narrative:

"The northern seas," said Mr. Barlow, "are frequently so full of ice as to render it exceedingly hazardous to ships, which are exposed to the danger of being crushed between two bodies of ice, or of being so surrounded, as to deprive them of every power of moving from the spot.

"In this latter alarming situation were the crew of a Russian ship. A council was immediately held, when the mate mentioned, what he recollected to have heard, that a ship's crew from Mesen, some time before, had formed a resolution of passing the winter upon this island, and for that purpose had carried timber proper for building a hut at a little distance from the shore. This information led the whole company to form the resolution of wintering there, should the hut be fortunately remaining. They were induced to adopt this measure, from the certainty of perishing should they remain in the ship. They therefore deputed four of their crew to go in search of the hut, and make what further discoveries they could. These were Alexis Himkof the mate, Iwan Himkof his god-son, Stephen Scharossof, and Feoder Wetegin.

"As no human creature inhabited the shore on which they were to land, it was absolutely necessary for them to carry some provisions with them for their support. They had to make their way for nearly two miles, over loose heaps of ice, which the water had raised, and the wind had driven against each other; and this made it equally difficult and dangerous. From this consideration, they avoided loading themselves too much with provisions, lest their weight might sink them between the pieces of ice, where they must inevitably perish. Having previously considered all these matters, they provided themselves only with a musket and powder-horn, containing twelve charges of powder and ball; an axe, a small kettle, a bag with about twenty pounds of flour, a knife, a tinder box and tinder, a bladder filled with tobacco, and every man his wooden pipe. Thus poorly equipped, these four sailors reached the island, little thinking what they were to endure while they remained on it.

"After exploring some small part of the country, they discovered the hut they were in pursuit of, at the distance of about an English mile and a half from the shore.—Its length was about thirty-six feet, and its height and breadth eighteen. It consisted of a small antichamber, about twelve feet broad; and a large room, in which was an earthen stove, constructed in the Russian manner. They rejoiced exceedingly at this discovery, though they found the hut had suffered very much from the severity of the weather. However, they contrived to make it supportable for that night.

"The next morning early they repaired to the shore, in order to acquaint their comrades with their success. But what pen can properly describe the terrible situation of their minds, when, coming to the place at which they landed, they discovered nothing but an open sea, clear of all ice, though but a day before it had covered the ocean! During the night, a violent storm had arisen, which had been the cause of this change of appearance in the ocean. Whether the ice had crushed the ship to pieces, or whether she had been carried by the current into the main ocean, it was impossible for them to determine. However, they saw the ship no more, and as she was never afterwards heard of, it is most likely that she went to the bottom with every soul on board.

"This dreadful event deprived the poor unhappy wretches of all hopes of ever again seeing their native country. They returned to their hut, and there bewailed their deplorable lot.

"Their thoughts were, in course, first directed to procure subsistence, and to repair their hut. Their twelve charges of powder and shot soon produced them as many rein-deer, of which there fortunately happened to be many on the island. They then set about repairing their hut, and filled up all the crevices, through which the air found its way, with the moss that grew there in plenty. As it was impossible to live in that climate without fire, and as no wood grew upon the island, they were much alarmed on that account. However, in their wanderings over the beach, they met with plenty of wood, which had been driven on shore by the waves. This principally consisted of the wrecks of ships; but sometimes whole trees with their roots came on shore, the undoubted produce of some more hospitable clime, which were washed from their native soil by the overflowings of rivers, or some other accident.

"As soon as their powder and shot were exhausted, they began to be in dread of perishing with hunger; but their own ingenuity, to which necessity always gives a spur, removed these dreadful apprehensions. In the course of their traversing the beach, they one day discovered some boards, in which were large hooks and nails in abundance. By the assistance of these they made spears and arrows, and, from a yew tree, which had been thrown on shore by the waves, they formed plenty of bows. With these weapons, during the time of their continuance on the island, they killed upwards of two hundred and fifty rein-deer, besides a great number of blue and white foxes, whose flesh served them for food, and their skins were equally useful in supplying them with warm clothing. The number of white bears they killed was only ten; for these animals being very strong, defended themselves with great vigour and fury, and even ventured to make their appearance frequently at the door of their hut, from whence they were driven with some difficulty and danger. Thus these three different sorts of animals were the only food of these miserable mariners, during their long and dreary abode on this island.

"The intenseness of the cold, and the want of proper conveniencies, rendered it impossible for them to cook their victuals properly, so that they were obliged to eat their provisions almost raw, and without bread or salt. There was but one stove in the hut, and that being in the Russian manner, was not proper for boiling. However, to remedy this inconvenience, they dried some of their provisions during the summer, in the open air, and then hung them up in the upper part of the hut, which being continually filled with smoke, they thus became thoroughly dried. This they used instead of bread, which made them relish their half-boiled meat the better.

"They procured their water in summer from the rivulets that fell from the rocks, and in the winter from the snow and ice thawed. This was their only drink, and their small kettle was the only convenience they had to make use of, for this and many other purposes. As it was necessary to keep up a continual fire, they were particularly cautious not to let the light be extinguished; for, though they had both steel and flints, yet they had no tinder, and it would have been a terrible thing to be without light, in a climate where darkness reigns so many months during winter. They therefore fashioned a kind of lamp, which they filled with rein-deer fat, and stuck into it some twisted linen, shaped in the form of a wick. After many trials, they at last made their lamp so complete as to keep burning without intermission. They also found themselves in want of shoes, boots, and other necessary articles of dress, for all which they found wonderful resources in that genius, to which necessity gives birth.

"Having lived more than six years upon this dreary and inhospitable island, a ship happened to arrive there, which took three of them on board, and carried them back to their native country. The fourth man was seized with the scurvy, and being naturally indolent, and not using proper exercise, he died, after lingering for some time, when his companions buried him in the snow.

"These," said Mr. Barlow, "are the principal particulars of this extraordinary story, and which are sufficient to show how many accidents mankind are exposed to, and the wonderful expedients, which ingenuity and necessity can find out, under the most dreadful circumstances."

Tommy was going to make some remarks on this singular adventure, when he was interrupted by the appearance of Harry, who brought with him the chicken he had saved, as before mentioned, from the claws of the kite. The animal was perfectly recovered of its wounds, and was so grateful to its preserver, that whenever it saw Harry, it would hover about him, hop on his shoulder, and shew every other mark of tenderness and gratitude.

Tommy was vastly delighted with this scene, and enquired by what means he had made it so tame and gentle. Harry replied, that he had taken no pains about the matter; but that he had treated the animal kindly, and that every creature would always be friendly with those who treated them well. Mr. Barlow here interfered, and told Tommy, that if he wanted to tame animals, he must be good to them, and treat them with kindness.

This conversation between Mr. Barlow, Tommy, and Harry, lasted some time, after which Tommy resolved to try his skill in taming animals. He accordingly took a large slice of bread in his hand, and sallied forth in pursuit of some animal on which he might make the experiment.

The first object he met with was a sucking pig, which had wandered some distance from the sow, and was basking in the sun. Tommy immediately began to put his skill to the trial, and called out, "Piggy, piggy, piggy, come hither, little piggy!" The pig, however, not understanding his meaning or intentions, ran away grunting. Tommy accused the pig of ingratitude, in thus running away from him when he meant him a kindness. "And since," said the little gentleman, "you do not know what is good manners, I will teach you to behave better for the future." So saying, he sprung at the pig, and caught him by one of his hind legs, intending to make him eat the bread he had in his hand; but the uncomplaisant animal, who was not used to such kind of treatment, began struggling and squeaking so violently, that the old dam, who was within hearing, instantly ran to the assistance of her pig, attended by all her young family. As Tommy apprehended the old sow would be less complaisant than even her pig, he thought it advisable to let the young one go, when the pig, in endeavouring to get away with all possible speed, ran between his legs, and threw him down.

The scene of this action being in a very dirty place, Tommy was covered with mud and mire from head to foot, and the sow, who reached the spot at that instant, ran over him as he was rising, and increased his dirty condition. As Tommy, though naturally good-natured, was not remarkably cool in his temper, he was sadly irritated at these ungrateful returns for his intended kindness. He instantly seized the sow by one of the hind legs, and began beating her with a stick, which he picked up in the mire. We may naturally suppose, that the sow did not like this kind of treatment, but endeavoured to escape. Tommy, however, kept his hold, still beating the sow, who dragged him several yards, squeaking all the time in the most pitiful manner, to which the young pigs added the music of their pipes.

The noise alarming Mr. Barlow, he hastened to the spot, and found his pupil in a dirty plight. He enquired into the cause of this disaster, when Tommy, as soon as he was able to speak, told him every thing that had happened, and concluded with saying, "All this, Sir, is the consequence of what you have told me concerning the taming of animals."

Mr. Barlow told him, that before he attempted to make free with any animal, he should make himself acquainted with its nature and disposition. He then advised Tommy to go into the house and get himself cleaned, after which they would talk over the matter more fully.

CHAPTER VI

TOMMY AND HARRY went the next day into the garden, to sow some wheat, which Harry had brought with him from his father's, on a piece of ground which Tommy had dug and prepared for the purpose. After they had finished their labour, they returned into the house, when Mr. Barlow desired Tommy to read the following History of the Good-natured Boy, which he accordingly did, in a very clear and distinct voice.

"One morning, a little boy set out from his own home, to go to a village at a small distance, and took with him a basket of provisions sufficient to serve him the whole day. In the course of his journey, a half-starved dog came up to him wagging his tail, and seem-

ingly to implore his compassion. The little boy at first took no notice of him; but seeing the dog still follow him, and observing how lean and meagre he looked, he gave him part of his victuals, though he had no more than what he should want for himself.

"The little boy then pursued his journey, the dog still attending him, and fawning upon him with gratitude and affection. Presently he saw a poor old horse lying upon the ground, and groaning bitterly. He went up to him, and perceived he was in a starving condition. Though he was afraid of being benighted before he should get back, he went and gathered some grass, which he put to the horse's mouth, who began to eat it in such a manner as plainly showed that his principal disorder was hunger. He then fetched some water in his hat, which the animal having drank up, seemed to be so much refreshed, that it soon got on its legs, and began grazing.

"He then continued his journey, and presently saw a man wading about in a pond of water, and seemingly incapable of finding his way out of it. The little boy asked him, why he did not get out of the pond; to which the poor man replied, that he was blind, and having fallen into it, he could not get out again. The little boy told him, that if he would throw him his stick, he would endeavour to get at him. The blind man threw his stick, and the good boy groped his way into the pond, taking care not to get out of his depth. At length he reached the blind man, and conducted him safely out. The blind man blessed him repeatedly, and the little boy again resumed his journey.

"He had not got a great way from hence, when he met a poor sailor, who had lost both his legs in an engagement, and was hobbling along upon crutches. The poor sailor begged charity of the little boy, saying he had neither victuals nor money, and was almost famished. The tender-hearted child immediately gave him all the victuals he had left, telling him he had nothing else to give him. He then ran the rest of the way, and getting to the place he was going to, he did his business, and set out for home with all possible speed.

"He had not got far on his return before night commenced, which proved exceedingly dark, neither moon nor stars making their appearance. The poor boy missing his way, turned down a lane, which brought him into a wood, where he lost himself. Overcome with fatigue and hunger, he sat himself down upon the ground, crying bitterly. At last, the little dog, who had never left him, came to him, wagging his tail, and holding something in his mouth. He soon found it was a handkerchief nicely pinned together, which somebody had dropped, and the dog had picked up. The contents of it, which were bread and meat, he eat most heartily, and then found himself much refreshed. Thus the dog, to whom the little boy had given a breakfast, provided him with a supper.

"He again attempted to make his way through the wood, but in vain, and was almost giving himself up to despair, when he saw, by the light of the moon, which was just beginning to shine, the horse he had fed in the morning. He thought, if he would permit him to get on his back, he might probably carry him out of the wood into the road. He then went up to the horse, stroked him, and spoke to him kindly, and he let him get quietly on his back. The horse then proceeded on slowly till he got into the main road, when the little boy got off his back, stroked and patted him by way of kindness, and then proceeded towards his own home.

"He had not, however, gone a great way before he met with another danger to encounter. As he was passing through a solitary lane, two men rushed out upon him, and were preparing to strip him of his clothes, when the little dog bit the leg of one of the men so violently, that he left the little boy to pursue the dog, who ran away howling and barking. In this critical moment a voice was heard crying out, 'There the villains are, knock them down!' This frightened the thieves so much, that they instantly decamped.

"The little boy then saw it was the sailor he had relieved in the morning, supported on the shoulders of the blind man, whom he had conducted out of the pond. 'Thank God, my little dear,' said the sailor, 'I have now been able to return your kindness to me in the morning. As I was sitting in a ditch, I heard these two fellows lay the plan of robbing you; and, as I was unable to follow them, I got this blind man to let me sit on his shoulders, while he carried me to the spot where they intended to attack you.'

"The little youth thanked them kindly, and from what had passed that day, was fully convinced that a good action never goes unrewarded. He then invited them home to his father's house, where they were kindly treated for the night, and he took care of his favourite dog as long as he lived."

Tommy, having thus finished the story, was vastly pleased with it, and particularly of that part which speaks of the fidelity of the dog. Upon this occasion Mr. Barlow observed to him, that those animals would be equally fond of him, provided he were kind to them, and allowed them some little time to be acquainted with him; for, as he justly observed, nothing equals the gratitude and sagacity of a dog. "But," added Mr. Barlow, "since you have been so well pleased with this story, Harry shall read you the adventures of an Ill-natured Boy, and he accordingly proceeded as follows:

"It is a great misfortune for children to have bad parents, who take no care of them, and such was the unhappy lot of a little youth, who might have been happier and better under a good parent. He drew on himself the name of the Ill-natured Boy, and, as he was quarrelsome, he became disagreeable to every one. This little boy had a dog, which in temper resembled himself, as he was always barking at the heels of every horse, and worrying every sheep he met with.

"One holiday, his father got up early in the morning, in order to go to the ale-house.

Before he went out, he gave his son some provisions and six-pence, telling him, that he might amuse himself that day as he liked. The boy was very much pleased with this liberty, and taking with him his dog Tiger, he set out on his ramble.

"He had not gone far, before he met a lad with a flock of sheep, which the youth wished to drive through a gate into a field adjoining to the road. The little shepherd begged of him to keep off his dog, that he might not frighten the sheep; but, instead of complying with so reasonable a request, he ordered his dog to seize them. Tiger, thus encouraged, sprung into the middle of the flock, when the affrighted sheep dispersed in different directions. The master and his dog equally enjoyed this ill-natured and inhuman sport. Tiger happened, however, to attack an old ram, who, having more courage than the rest, handled him very roughly, and obliged him at last to run away howling. In the mean time, the little shepherd, taking up a stone, threw it with so good an aim, that he gave the ill-natured boy such a blow upon the temple as almost brought him to the ground. Then he walked off crying, both he and his dog being sick of the business.

"He had hardly recovered from the smart the blow had occasioned, than he began to think of fresh mischief. He saw a little girl standing by a stile, with a large pan of milk by her side. She begged him to help her to put it on her head, for she wished to get home as soon as she could, as it was to make a pudding for the family, who had not had a good meal for some days. The wicked boy, taking up the jug, pretended to put it on her head, but just as she had got hold of it, he feigned to make a stumble, gave her a push, and overturned the milk upon her, and then ran away laughing.

"He presently afterwards came to a green, where several boys were playing, and, on his asking to be permitted to make one of them, they readily consented. His mischievous disposition was still at work, and taking an opportunity when the ball came to him, instead of throwing it the right way, he struck it into a muddy ditch: the little boys ran to find it, and as they were standing on the brink, he gave the boy furthest behind a violent push, and he pressing on the rest they tumbled into the ditch. As soon as they got out, covered with mud and mire, they were preparing to give him a drubbing; but he got Tiger between his legs, whom he clapped on his sides, and on the dog's shewing his teeth and grinning, they were afraid to proceed. Thus he again escaped without punishment.

"He soon afterwards met with a jack-ass, quietly feeding, and he determined to have, as he called it, some fun with the animal. He accordingly cut a large bunch of thorns, which he contrived to fix to the poor beast's tail, and then setting Tiger at him, he was greatly diverted with the fright and agony of the animal. Tiger, however, paid dear for his master's sport; for as he was biting the animal's heels, he received so violent a kick as laid him dead on the spot. As this sad boy had no feelings of compassion, he did not care much for the fate of his dog, whom he left with the utmost unconcern, and then sat down to regale himself.

"Shortly after he saw a lame beggar walking on crutches. The beggar craved his charity, when the mischievous little boy, pulling out his six-pence, threw it on the ground, and bid him take it; but, as the poor man was stooping to pick it up, this wicked boy knocked his crutches from under him, and the beggar fell upon his face, when he snatched up the sixpence, and ran away laughing.

"His career of wickedness was, however, now at an end; for, observing two men coming up to the beggar, he ran away as fast as he could, over several fields. At last he came to a farmer's orchard, and, as he was clambering over the fence, a large dog seized him, and held him fast. Being terribly frightened, he roared out lustily, which brought out the farmer, who instantly called off his dog, but seized hold of the boy, saying, 'So, my lad, I have caught you at last. You thought you might steal my apples when you pleased; but you are mistaken, and you shall now suffer for all.' So saying, he laid a whip he had in his hand very smartly on his back and shoulders. In vain did the Ill-natured Boy roar and cry as loud as he could; for the farmer did not let him go till he had given him a severe whipping.

"He now began to be sensible that punishment does not fail at last to overtake the wicked; but the measure of his misfortunes was not yet completed, as he jumped down from a stile, he found himself in the hands of the lame beggar he had thrown on his face. He cried and begged pardon, but the lame man gave him a severe thrashing before he let him depart.

"He again pursued his journey, roaring and crying most bitterly with pain; but he had not gone much further, before he found himself surrounded by the boys he had so ill-treated in the morning. As soon as they saw him without his dog, they set up a shout, and began to torment him different ways. Some pulled his hair, and others pinched him; some pelted him with dirt, and others snapped their handkerchiefs at his legs. He endeavoured in vain to make his escape, as they were deaf to his tears and entreaties. At last, however, he happened to see the jack-ass he had tormented in the morning, when he sprang upon his back, hoping, by that means, to escape. The ass instantly galloped away with him, and soon bore him from his enemies; but, the animal still keeping his pace, in spite of the efforts of the Ill-natured Boy to prevent him, on a sudden stopped short at the door of a cottage, and began kicking and prancing with such violence, that he threw the little boy from his back, and in the fall bruised his leg so much that he could not walk.

"His cries brought out the family, and among them the little girl, whose milk he had spilled in the morning. However, they took him in, laid him on the bed, and there this unfortunate boy had leisure to recollect himself, and reflect on the evils which his bad behaviour had brought on him in the course of one day. He determined, should he recover from this accident, he would in future study to do good, and injure no person or animal any more."

Tommy was vastly pleased with this story, as it showed the difference between being good and naughty. Every one loved and assisted the little good-natured boy, but every one punished and despised the other.

CHAPTER VII

Tommy and harry having taken it into their heads, that they would build them a house at the bottom of the garden, Mr. Barlow not only gave his consent, but went into the copse, to cut down poles proper for the purpose. These poles, which were about as thick as a man's wrist, and about eight feet long, he brought to a point at one end, in order to run into the ground. So eager were the two little boys at their business, that they soon conveyed all the poles to the bottom of the garden, and Tommy seemed to have entirely forgotten that he was a gentleman.

Harry then took the stakes, and drove them into the ground, at the distance of about a foot, and thus he enclosed a piece of land, about ten feet long, and eight wide. This being done, they gathered up the brushwood they had cut off, and interwove it between the poles, so as to form a kind of fence. They worked so hard at this business, that Mr. Barlow, in order to encourage them, told them the following story of the Grateful Turk.

"At a time when the Venetians and Turks were at war, one of the ships of the latter was taken and carried into Venice, where the crew were all sold as slaves. One of these unhappy people happened to live opposite the house of a rich Venetian, who had an only son, then in the twelfth year of his age. The little youth used frequently to stop and gaze at Hamet, for such was the name of the slave, and at last, an acquaintance commenced between them.

"Though Hamet seemed always delighted with the tender regards of his little friend, yet the latter frequently observed, that involuntary tears trickled down the cheeks of Hamet. The little youth at last spoke of it to his father, and begged of him, if he could, to make Hamet happy.

"Hereupon the father determined to see the slave, and to talk to him himself. He went to him the next day, and asked him if he were the Hamet, whom his son had spoken so kindly of. He replied that he was the unfortunate Hamet, who had been three years a captive; and that during that time, his little son was the only person who had in the least pitied his misfortunes. 'And I, night and morning,' added he, 'offer up my praise to that power, who is equally the God of Turks and Christians, to shower down upon his head every blessing he deserves, and to preserve him from miseries like mine.'

"The Venetian merchant then entered into closer conversation with Hamet, and could not help admiring his generous sentiments and manly fortitude. He asked him what he would do to regain his liberty. 'What would I do?' answered Hamet, 'I would cheerfully face every danger, and even death itself, in whatever shape it might appear!'

"The merchant then told him, that the means of his deliverance were in his own hands. 'Hear me attentively,' said the merchant: 'an inveterate foe of mine lives in this city, and has heaped upon me every injury that can sting the heart of man. He is as brave as he is haughty, and I must confess that his strength and valour prevent my attempting personally to revenge my wrongs. Now, Hamet, take this dagger, and as soon as the shade of night shall envelope the city, I will lead you to the place, where you may at once revenge the injuries of your friend, and regain your own freedom.'

"Scorn and contempt now flamed in the eyes of Hamet, and, as soon as his passion had a little subsided, he exclaimed, 'Go, wicked Christian, and be assured, that Hamet would not become an assassin for all the riches of Venice, or to purchase the freedom of his whole race!' The merchant coolly replied, that he was sorry he had offended him, but thought that he prized his freedom at a higher rate: and added, as he turned his back, 'You will perhaps change your mind to-morrow, after you shall have more maturely reflected on the matter,' and then left him.

"The next day, the merchant, accompanied by his son, returned to Hamet, and was going to renew his former conversation, when the honest Turk exclaimed, with a severe and fixed countenance, 'Christian! cease to insult the miserable with proposals more shocking than death itself! The Christian religion may tolerate such acts, but to a Mahometan they are an abomination!'

"Francisco, for that was the name of the Venetian merchant, now tenderly embraced Hamet, and begged he would forgive the trial to which he put his virtue, assuring him at the same time, that his soul abhorred all deeds of blood and treachery, as much as Hamet himself. 'From this moment,' said the merchant, 'you are free; your ransom is paid, and you are at liberty to go where you please. Perhaps, hereafter, when you see an unhappy Christian groaning in Turkish fetters, your generosity may bring Venice to your remembrance.'

"The feelings of Hamet at this unexpected deliverance are not to be described. Francisco put him on board a ship, which was bound to one of the Grecian islands, and gave him a purse of gold to pay his expences. Affectionate was the parting of Hamet with his little friend; he embraced him in an agony of tenderness, wept over him, and implored Heaven to grant him all the blessings of this life.

"About six months afterwards, one morning while the family were all in bed, Francisco's house was discovered to be on fire, and [a] great part of the house was in flames before the family was alarmed. The terrified servants had but just time to awaken Francisco, who was no sooner got into the street, than the whole staircase gave way, and fell into the flames.

"If the merchant thought himself happy in having saved himself, it was only for a moment, as he soon recollected that his beloved son was left behind to the mercy of the flames. He sunk into the deepest despair, when upon enquiry he found, that his son, who slept in an upper apartment, had been forgotten in the general confusion. He raved in agonies of grief, and offered half his fortune to any one who would save the child. As he was known to be very rich, several ladders were instantly raised by those who wished to obtain the reward; but the violence of the flames drove every one down who attempted it.

"The unfortunate youth then appeared on the top of the house, and calling out for aid, the unhappy father became motionless, and remained in a state of insensibility. At this critical moment a man rushed through the crowd, and ascended the tallest ladder, seemingly determined to rescue the youth, or perish in the attempt. A sudden gust of flame bursting forth, led the people to suppose he was lost; but he presently appeared, descending the ladder with the child in his arms, without receiving any material injury. A universal shout attended this noble action, and the father, to his inexpressible surprise, on recovering from his swoon, found his child in his arms.

"After giving vent to the first emotions of tenderness, he enquired after his generous deliverer, whose features were so changed with the smoke, that they could not be distinguished. Francisco immediately presented him with a purse of gold, promising the next day to give him the reward he had offered. The stranger replied, that he should accept of no reward. Francisco started, and thought he knew the voice, when his son flew to the arms of his deliverer, and cried out, 'It is my dear Hamet!'

"The astonishment and gratitude of the merchant were equally excited, and retiring from the crowd, he took Hamet with him to a friend's house. As soon as they were alone, Francisco enquired by what means he had been a second time enslaved.

"I will tell you in a few words," said the generous Turk. "When I was taken by the

Venetian gallies, my father shared in my captivity. It was his fate, and not my own, which so often made me shed those tears which first attracted the notice of your amiable son. As soon as your bounty had set me free, I flew to the Christian who had purchased my father. I told him, that as I was young and vigorous, and he aged and infirm, I would be his slave instead of my father. I added too the gold which your bounty had bestowed on me, and by these means I prevailed on the Christian to send back my father in that ship you had provided for me, without his knowing the cause of his freedom. Since that time I have staid here a willing slave, and Heaven has been so gracious as to put it in my power to save the life of that youth, which I value as my own.

"The merchant, astonished at such an instance of gratitude and affection, pressed Hamet to accept of half of his fortune, and to settle in Venice for the remainder of his days. Hamet, however, with a noble magnanimity, refused the offer, saying, he had done no more than what every one ought to do in a similar situation. Though Hamet seemed to under-rate his past services to the merchant, yet the latter could not suffer things to pass in this manner. He again purchased his freedom, and fitted a ship out on purpose to take him back to his own country. At parting, they mutually embraced each other, and, as they thought, took a last farewell.

"After many years had elapsed, and young Francisco was grown up to manhood, beloved and respected by every one, it so happened, that some business made it necessary for him and his father to visit a neighbouring city on the coast, so they embarked in a Venetian vessel, which was bound to that port and ready to sail.

"A favourable gale soon wafted them out of sight; but, before they had proceeded half their voyage, they were met by some Turkish vessels, who, after an obstinate resistance from the Venetians, boarded them, loaded them with irons, and carried them prisoners to Tunis. There they were exposed in the market-place in their chains, in order to be sold as slaves.

"At last, a Turk came to the market, who seemed to be a man of superior rank, and after looking over the prisoners, with an expression of compassion, he fixed his eyes upon young Francisco, and asked the captain what was the price of that young captive. The captain replied, that he would not part with him for less than five hundred pieces of gold. The Turk considered that as a very extraordinary price, since he had seen him sell others, that exceeded him in strength and vigour, for less than a fifth part of that money.

"'That is true,' replied the captain, 'but he shall either fetch me a price that will repay me the damage he has occasioned me, or he shall labour all the rest of his life at the oar.' The Turk asked him, what damage he could have done him more than the rest of the crew. 'It was he,' replied the captain, 'who animated the Christians to make a desperate resistance, and thereby proved the destruction of many of my bravest seamen. We three times boarded them, with a fury that seemed invincible, and each time did that youth attack us with a cool and determined opposition; so that we were obliged to give up the contest, till other ships came to our assistance. I will therefore have that price for him, or I will punish him for life.'

"The Turk now surveyed young Francisco more attentively than before; and the young man, who had hitherto fixed his eyes in sullen silence on the ground, at length raised them up; but he had no sooner beheld the person who was talking to the captain, than, in a loud voice, he uttered the name of Hamet. The Turk, struck with astonishment, surveyed him for a moment, and then caught him in his arms.

"After a moment's pause, the generous Hamet lifted up his hands to heaven, and thanked his God, who had put it in his power to show his gratitude; but words cannot express his feelings, when he found that both father and son were slaves. Suffice it to say, that he instantly bought their freedom, and conducted them to his magnificent house in the city.

"They had here full leisure to discourse on the strange vicissitudes of fortune, when Hamet told his Venetian friends, that after their generosity had procured him liberty, he became an officer in the Turkish army, and happening to be fortunate in all his enterprises, he had been gradually promoted, till he arrived at the dignity of bashaw of Tunis. That in this situation, he found the greatest consolation in alleviating the misfortunes of the Christian prisoners, and always attended the sales of those unhappy slaves, to procure liberty to a certain number of them. 'And gracious Allah,' added he, 'has this day put it in my power, in some measure, to return the duties of gratitude.'

"They continued some days with Hamet, who did every thing in his power to amuse and divert them; but as he found their desire was to return to their own country, he told them that he would not wish to detain them against their wishes, and that they should embark the next day in a ship bound for Venice, which should be furnished with a passport to carry them safe there.

"The next day, he dismissed them with every mark of tenderness and affection, and ordered a party of his own guards to attend them to the vessel. They had no sooner got on board, than they found, to their inexpressible surprise and joy, that they were in the very ship in which they had been taken, and that by the generosity of Hamet, not only the ship, but even the whole crew, were redeemed and restored to freedom. Francisco and his son, after a quick passage, arrived in their own country, where they lived beloved and respected, and endeavoured to convince every one they knew, however great were the vicissitudes of fortune, that God never suffers humanity and generosity to go unrewarded, here or hereafter."

The story being now ended, Mr. Barlow with pleasure saw the tear[s] stealing down the cheeks both of Tommy and Harry, when he led them into the garden to amuse them.

CHAPTER VIII

THEIR NEXT BUSINESS was to go to look at the house they had begun building, when they found, that a hurricane which had happened the preceding night, had levelled every stick with the earth. Tommy shook his head, but Harry only observed, that they had not built it strong enough, and that they must drive their posts further into the ground. They therefore set about repairing it, and in the course of a few days completed the whole, so as to make it capable of affording them shelter from the severest shower.

The winter had now set in with its usual severity, so that the two youths were at present no longer able to pursue their labours in the garden; but they now and then took a walk in the air. One day, when the snow which had fallen was a good deal gone off, Tommy and Harry took their usual walk. They were so deep in conversation, that they wandered much further than they intended, and got into paths, with which they were not well acquainted. They therefore thought it prudent to return as fast as possible; but in passing through a wood, they wandered from the right path, and could not tell where they were. To add to their distress, the wind from the north began to blow with great fury, and so violent a fall of snow came on, as obliged them to seek shelter. The hollow of an aged oak afforded them a comfortable asylum, and they exerted all their youthful abilites to keep themselves warm.

Tommy had never before experienced hardships of this nature, and for some time, showed an heroic courage; but hunger and fear at last got the better of him, when, with tears in his eyes, he asked Harry what they should do.—"Why," replied Harry, with great courage, "we must stay here till the storm is over, and then endeavour to get home."

After remaining some time in the hollow of the tree, the storm greatly abated, when they began their march through the snow, which had completely covered every track, and what was worst of all, the day began to close. Harry had great difficulty to persuade his companion, who was up to his knees in snow every step he took, to pursue his march.

At length, however, they came to some lighted embers, which probably some labourers had just quitted. Harry then got together all the dry pieces of wood he could find, and placing them on the embers, they soon caught fire, which afforded them a comfortable warmth. Tommy, as they were warming themselves, observed to Harry, that it was a terrible thing to be cold and hungry, and more so to a gentleman than to a common person.

Harry replied, that what he had felt from the storm might be disagreeable to a gentleman, but it was nothing more than common to country farming people, who were of more use to the community than gentlemen, who were ready to die under the least degree of fatigue. For his part, he thought it much better to be a plain countryman, than a fine laced gentleman.

While they were conversing together on such subjects as these, a little boy came along singing, with a bundle of sticks on his shoulder, whom Harry happened to know. In fact, he was the very little ragged boy, to whom Tommy had given the clothes in the summer. Harry instantly spoke to him, and desired him to show them the way out of the wood, which he readily consented to, but advised them to go first to his father's house, and, while they warmed themselves, they would send to Mr. Barlow, to acquaint him where they were. Tommy joyfully accepted the offer, and the little boy led them to his father's cottage.

As soon as they arrived there, the good woman, who knew them again, gave them a hearty welcome, and threw a large faggot on the fire, to give them a comfortable warm. She said she had not any thing in the house worth asking Tommy to eat, as she had nothing better than brown bread and bacon. Tommy, however, was so hungry, that he said he could eat any thing.

The good woman laid a clean coarse cloth, and soon brought some bacon on an earthen plate, together with some coarse brown bread. The two youths, having ate nothing since the morning, made a most hearty meal, while the honest farmer went to acquaint Mr. Barlow of the safety of his pupils, which gave infinite satisfaction to that reverend gentleman; as he had dispatched people every where in pursuit of them.

The next morning, after they had related all the particulars of their expedition, Mr.

Barlow desired Tommy to read the following account of some people who were buried in the snow, when he began as follows:

"In the neighbourhood of those vast mountains called the Alps, the tops of which are perpetually covered with snow, on the nineteenth of March, 1755, a small cluster of houses were entirely buried by two immense bodies of snow, which fell upon them from a higher part of the mountain. All the inhabitants were then within doors, except one Joseph Rochia, and his son, a lad of fifteen years of age, who were on the roof of their house, removing the snow which had fallen for three days successively.

"A priest, who happened to be going by, advised them to come down, having just before observed a body of snow tumbling from the mountain towards them. The man and his son descended with all possible haste, and fled they knew not whither. At last turning round to look back, he saw his own and his neighbours' houses, in which were twenty-two persons, covered with a high mountain of snow. After viewing this sorrowful sight, he hastened to a friend's house at some distance.

"Five days afterwards, Joseph got upon the snow, accompanied by his son and two of his wife's brothers, with an intent to discover whereabouts his house lay buried: but after various trials, they were obliged to give up the pursuit. The month of April proving hot, and the snow beginning to give way, Joseph again made a second effort, in order to recover his effects, and bury the unfortunate victims. On the 24th of April the snow was greatly diminished, when he broke through ice the thickness of six English feet, and with a long pole, touched the ground; but the night coming on, obliged him to desist for that time.

"His wife's brother, who had been informed of this misfortune, came the next day to the house where Joseph was, and after resting himself a little, they both went to work on the snow. They then made another opening, which led them to the house they were in search of. As they found no dead bodies in the ruins, they searched for the stable, which was at the distance of about two hundred and forty English feet. Having found the stable, they heard a cry of, 'Help, my dear brother?' Equally surprised and encouraged by these words, they laboured with additional ardour, till they had made a large opening, through which the brother immediately descended, where the sister, with a faint and feeble voice, said to him, 'I have always trusted in God and you, and knew that you would not forsake me.'

"The husband and the other brother then went down, and found the wife, about forty-five, the sister, about thirty-five, and the daughter, all still alive. These they raised on their shoulders to men above, who pulled them up as from a deep pit, and carried them to a neighbouring house; for they were unable to walk, being so wasted that they appeared like skeletons.

"The magistrates of the place came some days afterwards to visit them, and found the wife still unable to use her feet, or rise from the bed, owing to the severity of the cold she had endured, and the posture to which she had been confined. The sister, whose legs they had bathed with hot wine, was a little recovered, and could walk with some difficulty. The daughter stood in no need of any further remedies.

"The woman gave the following account of their situation while buried in the snow. On the morning of the nineteenth of March they were in the stable, with a boy about six years old, and a girl of thirteen. There were six goats in the stable, one of which having brought forth two dead kids the night before, they went to carry her a mess of rye flour gruel. There were also an ass and five or six fowls.

"They had got into a warm corner of the stable, waiting there till the church bell should ring, as they proposed to attend divine service. Joseph's wife related, that having occasion to go and kindle a fire in the house, while her husband was clearing away the snow from the top of it, she perceived a body of snow breaking down towards her, when she immediately went back into the stable, shut the door, and mentioned to her sister what she had seen. Three minutes had scarcely elapsed, when they heard the roof break over their heads, together with part of the ceiling. They immediately got into the manger, to which was tied the ass, who got loose, kicking and struggling, and threw down a small vessel, which they afterwards found, and used to hold the melted snow, the principal liquor they had to drink.

"The main prop of the stable being fortunately over the manger, it resisted the weight of the snow. Their first care was to consider what they should live upon. The sister said she had fifteen chesnuts in her pocket; the children said they had breakfasted, and therefore could do without any thing more till the next day. They recollected, that there were between thirty and forty biscuits in a place near the stable; but they were not able to get at them, on account of the snow. They frequently called for help, but in vain.

"They eat part of the chesnuts the first day, and drank some snow water. The ass was restless, and the goats kept bleating for some days, after which they heard nothing more of them. Two of the goats, however, were still living, and being near the manger, they felt them. They found that one of them was big, and they recollected it would kid about the middle of April. The milk of the other preserved their lives. Not the least ray of light was to be seen, though the crowing of the fowls, for about twenty days, gave them some notice of night and morning; but when the fowls died, they could no longer make any distinction.

"Being very hungry the second day, they eat all the chesnuts, and drank what milk the goat yielded, being at first about two pounds a day, but that soon decreased. On the third day, they made another vain attempt to get at the cakes. They therefore resolved to take all possible care to feed the goats, which they were enabled to do by means of the hay-loft being just above the manger, from whence the sister pulled some down, through a hole into the rack, and gave it the goats as long as she could reach it; and when it got beyond her reach, the goats got at it themselves, by climbing on her shoulders.

"On the sixth day, the poor little boy grew sick, and six days after that, desired his mother, who had kept him in her arms all the time, to lay him at length in the manger. She complied with his desire, and then taking him by the hand, found it was cold as well as his mouth. She then gave him a little milk, when the poor boy cried, 'Oh, my father is in the snow; O father! father:' and then expired.

"The goat's milk began to diminish daily; but according to the woman's recollection, it could not be long before the other goat would kid, which she soon did, and the young one dying immediately, they in course had all the milk for their own nourishment. The circumstance of the goat's kidding, led them to suppose, that the middle of April was come. As soon as they called the goat to them, it would come, and lick their hands and faces, and every day afforded them about two pounds of milk, which saved them from perishing, and preserved their existence till they were relieved in the manner before related. It is no wonder, if the goats were properly taken care of, for the rest of their lives, in the manner which gratitude would dictate."

The story being now ended, Tommy could not help exclaiming, "O dear Sir! what a variety of accidents people are exposed to in this world!" Mr. Barlow replied, that it was very true; but that, in such cases, it was necessary for us to improve ourselves in such a manner as to be able to struggle with them, and not to suffer them to conquer us.

CHAPTER IX

Tommy, during his residence with Mr. Barlow, had lost a great part of his West-Indian pride, and had contracted many acquaintances among poor families. In imitation of Mr. Barlow, he went about from house to house, enquiring after the health and welfare of their families, and the returns of civility and gratitude he met with, amply rewarded his tenderness and humanity. He began to reflect on every thing he heard, and to imitate whatever he saw that appeared laudable and praise-worthy.

Mr. Barlow had a large Newfoundland dog, which was exceedingly good-natured, and very fond of the water. Tommy had by this time learned to make even animals respect him, and he and Cæsar were upon exceeding good terms. He would sometimes divert himself with throwing a stick into the water, which the dog would instantly fetch in his mouth, and lay it down at his feet, when he would stroke and pat him by way of encouragement.

Tommy had heard Mr. Barlow give an account in what manner the Kamtschatkan dogs drew their sledges, and he determined to make an experiment of that nature. Being one day perfectly disengaged from business, he furnished himself with some rope, and a kitchen chair, which he intended to make use of instead of a sledge. He then coaxed Cæsar into a large yard behind the house, and placing the chair flat upon the ground, he fastened the dog into it, with great care, and no small share of ingenuity. Cæsar, however, did not understand being harnessed, and was ignorant of the part he was to act. At last Tommy mounted his seat triumphantly, with a whip in his hand, and began his career.

A number of the neighbouring little boys gathered round the young gentleman, which made him the more anxious to distinguish himself. Tommy began to make use of those expressions to his dog, which he had heard coachmen apply to their horses, and smacked his whip with great consequence. Cæsar, who had not been used to this kind of language, grew rather impatient, and showed his dislike to his present situation, by endeavouring to get rid of his harness. This drew on Tommy the laugh of the spectators, which made him more eager to perform his exploit with honour, and, after having tried many experiments with his steed, and being a little angry with him, he applied a pretty severe lash to his hinder parts. Cæsar was very angry at this, and instantly set off in full speed, dragging the chair, with the driver upon it, at a prodigious rate.

Tommy now looked about him with a triumphant air, and maintained his seat with great firmness and address. Unfortunately, however, at no great distance was a large horse-pond, which gradually shelved to the depth of three or four feet. The affrighted Cæsar, by a kind of natural instinct, ran thither in hopes of getting rid of his tormentor; while Tommy, who began not much to like his situation, in vain endeavoured to pacify and restrain his steed. Cæsar, without paying any regard to his driver, precipitately rushed into the pond, and carried both carriage and driver into the middle of it. The boys who were spectators, now received fresh matter of diversion, and, notwithstanding their respect for Tommy, they could not help uttering loud shouts of derision. The unmannerly exultations of the spectators, very much discomposed our little hero; but his misfortunes had not yet reached their summit. Cæsar, by floundering about the pond, and by making a too sudden turn, over-turned the car, and threw poor Tommy into the water.

A sudden thaw having commenced the day before, occasioned the pond to be a mixture of ice and water, and mud and mire. Through this he struggled as well as he was able, his feet sometimes slipping, and then down he tumbled. At last, however, he got safe through the ice, mud, and water, with the loss of both his shoes. Such was the appearance of poor Tommy when he got out of the pond, that the whole troop of spectators, who were incapable of stifling their laughter, broke forth in redoubled peals, which irritated the unfortunate hero to a violent degree of rage. As soon as he had struggled to the shore, forgetting the situation he was in, he fell upon the boys with great fury, and so liberally dealt his blows on every side, that he put them all to flight.

While Tommy was thus revenging the affronts he thought he had received, and pursuing the vanquished about the yard, the uproar brought Mr. Barlow to the door, who could hardly help laughing at the sorrowful figure of his pupil, with the water dropping from every part of his body, and the violent attacks he was making.

Such was the agitation of Tommy's mind, that it was some little time before he could listen to the calls of Mr. Barlow. At last, having heard his precepter's voice, he respectfully approached him, and related every thing that had happened. Mr. Barlow immediately led him into the house, and having advised him to undress himself and go to bed, he carried him a little warm wine to drink, and thus this unfortunate affair ended without any evil consequences.

Not long after this, Tommy was to pay a visit to his parents, and Harry was to accompany him. They no sooner arrived at Mr. Merton's, than they found a crowded assembly to receive them. It is impossible to describe the many flattering encomiums that were passed upon Tommy, not even his hair or his teeth passed without some compliment, while nobody took the least notice of Harry, except Mr. Merton, who treated him in the most tender and affectionate manner.

Among the company, however, was an amiable young lady, Miss Simmons, who advanced towards Harry, with the greatest affability, and entered into conversation with him. This young lady had the misfortune to lose her father and mother in her infancy, and was then under the care of an uncle, who brought her up in such a manner, as contributed to inform her mind, without suffering her to acquire those fashionable talents which are so pernicious to the fair of the rising generation.

This young lady, whose character was singularly benevolent, addressed Harry in such a manner, as set him perfectly at ease. He possessed such a natural politeness and good-nature as is infinitely preferable to all the artificial graces of society. He indeed had not that vivacity, or rather impertinence, which renders a boy the darling of the ladies, and passes for wit among superficial people; but he paid the strictest attention to what was said to him, and always answered to the purpose: it was for these reasons, that Miss Simmons, who though much older, and more improved than Harry, was highly pleased with his conversation, and thought it preferable to any thing of the kind she had met among the number of smart young gentlemen, with whom she had conversed at Mr. Merton's house.

At dinner time, when Harry saw so many fine gentlemen and ladies, so many powdered servants to stand behind them, such a multitude of dishes, and such pomp and solemnity about merely satisfying the appetite, he could not help envying the condition of his father's labourers, who, when they find themselves hungry, sit perfectly at ease under a hedge, and make a hearty meal without tablecloth, plates, or compliments.

Tommy never opened his mouth, but his words were caught by the whole company, who considered them as so many marks of the most brilliant wit, while little or no notice was taken of Harry.

The time was passed in all these fashionable amusements, which tend only to corrupt the morals of youth, and had such an influence on the mind of Tommy, that he began almost to hate the name of Mr. Barlow, and no longer paid any respect to his friend Harry, who received very little satisfaction from this visit, except in his conversation with Miss Simmons.

One day, a bull was to be baited in the neighbourhood, when Tommy and all his gay and flighty companions, stole away to see it, and Harry reluctantly followed them at a distance; for he had received very singular ill-treatment, not only from the young visitors at Mr. Merton's house, but even from Tommy himself.

While this inhuman spectacle was going forward, a poor half naked black came to them, and humbly implored their charity. The poor black, finding he could get nothing from them, (for Tommy had spent all his money in trifles, and the rest of the young gentlemen only made a laugh of the poor man) he approached the place where Harry stood, holding out the remains of his tattered hat, and imploring charity. Harry put his hand in his pocket, and gave him the only six-pence he had.

The dog now attacked the bull with such fury, that the animal became mad and outrageous; he killed two of the dogs presently, and soon after snapped the rope that held him. It is impossible to describe the terror and confusion that followed. Those who had but just before been rejoicing in the torments of the poor animal, now fled with precipitation, and were pursued by the enraged bull, who trampled over some, gored others, and thus took ample vengeance for the injuries he had received.

The furious animal, then changing its course, ran towards the spot where Tommy and his associates stood, and put them to flight; but the bull was too swift for them, and Tommy stumbling and falling to the ground, lay directly in the way of his pursuing enemy. Master Merton was now given over for lost.

Harry had all this time kept his ground, but now seeing his little friend in extreme danger, he determined to rescue him, or lose his life in the attempt. With a courage and presence of mind above his years, he catched up a prong, which had been dropped by one of the fugitives, and at the very instant the bull was stooping to revenge himself on the defenceless Tommy, he gave him a deep wound in the flank. The wounded animal instantly turned round to attack a more formidable enemy; and it is highly probable that, notwithstanding Harry's courage and resolution, his life would have paid for the salvation of his friend, had not the generous black, to whom he had just before given six-pence, instantly fled to his assistance. With a large stick he had in his hand, he gave the bull so violent a blow as called off his attention from Harry. He instantly turned round to his new enemy, who with the greatest dexterity shifted from him, and caught hold of his tail, by which he held fast, and so belaboured the bull with his stick, that he was at last obliged to lie down, when they threw a rope over his horns, and fastened him to a tree.

While these matters were transacting, Mr. Merton had sent out his servants to see after the young gentlemen. They flew to the spot where their young master lay, who, though he had not received any injury, was half dead with fear and terror. As soon as Harry saw that Tommy was safe in the hands of his servants, he asked the black to go along with him; but he took the road which led to his father's house, instead of returning to Mr. Merton's.

CHAPTER X

M<small>RS.</small> M<small>ERTON</small> was looking out at the window, when she saw her son in the arms of one of the servants, who was bringing him home. Judge what were the feelings of so fond a mother! she fainted at the sight, and was some time before she recovered. At length coming to herself, and finding he had received no injury, she embraced him with the greatest tenderness, and accused the absent Harry with enticing him, and the rest of the young gentlemen, to the bull-baiting. However, when the matter came to be cleared up, and she found that her son owed his life to his valour, she was ashamed of her partiality.

At this instant Mr. Barlow, who knew nothing of what had passed, arrived at Mr. Merton's, where he was received by that gentleman with every mark of hospitality. Mr. Merton related to him every thing that had passed, and concluded with lamenting how much unlike his son was to the amiable little Harry. A long and interesting discourse took place between the two gentlemen, when Mr. Barlow prevailed on Mr. Merton to believe, that, in a little time, his son Tommy might be brought to forget all his pride, and become an amiable young gentleman, however poisoned his mind might have been by too much indulgence, and the flattery of the visitors at home.

This conversation being ended, Mr. Merton conducted Mr. Barlow into another room, and introduced him to the company, who received him with great politeness, and particularly Mrs. Merton, who began to think, that her conduct to her son was not entirely rational and prudent.

Tommy, who was so lately the idol of this flattering circle, appeared to be much humbled. He indeed approached Mr. Barlow with every appearance of modesty and gratitude, and answered all his questions in the most respectful manner; but he could not conceal that dejection of mind, which evidently appeared on his countenance. Mr. Barlow was too sensible a man not to see these marks of contrition, and drew from them the most pleasing omens.

The company now began to depart for their respective homes; and Tommy, who before was so fond of the company of the young gentlemen, seemed not a little pleased at their departure. Mr. Merton's house, which had for some days been a scene of noise, bustle, and festivity, was become the abode of tranquillity and repose. As Mr. Barlow was

not fond of cards, an amusement in which too much time is frequently spent, he proposed that Miss Simmons should read a story for the entertainment of the company;
which she instantly complied with, and accomplished the task with great accuracy, pre-
cision, and judgment.

The time for retiring to rest being now come, the company broke up for the evening.
The next day Tommy rose before his father and mother, and as his mind was much
impressed with the story read by Miss Simmons the preceding evening, in which she had
described the wonderful exploits of some Arabian horsemen, he imagined that nothing
could be so great as guiding a high-mettled steed over dreary and desolate wastes, such as
he had heard Miss Simmons describe. He therefore chose the common before his father's
house as the proper field of action, that being the most rugged part in the neighbourhood. He accordingly put on his boots, and ordered William to saddle his poney and
attend him. This servant had been accustomed to humour him in whatever he took into
his head, and indeed he might have endangered the loss of his place, had he shown the
least reluctance to obey his commands. Mrs. Merton had strictly forbidden her son ever
to ride with spurs, and had ordered all the servants never to suffer him to put on those
dangerous implements. Tommy had long complained of this severe restriction, which
seemed to lessen his abilities as a horseman, and very much wounded his pride; but as
he had now taken it into his head to be an Arabian horseman, he could no longer submit to that restraint. However, as he dared not ask for spurs, he went to one of the maids,
and got from her two large pins, which he very ingeniously stuck into his boots, and
then mounted his horse.

He had not ridden far, before he thought of putting his horsemanship to the trial,
and accordingly gave his horse a very sharp prick with his pins. The animal being a
spirited creature, set off with him at full gallop, and William knew not whether this
sudden start was from accident or design. Seeing, however, that the horse galloped over
the roughest part of the common, while Tommy used all his efforts to stop him, he
thought it prudent to endeavour to overtake him, and therefore pursued him with all
possible speed. The poney, hearing another horse behind him, rather increased his pace;
so that while Tommy was carried over the common with such violent speed, William was
in vain pursuing him. Just as the servant thought he had reached his master, his horse
exerted all his strength to push forward, and left his pursuer at a distance behind him.

The young gentleman maintained his seat admirably well; but he began seriously to
reflect on his own ungovernable ambition, and would have been happy to exchange his
high-mettled steed for the dronest ass in England. The race continued without any
appearance of abatement, when the poney turned short on a sudden, upon an attempt of
his master to stop him, and rushed into a quagmire. This stopped him for a moment, and
gave Tommy an opportunity of slipping off his back into a soft bed of mire.

The servant had now time to get up to Tommy, and rescue him from his disagreeable
situation, where he had received no other damage than that of daubing his clothes. The
servant was very much frightened at the situation of his young master, while the horse
was running away with him; but finding he had received no injury, he left Tommy
to walk home on foot, while he went in pursuit of the poney.

Tommy, in the mean time, walked pensively along, thinking of the different accidents
he had encountered, and of the various disappointments he had met with in his pursuit

of glory. While his mind was thus employed, a poor and ragged figure made his appearance. He was a Scotch Highlander, dressed in a tattered plaid, and a large broad-sword by his side. He was leading two poor children, and carried a third in his arms. Tommy immediately took notice of him, which the poor man seeing took off his hat, and begged his charity. Our little gentleman, after some conversation with him, put his hand in his pocket, and gave him a shilling to buy himself and his children some bread. The poor man gratefully thanked him, and pursued his journey.

Tommy had not proceeded a great way before he met with another adventure. A flock of sheep was running with all possible speed from the pursuit of a large dog. As he was an enemy to all cruelty, he endeavoured to drive the dog from his prey. The dog, however, probably despising the size of little Tommy, after growling and showing his teeth for a little time, at last seized upon the skirt of Tommy's coat, shaking it with every appearance of rage; but the youth neither attempted to run, nor showed any marks of fear, only endeavouring to disengage himself from his enemy.

It is probable that Tommy would have suffered much from the teeth of the enraged animal, had not the man whom he had just relieved ran to his assistance, and laid the dog sprawling on the ground with a stroke of his broad-sword. Tommy thanked his deliverer in the most grateful manner, and desired him to attend him to his father's house, where he and his children should receive every refreshment their house could afford.

Tommy being arrived within a short distance of the house, met his father and Mr. Barlow, who were walking to enjoy the morning air before breakfast. They were surprised at the appearance Tommy made, he being bespattered with mud from head to foot. The youth, however, without giving time to make any enquiries, ran up to the gentlemen, and wished them a good morning. Mr. Merton was very glad to find his son was not hurt, for he doubted not, from the situation of his clothes, that he had fallen from a horse, which was presently confirmed by the appearance of William, who was leading the poney.

On the servant telling Mr. Merton, that the poney had run away with Tommy, he seemed very much surprised, as it was the most quiet and easy horse he had. He then asked William, if he had not been so imprudent as to let his young master have spurs, which the servant positively denied. Mr. Merton, who was convinced there was something more in the business than he could get at, surveyed Tommy very attentively, and soon found out his ingenious contrivance to supply the place of spurs. Though his father could hardly keep his countenance at this discovery, he endeavoured to convince him of his imprudence, which might have been attended with very disagreeable consequences, such as a broken limb, and even the loss of life. He therefore desired him for the future to be more cautious, and they then returned to the house, where Mr. Merton gave orders, that proper nourishment might be administered to the beggar and his children, whom Tommy had brought home with him, and then dismissed the poor man with a valuable present.

After dinner, a very interesting conversation took place between Mr. Barlow and his pupil Tommy, who confessed that he had been a very unthinking boy, and that he had forfeited all kind of pretensions to the kindness of his worthy preceptor. Mr. Barlow told him, that to be sensible of his fault was half way to a reformation, and therefore begged that he would open his mind without the least reserve.

Encouraged by this kind declaration, Tommy thus proceeded. "Since I have been at home, Sir, I have been surrounded by a number of young gentlemen and iadies, who, because their parents are rich, thought they had a right to despise every one who was poor. Indeed, they at last taught me to think so too, and to forget all your wise admonitions. As they told me every thing centered in politeness, I imitated them on all occasions, and soon became as bad as themselves. They were always laughing at poor Harry Sandford, and at last brought me to slight his company."

"I am very sorry for that, (replied Mr. Barlow) because I am sure he loves you. That, however, is of no great consequence, for he finds sufficient employment among his father's labourers in the fields, and I am sure he would be rather there, than in any gentleman's house whatever. I will inform him, that you have got other acquaintance, and do not wish him to interrupt you in future."

Tommy replied, with tears in his eyes, "I did not think, Sir, you could be so cruel! I love him better than all the company I have lately seen put together, and I shall never more be happy till he forgives all my past unfriendly behaviour." Tommy then went on to acquaint Mr. Barlow with all the ill treatment he had been guilty of to his friend Harry, and concluded with asking, if he thought it possible that Harry would ever forgive him.

Our little gentleman here burst into a flood of tears, and Mr. Barlow after having suffered him to ease his mind that way, told him, he must ask Harry's pardon. To this Tommy had no objection, and begged that Mr. Barlow would bring him to their house. To this the reverend gentleman objected, saying it was his place to go to Harry, and not Harry's to come to him. Tommy's pride was not yet quite conquered, and he replied, that he thought it would be very unbecoming a gentleman to go to a farmer's son to ask his pardon. Mr. Barlow told him he might do as he pleased, and then got up to go away.

Hereupon Tommy again burst into tears, and begged Mr. Barlow would not leave him. He promised to go directly, and beg Harry's forgiveness. As his preceptor was now sensible of his contrition, he said he would go to young Sandford, and hear what he thought of the meeting.

He accordingly set out for Mr. Sandford's on foot, for he would not accept of the carriage Mr. Merton offered him, nor even of any servant to attend him. He found Harry driving the team in the field, more happy than a prince. He no sooner saw Mr. Barlow, then he stopped his team, and ran to him with every expression of joy in his countenance.

Mr. Barlow told him, that he was sorry to hear of the difference that had happened between him and Tommy, and desired that he would acquaint him with every particular. Harry hereupon told him the whole of the transaction, omitting only, out of modesty, the circumstance of saving Tommy's life. On Mr. Barlow's asking him why he did not mention that matter, he replied, he would have done as much for any one else, and therefore could not do less for his little friend, whom he loved.

The good preceptor then desired to know, what was become of the black, who had in fact saved his life. Harry replied, that he invited him home with him; and, when he informed his father of what service he had been to him, he ordered a decent bed to be made for him over the stable; that he gave him victuals every day, and that he appeared very thankful and industrious, saying, he should be very glad to put his hand to any thing that might enable him to get his living.

Mr. Barlow hereupon returned to Mr. Merton's house, and in the presence of Tommy related the whole of the conversation between him and Harry. Our little gentleman, who had attentively listened to all his preceptor had said, for some time hung down his head in silence. At last, in a faint voice, he owned, that he was become unworthy of the affection of his real friends; but he hoped that his father and Mr. Barlow would not give him up entirely; and that, should he be ever guilty of the same faults again, he would never more entreat for their favour and forgiveness. He had no sooner uttered these words, than he silently withdrew from the presence of his father and preceptor.

Mr. Merton was at a loss to guess what could be the motive of this abrupt departure, and said that his son appeared to him like a weather-cock, which changes its position with every varying gust of wind. But Mr. Barlow gave him great hopes, from the sorrow and contrition which at present evidently marked the countenance of his son.

Tommy presently returned, but in a very different kind of dress. He had destroyed all the gaiety of his curls, and combed all the powder out of his hair. Every appearance of finery was vanished, and even his darling buckles were changed for others of the plainest sort. His mother, seeing him thus strangely altered, could not help exclaiming, "What has the boy been doing to himself! Why, Tommy, I declare you look more like a country clown than like a young gentleman of fortune."

To this observation of Mrs. Merton, who still considered the parade of grandeur as the summit of all human happiness, Tommy gravely replied, that he was then only what he ought always to have been; and that, had he been accustomed to that dress, he should never have treated his dear friend Harry in so shameful a manner. "From this time, (said he) I shall spend my life in rational pursuits, and shall no longer give up myself to the false parade of finery and grandeur."

Mr. Merton and Mr. Barlow could hardly keep their countenance at this solemn speech, which Tommy delivered with uncommon gravity. However, they endeavoured to put on a serious countenance, and advised him to persevere in so commendable a resolution. As the night was pretty far advanced, and the gentlemen did not wish to tire Tommy with too many moral reflexions at one time, they retired to their different chambers.

CHAPTER XI

Tommy rose early the next morning, and dressed himself in his new habit of simplicity; and, after they had all breakfasted together, he begged of Mr. Barlow to go with him to Harry Sandford's. When they drew near to the house, Tommy saw at some distance his friend, who was driving his father's sheep home. At this sight, he took to his heels, and ran so hastily to meet Harry, that he was quite out of breath when he reached him. Harry met him with open arms, and a reconciliation immediately took place.

As soon as Mr. Barlow got up, he told Harry that he had brought him his little friend, who was very sorry for the faults he had committed, and was come to ask his pardon. "Indeed, (said Tommy,) I am sincerely ashamed of the affronts I have given you, and I am afraid, as I have been such an ungrateful boy, you will not easily pardon me."

"Indeed, (answered Harry,) you are very much mistaken in the matter; for I have long since forgot every thing but your former friendship and affection." After several endearing expressions had passed between them, Harry took his companion by the hand, and led him to his father's house, where he was received with the greatest civility by the family.

As soon as the first civilities were over, Tommy cast his eyes on the black, who had done such singular services for him at the bull-baiting, and who was sitting in the chimney corner. "I see (said Tommy) that I am to receive favours from all the world, and to return them by neglect and ingratitude." He then took the black by the hand, and kindly thanked him for the important service he had done him. The black replied, that he was happy in what he had done, and for his trifling services he had been amply repaid by Mr. Sandford and his hospitable family. Tommy said he had not yet been sufficiently rewarded, and he had still something to expect from his father.

Dinner being ready, Tommy sat down, in company with Mrs. Sandford, a venerable, decent, middle aged woman, and her two daughters, plain, modest, healthy-looking girls, a little older than Harry, who also was one of the company. Though the table was not covered with dainties, yet the provisions were of the best kind, plenty in quantity, but sparing in variety. Every thing was hot and well dressed, and neatness was visible in every part of the rustic banquet.

After Tommy had made a very hearty dinner, and the cloth was removed, he begged the black would give him some information concerning bull-baiting, with which he seemed to be so well acquainted. "I do suppose, (said Tommy,) that it was in your own country you learned to encounter such a furious animal."

The black replied, that it was not in his own country he had learned to encounter these creatures. "I lived for some time, (said he,) as a slave, among the Spaniards at Buenos Ayres, where it was a common practice of the people to hunt down cattle in the woods for their subsistence." He then related the following story, to which he had been an eye-witness.

"A native of that country (continued the black) having committed some offence, was condemned to labour in the gallies for several years. He sent a petition to the governor of the town, praying that his punishment might be changed. Being bred a warrior, he stood more in dread of dishonour than death. He therefore implored, that he might not be suffered to consume his strength and spirits in such an ignominious employment, but have an opportunity given him of performing something worthy of a man, or of perishing in the attempt. 'At the approaching festival, (said he,) I will encounter the most furious bull you can procure, I will throw him down, bridle him, saddle him, and ride him. At the same time you shall turn out two more, when I will attack them and put them to death with my dagger.'

"The emperor consented to this proposal, and when the appointed day arrived, all the inhabitants of the city assembled in a kind of amphitheatre, erected for the purpose. The brave American made his appearance on horseback, with nothing but a cord in his hand. Soon after an enormous bull was let loose, who hastened to attack the man; but with great agility he galloped round his antagonist, who in his turn, betook himself to flight. The horseman then pursued his flying enemy, and throwing the noose, which he held ready in his hand, he caught the bull in his flight by one of his hind legs. Then galloping two or three times round the animal, he so entangled him in the snare, that after a few violent efforts to disengage himself, he fell to the ground. The American then leaped from his horse, and put the animal to death in an instant, by stabbing him with his dagger behind the horns. The air resounded with the applauses of the spectators, while he was employed in taking the rope from the slaughtered animal, and prepared for a more furious enemy.

"As soon as he was prepared, a bull much more furious than the first, was let loose, and this he was ordered, according to his engagement, to bridle and saddle. The champion waited the attack of this furious enemy with an undaunted resolution, and making his horse wheel nimbly round the bull, he by that means baffled his fury, and put him to flight. He then chased him as he had done the former, till he got him into the middle of the enclosed space, where a strong post was fixed into the ground. Here he threw the unerring noose round the horns of the bull, and therewith dragged him to the stake, to which he bound him down closely. Then taking a saddle, he girded it on firmly to the back of the bull; and through his nostrils he thrust an iron ring, to which was fixed a cord; this, which he brought over his neck, served as a bridle. Then taking a short pike in his hand, he nimbly jumped on the back of the bull.

"All this time the creature bellowed with rage, without producing any effect on the mind of its rider, who coolly taking a knife, cut the cord that confined him to the stake, and gave him his liberty. The bull being thus disengaged, tried every expedient that rage and fury could dictate to throw his rider, who maintained his seat with wonderful dexterity.

"Two other furious bulls were then let loose, to attack the champion; but, as soon as they saw in what manner he was mounted, terror seized them and they precipitately fled away. The bull on which he was mounted followed the others, and carried his rider several times round the amphitheatre. The governor then called to the champion to complete his business, by putting all the bulls to death; when he instantly dispatched that on which he rode, by plunging in his knife behind the horns. After this he mounted his horse, and destroyed the other two bulls, in the same manner as he had dispatched the first."

Tommy was vastly pleased with this narration; but, as the evening was approaching, Mr. Barlow reminded him that it was time to return. Tommy, however, taking his kind preceptor by the hand, begged he might be permitted to stay some time with his friend Harry. "I assure you, Sir, (said Tommy,) that I am entirely ashamed of my past conduct, and in your presence, as well as before all this worthy family, I do most sincerely ask my friend Harry's pardon for all my past offences, most sincerely promising that I will do my endeavours for the future to act otherwise." Harry embraced his friend with all imaginable tenderness, and begged no more might be said about the matter. The whole family regarded this conversation with wonder, as they had no idea that Tommy's pride would suffer him to act upon such humiliating principles.

Tommy's proposal of staying some time with Harry was highly approved of by Mr. Barlow, who took upon himself to answer for the consent of Mr. Merton; and then, after taking a complaisant leave of the company, he went to his own house.

Our young gentleman was now embarked in a new scene of life, very different from that he had been hitherto engaged in. He supped heartily that night on the rustic fare he met with, went to bed early, and slept soundly. When Harry called him at five the next morning, according to agreement the overnight, he found some difficulty in complying with the summons; but when he recollected that his word and honour were at stake, he immediately jumped out of bed, dressed himself, and accompanied Harry in all his rustic employments.

In a short time Tommy became perfectly reconciled to his new mode of life, though it appeared a little awkward to him at first. The increase of exercise greatly contributed to improve his health and strength, and so much assisted his appetite, that the rustic food of farmer Sandford's table appeared to him more pleasing than all the luxuries he met with at home. From being accustomed to view scenes of distress, his heart began to be more sensible of the tender feelings of humanity; and from the observations he had daily occasion to make, he learned to know of what utility the labourer was to the community. Mr. Barlow paid him frequent visits, and pointed out every thing to him that was most worthy of his notice; and one day thus addressed his little friend. "You are now, Tommy, learning the practice of those virtues, which have rendered the sages of antiquity so conspicuous. It is not by finery, indolence, or the gratification of our appetites, that we must expect to establish our reputation in the world; for no man could ever derive the abilities of commanding armies in the field, or acting as a good legislator at home, who had been nursed in the lap of indolence or luxury. When the Roman people were pushed hard by their enemies, and the greatest generals were necessary to check them, it was not in the circles of the gay, elegant, and dissipated, nor at banquets, nor in gilded palaces, that they sought such commanders; they visited the poor and homely cottage, such as your late companions would view with the utmost contempt. But it was in such a situation they found Cincinnatus, whose virtues and abilities rendered him superior to the rest of his fellow citizens; they found him ploughing his field, and driving his oxen himself. Though this great man had passed his youth in the study of civil government and the use of arms, yet, when his country had no more commands on his service, he withdrew from the bustle of affairs, and, in a retired, humble situation, owed his subsistence to his labour. Tell me, my little friend, since chance seems to have more the direction of human affairs than merit, would you rather appear to the world in an elevated station, and as unworthy of the advantages you enjoy; or in a humble condition, be esteemed as worthy, from your virtues and abilities, of the most exalted places of honour and trust?"

Tommy frequently received such lessons as these from Mr. Barlow, and the young gentleman attended to them with every mark of gratitude and sensibility. The behaviour of Harry was truly great and noble; for after he had finished his labour of the day, he employed all the rest of his time to the amusement of Tommy, and this he did with such affection and pleasure, that they loved each other infinitely beyond what they had before.

In the course of the evenings, Tommy frequently conversed with the negro, and asked him many questions concerning his own country. The young gentleman being one night particularly inquisitive, the black man gave him the following history of himself.

"A town on the river Gambia, in Africa, (said he,) gave me birth. In this part of the world where I now am, people look upon me as a being of a different species; and the inhabitants of my country look with equal surprise on the white Europeans. I have seen men in some parts of the world of a yellow hue, in other parts the copper colour prevailed, and each have considered the rest as beings beneath them. This opinion, however, arises from ignorance, and I have often been surprised to see the people of so enlightened a nation as this, give way to such idle prejudices. Do you make any difference between a white and a black horse, in point of strength and agility? Is a white cow more valuable on account of its colour, or is a white dog more useful in your houses or in the chase, than that of any other colour? It has, on the contrary, been the general opinion that light-coloured animals are more feeble and less active.

"In my own country, there is a difference, not only in the colour of men, but also in a variety of other circumstances. In England, for a great part of the year, you are chilled with frosts and snows, and sometimes do not see the sun for whole days together. It is the contrary with us, for the sun never leaves us. Our days and nights are equal, and we are consequently strangers to that diversity of seasons you experience in this climate. Snow, frost, and ice, are unknown to us, a perpetual verdure prevails, and every season of the year produces us fruits. There are indeed some months in the year, when we are scorched with intolerable heat; in those seasons vegetation appears to be destroyed, the rivers fail in their salutary streams, and men and animals are parched with thirst.

"Tigers, lions, elephants, and other animals of prey, in those seasons, are driven from their dreary abodes, in forests impenetrable to men, and skulk about the borders of rivers. We are then frequently disturbed by the nocturnal yells and savage roarings of these fero-cious animals, which frequently interrupt our repose in our peaceful cottages.

"In this country I am now in, however melancholy may be the truth, you seem to have more to fear from each other, than from the savage inhabitants of the woods. Your houses are built so as to defy the utmost fury of the winds and weather, and which seem almost to resist the efforts of time. With us, reeds, twisted together, and cemented with slime or mud, form our contented, though humble dwellings. Wretched as these habitations may appear to you, an African enjoys in them all the felicities of life, till you white Christians drag him from thence, and export him from his native country into foreign climes, where he is exposed to all the calamities of slavery and cruelty.

"A few stakes set in the ground, interwoven with reeds, and whose covering was nothing more than the spreading leaves of the palm, were the compositions of that mansion, in which I first learned to know that I was a human creature. A few earthen vessels, which served to dress our provisions, composed the whole of our kitchen utensils. Our chamber furniture was nothing more than a few mats woven with soft grass, and these supplied us with a luxurious bed. The few tools we used in turning up the ground, the arrows and javelins which we employed in hunting, and our lines necessary for fishing, completed the catalogue of all our earthly possessions.

"In your country, men seem to place their happiness in obtaining a thousand things more than nature requires, and more than they can ever make use of. Your houses are sufficiently extensive to contain a whole tribe of our people, and you so load yourselves with clothes, that your limbs cannot perform their offices. Your tables at meal times are covered with a profusion of victuals, sufficient to serve a whole village, and I have fre-quently seen a poor wretch perishing with hunger at the gates of a rich man, while he was at his dinner, composed of many sumptuous dishes, without the least appetite for any.

"Yams, a root resembling your potatoe, Indian corn, and rice in particular, form all the natural luxuries of our tables, excepting what nature spontaneously produces in our woods, and the produce of hunting and the fishery. Yet this simple diet contents us more, and affords us a greater degree of satisfaction, than what you derive from your most splen-did tables.

"In the cool of the evening, we enjoyed ourselves under the wide-spreading palm-trees, and every traveller that chanced to pass through our village, found a home at every house he came to. No door was shut against him, no saucy insolent servant disputed his admission: he entered every house freely, was welcome to partake of what the table produced, and then pursued his journey.

"In almost every town there is a large building, where the aged people meet, in the cool of the evening, and converse on different subjects. Here the sturdy youths amuse themselves in manly exercises: while the children of the rising generation divert themselves with their innocent gambol. Some throw little arrows at marks, and dart at each other their light, blunted javelins, in order to prepare themselves to join in the chase, or to perform their duty when called forth to feats of war. Some wrestle, others run races, with a degree of activity little known to Europeans. Among us, every man is his own architect, for our buildings are plain and simple. Our little towns, which generally consist of a hundred or two of such houses as I have just described, are surrounded by thick hedges of thorns, which guard us against any nocturnal attacks of the wild beasts."

Tommy had hitherto listened in profound silence, to a narrative so novel to him; but now he interrupted the honest negro, by asking him, if his country was much infested with wild beasts.

"Yes, master, (replied the black,) we have every species of them, equally ferocious and dreadful. We have the powerful lion, who has so much strength in his paw, that he will level a man to the earth with a single blow, and his paws are armed with such claws, that no creature can resist their sharpness and violence. His roar is like that of thunder, at which the boldest hunter frequently trembles. When our valiant youths resolve to attack this noble, dreadful animal, they assemble in troops, arm themselves with javelins and arrows, and surround his dreadful abode. Their shouts and cries, accompanied with the clashing of their arms, bring him out of his den, and rouse him to resistance. He no sooner views his enemies, than he shakes his majestic mane, and looks round upon his host of foes with the utmost contempt and indifference. He regards neither their numbers, their horrid shouts, nor the glittering of their shining arms.

"He remains undaunted, and despises the weakness of all their vain boastings.

"After a little time he begins lashing his sides with a long and ponderous tail, which is a certain emblem of his rising fury; his eyes sparkle like consuming fire, and, when he perceives that his hunters are numerous, he generally moves towards them with a slow and awful step. This, however, he is not permitted long to do, for those in his rear wound him in the flank with a javelin, which makes him face about. Then commences his rage and fury, when neither a torrent of blood issuing from his wound, nor a combined number of spears opposed to him, can prevent his rushing on the man he supposes to have first wounded him. Death is the inevitable lot of his devoted enemy, should he reach him in his first spring; but it generally happens that the hunter, who has glory and his own life at stake, avoids him by a nimble leap, when the whole troop rush on to his assistance. The rage of this furious animal then avails him but little, his strength is gradually exhausted, and his life hastily steals away through every fresh wound he receives.

"The conquerors, as a trophy of their victory, carry him home in triumph, when all the villagers, young and old, meet them with joyful shouts, and celebrate the valour of the conquerors. Every part of the slain animal is surveyed, his enormous size, his wonderful limbs, and his dreadful fangs. The men repeat tales of their former exploits, while the

children are brought forward to survey the victim, and are taught to examine the most terrible parts of him, that they might become familiar to scenes of danger. Joyful acclamations are echoed from every part of the village, and a feast is prepared for the entertainment of the conquerors."

Tommy here said, that this relation almost made him tremble. He observed, that should a lion meet a man singly, he supposed his death would be unavoidable.

"That is not always the case, (replied the black,) as I was myself once witness to the contrary. My father, who, besides having had the reputation of being a skilful hunter, was considered as the bravest in our village, and many trophies of his valour are there to be seen at this day. The inhabitants of the whole village being one day assembled at their sports and pastimes, an enormous lion, perhaps attracted by the smell of roasted flesh, unexpectedly rushed in upon them with a horrid roaring. The villagers, being all unarmed, fled away with the utmost precipitation, when none but my father remained. As he had never yet turned his back on any beast of the forest, he drew from his side a short dagger, which he always carried with him, and placing one knee and hand on the ground, serenely waited the attack of this formidable enemy. It is not in the power of words to express the fury with which the lion rushed towards my father; but he received him on the point of his dagger, in so steady and composed a manner, that he sunk it several inches into his belly. The beast then made a second attack, and received another wound more dreadful than the first, after having given my father so severe a blow with his paw, as laid one of his sides bare. By this time, the villagers had armed themselves, and rushing to the assistance of my father, they soon dispatched this furious animal. This action appeared so wonderful to every one, that his fame was spread over the whole country, and he gained the most honourable marks of distinction."

A gentleman now entering Mr. Sandford's house, about some particular business, Tommy desired the honest black to defer the remainder of his story till the gentleman's departure.

CHAPTER XII

As soon as the gentleman was gone, Tommy desired the black to proceed in his entertaining narrative, with which he instantly complied. "It is no wonder, (said he,) under such a parent I learned every species of the chase. I was first taught to pursue stags and other feeble animals, and accompanied other children and young men to defend our rice-fields from the depredations of the river-horse. Rice being a plant that requires great moisture, our plantations are for the most part made by the sides of rivers, where the soil, being overflowed in the rainy season, becomes soft and fertile. As soon as it nearly approaches perfection, we are obliged to defend it from different kinds of destructive animals, of which the principal is the river-horse. It is a prodigious animal, being twice the size of your English oxen. He has four short, thick legs, an enormous head, and jaws armed with prodigiously long and strong teeth, besides two prominent tusks, which make a most formidable appearance.

"Notwithstanding the strength and size of this animal, his principal abode is in rivers, where he lives upon the produce of the waters. It is a curious, though dreadful sight, to behold this monstrous creature travelling along the bottom, several yards below the surface, over which you are gently gliding in a boat, and can see every thing that passes in the transparent mirror beneath you. The boatman always endeavours to get out of his way; for so strong is this animal, that he can overset a tolerably large bark, or tear out a plank with his enormous fangs. During the day, he generally conceals himself in the water, and preys on the inhabitants of that element; but when the gloom of night approaches, he quits the river, and entering the fields, commits depredations on the standing corn, which he would totally destroy, were not people set to watch his motions, and drive him away by their shouts and clamours.

"Among these parties I have frequently made one, and have watched several successive nights. At length, one of our most enterprising youths proposed that we should boldly attack the enemy, and punish him for his depredations. For this purpose we concealed ourselves in a proper place, and when we saw him some way into the plantation, we rushed from our concealment, and endeavoured to intercept his return. This monster was so sensible of his own strength, that he slowly retreated, snarling horribly, and gnashing his dreadful tusks. Our darts and arrows had no power on his sides, every weapon rebounding as from a wall, or glancing aside, without making the least wound.

"One of our boldest youths then unguardedly approached him, and endeavoured to wound him at a shorter distance; but the enraged animal, running at him with a degree of swiftness he was not before supposed to possess, he seized him, ripped up his body with his tusk, and left him dead upon the spot. His companions instantly fled with terror, and every one but myself declined the dangerous conflict. Inflamed with grief and rage for the loss of my comrade, I resolved, at the hazard of my life, to attempt to revenge his death. As I found his hide was impenetrable to any weapon, I selected one [of] my sharpest arrows, fitted it to my bow-string, and with a cool and steady aim, while the animal was hastening to the borders of the river, I hit him so directly in the ball of one of his enormous eyes, that the point penetrated to his brain, when he fell to the ground with a dismal groan, and instantly expired.

"Though there was in fact nothing very great in this action, from that time I was regarded as the first among the youths of our hamlet. I was received with joy and congratulation, and was ever afterwards chosen as the leader of every dangerous exploit. But what flattered my ambition more than all the rest, my father received me with transport; he pressed me to his bosom with tears of joy, and told me, that he could now resign his breath without reluctance, since he had lived to see that I was not unworthy of being called his son. 'I have not, (continued my father,) passed my youth in an inglorious inactivity: I have laid many a tiger dead at my feet: I have compelled the lion, the terror of the woods, and the fiercest of all animals, to yield to my courage, and many an elephant has been obliged to flee from me, but I do not remember that I ever achieved such an action as what you have just now performed.'

"My father then went into his cabin, and brought out the bows and arrows he had so successfully used in the chase. 'Take these, my son, (said he to me,) for now you are worthy of them. Age now creeps on me apace, and I have no longer strength sufficient properly to use them in the chase. I must now transfer that business to you, and leave to your youthful and nervous arm, the protection of your country from the furious beasts of the forest.' "

Tommy's curiosity was much gratified with the recital of these adventures, and, as his knowledge increased, so his generous heart expanded. He reflected on his former prejudices with shame and contempt, began to consider all mankind as his equals, and ceased to make those foolish distinctions, which pride and vanity had before suggested to his mind. This happy change in his sentiments made him respected by every one in Mr. Sandford's family, and Harry and Tommy loved each other more than ever.

Our young gentleman was one day surprised by an unexpected visit from his father. The meeting was equally affectionate on both sides, for Tommy was become another boy. His father told him, he was come to take him back to his own house, having heard such an account of his present behaviour, that all his former errors were forgiven; and Tommy mutually met the embraces of his father, and consented to return home to his mother, that he might, by his future conduct, convince her of the happy alteration made in his temper.

Farmer Sandford was at this instant returning from the fields, and very respectfully invited Mr. Merton to walk in, when the latter called the former aside; as if he had something to say to him in private. When they were alone, Mr. Merton thanked the farmer for the infinite services he and his family had been of to his son, in working so happy a reformation. He then pulled out a pocket-book, and begged Mr. Sandford would accept of it and its contents. The farmer taking the book, and looking into it, found it contained bank-notes of great value. He therefore shut it up again, and politely returned it to Mr. Merton, begging to be excused the acceptance of it.

Mr. Merton was very much surprised at this mark of modesty and moderation. He reminded Mr. Sandford of the state of his family; his daughters unprovided for, his amiable son brought up to labour, and himself hastening to old age, which required a respite from the toils and fatigues of life. "I remember the time was, (replied the farmer,) when people in my station thought of nothing but doing their duty towards God, and working hard. When I was a youth, I rose with the sun, and could turn a furrow as straight as any ploughman in this or any neighbouring county. My father used to say, that a farmer was good for nothing who was not in the fields by four in the morning, and my mother always began milking by five. In those times women knew something of the management of a house, and did not give themselves up to indolence and the pride of dress."

Mr. Merton here interrupted the farmer, and earnestly pressed him to accept of his present; but he persisted in his refusal, saying, "Formerly, Sir, farmers were a healthy and happy set of people, because they gave themselves no concern about the parade of life; but now nothing else is talked of. One of my neighbours, a farmer like myself, suffers his son to go a shooting with gentlemen; another sends his to market on a blood horse, with a plated bridle and a fine saddle. And then the girls! the girls!—There is pretty work indeed. They must have their hats and feathers and riding habits. What a profusion of pomatum, powder, and pasteboard, and cork! Hardly any one of them knows any thing of the common duties of a family; so that, unless our wise ministers of state will send them all to this new settlement, of which I have heard so much talk, and bring us a cargo of plain and industrious housewives, who have not been brought up at boarding schools, I cannot see how we plain farmers are to get wives."

Mr. Merton could not help laughing at this honest declaration, and observed, that he would venture to pronounce, that things were not conducted in that manner at his house.

"I cannot say quite so bad, (replied Sandford.) My wife was brought up by an industrious mother, and, though she wishes to have her tea every afternoon, she is, nevertheless, a good wife. Her daughters are brought up in a little higher mode than she was; but my wife and I have sometimes a serious conversation on that matter. She indeed employs them in milking, spinning, and making themselves useful in the family; and yet she lets them run into, what they call, a little of the genteel mode. Every woman now-a-days, runs mad after gentility, and when once gentility begins, good-bye to industry. Were such a sum mentioned to them, as you have been pleased generously to offer me, there would be an end to all peace in the family. It would be no longer Deb and Kate, but Miss Deborah and Miss Catherine. The next thing would be, they must be sent to a boarding-school, to learn French and music, and to cut capers about the room. When they came back, there would be a dispute about who was to look after the boiling of the pot, make the puddings, sweep the house, and feed the chickens and pigs; for such vulgar things as these are not to be done by a delicate Miss."

Mr. Merton could not avoid being struck with this reasonable mode of arguing, and sensibly felt the truth of his observations. However, he still pressed him to accept of his offer, telling him how far it would enable him to improve his farm, and cultivate his lands.

"I return you a thousand thanks, (replied the farmer,) but all our family, time immemorial, have been brought up to industry, and to live by the labour of our hands. I have been told by my father, that there has not been a dishonest person, a gentleman, or a nobleman, or a madman among us. I will not be the first to break through the long-established custom of the family. I could not be more happy, were I a lord, or a macaroni, as I think you call them. I want for neither victuals nor work, good firing, clothes, a warm house, a little to give to the poor, and between you and I, perhaps, I have something by me to give to my children, to put them into the world, if they behave well. Ah! my good neighbour, if you did but know the pleasure of following a plough, drawn by a good team of horses, and then going tired to bed, I think you would wish you had been brought up a farmer. Certain I am, I shall never forget the kind offer you have made me; but if you do not wish to make an innocent and industrious family miserable, I am sure you will consent to leave us in the condition in which you at present find us."

Mr. Merton no longer pressed him to accept the present, as he found it was to no purpose; and Mrs. Sandford coming at this instant to invite them in to dinner, they went immediately into the house, and after Mr. Merton had paid his respects to the family, they all sat down to dinner.

As soon as dinner was over, the cloth was removed, and the silver mug, the only article of luxury in [t]his house, had been two or three times replenished, when little Harry Sandford came running in, crying, "Father! father! here is the sweetest team of horses, all of a size and colour, with new harness, and make the finest figure I ever saw in my life. They are stopped at our door, and the man says he has orders to deliver them to you."

Farmer Sandford was then relating the history of the ploughing match, where he won the silver mug they were then drinking out of; but this account of his son had such an effect on him, that he started up immediately, and after making an apology to Mr. Merton, ran out to see what sort of horses these were.

On his return, surprised as well as his son, "Mr. Merton, (said he,) I suppose these horses are a new purchase, and that you want to have my opinion of them. I can assure you, that they are the true Suffolk sorrels, the finest breed of working horses in the kingdom, and these appear to me to be some of the best of that sort."

Mr. Merton replied, that such as they were, they were at his service. "I cannot think, (said he,) after the singular favours I have received from your family, you will so far displease me as to refuse this mark of my gratitude." Mr. Sandford was lost in astonishment, and knew not what answer to make. At length, however, recovering himself, he was going to make the politest refusal he could think of, when Tommy coming in, took Mr. Sandford by the hand, and begged he would not be so unkind as to refuse his father and himself the first favour they ever asked him to grant them. He also reminded him, that this present was less to him, than it was to little Harry, his dear companion; and, after having lived so long in his family, he hoped he would not treat him as if his conduct had been improper.

Harry himself here interposed, and considering the feelings and intentions of the giver, more than the value of the present, he took his father by the hand, and begged him to oblige Mr. Merton and his son. "I would not say a word (added he) were it any person else; but I so well know the generosity of Mr. Merton, and the benevolence of Tommy, that they will receive more pleasure in your accepting, than in their giving the horses." Mr. Sandford's delicacy was now quite conquered, and he at last consented that the horses should be led into his stables.

Mr. Merton, having expressed every mark of tenderness and affection to this worthy family, not even forgetting the honest black, for whom he promised to provide, he desired his son to accompany him home. Tommy arose, and with the sincerest gratitude and affection, took his leave of his friend Harry, and of all the rest of the family. "It will not be long before I shall see you again, (said he to Harry,) for to your example I owe the little good I have to boast of. You have made me sensible, how much better it is to be useful than to be rich or fine, and that it is more amiable to be good than great. Should I ever be tempted to return to my former errors, and to relapse into my late habits, I will return here to be taught better, and I hope I shall not be so unhappy as to be unworthy of your instructions." Tommy and Harry then most affectionately embraced each other, shed the tear of sincere friendship, and then parted, when Mr. Merton conducted his son home.

THE END.

6

The Adventures of a Pincushion

By MARY ANN KILNER

The
ADVENTURES
of a
Pincushion
designed chiefly
for the use of Young Ladies.

VOL. I

Imagination here Supplies.
What Nature's sparing Hand denies.
And, by her magic powers dispense.
To meanest objects, thought & sense.

LONDON.
Printed & sold by John Marshall.
140 Fleet Street.

Mary Maze Kilner *(1753–1831) was the sister-in-law of Dorothy Kilner. According to Jill E. Grey* (The Book Collector, Winter 1969, p. 519), *her middle name was Ann, not Jane, as usually given. Though the sisters-in-law never co-authored, their books for children are often confused with one another because they came out anonymously. Mary Ann used S. S. or Sarah Slinn for her pseudonym. Her books include* A Course of Lectures for Sunday Evenings *(4 vols, 1783–1790),* Jemima Placid; or The Advantage of Good-Nature, Exemplified in a Variety of Familiar Incidents *(ca. 1783), and* William Sedley; or, The Evil Day Deferred *(1783).*

Jemima Placid *was reprinted (1870) in the first of Charlotte Yonge's* A Storehouse of Stories, *and in E. V. Lucas's* Forgotten Tales of Long Ago *(1906).* Memoirs of a Peg-Top *(ca. 1783) and* The Adventures of a Pincushion *(2 vols., ca. 1780) derive their form from adult literature: Charles Johnstone's novel* Chrysal; or, The Adventures of a Guinea *(1769) and Thomas Bridges'* The Adventures of a Bank-Note *(1770). There were plenty of imitations of the form in children's literature, such as Mr. Truelove's* Adventures of a Silver Three-Pence *(pre 1800),* The History of a Pin *(1798), and Richard Johnson's* The History of a Doll *(1794?)*

In The Adventures of a Pincushion Designed Chiefly for the Use of Young Ladies *there is true suspense — a child has to read the second volume to find out how the pincushion gets out from under the bookcase. Early in the tale Mary Ann Kilner warns the child reader:*

> *As I would not willingly mislead your judgment, I would, previous to your reading this work, inform you, that it is to be understood as an imaginary tale; in the same manner as when you are at play, you sometimes call yourselves gentlemen and ladies, though you know you are only little boys and girls.*

She warns children that they have to pretend that pincushions can think and feel. At the same time she feels obliged to be truthful lest she mislead.

Some critics see Mary Ann as kinder to her child characters than her sister-in-law was, but in Memoirs of a Peg-Top *(the boys' companion to the pincushion volume), George Mealwell fakes a robbery by rolling in brambles. Unluckily, he is almost blinded when he gets a thorn in his eye. Ready to whip him, the father bellows: "And as for your eye, if you had quite lost it, it would have been what you deserved." Lex talionis may have been merciful in savage times; in the rational eighteenth century, it seems cruel. Despite their strict punishments, Mary and Dorothy Kilner have been praised by Gillian Avery (in* Nineteenth-Century Children) *for their "earthy robustness." Avery judges them the only writers outside of Maria Edgeworth who succeeded in animating the moral tale.*

The Adventures of a Pincushion *is reprinted from a two-volume (ca. 1783) edition from the University of Chicago Regenstein Library.*

PREFACE

THE AUTHOR of the following sheets is well aware of the objections which may be made to the performance; but hopes the candour of the public will excuse those defects, which the nature of the undertaking rendered it almost impossible to avoid. The pointed satire of ridicule, which would perhaps have given a zest to those scenes in which the subject of these pages was engaged, was not, in the opinion of the writer, at all proper for those readers for whom it was solely designed: to exhibit their superiors in a ridiculous view, is not the proper method to engage the youthful mind to respect: to represent their equals as the objects of contemptuous mirth, is by no means favourable to the interest of good-nature: and to treat the characters of their inferiors with levity, the author thought was inconsistent with the sacred rights of humanity. Circumscribed therefore to the narrow boundaries of simple narrative, it has been the design of the following pages, carefully to avoid exciting any wrong impression, and, by sometimes blending instruction and amusement, to make it the more easily retained.

To multiply incidents in these circumstances, was a very difficult task, especially, as it was wished to make them arise naturally from the subject; and not obtrude unnecessarily without any seeming cause to produce them. The avidity with which children peruse books of entertainment, is a proof how much publications proper for their attention are required. Though the sentiments should be suited to their simplicity, they ought to be expressed with propriety; since a taste for elegance may be insensibly acquired; and we should always endeavour to present them with proper models of imitation. Conscious of the difficulty of the undertaking, the Author of these adventures would gladly have declined the task, in the expectation of such a work's engaging the attention of those, whose genius were more equal to its accomplishment. With the hope, therefore, of inspiring others to excel the example, it is now submitted to the world "with all its imperfections on its head," trusting for a candid reception to the motive which first suggested the idea: That of presenting the juvenile reader with a few pages which should be innocent of corrupting, if they did not amuse.

It happened one very fine afternoon in the latter end of May, that Mrs. Airy had been collecting together a great number of different pieces of silk, in order to make a work-bag; which she intended as a present to one of her nieces. Miss Martha Airy, her eldest daughter, was about ten years old, and had been for some time indolently lolling with both her elbows on the table, looking at her mamma while she was choosing the prettiest pattern for the purpose I just mentioned. Her chin rested on her two hands, which were crossed over each other, and she was seated on the back of her brother's chair, which he had turned down in that manner for the purpose of serving him as a horse. At last, however, her weight proving too great from the seat she had chosen, as she did not keep still, the upper part of the chair-back came to the ground, while the other end mounted up like a piece of board for a see-saw; and in her fall tumbling down backwards, proved the occasion of a great deal of mischief, by oversetting a curious set of tea-china, which her sister Charlotte was playing with; and which she had received as a present the day before from her grand-papa. Charlotte was so enraged at the loss of her play-things, that, without offering to help her sister, she gave her a slap on the face, and told her, she was very naughty to spoil things in such a manner by her carelessness; and that she would break her plates whenever they came in her way. She was proceeding in this manner when Mrs. Airy thought it time to interfere, and was extremely angry with Charlotte for her warmth. "Martha was not to blame," added she, "as she had no intention of doing the least mischief to your cups and saucers. I think, as I told her once before, she was not sitting in a graceful attitude, and had she moved at the time I spoke to her, it would have prevented her fall; but that is no justification of your behaviour to your sister. She has not deserved your reproaches, and I did not think you could have behaved so improperly, as well as unkindly, as to strike any one, especially your elder sister. Indeed I am much displeased with you, and the threat you made of breaking her plates in return, is so very naughty and wicked, that I think you deserve to be punished; and I desire you will ask Martha's pardon for the blow you have given

her." Charlotte coloured with indignation and anger, at the thoughts of submitting in such a manner to humble herself. She had heard some silly girls declare, they would never own their being in the wrong, and was withheld from acting in the noblest manner, by the false shame of confessing an error. At length, however, upon her mamma coming towards her with an avowed intention of inflicting some further punishment, she mumbled out, in a low voice, which was very difficult to be understood, "That she was sorry that she had struck her sister." Martha, who was extremely generous, and uncommonly good-natured, very affectionately kissed her sister; and told her, she was much concerned at the mischief she had occasioned; though she could not have helped it; as she fell down before she was aware of it, and did not see that her tea-things were near her. Charlotte grew reconciled by degrees; but it was a long time before she regained her usual cheerfulness. After some time, however, the sisters seated themselves in a window by the table, and solicited their mamma for a bit of silk to make a Pincushion. Mrs. Airy gave them several pieces to choose which they liked best; and after they had taken them up a dozen times, or perhaps as many more, had they been reckoned, Martha made a choice of a square piece of pink sattin, which she neatly sewed and stuffed with bran, and which, gentle reader, when it was finished, was the identical Pincushion whose adventures form the subject of this little volume. Assuming, therefore, the title of an Historian, or Biographer, which is generally understood to mean a person who is writing an account of his own, or another's actions, I shall take the liberty to speak for myself, and tell you what I saw and heard in the character of a Pincushion. Perhaps you never thought that such things as are inanimate, could be sensible of any thing which happens, as they can neither hear, see, nor understand; and as I would not willingly mislead your judgment, I would, previous to your reading this work, inform you, that it is to be understood as an imaginary tale; in the same manner as when you are at play, you sometimes call yourselves gentlemen and ladies, though you know you are only little boys and girls. So, when you read of birds and beasts speaking and thinking, you know it is not so in reality, any more than your amusements, which you frequently call making believe. To use your own style, and adopt your own manner of speaking, therefore, you must imagine, that a Pincushion is now making believe to address you, and to recite a number of little events, some of which really have happened, and others might do so with great probability: and if any of the characters here represented should appear to be disagreeable, the author hopes you will endeavour to avoid their failings, and to practise those virtues or accomplishments, which render the contrary examples more worthy of imitation. And now, if you please, we will return to the account of what further befel me in the family of Mrs. Airy.

After the young ladies had amused themselves a great while with the pieces of silk I have so often had occasion to mention, and Miss Martha had completed me to her entire satisfaction; she took all the pins out of an old green one, which was originally in the shape of a heart, but had, by losing a great part of its inside, through various little holes, quite lost its form: and which, that she might find those pins which had gone through the silk, she cut open on an old news-paper, and then stuck all she could find upon my sides in the shape of letters, which she afterwards changed to flowers, and a third time altered to stars and circles; which afforded her full amusement till bed-time. Miss Charlotte, though her mamma had given her as much silk as her sister, had only cut it into waste; while Martha, after she had furnished me, had saved the rest towards making a housewife for her doll. I could not help reflecting when I saw all Charlotte's little shreds and slips littering the room, what a simple method many little girls are apt to get into, of wasting every thing which their friends are so kind as to give them, and which properly employed, might make them many useful ornaments for their dolls, and sometimes pretty trifles for themselves. Charlotte Airy, as such children usually are, was desirous of having every thing she saw; so that her drawers were always filled with bits of ribbon, pieces of silk, cuttings of gauze, catgut, and muslin: and if she wanted to find her gloves, tippet, tuckers, or any part of her dress, she was obliged to search for them in twenty different places, and frequently to go without what she was looking for. Martha, on the contrary, by taking care of what might be of use, and laying it by in a proper place, always knew where to find what she had occasion for directly. So that it frequently happened that she went out with her mamma, when her sister was forced to stay at home; because she had lost something which had delayed her so long to look for, that she could not get ready in time. This very circumstance happened the day after I became acquainted with her, to her no small mortification. Mrs. Airy was going to see the exhibition of pictures, at the Royal Academy, and told her daughters if they behaved well they should accompany her; as Mrs. Gardner and her niece Miss Lounge would call at one o'clock. After breakfast, Charlotte, who had found the mould of an old button in one of her papa's waistcoat pockets which she had been rummaging, had cut to pieces an axle-tree of a little cart, which belonged to her brother, to make a spindle, in order to convert it into a tea-totum; with which she was so much entertained, that she was very unwilling to leave it to go to work, though her mamma repeatedly told her, she would not be ready against Mr. Gardner's coach came. "Yes, I shall, madam!" said she, and played on. "Do pray go to work, Charlotte!" "Presently, madam." But still she thought she would give it another twirl. "You shall not go if you have not finished your morning business!" "In a minute I will!" And so she simply idled away her time, without heeding her mamma's admonition, till near an hour beyond her usual time of beginning. This put her into such a hurry to finish when she found it was so late, that she stitched some wristbands she was about, and which were intended for her grand-papa, so very badly, they were obliged to be undone; which made her so cross, that in pulling out the work, she broke

the threads of the cloth, and entirely spoiled it. Charlotte was a very fair complexioned pretty girl; but you cannot imagine how ugly her ill-humour made her appear; nor how much more agreeable her sister looked, who was much browner, was pitted with the small-pox, and a much plainer child. I surveyed them both as I lay on the table, where my mistress had placed me to stick her pins as she took out of the shirt collar which she was putting on; Martha looked so placid and cheerful, and seemed to speak so kindly when she asked a question, that it made her really charming; while Charlotte, who had a very pretty mouth, and very regular features, stuck out her lips in a manner so unbecoming, and tossed about her head with such very illiberal jerks that she lost all natural advantages in her wilful ill-humour.

A person happening to call on Mrs. Airy, to speak about some particular business, she left the children to attend him; and Martha, who pitied her sister's distress, and saw the impossibility of her finishing the task she was ordered to do, very kindly offered to assist her, without which, she never could have accomplished it. But their mamma, at her return, immediately suspected the case to be as I have told you, and inquired what help Charlotte had received in her absence? They were both girls of too much honour to deny the truth, and in consequence of her frankly owing her sister's kindness, Mrs. Airy permitted her to retire, in order to prepare for the intended expedition; but alas! poor Charlotte, who indeed was not always so good as she ought to have been, was not to go that morning, although her mamma had consented to it. Betty, who came to put on her frock, was not very fond of her, for she was sometimes apt, when her mamma was not in the way, to speak very haughtily, and in a manner quite unbecoming a young lady. Unfortunately she forgot herself on the present occasion, and very rudely said, "You must come and dress me, and you must make haste, or I shall not be ready." Must I? replied Betty, That is if I please, Miss Charlotte, though you forgot to put that in: and unless you speak in a prettier way, I will not help you at all. "Then you may let it alone, for I will not ask you any otherwise," and away she went, banging the door after her, to call her sister, who was ready and waiting for the coach in her mamma's room. Martha ran directly, and began to pin her frock as she desired. But a new distress arose, for as she was too careless ever to retain any of my fellow-servants (commonly called a Pincushion) in her service, so she had not one pin to proceed with after three, which

had stuck at one end of me, had been employed. Neither of them chose to apply to Betty, because they were sure from Charlotte's ill-behaviour to be denied: and she would not permit her sister to ask her mamma, for fear of an inquiry which might not turn out to her credit. So, in short, they both traversed the room backwards and forwards, and were quite overjoyed when they found two, (one of which proved to be crooked) between the joining of the floor. Then they each returned and took me up repeatedly, and examined me over and over, though they were convinced I had been empty long ago. At last a loud rap at the door announced Mrs. Gardner's arrival. The ladies were called, and Martha obeyed, though with reluctance to leave her sister: and Charlotte, with conscious shame and remorse for her past conduct, and heart-heaving sobs of disappointment, saw them drive away without her. I was left upon the table in the hurry of my mistress's departure, and Charlotte took me up, and earnestly wished she had had a Pincushion of her own: and so I should think would any one, who had experienced the want of such an useful companion; though unless well furnished with pins, it is in itself but of little assistance, as she had but too unfortunately found. The slatternly appearance, and real inconvenience, which many ladies suffer from neglecting to provide themselves with, and retaining a few such necessary implements of female œconomy about them is really inconceivable by any person accustomed to a proper degree of attention. Trifles are frequently regarded by the giddy and thoughtless as of no moment, when essentials are taken care of: but it is the repetition of trifles which constitutes the chief business of our existence. In other words, people form their opinion of a young lady from her personal appearance; and if, because she is at work, and in want of pins, and destitute of a Pincushion, she has quite undressed herself, and her clothes are dropping off, she will be thought a negligent slattern; which, I suppose, is what no one would chuse to be esteemed: so, when children accustom themselves to loll their elbows, stoop their heads, stand upon one foot, bite their nails, or any other ungraceful actions, it makes them disagreeable, and the object of dislike to all their friends, and every one who is acquainted with them. And it is very foolish to imagine, that because they are not in company with strangers it does not signify; for ill habits, when once they are acquired, are very difficult to leave off; and by being used to do an unpolite action frequently, they will do it without recollecting the impropriety; when if they thought, perhaps,

they would have on no account been guilty of it.

Miss Lounge, the young lady who accompanied Mrs. Airy to the exhibition, was a striking example of what I mention above. She was about sixteen, and very tall of her age; so that she appeared quite womanly in person, though her manners were to the highest degree remarkable and unpleasing, she had a strange way of tossing her legs round at every step, as if she was making circles, and her arms were crossed over each other in so aukward a manner, and unfashionably low, that it made her still more ungraceful in her appearance: besides this, she had acquired a drawling tone in conversation, which made her completely an object of disgust; as it was entirely the consequence of her own neglect, and therefore was by no means deserving of that pity which is due to every natural defect, or accidental deformity. She returned with her aunt to dinner.

Miss Charlotte was quite ashamed of entering the drawing-room, though she was now dressed, and had promised Mrs. Betty she would behave with more civility for the future. But the fear of mamma's exposing her folly to Mrs. Gardner, had made her dislike to show herself in company; and the consciousness of having deserved reproof, made her justly apprehensive of receiving it. She did not venture down stairs, therefore, till dinner was on the table; and then, with her neck and face as red as blushes could make them, she paid her compliments to the company, without daring to look at her mamma. So cowardly and uncomfortable does the thought of a wrong action make those who have committed it, even when they are not certain it will be publicly known. And this reminds me of a few stanzas I found in Miss Martha's work-bag one day, when she put me into it with her scissars, (by mistake I suppose) as my proper place was certainly in her pocket. But as they are so very a-propos to my present subject, I will present my readers with them: and as the author is quite unknown, if they should not be thought deserving of a favourable reception, they will not at least subject the writer to any mortification.

'TIS innocence only true courage can give,
    Or secure from the fear of disdain;
To be conscious of guilt all affiance destroys,
    And the hope of enjoyment is vain.

If to error betrayed, then delay not to own
  The crime which has robb'd you of peace;
As penitence only can wash out the stain,
  Or cause your vexation to cease.

When the ermine of conscience is spotted by guilt,
  Most severe are the pangs of the mind;
'Tis a woe which no sympathy e'er can relieve,
  Nay, is hurt by a treatment too kind.

To feel undeserving of friendly esteem,
  Is the worst of all evils below:
We may suffer from pain, but the sting of remorse
  Is the heaviest grief we can know.

Then careful your innocence ever maintain,
  Be assured, it is worthy your care;
Since no other distress so deprives us of hope,
  Or so soon sinks the soul in despair.

There was another short piece by the same hand, which my mistress had transcribed, to give her sister on occasion of a little quarrel which had happened between them: Miss Martha having mentioned to her the impropriety of speaking rudely to servants, and behaving in a different manner when her mamma was absent, to what she could dare to do in her presence; which reproof Charlotte highly resented, and was very angry that her sister should find fault with her: as the following verses were applicable to the circumstance, she adopted them as her own on the occasion.

NAY, Charlotte, why so much displeas'd to be told,
  That your friends have discernment to see?
If you could descend to deserve *my reproach,*
  The error lies sure not in me.

I mention'd the fault that in future your care
  Might secure from unguarded surprize;
I thought you had sense to rely on my love;
  To resent it I deem'd you too wise.

The freedom of friendship should never displease,
  Tho' harsh its reproofs may appear;
Since often in public who flatter us most,
  Are the first at our weakness to sneer.

Then should you not gladly, with candour receive
  The advice which affection bestows;
For sincerity rarely we meet with in life,
  Few will aid us, but numbers oppose.

As to you, I am bound by the dearest of ties,
  My sister, *as well as my* friend:
No undue command did I mean to usurp,
  Nor ever design to offend.

Then let us united in harmony live,
  For sisters should ne'er disagree;
And when I am wrong, equal freedom exert;
  To complain of these errors to me.

Mrs. Airy was so generous as not to expose her daughter's folly before Mrs. Gardner; and as she had met with a severe punishment in the consequence of her fault, and had promised amendment for the future, after a gentle reprimand, when she came down the next morning, nothing further passed on the subject.

Charlotte was conscious of her late misbehaviour, that she had scarce courage to enquire what entertainment they had received from a sight of pictures at the exhibition; and Martha, who was extremely delicate and attentive, very cautiously avoided the subject, from fear of appearing to insult her sister, or to remind her mamma of the reason which had occasioned her absence from the party. Mrs. Airy inquiring whether Martha had not particularly taken notice of a large picture, which represented the death of Earl Goodwin; she replied, that Mrs. Gardner had pointed it out to her observation; but that she had not remarked any particulars, except the figure of a King, and a large company at dinner. I will tell you the story then, my dear, to which this picture refers, said Mrs. Airy.

In the reign of Edward the Confessor, in the year 1042; Earl Goodwin, who had been accessary to the murder of Prince Alfred, was at dinner with the King at Windsor; and taking a piece of bread, called God to witness his innocence, and wished, if he uttered any but the truth, that the next mouthful he ate might choak him: Which accordingly happened, and the bread stuck in his throat, and he died immediately at the table. Do not you think, my dear, added Mrs. Airy, it was a just punishment for his untruth, and an awful judgment for calling God to witness a falsehood? Indeed, Madam, I think it

was quite dreadful: but are you sure that this account is true? for though it is certainly very wicked to tell a lie on any occasion, yet, as sometimes many people are thus guilty, I wonder that such events do not more frequently happen! You know that Miss Riby said she had not been writing last week, although you saw that her fingers were inked; and Charlotte had seen her doing it; why then did not the same accident happen to her? "Because, my love, the punishment of such crimes does not always immediately follow the commission of them; but you may be sure that the remorse of conscience, and the secret uneasiness of mind which the guilty suffer, is a very great unhappiness; and the apprehension and the fear of a future account after death, besides the idea of present detection, is such a degree of misery as no other punishment can equal. As to your question, whether I believe this account to be true? I certainly do! It was an extraordinary event which was recorded at the time it happened, and which every history has mentioned since, and faithfully transmitted to us. This is the best authority we can have for any fact which happened before our own time, and is therefore entitled to our belief. But why such examples are so rare, is not to be wondered at; because you know that wicked people will be punished hereafter; and though such instances sometimes happen, to teach others to be good, and to make them afraid of doing what might make them liable to such terrible vengeance, yet, in general, a crime of this kind does not meet with immediate chastisement; because, after death, as I have before told you, those who have been wicked, will suffer such misery as their sins deserved. Besides which, the liar is at present detested by every one, and loses all the advantage of confidence, and the pleasure of being believed: even when he does speak truth, he is liable to be suspected, and his word is doubted on all occasions." The conversation was here interrupted by the arrival of two young ladies and their mamma, who came to pay a morning visit to Mrs. Airy. But as they did not say any thing worth the attention of my readers, I shall not trouble myself to repeat more of what passed than may be imagined, from the comments of my mistress and her sister, with which I shall present them.

Martha, before the room door was well shut after them, began to observe that the eldest Miss Chantillon was very ugly, and very stupid; and the youngest a good pretty girl, and talked a great deal indeed. I wish, added she, I could speak as fast as she does. To talk so fast, my love, said her mamma, is by no means any accomplishment; and I am far from

your opinion, in so highly admiring the merits of Miss Lucy. She chatters so fast, as frequently not to be understood; and has a very silly trick of beginning every sentence with a laugh, than which nothing can be more ill-bred. The person who is speaking, should never laugh, if she can help it, at her own wit, if she design to excite mirth, or to meet with approbation from others. But without any such intention, Lucy assumes an affected giggle whenever she attempts to speak. She has likewise a very unbecoming pertness in her manner, and, by frequent interruptions, when her elders are otherwise engaged, renders herself extremely disagreeable. I would have you, my good girls, possess that desirable degree of proper courage, as never to feel ashamed of speaking when it is necessary; but I think it is an unpleasing sight to perceive a young woman, or child I should say, for Lucy is young enough for that epithet, affecting to understand every thing, and giving her opinion unasked, upon subjects which frequently expose her ignorance and presumption. This is aiming at a character to which she has no pretensions; and by wishing to rise into a woman, before she has reached the age of understanding, she is despised for her vanity, and loses that esteem she might have attained by a proper degree of humility, and her better knowledge of her station. This observation, my dear Martha, I would particularly address to you; as you are generally thought uncommonly tall, and are usually imagined to be much older than you are. This I know you fancy to be a compliment, which always appears to give you pleasure; but remember, that, if you assume airs of womanhood, and affect to be thought further advanced in age, you will have the less allowance made for any errors you may commit, and consequently meet with contempt where you might otherwise have escaped censure. Youth, and inexperience, are justly allowed to excuse any slight inadvertence in manners, or want of grace in appearance; but if you choose to be thought of more consequence, you must likewise expect, that the notice you may attract will not always be favourable to your vanity. I assure you, I think Miss Jenny Chantillon is much more agreeable than her sister, as she has courage sufficient to reply to any question, and to speak distinctly when she is particularly addressed, without enquiring, in Lucy's manner, into the reason of every word which is uttered, and deciding every argument according to her own fancy: and, I dare say, if you will be careful to observe, you will find that Jenny always meets with attention from the company, while Lucy is frequently insulted, by being enjoined to silence, and by her hearers turning from her with disdain. In short, my dear, it requires a great deal of thought and propriety, to behave in an agreeable manner at your age. It is best not to be anxious to be taken notice of, since that eagerness always defeats its aim. Girls have not had the advantage of experience to teach them wisdom; and when once they are engaged in conversation, and find themselves attended to, their volatile spirits hurry them on, with the desire of obtaining applause for their wit, to say things which are sometimes neither delicate nor prudent; and which they may, when they have time to reflect, long have reason to repent having imprudently uttered. Any restraint at such a time, is, I know, always esteemed an ill-natured interruption, and is apt to damp their harmony, and lower their spirits. I would therefore warn you of the danger beforehand, that your own prudence may be a check to that unlimited indulgence, which at such a period is liable to excess: and I dare say, that your good sense will teach you, that my admonitions are always intended for your advantage. To impress this deeper upon your mind, I will repeat to you a few lines which were written to me, when I was young, by my aunt, and which, as they frequently occurred to my memory, I found to be singularly useful.

RECOLLECT, my sweet girl, ere you mix with the world,
There is need for some caution to guide;
Then wisely remember to govern your tongue,
As silence much folly may hide.

Most useful, I think, you this maxim will find,
And never its precepts neglect;
That who giddy and thoughtless will chatter away,
Shall ne'er gain applause or respect.

Like the Parrot, awhile they may please and amuse;
But no real esteem will acquire;
And I trust that your wish when in converse you join,
Is a nobler regard to inspire.

Remember that memory long may record
The folly you utter'd in jest;
And a secret unmark'd, when escaped from your lips,
May long rob your bosom of rest.

Then conscious of error 'tis vain to repent,
As the mischief admits no relief;
And surely 'tis simple so thoughtless to lay
The dismal foundation of grief.

The ladies now all retired to dinner: but I am ignorant of what passed there, as I was left upon a piece of embroidery, which my mistress was covering with some white paper to

keep it clean: and she did not fetch me till after tea; when she carried me in her hand down stairs with her work, to show some ladies who were assembled in the drawing-room. I then accompanied her into what was usually called the green parlour, as the furniture was all of that colour; whither she went to play with her young visitors, whose names were Eliza Meekley and Julia Norris.

They amused themselves with playing on the harpsichord, while Miss Martha person-ated the music-master, and Charlotte chose to teach them dancing. Some part of the evening they played at going to the exhibition; and just as they determined to visit the pictures, the footman came to acquaint the young ladies, that their coach was ready. Miss Meekley's bib was unpinned, and Martha gave me into her hand in a hurry while she was looking for her cloak. So without recollecting that I was another's property, Eliza put me into her pocket, made a very elegant curtsey, and stepped into the carriage. I felt really very sorry to part from a family with which I had been some time connected, and to one of whom I owed my being as a Pincushion. But my new mistress was so very engaging, that I was in hopes she would take care of me, and not leave me about to the mercy of a little kitten, who jumped into her lap the moment she got home; and who afterwards frisked away with a little tassel which dropped off, from one corner of a workbag which lay on the table. But before I proceed with my history, it will be necessary to introduce my readers to Miss Meekley and her companions, and to make them better acquainted with this new family, who are all of them deserving their notice.

Mrs. Stanley, to whom the house belonged, was the widow of a clergyman, who had at his death left her in rather indigent circumstances; and she had been advised (to sup-port herself and two younger sisters who lived with her) to take a small number of young ladies to board. Her number was confined to six; two of whom were those I have before mentioned. The others were three sisters, whose name were Saxby, and a Miss Una, who for her sweetness of temper, and excellence in every accomplishment, was esteemed superior to all the rest of her companions. Harriet Una was cousin to Miss Meekley, and they usually slept together. She was just turned of thirteen, was tall and large; had light brown hair, blue eyes, and a fine complexion: but her good-nature and willingness to oblige every one, made her the general favourite, and recommended her to universal esteem.

When the young ladies retired to bed, Eliza found me in her pocket, and told Harriet, she was afraid Miss Airy would want her Pincushion; and she was the more concerned, as the family were to go into the country very early the next morning, and she should have no opportunity to return it. However, continued she, I will make a new one to present to Miss Airy when I see her; and I will keep this, as I have not one at present, my kitten having pulled mine to pieces this morning: but I will take care this shall not come to the same mischance. I was glad to hear that was her intention, as I should by no means have liked the thought of sharing the fate of my predecessor. At this time Mrs. Stanley entered the room to wish them a good night, and to see whether they were properly taken care of. I am very unhappy to-night, said Eliza, as soon as she was gone; and I feel ashamed of receiving Mrs. Stanley's kisses, because I behaved in a manner I am sure she would not approve. What have you done, my dear cousin, replied Harriet, to make you so uneasy? I will tell you, answered Miss Meekley, though I do not like to confess my weakness. Just before dinner, Miss Charlotte Airy asked me to eat some preserved plums, which she said had been made a present of to her mamma, and which came from Portugal. They were very sweet and luscious; and as I am not allowed to have any thing of that kind, I refused her offer. But when we had dined, she pressed me again, and laughed at me very much for being so foolish, as to imagine any thing so innocent could hurt me; but supposed, as I went to school, my mistress, for so she sneeringly called Mrs. Stanley, would whip me if I did. At last overcome with her persecutions, and vexed to be treated so much like a baby, and as if I was afraid of punishment, I took the plum, and have not been easy since. And now, my dear Harriet, what shall I do? Suppose Mrs. Stanley should ask me whether I have eaten any thing lately which I ought not: and if she does not put that question, I feel so undeserving of her caresses, that she will see by my looks I have behaved improperly. I am very sorry, replied Miss Una; but as you are so sensible it was wrong, I may spare my recriminations. However, I think the noblest reparation you can now make, would be honestly to inform Mrs. Stanley of the crime, and the sincerity of your regret for having been guilty of it: should it be discovered by any other means, you will forfeit her esteem, and lose that confidence, with which you are at present favoured; by such an unsolicited confession, you will restore satisfaction to your own conscience, and be certain of her approbation.

Eliza was convinced of the propriety and justice of her friend's advice, and promised to comply with it the next morning. But her excessive timidity prevented her making use of several opportunities which presented, though the subject occupied all her attention, and she could scarce think of any thing else. She again applied therefore to Harriet, and told her it was impossible for her to summon up courage to do as she had desired; and begged she would, from her, acquaint Mrs. Stanley with what had happened. Miss Una, in the mildest terms, complied with her request; at the same time very generously commended her honour on every occasion, and urging her present uneasiness to engage Mrs. Stanley's compassion. Miss Meekley, when she was acquainted with her cousin's having revealed this secret, which had oppressed her mind, was very unwilling to attend her to the lady above mentioned. Mrs. Stanley received her with the greatest affection and tenderness; and after expressing in the warmest terms her approbation of such a generous confession, added, "You need never, my dear girl, be afraid either of anger or punishment, when with such a degree of frankness you acknowledge any fault you have committed. Be assured, your friends will be always willing to pardon those errors which you promise to amend: but let the present instance warn you, my Eliza, never to be led into actions which you know are improper, because the company you are with may ridicule your refusal. Miss Charlotte Airy is, in my opinion, a very naughty girl, to endeavour to persuade you to do any thing which you have been forbidden. And I hope from the remorse you have suffered, you will reflect on the folly of complying with any proposals, which your conscience suggests to you is wrong. Do not be afraid of being laughed at for being good. Every person of real sense will esteem you for your resolution: and because a silly girl may sneer at your apprehension of punishment, it will be much more ridiculous, and wicked at the same time, to be guilty of what you are conscious is a crime, for which you will deserve, and perhaps receive, correction. Besides, one bad action is but too often the cause of the commission of others; and when once we have deviated from what is right in a small instance, it is frequently the occasion of accumulated guilt. I will tell you an instance of this kind that may illustrate my meaning, and which, as I was acquainted with the person who is the subject of it, will perhaps make a deeper impression on your mind.

A young lady whose real name I shall (for the sake of charity) conceal under that of Lloyd, and who was, my dear Eliza, nearly of the same age with yourself, was educated with the utmost attention; and as she was an only child, was the darling of her parents, and the centre of all their future expectations. Betsey, which was the usual appellation, went one day to visit a companion, with whom she was extremely intimate; but who, unfortunately for her, was not possessed of that strict honour which should be the basis and foundation of friendship. When they had been for some time at play in the garden, she proposed to go back to a little shop in the neighbourhood to make a purchase of some gingerbread; and though Miss Lloyd for a time objected to the proposal without leave, against her mamma's repeated command; yet, her companion, laughing at her squeamishness (as she wickedly called an adherence to her duty), prevailed over her better resolutions, and she accompanied her to the place I mentioned. As it was the only shop of the kind which the village afforded, the boys of an adjacent school very frequently went there for the same purpose as the two young ladies who now entered; and two of the most unlucky of their number, happened at that time to be bargaining for some balls.

They staid very soberly till Miss Lloyd had taken out her purse to pay for the cakes she had purchased; but as the lock of her pocket-book was entangled in it, it came out of her pocket at the same time, when one of the boys snatched it from her hand, and rudely declared he would see its contents, and know all the girl's secrets. This vexed her extremely, and she thoughtlessly pursued him, as he ran away with the prize, till she was a good way from home. He was joined by several of his school-fellows, who took part with him, and behaved in so wild a manner as to terrify her greatly. At length, however, she got away from them, and ran back with all the speed in her power; but as it was later than her usual time of returning, her parents were uneasy, and questioned her with great tenderness and anxiety, as to the reason of her stay. She told them, she had been out with Miss Hannah (the companion she had really visited) and her maid, and that a horse had been near running over her, which had frightened her so much, as to prevent her return.

This story was believed by Mr. and Mrs. Lloyd for some time, and Betsey, who had at first been very unhappy at the thoughts of such a wicked deceit, at length grew reconciled as she found herself undetected. She therefore ventured upon a second transgression, from the encouragement which she foolishly imagined the secresy of her first fault had given her; and with her intimate Mrs. Hannah, took another walk, without any person to have the care of them. But during their absence from home, an unexpected accident punished the imprudent Miss Lloyd for her disobedience and untruth, in a manner which will give her cause for repentance to the latest period of her life; for as she was crossing a road in her return, a horse, which had been tied to the rails of a house at a little distance, broke the bridle which confined him, and galloped away full speed, unrestrained by any opposition, till in his passage the unfortunate Miss Lloyd, who did not perceive his approach, was thrown down, and broke her leg in such a terrible manner, as to occasion her being a cripple ever after. She has since confessed, the consciousness of her falsehood was such a conviction to her mind of the wickedness of her conduct (when she was made sensible that the accident was the consequence of her disobedience to her parents) that it was more difficult to support, than any bodily uneasiness she had suffered, and the reflection that they would never be able to confide in her for the future, was the occasion of so much self-reproach, as to deprive her of every enjoyment. This in-

stance may serve to convince you, that a slight error is very frequently, without any previous intention, and when least expected, the occasion of such crimes, as in the cooler
moments of thought (that is, when you have time to reflect on the wickedness of the
action) you would never be capable of committing; and as none can be sure they would
be able to resist temptation, it is best never to do any thing which you know to be wrong,
though it may appear to be in the smallest instance, since the desire of concealing a
trifling fault, may lead you to hide it by a falsehood, which is one of the greatest you
can be guilty of.

Miss Meekly was convinced of the truth and propriety of this argument, and promised
to be more attentive in her future conduct. She then joined her companions with that
cheerful good humour, which distinguished her character, and attended them into the
great parlour, where they usually spent the morning. When they had concluded their
work, writing, &c. Mrs. Stanley always made them read to her, and encouraged them to
ask any question which occurred to them; to make their own observations upon those
passages in history which struck their imaginations; or to propose to her any objection
which arose in their minds. She desired them to ask the meaning and origin of those
customs they did not comprehend, and by so doing had frequent opportunities of improving their understandings. Instances of this kind very frequently occurred, and supplied them with subjects of conversation. Miss Una was working a map of England, and
inquired one day how long the island had been divided into shires and counties. Mrs.
Stanley applied to the young ladies to know if any of them could resolve the question,
but as they were all silent, "you should endeavour, my dears, said she, to remember what
you read, or it will be of very little advantage. I believe, Harriet, you read an account of
this division, a few months ago, when you were going through the reigns of the Saxon
Monarchs. Do not you remember that the great King Alfred, in the year 886 repaired the
city of London, which had been burnt by the Danes in 839, and that he afterwards divided
the kingdom into shires, hundreds, and tithings?" "I did not recollect it," said Miss Una.
"But pray," added Miss Saxby, "did the same king set up all the crosses? for I remember
something about their being erected, though I have forgotten when it happened."
"Your memory is very short, I am afraid, replies Mrs. Stanley; but if you were to write
down such particulars, you would find it of great assistance: as it appears very illiterate to
be unacquainted with those facts which have occurred in the history of your native
country. All the crosses you mention, were erected by King Edward the First, in every
place where the funeral procession of his Queen stopped, from Lincolnshire (w[h]ere she
died) to Westminster. There were in all ten, I think. One at Lincoln, Grantham, Stam-
ford, Geddington, Northampton, Stoney Stratford, Dunstable, St. Albans, Waltham, and
Westminster, called Charing Cross. You should always endea[vour] to observe what you
read; but those things which relate to the island in which you live, have a particular
claim to your remembrance. For this purpose I think your present work is singularly
useful, as it will so strongly impress the geography of your country upon your mind, that
I hope, my dear Harriet, you will never forget it." As nothing material happened to my
mistress, and very little variation occurred in her manner of living, I shall pass over the
usual events of every day, which my readers can easily imagine; such as her taking me out
of her pocket during the time of dressing, and restoring me to that place of confinement
when she had concluded, and proceed to relate an accident in which I was very nearly
concerned.

The kitten I have before mentioned, who was a great favourite with Miss Meekly, was never allowed to enter into her bed-chamber; but one day, the weather being extremely warm, and the door left open, it walked in, and laid itself down at a little distance from the window, in a spot where the sun shone; the shutters being half closed to exclude the heat. Eliza was employed in putting a pair of ruffles into her jacket, and I lay in her lap securely, as I imagined, till a carriage stopping at the gate, she precipitately jumped up to look out at the visitors, and in her haste let me fall upon the floor. Her motion was so sudden and unexpected that I could not save myself, or check the velocity with which I was impelled. So that I unfortunately rolled on, till I touched the edge of a book-case, and discovered myself to Mrs. Puss, who hooked me with her claws, and twisted me round several times with as much dexterity as if I had been spinning; or, to use a more proper simile, as if I had represented a mouse. I afforded her great entertainment for some time, till at last I found myself a second time under one of the feet of the book-case, and so fast wedged in, that it was beyond the art of even a kitten's invention to extricate me from my situation. Mrs. Stanley coming up stairs, Miss Meekly turned out my antagonist, and with unavailing care searched for me in every drawer, on every table, and upon the bed.

Long have I remained in this dull state of obscurity and confinement, unable to make known my distress, as I want the power of articulation: at least my language can be only understood to things inanimate as myself. A pen, however, which fell down near me, engaged to present these memoirs to the world, if ever it should be employed by the hand of kindness, to rescue my name from oblivion. Should the eye of youth read this account with any pleasure, it is hoped the candour of generosity will overlook its imperfections: and should fate, in some fortunate moment of futurity, again restore me to the possession of Miss Meekly, or any of her companions, my gratitude will engage me to thank the public for its indulgence, and to continue the account of my adventures.

If I am not so happy as to meet with approbation, I shall at least have the consolation to reflect that these pages have suggested no wrong ideas to the youthful mind, have given no encouragement to vanity, nor exhibited any improper example with commendation; which is what better authors and works of higher genius cannot always be happy enough to boast. Such as it is, I submit this account of myself to the world, and only desire them to remember, in the words of the admired Gay, that,

> *"From objects most minute and mean,*
> *"A virtuous mind may morals glean."*

END OF VOL. I.

I HAD LAIN so long in my dismal confinement, that I began to despair of ever presenting the world with any second part of my adventures. And yet, thought I, it is very hard that a Pincushion so new, so clean, and so beautiful, that might have a thousand opportunities of seeing the different manners of mankind, should be thus secluded from company, and condemned by the playful freaks of an insignificant kitten thus to pass away its best days in obscurity. And here let me take this opportunity to suggest a useful hint to my young readers, which, as my inactive situation allowed me sufficient time for reflection, I had frequently reason to feel the force of: namely, That although I fretted and fumed every day at my unfortunate condition, I never found it was at all improved by it, or that my ill-humour in the least degree made me happier or assisted my escape.

When I determined to submit quietly, I was as happy as any Pincushion in such a state of retirement could be. But when in a cross fit I tried to roll myself from under the book-case, I found the attempt was impossible to accomplish, and I hurt my sides against the foot of it. The space was so small between the bottom of my prison and the floor, that I had no hopes of escape, as it was impossible for any broom to find its way under: or otherwise the cleanliness of Mrs. Stanley's maid would certainly have effected my deliverance. But alas! of this I had no prospect; and though my endeavours were fruitless, it taught me such a lesson of contentment, as I wish every little reader of my memoirs may remember, and copy in their own conduct. For if they are tired of working, reading, music, drawing, or any other employment at home; or, what is frequently the case, are impatient of the confinement of being at school; I would have them take my advice, and try to amuse themselves when they have opportunity, and wait with patience till they are of a proper age, either to leave the place they dislike, or have overcome the difficulty of learning those accomplishments which are necessary to be acquired. For they

may depend upon it, that fretfulness and ill-humour will make every condition unhappy; while a resolution to be pleased, and make the best of every thing, is the only method to be agreeable to others, or comfortable themselves. The foot of the bookcase will press closer, when we petulantly try to escape: and though children are not Pincushions, yet they will find, that whenever they are fretful and dissatisfied, they will be unhappy, and never succeed in any thing they undertake. I hope I shall be pardoned for this digression; but as the event of my escape was so strong in my mind, I could not pass it by without a pause of observation.

Let me now, however, proceed to inform my readers, that one fine day, when I had determined to make myself contented, and when from the quietness in which I had been for some days, I had reason to believe the family were absent, and had therefore little hope for release, on a sudden I felt the book-case move, and heard the sound of men's voices, who, after much pushing and hoisting, took away what had so long covered me from the eye of every beholder. In short I found that Mrs. Stanley had taken another house, as her lease was expired: and in consequence of the removal of her furniture, I regained my liberty. One of the porters took me up, and blew off the flue with which so long a confinement had covered me; and, taking me down stairs, presented me to a chair-woman, who was hired to clean the house. There, mother Trusty, said he, is a present for you, which, if you please, you may give to little Jenny: it will make her as fine as a lady. Thank you, returned she, I will keep it safe for my girl; and if you have a bit of paper, I will wrap it up, for my hands are wet and dirty, and when I take any thing out of my pocket I may spoil it, you know. But as to making her fine, Jacob, indeed I do not desire it; and were you to present any thing to wear, she could not have it, for I think finery is not suitable for us. She is a good child, Jacob, and that is better than being a lady. Well, mother Trusty, do as you please, replied Jacob; I do not know who the Pincushion belonged to; so if you like Jane should have it, why I am glad I found it. So saying, he complained that the weather was very hot, and after wiping his face with a coarse apron, which was tied round him, he drank Mrs. Trusty's health; and took a good draught of porter, which stood on the table. He then sat down to eat some bread and cheese, and, calling a great dog which lay in one corner of the kitchen, made him sit up on his hind legs to beg for some victuals, and afterwards bring him his knot, which he very dexterously did, by taking the buckle of it in his mouth, and dragging it after

him to his master. Another trick which this animal had been taught, was to shut the door at word of command; and his last performance to the entertainment of my new Mistress and Mr. Jacob, was to pick up his master's wig and bring it upon his head, which made indeed a very droll figure to the spectators. At the conclusion of his meal, Jacob bade adieu to mother Trusty, and they each separated to pursue their different employments. I was in the mean time laid on one of the shelves, curiously wrapped up in a bit of paper, which had fallen from the back of that very book-case under which I had so long resided: it was torn in two by Jacob, who took one half to put up some bits of cheese rinds for his dog; and I found it was a fragment of poetry, which I suppose had been sent to Miss Saxby, as her name was Martha. I amused myself with the perusal of the lines, which were as follow:

Fragment.

'Tis a folly, my friend, thus to envy the great,
Since content may be found in the lowest estate;
Tho' Miss *** exults that she's splendidly drest,
Of true happiness, Martha, *she ne'er was possess'd.*

I have seen her, my friend, when no art could assuage
Her anger, vexation, and petulant rage;
Because an inferior had treated with scorn,
Those trinkets and gauze which her person adorn.

But believe me, esteem from true merit must rise,
Or the world will the pageants of fortune despise;
'Tis ridiculous, surely, for pride to expect
Any better return than disdain and neglect.

Let us, then, my Martha, *more prudent and wise,*
Endeavour with nobler ambition to rise:
Let kind emulation our bosoms expand,
The foolish suggestions of pride to withstand.

Let us trust that perfection *each effort shall bless,*
As industry e'er is crown'd with success:
Tho' hard is the task, yet 'tis great to aspire,
And the deep-buried embers of genius *to fire.*

'Tis a laudable aim, when we seek to excel,
And conquer that sloth which is apt to rebel:
Then let us attentive each precept obey,
And snatch the proud laurels of glory away.

The business of the day being concluded, the good mother Trusty shut up the house; and taking me down from the shelf, put me carefully in her pocket. We were not long before we arrived at her habitation, which consisted of two neat little rooms in a small house, about the middle of a very pleasant lane. A clean looking boy and girl were sitting at the door, with a coloured apron full of peas, which they were very busily shelling. They expressed great pleasure at the sight of Mrs. Trusty, whom I found to be their grandmother, and with much good humour told her they had each earned a halfpenny; for that Mrs. Traffic, at the chandler's shop, had given them one penny, and promised them a farthing's worth of gingerbread, or a stale roll, for getting her peas ready for supper. Well, and I have brought you home something, replied Mrs. Trusty, unfolding me to the child, who eagerly getting up to receive her present, had nearly overset the apron and its contents; but her brother luckily caught it, so as to prevent the peas from falling into the dirt. But pray, Jenny, stay till you have done, and have washed your hands, said her grandmother; for it would be a pity to spoil this nice satin Pincushion: And what have you brought for me? cried rosy Dick, as he emptied a handful of peas into the bason. Why, nothing at all, my good boy, replied Mrs. Trusty, but a piece of bread and cheese: but I hope you are not jealous that your sister should have any thing, when you cannot partake of it? Jealous! said he: No, I would go without any thing in the world for the sake of my Jenny; and I will give her my half-penny with all my heart, though I have staid away from a nice game at cricket on the green to earn it. When

I am a man, you shall see how hard I will work, and take care of all the money I get, and give it to you, grandmother, to buy us victuals, and drink, and clothes; and you shall stay at home and knit; but never, while I have any health, shall you go out to such hard labour as you now do. Blessings on my generous boy, exclaimed the tender-hearted mother Trusty, while the tears of affection rolled down her aged cheeks. Just such a man was thy father Dick. While he was alive, we never wanted for any thing. He was a good man, indeed he was; and I hope that you will resemble him. But go, my boy; carry home your work, and bring the stale roll which you was promised: it will be much better for you than gingerbread.

Jenny kissed her brother, and thanked him for his kind intention; but we will give the penny to our grandmother, said she; you know she has got five-pence three-farthings which we have had given us already; and when there is enough, we will ask her to buy you a pair of new shoes; because those are too bad to walk with. Away ran Richard with the peas, and returned in triumph with the roll, when the little party sat down to supper, with that smiling good-humour and cheerful contentment, which is not always an attendant on the meals of the rich and great. But when I saw how very little was sufficient (or was obliged to be so) for a woman who had been hard at labour all day, and two little hungry children, I could not help reflecting, how wicked it is in those who are blessed with plenty, to be dissatisfied with their food, and idly waste, when they are not disposed to eat it, that which would keep the poor from starving, and which many an unhappy child would be highly thankful to receive. When they had concluded the meal which their grandmother had brought them, Dick ran to a neighbouring pump, to replenish a broken red pitcher which had lost its handle and a piece out of the top: and after they had each of them drank with thirsty eagerness, he kissed his grandmother and sister, and wishing them a good night, went quietly to bed. Little Jenny followed her brother's example, as soon as she had laid me in a drawer with great care, where all her treasures were deposited. Among that number was a little paper, which was nearly worn out with frequent perusal, and with which I shall beg leave to present my readers.

Dick To His Sister.

THO I am but a boy, yet I'll do the best I can,
And I'll try to earn something, although I'm not a man;
But when I am older, nay, Jenny, do not cry,
For the loss of thy father and mother I'll supply.

I'll go to yon farm-house, and beg a bit of bread;
And if I get a morsel, my Jenny shall be fed;
Then do not weep so sore, for I hope we know the worst,
And to see you look so dismal, my heart it will burst.

Old grannam she will help us, and work for to maintain;
And when I am bigger, I will pay it all again.
Tho' as yet I cannot dig, yet a gleaning I may go;
Then stop your tears, my Jenny, for I cannot see them flow.

When I pass thro' the church-yard, where Daddy is at rest;
I cannot help sobbing, and a sigh will heave my breast:
And I think to myself, if my Jenny too should die,
Ah! who would her place to her Richard e'er supply?

Then, my sister, cheer thine heart, and do not look so sad:
If we can but live together, matters will not be so bad.
Now the blackberries are ripe, and I'll gather some for thee;
And we'll eat them, my Jenny, beneath yon hollow tree.

I know too, my love, where some honey may be found;
For I have oft mark'd the place, which the bees do surround;
And I'll take some for thee, for young Robin taught me how,
One day when he followed in the field with his plough.

Then, my Jenny, be but happy, and cheer us with a smile;
For I fain would make thee blest, and thy sorrows all beguile.
Tho' poor Daddy is no more, yet Richard loves his Jane,
And all thy tears, my sister, can't bring him back again.

Perhaps it may be thought an uncommon effort for little Dick to turn poet at so early an age, and with so few advantages from education. But there is no answering for the powers of natural genius, and many a one may regard the attempt as impossible, merely because they are too indolent to exert their faculties. Richard had been taught to read and write at the charity school of the parish where he lived: and as no application had been wanting on his part, the progress he made did equal credit to his own abilities and the attention of his master, with whom his merit made him a great favourite.

Jenny was likewise put to a small school at a little distance, by the benevolence of the

vicar's wife, (with whom such instances were very frequent) and by her assiduity recommended herself to her mistress, who would often propose her example as a pattern to the rest of her scholars.

The next morning, when mother Trusty got up to her daily labour, she kissed her grand-children, and told them to go to school early, and not stay and play afterwards; but to return back again, for she would probably come home to dinner. This they promised to do; and after they had learned their lessons they affectionately hugged each other, and diligently set forward with their books in their hands. But Jenny in a few minutes returned to fetch me, in order to exhibit her new present to her school-fellows. We soon arrived at a cottage, the apartments of which were neither large nor numerous; but the exquisite cleanness of it was truly admirable. The mistress, whose name was Markall, was dressed in a blue and white striped gown, which was rather of the coarsest materials; but was put on with the neatness of a Quaker, as was a plain bordered mob, with a white cloth binder, and a coloured silk handkerchief; which, with the addition of a checked apron, and a black petticoat, will give a pretty good idea of her appearance. She commended Jenny for coming early, and having inquired after her grandmother and brother, heard her read, and repeat the lesson she had the day before given her to learn. Soon after which, Betsy Field, Nanny Hay, and the rest of the scholars arrived; among which number were likewise several boys. As the room door (which indeed was the door of the house too) was left open for the benefit of the air, and as one of the forms where the girls were at work was placed on that side, they were many of them better disposed to watch the passing of a cart or a wheel-barrow, or to attend the flight of birds and butterflies, than to mind their works: and Mrs. Markall punished several of them with a few strokes of a little cane, which lay on her table for that purpose.

After she had heard them read, they stood round her in a circle to spell; and those who were so negligent as to mistake, lost their place in the set, and exchanged with their more attentive companions. A precedency in the ring was coveted with great ardour, and encouraged a spirit of emulation among them, as to stand first, (which was my mistress's distinction) was regarded as an acknowledgment of superior excellence. When they had finished their business, and the wished-for hour of twelve struck from the church clock, which was very near Mrs. Markall's house, they all made their rustic curtsies and bows to the Dame, and poured like a swarm of summer flies into the lane. The whole body of them stood for a few moments to interchange their mutual salutations: when some divided to the right hand, and the other party to the left, which led to the church porch; where they seated themselves to be sheltered from the intense heat of the sun; and Jenny, with a smile of conscious satisfaction, produced me to her companions. Though she was anxious to display what she was so well pleased with herself, yet she began to be apprehensive for my safety, when the girls, with unpolished rudeness, all scrambled for a sight of her present at the same time. At last the two whose names are above mentioned, pursued Polly Chaunt, who was in possession of me, and after scuffling on the grass, till Nanny Hay knocked her head with great violence against one of the tomb-stones, and Betsy sprained her wrist in trying to wrench me from Polly, she ran home with the prize with so much swiftness, as to outstrip all her competitors. What became of poor Jenny I cannot tell, nor how she bore the loss of me; but I could not help reflecting how much better it would have been, had these girls been sufficiently polite, to have each satisfied their own curiosity and then have resigned me to the inspection of others. Whereas, by all eagerly snatching me at once, they dirtied my outside, and pulled me quite out of shape; together with making them all very angry, and foolishly commencing a quarrel, of which the first consequences were the wounds I have mentioned. Polly Chaunt, whose property I so unjustly became, was the daughter of the parish clerk. He was by trade a shoemaker, and had three children, two girls and a boy. His wife was a notable little woman, who took care of some poultry, pigs, and asses, which were allowed to feed upon a green before the house.

As soon as my new Mistress arrived at home, her mother ordered her to prepare what was wanted for dinner, at the same time telling her, she was much displeased that she did not return from school sooner. Polly answered in a manner which convinced me, she was more pert than prudent; and ran into a little back wash-house to her sister, who was taking a piece of bacon out of the saucepan, and who likewise chid her delay; adding, that dinner was ready, and she had been wanted to lay the table-cloth. In reply to this, she told the history I have just related, and produced me to her sister, who wiping her hands on a bit of rag which hung upon a nail in the window, took me up to examine: when lo! Polly, who was at all times too hasty to attend to reason, not chusing that Sukey should touch me for fear of spoiling my beauty, hastily snatched me from her, and dropped me, not into the saucepan, which I escaped, but into a bason of soap and water which stood near it, and in which Mrs. Chaunt had just been washing her hands. Upon this arose a quarrel between the sisters, which was terminated by the entrance of their father, who insisted on their bringing his dinner immediately; and Polly, after having carefully wiped, laid me on a clean handkerchief to dry. I staid with this family some days, and was witness to many disagreements betwen the different parties which composed it; but as I do not think the recital of illiberal abuse could afford any entertainment to my readers, I shall not trouble myself to repeat it. But the folly of such behaviour must be evident to every reflecting mind, when it is considered, that although the scenes I have mentioned passed in the low life of poverty, yet the same ill-humour would occasion equal animosity in the most affluent circumstances. And though no situation can justify fretful petulance, yet it was certainly more excusable in girls who were untaught by education, and unpolished by politeness, than in those with whom the utmost care has been exerted, and who have had all the advantages of reading and instruction to contribute to their improvement. That it is possible for good-humour, and a determined endeavour to please, in a great measure to supply the deficiency of acquired graces, may be seen in the characters of Richard and Jenny, whose affection to each other must interest every one in their favour: and the same sweetness of temper will likewise recommend to my readers' esteem the agreeable Hannah Mindful, to whom I was given one Sunday afternoon by Polly Chaunt, in a walk which they took together after church. And sincerely glad was I to exchange mistresses, as my last had been so ill-tempered and quarrelsome, and had taken me in so unjustifiable a manner from the good-natured little Jenny. Hannah was near fourteen years old, and the eldest of six children. Her mother was a very worthy woman, but was afflicted with such bad health, that she was seldom able to leave her bed. Her father had a small farm, and was very industrious in his business, and very careful of his family; and I was quite astonished to think of how much service Hannah's attention proved to her brothers and sisters; and what a comfort it was to her sick mother to have such a good girl, in whom she could confide, and to whose care she could entrust them.

After she had parted from my late owner, she was met in her way home by the vicar, whose lady was mentioned as the benefactress of my favourite Jenny, and who with her husband was returning to his house. He stopped at the gate, and desired Hannah to wait there, or amuse herself in the garden, while he went to fetch a medicine which he had promised to send to her mother; and at his return presented her with a couple of fine peaches, which he told her to eat, as she was a good girl. She thanked him very civilly, and, after wishing him good night, ran home as fast as possible, for fear her mother should want her; to whom she immediately presented her present, without offering to taste them herself. A niece of Mr. Mindful's lived at this time in his house, whose name was Sally Flaunt; and who had been a half-boarder at a great school near London, where she was put by a relation, whose death had left her no friend but her uncle. She was entirely unprovided for; yet was so inconsiderately proud as to make herself a burden to the family, instead of trying to be of any service; which she might have had a sufficient opportunity of being, as she was near fifteen, and very tall of her age. When Hannah rose in the morning to assist in getting breakfast, dressing her sisters, and making the beds, Sally would disdainfully turn round to sleep, because it was in her silly opinion, unlike a lady to get up early. Without any fortune, or the slightest recommendation but her industry, she was ever foolishly aiming at a rank in life to which she had no pretensions; and without sense to distinguish, that it is gracefulness of manners and superior learning that form the essential difference between high life and poverty; and that merit is as much entitled to respect in the lowest circumstances of indigence, as in the most exalted station, she was so weak as to imagine, that by imitating some of those foibles she had seen in girls who had more fortune than understanding, she should be thought to resemble them, and meet with that regard which is not bestowed on riches, but on the supposed worth of those who possess them. While Hannah went up stairs to carry some water-gruel to her mother, she dispatched one of her little sisters to tell Sally that breakfast was ready; but as she had slept so long, it was some time before she could make her appearance; and Mr. Mindful, who was justly displeased with her indolence, told one of his children to carry her milk away; for that those who were too lazy to provide for themselves, and to be ready at the proper time, might go without food. When Sally therefore came down, she was much disappointed to hear, that a fast was for the present enjoined as her portion; and looking

very much out of humour, she walked into the garden. He followed her out; and as he was
turning round a little yew hedge which fronted a field, he took hold of her hand, and pulling her into the kitchen, told her he was displeased at her behaviour. "You are very foolish, Sally, said he, because you have been to school to imagine that you have nothing further to do than sit with your hands before you, and play the fine lady. You have no money
to provide for yourself, and there is no person will take care of you if you do not work
hard to get your bread. Behave as you should, and I will treat you as my own child; but
if you have too much pride to know your duty, and will not mind my advice, I will turn
you out, to try where you can live better than with me." Sally knew she durst not reply
to this positive speech; and fearing her uncle should become more angry, she promised to
behave better, and walked up stairs to Hannah, who was dusting the furniture in her own
room. To her she related the above particulars, with the tears running down her cheeks,
and with the most dismal sobs of distress and passion. My good-natured Mistress compas-
sionately kissed her, and wept to see her disturbance; but indeed, my dear Sally, said she,
I wish you would try to exert yourself, and as you cannot be a lady, you had better
endeavour to please my father. You see we all live very happily, and I am sure I would do
all in my power to make you do so too; so cheer up your spirits, and do not weep so sadly.
"I cannot, replied Sally, very crossly! indeed you may, who have never seen any higher life;
but where I was at school do you think any of the ladies scoured the rooms, or milked the
cow, or went to such work as washing and ironing? O! Hannah, had you seen the caps, and
feathers, and muslin and gauze frocks, which they used to wear on a dancing day, and how
smart they looked in their silk shoes, or else red morocco ones, you would not wonder that
I do not like these great black leather things, (and she scornfully tossed out her foot as she
spoke.) Indeed, Hannah, I could cry whenever I see you and your sisters clothed in such
coarse gowns, with your black worsted stockings, and with that check handkerchief on your
neck, and your round cloth caps, with that piece of linen for a ribbon. I cannot bear it!
and I wish I was any thing but what I am." "O fie, Sally! said Hannah, that is quite
ungrateful for the good things which you are blessed with, to talk in such a manner as
that." "What good things?" retorted the haughty girl, raising her voice, and growing more
angry. "Do you call this dowlas shift, this coarse apron, this linsey-woolsey gown, good
things? Or do you call the brown bread we eat, or the hard dumplings you were making

just now, good things? And pray this old worm-eaten bed, without any curtains to it, and this little window which is too small to admit one's head out, and what a little hole there is, is quite crammed full of honey-suckles; or this propped-up chest of drawers, or that good-for-nothing chair with a great hole in the bottom, which you know Bet nearly fell through yesterday, when she got upon it to reach the box which holds her Sunday straw hat; do you call these good things? because, if you do, I am sorry you know no better."

"I should be sorry indeed, rejoined Hannah, with rather more displeasure than was usual to her, if I knew so much of high life as to be discontented with what my father and mother can afford. I think our bread is as good as any body need wish for; and I am sure the dumplings you so scornfully mention, will be very well tasted and wholesome. As to the furniture, if it is old, I will answer for its being clean, Sally; and my father says, he can nail on a piece of board over that chair, which will last as many years as the back does. And as to our clothes, I am sure they are whole and tight; for I would work my fingers to the bone before I would see them otherwise. They are coarse to be sure; but they are as good as our neighbours, and many a one would be thankful to have such to put on: and though you speak so proudly of the house and every thing in it, I have seen the ladies at Oakly Hall, who are worth as much money as would buy all the villages for twenty miles round, come as kindly and sit down in my mother's room, and take hold of my hand, and my sisters, and speak as prettily as if I had been a lady too; without looking at the chairs, or finding fault with the bed. And Miss Goodall, although she is dressed so handsomely, never seems to think about it, and the last time she stopped here, took the loaf out of my father's hand, and said, let me cut Mrs. Mindful a piece of bread and butter! I can do it very well, and it shall be thin, such as I know she can eat. And she brought with her a cannister of sago, and went herself to the fire, and poured the water to mix it, and put some wine into it, which she brought with her; and showed me the way to do it, with so much good-nature, that I do not think you need be so very proud, Sally, and look so unhappy about your situation. And I assure you she has sometimes eaten our bread, and always said it was very good." Hannah was here interrupted by one of her sisters, who came to call her to assist her mother, who was going to get up. She attended her immediately, and taking me out of her pocket, into which she hastily put me at the conclusion of the above conversation, she placed me on the table, while she assisted Mrs. Mindful in putting on a clean cap and bed-gown; and after she had helped her to an old elbow chair, she made the bed; which, as soon as she had finished, she went into the garden, and returning with a nice nosegay of flowers placed them in a little white stone mug, upon the table, in order, by their sweetness, to refresh and please her mother, as she was very fond of them. She then kissed her with great tenderness, and begged her to take an egg beat up with some milk, which she immediately got ready. These little services were all performed with so much alacrity and good-nature, and such visible pleasure in her countenance, as doubled the merit of all her actions. It was impossible indeed to see her, without thinking how very agreeable it is in the power of good-nature and industry to make those who have no other advantages to recommend them.

Hannah Mindful was a healthy-looking country girl, her complexion was burnt by the sun, and her hands hardened by laborious toil; she was not ornamented by dress, though her person was at all times made agreeable by neatness: she had never been taught those graces, which so forcibly recommend the possessor to general observation; but a constant cheerfulness, and a desire of obliging, which was never interrupted by petulance, made her beloved by every one who knew her. To be as good-natured as Hannah Mindful, was the highest praise of every girl in the village; and every mother was ready to propose her conduct as an example to her own children. If there was a piece of bread which her sisters liked better than the rest of the loaf, she would save it for them by turns, whenever she had opportunity. If any of them went to play, and forgot the business which fell to their share, or which their mother had ordered them to do, she would either fetch them home again, (or if in her power) do it for them herself. By this she often saved them from punishment. One day when her father had brought two ribbons from a fair, for her sister Molly and herself, he gave Hannah the liberty of chusing first. She directly took a pink, which was her favourite colour, and left a dark green, which was what she most disliked; but afterwards finding her sister wished for the one she had chosen, she gave it to her immediately, with as much readiness as if she had approved of the exchange from the preference to the colour she disliked. Sally told her she thought it was foolish to give up what she had in her possession; but Hannah, with a generosity which did great credit to the goodness of her disposition, replied, that she should never have worn with comfort, what she evidently saw her sister was desirous to obtain: and I declare, added she, I feel a much higher gratification in the idea of giving pleasure to my dear Molly, than I should receive from any difference of colour, or from a present of much greater value. Sally was not of that opinion; for, the indulgence of pride is the occasion of selfishness, and the cause of the most despicable meanness. By wishing for greater riches and despising that way of life to which she was destined, her heart was constantly agitated by anxious vexation. Whereas, Hannah was always cheerful, good-humoured, and contented: and the same incidents, which to the one were the occasion of dissatisfaction and complaint, the other submitted to without repining, and rejoiced with gratitude at the felicity of her lot. And thus, my young readers, will it be with persons of higher rank than those of whom I am now writing. If you make yourself unhappy because some of your companions have more elegant clothes, or a greater variety than yourself; or because it may suit the fortune of their parents to make more splendid entertainments than the choice or circumstances of yours will admit: if they ride in their father's carriage, while you walk on foot and unattended, remember, that is no rational cause of uneasiness. It is not the station, but the propriety with which it is

sustained, that is the real matter of concern. A beggar may be more respectable than a prince, if he is sunk to indigence by misfortune; and exerts his utmost powers to act with industry, and maintain the proper conduct which his situation requires. Let me advise you, then, not to wish for that finery, which would be unsuitable to your circumstances; but to submit to the discretion of your parents, because they must know best what is proper for you. Sally Flaunt had not the power to make her uncle's brown bread in the least degree whiter, although she was too fretful to eat it with satisfaction. She could not enlarge the rooms, or repair the furniture, by her discontent; but she might have been as happy as her cousin, had she been disposed to be good humoured. When any business is necessary to be performed, if it is done with sullenness and ill-will, it becomes the most laborious toil and most irksome employment; but if it is executed with cheerfulness, it is much sooner dispatched, and the fatigue is considerably abated. It is time, however, to return to my own adventures, without trespassing longer on your patience by my advice.

I had continued some time with my mistress, when Mr. Goodall (whose daughter I believe I have before mentioned,) gave an entertainment to his tenants, on account of her attaining her eighteenth year. Mr. Mindful, out of kindness to his family, determined to stay at home himself, and take care of his wife, while he dispatched all the young ones who were of a proper age, to enjoy an amusement which would afford them so much pleasure. Hannah dressed herself and two sisters, as neat as rustic simplicity could adorn them. They had each of them light brown stuff gowns, white aprons and handkerchiefs, with straw hats; her own with green, and her sisters with pink ribbons. They had all a nosegay of flowers in their bosoms, and with the freshness of innocence and health glowing in their cheeks, prepared to set out for Oakly Hall. Hannah did not forget to get ready every thing she thought her mother might want in her absence; and with a kiss of filial affection bade her adieu.

Jack Mindful, her brother, was a lad of about thirteen, very active and sprightly, and sometimes apt to be extremely mischievous. I have had no opportunity before this to introduce him to the notice of my readers; but the part he took in dressing his cousin for the intended sport, will make it necessary to exhibit him on the present occasion. Sally, whose attention was wholly engrossed by the pride of excelling her companions in the finery of clothes, had been for some days busily employed in mending an old silk coat,

which had been given her during her stay at school. It had originally been ornamented with gauze cuffs, which were grown dirty and yellow with keeping: the rest of the trimming was sufficiently decayed, to make it a rather despicable garb: and Mrs. Mindful, who justly thought such shabby finery very improper for her niece's situation, insisted upon her going in a new garnet-coloured stuff, which she had lately bought her. This Sally was much distressed at, and communicated her intention to her cousin Jack, who promised to assist her in her design; which was, after she had taken leave of Mrs. Mindful, to carry her clothes to a barn at some distance, and there put on the silk coat, which she imagined would make her so much better respected by the family at Oakly Hall. To this place she then repaired, her heart beating with expectation, and flattered with the imagination of outshining all her companions. She had made up a new cap for the occasion; and as she was very tall and womanly in her appearance, thought if she could form any substitute for a cushion, it would much improve her fashionable appearance. On this great occasion, she borrowed me of Hannah, who went before her cousin; as she did not chuse to have any witness but Jack, who was the only person entrusted with this important secret. At the barn then we soon arrived, and her stuff gown was thrown off with disdain, while she prepared, with the assistance of an old triangular bit of a broken looking glass, to equip for the desirable expedition. After placing the cushion, which she had taken great pains to complete, and pinning her hair over it with a piece of black ribbon, she put on her cap; which exhibited the most tawdry collection of old gauze, bits of ribbon, and slatternly tassels, that can well be imagined. At last came the trial of the coat, which as it had been made very long behind, was in that respect tolerable; but its appearance in front was so short, as to be really ridiculous. During the time she was looking at her head in the glass, Jack in turning round hastily threw it down a hole which he had purposely contrived, and where it was impossible to regain it, as it was so instantly out of sight, that Sally had not an idea where it had vanished, her search was totally in vain, and she could only finish her dress by Jack's direction. He pretended to admire her appearance extremely, and, to make it the more complete, he had before tied a couple of sheep's feet to a piece of ribbon, which he now pinned to her shoulders, fastening them close to her back with another string which he likewise pinned down; and by way of addition to the streamers in her cap, he suspended a number of bits of straw, which he had tied together with a piece of packthread. With these burlesque ornaments she hurried with him to the Hall; and as she was entering the door which led to the house, under pretence of fastening a piece of the trimming which he said he could improve, he undid the lower pins, and let the sheep's feet dance about on her back, to the unspeakable entertainment of every beholder. The laugh which her appearance occasioned covered her with confusion: and her pride was mortified in the highest degree, to find her finery treated with such a degree of contemptuous mirth: instead of that admiration, with which she had flattered herself. The boys were eager to dissect her head-dress, and Polly Chaunt, who was of the party, very maliciously pinned one of her cuffs to the table cloth, as she was lolling her head on her hand to hide those tears of vexation which she could not forbear. Unfortunately she rose in some haste, upon the appearance of Mr. Goodall, who entered the room to welcome his guests, and dragged down the saltseller, and several plates, knives, forks, and spoons; which had they been brittle materials would have been certainly demolished; but as the whole service was of pewter, they escaped unhurt. The bustle which this accident occasioned, still more disconcerted the unfortunate Sally Flaunt; who bursting into tears very hastily left the room. In the angry jerk, with which she walked away from the company, her two shoulders were saluted with the sheep's feet, in such a manner, as to make her imagine she had received a blow, which she turned round very quickly in order to resent: but the agility of her motions, only served to repeat the imagined offence, the author of which, however, she found it impossible to discern. But as she was going through an apartment which led to the garden, she discovered her own figure in a large pier-glass; the sight of which so fully completed her vexation, that she determined to hurry home immediately; and snatching her handkerchief from her pocket to wipe her eyes, she whirled me out with it to a considerable distance, and without perceiving her loss, left me to enjoy my own reflections. The thought of Sally's ridiculous vanity entirely took up my attention. How happily might she have passed the day, had she been contented to do so in her proper character! But, by assuming a superiority to her companions, she excited the contempt of Jack Mindful, who was determined to mortify her pride, by making her an object of ridicule; and though his mischievous intention was certainly extremely blameable, yet it was her own folly which put the execution of it into his power. Had she not determined so meanly to deceive, and disobey her aunt, by pretending to comply with her advice at the very moment she was preparing to act in opposition to it, she would have escaped that mortification; which was undoubtedly deserved.

I lay unperceived by the door of a little closet till the next morning; when Mrs. Betty, who came to sweep the room, picked me up, and laid me some time on a marble slab; after she had finished her business, I accompanied her to breakfast. My new mistress was a pleasing young woman, who was a housemaid in Mr. Goodall's family. She sat down with the laundry-maid, whose name was Joice, and who complained very much of the heat of the weather. I have been so ill for some days past, said she, that I can with difficulty stand to wash; and the heat of the fire when I am ironing makes me much worse than I should otherwise be: and then Miss Sophy is so careless, she never considers what will dirt her cloaths, nor how much work she occasions. I am sure her sister at her age was always neat and nice, with half the number of frocks and petticoats which she requires. I wonder that a young lady should not have more compassion for a poor servant. "That is because they do not know the trouble it is, replied Betty; but indeed, Joice, Miss Sophy is the same in

every thing. If she is cutting a piece of gauze, or paper, she is sure to make a litter all over the room; and I have often seen her cut a card into a thousand bits on the carpet, without making any use of it at all: and if she is undoing her work or picking her doll's clothes to pieces, she will strew the threads on the floor without thinking how much trouble it gives me to take them up again. But if she would but put the bits of rubbish into a piece of paper, it might be taken away without any difficulty." She will never be beloved like her sister, said Joice. And then she does not look so much like a young lady; for Jerry says that when he is waiting at dinner, he cannot help looking at her, to see how she leans against the table, (that is one way in which she makes her frock so dirty) and takes such great mouthfuls, and eats so exceedingly fast, as if she were starving, and thought she should lose her dinner; and sometimes she drinks without wiping her mouth, and very frequently when it is not empty. "O! I have seen her myself, interrupted Betty; I have seen her, when I have been at breakfast, grasp the spoon in her hand, quite down to the bowl of it, and my mistress has told her it looked very unmannerly: and then she altered it for a minute, but as soon held it as awkwardly as ever. But what I am most angry with her for, is slopping her milk, or tea, on the tables, just after I have rubbed them till they are as bright as looking-glasses; and then she smears her hands across, and all my labour goes for nothing. I wonder how she would like this hot day to have such violent exercise. But ladies have often little consideration for their servants feelings." To be sure, said Mrs. Joice, my master and mistress and Miss Goodall, are very good-natured, Betty; and Miss Sophy will, I hope, think more of the consequence of her actions when she is older. I would do any thing in the world for my mistress, she speaks so kindly; and when I am ill, she says, "Take your time, Joice, and do not fatigue yourself to-day, I hope you will be better to-morrow." I do not care how I slave when people are considerate, and seem to think I do my duty. During the latter part of this conversation, Mrs. Betty had laid me on the table, and was pinning her gown close, which had before hung loose, only fastened with one pin at the top, and the two sides turned behind; and at the conclusion of it, Mrs. Joice, who had been clearing away the breakfast things, folded me up in the table cloth, and carrying me under her arm to the poultry yard, shook me out with the crumbs. She turned round at the same time, to speak to a gardener, who was emptying some weeds out of his apron upon the dunghill, and did not see my fall. After her departure, I was pecked at alternately by almost all the fowls, till at last I was tossed by a bantam hen, under the little water-tub, where I have lain ever since. My last unfortunate adventure has so dirtied my outside, that I should not now be known. But if the recital of what has hitherto befallen me has at all engaged the readers regard, I hope I shall not lose their approbation, from a change of situation or appearance.

The catastrophe which has thus reduced me, was entirely unexpected; and should teach them, that no seeming security can guard from those accidents, which may in a moment reduce the prospect of affluence to a state of poverty and distress; and therefore it is a mark [of] folly, as well as meanness, to be proud of those distinctions, which are at all times precarious in enjoyment, and uncertain in possession.

THE END.

The Life and Perambulation of a Mouse

By DOROTHY KILNER

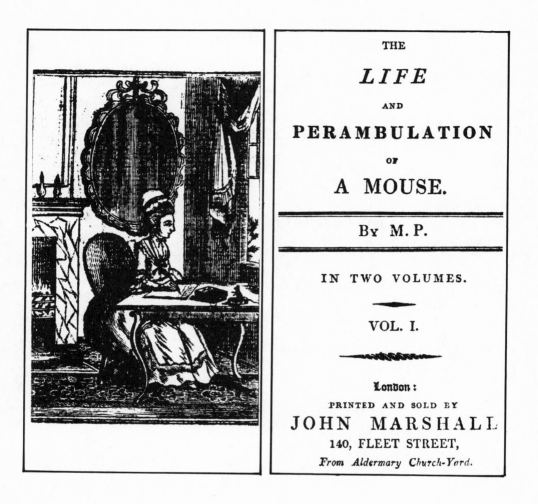

THE
LIFE
AND
PERAMBULATION
OF
A MOUSE.

By M. P.

IN TWO VOLUMES.

VOL. I.

London:

PRINTED AND SOLD BY

JOHN MARSHALL

140, FLEET STREET,

From Aldermary Church-Yard.

Dorothy Kilner (1755–1836) signed her books Mary Pelham or M. P. for Maryland Point, a village in which she lived from the age of four until her death at eighty-one. A friend of Sarah Trimmer, she never married but wrote stories initially for her brother's children.

The Life and Perambulation of a Mouse (2 vols., 1783–1784) is her best-known work. Other titles by her include The Village School (ca. 1795), The Histories of More Children Than One (1795), The Holiday Present (ca. 1780), Anecdotes of a Boarding School (1790), and The Rational Brutes (1799).

Charlotte Yonge (b. 1823) testified that her father read The Life and Perambulation of a Mouse to her on a journey. She remembered it fondly and published it in A Storehouse of Stories (1870). Like her sister-in-law Mary Kilner, Dorothy apologizes for her invention, assuring the reader "in earnest, I never heard a mouse speak in all my life. . . ." The first-person account of the four mice is adventuresome and interesting. Even though the mouse narrator seems too literary, Dorothy Kilner's mouse book was as close, Gillian Avery notes, as the matter-of-fact Georgians could come to fantasy before The Butterfly's Ball.

The text of The Life and Perambulation of a Mouse is reprinted from a two-volume edition (ca. 1805) published by John Marshall.

TO THE READER

BEFORE YOU BEGIN the following history, which is *made believe* to be related by a MOUSE, I must beg you will be careful to remember, that the Author's design in writing it, was no less to *instruct* and *improve*, than it was to *amuse* and *divert* you. It is, therefore, earnestly hoped that, as you read it, you will observe *all* the good advice therein delivered, and endeavour to profit from it; whilst, at the same time, you resolve to shun all actions which render those who practise them not only *despicable*, but really *wicked*. Sincerely wishing that the MOUSE may prove neither wholly *unentertaining* nor *uninstructive* to you, I subscribe myself

A very sincere well-wisher
to all my little readers,
M. P.

INTRODUCTION

DURING A REMARKABLY severe winter, when a prodigious fall of snow confined every body to their habitations, who were happy enough to have one to shelter them from the inclemency of the season, and were not obliged by business to expose themselves to its rigour, I was on a visit to *Meadow Hall;* where had assembled likewise a large party of young folk, who all seemed, by their harmony and good humour, to strive who should the most contribute to render pleasant that confinement which we were all equally obliged to share. Nor were those further advanced in life less anxious to contribute to the general satisfaction and entertainment.

After the more serious employment of reading each morning was concluded, we danced, we sung, we played at blind-man's buff, battledore and shuttlecock, and many other games equally diverting and innocent; and when tired of them, drew our seats round the fire, while each one in turn told some merry story to divert the company.

At last, after having related all that we could recollect worth reciting, and being rather at a loss what to say next, a sprightly girl in company proposed that every one should relate the history of their own lives; 'and it must be strange indeed,' added she, 'if that will not help us out of this difficulty, and furnish conversation for some days longer; and by that time, perhaps, the frost will break, the snow will melt, and set us all at liberty. But let it break when it will, I make a *law,* that no one shall go from Meadow Hall till they have told their own history: so take notice, ladies and gentlemen, take notice, every body, what you have to trust to. And because,' continued she, 'I will not be unreasonable, and require more from you than you can perform, I will give all you who may perhaps have forgotten what passed so many years ago, at the beginning of your lives, two days to recollect and digest your story; by which time if you do not produce something pretty and entertaining, we will never again admit you to dance or play among us.' All this she spoke with so good-humoured a smile, that every one was delighted with her, and promised to do their best to acquit themselves to her satisfaction; whilst some (the *length* of whose lives had not rendered them *forgetful* of the transactions which had passed) instantly began their *memoirs,* as they called them: and really some related their narratives with such spirit and ingenuity, that it quite distressed us older ones, lest we should disgrace ourselves when it should fall to our turns to hold forth. However, we were all determined to produce *something*, as our fair directress ordered. Accordingly, the next morning I took up my pen, to endeavour to draw up some kind of a history, which might satisfy my companions in confinement. I *took up my pen*, it is true, and laid the paper before me; but not one word toward my appointed task could I proceed. The various occurrences of my life were such as, far from affording entertainment, would, I was certain, rather afflict; or, perhaps, not *interesting* enough for that, only *stupify*, and render them more weary of the continuation of the frost than they were before I began my narration. Thus circumstanced, therefore, although by myself, I broke silence by exclaiming, 'What a task has this sweet girl imposed upon me! One which I shall never be able to execute to my *own satisfaction* or *her amusement*. The adventures of my life (though deeply interesting to myself) will be insipid and unentertaining to others, especially to my young hearers: I cannot, therefore, attempt it.'—'Then write mine, which may be more diverting,' said a little squeaking voice, which sounded as if close to me. I started with surprise, not knowing any one to be near me; and looking round, could discover no object from whom it could possibly proceed, when casting my eyes upon the ground, in a little hole under the skirting-board, close by the fire, I discovered the head of a Mouse peeping out. I arose with a design to stop the hole with a cork, which happened to lie on the table by me; and I was surprised to find that it did not run away, but suffered me to advance quite close, and then only retreated a little into the hole, saying in the same voice as before, 'Will you write my history?' You may be sure that I was much surprised to be so addressed by such an animal; but, ashamed of discovering any appearance of astonishment, lest the Mouse should suppose it had frightened me, I answered with the utmost composure, that I would write it willingly if it would dictate to me. 'Oh, that I will do,' replied the Mouse, 'if you will not hurt me.'—'Not for the world,' returned I; 'come, therefore, and sit upon my table, that I may hear more distinctly what you have to relate.' It instantly accepted my invitation, and with all the nimbleness of its species, ran up the side of my chair, and jumped upon my table; when, getting into a box of wafers, it began as follows.

———

But, before I proceed to relate my new little companion's history, I must beg leave to assure my readers that, *in earnest*, I never heard a mouse speak in all my life; and only wrote the following narrative as being far more entertaining, and not less instructive, than my own life would have been: and as it met with the high approbation of those for whom it was written, I have sent it to Mr. MARSHALL, for him to publish it, if he pleases, for the equal amusement of his little customers.

Lᴵᴷᴇ ᴀʟʟ ᴏᴛʜᴇʀ new-born animals, whether of the human, or any other species, I cannot pretend to remember what passed during my infant days. The first circumstance I
can recollect was my mother's addressing me and my three brothers, who all lay in the same
nest, in the following words:—'I have, my children, with the greatest difficulty, and at the
utmost hazard of my life, provided for you all to the present moment; but the period is
arrived, when I can no longer pursue that method: snares and traps are every where set
for me, nor shall I, without infinite danger, be able to procure sustenance to support my
own existence, much less can I find sufficient for you all; and, indeed, with pleasure I
behold it as no longer necessary, since you are of age now to provide and shift for yourselves; and I doubt not but your agility will enable you to procure a very comfortable
livelihood. Only let me give you this one caution—Never (whatever the temptation may
be) appear often in the same place; if you do, however you may flatter yourselves to the
contrary, you will certainly at last be destroyed.' So saying, she stroked us all with her
fore paw, as a token of her affection, and then hurried away, to conceal from us the
emotions of her sorrow, at thus sending us into the wide world.

She was no sooner gone, than the thought of being our own directors so charmed our
little hearts, that we presently forgot our grief at parting from our kind parent; and,
impatient to use our liberty, we all set forward in search of some food, or rather some
adventure, as our mother had left us victuals more than sufficient to supply the wants of
that day. With a great deal of difficulty, we clambered up a high wall on the inside of a
wainscot, till we reached the story above that we were born in, where we found it much
easier to run round within the skirting-board, than to ascend any higher.

While we were there, our noses were delightfully regaled with the *scent* of the most
delicate food that we had ever smelt; we were anxious to procure a taste of it likewise,
and after running round and round the room a great many times, we at last discovered
a little crack, through which we made our entrance. My brother Longtail led the way; I
followed; Softdown came next; but Brighteyes would not be prevailed upon to venture.
The apartment which we entered was spacious and elegant; at least, differed so greatly
from any thing we had seen, that we imagined it the finest place upon earth. It was
covered all over with a carpet of various colours, that not only concealed some bird-seeds
which we came to devour, but also for some time prevented our being discovered; as we
were of much the same hue with many of the flowers on the carpet. At last a little girl,
who was at work in the room, by the side of her mamma, shrieked out as if violently
hurt. Her mamma begged to know the cause of her sudden alarm. Upon which she called
out, 'A Mouse! a Mouse! I saw one under the chair!' 'And if you did, my dear,' replied
her mother, 'is that any reason for your behaving so ridiculously? If there were twenty
mice, what harm *could* they possibly do? *You* may easily hurt and destroy *them;* but,
poor little things! they cannot, if they would, hurt *you*.' 'What, could they not *bite* me?'
inquired the child. 'They may, indeed, be *able* to do that; but you may be *very* sure
that they have no such inclination,' rejoined the mother. 'A mouse is one of the most
timorous things in the world; every noise alarms it: and though it chiefly lives by plunder,
it appears as if punished by its fears for the mischiefs which it commits among our

property. It is therefore highly ridiculous to pretend to be alarmed at the sight of a creature that would run from the sound of your voice, and wishes never to come near you, lest, as you are far more *able*, you should also be disposed to hurt it.' 'But I am sure, Madam,' replied the little girl, whose name I afterwards heard was Nancy, 'they do not *always* run away; for one day, as Miss Betsy Kite was looking among some things which she had in her box, a mouse jumped out and ran up her frock sleeve—she felt it quite up on her arm.' 'And what became of it then?' inquired the mother. 'It jumped down again,' replied Nancy, 'and got into a little hole in the window seat; and Betsy did not see it again.' 'Well, then, my dear,' resumed the lady, 'what *harm* did it do her? Is not that a convincing proof of what I say, that you have no cause to be *afraid* of them, and that it is very silly to be so? It is certainly foolish to be afraid of *any* thing, unless it threatens us with immediate danger; but to pretend to be so at a *Mouse*, and such like inoffensive things, is a degree of weakness that I can by no means suffer any of my children to indulge.' 'May I then, Madam,' inquired the child, 'be afraid of cows and horses, and such great beasts as those?' 'Certainly not,' answered her mother, 'unless they are likely to hurt you. If a cow or an horse runs after you, I would have you fear them so much as to get out of the way; but if they are quietly walking or grazing in a field, then to fly from them, as if you thought they would eat *you* instead of the grass, is most absurd, and discovers great want of sense. I once knew a young lady, who, I believe, thought it looked *pretty* to be terrified at every thing, and scream if a dog or even a *mouse* looked at her: but most severely was she punished for her folly, by several very disagreeable accidents she by those means brought upon herself.

One day when she was drinking tea in a large company, on the door being opened, a small Italian greyhound walked into the drawing-room. She happened to be seated near the mistress of the dog, who was making tea: the dog, therefore, walked toward her, in order to be by his favourite; but, upon his advancing near her, she suddenly jumped up, without considering what she was about, overturned the water-urn, the hot iron of which rolling out, set fire to her clothes, which instantly blazed up, being only muslin, and burnt her arms, face, and neck, most dreadfully: she was so much hurt as to be obliged to be put immediately to bed; nor did she recover enough to go abroad for many months. Now, though every one was sorry for her sufferings, who could possibly help blaming her for her ridiculous behaviour, as it was entirely owing to her own folly that she was so hurt? When she was talked to upon the subject, she pleaded for her excuse, that she was so frightened she did not *know* what she did, nor whither she was going; but as she *thought* that the dog was coming to her she could not *help* jumping up, to get out of his way. Now what ridiculous arguing was this! Why *could* not she *help* it? And if the dog had really been going to her, what harm would it have done? Could she suppose that the lady whose house she was at, would have suffered a beast to walk about the house loose, and go into company, if he was apt to *bite* and *hurt* people? Or why should she think he would more injure *her*, than those he had before passed by? But the real case was, she did not think at all; if she had given herself time for that, she could not have acted so ridiculously. Another time, when she was walking, from the same want of reflection, she very nearly drowned herself. She was passing over a bridge, the outside rails of which were in some places broken down: while she was there, some cows, which a man was driving, met her: immediately, without minding whither she went, she shrieked out, and at the same time jumped on one side just where the rail happened to be broken, and down she fell into the river; nor was it without the greatest difficulty that she was taken out time enough to save her life. However, she caught a violent cold and fever, and was again, by her own foolish fears, confined to her bed for some weeks. Another accident she once met with, which though not quite so bad as the two former, yet might have been attended with fatal consequences. She was sitting in a window, when a wasp happened to fly toward her; she hastily drew back her head, and broke the pane of glass behind her, some of which stuck in her neck. It bled prodigiously; but a surgeon happily being present, made some application to it, which prevented its being followed by any other ill effects than only a few days weakness, occasioned by the loss of blood. Many other misfortunes of the like kind she frequently experienced; but these which I have now related may serve to convince you how extremely absurd it is for people to give way to and indulge themselves in such groundless apprehensions, and, by being afraid when there is no danger, subject themselves to real misfortunes and most fatal accidents. And if being afraid of *cows*, *dogs*, and *wasps* (all of which, if they please, *can* certainly hurt us) is so ridiculous, what must be the folly of those people who are terrified at a little silly *mouse*, which never was known to hurt any body.

Here the conversation was interrupted by the entrance of some gentlemen and ladies; and we having enjoyed a very fine repast under one of the chairs during the time that the mother and daughter had held the above discourse, on the chairs being removed for some of the visitors to sit upon, we thought it best to retire; highly pleased with our meal, and not less with the kind goodwill which the lady had, we thought, expressed towards us. We related to our brother Brighteyes all that had passed, and assured him he had no reason to apprehend any danger from venturing himself with us. Accordingly he promised, if such was the case, that the next time we went and found it safe, if we would return back and call him, he would certainly accompany us. 'In the mean time, do pray, Nimble,' said he, addressing himself to me, 'come with me to some other place, for I long to taste some more delicate food than our mother has provided for us; besides, as perhaps it may be a long while before we shall be strong enough to bring any thing away with us, we had better leave that, in case we should ever be prevented from going abroad to seek for fresh supplies.' 'Very true,' replied I, 'what you say is quite just and wise, therefore I will with all my heart attend you now, and see what we can find.' So saying, we began to climb; but not without difficulty, for very frequently the bits of mortar which we stepped upon gave way beneath our feet, and tumbled us down together with them lower than when we first set off. However, as we were very light, we were not much hurt by our falls; only indeed, poor Brighteyes, by endeavouring to save himself, caught by his nails on a rafter, and tore one of them from off his right fore-foot, which was very sore and inconvenient. At length we surmounted all difficulties, and, invited by a strong scent of plum-cake, entered a closet, where we found a fine large one, quite whole and entire. We immediately set about making our way into it, which we easily effected, as it was most deliciously nice, and not at all hard to our teeth.

Brighteyes, who had not before partaken of the bird-seed, was overjoyed at the sight. He almost forgot the pain of his foot, and soon buried himself withinside the cake; whilst I, who had pretty well satisfied my hunger before, only ate a few of the crumbs, and then went to take a survey of the adjoining apartment. I crept softly under the door of the

closet into a room, as large as that which I had before been in, though not so elegantly furnished; for, instead of being covered with a carpet, there was only a small one round the bed; and near the fire was a cradle, with a cleanly-looking woman sitting by it, rocking it with her foot, whilst at the same time she was combing the head of a little boy about four years old. In the middle of the room stood a table, covered with a great deal of litter; and in one corner was the little girl whom I had before seen with her mamma, crying and sobbing as if her heart would break. As I made not the least noise at my entrance, no one observed me for some time; so creeping under one of the beds, I heard the following discourse.

'It does not signify, miss,' said the woman, who I found was the children's nurse, 'I never will put up with such behaviour: you know that I always do every thing for you when you speak *prettily;* but to be *ordered* to dress you in such a manner, is what I never will submit to: and you shall go *undressed* all day before I will dress you, unless you ask me as you *ought* to do.' Nancy made no reply, but only continued crying. 'Aye! you may cry and sob as much as you please,' said the nurse; 'I do not care for that: I shall not dress you for *crying* and *roaring*, but for being *good* and speaking with civility.' Just as she said these words, the door opened, and in came the lady whom I before saw, and whose name I afterwards found was Artless. As soon as she entered, the nurse addressed her, saying, 'Pray, madam, is it by your desire that Miss Nancy behaves so rudely, and bids me dress her directly, and change the buckles in her shoes, or else she will slap my face? Indeed she did give me a slap upon my hand; so I told her, that I would not dress her at all; for really, madam, I thought you would not wish me to do it, whilst she behaved so; and I took the liberty of putting her to stand in the corner.' 'I do not think,' replied Mrs. Artless, 'that she deserves to stand in the *room* at all, or in the *house* either, if she behaves in that manner: if she does not speak civilly when she wants to be assisted, let her go without help, and see what will become of her then. I am quite ashamed of you, Nancy! I could not have thought you would behave so; but since you have, I promise that you shall not be dressed to-day, or have any assistance given you, unless you speak in a very different manner.

Whilst Mrs. Artless was talking, nurse went out of the room. Mrs. Artless then took her seat by the cradle, and looking into it, found the child awake, and I saw her take out a fine little girl, about five months old: she then continued her discourse, saying, 'Look here, Nancy, look at this little baby, see how unable it is to help itself; were we to neglect attending to it, what do you think would become of it? Suppose I were now to put your sister upon the floor, and there leave her, tell me what do you think she could do, or what would become of her?' Nancy sobbed out, that she would die. 'And pray, my dear,' continued Mrs. Artless, 'if we were to leave *you* to yourself, what would become of *you?* It is true, you talk, and run about better than Polly: but not a bit better could you provide for, or take care of yourself. Could you buy or dress your own victuals? could you light your own fire? could you clean your own house, or open and shut the doors and windows? could you make your own clothes, or even put them on without some assistance, when made? And who do you think will do any thing for you, if you are not good, and do not speak civilly? Not *I*, I promise you, neither shall nurse, nor any of the servants; for though I pay them wages to help to do my business for me, I never want them to do any thing unless they are desired in a pretty manner. Should you like, if when I want you to pick up my scissars, or do any little job, I were to say, *Pick up my scissars this moment, or I will slap your face?* Should not you think that it sounded very *cross* and disagreeable?' 'Yes, madam,' replied Nancy. 'Then why,' rejoined Mrs. Artless, should *you* speak cross to any body, particularly to *servants* and *poor* people? for to behave so to them, is not only *cross*, but *insolent* and *proud:* it is as if you thought that because they are rather poorer, they are not so good as yourself, whereas, I asure you, *poverty* makes no difference in the merit of people; for those only are deserving of respect who are truly *good;* and a *beggar* who is *virtuous*, is far better than a *prince* who is *wicked*. I was prevented from hearing any more of this very just discourse, by the little boy's opening the door and letting in a cat; which, though it was the first that I had ever seen in my life, I was certain was the same destructive animal to our race, which I had frequently heard my mother describe. I therefore made all possible haste back to the closet, and warning Brighteyes of our danger, we instantly returned by the same way which we came, to our two brothers, whom we found waiting for us, and wondering at our long absence. We related to them the dainty cheer which we had met with, and agreed to conduct them thither in the evening. Accordingly, as soon as it grew towards dusk, we climbed up the wall, and all four together attacked the plum-cake, which no one had touched since we left it; but scarcely had we all seated ourselves round it, than on a sudden the closet-door opened, and a woman entered. Away we all scampered as fast as possible, but poor Brighteyes, who could not move quite so fast on account of his sore toe, and who likewise having advanced farther into the cake, was discovered before he could reach the crack by which we entered. The woman, who had a knife in her hand, struck at him with it, at the same time exclaiming, 'Bless me, nurse, here is a mouse in the closet!' Happily she missed her aim, and he only received a small wound on the tip of his tail. This interruption sadly alarmed us, and it was above an hour before we could have courage to venture back, when finding every thing quiet, except Mrs. Nurse's singing to her child, we again crept out, and once more surrounded the cake. We continued without any further alarm till we were perfectly satisfied, and then retired to a little distance behind the wainscot, determined there to sleep, and to breakfast on the cake the next day.

Early in the morning I waked, and calling my brothers, we all marched forward, and soon arrived at the delightful cake, where we highly enjoyed ourselves without the least disturbance, till our appetites were fully satisfied. We then retired, took a little run round some other parts of the house, but met with nothing worth relating. At noon we again made our way into the closet, intending to dine on the dish on which we breakfasted; but, to our no small mortification, the delicious dainty was removed. This you may be sure was a sad disappointment; yet as we were not extremely hungry, we had time to look about for more. We were not long in finding it; for upon the same shelf from which the cake was removed, there was a round tin box, the lid of which was not quite close shut down; into this we all crept, and were highly regaled with some nice lumps of sugar.— But it would be endless to enumerate all the various repasts which we met with in this closet, sometimes terrified by the entrance of people, and sometimes comfortably enjoying ourselves without alarm: it is sufficient to inform you, that, unmindful of our mother's advice, we continued to live upon the contents of the same cupboard for above a week; when, one evening, as we were as usual hastening to find our suppers, Softdown, who happened to be first, ran eagerly to a piece of cheese, which he saw hanging before him. Come along, said he, here is some nice cheese, it smells most delightfully good! Just as he spoke these words, before any of us came up to him, a little wooden door on a sudden dropped down, and hid him and the cheese from our sight.

It is impossible to describe our consternation and surprise upon this occasion, which was greatly increased when we advanced near the place, at seeing him (through some little wire bars) confined in a small box, without any visible way for him to get out, and hearing him in the most moving accents beg us to assist him in procuring his liberty. We all ran round and round his place of confinement several times; but not the least crack or opening could we discover, except through the bars, which being of iron, it was impossible for us to break or bend. At length we determined to try to gnaw through the wood-work close at the edge, which being already some little distance from one of the bars, we hoped, by making the opening a little wider, he would escape: accordingly we all began, he on the inside, and we all on the out, and by our diligence had made some very considerable progress, when we were interrupted by the entrance of Mrs. Nurse with the child in her arms.

Upon the sight of her, though much grieved to leave our brother in his distress, yet fearing instant death would be the fate of all of us if we stayed, to preserve our own existence, we retired as quick as possible, but not without her seeing some of us, for we heard her say to herself, or to the babe in her arms, 'I declare, this closet *swarms* with mice, they spoil every things one puts here.' Then taking up the box in which was poor Softdown (and which I afterwards learned was called a *trap*) she carried it into the room. I crept softly after her, to see what would be the fate of my beloved brother. But what words can express my horror, when I saw her holding it in one hand close to the candle, whilst in the other she held the child, singing to her with the utmost composure, and bidding her to look at the *mousy! mousy!*

What were the actions or sensations of poor Softdown at that dreadful moment I know not; but my own anguish, which it is impossible to describe, was still augmented every moment by seeing her shake the trap almost topsy-turvy, then blow through the trap at one end, at which times I saw the dear creature's tail come out between the wires on the contrary side, as he was striving, I suppose, to retreat from her. At length, after she had thus tortured him for some time, she set the trap on the table, so close to a large fire, that I am sure he must have been much incommoded by the heat, and began to undress her child.

Then hearing somebody go by the door, she cried out, 'Who is there? is it you, Betty? if it is, I wish you would come and take down the mouse-trap, for I have caught a mouse.' Betty instantly obeyed her call, and desired to know what she wanted. 'I want you to take down the mouse-trap,' she replied, 'for I cannot leave the child. I am glad that I have got it, I am sure, for the closet swarms so, there is no such thing as bearing it. They devour every thing: I declare they have eaten up a whole pound of sugar, which cost me eleven-pence, sugar is now so *monstrously* dear! indeed the man made a favour to let me have it for that; only, he said, as our family were good customers, and I was but a servant, he would take no more. And enough too I thought it was, to have only a penny back in change out of a whole shilling for one pound of sugar: and then to think of the *poison* mice to have it all; but I will break their filthy necks. Do, Betty, pray take the trap down, and return with it as soon as you can, and I will set it again: for I dare say I shall catch another before I go to bed, for I heard some more rustling among the things.' '*O lauk!*' replied Betty, 'you do not think that *I* will take down the trap, do you? I would not touch it for twenty pounds. I am always frightened, and ready to die at the sight of a mouse. Once, when I was a girl, I had one thrown in my face, and ever since I have always been scared out of my wits at them; and if ever I see one running loose, as I did one night in the closet below stairs, where the candles are kept, I *scream* as if I was being killed.' 'Why then,' answered Nurse, 'I think you behave like a great fool, for what harm could a mouse do to you?' '*O la!* I hate them,' returned she, and then ran away without the trap. Greatly was I rejoiced at her departure, as I hoped that, by some means, Softdown might still be able to make his escape. But, alas! no such good fortune attended him. Some person again passing the door, Nurse once more called out, 'Who is there? John is it you?' 'Yes,' replied a man's voice. 'Then do you step in, will you, for a moment?' rejoined Mrs. Nurse; and instantly entered a man whom I had never before seen. 'What do you want, Nurse?' said he. 'I only want to get rid of a mouse,' returned she; 'and, do you know, Betty is such a fool that she is afraid of taking it, and I want the trap to set it again, for they swarm here like bees in a hive, one can have no peace for them: they devour and spoil every thing; I say sometimes that I believe they will eat *me* up at last.' While she was saying this, John took the trap in his hand, held it up once more to the candle, then taking a piece of thread out of a paper, that lay bound round with a dirty blue ribband upon the table, he shook the trap about till he got my brother's tail through the wires, when catching hold of it, he tied the thread tight round it and dragged him by it to the door of the trap, which he opened, and took him out, suspending the weight of his body upon his tail.

Softdown, who till the thread was tied had patiently continued perfectly quiet, could no longer support the pain without dismal cries and anguish: he squeaked as loud as his little throat would let him, exerting at the same time the utmost of his strength to disengage himself. But in such a position, with his head downward, in vain were all his efforts to procure relief; and the barbarous monster who held him discovered not the smallest emotions of pity for his sufferings. Oh! how at that moment did I abhor my own existence, and wish that I could be endowed with size and strength sufficient, at once both to rescue him, and severely punish his tormentors. But my wish was ineffectual, and I

had the inexpressible affliction of seeing the inhuman wretch hold him down upon the hearth, whilst, without remorse, he crushed him beneath his foot, and then carelessly kicked him into the ashes, saying, 'There! the cat will smell it out when she comes up.' My very blood runs cold within me at the recollection of seeing Softdown's as it spirted from beneath the monster's foot; whilst the craunch of his bones almost petrified me with horror. At length, however, recollecting the impossibility of restoring my beloved brother to life, and the danger of my own situation, I, with trembling feet and palpitating heart, crept softly back to my remaining two brothers, who were impatiently expecting me behind the closet. There I related to them the horrid scene which had passed before my eyes, whilst the anguish it caused in their gentle bosoms far exceeds my power to describe.

After having mingled our lamentations for some time, I thus addressed them: 'We have this night, my brothers, tasted the severest affliction in the cruel death of our dear brother, companion, and friend; let us not, however, only *mourn* his loss, but also gather wisdom from our misfortune, and return to that duty which we have hitherto neglected. Recollect, my dear friends, what were the last words which our good mother spoke to us at parting. She charged us, upon no account, for no temptation whatever, to return frequently to the same place; if we did, she forewarned us that death and ruin would certainly await us. But in what manner have we obeyed this her kind advice? We have not even so much as once recollected it since she left us; or, if we thought of it for a moment, we foolishly *despised* it as unnecessary. Now, therefore, we sincerely feel the consequence of our disobedience; and, though our sufferings are most distressing, yet we must confess that we amply deserve them. Let us therefore, my brothers, instantly fly from a place, which has already cost us the life of our beloved Softdown, lest we should all likewise fall a sacrifice to our disobedience.—And here the writer cannot help observing how just were the reflections of the Mouse on the crime which they had been guilty of; and begs every reader will be careful to remember the fatal consequences that attended their disobedience of their mother's advice, since they may be assured that equal if not the same misfortune will always attend those who refuse to pay attention to the advice of their parents. But, to return to the history—

To this proposal (continued the Mouse) my brothers readily agreed; and we directly descended to the place we were in when we discovered the crack that led us to the room in which we feasted on bird-seed. Here we determined to wait, and when the family were all quiet in bed, to go forth in search of provision, as we began to be rather hungry, not having eaten any thing a long while. Accordingly we stayed till after the clock struck twelve, when peeping out, we saw that the room was empty: we then ventured forth, and found several seeds, though not enough to afford a very ample meal for three of us.

After we had cleared the room, we again returned to our hiding-place; where we continued till after the family had finished their breakfast. They all then went to take a walk in the garden; and we stepped out to pick up the crumbs which had fallen from the table. Whilst we were thus employed, at a distance from our place of retreat, we were alarmed by the entrance of two boys, who appeared to be about twelve or thirteen years of age. We directly ran towards the crack; but alas! we were not quick enough to escape their observation; for, seeing us, they both at once exclaimed, 'Some mice! some mice!' and at the same time took off their hats, and threw at us. Longtail happily eluded the blow, and safely got home; but poor Brighteyes and myself were less fortunate; and though we for a considerable time, by our quickness, prevented their catching us, at length, being much disabled by a blow that one of them gave me with a book which he threw at me, I was unable any longer to run, and hobbling very slowly across the room, he picked me up. At the same moment Brighteyes was so entangled in a handkerchief which the other boy tossed over him, that he likewise was taken prisoner. Our little hearts now beat quick with fear of those tortures we expected to receive; nor were our apprehensions lessened by hearing the boys consult what they should *do* with us, 'I,' said one, 'will throw mine into the pond, and see how he will swim out again.' 'And I,' said the other, 'will keep mine and *tame* it.' 'But *where* will you keep it?' inquired his companion. 'Oh,' replied he, 'I will keep it under a little pan till I can get a house made for it.' He then, holding me by the skin at the back of my neck, ran with me into the kitchen to fetch a pan. Here I was not only threatened with death by three or four of the servants, who all blamed Master Peter for keeping me; but likewise two or three cats came round him, rubbing themselves backward and forward against his legs, and then standing upon their hind feet to endeavour to make themselves high enough to reach me. At last, taking a pan in his hand, he returned to his brother with one of the cats following him. Immediately upon our entrance, the boy exclaimed, 'Oh, now I know what I will do: I will tie a piece of string to its tail, and teach the cat to jump for it.' No sooner did this thought present itself than it was put into practice, and I again was obliged to sustain the shocking sight of a brother put to the torture. I, in the mean time, was placed upon the table, with a pan put over me, in which there was a crack, so that I could see as well as hear all that passed: and from this place it was that I beheld my beloved Brighteyes suspended at one end of a string by his tail; one while swinging backward and forward, at another pulled up and down, then suffered to feel his feet on the ground, and again suddenly snatched up as the cat advanced, then twisted round and round as fast as possible at the full length of the string: in short, it is impossible to describe all his sufferings of body, or my anguish of mind. At length a most dreadful conclusion was put to them, by the entrance of a gentleman booted and spurred, with a whip in his hand. 'What in the world, Charles!' said he, as he came in, 'are you about? What have you got there?' 'Only a mouse, sir,' replied the boy. 'He is teaching the cat to jump, sir,' said Peter, 'that is all.'

Brighteyes then gave a fresh squeak from the violence of his pain. The gentleman then turning hastily round, exclaimed eagerly, 'What, is it *alive?*' 'Yes, sir,' said the boy.— 'And how can you, you *wicked, naughty, cruel* boy, replied the gentleman, 'take delight in thus torturing a little creature that never did you any injury? Put it down this *moment,*' said he, at the same time giving him a severe stroke with his horse-whip across that hand by which he held my brother: 'let it go directly,' and again repeated the blow: the boy let go the string, and Brighteyes fell to the ground; and was instantly snapped up by the cat, who growling, ran away with him in her mouth, and, I suppose, put a conclusion to his miseries and life together, as I never from that moment have heard any account of him.

As soon as he was thus taken out of the room, the gentleman sat down, and, taking hold of his son's hand, thus addressed him: 'Charles, I had a much better opinion of you, than to suppose you were capable of so much cruelty. What right, I desire to know, have you to torment any living creature? If it is only because you are larger, and so have it in your power, I beg you will consider, how you would like, that either myself, or some great giant, as much larger than you as you are bigger than the mouse, should hurt and torment you? And I promise you, the smallest creature can feel as acutely as you, nay, the smaller they are, the more susceptible are they of pain, and the sooner they are hurt: a less touch will kill a *fly* than a *man,* consequently a less wound will cause it pain; and the mouse which you have now been swinging by the tail over the cat's mouth, has not, you may assure yourself, suffered less torment or fright than you would have done, had you been suspended by your leg, either over water, which would drown you, or over stones, where if you fell you must certainly be dashed to pieces. And yet you could take *delight* in thus torturing and distressing a poor inoffensive animal. Fie upon it, Charles! fie upon it! I thought you had been a better boy, and not such a *cruel, naughty, wicked* fellow.' '*Wicked!*' repeated the boy, 'I do not think that I have been at all *wicked.*' 'But I think you have been extremely so,' replied his father; 'every action that is cruel, and gives pain to *any* living creature, is wicked, and is a sure sign of a *bad* heart. I never knew a man, who was cruel to *animals,* kind and compassionate towards his fellow-creatures: he might not perhaps treat them in the same shocking manner, because the laws of the land would severely punish him if he did; but if he is restrained from bad actions by no *higher* motive than fear of *present punishment,* his goodness cannot be very great. A good man, Charles, always takes delight in conferring happiness on all around him; nor would he offer the smallest injury to the meanest insect that was capable of feeling. 'I am sure,' said the boy, 'I have often seen you kill wasps, and spiders too; and it was but last week that you bought a mouse-trap yourself to catch mice in, although you are so angry now with me.' 'And pray,' resumed his father, 'did you ever see me *torment* as well as kill them? Or did I ever keep them in pain one moment longer than necessary? I am not condemning people for killing vermin and animals, provided they do it expeditiously, and put them to death with as little pain as possible; but it is putting them to needless torment and misery that I say is wicked. Had you destroyed the mouse with one blow, or rather given it to somebody else to destroy it (for I should not think a tender-hearted boy would delight in such operations himself), I would not have condemned you; but, to keep it hanging the whole weight of its body upon its tail, to swing it about, and, by that, to hold it terrifying over the cat's jaws, and to take *pleasure* in hearing it squeak, and seeing it struggle for liberty, is such *unmanly*, such *detestable* cruelty, as calls for my utmost indignation and abhorrence. But, since you think pain so very trifling an evil, try, Charles, how you like *that*,' said he, giving him at the same time some severe strokes with his horsewhip. The boy then cried, and called out, '*I* do not like it at all, I do not like it at all.' 'Neither did the *mouse*,' replied his father, 'like at all to be tied to a string, and swung about by his tail; he did not *like* it, and told you so in a language which you perfectly well understood; but you would not attend to his cries; *you* thought it pleasure to hear it squeak, because you were *bigger*, and did not feel its torture. *I* am now bigger than *you*, and do not feel *your* pain, I therefore shall not yet leave off; as I hope it will teach you not to torment any thing another time.' Just as he said these words, the boy, endeavouring to avoid the whip, ran against the table on which I was placed, and happily threw down the pan that confined me. I instantly seized the opportunity, jumped down, and once more escaped to the little hole by which I first entered. There I found my *only* brother waiting for me, and was again under the dreadful necessity of paining his tender heart with the recital of the sufferings which I had been witness to in our dear Bright-eyes, as well as the imminent danger I myself had been exposed to. 'And, surely,' said I, 'we have again drawn this evil upon ourselves by our disobedience to our mother's advice; she, doubtless, intended that we should not continue in the same *house* long together; whereas from the day of her leaving us, we have never been in any other but this, which has occasioned us such heavy affliction. Therefore, upon no account, let us continue another night under this roof; but, as soon as the evening begins to grow dark enough to conceal us from the observation of any one, we will set off, and seek a lodging in some other place: and should any misfortune befal us on our passage, we shall at least have the consolation of thinking, that we were doing our duty by following the advice of our parent.' 'It is true,' said my brother, 'we have been greatly to blame; for the future we will be more careful of our conduct: but do, my dear Nimble,' continued he, 'endeavour to compose yourself, and take a little rest, after the pain and fatigue which you have gone through, otherwise you may be sick; and what will become of me, if any mischief should befal you? I shall then have no brother to converse with, no friend to advise me what to do.' Here he stopped, overpowered with his grief for the loss of our two murdered brothers, and with his tender solicitude for my welfare. I endeavoured all in my power to comfort him, and said, I hoped that I should soon recover from the bruises I had received both from the boy's hat and book, as well as the pinches in my neck with his finger and thumb, by which he held me, and promised to compose myself. This promise I fulfilled by endeavouring to sleep; but the scene that I had so lately been witness to was too fresh in my imagination to suffer me to close my eyes: however, I kept for some time quiet.

The rest of the day we spent in almost total silence, having no spirits for conversation; our hearts being almost broken with anguish. When it grew toward evening, we agreed to find our way out of that detested house, and seek for some other habitation, which might be more propitious. But we found more difficulty in this undertaking than we were at all aware of; for though we could with tolerable ease go from room to room *within* the house, still, when we attempted to quit it, we found it every way surrounded with so thick a brick wall, that it was impossible for us to make our way through it: we therefore ran round and round it several times, searching for some little crevice through which we might escape; but all to no purpose, not the least crack could we discover: and we might have continued there till this time, had we not at length, after the family were in bed, resolved to venture through one of the apartments into the hall, and so creep out under the house-door. But the dangers we exposed ourselves to in this expedition were many and great; we knew that traps were set for us about the house, and where they might chance to be placed we could not tell. I had likewise been eye-witness to no less than four cats, who might, for ought we knew to the contrary, at that hour of darkness, be prowling in search of some of our unhappy species.

But, in spite of every difficulty and hazard, we determined to venture rather than continue in opposition to our mother's commands; and, to reward our obedience, we escaped with trembling hearts, unobserved, at least unmolested, by any one. And now, for the first time since our birth, we found ourselves exposed to the inclemency of the weather. The night was very dark and tempestuous; the rain poured down in torrents; and the wind blew so exceedingly high, that, low upon the ground as we were, it was with difficulty that we could keep our legs: added to which, every step we took, we were in water up to our stomachs. In this wretched condition we knew not which way to turn ourselves, or where to seek for shelter. The spattering of the rain, the howling of the wind, together with the rattling and shaking of the trees, all contributed to make such a noise as rendered it impossible for us to hear whether any danger was approaching us or not.

In this truly melancholy situation we waded on for a considerable time, till at length we reached a small house, and very easily gained admittance through a pretty large hole on one side of the door. Most heartily did we rejoice at finding ourselves once more under shelter from the cold and rain, and for some time only busied ourselves in drying our hair, which was as thoroughly wet as if we had been served as the boy threatened my brother Brighteyes, and we had really been drawn through a pond. After we had done this, and had a little rested ourselves, we began to look about in search of food, but we could find nothing, except a few crumbs of bread and cheese in a man's coat-pocket, and a piece of tallow-candle stuck on the top of a tinder-box. This, however, though not such delicate eating as we had been used to, yet served to satisfy our present hunger; and we had just finished the candle when we were greatly alarmed by the sight of a human hand (for we mice can see a little in the dark) feeling about the very chair on which we stood. We jumped down in an instant, and hid ourselves in a little hole behind a black trunk that stood in one corner of the room.

We then heard very distinctly a man say, 'Betty, did you not put the candle by the bedside?' 'Yes, that I am very sure I did,' replied a female voice.' 'I thought so,' answered the man; 'but I am sure it is not here now. Tom! Tom! Tom!' continued he. 'What, father?' replied a boy, starting up, 'what is the matter?' 'Why, do you know any thing of the candle? I cannot find it, my dear; and I want it sadly, for I fancy it is time we should be up and be jogging. Dost know any thing of it, my lad?' 'Not I, truly, father,' said the boy, 'I only know that I saw mother stick it in the box-lid last night, and put it upon the chair, which she set by the bedside, after you had put your clothes upon the back of it; I know I saw her put it there, so it must be there now, I fancy.' 'Well, I cannot find it,' replied the father; so we must e'en get up in the dark, for I am sure it must be time.' The

father and son then both dressed themselves; and the man, taking a shilling out of his pocket, laid it upon the chair, saying at the same time, 'There, Betty, I have left a shilling for you; take care it does not go after the candle, for where that is I *cannot* tell any more than the carp at the bottom of the squire's fish-pond.' He then unlocked the door, and went away, accompanied by his son.

After their departure, we again came out, and took another walk round the room, and found our way into a little cupboard, which we had not before observed. Here we discovered half a loaf of bread, a piece of cold pudding, a lump of salt butter, some soft sugar in a bason, and a fine large slice of bacon. On these dainties we feasted very amply, and agreed that we should again hide ourselves behind the black trunk all day, and at night, when the family were in bed, return to take another meal on the plenty of nice provision which we so happily discovered. Accordingly, we crept back just as the woman went to fill her tea-kettle at a pump, which stood between her house and the next neighbour's. When she returned, she put it upon the fire she had just lit, and, taking a pair of bellows in her hand, sat down to blow it.

While she was so employed, a young gentleman, about ten years of age, very genteelly dressed, entered the room, and in a familiar manner asked her how she did. 'I am very well, thank you, my dear,' replied she: 'and pray, Master George, how does your mamma and papa do; and all your brothers and sisters?' 'They are all very well, thank you,' returned the boy: 'And I am come to bring you a slice of cake, which my grandpapa gave me yesterday.' Then throwing his arms round her neck, he went on saying, 'Oh! my dear, dear Betty Flood, how I do love you! I would do any thing in the world to serve you. I shall save all my Christmas-boxes to give to you; and when I am a man, I will give you a great deal of money. I wish you were a lady, and not so poor.' 'I am much obliged to you, my dear,' said she, 'for your kind good-wishes; but, indeed, *love*, I am very well contented with my station: I have a good husband, and three good children, and that is more than many a *lady* can say; and *riches*, Master George, unless people are *good*, and those one lives with are *kind* and *obliging*, will never make any body happy. What comfort, now, do you think a body could ever have at Squire Stately's? I declare, if it was put to my choice, I would rather a thousand times be as I am. To be sure, they are very rich; but what of that? they cannot eat gold; neither can gold ease their hearts when they are bursting almost with pride and ill-nature. They say, indeed, that Madam Stately would be kind enough, if they would let her rest; but what with the Squire's drinking and swearing, and the young gentleman's extravagance, and her daughter's pride and quarrelling, she is almost tired out of her life. And so, Master George, I say I had rather be poor Betty Flood, with honest Abraham for my husband, than the finest lady in the land, if I must live at such a rate. To be sure, nobody can deny but that money is very desirable, and people that are rich can do many agreeable things which we poor ones cannot; but yet, for all that, *money* does not make people happy. Happiness, Master George, depends greatly upon people's own tempers and dispositions: a person who is fretful and cross will never be happy, though he should be made king of all England; and a person who is *contented* and good-humoured will never be wretched, though he should be as poor as a beggar. So never fret yourself, *love*, because Betty Flood is *poor*; for though I am *poor*, I am *honest*: and whilst my husband and I are happy enough to be blessed with health, and the use of our limbs, we can work for our living; and though we have no great plenty, still we have sufficient to support us. So pray, dear, eat your cake yourself, for I would not take it from you for ever so much.' They then disputed for some time who should have it: at last, George scuffled away from her, and put it into the closet, and then, nodding his head at her, ran away, saying, he must go to school that moment.

Betty Flood then ate her breakfast; and we heard her say *something* about the *nasty mice*, but *what* we could not make out, as she muttered softly to herself. She then came to the trunk behind which we lay, and taking out of it a roll of new linen, sat down to needle-work. At twelve o'clock her husband and son returned; so moving her table out of the way, she made room for them at the fire, and, fetching the frying-pan, dressed some rashers of the nice bacon we had before tasted in the cupboard. The boy, in the mean time, spread a cloth on the table, and placed the bread and cold pudding on it likewise: then, returning to the closet for their plates, he cried out, '*Lauk!* father, here is a nice *hunch* of plum-cake; can you tell how it came?' 'Not I, indeed, Tom,' replied his father; 'I can tell no more than the carp at the bottom of the squire's fish-pond.' 'Oh, I will tell you,' said Mrs. Flood; 'I know how it came. Do you know, that dear child, Master George Kendall, brought it for me: he called as he went to school this morning. I told him I would not have it; but the dear little soul popped it into the cupboard, and ran away without it. *Bless* his little heart! I do think he is the sweetest child that ever was born. You may laugh at me for saying so; but I am sure I should have thought the same if I had *not* nursed him myself.' 'Indeed,' replied her husband, 'I do not laugh at you for saying so, for I think so too, and so must every one who knows him; for when young gentlemen behave as he does, every body must love and admire them. There is nothing I would not do to help and serve that child, or any of his family; they always are so kind, and speak as civilly to us poor folk as if we were the first lords or ladies in the land. I am sure, if it were needful, I would go through fire and water for their sakes; and so would every man in the parish, I dare say. But I wonder who would do as much to help Squire Stately or any of his family, if it was not that I should think it my *duty* (and an honest man ought always to do *that*, whether he likes it or not); but I say, if it was not that it would be my *duty* to help my fellow-creature, I would scarcely be at the trouble of stepping over the threshold to serve them, they are such a set of cross good-for-nothing gentry. I declare, it was but as we came home to dinner now, that we saw Master Sam throwing sticks and stones at Dame Frugal's ducks, for the sake of seeing them waddle; and then, when they got to the pond, he sent his dog in after them to bark and frighten them out of their wits. And as I came by, nothing would serve him but throwing a great dab of mud all over the sleeve of my coat. So I said, "Why, Master Sam, you need not have done that; I did nothing to offend you: and however amusing you may think it to insult poor people, I assure you it is very wicked, and what no good person in the world would be guilty of." He then set up a great rude laugh, and I walked on and said no more. But if all gentlefolk were to behave like that family, I had rather be poor as I am, than have all their *riches*, if that would make me act like them.' 'Very true, Abraham,' replied his wife, 'that is what I say, and what I told Master George this morning; for to be poor, if people do not become so through their own *extravagance*, is no disgrace to any body; but to be *haughty, cruel, cross*, and *mischievous*, is a disgrace to all who are so, let their rank be as exalted as it may.'

Here the conversation was interrupted by the entrance of a man, who begged Mr. Flood to assist him in unloading his cart of flour, as his man was gone out, and he could not do it by himself. 'Well, I will come and help you, with all my heart,' said Flood; 'and so shall Tom too: will you, my lad? I cannot live without help myself; and if I do not assist others, I am sure I shall not deserve any when I want it.' So saying, he left his house; and his wife, after cleaning and putting in their proper places those things which had been used at dinner, again sat down to her sewing.

Soon after the clock had struck six, the man and his son returned; and, sitting round the fire, they passed the evening in social conversation, till they went to bed, which was a little after eight: and they convinced me, by their talk and behaviour, that happiness in this world depends far more upon the *temper* and disposition of the *heart*, than upon any external possessions; and that *virtue*, and a desire to be *useful* to others, afford far greater satisfaction and peace of mind than any riches and grandeur can possibly supply without such necessary qualifications. After they were all fallen asleep, we crept out; and, leaving the candle unmolested, which was again placed on the tinder-box by the bed-side, we hastened into the closet, where we regaled heartily, and devoured that part of the plum-cake which Tom had very generously left for his sister Polly, who we found was expected home the next day.

We then retired to our safe retreat, and thought we might venture to stay for one more night's provisions without running any danger from our too frequent return to the same place. But in the morning we found our scheme frustrated; for, on the woman's going to the closet to get her breakfast, she observed the robbery which we had committed, and exclaimed, 'Some teazing mice have found their way into the closet: I will borrow Neighbour Savewell's trap to-night, and catch some of the little toads; that I will!' After hearing this, it would have been madness to make any further attempts; we therefore agreed to watch for an opportunity, and escape on the very first that offered. Accordingly, about noon, when Mrs. Flood was busily employed in making some pancakes, we slipped by her unobserved, and crept out at the same hole by which we first entered. But no sooner were we in the open road, than we repented our haste, and wished that we had continued where we were till the darkness of the night might better have concealed us from the observation of any one. We crept as close to the wall of the house (as far as it reached, which was but a few paces) as we possibly could, and then stepped into a little ditch,

which we were soon obliged to leave again, as the water ran in some parts of it almost up to the edge.

At length we reached a little cottage, which we were just entering, when a cat that was sleeping unnoticed by us upon a chair, jumped down, and would certainly have destroyed me (who happened to go first) had she not at the same moment tried to catch my brother, and by that means missed her aim, and so given us both an opportunity to escape, which we did by scrambling behind a brick that a child had been playing with by the side of the door. Fortunately, the brick lay too close to the house for the cat to get her paw behind it, so as to be able to reach us; though to avoid it we were obliged to use the greatest precaution, as she could thrust it in a little way, so that if we had gone one inch too near either end, she would certainly have dragged us out by her talons. In this dreadful situation did we spend some hours, incessantly moving from one end of the brick to the other; for the moment she had, by the entrance of her paw at one end, driven us to the other, she stepped over, and again made us retreat. Think with what dreadful terror our little hearts must have been oppressed, to see our mortal enemy so closely watching us, expecting every moment when she shook the brick with her two fore-paws in searching, and with her mouth endeavoured to lift it up, that she would be so far able to effect her purpose, as to make it impossible for us to escape her jaws. But, happily for us, it had somehow or other got so wedged that she could not move it to any distance; though it kept momentarily increasing our terrors, by shaking as she strove to turn it.

From this state of horror, however, we were at length delivered by a little boy of about two years old, who came out of the house, and taking the cat up round its body with both hands, tottered away with it, and shut the door.

Finding ourselves thus unexpectedly once more at liberty, we determined to make use of it, by seeking some safer retreat, at least, till night should better hide us from public view. Terrified almost out of our senses, we crept from behind the brick, and, after running a few yards, slipped under the folding doors of a barn, and soon concealed ourselves amidst a vast quantity of threshed corn. This appeared to us the most desirable retreat that we had yet found; not only as it afforded such immense plenty of food, but also as we could so easily hide ourselves from the observation of any one: beside, as it did not appear to be a dwelling-house, we could in security reside, free from any danger of traps, or the cruelty of man. We therefore congratulated each other, not more on account of the wonderful escape which we had, than upon our good fortune in coming to a spot so blessed with peace and plenty.

After we were a little recovered from the fatigue of mind, as well as of body, which we had lately gone through, we regaled very heartily upon the corn that surrounded us, and then fell into a charming sleep, from which we were awakened the next morning by the sound of human voices. We very distinctly heard that of a boy, saying, 'Let us mix all the threshed corn with the rest that is not threshed, and that will make a *fine fuss*, and set John and Simon a *swearing* like *troopers* when they come and find all their labour lost, and that they must do all their work over again.' 'And do you think there is any thing so *agreeable* in giving people trouble, and hearing them swear,' replied another voice, 'that you can wish to do it? For my part, I think it is so wicked a thing, that I hate to hear any body guilty of it, much less would I be the cause of making them commit so great a sin: and as for giving them all their trouble over again, so far would it be from affording me any *pleasure*, that on the contrary it would give me great *pain;* for however you may think of it, Will, I assure you, it always gives me much uneasiness to see people labouring and working hard. I always think how much *I* should dislike to be obliged to do so myself, and therefore very sincerely pity those who must. On no account therefore will I do any thing to add to their labour, or that shall give them unnecessary work.'

'Pough!' answered Will, 'you are wonderfully *wise;* I, for my part, hate such superabundant wisdom: I like to see folk *fret,* and *stew,* and *scold,* as our maids did last week when I cut the line, and let all the *sheets,* and *gowns,* and *petticoats,* and *frocks,* and *shirts,* and *aprons,* and *caps,* and what not, fall plump into the dirt. O! how I did laugh! and how they did mutter and scold! And do you know, that just as the wash *ladies* were wiping their coddled hands, and comforted themselves with the thought of their work being all over, and were going to *sip* their tea by the fire-side, I put them all to the *scout;* and they were obliged to wash every rag over again. I shall never forget how cross they looked, nay, I verily believe Susan *cried* about it; and *how* I did laugh!'

'And pray,' rejoined the other boy, 'should you have laughed equally hearty if, after you had been at school all day, and had with much difficulty just got through all your writing, and different exercises, and were going to play, should you *laugh,* I say, if somebody was to run away with them all, and your master oblige you to do them all over again? Tell me, Will, should you *laugh,* or *cry* and look *cross?* And even that would not be half so bad for you, as it was for the maids to be obliged to wash their clothes over again; washing is very hard labour, and tires people sadly, and so does threshing too. It is very unkind, therefore, to give them such unnecessary trouble; and every thing that is *unkind,* is *wicked:* and I would not do it upon any account, I assure you.' 'Then I *assure* you, replied Will, you may let it alone: I can do it without your assistance.' He then began mixing the grain and the chaff together, the other boy strongly remonstrating against it, to which he paid no attention; and whilst he was so employed, two men, Simon and John, entered the barn.

'Why, how now, Master Billy,' said Simon, 'what are you about? What business have you to be here? You are always doing some mischief or other! I wish, with all my heart, that you were kept chained like a dog, and never suffered to be at liberty, for you do more harm in an hour, than a body can set right again in a month!' Will then took up hats full of the corn and chaff, and threw it in the two men's faces; afterwards taking up a flail, he gave Simon a blow across his back, saying, at the same time, I will shew you the way to thresh, and separate the flesh from the bones.' 'O! will you so, young squire?' said John, 'I will shew you the way to make naughty boys good.' He then left the barn, but presently returned accompanied by a gentleman, upon the sight of whom Will let fall the flail, which he was till then brandishing over Simon's head, and was going away, when the gentleman taking hold of his hand, said, 'You do not *stir* from *this* place, Master William, nor have one mouthful of breakfast, till you have asked the men pardon for your behaviour, and likewise sifted every grain of corn from the chaff which you have mixed with it. When you have done that, you may have some food, but not before; and afterward you may spend the rest of the day in threshing, then you will be a better judge, my boy, of the fatigue and labour of it, and find how you should like, after working hard all day, to have it rendered useless by a mischievous boy. Remember, William, what I have now said to you, for I do insist upon being minded: and I promise you, that if you offer to play, or do any thing else to day, you shall be punished very severely.' The gentleman then went away. Will muttered something, I could not exactly hear what, began to sift the corn, and so much had he mixed together, that he did not go in for his breakfast till after I had heard the church clock strike one, though it was before eight when he came into the barn. In about an hour he returned, and the other boy with him, who addressed him, saying: 'Ah! Will, you had better have taken my advice, and not have done so: I thought what you would get by your *nice fun* as you called it. I never knew any good come of mischief; it generally brings those who do it into disgrace; or if they *should* happen to escape unpunished, still it is always attended with some inconvenience: it is an *ill-natured* disposition which can take pleasure in giving trouble to any one.' 'Do *hold* your tongue, James,' replied Will, 'I declare I have not patience to hear you preach, you are so prodigiously *wise,* and *prudent,* and *sober!* you had better go in doors and *sew* with your mamma, for you talk just as if you were a *girl,* and not in the least like a boy of spirit.' 'Like a *girl!*' resumed James, 'are *girls* then the only folk who have any sense, or good-nature? Or what proof does it shew of spirit to be fond of mischief, and giving people trouble? It is like a *monkey* of spirit indeed; but I cannot say, that I see either *spirit* or sense in making the clean clothes fall into the dirt, or mixing the corn and chaff, for the sake of making the poor servants do them all over again: if these things are a sign of any spirit, I am sure it is of an *evil* one, and not at all such as I wish to possess, though I no more want to sit still, or *work* with a *needle,* than you do; but I hope there are other ways of shewing my *spirit,* as you call it, than by doing *mischief,* and being *ill-natured.* I do not think my papa ever seems to be effeminate, or want sufficient *spirit;* but he would *scorn* to give unnecessary trouble to any body: and so will Tom Vaulter, though no boy in the world loves play better than he does; he plays at cricket the best of any boy in the school, and I am sure none can beat him at tennis; and as for skipping, I never saw a boy skip so well in all my life; and I am sure he would beat you, with all your *spirit,* out and out twenty times, either at running, or sliding, or swimming, or climbing a tree. And yet he never gives trouble to any body for the sake of *fun;* he is one of the best-tempered boys in the world; and whether it is like a *girl* or not, he always does what he knows to be right and kind; and if that is being like girls, why? with all my heart; I like girls well enough, and if they behave well I do not see why you should speak so contemptuously of them. My papa always says that he loves girls just as well as boys, and none but foolish and naughty boys despise and teaze them.' Just as he said these words, Simon and John entered the barn, and seeing Will stand idle, 'Come, come, young gentleman,' said John, 'take up your flail and go to work, Sir, to work! to work! night will be here presently, and you have done nothing yet.' Presently after the gentleman returned, and enforced John's advice for him to mind his work.

After Master Will had continued his employment some little time, he began to cry, saying, his arms ached ready to drop off, and his hand was so sore he could not *bear* it. 'Then doubtless,' replied his father, 'you would prodigiously like, after you have been labouring all day, to have your work to do over again, for the sake of diverting a foolish boy. But go on, William, I am determined that you shall, for one day, know what it is to work hard, and thereby be taught to pity, and *help,* not add to the fatigue of those who do.' The boy then went on with his business, though not without making great complaints, and shedding many tears. At length, however, evening came; and the gentleman, his son, and the two men, all went away, leaving Longtail and myself to enjoy our abundance. We passed another night in the sweetest undisturbed repose, and in the day had nothing to alarm our fears. In short, our situation was every way so perfectly happy and desirable, that we thought, although our mother had charged us not to *return* frequently to the same place, yet she could not mean that we should not take up our abode in a spot so secure and comfortable. We therefore determined to continue where we were, till we should find some cause for removing. And happy had it been for us if we had kept to this resolution, and remained contented when we had every thing requisite to make us so. Instead of which, after we had thus, free from care, passed our time about seven months, like fools as we were, we began to grow weary of our retirement, and of eating nothing but the same food; and agreed that we would again venture forth and seek for some other lodging, at the same time resolving, in case we could find no habitation that suited us, to return to the barn where we had enjoyed so many days of plenty and repose.

Accordingly, one fine moon-light *Monday* night, after securing our supper on the corn, we set forth, and travelled for some distance without any further molestation than our own natural fears created. At length we came to a brick house, with about five or six windows in front, and made our way into it through a small latticed window which gave air into the pantry; but on our arrival here we had no opportunity of so much as observing what it contained, for on our slipping down a cat instantly flew at us, and by the greatest good luck in the world, there chanced to be a hole in one of the boards of the floor close to the spot where we stood, into which we both were happy enough to pop, before she could catch us. Here we had time to reflect, and severely blame ourselves for not being satisfied with our state in the barn. 'When,' said I, addressing myself to my brother 'when shall we grow wise, and learn to know *that certain evil always attends every deviation from what is right.* When we disobeyed the advice of our mother, and, tempted by cakes and other da[i]nties, frequently returned to the same dangerous place, how severely did we suffer for it? And now, by our own *discontent,* and not being satisfied when so safely, though more humbly lodged, into what trouble have we not plunged ourselves? How securely have we lived in the barn for the last seven months, and how happily might we still have continued there, had it not been for our restless dispositions? Ah! my brother, we have acted foolishly. We ought to have been contented when we were at peace, and should have considered

that if we had not every thing we could wish for, we had every thing that was *necessary;* and the life of a mouse was never designed for *perfect* happiness. Such enjoyment was never intended for our lot: it is the portion only of beings whose capacities are far superior to ours. We ought then to have been *contented;* and had we been so, we should have been as happy as our state of life would have admitted of.' 'What you say is certainly very true,' replied Longtail, 'and I sincerely wish that we had thought of these things before. But what must we now do? we *said* we would return to the barn in case of difficulties, but that is now impossible, as, if we attempt to retreat, the cat that drove us in here, will certainly destroy us: and yet in proceeding, what difficulties must we encounter, what dangers may we not run! Oh! my beloved Nimble,' continued he, 'what a life of hazard is ours! to what innumerable accidents are we hourly exposed! and how is every meal that we eat at the risk of our very existence.

'It undoubtedly is,' replied I; 'but with all its troubles we still are very desirous of preserving it: let us not then, my brother, indulge our hearts with murmuring and finding fault with that life, which, notwithstanding all its evils, we value so highly. Rather let us endeavour to learn experience, and, by conducting ourselves better, escape many of those troubles which we now suffer.' So saying, I advised him to follow me: 'for,' added I, 'it is impossible for us to exist in the spot in which we are at present; we must therefore strive to work our way into some other house or apartment, where we can at least find some food. To this Longtail agreed; the rest of the night, and all the next day, we spent in nibbling and finding our way into a closet in the house, which richly repaid us for all our toil, as it contained *sugar-plums, rice, millet,* various kinds of *sweetmeats,* and what we liked better than all the rest, a paper of nice *macaroons.* On these we feasted most deliciously till our hunger was fully satisfied, and then creeping into a little hole, just big enough to contain us both, behind one of the jars of sweetmeats, reposed ourselves with a nap, after our various and great fatigues which we had gone through. I never was a remarkably sound sleeper, the least noise disturbs me, and I was awakened in the morning by the servant-maid's coming into the room to sweep it, and get it ready for the reception of her mistress and family, who soon after entered. As I wanted to know from whom the voices I heard proceeded, I stepped softly from behind the jar, and just peeped under the door into the room, where I discovered a gentleman, two ladies, and a little boy and girl.

As I was totally unacquainted with all places of retreat, and did not know how soon any of them might have occasion to open the closet-door, I instantly returned to my brother; and, awaking him, told him it was time for us to be upon our guard, as the family were all up and about.

Whilst we were thus situated, the first words I heard distinctly were those of the gentleman, saying, 'No, Frank, I can never have a good opinion of him; the boy who could *once* deceive may, for aught I know, do so *again;* he has, by breaking his word, forfeited the only dependence one could possibly have in him. A person who has once lost his *honour* has no means left of gaining credit to his assertions. By *honour,* Frank, I would be understood to speak of *veracity,* of *virtue,* of *scorning* to commit a *mean* action, and not that brutish sense in which some understand it, as if it consisted in a readiness to *fight* and resent an injury; for so far am I from considering such behaviour as any proof of honour, that, on the contrary, I look upon it as a sure sign of want of *proper spirit* and *true honour. Fools, bullies,* and even *cowards,* will *fight;* whereas none but men of *sense* and *resolution* and *true magnanimity* know how to *pardon* and *despise* an insult.' 'But, indeed, Sir,' replied the boy, 'at school, if one did not fight, they would laugh at one so, there would be no such thing as bearing it.' 'And for that very reason it is, my dear, that I say, to pass by and pardon an insult requires more *resolution* and *courage* than mere *fighting* does. When I wish you to avoid quarrelling and fighting, I by no means want you to become a *coward,* for I as much abhor a *dastardly spirit* as any boy in your school can possibly do; but I would wish you to convince them that you merited not that appellation, by shewing, through the whole of your behaviour, a resolution that despised accidental pain, and avoided revenging an affront for no other reason than because you were convinced it shewed a much nobler spirit to *pardon* than to *resent.* And you may be assured, my dear, few are the days that pass without affording us some opportunity of exerting our patience, and shewing that, although we disdain quarrelling, still we are far from being *cowards.*

'I remember, when I was at school, there was one boy, who, from his first coming, declined upon all occasions engaging in any battle; he even gave up many of his just rights to avoid quarrelling: which conduct, instead of gaining (as it justly deserved) the approbation of his companions, drew upon him the insult and abuse of the whole school; and they were perpetually teazing him with the opprobrious title of *coward.* For some time he bore it with great good-humour, and endeavoured to laugh it off; but, finding that had no effect, he one day thus addressed us— "If you suppose that I like to be called a *coward,* you are all very much mistaken; or if you think me one, I assure you that you are not less so; for no boy in the school should, if put to the trial, shew greater resolution than myself. Indeed, I think it no small proof of patience that I have borne your repeated insults so long; when I could, by behaving more like a savage beast, and less like a reasonable creature, have established my character at once: but I *abhor* quarrelling, my soul detests to treat my fellow-creatures as if they were brutes, from whose fangs I must defend myself; but if nothing else but *fighting* will convince you that I possess not less courage than yourselves, I will now offer, in cold blood, to engage with the biggest boy in the school. If I conquer him, it will be a sign that I *know* how to defend myself; and if he conquers me, I will, by my behaviour, give a proof that I am not wanting in resolution to suffer pain, although

I never will so far demean the character of a *reasonable creature* and a *Christian,* as to *fight* upon every trifling disagreement or insult." No sooner had he uttered these words, than every boy present was loud either in his commendation or condemnation. One quarter of them, convinced of the justness of his arguments, highly extolled his forbearance; whilst the other three parts, with still greater noise, only called him a *bully* and a *mean-spirited coward,* who dared not fight, and for that reason made such a fine speech, hoping to intimidate them. "Well then," said he, "if such is your opinion, why will none of you accept my offer? you surely cannot be afraid, *you* who are such brave fellows, of such *true courage,* and such *noble spirits,* cannot be afraid of a *coward* and a *bully!* Why, therefore, does not one of you step forward, and put my *fine speech* to the test? Otherwise, after I have thus challenged you *all,* I hope *none* for the future will think they have any right to call me *coward;* though I again declare my fixed resolution against fighting."

'Just as he said this, a voice calling for *help,* was heard from a lane adjoining to the play-yard. Immediately we all flocked to the side nearest whence it proceeded; and, clambering upon benches, watering-pots, or whatever came first in our way, peeped over the wall, where we discovered two well-grown lads, about seventeen or eighteen, stripping a little boy of his clothes, and beating him for his outcries in a most cruel manner: and at a little distance farther down the lane, sat a company of gypsies, to whom the two lads evidently belonged. At the sight of this we were all much distressed, and wished to relieve the boy; though, discovering so large a party, we were too much afraid to venture, till Tomkins (the boy I before spoke about) instantly jumped from the wall, and only saying, "Has nobody courage to follow me?" ran toward them as fast as possible, and with uncommon strength and agility placed himself between them and the boy, and began defending himself in the best manner he could; which he did for some time with great dexterity, none of his *fighting* schoolfellows having courage to go to his assistance. At length, however, seeing it impossible for him to stand out any longer against two so much stronger than himself, the boys agreed to secure themselves by numbers, and to sally forth to his assistance altogether. This scheme succeeded, and very shortly rescued Tomkins from his antagonists. He thanked them for their assistance, saying, at the same time, "I hope you will no longer doubt my *courage,* or my abilities to fight, when it is necessary or in a good cause." After so signal a proof of his valour, his greatest enemies could no longer doubt it; and, without ever engaging in foolish battles, he passed through school as much respected as any boy, and his magnanimity was never again called in question.'

As the gentleman stopped speaking, the little girl called out, 'O, papa, the coach is at the door.' 'Is it, my dear?' returned the father. 'Well then, stop, my love,' said one of the ladies, 'I have got a few cakes for you; stay, and take them before you go.' She then unlocked the closet where we were, and took down the paper of macaroons, among which we had so comfortably regaled ourselves; when, observing the hole in the paper through which we entered, 'O dear!' she exclaimed, 'the mice have actually got into my cupboard. I will move all the things out this very morning, and lock the cat up in it; for I shall be undone if the mice once get footing here: they will soon spoil all my stores, and that will never do.' She then kissed both the children; and, giving them the cakes, they, the gentleman, and another lady, all departed: and she instantly began to move the boxes and jars from the closet; whilst we, terrified almost out of our wits, sat trembling behind one of them, not daring to stir, yet dreading the cat's approach every moment.

We were soon, however, obliged to move our quarters, for the lady taking down the very jar which concealed us, we were forced (without knowing where we were) to jump down instantly. In vain we sought all round the room for some avenue whereat we might escape; the apartment was too well fitted up to admit the smallest crack: and we must then certainly have been destroyed, had we not, with uncommon presence of mind, ran up the back of the lady's gown, by which means she lost sight of us, and gave us an opportunity to make our escape, as she opened the door to order the cat to be brought in. We seized the lucky moment, and, dropping from her gown, fled with the utmost haste out at the house-door, which happened to be wide open; and I, without once looking behind me, ran on till I discovered a little crack in the brick wall, which I entered, and which, after many turnings and windings, brought me to this house, where I have now continued skulking about in its different apartments for above a month; during which time I have not heard the least tidings of my beloved brother Longtail. Whether, therefore, any mischief befel him as he followed me, or whether he entered the crack with me and then lost sight of me, I know not; but in vain have I sought him every day since my arrival within these walls: and so anxious am I to learn what is become of him, that I am now come forth, contrary to my nature, to engage your compassion, and to beseech you, in case—

———————

At this moment, the door of my room opened, and my servant coming hastily in, the Mouse jumped from my table, and precipitately retreated to the same hole from whence it first addressed me; and though I have several times peeped into it, and even laid little bits of cake to entice it back again, yet have I never been able to see it any where since. Should either that, or any other, ever again favour me so far with their confidence, as to instruct me with their history, I will certainly communicate it with all possible speed to my little readers; who I hope have been wise enough to attend to the advice given them in the preceding pages, although it was delivered to them by one as insignificant as a MOUSE.

END OF VOLUME I.

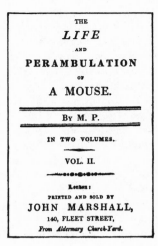

THE
LIFE
AND
PERAMBULATION
OF
A MOUSE.

By M. P.

IN TWO VOLUMES.

VOL. II.

London:
PRINTED AND SOLD BY
JOHN MARSHALL,
140, FLEET STREET,
From Aldermary Church-Yard.

DEDICATION

To MASTER * * * * * *. As you were pleased to express so much pleasure at reading *The Life and Perambulation of a Mouse,* and so ardently to wish to know what became of it afterwards, I have endeavoured to gratify your innocent curiosity by again taking up the pen; and for a little while longer making believe the MOUSE once more came and talked to me. You, I know, have too much good sense ever to refuse *instruction,* because it is conveyed to you through the channel of an *entertaining* little book, but are wise enough to receive it with pleasure, and have the gratitude to acknowledge yourself obliged to every one who will take the trouble to give it you, and on that account confess some few thanks due to

Your most sincere Friend,
M. P.

INTRODUCTION

It is now some months ago since I took leave of my little readers, promising, in case I should ever hear any further tidings of either Nimble or Longtail, I would certainly communicate it to them; and, as I think it extremely wrong not to fulfil any engagement we enter into, I look upon myself bound to give them all the information I have since gained, relating to those two little animals; and I doubt not but they will be glad to hear what happened to them, after Nimble was frightened from my writing-table by the entrance of my servant. If I recollect right, I have already told you, that I frequently peeped into the hole in the skirting-board, and laid bits of cake to try to entice my little companion back, but all to no purpose: and I had quite given over all hopes of ever again seeing him, when one day, as I was putting my hand into a large jar, which had some Turkey figs in it, I felt something soft at the bottom, and taking it out, found it to be a poor little mouse, not quite dead, but so starved and weak, that upon my placing it upon the table, it had not strength sufficient to get from me. A little boy happened to be standing by me, who, upon the sight of the mouse, began to beg me to give it to the cat, or kill it, "for I don't like mice," said he; "pray, Ma'am, put it away." "Not like mice," replied I; "what can be your objection to such a little soft creature as this?" and taking advantage of its weakness, I picked it up, and held it in the palm of one hand, whilst I stroked it with the fingers of my right.— "Poor little mouse," said I, "who can be afraid of such a little object as *this*? Do you not feel ashamed of yourself, Joe, to fear such a little creature as *this*? Only look at it, observe how small it is, and then consider your own size, and surely, my dear, you will blush to think of being no more of a *man* than to fear a *mouse!* Look at me, Joe," continued I, "see, I will kiss it, I am not at all afraid that it will hurt me." When, lifting it up toward my face, I heard it say, in the faintest voice possible. "Do you not know me?" I instantly recollected my little friend Nimble, and rejoiced at so unexpectedly finding him.— "What, is it you, little Nimble," exclaimed I, "that I again behold? Believe me, I am heartily rejoiced once more to find you; but tell me, where have you been, what have you done, whom have you seen, and what have you learned since you last left me?" "Oh!" replied he, in a voice so low I could scarcely hear him, "I have seen many things; but I am so faint and weak for want of food and fresh air, that I doubt I shall never live to tell you; but, for pity's sake have compassion on me, either put me out of my present misery by instantly killing me, or else give me something to eat; for, if you knew my sufferings, I am sure it would grieve your heart." "*Kill* you!" returned I, "no, that I will not: on the contrary, I will try by every method to restore you to health, and all the happiness a mouse is capable of feeling." I then instantly sent for some bread, and had the satisfaction of seeing him eat very heartily of it, after which he seemed much refreshed, and began to move about a little more suitable to his *name*; for, in truth, when I first found him, no living creature in the world could appear less deserving of the appellation of Nimble. I then fetched him a little milk, and gave him a lump of sugar to nibble; after eating of which he begged to retire into some safe little hole to take a nap, from whence he promised to return as soon as he should wake; and accordingly, in about an hour he again appeared on my table, and began as follows:

I WAS FRIGHTENED away from you just as I was going to implore your compassion for any unfortunate mouse that might happen to fall within your power; lest you should destroy my dear and only surviving brother, Longtail; but somebody entering the room, prevented me, and after I had regained my hiding place, I resolved to quit the house, and once more set out in search of my beloved brother. Accordingly, with great difficulty I made my way out of the house; but my distress was much increased upon finding the snow so deep upon the ground, that it was impossible for me to attempt to stir, as upon stepping one foot out to try, I found it far too deep for me to fathom the bottom. This greatly distressed me. Alas! said I to myself, what shall I do now? To proceed is impossible; and to return is very melancholy, without any tidings of my dear, dear Longtail! But I was interrupted in the midst of these reflections, by the appearance of two cats, who came running with such violence as to pass by without observing me: however, it put me in such consternation, that regardless where I went, I sprung forward, and sunk so deep in the snow that I must inevitably soon have perished, had not a boy come to the very place where I was, to gather snow for making snow-balls to throw at his companions. Happily for me, he took me up in his hand, in the midst of the snow, which not less alarmed me, when I considered the sufferings I had before endured, and the cruel death of my brother Brighteyes, from the hands of boys. Oh! thought I to myself, what new tortures shall I now experience? Better had I perished in the cold snow, than be spared only to be tormented by the cruel hands of unthinking children.

Scarcely had I made this reflection, when the boy called out, upon seeing me move, "*Lud!* what have I got here?" at the same instant tossing the handful of snow from him in a violent hurry, without attempting to press it into a ball. Over I turned head and heels, wondering what further would be my fate, when I was happy to find I fell unhurt upon some hay, which was laid in the yard to fodder the cows and horses. Here I lay some time, so frightened by my adventure, as to be unable to move, and my little heart beat as if it would have burst its way through my breast: nor were my apprehensions at all diminished by the approach of a man, who gathered the hay up in his arms, and carried it (with me in the midst of it) into the stable; where, after littering down the horses, he left me once more to my own reflections.

After he had been gone some time, and all things were quiet, I began to look about me, and soon found my way into a corn-bin, where I made a most delicious supper, and slept free from any disturbance till the morning, when fearing I might be discovered, in case he should want any of the oats for his horses, I returned by the same place I had entered, and hid myself in one corner of the hay-loft; where I passed the whole of the day more free from alarm than often falls to the lot of any of my species; and in the evening again returned to regale myself with corn, as I had done the night before. The great abundance with which I was surrounded, strongly tempted me to continue where I was; but then the thoughts of my absent brother imbittered all my peace, and the advice of my mother came so much across my mind, that I determined before the next morning I would again venture forth and seek my fortune and my brother. Accordingly, after having eaten a very hearty meal, I left the bin, and was attempting to get out of the stable, when one of the horses being taken suddenly ill, made so much noise with his kicking and struggling, as to alarm the family, and the coachman entering with a lantern in his hand, put me into such consternation, that I ran for shelter into the pocket of a great coat, which hung up upon a peg next the harness of the horses. Here I lay snug for some hours, not daring to stir, as I smelt the footsteps of a cat frequently pass by, and heard the coachman extol her good qualities to a man who accompanied him into the stable; saying she was the best mouser in the kingdom. "I do not believe," added he, "I have a mouse in the stable or loft, she keeps so good a look out. For the last two days I lent her to the cook, to put into her pantry, but I have got her back again, and I would not part with her for a crown; no, not for the best silver crown that ever was coined in the Tower." Then, through a little moth-hole in the lining of the coat, I saw him lift her up, stroke her, and put her upon the back of one of the horses, where she stretched herself out, and went to sleep.

In this situation I did not dare to stir, I had too often seen how eager cats are to watch mice, to venture out of the pocket, whilst she was so near me, especially as I did not at all know the holes or cracks round the stable, and should, therefore, had she jumped down, been quite at a loss where to run. So I determined to continue where I was till either hunger forced me, or the absence of the cat gave a better opportunity of escaping. But scarce had I taken up this resolution when the coachman again entered, and suddenly taking the coat from the peg, put it on, and marched out with me in his pocket.

It is utterly impossible to describe my fear and consternation at this event, to jump out whilst in the stable exposed me to the jaws of the cat, and to attempt it when out of doors was but again subjecting myself to be frozen to death, for the snow continued still on the ground: yet to stay in his pocket was running the chance of suffering a still more dreadful death by the barbarous hands of man; and nothing did I expect, in case he should find me, but either to be tortured like *Softdown*, or given to be the sport of his favorite cat, a fate almost as much dreaded as the other. However it was soon put out of my power to determine, for whilst I was debating in my own mind what course I had better take, he mounted the coach-box, and drove away with me in his pocket, till he came to a large house, about a mile distant from this place; there he put down the company he had in the coach, and then drove into the yard. But he had not been there many moments before the coachman of the family he was come to, invited him into the kitchen to warm himself, drink a mug of ale, and eat a mouthful of cold meat. As soon as he entered, and had paid the proper compliments to the *Mrs. Betties* and *Mollies* at the place, he pulled off his great coat, and hung it across the back of his chair. I instantly seized the first opportunity, and whilst they were all busy assembling round the *luncheon* table, made my escape, and ran under a cupboard door close to the chimney, where I had an opportunity of seeing and hearing all that passed, part of which conversation I will relate to you.

"Well, Mr. *John*," said a footman, addressing himself to the man whose pocket I had just left, "How fare you? are you pretty hearty? You look well I am sure." "Aye, and so I am," replied he. "I never was better in all my life; I live comfortably, have a good master and mistress, eat and drink bravely, and what can a man wish for more? For my part I am quite contented, and if I do but continue to enjoy my health, I am sure I shall be very ungrateful not to be so." "That's true," said the other, "but the misfortune of it is, people never know when they are well off, but are apt to *fret* and *wish* and *wish* and *fret*, for something or other all their lives, and so never have any enjoyment. Now for my own part, I must needs confess, that I cannot help *wishing* I was a gentleman, and think I should be a deal happier if I was." "Pshaw!" replied *John*, "I don't like now to hear a man say so; it looks as if you are discontented with the state in which you are placed, and depend upon it, you are in the one that is fittest for you, or you would not have been put into it. And as for being *happier* if you were a gentleman, I don't know what to say to it. To be sure, to have a little more money in one's pocket, nobody can deny that it would be very *agreeable*; and to be at liberty to come in and go out when one pleased, to be sure would be very comfortable. But still, *Bob*, still you may assure yourself, that no state in *this* world is free from care, and if we were turned into *Lords*, we should find many causes for uneasiness. So here's you good health," said he, lifting the mug to his mouth, "wishing, my lad, you may be *contented, cheerful,* and *good humoured*; for without these three requisites, *content, cheerfulness,* and *good humour,* no one person upon earth, rich or poor, old or young, can ever feel comfortable or happy; and so here's to you, I say." "And here's the same good wishes to *you*," said a clean decent cook-woman servant, who took up the mug upon *John's* putting it down. "*Content, cheerfulness,* and *good humour,*" I think was the toast. Then wiping her mouth, as she began her speech, she added, "and an excellent one it is: I wish all folks would mind it, and endeavour to acquire three such good qualifications." "I am sure," rejoined another female servant, whose name I heard was *Sally*, "I wish so too: at least I wish Miss *Mary* would try to gain a little more of the *good-humour*; for I never came near such a cross *crab* in my life as it is. I declare I hate the sight of the girl, she is such a proud little *minx* she would not vouchsafe to speak to a poor servant for the world; as if she thought because we are *poorer*, we were therefore not of the same nature: her sisters, I think are worth *ten* of her, they always reply so civilly if a body speaks to them, and say, Yes, if you *please*, Mrs. *Sally*, or no *thank* you Mr. *Bob*; or I should be obliged to you if you would do so and so, Mrs. *Nelly*; and not plain *yes* or *no*, as she does; and well too if you can get even that from her; for sometimes I declare she will not deign to give one any answer at all." "Aye, that is a sure thing she won't," replied the maid servant who first drank, "it is a sad thing she should behave so; I can't think, for my part, where she learns it; I am sure neither her papa nor mamma set her the example of it, for they always speak as pretty and as kind as it is possible to do: and I have heard, with my own ears, my mistress tell her of it twenty and twenty times, but she *will* do so. I am sure it is a sad thing that she should, for she will always make people dislike her. I am sure, if young gentlemen and ladies did not know how it makes people love them to speak civilly and kind, they would take great care not to behave like Miss Mary. Do you know, the other day, when Mrs. Lime's maid brought little Miss Peggy to see my mistress, when she went away, she made a courtesy to Miss Mary, and said good morning to you Miss. And would you think it, the child stood like a stake, and never returned it so much as by a nod of the head, nor did she open her lips. I saw by her looks the maid took notice of it, and I am sure I have such a regard for the family, that I felt quite ashamed of her behaviour."

"Oh! she served me worse than that," resumed Sally, "for, would you believe it, the other day I begged her to be so kind as to let her mamma know I wanted to speak with her; and I did not choose to go into the room myself, because I was dirty, and there was company there; but for all I desired her *over* and *over* only just to step in (and she was at play *close* to the door) yet, could you suppose it possible, she was ill-natured enough to refuse me, and would not do it at last." "Well, if ever I heard the like of that!" exclaimed John, whose pocket I had been in, "I think that was being cross indeed, and if a child of mine was to behave in that surly manner, I would whip it to death almost. I abominate such unkind doings, let every one, I say, *do* as they like to be done *by*, and that is the only way to be happy, and the only way to *deserve* to be so; for if folks will not try to be kind, and oblige others, why should any body try to please them? And if Miss Mary was my girl, and chose to behave rude and cross to the servants, if I was her papa, I would order them to refuse doing any thing for her. I would soon humble her pride I warrant you, for nobody should make her *puddings*, or cut her bread, or do any thing for her till she learned to be *kind,* and *civil,* and *thankful* too, for all that was done for her. I have no notion, for my part, for a *child* to give herself such airs for nothing! and because her parents happen to have a little more money in their pockets, for that reason to think she may be *rude* to *poor* folks; but though servants are *poor*, still surely they are richer than *she* is; I should like to ask her how much she has got? and which way she came by it? A *child* I am sure is no richer than a *beggar*, for they have not a farthing that is not *given* them through mere bounty; whereas a servant who works for his living, has a *right* and *just claim* to his wages, and may truly call them his *own;* but a *child* has not one farthing that is not its parents. So here's my service to you, Miss," said he, (again lifting the ale-mug to his mouth) "and wishing her a speedy reformation of manners, I drink to her very good health."

John drank to the bottom of the mug, and then shaking the last drop into the ashes under the grate, he told the following story, as he sat swinging the mug by its handle across his two fore-fingers, which he had joined for that purpose.

"When my father was a young man he lived at one Mr. Speedgo's, as upper footman: they were vastly rich. Mr. Speedgo was a merchant, and by good luck he gathered gold as fast as his neighbours would pick up stones (as a body may say.) So they kept two or three carriages, there was a *coach,* and a *chariot,* and a *phæton,* and I can't tell what besides, and a *power* of servants you may well suppose to attend them all; and very well they lived, with plenty of victuals and drink. But though they wanted for nothing still they never much loved either their master or mistress, they used to give their orders in so *haughty* and *imperious* a manner; and if asked a civil question, answer so *shortly,* as if they thought their servants not worthy of their notice: so that, in short, no one loved them, nor their children either, for they brought them up just like themselves, to despise every one poorer than they were; and to speak as cross to their servants as if they had been so many adders they were afraid would *bite* them.

"I have heard my father say, that if Master Speedgo wanted his horse to be got ready, he would say, '*Saddle my horse!*' in such a displeasing manner as made it quite a burthen to do any thing for him. Or if the young ladies wanted a piece of bread and butter, or cake, they would say, '*Give me* a bit of cake;' or, if they added the word *pray* to it, they spoke in such a *grumpy* way, as plainly shewed they thought themselves a deal better than their servants; forgetting that an *honest* servant is just as worthy a member of society as his master, and whilst he behaves well, as much deserving of *civility* as any body. But to go on with my story. I have already told you Mr. Speedgo was very *rich* and very *proud*, nor would he on any account suffer any one to visit at his house whom he thought *below* him, as he called it; or at least, if he did, he always took care to behave to them in such a manner, as plainly to let them know he thought he shewed a *mighty favour* in conversing with them.

"Among the rest of the servants there was one Molly Mount, as good a hearted girl, my father says, as ever lived: she had never received much education, because her parents could not afford to give her any, and she learned to read after she was at Mr. Speedgo's, from one of the housemaids, who was kind enough to teach her a little; but you may suppose, from such sort of teaching, she was no very good scholar. However, she read well enough to be able to make out some chapters in the Bible; and an excellent use she made of them, carefully fulfilling every duty she there found recommended as necessary for a Christian to practise. She used often to say she was perfectly contented in her station, and only wished for more money that she might have it in her power to do more good. And sometimes, when she was dressing and attending the young ladies of the family, she would advise them to behave prettier than they did; telling them, 'That by kindness and civility they would be so far from *losing* respect, that, on the contrary, they would much gain it. For we cannot (she would very truly say) have any respect for those people who seem to forget their human nature, and behave as if they thought themselves superior to the rest of their fellow-creatures. Young ladies and gentlemen have no occasion to make themselves very *intimate* or *familiar* with their servants; but every body ought to speak *civilly* and *good-humouredly*, let it be to whom it may: and if I was a lady I should make it a point never to *look cross* or *speak gruffly* to the poor, for fear they should think I forgot I was of the same human nature as they were. By these kind of hints, which every now and then she would give to the misses, they were prodigiously offended, and complained of her *insolence*, as they called it, to their mamma, who very wrongly, instead of teaching them to behave better, joined with them in blaming Molly for her freedom, and, to shew her displeasure at her conduct, put on a still haughtier air, whenever she spoke to her, than she did to any other of the servants. Molly, however, continued to behave extremely well, and often very seriously lamented in the kitchen the wrong behaviour of the family. 'I don't mind it,' she would say, 'for my own part; I know that I do my duty; and their cross looks and proud behaviour can do me no real harm: but I cannot help grieving for their sakes;

it distresses me to think that people who ought to know better, should, by their ill conduct, make themselves so many enemies, when they could so easily gain friends—I am astonished how any body can act so foolishly.'

In this sensible manner she would frequently talk about the *sin* as well as the *folly* of pride. And one day, as she was talking to her fellow-servants, rather louder than in prudence she ought to have done, her two young ladies overheard her; and the next time she went to dress them, they enquired what it was she had been saying to the other maids. 'Indeed, ladies,' said she, 'I hope you will excuse my telling you. I think, if you give yourselves time to reflect a little, you will not insist upon knowing, as it is beneath such *rich ladies* as you are, to concern yourselves with what poor servants talk about.' This answer did not, however, satisfy them, and they positively commanded her to let them know. Molly was by far too good a woman to attempt to *deceive* any one; she therefore replied, 'If, ladies, you insist upon knowing what I said, I hope you will not take any thing amiss that I may tell you, thus *compelled* as I am by your *commands*. You must know then, Miss Betsy and Miss Rachael, that I was saying how sad a thing it was for people to be *proud* because they are rich; or to fancy, because they happen to have a little more money, that for that reason they are better than their servants, when in reality the whole that makes one person *better* than another is, having superior *virtues*, being *kinder* and more *good natured*, and readier to *assist* and *serve* their fellow-creatures; these are the qualifications, I was saying, that make people beloved, and not being possessed of money. Money may, indeed, procure servants to do their business for them, but it is not in the power of all the riches in the world to purchase the *love* and *esteem* of any one. What a sad thing then it is, when gentlefolks behave so as to make themselves *despised;* and that will ever be the case with all those who, like (excuse me, ladies, you insisted upon my telling you what I said) Miss Betsy, and Miss Rachael, and Master James, shew such contempt to all their inferiors. Nobody could wish children of their fortunes to make themselves too free, or play with their servants; but if they were little kings and queens, still they ought to speak *kind* and *civil* to every one. Indeed our King and Queen would scorn to behave like the children of this family, and if——' She was going on, but they stopped her, saying, 'If you say another word, we will push you out of the room this moment, you *rude, bold, insolent woman;* you ought to be ashamed of speaking so disrespectfully of your *betters;* but we will tell our mamma, that we will, and she won't suffer you to allow your tongue such liberties.' 'If,' replied Molly, 'I have offended you, I am sorry for it, and beg your pardon, ladies; I am sure I had no wish to do so; and you should remember that you both insisted upon my telling you what I had been saying.' 'So we did,' said they, 'but you had no *business* to say it *all;* and I promise you my mamma shall know it.'

"In this manner they went on for some time; but, to make short of my story, they represented the matter in such a manner to their mother, that she dismissed Molly from her service, with a strict charge never to visit the house again. 'For,' said Mrs. Speedgo, 'no servant who behaves as you have done, shall ever enter my doors again, or eat another mouthful in my house.' Molly had no desire so suddenly to quit her place; but as her conscience perfectly acquitted her of any wilful crime, after receiving her wages, respectfully wishing all the family their health, and taking a friendly leave of her fellow-servants, she left the house, and soon engaged herself as dairy-maid in a farmer's family, about three miles off; in which place she behaved so extremely well, and so much to the satisfaction of her master and mistress, that, after she had lived there a little more than two years, with their entire approbation, she was married to their eldest son, a sober, worthy young man, to whom his father gave a fortune not much less than three thousand pounds, with which he bought and stocked a very pretty farm in Somersetshire, where they lived as happy as virtue and affluence could make them. By industry and care they prospered beyond their utmost expectations, and, by their prudence and good behaviour, gained the esteem and love of all who knew them.

"To their servants (for they soon acquired riches enough to keep three or four, I mean household ones, besides the number that were employed in the farming business) they behaved with such *kindness* and *civility*, that had they even given less wages than their neighbours, they would never have been in want of any; every one being desirous of getting into a family where they were treated with such kindness and condescension.

"In this happy manner they continued to live for many years, bringing up a large family of children to imitate their virtues: but one great mortification they were obliged to submit to, which was that of putting their children very early to boarding-school, a circumstance which the want of education in Mrs. and indeed I may add Mr. Flail, rendered absolutely necessary.

"But I am afraid, Mrs. Sally and Mrs. Nelly, you will be tired, as I have but half told my story; but I will endeavour to make short work of it, though indeed it deserves to be noticed, for it will teach one a great deal, and convince one how little the world's riches are to be depended on.

"I have said, you know, that Mr. Speedgo was a merchant, and a very rich one too. It is unknown what vast sums of money he used to spend! When, would you think it, either through spending it too fast, or some losses he met with in trade, he broke all to nothing, and had not a farthing to pay his creditors. I forgot how many thousand pounds it was he owed; but it was a *vast great* many. Well! this you may be sure was a great mortification to them; they begged for mercy from their creditors; but as in their prosperity they had never shewn much mercy themselves to those they thought *beneath* them, so now they met with very little from others: the *poor* saying they *deserved* it for their *pride;* the *rich* condemning them for their *presumption,* in trying to *vie* with those of superior birth; and those who had been less successful in business, blaming them for their *extravagance,* which, they said, had justly brought on them their misfortunes.

In this distress, in vain it was they applied for assistance to those they had esteemed their *friends*; for as they never had been careful to form their connections with people of *real merit,* only seeking to be acquainted with those who were *rich* and *prosperous,* so now they could no longer return their civilities, they found none were ready to shew them any; but every one seemed anxious to keep from them as much as possible. Thus distressed, and finding no one willing to help them, the young squire, Master James, was obliged to go to sea: while Miss Betsy and Miss Rachael were even forced to try to get their living by service, a way of life they were both ill qualified to undertake, for they had always so accustomed themselves to be waited on and attended, that they scarcely knew how to help themselves, much less how to work for others. The consequence of which was, they gave so little satisfaction to their employers, that they staid but a little time in a place, and from so frequently changing, no family, who wished to be well settled, would admit them, as they

thought it impossible they could be good servants whom no one thought worthy of keeping.

"It is impossible to describe the many and great mortifications those two young ladies met with. They now frequently recollected the words of Molly Mount, and earnestly wished they had attended to them whilst it was in their power, as by so doing they would have secured to themselves *friends*. And they very forcibly found, that, although they were *poor* and servants, yet they were as sensible of *kind treatment* and *civility*, as if they had been richer.

"After they had been for some years changing from place to place, always obliged to put up with very low wages, upon account of their being so ill qualified for servants, it happened that Miss Betsy got into service at Watchet, a place about three miles distant from Mr. Flail's farm. Here she had a violent fit of illness, and not having been long enough in the family to engage their generosity to keep her, she was dismissed upon account of her ill health rendering her wholly incapable of doing her business for which she was hired. She then, with the very little money she had, procured a lodging in a miserable little dirty cottage; but through weakness being unable to work, she soon exhausted her whole stock, and was even obliged to quit this habitation, bad as it was, and for some days support herself wholly by begging from door to door, often meeting with very unkind language for so idle an employment; some people telling her to go to her parish, when, alas! her parish was many miles distant, and she, poor creature, had no means of getting there.

"At last she wandered, in this distressful situation, to the house of Mr. Flail, and walked into the farm-yard just at the time the cows were being milked. She, who for a long time had tasted nothing but bits of broken bread, and had no drink besides water she had scooped up in her hands, looked at the quantity of fresh milk with a most wishful eye: and, going to the women who were milking, she besought them in a moving manner to give her a draught, as she was almost ready to perish. 'For pity sake,' said she, 'have compassion upon a poor wretch, dying with *sickness, hunger,* and *thirst;* it is a long time since I have tasted a mouthful of wholesome victuals, my lips are now almost parched with thirst, and I am so faint for want, that I can scarcely stand; my sufferings are very great indeed, it would melt a heart of stone to hear the story of my woes. Oh! have pity upon a fellow-creature then, and give me one draught of that milk, which can never be missed out of so vast a quantity as you have there, and may you *never, never,* know what it is to suffer as I now do.' To this piteous request, she received for answer, the common one of 'Go about your business, we have nothing for you, so don't come here.' 'We should have enough to do indeed,' said one of the milkers, 'if we were to give every idle beggar who would like a draught of this delicious milk; but no, indeed, we shall not give you a drop; so go about your business, and don't come *plaguing us here.*' Mrs. Flail, who happened to be in the yard, with one of her children who was feeding the chickens, overheard enough of this to make her come forward, and enquire what was the matter. 'Nothing, ma'am,' replied the milk-maid, 'only I was sending away this nasty dirty creature, who was so bold as to come asking for milk indeed! But beggars grow so impudent now a-days there never was the like of it.' 'Oh *fie!* returned Mrs. Flail, shocked at her inhuman way of speaking, '*fie* upon you, to speak in so unkind a manner of a poor creature in distress.' Then turning to the beggar, she inquired what she wanted, in so mild a tone of voice, that it encouraged her to speak and tell her distress.

"Mrs. Flail listened with the greatest attention, and could not help being struck with her speech and appearance; for though she was clothed in rags (having parted with all her better cloaths to pay for lodging and food) still there was a *something* in her *language* and *manner* which discovered that she was no *common* beggar. Betsy had stood all the time with her eyes fixed upon the ground, scarcely once lifting them to look at the face of Mrs. Flail; and she was so changed herself by her troubles and sickness, that it was impossible for any one who had ever seen Miss Speedgo, to recollect her in her present miserable state. Mrs. Flail, however, wanted no farther inducement to relieve her than to hear she was in want. 'Every fellow-creature in distress,' she used to say, 'was a proper object of her bounty; and whilst she was blest with plenty she thought it her duty to relieve, as far as she prudently could, all whom she knew to be in need.' She therefore fetched a mug, and, filling it with milk herself, gave it to the poor woman to drink. 'Here,' said she, 'take this, good woman, and I hope it will refresh and be of service to you.' Betsy held out her hand for it, and, lifting her eyes up to look at Mrs. Flail, whilst she thanked her for her kindness, was greatly astonished to discover in her benefactress, the features of her old servant, Molly Mount. 'Bless me!' said she, with an air of confusion, 'What do I see? Who is it? Where am I? Madam, pardon my boldness, but pray *forgive* me, ma'am, but is not your name Mount?' 'It was,' replied Mrs. Flail, 'but I have been married for thirteen years to a Mr. Flail, and that is my name now. But, pray, where did you ever see me before? or how came you to know any thing of me?' Poor Betsy could return no answer, her *shame* at being seen by her servant that was, in her present condition, and the *consciousness* of having so ill-treated that *very* servant, to whose kindness she was now indebted; all together were too much for her in her weak state, and she fell senseless at Mrs. Flail's feet.

"This still added to Mrs. Flail's surprize, and she had her carried into the house and laid upon a bed, where she used every means to bring her to herself again: which, after a considerable time, succeeded; and she then (covered with *shame* and *remorse*) told her *who* she was, and how she came into that miserable condition. No words can describe the astonishment Mrs. Flail was in, at hearing the melancholy story of her sufferings: nor is it possible to tell with what generosity and kindness she strove to comfort her, telling her to compose herself, for she should no longer be in want of any thing. 'I have, thank Heaven,' said she, 'a most worthy good man for my husband, who will rejoice with me in

having it in his power to relieve a suffering fellow-creature. Do not, therefore, any longer distress yourself upon what passed between us formerly. I had, for my part, forgotten it, if you had not now told it me; but, however I might then take the liberty to censure you for too much haughtiness, I am sure I have no occasion to do so now. Think no more, therefore, I beseech you, upon those times which are now past; but be comforted, and make yourself as happy as in my humble plain manner of living you can possibly do.'

"She then furnished her with some of her own clothes, till she could procure her new ones, and sent immediately for a physician from the next town; by following of whose prescription, together with good nursing, and plenty of all necessaries, she soon recovered her health; but she was too deeply affected with the thoughts of her former misconduct ever to feel happy in her situation, though Mrs. Flail used every method in her power to render her as comfortable as possible. Nor did she confine her goodness only to this one daughter, but sent also for her sister and mother (her father being dead), and fitted up a neat little house for them near their own. But as the Flails could not afford wholly to maintain them for nothing, they entrusted the poultry to their care; which enabled them to do with one servant less; and by that means they could, without any great expence, afford to give them sufficient to make their lives comfortable, that is, as far as their own *reflections* would let them: for the last words Mrs. Speedgo said to Molly, when she parted from her, dwelt continually upon her mind, and filled her with shame and remorse.

'I told her,' said she, 'that she should never again come into my doors, or eat another mouthful in my house; and now it is *her* bounty alone which keeps us all from perishing. Oh! how unworthy are we of such goodness! True, indeed, was what she told you, that *kindness* and *virtue* were far more valuable than *riches*. Goodness and kindness no time or change can take from us; but *riches* soon fly as it were away, and then what are we the better for having been once possessed of them?'

Here Mr. John stopped, and jumping hastily up, and turning round to Mrs. Sally, Mrs. Nelly, and Mr. Bob, exclaimed, rubbing his hands— "There ladies, I have finished my story; and, let me tell you, so long preaching has made my throat dry, so another mug of ale, if you please, Master Bobby (tapping him at the same time upon the shoulder), another mug of ale, my boy; for *faith*, talking at the rate I have done, is enough to wear a man's lungs out, and, in truth, I have need of something to *hearten* me after such fatigue."

"Well, I am sure," replied Mrs. Sally and Mrs. Nelly, in the same breath, "we are greatly obliged to you for your history; and I am sure it deserves to be framed and glazed, and it ought to be hung up in the hall of every family, that all people may see the sad effects of pride, and how little cause people have, because they are *rich,* to despise those who are *poor;* since it frequently happens, that those who this year are like little kings, may the next be beggars; and then they will repent, when it is too late, of all their *pride* and unkindness they shewed to those beneath them."

Here the conversation was put a stop to by the bell ringing, and John being ordered to drive to the door. I, who during the whole of the history had been feasting upon a mince-pie, now thought it safer to conceal myself in a little hole in the wainscot of the closet, where, finding myself very safe, I did not awake till midnight. After the family were all retired to rest, I peeped out of the hole, and there saw just such another frightful trap as that which was the prelude to poor Softdown's sufferings. Startled at the sight, I retreated back as expeditiously as possible, nor ever stopped till I found my way into a bed-chamber, where lay two little girls fast asleep.

I looked about for some time, peeping into every hole and corner before I could find any thing to eat, there being not so much as a candle in the room with them. At last I crept into a little leathern trunk, which stood on a table, not shut down quite close: here I instantly smelt something good; but was obliged to gnaw through a great deal of linen to get at it; it was wrapped up in a *lap-bag,* amongst a vast quantity of work.—However, I made my way through half a hundred folds, and at last was amply repaid, by finding out a nice piece of plum-cake, and the pips of an apple, which I could easily get at, one half of it having been eat away.—Whilst I was thus engaged I heard a cat mew, and not knowing how near she might be, I endeavoured to jump out; but in the hurry I somehow or other entangled myself in the muslin, and pulled that, trunk and all, down with me: for the trunk stood half off the table, so that the least touch in the world overset it, otherwise my weight could never have tumbled it down.

The noise of the fall, however, waked the children, and I heard one say to the other,— "Bless me! Mary, what is that noise?— What *can* it be! I am almost frightened out of my wits; do, pray, sister, hug me close!" "Pough!" replied the other, "never mind it! What in the world need you be frightened at? What do you suppose will hurt you? It sounded as if something fell down; but as it has not fallen upon us, and I do not hear any body stirring, or speaking as if they were hurt, what need we care about it? So pray, Nancy, let us go to sleep again; for as yet I have not had half sufficient, I am sure; I hope morning is not coming yet, for I am not at all ready to get up." "I am *sure,*" answered the other, "I *wish* it was morning, and day-light now, for I should like to get up vastly, I do not like to lay here in the dark any longer; I have a great mind to ring the bell, and then mamma or somebody will come to us with a candle." "And what in the world," rejoined Mary, "will be the use of that? Do you want a candle to light you to look for the wounds the *noise* has given you; or what can you wish to disturb my mamma for? Come, let me cuddle you, and do go to sleep, child, for I cannot think what occasion there is for us to keep awake because we heard a noise; I never knew that *noise* had *teeth* or *claws* to hurt one with; and I am sure this has not hurt me; and so, whether you chuse to lie awake or not, I will go to sleep, and so good-bye to you, and pray do not disturb me any more, for I *cannot* talk any longer." "But, Mary," again replied the other, "*pray* do not go to sleep yet, I want to speak to you." "Well, what do you want to say?" inquired Mary. "Why, pray have you not very often," said Nancy, "heard of *thieves* breaking into people's houses and robbing them; and I am sadly afraid that noise was some rogues coming in; so pray, Mary, do not go to sleep, I am in such a fright and tremble you cannot think. *Speak,* Mary, Have not you, I say, heard of thieves?" "Yes," replied Mary, in a very sleepy voice, "a great many times." "Well, then, *pray* sister, do not go to sleep," said Nancy, in a peevish accent, "suppose, I say, that noise I heard should be thieves, what should we do? What will become of us? O! what shall we do?"—"Why, go to sleep, I tell you," said Mary, "as fast as you can! at least, do pray let me, for I cannot say I am in the smallest fear about *house-breakers* or *house-makers* either; and of all the robberies I ever heard of in all my life, I never heard of *thieves* stealing little *girls;* so do, there's a dear girl, go to sleep again, and do not so foolishly frighten yourself out of your wits for nothing." "Well," replied Nancy, "I will not keep you awake any longer; but I am sure *I* shall not be able to get another *wink* of sleep all night."

Here the conversation ended, and I could not help thinking how foolish it was for people to permit themselves to be terrified for nothing. Here is a little girl, now, thought I, in a nice clean room, and covered up warm in bed, with pretty green curtains drawn round her, to keep the wind from her head, and the light in the morning from her eyes; and yet she is distressing herself, and making herself really uncomfortable, and unhappy, only because *I*, a poor, little, harmless *mouse,* with scarcely strength sufficient to gnaw a nutshell, happened to jump from the table, and throw down, perhaps, her own box—Oh! what a pity it is that people should so destroy their own comfort! How sweetly might this child have passed the night, if she had but, like her sister, wisely reflected that a *noise* could not possibly hurt them; and that, had any of the family occasioned it, by falling down, or running against any thing in the dark which hurt them, most likely they would have heard some more stirring about.

And upon this subject the Author cannot help, in *human* form (as well as in that of a *mouse*), observing how extremely ridiculous it is for people to suffer themselves to be terrified upon every trifling occasion that happens; as if they had no more resolution than a *mouse* itself, which is liable to be destroyed every meal it makes. And, surely, nothing can be more absurd than for children to be afraid of *thieves* and *house-breakers*; since, as little Mary said, they never want to seek after *children.* Money is all they want; and as children have very seldom much of that in their possession, they may assure themselves they are perfectly safe, and have therefore no occasion to alarm themselves if they hear a noise, without being able to make out what it is; unless, indeed, like the child I have just been writing about, they would be so *silly* as to be frightened at a little *mouse*; for most commonly the noises we hear, if we lay awake in the night, are caused by mice running about and playing behind the wainscot; and what reasonable person would suffer themselves to be alarmed by such little creatures as those? But it is time I should return to the history of my little *make-believe* companion, who went on, saying—

The conversation I have been relating I overheard as I lay concealed in a *shoe* that stood close by the bedside, and into which I ran the moment I jumped off the table, and where I kept snug till the next morning; when, just as the clock was striking eight, the same Mrs. Nelly, whom I saw the day before in the kitchen, entered the apartment, and accosted the young ladies, saying, "Good morning to you, ladies, do you know that it is time to get up?" "Then, pray, Nelly, lace my stays, will you?" said Miss Nancy." "But lace *mine* first, and give me my other shoes; for those I wore yesterday *must* be brushed, because I stepped in the dirt, and so when you go down you *must* remember, and take and brush them, and then *let* me have them again," said Mary; "but come and dress me *now*."

Well, thought I, this is a rude way of speaking, indeed, something like Miss Nancy Artless, at the house where my poor dear Softdown was so cruelly massacred; I am sure I hope I shall not meet with the like fate here, and I wish I was safe out of this shoe; for, perhaps, presently it will be wanted to be put on Mary's foot: and I am sure I must not expect to meet any mercy from a child who shows so bad a disposition as to speak to a servant in so uncivil a manner, for no *good-natured* person would do that."

With these kind of reflections I was amusing myself for some little time, when, all on a sudden, they were put an end to, by my finding the shoe in which I was concealed, hastily taken up; and before I had time to recollect what I had best do, I was almost killed by some violent blows I received, which well nigh broke every bone in my skin. I crept quite up to the toe of the shoe, so that I was not at all seen, and the maid, when she took up the shoes, held one in one hand, and the other in the other, by their heels, and then slapped them hard together, to beat out of some of the dust which was in them. This she repeated three or four times, till I was quite stunned; and how or which way I tumbled or got out, I know not; but when I came to myself, I was close up behind the foot of a table, in a large apartment, where were several children, and a gentleman and a lady, all conversing together with the greatest good humour and harmony.

The first words I heard distinctly enough to remember, were those of a little boy, about five years old, who, with eagerness exclaimed— "*I* forget you! no that *I* never shall. If I was to go a *hundred thousand* miles off, I am sure I shall never forget you. What! do you think I should ever, as *long* as I *live*, if it is a *million* of years, forget my own dear papa and mamma? No; that I should not, I am *very, very sure* I never should." "Well, but Tom," interrupted the gentleman, "if in a *million* of years you should not forget *us*, I dare say, in less than two *months* you will forget our *advice*, and before you have been at school half that time, you will get to squabbling with and tricking the other boys, just as they do with one another; and instead of playing at all times with the strictest openness and honour, you will, I sadly fear, learn to *cheat*, and *deceive*, and pay no attention to what your mother and I have been telling you." "No! that I am *sure* I sha'n't!" replied the boy. "What! do you think I shall be so *wicked* as to turn a *thief*, and *cheat* people?" "I dare say, my dear," resumed the father, "you will not do what we call *thieving*; but as I know there are many naughty boys in all schools, I am afraid they will teach you to commit *dishonourable* actions, and to tell you there is no *harm* in them, and that they are signs of *cleverness* and *spirit*, and qualifications very necessary for every boy to possess." "Aye, that's sure enough," said the boy, who appeared about ten years old, "for they almost all declare, that if a boy is not *sharp* and *cunning*, he might almost as well be out of the world as in it. But, as you say, papa, I *hate* such behaviour, I am sure there is one of our boys, who is so wonderfully *clever* and *acute*, as they call him, that I detest ever having any thing to do with him; for unless one watches him as a cat would watch a mouse, he is sure to cheat or play one some trick or other." "What sort of tricks do you mean?" inquired the little boy. "Why, I will tell you," replied the other. "You know nothing of the games we have at school, so if I was to tell you how he plays at them, you would not understand what I meant. But you know what walking about blindfold is, don't you? Well! one day, about a dozen boys agreed to have a blind race, and the boy who got nearest the goal, which was a stick driven in the ground with a shilling upon the top of it, was to win the shilling, provided he did it fairly without seeing." "I suppose," interrupted Tom, "you mean the boy who got to the stick first." "No, I do not," replied his brother, "I *mean* what I *say*, the boy who got *nearest* it, no matter whether he came first or last; the fun was to see them try to keep in a straight path, with their eyes tied up, whilst they wander quite in the wrong, and not to try who could run *fastest*. Well! when they were all blinded, and twisted round three or four times before they were suffered to set off, they directed their steps the way they thought would directly conduct them to the goal; and some of them had almost reached it, when Sharply (the boy I mentioned) who had placed a shilling upon the stick, for they drew lots who should do that, and he who furnished the money was to stand by it, to observe who won it by coming nearest.—Well, Sharply, I say, just as they came close to it, moved away *softly* to another place, above three yards distant from any of them! (for I should have told you, that if none of them got within three yards, the shilling was to remain his, and they were each to give him a penny.) So then he untied their eyes, and insisted upon it they had all of them lost. But two or three of us happened to be by, and so we said he had cheated them, and ought not to keep the money, as it had fairly been won by Smyth. But he would not give it up, so it made a quarrel between him and Smyth, and at last they fought, and Mr. Chiron confined them both in the school all the rest of the afternoon, and when he heard what the quarrel was about, he took the shilling from Sharply, and called him a *mean-spirited cheat;* but he would not let Smyth have it, because he said he deserved to lose it for *fighting* about such a trifle, and so it was put into the forfeit-money.

"But pray do not you think Sharply behaved extremely wrong?" "Shamefully so, indeed," said the gentleman. "I never could have any opinion of a boy who could act so dishonour-ably," said the lady, "let his *cleverness* be what it would." "Pray, Frank, tell me some more," said the little boy. "*More!*" replied Frank, "I could tell you an hundred such kind of things. One time, as Peter Light was walking up the yard, with some damsens in his hat, Sharply ran by, and as he passed, knocked his hat out of his hand, for the sake of scram-bling for as many as he could get himself. And sometimes, after the pie-woman has been there, he gets such heaps of tarts you cannot think, by his different tricks: perhaps he will buy a currant tart himself; then he would go about, calling out, "Who'll change a cheese-cake for a currant tart?" and now-and-then he will add, "and half a bun into the bargain!" Then two or three of the boys call out, "I will, I will!" and when they go to hold out their cheesecakes to him, he snatches them out of their hands before they are aware, and runs away in an instant; and whilst they stand for a moment in astonishment, he gets so much ahead of them that he eats them up before they can again overtake him. At other times, when he sees a boy beginning to eat his cake, he will come and talk carelessly to him for a few moments, and then all of a sudden call out, "Look! look! look!—there!" pointing his finger as if to shew him something wonderful; and when the other, without suspecting any mischief, turns his head to see what has so surprised him, away he snatches the cake, and runs off with it, cramming it into his mouth in a moment.

"And when he plays at handy, dandy, Jack-a-dandy, which will you have, upper hand or lower? if you happen to guess right, he slips whatever you are playing with into his other hand; and that you know is not playing fair; and so many of the boys tell him; but he does not mind any of us. And as he is clever at his learning, and always does his exercise quite right, Mr. Chiron (who indeed does not know of his tricks) is very fond of him, and is for ever saying what a clever fellow he is, and proposing him as an example to the rest of the boys; and I do believe many of them imitate his deceitful, cheating tricks, only for the sake of being thought like him."

"Aye! it is a sad thing," interrupted the gentleman, "that people who are blessed with sense and abilities to behave well, should so misuse them as to set a bad, instead of a good example to others, and by that means draw many into sin, who otherwise, perhaps, might never have acted wrong. Was this Sharply, you have been speaking of, a dunce and block-head at his book, he would never gain the commendations that Mr. Chiron now bestows upon him; and, consequently, no boy would wish to be thought like him; his bad example, therefore, would not be of half the importance it now is.

"Only think, then, my dear children, how extremely wicked it is, for those who are blessed with understandings capable of acting as they should do, and making people admire them, at the same time to be guilty of such real and great sin. For, however children at play may like to trick and deceive each other, and call it only *play* or *fun*, still, let me tell you, they are much mistaken if they flatter themselves there is no *harm* in it. It is a very *wrong* way of behaviour; it is *mean*, it is *dishonourable*, and it is *wicked;* and the boy or girl who would ever permit themselves to act in so unjustifiable a manner, however they may excel in their *learning*, or *exterior* accomplishments, can never be deserving of *esteem*, *confidence*, or *regard*. What *esteem* or respect could I ever entertain of a person's sense or learning, who made no better use of it than to practise wickedness with more *dexterity* and *grace* than he otherwise would be enabled to do? Or, what *confidence* could I ever place in the person who, I knew, only wanted a convenient opportunity to *defraud, trick*, and *deceive* me? Or, what regard and love could I possibly entertain for such a one, who, unless I kept a constant watch over, as I must over a wild beast, would, like a wild beast, be sure to do me some injury!—Would it be possible, I say, to love such a character, whatever shining abilities or depth of learning he might possess? Ask your own hearts, my dears, whether you think you could?"

To this they all answered at once, "No, that I could not," and "I am sure I could not." "Well, then," resumed the father, "only think how odious that conduct must be, which robs us of the *esteem, confidence*, and *love* of our fellow-creatures; and that too, notwithstanding we may at the same time be very *clever*, and have a great deal of *sense* and *learning*. But, for my part, I confess I know not the least advantage of our understanding or our learning, unless we make a proper use of them. *Knowing a great deal*, and having *read a great many books*, will be of no service to us, unless we are careful to make a proper *use* of that knowledge, and to improve by what we read, otherwise the time we so bestow is but lost, and we might as well spend the whole of our lives in idleness.

"Always remember, therefore, my loves, that the whole end of our taking the trouble to instruct you, or putting ourselves to the expence of sending you to school, or your attending to what is taught you, is, that you may grow better men and women than you otherwise would be; and unless, therefore, you do improve, we might as well spare ourselves the pains and expence, and you need not take the trouble of learning; since, if you will act wickedly, all our labour is but thrown away to no manner of purpose.

"Mr. and Mrs. Sharply, how I pity them! What sorrow must they endure, to behold their son acting in the manner you have described; for nothing can give so much concern to a fond parent's heart, as to see their children, for whom they have taken so much pains, turn out naughty; and to *deceive* and *cheat!* What can be worse than that? I hope, my dear children, you will never, any of you, give us that dreadful misery. I hope, my dear Tom, I hope you will never learn any of those detestable ways your brother has been telling you of. And if it was not that you will often be obliged to see such things when you mix with other children, I should be sorry you should even hear of such bad actions, as I could wish you to pass through life without so much as knowing such wickedness ever existed; but that is impossible. There are so many naughty people in the world, that you will often be obliged to see and hear of crimes which I hope you will shudder to think of committing yourselves; and being warned of them beforehand, I hope it will put you more upon your guard, not to be tempted, upon any consideration, to give the least encouragement to them, much less to practise them yourselves.

"Perhaps, Tom, if your brother had not, by telling us of Sharply's tricks, given me an opportunity of warning you how extremely *wrong* and *wicked* they are, you might when you were at school, have thought them very *clever,* and marks of *genius;* and therefore, like others of the boys, have tried to imitate them, and by that means have become as *wicked, mean,* and *dishonourable* yourself. And only think how it would have grieved your mamma and me, to find the next holidays, our dear little Tom, instead of being that *honest, open, generous-hearted* boy he now is, changed into a *deceiver,* a *cheat,* a *liar,* one whom we could place no trust or confidence in; for, depend upon it, the person who will, when at *play,* behave unfair, would not scruple to do so in every other action of his life. And the boy who will deceive for the sake of a marble, or the girl who would act ungenerously, for the sake of a doll's cap or a pin, will, when grown up, be ready to *cheat* and *over-reach* in their *trades,* or any affairs they may have to transact. And you may assure yourselves that numbers of people who are every year hanged, began at *first* to be wicked by practising those little *dishonourable* mean actions, which so many children are too apt to do at play, without thinking of their evil consequences.

"I think, my dear," said he, turning to his wife, "I have heard you mention a person who you were acquainted with when a girl, who at last was hanged for stealing, I think, was not she?" "No," replied the lady, "she was not *hanged,* she was transported for one-and-twenty years."— "Pray, madam, *how transported?* what is that?" inquired one of the children. "People, my dear," resumed the lady, "are transported when they have committed crimes, which, according to the laws of our land, are not thought quite wicked enough to be hanged for; but still too bad to suffer them to continue amongst other people. So, instead of hanging them, the judge orders that they shall be sent on board a ship, built on purpose to hold naughty people, and carried away from all their friends, a great many miles distant, commonly to America, where they are sold as slaves, to work very hard for as many years as they are transported for. And the person your papa mentioned was sold for twenty-one years; but she died before that time was out, as most of them do: they are generally used very cruelly, and work very hard; and besides, the heat of the climate seldom agrees with any body who has been used to live in England, and so they generally die before their time is expired, and never have an opportunity of seeing their friends any more, after they are once sent away. How should any of you, my dears, like to be sent away from your papa and me, and your brothers and sisters, and uncles and aunts, and all your friends, and *never, never* see us any more; and only keep company with naughty, cross, wicked people, and labour very hard, and suffer a great deal of sickness, and such a number of different hardships, you cannot imagine? Only think how shocking it must be! How should you like it?" "Oh! not at all, not at all," was echoed from every one in the room.

"But such," rejoined their mother, "is the punishment naughty people have; and such was the punishment the person your papa spoke of had; who, when she was young, no more expected to come to such an end than any of you do. I was very well acquainted with her, and often used to play with her, and she (like the boy Frank has been talking of) used to think it a mark of *cleverness* to be able to deceive; and for the sake of winning the game she was engaged in, would not scruple committing any little unfair action, which would give her the advantage.

"I remember one time, at such a trifling game as *pushpin,* she gave me a very bad opinion of her; for I observed, instead of pushing the pin as she ought to do, she would try to lift it up with her finger a little, to make it cross over the other.

"And when we were all at cards, she would peep, to find out the pictured ones, that she might have them in her own hand.

"And when we played at any game which had forfeits, she would try, by different little artifices, to steal back her own before the time of *crying them* came; or, if she was the person who was to *cry them,* as you call it, she would endeavour to see whose came next, that she might order the penalty accordingly.

"Or if we were playing at *hide and seek,* she would put what we had to hide either in her own pocket, or throw it into the fire, so that it would be impossible to find it; and then, after making her companions hunt for it for an hour, till their patience was quite tired, and they *gave out;* she would burst out in a loud laugh! and say she only did it for *fun.* But, for my part, I never could see any joke in such kind of things: the *meanness,* the *baseness,* the *dishonour,* which attended it always, in my opinion, took off all degree of *cleverness,* or *pleasure* from such actions.

"There was another of her *sly* tricks which I forgot to mention, and that was, if at tea, or any other time, she got first to the plate of cake or bread, she would place the piece she liked best where she thought it would come to her turn to have it: or if at breakfast she saw her sisters' bason have the under crust in it, and they happened not to be by, or to see her, she would take it out, and put her own, which she happened not to like so well, in the stead.

"Only think, my dears, what frightful, sly, naughty tricks to be guilty of! And from practising these, which she said there was no *harm* in, and she only did them in *play,* and for a *bit of fun,* at last she came, by degrees, to be guilty of greater. She two or three different times, when she was not seen, stole things out of shops; and one day, when she was upon a visit, and thought she could do it *cleverly,* without being discovered, put a couple of table-spoons into her pocket. The footman who was waiting happened to see her; but fearing to give offence, he took no notice of it till after she was gone home, when he told his master, who, justly provoked at being so ill-treated, by a person to whom he had

shewn every civility, went after her, called in her own two maids, and his footman, as witnesses, and then insisted upon examining her pockets, where he indeed found his own two
spoons. He then sent for proper officers to secure her, had her taken into custody, and for
that offence it was that she was transported.

"Thus, my dear children, you see the shocking consequence of ever suffering such vile
habits to grow upon us; and I hope the example of this unhappy woman (which I assure
you is a *true* story) will be sufficient to warn you for ever, for a single time, being guilty of
so detestable a crime, lest you should, like her, by degrees come to experience her fatal
punishment."

Just as the lady said these words a bell rang, and all getting up together, they went out
of the room, the young one calling out, "To dinner! to dinner! to dinner! here we all go
to dinner!"

And I will seek for one too, said I to myself, (creeping out as soon as I found I was alone)
for I feel very faint and hungry. I looked and looked about a long while, for I could move
but slow, on account of the bruises I had received in the shoe. At last under the table,
round which the family had been sitting, I found a pincushion, which, being stuffed with
bran, afforded me enough to satisfy my hunger, but was excessively dry and unsavoury; yet,
bad as it was, I was obliged to be content at that time with it; and had nearly done eating
when the door opened, and in ran two or three of the children. Frightened out of my
senses almost, I had just time to escape down a little hole in the floor, made by one of the
knots in the wood slipping out, and there I heard one of the girls exclaim:

"O dear! who now has cut my pincushion? it was you did it, Tom." "No, indeed I did
not," replied he. "Then it was *you*, Mary." "No, I know nothing of it," answered she.
"Then it was *you*, Hetty." "That I am *sure* it was not," said she; "I am *sure*, I am *certain*
it was not me; I am *positive* it was not." "Ah!" replied the other, "I dare say it was." "Yes,
I think it is most *likely*," said Mary. "And so do I too," said Tom. "And pray *why* do you
all think so?" inquired Hetty, in an angry tone. "Because," said the owner of the pincushion, "you are the only one who ever tells fibs; you told a story, you know, about the
fruit; you told a story too about the currant jelly; and about putting your fingers in the
butter, at breakfast; and therefore there is a very great reason *why* we should suspect you
more than any body else." "But I am *sure*," said she, bursting into tears, "I am *very* sure
I have not meddled with it." "I do not at all know that," replied the other, "and I do
think it was you; for I am certain if any one else had done it they would not deny it; and
it could not come into this condition by itself, *somebody* must have done it: and I dare
say it was you; so say no more about it."

Here the dispute was interrupted by somebody calling them out of the room; and I
could not help making some reflections on what had passed. How dreadful a crime,
thought I, is lying and falsity; to what sad mortifications does it subject the person who is
ever wicked enough to commit it; and how does it expose them to the contempt of every
one, and make them to be suspected of faults they are even perfectly free from. Little
Hetty now is innocent, with respect to the pincushion with which her sister charges her,
as any of the others; yet, because she has before forfeited her *honour*, she can gain no
credit: no one believes what she says, she is thought to be guilty of the double fault of
spoiling the pincushion, and what is still worse, of lying to conceal it; whilst the other
children are at once believed, and their words depended upon.

Surely, surely, thought I, if people would but reflect upon the *contempt*, the *shame*, and the *difficulties* which lies expose them to, they would never be guilty of so terrible a vice, which subjects them to the scorn of all they converse with, and renders them at all times suspected, even though they *should*, as in the case of Hetty, really speak the truth. Such were my reflections upon *falsehood*, nor could I help altogether blaming the owner of the pincushion for her hasty judgment relating to it. *Somebody*, she was certain, *must* have done it; it was impossible it could come so by itself. That, to be sure, was very true; but then she never recollected that it *was possible* a little Mouse might put it in that condition. Ah! thought I to myself, what pity is it, that human creatures, who are blest with understanding and faculties so superior to any species, should not make better use of them; and learn, from daily experience, to grow wiser and better for the future. This one instance of the pincushion, may teach (and surely people engaged in life must hourly find more) how dangerous it is to draw hasty conclusions, and to condemn people upon suspicion, as also the many, great, and bad consequences of *lying*.

Scarcely had I finished these soliloquies when a great knock at the house door made me give such a start that I fell off the joist on which I was standing, and then ran straight forwards till I came out at a little hole I found in the bricks above the parlour window: from that I descended into the road, and went on unmolested till I reached a malt-house, about whose various apartments, never staying long in the same, I continued to live; till one night, all on a sudden, I was alarmed by fire, which obliged me to retreat with the greatest expedition.

I passed numberless rats and mice in my way, who, like myself, were driven forth by the flames; but, alas! among them I found not my brother. Despairing, therefore, of ever seeing him again, I determined, if possible, to find my way back to you, who before had shown me such kindness. Numberless were the fatigues and difficulties I had to encounter in my journey here; one while in danger from hungry cats, at another almost perished with cold and want of food.

But it is needless to enumerate every particular; I should but tire your patience was I to attempt it: so I will hasten to a conclusion of my history, only telling you how you came to find me in that melancholy condition from which your mercy has now raised me.

I came into your house one evening concealed in the middle of a floor-cloth, which the maid had rolled up and set at the outside of the back door, whilst she swept the passage, and neglected to take it in again till the evening. In that I hid myself, and upon her laying it down, ran with all speed down the cellar-stairs, where I continued till the family were all gone to bed. Then I returned back, and came into your closet, where the scent of some figs tempted me to get into the jar in which you found me. I concealed myself among them, and after feasting most deliciously, fell asleep, from which I was awakened by hearing a voice say, "Who has left the cover off the fig-jar?" and at the same time I was involved in darkness by having it put on. In vain I endeavoured to remove it, the figs were so low, that when I stood on them I could but just touch it with my lips, and the jar being stone I could not possibly fasten my nails to hang by the side.

In this dismal situation therefore I was constrained to stay, my apprehensions each day encreasing as my food diminished, till at last, after feeding very sparingly for some days, it was quite exhausted: and I had endured the inexpressible tortures of hunger for three days and three nights, when you happily released me, and by your compassion restored me once more to life and liberty. Condescend, therefore, to preserve that life you have so lengthened, and take me under your protection.

"That most gladly," interrupted I, "I will do: you will live in this large green-flowered tin canister, and run in and out when you please, and I will keep you constantly supplied with food. But I must now shut you in, for the cat has this moment entered the room."

And now I cannot take leave of all my little readers, without once more begging them, for their own sakes, to endeavour to follow all the good advice the *Mouse* has been giving them: and likewise warning them to shun all those vices and follies, the practice of which renders children so *contemptible* and *wicked*.

8

Fabulous Histories, or, The History of the Robins

By SARAH KIRBY TRIMMER

"Mifs Harriet with great delight called
her brother to see two robin redbreasts." p. 4.

Frontisp.

FABULOUS HISTORIES,

BY MRS. TRIMMER;

OR, THE

HISTORY OF THE ROBINS.

DESIGNED FOR THE

INSTRUCTION OF CHILDREN,

RESPECTING

THEIR TREATMENT OF ANIMALS.

ILLUSTRATED WITH TWELVE PLATES.

LONDON:

PRINTED FOR J. F. DOVE, PICCADILLY;
OPPOSITE BURLINGTON HOUSE.
1833.

SARAH KIRBY TRIMMER *(1741–1810), the mother of twelve, somehow found time to write* Fabulous Histories *(1786),* An Easy Introduction to the Knowledge of Nature *(1780), and* Sacred History selected from the Scriptures *(6 vols., 1782–1786). She also founded the* Family Magazine *(1788–1789) for cottagers and servants and* The Guardian of Education *(1802–1806), in which she reviewed many juvenile books. Though she found "Cinderella" and "Fortunatus" "full of romantic nonsense," she showed sound judgment in catching defects even in books she liked, such as Barbauld's* Lessons for Children. *She justly labelled the story of the boy eaten by bears "too terrific," and refused to go as far as Kendall and others in the adulation of animals. Her love for the early Newbery books probably aided her own fiction. She took the names of Pecksy and Flapsy from two rooks in* The Valentine's Gift *(John Newbery, 1765), which she preferred to Kendall's* Keeper's Travels.

The Lady's Monthly Museum *(November 1798) praised Trimmer because "in the fictitious fabrications of fancy, she has very judiciously been sparing."* Fabulous Histories *might seem ordinary today, but Robert Southey called it "the prettiest fiction that ever was composed for children." Inspiring many animal tales, it endured in print up until the time of World War I.*

Fabulous Histories *is reprinted from an 1833 London edition.*

ADVERTISEMENT

IT CERTAINLY comes within the compass of *Christian Benevolence,* to shew compassion to the *Animal Creation;* and a good mind naturally inclines to do so. But as through an erroneous education, or bad example, many children contract habits of *tormenting* inferior creatures, before they are conscious of giving them pain; or fall into the contrary fault of *immoderate tenderness* to them; it is hoped, that an attempt to point out the line of conduct, which ought to regulate the actions of *human* beings, towards those, over whom the SUPREME GOVERNOR has given them dominion, will not be thought a useless under taking: and that the mode of conveying instruction on this subject, which the Author of the following sheets has adopted, will engage the attention of young minds, and prove instrumental to the happiness of many an innocent animal.

INTRODUCTION

MANY YOUNG Readers, doubtless, remember to have met with a Book, entitled, "AN EASY INTRODUCTION TO THE KNOWLEDGE OF NATURE," which gives an account of a little boy, named Henry, and his sister Charlotte, who were indulged by their Mamma, with walking in the fields and gardens, where she taught them to take particular notice of every object that presented itself to their view. The consequence of this was, that they contracted a great fondness for Animals; and used often to express a wish, that their Birds, Cats, Dogs, &c. could *talk,* that they might hold conversations with them. Their Mamma, therefore, to amuse them, composed the following Fabulous Histories; in which the sentiments and affections of a good Father and Mother, and a Family of Children, are *supposed* to be possessed by a *Nest of Red-breasts;* and others of the feathered race, are, by the force of imagination, endued with the same faculties: but, before Henry and Charlotte began to read these Histories, they were taught to consider them, not as containing the real conversations of Birds (for that it is impossible we should ever understand), but as a series of FABLES, intended to convey a moral instruction applicable to themselves, at the same time that they excite compassion and tenderness for those interesting and delightful creatures, on which such wanton cruelties are frequently inflicted, and recommend *universal Benevolence.*

Having given this account of the origin of the following little work, the Author will no longer detain her young Readers from the perusal of it, as she flatters herself, they will find ample instruction respecting the proper treatment of Animals, in the course of her Fabulous Histories, which now invite their attention.

CHAPTER I

IN A HOLE, which time had made in a wall covered with ivy, a pair of REDBREASTS built their nest. No place could have been better chosen for the purpose; it was sheltered from the rain, skreened from the wind, and in an orchard belonging to a gentleman, who had strictly charged his domestics not to destroy the labours of those little songsters, who chose his ground as an asylum.

In this happy retreat, which no idle school-boy dared to enter, the Hen Redbreast laid four eggs, and then took her seat upon them; resolving, that nothing should tempt her to leave the nest, till she had hatched her infant brood. Her tender mate every morning brought her food, before he tasted any himself, and then cheered her with a song.

At length the day arrived, when the happy mother heard the chirping of her little ones; pleasing to her ears, as the prattle of a beloved child to its fond parent: with inexpressible tenderness she spread her maternal wings to cover them, threw out the egg-shells in which they before lay confined, then pressed them to her bosom, and presented them to her mate, who viewed them with rapture, and seated himself by her side, that he might share her pleasure.

We may promise ourselves much delight in rearing our little family, said he, but it will occasion us a great deal of trouble; I would willingly bear the whole fatigue myself, but it will be impossible for me, with my utmost labour and industry, to supply all our nestlings with what is sufficient for their daily support; it will therefore be necessary for you, to leave the nest occasionally, in order sometimes to seek provisions for them. She declared her readiness to take a flight whenever it should be requisite; and said, that there would be no necessity for her to be long absent, as she had in her last excursion discovered a place near the orchard, where food was scattered on purpose for such birds as would take the pains of seeking it; and had been informed by a Chaffinch, that there was no kind of danger in picking it up. This is a lucky discovery indeed, replied he, and we must avail ourselves of it; for this great increase of family, renders it prudent to make use of every expedient for supplying our necessities; I myself must take a larger circuit, for some insects that are proper for the nestlings, cannot be found in all places: however, I will bear you company whenever it is in my power. The little ones now began to feel the sensation of hunger, and opened their gaping mouths for food: on which, their kind father instantly flew forth to find it for them, and in turns supplied them all, as well as his beloved mate. This was a hard day's work, and when evening came on, he was glad to seek repose; and turning his head under his wing, he soon fell asleep; his mate followed his example; the four little ones had before fallen into a gentle slumber, and perfect quietness for some hours reigned in the nest.

The next morning they were awakened at the dawn of day, by the song of a Skylark, who had a nest near the orchard; and as the young Redbreasts were impatient for food, their father cheerfully prepared himself to renew his toil, but first requested his mate to accompany him to the place she had mentioned. That I will do, replied she, at a proper hour, but it is too early yet; I must, therefore, entreat that you will go by your-self, and procure a breakfast for us, as I am fearful of leaving the nestlings before the air is warmer, lest they should be chilled. To this he readily consented, and fed all his little darlings, to whom, for the sake of distinction, I shall give the names of Robin, Dicky, Flapsy, and Pecksy. When this kind office was performed, he perched on an adjacent tree, and there, while he rested, entertained his family with his melody, till his mate, springing from the nest, called on him to attend her; on which he instantly took wing, and followed her to a court-yard, belonging to an elegant mansion.

No sooner did they appear before the parlour window, than it was hastily thrown up by Miss Harriet Benson, a little girl about eleven years old, the daughter of the Gentleman and Lady to whom the house belonged.

Miss Harriet, with great delight, called her brother to see two Robin Redbreasts: her summons was instantly complied with, and she was joined by Master Frederick, a fine chubby rosy-cheeked boy, about six years of age, who, as soon as he had taken a peep at the feathered strangers, ran to his mamma, and entreated her to give him something to feed the birds with. I must have a great piece of bread this morning, said he, for there are all the Sparrows and Chaffinches that come every day, and two Robin Redbreasts besides. Here is a piece for you, Frederick, replied Mrs. Benson, cutting a roll that was on the table; but if your daily pensioners continue to increase, as they have done lately, we must provide some other food for them, as it is not right to cut pieces from a loaf on purpose for birds, because there are many children that want bread, to whom we should give the preference. Would you deprive a poor little hungry boy of his breakfast, to give it to birds? No, said Frederick, I would sooner give my own breakfast to a poor boy, than he should go without. But where shall I get victuals enough for my birds? I will beg the cook to save the crumbs in the bread-pan, and desire John to preserve all he makes, when he cuts the loaf for dinner, and those which are scattered on the table-cloth. A very good scheme, said Mrs. Benson, and I advise you, my dear, to put it in execution; for I make no doubt it will answer your purpose, if you can prevail on the servants to indulge you. I cannot bear to see the least fragment of food wasted, which may conduce to the support of life in any creature.

Miss Harriet being quite impatient to exercise her benevolence, requested her brother to remember that the poor birds, for whom he had been a successful solicitor, would soon fly away, if he did not make haste to feed them; on which, he ran to the window with his treasure in his hand.

When Miss Harriet first appeared, the winged suppliants approached with eager expectation of the daily handful, which their kind benefactress made it a custom to distribute, and were surprised with the delay of her charity. They hopped around the window—they chirped—they twittered, and employed all their little arts to gain attention; and were on the point of departing, when Master Frederick, breaking a bit from the piece he held in his hand, attempted to scatter it among them, calling out at the same time, Dicky! Dicky! On hearing the well-known sound of invitation, the little flock immediately drew near—Master Frederick held a short contest with his sister, in order to prevail with her to let him feed all the birds himself; but finding that he could not fling the crumbs far enough for the Redbreasts, who, with the timidity of strangers, kept at a distance, he resigned the task, and Miss Harriet, with dexterous hand, threw some of them to the very spot where the affectionate pair stood, waiting for an opportunity of attracting her notice, and with grateful hearts picked up the portion assigned them; and in the mean while, the other birds having satisfied their hunger, successively withdrew, and they were left alone. Master Frederick exclaimed with rapture, that the two Robin Redbreasts were feeding! and Miss Harriet meditated a design of taming them, by repeated instances of kindness. Be sure, my dear brother, said she, not to forget to ask the cook and John for the crumbs; and do not let the least little morsel of any thing you have to eat, fall to the ground. I will be careful in respect to mine, and we will collect all that papa and mamma crumble; and if we cannot by these means get enough, I will spend some of my money in grain for them.—O, said Frederick, I would give all the money I have in the world to buy victuals for my dear, dear birds. Hold, my love, said Mrs. Benson, though I commend your humanity, I must remind you again, that there are poor people as well as poor birds.—Well, mamma, replied Frederick, I will only buy a little grain then. As he spake the last words, the Redbreasts having finished their meal, the mother bird expressed her impatience to return to the nest: and having obtained her mate's consent, repaired with all possible speed to her humble habitation, whilst he tuned his melodious pipe, and delighted their young benefactors with his music: he then soared into the air, and took his flight to an adjoining garden, where he had a great chance of finding worms for his family.

CHAPTER II

MASTER BENSON expressed great concern that the Robins were gone; but was comforted by his sister, who reminded him, that in all probability his new favourites, having met with so kind a reception, would return on the morrow. Mrs. Benson then bid them shut the window, and taking Frederick in her lap, and desiring Miss Harriet to sit down by her, thus addressed them.

I am delighted, my dear children, with your humane behaviour towards the animal creation, and wish by all means to encourage it. But though a most commendable propensity, it requires regulation; let me therefore recommend to you, not to suffer it to gain upon you to such a degree, as to make you unhappy, or forgetful of those who have a superior claim to your attention; I mean poor people: always keep in mind the distresses which they endure, and on no account waste any kind of food, nor give to inferior animals what is designed for mankind.

Miss Harriet promised to follow her mamma's instructions; but Frederick's attention was entirely engaged by watching a Butterfly, which had just left the chrysalis, and was fluttering in the window, longing to try its wings in the air and sunshine. This Frederick was very desirous of catching, but his mamma would not permit him to attempt it; because (she told him) he could not well lay hold of it[s] wings without doing it an injury, and it would be much happier at liberty. Should you like, Frederick, said she, when you are going out to play, to have any body lay hold of you violently, scratch you all over, then offer you something to eat which is very disagreeable, and perhaps poisonous, and shut you up in a little dark room? And yet this is the fate to which many an harmless insect is condemned by thoughtless children. As soon as Frederick understood that he could not catch the Butterfly without hurting it, he gave up the point, and assured his mamma he did not want to keep it, but only to carry it out of doors. Well, replied she, that end may be answered by opening the window, which at her desire was done by Miss Harriet;

the happy insect seized the opportunity of escaping, and Frederick had soon the pleasure of seeing it in a rose-tree.

Breakfast being ended, Mrs. Benson reminded the young lady and gentleman, that it was almost time for their lessons to begin; but desired their maid to take them into the garden before they applied to business, whilst she gave some directions in the family; and Master Frederick, during his walk, amused himself with watching the Butterfly, as it flew from flower to flower, which gave him more pleasure than he could possibly have received from catching and confining the little tender creature.

Let us now see what became of our Redbreasts, after they left their young benefactors.

The hen bird, as I informed you, repaired immediately to the nest; her heart fluttered with apprehension as she entered it, and she eagerly called out, "Are you all safe, my little dears?" All safe, my good mother, replied Pecksy, but a little hungry and very cold. Well, said she, your last complaint I can soon remove; but in respect to the satisfying your hunger, that must be your father's task, for I have not been able to bring any thing good for you to eat; however, he will soon be here, I make no doubt. Then spreading her wings over them all, she soon communicated warmth to them, and they were again comfortable.

In a very short time her mate returned, for he only staid at Mr. Benson's to finish his song, and refresh himself with some clear water, which his new friends always kept in the place where they fed the birds, on purpose for their little pensioners. He brought in his mouth a worm, which was given to Robin; and was going to fetch one for Dicky, but that his mate reminded him of their agreement, to divide betwixt them the care of providing for the family. My young ones are now hatched, said she, and you can keep them warm as well as myself; take my place therefore, and the next excursion shall be mine. I consent, answered he, with the more pleasure, because I think a little flying now and then will do you good; but to save you the trouble of a painful search, I can direct you to a spot, where you may be certain of finding worms enough for this morning's supply. He then described the place; and immediately, on her quitting the nest, entered it, and gathered his young ones under his wings.—Come, my dears, said he, let us see what kind of a nurse I can make; but an awkward one I fear; even every mother-bird is not a good nurse: but you are very fortunate in yours, for she is an exceedingly tender one, and I hope you will make her a dutiful return for her kindness. They all promised him they would: Well, then, said he, I will sing you a song. He did so, and it was a very merry one, and delighted the nestlings extremely; so that, though they laid a little inconveniently under his wings, they did not regard it, nor think the time of their mother's absence long; she had not succeeded in the place she first went to, as a boy was picking up worms to angle with, of whom she was afraid, and therefore flew farther: but as soon as she obtained what she went for, she returned with all possible speed; and notwithstanding she had repeated invitations from several gay birds which she met, to join their sportive parties, she kept a steady course, preferring the pleasure of feeding little Dicky to all the diversions of the fields and groves. As soon as she came near the nest, her mate started up to make room for her, and take his turn of providing for his family. Once more adieu! said he, and was out of sight in an instant.

My dear nestlings, said the mother, how do you do? Very well, thank you, replied all at once; and we have been exceedingly merry, said Robin, for my father has sung us a sweet song. I think, said Dicky, I should like to learn it. Well, replied the mother, he will teach it you, I dare say; here he comes, ask him. I am ashamed, said Dicky. Then you are a silly bird; never be ashamed, but when you commit a fault: asking your father to teach you to sing, is not one; and good parents delight to teach their young ones every thing that is proper and useful. Whatever so good a father sets you an example of, you may safely desire to imitate. Then addressing herself to her mate, who for an instant stopped at the entrance of the nest, that he might not interrupt her instructions, Am I not right, said she, in what I have just told them? Perfectly so, replied he; I shall have pleasure in teaching them all that is in my power; but we must talk of that another time. Who is to feed poor Pecksy? Oh! I, I, answered the mother, and was gone in an instant. And so you want to learn to sing, Dicky? said the father. Well, then, I will repeat my song, so pray listen very attentively; you may learn the notes, though you will not be able to practise them till your voice is stronger. He then sung with the same approbation as before.

Robin now remarked, that it was very pretty indeed, and expressed his desire to learn it also. By all means, said his father, I shall sing it very often, so you may learn it if you please. For my part, said Flapsy, I do not think I could have patience to learn it, it will take so much time.—Nothing, my dear Flapsy, answered the father, can be acquired without patience, and I am sorry to find yours begin to fail you already: But I hope if you have no taste for music, that you will give the greater application to things that may be of more importance to you. Well, said Pecksy, I would apply to music with all my heart, but I do not believe it possible for me to attain it. Perhaps not, replied her father, but I do not doubt your application to whatever your mother requires of you, and she is an excellent judge both of your talents, and of what is suitable to your station in life. She is no songster herself, and yet she is very clever, I assure you. Here she comes. Then rising to make room for her, Take your seat, my love, said he, and I will perch upon the ivy. The hen again covered her brood, whilst her mate amused her with his singing and conversation, till evening reminded them of repose; excepting, that each made alternate excursions, as the appetites of their young ones required.

In this manner several days passed with little variation, the nestlings were very thriving, and daily gained strength and knowledge, through the care and attention of their indulgent parents, who every day visited their friends, Master and Miss Benson. Frederick had been successful in his application to both the cook and footman, by whose assistance he obtained enough for his dear birds, as he called them, without infringing on the rights of the poor; as he was still able to produce a penny, whenever his papa or mamma pointed out to him a proper object of charity.

CHAPTER III

It HAPPENED ONE DAY, that both the Redbreasts, who always went together to Mr. Benson's (because if one had waited for the other's return, it would have missed the chance of being fed), it happened, I say, that they were both absent longer than usual, for their little benefactors having been fatigued with a very long walk the evening before, lay late in bed that morning; but as soon as Frederick was dressed, his sister, who was

waiting for him, took him by the hand, and led him down stairs, where he hastily demanded of the cook the collection of crumbs reserved for him. As soon as he entered
the breakfast parlour, he ran eagerly to the window, and attempted to fling it up. What
is the cause of this mighty bustle? said his mamma. Do you not perceive that I am in the
room, Frederick? Oh, my birds! my birds! cried he. I understand, rejoined Mrs. Benson,
that you have neglected to feed your little pensioners; how came this about, Harriet?
We were so tired last night, answered Miss Benson, that we overslept ourselves, mamma.
This excuse may satisfy you and your brother, added the Lady, but I fear your birds
would bring heavy complaints against you, were they able to talk our language. But make
haste to supply their present wants; and for the future, whenever you give any living
creature cause to depend on you for sustenance, be careful on no account to disappoint
it; and if you are prevented feeding it yourself, employ another person to do it for you.
But though it is very commendable, and indeed an obligation on your humanity, to be
attentive to your dependants, yet you must not let this make you forgetful of your duty to
your friends. It is customary for little boys and girls to pay their respects to their papas
and mammas, every morning, as soon as they see them. This, Frederick, you ought to have
done to me, on entering the parlour, instead of tearing across it, crying out, My birds!
my birds! It would have taken you but a very little time to have done so: however, I will
excuse your neglect now, my dear, as you did not intend to offend me; but I expect that
you will so manage the business you have undertaken, that it may not break in on your
higher obligations. You depend as much on your papa and me, for every thing you want,
as these little birds do on you: nay, more so, for they could supply their own wants, by
seeking food in other places; but children can do nothing towards their support: therefore,
it is particularly requisite, that they should be dutiful and respectful to those, whose
tenderness and care are constantly exerted for their benefit.

Miss Harriet promised her mamma, that she would, on all occasions, endeavour to
behave as she wished her to do; but I am sorry to say, Frederick was more intent on
opening the window, than on imbibing the good instructions that were given him: this
he could not effect, and therefore Harriet, by her mamma's permission, went to his
assistance, and the store of provisions was dispensed. As many of the birds had nests,
they ate their meal with all possible expedition; amongst this number were the Robins,
who dispatched the business as soon as they could, for the hen was anxious to return to her
little ones, and the cock to procure them a breakfast; and having given his young friends
a serenade before they left their bed-chambers, he did not think it necessary to stay to
sing any more: they therefore departed.

When the mother-bird arrived at the ivy wall, she stopt at the entrance of the nest,
with a palpitating heart; but seeing her brood all safe and well, she hastened to take
them under her wings. As soon as she was seated, she observed that they were not so
cheerful as usual. What is the matter? said she, how have you agreed during my absence?
To these questions all were unwilling to reply, for the truth was, that they had been
quarrelling almost the whole time. What, all silent? said she, I fear you have not obeyed
my commandments, but have been contending. I desire you will tell me the truth.
Robin, knowing that he was the greatest offender, began to justify himself, before the
others could have time to lay an accusation against him.

I am sure, mother, said he, I only gave Dicky a little peck, because he crowded me so;

and all the others joined with him, and fell upon me at once.

Since you have begun, Robin, answered Dicky, I must speak, for you gave me a very hard peck indeed, and I was afraid you had put out my eye. I am sure I made all the room I could for you; but you said you ought to have half the nest, and to be master, when your father and mother were out, because you are the eldest.

I do not love to tell tales, said Flapsy, but what Dicky says is very true, Robin; and you plucked two or three little feathers out of me, only because I begged you not to use us ill.

And you set your foot very hard upon me, cried Pecksy, for telling you that you had forgot your dear mother's injunction.

This is a sad story indeed, said the mother. I am very sorry to find, Robin, that you already discover such a turbulent disposition. If you go on in this manner, we shall have no peace in the nest, nor can I leave it with any degree of satisfaction. As for your being the eldest, though it makes me shew you a preference on all proper occasions, it does not give you a privilege to domineer over your brothers and sisters. You are all equally the objects of our tender care, which we shall exercise impartially amongst you, provided you do not forfeit it by bad behaviour. To shew you that you are not master of the nest, I desire you to get from under my wing, and sit on the outside, while I cherish those who are dutiful and good. Robin, greatly mortified, retired from his mother; on which Dicky, with the utmost kindness, began to intercede for him. Pardon Robin, my dear mother, I entreat you, said he, I heartily forgive his treatment of me, and would not have complained to you, had it not been necessary for my own justification. You are a good bird, Dicky, said his mother, but such an offence as this must be repented of before it is pardoned. At this instant her mate returned with a fine worm, and looked as usual for Robin, who lay skulking by himself. Give it, said the mother, to Dicky, Robin must be served last this morning; nay, I do not know whether I shall permit him to have any victuals all day. Dicky was very unwilling to mortify his brother, but on his mother's commanding him not to detain his father, he opened his mouth and swallowed the delicious mouthful. What can be the matter, said the good father, when he had emptied his mouth, surely none of the little ones have been naughty? But I cannot stop to inquire at present, for I left another fine worm, which may be gone if I do not make haste back.

As soon as he departed, Dicky renewed his solicitations that Robin might be forgiven; but as he sat swelling with anger and disdain, because he fancied that the eldest should not be shoved to the outside of his mother's wing, while the others were fed, she would not hear a word in his behalf. The father soon came and fed Flapsy, and then thinking it best for his mate to continue her instructions, he made another excursion; during which, Pecksy, whose little heart was full of affectionate concern for the punishment of her brother, thus attempted to comfort him.

Dear Robin, do not grieve, I will give you my breakfast, if my mother will let me. O, said Robin, I do not want any breakfast; if I may not be served *first*, I will have *none*. Shall I ask my mother to forgive you? I do not want any of your intercessions, replied he; if you had not been a parcel of ill-natured things, I should not have been pushed about as I am.

Come back, Pecksy, said the mother, who overheard them, I will not have you hold converse with so naughty a bird. I forbid every one of you even to go near him. The father then arrived, and Pecksy was fed. You may rest yourself, my dear, said the mother, your morning's task is ended. Why, what has Robin done? asked he. What I am sorry to relate, she replied; Quarrelled with his brothers and sisters. Quarrelled with his brothers and sisters! you surprise me: I could not have suspected he would have been either so foolish or so unkind.—O, this is not all, said the mother, for he presumes on being the eldest, and claims half the nest to himself when we are absent, and now is sullen because he is discharged, and not fed first as usual. If that is the case, replied the father, leave me to settle this business, my dear, and pray go into the air a little, for you seem to be sadly agitated. I am disturbed, said she, I confess; for after all my care and solicitude, I did not expect such a recompense as this. I am sorry to expose this perverse bird, even to you, but he resists my efforts to reform him. I will do as you desire, go into the air a little; so saying, she repaired to a neighbouring tree, where she waited, with anxious expectation, the event of her mate's interposition.

As soon as the mother departed, the father thus addressed the delinquent: And so, Robin, you want to be master of the nest? A pretty master you will make indeed, who do not know even how to govern your own temper! I will not stand to talk much to you now, because, in your present disposition, you would in all probability turn a deaf ear to my admonitions; but depend upon it, I will not suffer you to use any of the family ill, particularly your good mother; and if you persist in obstinacy, I will certainly turn you out of the nest before you can fly. These threatenings intimidated Robin, and he also began to be very hungry, as well as cold; he therefore promised to behave better for the future, and his brothers and sisters pleaded earnestly that he might be forgiven and restored to his usual place.

I can say nothing in respect to the last particular, replied the father, that depends upon his mother; but as it is his first offence, and he seems to be very sorry, I will myself pardon it, and intercede for him with his mother, who I fear is this time lamenting his obduracy. On this he left the nest to seek for her. Return, my dear, said he, to your beloved family; Robin seems sensible of his offence, and longs to ask your forgiveness. Pleased at this intelligence, the mother raised her drooping head, and closed her wings, which hung mournfully by her sides, expressive of the dejection of her spirits. I fly to give it him, said she, and hastened into the nest. In the mean while Robin wished for, yet dreaded her return.

As soon as he saw her, he lifted up a supplicating eye, and with feeble accents (for hunger and sorrow had made him faint) he chirped, "Forgive me, dear mother, I will not again offend you." I accept your submission, Robin, said she, and will once more receive you to my wing; but, indeed, your behaviour has made me very unhappy. She then made room for him, he nestled closely to her side, and soon found the benefit of her fostering heat; but the pain of hunger still remained, yet he had not confidence to ask his father to fetch him any victuals: but this kind parent waited not for solicitation, for seeing that his mother had received him into favour, he went with all speed to an adjacent field, where he soon met with refreshment for him, which with tender love he presented, and Robin swallowed with gratitude. Thus was peace restored to the nest, and the happy mother once more rejoiced that harmony reigned in the family.

CHAPTER IV

A FEW DAYS AFTER, a fresh disturbance took place. All the little Redbreasts, excepting Pecksy, in turn committed some fault or other, for which they were occasionally punished; but she was of so amiable a disposition, that it was her constant study to act with propriety, and avoid giving offence; on which account she was justly caressed by her parents with distinguishing kindness. This excited the envy of the others, and they joined together to treat her ill, giving her the title of the *favourite;* saying, that they made no doubt their father and mother would reserve the *nicest morsels* for their *darling.*

Poor Pecksy bore all their reproaches with patience, hoping that she should in time regain their good opinion by her gentleness and affection. But it happened one day, that in the midst of their tauntings their mother unexpectedly returned, who hearing an uncommon noise among her young ones, stopped on the ivy to learn the cause; and as soon as she discovered it, made her appearance at the entrance of the nest, with a countenance that indicated her knowledge of their proceedings, and her displeasure at them.

Are these the sentiments, said she, that subsist in a family, which ought to be bound together by love and kindness? Which of you has cause to reproach either your father or me, with partiality? Do we not, with the exactest equality, distribute the fruits of our labours among you? And in what respect has poor Pecksy the preference, but in that commendation which is justly her due, and which you do not strive to deserve? Has she ever yet uttered a complaint against you, though, from the dejection of her countenance, which she in vain attempted to conceal, it is evident that she has suffered your reproaches for some days past? I positively command you to treat her otherwise, for it is a mother's duty to succour a persecuted nestling; and I will certainly admit her next my heart, and banish you all from that place you have hitherto possessed in it, if you suffer envy and jealousy to occupy your bosoms, to the exclusion of that tender love which she, as the kindest of sisters, has a right to expect from you.

Robin, Dicky, and Flapsy, were quite confounded by their mother's reproof, and Pecksy felt an affectionate concern that they had incurred the displeasure of so tender a parent; and far from increasing it by complaining of them, endeavoured to soften her anger. That I have been vexed, my dear mother, said she, is true, but not to as great a degree as you suppose; and I am ready to believe that my dear brothers and sister were not in earnest in the severe things they said of me.—Perhaps they only meant to try my affection.—To spare them the trouble of any future trial, I now entreat them to believe my assurances, that I would willingly resign the greatest pleasure in life, could I by that means increase their happiness; and so far from wishing for the *nicest morsel,* would content myself with the humblest fare, rather than any of them should be disappointed. This tender speech had its desired effect; it recalled those sentiments of love, which envy and jealousy had for a time banished; each nestling acknowledged its fault, and having obtained the forgiveness of their mother, a perfect reconciliation took place, to the great joy of Pecksy, and indeed of all parties.

All the nestlings continued very good for several days, and no occurrence happened worth relating; the little flock were soon covered with feathers, which their mother taught them to dress, telling them, that neatness was a very essential thing, being conducive to health, and also to the rendering them agreeable in the eye of the world.

Robin was a very strong robust bird, not remarkable for his beauty, but there was a great briskness in his manner, which covered many defects, and he was very likely to attract notice. His father judged, from the tone of his chirpings, that he would be a very good songster.

Dicky had a remarkably fine plumage, his breast was of a beautiful red, his body and wings of an elegant mottled brown, and his eyes sparkled like diamonds.

Flapsy was also very pretty, but more distinguished for the elegance of her shape, than for the variety and lustre of her feathers.

Pecksy had no outward charms to recommend her to notice; but these defects were amply supplied by the sweetness of her disposition, which was amiable to the greatest degree. Her temper was constantly serene, she was ever attentive to the happiness of her parents, and would not have grieved them for the world; and her affection for her brothers and sister was so great, that she constantly preferred their interest to her own, of which we lately gave an instance.

The kind parents attended to them with unremitting affection, and made their daily visit to Master and Miss Benson, who very punctually discharged the benevolent office of feeding them. The Robin Redbreasts, made familiar by repeated favours, approached nearer and nearer to their little friends by degrees, and at length ventured to enter the room and feed upon the breakfast-table. Miss Harriet was delighted at this circumstance, and Frederick was quite transported; he longed to catch the birds, but his mamma told him, that it would be very mean to drive them away. Miss Harriet entreated him not to frighten them on any account, and he was prevailed on to forbear; but could not help expressing a wish that he had them in a cage, that he might feed them all day long.

And do you really think, Frederick, said Mrs. Benson, that these little delicate creatures are such gluttons, as to desire to be fed all day long? Could you tempt them to do it, they would soon die; but they know better, and as soon as their appetites are satisfied, always leave off eating. Many a little boy may learn a lesson from them. Do not you recollect one of your acquaintance, who, if an apple-pie, or any thing else that he calls nice, is set before him, will eat till he makes himself sick? Frederick looked ashamed, being conscious that he was too much inclined to indulge his love of delicacies. Well, said his mamma, I see you understand who I mean, Frederick, so we will say no more on that subject; only when you meet with that little Gentleman, give my love to him, and tell him, I beg he will be as moderate as his Redbreasts.

The cock bird having finished his breakfast, flew out at the window, followed by his mate; and as soon as they were out of sight, Mrs. Benson continued her discourse. And would you really confine these sweet creatures in a cage, Frederick, merely to have the pleasure of feeding them? Should you like to be always shut up in a little room, and think it sufficient if you were supplied with victuals and drink? Is there no enjoyment in running about, jumping, and going from place to place? Do not you like to keep company with little boys and girls? And is there no pleasure in breathing the fresh air? Though these little animals are inferior to you, there is no doubt but they are capable of enjoyments similar to these; and it must be a dreadful life for a poor bird to be shut up in a cage, where he cannot so much as make use of his wings—where he is excluded from his natural companions—and where he cannot possibly receive that refreshment, which the air must afford to him when at liberty to soar to such a height. But this is not all, for many a poor bird is caught, and separated from its family, after it has been at the trouble of building a nest, has perhaps laid its eggs, or even hatched its young ones, which are by this means exposed to inevitable destruction. It is likely that these very Redbreasts may have young ones, for this is the season of the year for their hatching; and I rather think they have, from the circumstance of their always coming together.

If that is the case, said Miss Harriet, it would be a pity indeed, to confine them. But why, mamma, if it is wrong to catch birds, did you at one time keep Canaries?

The case is very different in respect to Canaries, my dear, said Mrs. Benson. By keeping them in a cage, I did them a kindness. I considered them as little foreigners who claimed my hospitality. This kind of bird came originally from a warm climate; they are in their nature very susceptible of cold, and would perish in the open air in our winters: neither does the food which they feed on grow plentifully in this country; and as they are always here bred in cages, they do not know how to procure the materials for their nests abroad. And there is another particular which would greatly distress them were they to be turned loose, which is, the ridicule and contempt they would be exposed to from other birds. I remember once to have seen a poor Canary, which had been turned loose because it could not sing; and surely no creature could be more miserable. It was starving for want of victuals, famishing with thirst, shivering with cold, and looked terrified to the greatest degree; while a parcel of Sparrows and Chaffinches pursued it from place to place, twittering and chirping with every mark of insolence and derision. I could not help fancying the little creature to be like a foreigner just landed from some distant country, followed by a rude rabble of boys, who were ridiculing him because his dress and language were strange to them.

And what became of the poor little creature, mamma? said Miss Harriet. I was going to tell you, my dear, replied Mrs. Benson. I ordered the servant to bring me a cage, with seed and water in their usual places; this I caused to be hung on a tree, next to that in which the little sufferer in vain endeavoured to hide himself among the leaves from his cruel pursuers. No sooner did the servant retire, than the poor little wretch flew to it. I immediately had the cage brought into the parlour, where I experienced great pleasure in observing what happiness the poor creature enjoyed in her deliverance. I kept it some years, but not choosing to confine her in a *little* cage, had a *large* one bought, and procured a companion for her of her own species. I supplied them with materials for building, and from them proceeded a little colony, which grew so numerous, that you know I gave them to Mr. Bruce to put in his aviary, where you have seen them enjoying themselves. So now I hope I have fully accounted for having kept Canary birds in a cage. You have indeed, mamma, said Harriet.

I have also, said Mrs. Benson, occasionally kept Larks. In severe winters vast numbers of them come to this country from a colder climate, and many perish. Quantities of them are killed and sold for the spit, and the bird-catchers usually have a great many to sell, and many an idle boy has some to dispose of. I frequently buy them, as you know, Harriet, but as soon as the fine weather returns, I constantly set them at liberty. But come, my dears, prepare for your morning walk, and afterwards let me see you in my dressing-room.

I wonder, said Frederick, whether our Redbreasts have got a nest? I will watch to-morrow which way they fly, for I should like to see the little ones. And what will you do, should you find them out? said his mamma. Not take the nest, I hope? Why, replied Frederick, I should like to bring it home, mamma, and put it in a tree near the house, and then I would scatter crumbs for the old ones to feed them with.

Your design is a kind one, said Mrs. Benson, but would greatly distress your little favourites. Many birds, through fear, forsake their nests, when they are removed, therefore I desire you to let them alone if you should chance to find them. Miss Harriet then remarked, that she thought it very cruel to take birds' nests. Ah! my dear, said Mrs. Benson, those who commit such barbarous actions, are quite insensible to the distresses they occasion. It is very true, that we ought not to indulge so great a degree of pity and tenderness for such animals, as for those who are more properly our fellow-creatures; I mean men, women, and children; but as every living creature can feel, we should have a constant regard to those feelings, and strive to give happiness, rather than inflict misery. But go, my dear, and take your walk. Mrs. Benson then left them, to attend her usual morning employments; and the young Lady and Gentleman, attended by their maid, passed an agreeable half hour in the garden.

CHAPTER V

I N THE MEAN TIME, the hen Redbreast returned to the nest, while her mate took his flight in search of food for his family. When the mother approached the nest, she was surprised at not hearing as usual the chirping of her young ones; and what was her astonishment at seeing them all crowded together, trembling with apprehension: What is the matter, my nestlings, said she, that I find you in this terror?

Oh, my dear mother! cried Robin, who first ventured to raise up his head, is it you? Pecksy then revived, and entreated her mother to come into the nest, which she did without delay, and the little tremblers crept under her wings, endeavouring to conceal themselves in this happy retreat.

What has terrified you in this manner? said she. Oh! I do not know, replied Dicky, but we have seen such a monster as I never beheld before. A monster, my dear! pray describe it. I cannot, said Dicky, it was too frightful to be described. Frightful, indeed, cried Robin, but I had a full view of it, and will give the best description I can.

We were all lying peaceably in the nest, and very happy together; Dicky and I were trying to sing, when suddenly we heard a noise against the wall, and presently a great round red face appeared before the nest, with a pair of enormous staring eyes, a very large beak, and below that a wide mouth, with two rows of bones, that looked as if they could grind us all to pieces in an instant. About the top of this round face, and down the sides, hung something black, but not like feathers. When the two staring eyes had looked at us for some time, the whole thing disappeared. I cannot at all conceive, from your description, Robin, what this thing could be, said the mother, but perhaps it may come again.

O! I hope not, cried Flapsy, I shall die with fear if it does. Why so, my love? said her mother, has it done you any harm? I cannot say it has, replied Flapsy. Well, then, you do very wrong, my dear, in giving way to such apprehensions. You must strive to get the better of this fearful disposition. When you go abroad in the world, you will see many strange objects; and if you are terrified at every appearance which you cannot account for, will live a most unhappy life. Endeavour to be good, and then you need not fear any thing. But here comes your father, perhaps he will be able to explain the appearance which has so alarmed you to-day.

As soon as the father had given the worm to Robin, he was preparing to depart for another, but to his surprise, all the rest of the nestlings begged him to stay, declaring they had rather go without their meal, on condition he would but remain at home and take care of them. Stay at home and take care of you! said he. Why is that more necessary now than usual? The mother then related the strange occurrence that had occasioned this request. Nonsense! said he—a monster!—great eyes!—large mouth!—long beak!—I don't understand such stuff.—Besides, as it did them no harm, why are they to be in such terror now it is gone? Don't be angry, dear father, said Pecksy, for it was very frightful indeed. Well, said he, I will fly all round the orchard, and perhaps may meet this monster. Oh, it will eat you up! it will eat you up! said Flapsy. Never fear, said he, and away he flew.

The mother then again attempted to calm them, but all in vain, their fears were now redoubled by apprehensions for their father's safety; however, to their great joy, he soon returned. Well, said he, I have seen this monster; the little ones then clung to their mother, fearing the dreadful creature was just at hand. What, afraid again? cried he; a parcel of stout hearts I have in my nest, truly! Why, when you fly about in the world you will, in all probability, see hundreds of such monsters (as you call them), unless you choose to confine yourselves to a retired life: nay, even in woods and groves you will be liable to meet some of them, and those of the most mischievous kind. I begin to comprehend, said the mother, that these dear nestlings have seen the face of a man. Even so, replied her mate; it is a man, no other than our friend the gardener, who has so alarmed them.

A MAN! cried Dicky, was that frightful thing a man? Nothing more, I assure you, answered his father, and a good man too, I have reason to believe; for he is very careful not to frighten your mother and me, when we are picking up worms, and has frequently thrown crumbs to us, when he was eating his breakfast.

And does he live in this garden? said Flapsy. He works here very often, replied her father, but is frequently absent. O then, cried she, pray take us abroad when he is away, for indeed I cannot bear to see him. You are a little simpleton, said the father; and if you do not endeavour to get more resolution, I will leave you in the nest by yourself, when I am teaching your brothers and sister to fly and peck, and what will you do then? for you must not expect we shall go from them to bring you food. Flapsy, fearful that her father would be quite angry, promised to follow his directions in every respect, and the rest, animated by his discourse, began to recover their spirits.

CHAPTER VI

WHILST THESE TERRIBLE commotions passed in the nest, the *monster*, who was no other than honest Joe the gardener, went to the house, and inquired for his young master and mistress, having, as he justly supposed, a very pleasing piece of intelligence to communicate. Both the young gentleman and lady, who were accustomed to receive little civilities from Joe, very readily attended him, thinking he had got some fruit or flowers for them. Well, Joe, said Miss Benson, what have you to say to us? Have you got a peach or a nectarine? or have you brought me a root of Sweet William?

No, Miss Harriet, said Joe, but I have something to tell you, that will please you as much as *tho'f* I had. What's that? what's that? cried Frederick. Why master Frederick, said Joe, a pair of Robins have *come'd* mortal often to one place in the orchard lately; so, thinks I, these birds have got a nest. So, I watches, and watches, and at last I *see'd* the old hen fly into a hole in the ivy-wall. I had a fancy to set my ladder and look in, but as master ordered me not to frighten the birds, I staid till the old one flew out again, and then I mounted, and there I *see'd* the little creatures full fledged; and if you and Miss Harriet may go with me, I will shew them to you, for the nest is but a little way from the ground, and you may easily get up the step-ladder.

Frederick was in raptures, being, confident that these were the identical Robins he was so attached to, and (like a little thoughtless boy as he was) would have gone immediately with the gardener, had not his sister reminded him, that it was proper to ask mamma's leave first, for which purpose she accompanied him into the parlour.

Good news! good news! mamma, cried Frederick, Joe has found the Robin's nest. Has he, indeed? said Mrs. Benson. Yes, mamma, said Miss Harriet, and if agreeable to you, we should be glad to go along with Joe to see it. And how are you to get at it? said Mrs. Benson, for I suppose it is some height from the ground? Oh, I can climb a ladder very well, cried Frederick. You climb a ladder! You are a clever gentleman at climbing, I know, replied his mamma; but do you propose to mount too, Harriet? I think this is rather an indelicate scheme for a lady. Joe tells me that the nest is but a very little way from the ground, mamma, answered Harriet, but if I find it otherwise, you may depend on my not getting up. On this condition I will permit you to go; but pray, Mr. Frederick, let me remind you, not to frighten your little favourites. Not for all the world, said Frederick; so away he skipped, and got to Joe before his sister. We may go! we may go! Joe, cried he. Stay for me, Joe, I beg, said Miss Harriet, who presently joined him.

When the Redbreasts had quieted the fears of their young family, they fed them as usual, and then having a little private business, they retired to a tree, desiring their little nestlings not to be terrified if the monster should look in upon them again, as it was very probable he would do. They promised to bear the sight as well as they could.

When the old ones were seated in the tree, It is time, said the father, to take our nestlings abroad. You see, my love, how very timorous they are, and if we do not use them a little to the world, they will never be able to shift for themselves. Very true, replied the mother, they are now full fledged, and therefore, if you please, we will take them out to-morrow: but it will be necessary for me to prepare them for it; I will therefore return to the nest. One of the best preparatives, answered her mate, will be to leave them by themselves a little; therefore we will now take a flight together for a short time, and then go back. The mother complied, but not without reluctance, for she longed to be with her dear family. Let us now return to the happy party, whom we lately left setting off on their visit to the ivy wall.

CHAPTER VII

A s soon as Joe found, that the young *gentry*, as he called them, had obtained permission to accompany him, he took Frederick by the hand, and said, Come along, my young master, but, at Miss Harriet's request, stopped while she fetched her bonnet and tippet. Frederick's impatience was so great, that he could scarcely be restrained from running all the way, but that his sister entreated him not to make himself too hot.

At length they arrived at the desired spot; Joe placed the ladder, and his young master, with a little assistance, mounted it very dexterously: But who can describe his raptures when he beheld the nestlings! Oh, the sweet creatures, cried he, there are four of them, I declare! I never saw any thing so pretty in my life! I wish I might carry you all home! That you must not do, Frederick, said his sister; and I beg you will come away, for you will either terrify the little creatures, or alarm the old birds, which perhaps are now waiting somewhere near to feed them. Well, I will come away directly, said Frederick; and so good by, Robins! I hope you will come soon, along with your father and mother, to be fed in the parlour. He then, under the conduct of his friend Joe, descended.

Joe next addressed Miss Harriet: Now, my young mistress, said he, will you go up? *As the steps of the ladder were broad, and the nest was not high, Miss Benson ventured to go up*, and was equally delighted with her brother; but so fearful of terrifying the little birds, and alarming the old ones, that she would only indulge herself with a peep at the nest. Frederick inquired how she liked the young Robins? They are sweet creatures, said she, and I hope we shall soon find means to invite them to join our party of birds, for they appear to me ready to fly; but let us return to mamma, for you know we promised her to stay but a little while; besides, we hinder Joe from his work. Never mind that, said the honest fellow, master won't be angry, I am *sartain;* and if I thought he would, I would work an hour later to fetch up lost time. Thank you, Joe, replied Miss Harriet, but I am sure papa would not desire that.

At this instant, Frederick perceived the two Redbreasts, who were returning from their proposed excursion, and called to his sister to observe them. He was very desirous to watch whether they would go back to their nest, but she would on no account consent to stay, lest her mamma should be displeased; and lest the birds should be frightened: Frederick, therefore, with reluctance followed her, and Joe attended them to the house.

As soon as they were out of sight, the hen-bird proposed to return to the nest; she had observed the party, and though she did not see them looking into her habitation, supposed, from their being so near, that they had been taking a view of it, and communicated her suspicions to her mate. He agreed with her, that this had probably been the case, and said he now expected to hear a fine story from the nestlings. Let us return, however, said the mother, for perhaps they have been terrified again. Well, said he, I will attend you then; but let me caution you, my dear, not to indulge their fearful disposition, because such indulgence will certainly prove injurious to them. I will do the best I can, replied she, and then flew to the nest, followed by her mate.

She alighted upon the ivy, and peeping into the nest, inquired how they all did? Very well, dear mother, said Robin. What, cried the father (who now alighted), all safe? Not one eat up by the monster? No, father, cried Dicky, we are not devoured, and yet, I assure you, the monster we saw before, has been here again, and brought two others with him. Two others! what, like himself? said the father: I thought, Flapsy, you were to die with apprehension if you saw him again? And so I believe I should have done, had not you, my good father, instructed me to conquer my fears, replied Flapsy. When I saw the top of him, my heart began to flutter to such a degree, that I was ready to faint, and every feather of me shook; but when I found he staid but a very little while, I recovered, and was in hopes he was quite gone. My brothers and sister, I believe, felt as I did; but we comforted one another, that the danger was over for this day, and all agreed to make ourselves happy, and not fear this monster, since you had assured us he was very harmless. However, before we were perfectly come to ourselves, we heard very uncommon noises, sometimes a hoarse sound, disagreeable to our ears as the croaking of a raven, and sometimes a shriller noise, quite unlike the note of any bird that we know of, and immediately after, something presented itself to our view, which bore a little resemblance to the monster, but by no means so large and frightful. Instead of being all over red, it had on each side, two spots of a more beautiful hue than Dicky's breast; the rest of it was of a most delicate white, excepting two streaks of a deep red, like the cherry you brought us the other day, and between these two streaks were rows of white bones, but by no means dreadful to behold, like those of the great monster; its eyes were blue and white, and round this agreeable face, was something which I cannot describe, very pretty, and as glossy as the feathers of a Goldfinch. There was so cheerful and pleasing a look in this creature altogether, that notwithstanding I own I was rather afraid, yet I had pleasure in looking at it, but it staid a very little time, and then disappeared. While we were puzzling ourselves with conjectures concerning it, another creature, larger than it, appeared before us, equally beautiful, and with an aspect so mild and gentle, that we were all charmed with it; but, as if fearful of alarming us by its stay, it immediately retired, and we have been longing for your and my mother's return, in hopes you would be able to tell us what we have seen.

I am happy, my dears, said the mother, to find you more composed than I expected: for as your father and I were flying together, in order to come back to you, we observed the monster, and the two pretty creatures Pecksy has described; the former is, as your father before informed you, our friend the gardener, and the others are our young benefactors, by whose bounty we are every day regaled, and who, I will venture to say, will do you no harm. You cannot think how kindly they treat us; and though there are a number of other birds who share their goodness, your father and I are favoured with their particular regard.

Oh! said Pecksy, are these sweet creatures your friends? I long to go abroad that I may see them again. Well, cried Flapsy, I perceive that if we judge from appearances, we may often be mistaken; who would have thought that such an ugly monster as that gardener, could have had a tender heart? Very true, replied the mother; you must make it a rule, Flapsy, to judge of *mankind* by their *actions,* and not by their *looks.* I have known some of them, whose appearance was as engaging as that of our young benefactors, who were, notwithstanding, barbarous enough to take eggs out of a nest and spoil them; nay, even carry away nest and all, before the young ones were fledged, without knowing how to feed them, or having any regard to the sorrows of the tender parents. Yes, said the mother, last year it was my misfortune to be deprived of my nestlings in that manner, which occasions my being so timid; the anguish I suffered for their loss is not to be expressed.

A calamity of the same kind befel me, replied the father; I never shall forget it. I had been making an excursion into the woods, in order to procure some delicious morsels for one of my nestlings; when I returned to the place in which I had imprudently built (for being young and inexperienced, I did not foresee the danger of choosing an exposed situation), the first circumstance that alarmed me, was a part of my nest scattered upon the ground, just at the entrance of my habitation; I then perceived a large opening in the wall, where before there was only room for myself to pass. I stopped with a palpitating heart, in hopes of hearing the chirpings of my beloved family; but all was silence. I then resolved to enter; but what was my consternation, when I found that the nest, which my dear mate and I had with so much labour built, and the dear little ones, who were the joy of our lives, were stolen away; nay, I did not know but the tender mother also was taken captive. I immediately rushed out of the place, distracted with apprehensions for the miseries they might endure; lamented my weakness, which rendered me incapable of effecting their rescue; was ready to tear off my own feathers with vexation; but recollecting that my dear mate might in all probability have escaped, I resolved to go in search of her.

As I was flying along, I saw three boys, whose appearance was far from disagreeable; one of them held in his hand my nest of young ones, which he eyed with cruel exultation, while his companions seemed to share his joy.

The dear little creatures, insensible of their fate (for they were newly hatched), opened their mouths in expectation of the usual supply, but all in vain; to have attempted feeding them at this time, would have been inevitable destruction to myself; but I resolved to follow the barbarians, that I might at least see to what place my darlings were consigned.

In a short time the party arrived at a house, and he who before held the nest, now committed it to the care of another, but soon returned with a kind of victuals I was totally unacquainted with; and with this my young ones, when they gaped for food, were successively fed: hunger induced them to swallow it with avidity, but soon after missing the warmth of their mother, they set up a general chirp of lamentation, which pierced my very heart. Immediately after this the nest was carried away, and what became of my nestlings afterwards, I never could discover, though I frequently hovered about the fatal spot of their imprisonment, with the hope of seeing them.

Pray, father, said Dicky, what became of your mate? Why, my dear, said he, when I found there was no chance of assisting my little ones, I pursued my course, and sought her in every place of our usual resort, but to no purpose: at length I returned to the bush, where I beheld an afflicting sight indeed, my dear companion lying on the ground, just expiring! I flew to her instantly, and endeavoured to recall her to life: at the sound of my voice she lifted up her languid eyelids, and with feeble accents said, And are you then safe, my love? What is become of our little ones? In hopes of comforting her, I told her they were alive and well; but she replied, Your consolation comes too late; the blow is struck, I feel my death approaching. The horror which seized me when I missed my nest-lings, and supposed myself robbed at once of my mate and infants, was too powerful for my weak frame to sustain. Oh! why will the human race be so wantonly cruel! The agonies of death now came on, and after a few convulsive pangs, she breathed her last, and left me an unhappy widower. I passed the remainder of the summer, and a dreary winter that suc-ceeded it, in a very uncomfortable manner; though the natural cheerfulness of my disposi-tion, did not leave me long a prey to unavailing sorrow: and having paid a proper tribute to the memory of my first dear mate, I resolved the following spring to seek another; and had the good fortune to meet with one, whose amiable disposition has renewed my happi-ness; and now, my dear, said he, let me ask you what became of your former companion?

Why, replied the hen Redbreast, soon after the loss of our nest, as he was endeavouring to discover what was become of it, a cruel hawk caught him up and devoured him in an instant.

I need not say that I felt the bitterest pangs for his loss; it is sufficient to inform you, that I led a solitary life, till I met with you, whose endearing behaviour has made society again agreeable to me.

While the parent birds were thus relating the history of their past misfortunes, the young ones listened with the greatest attention; and when the tales were ended, Flapsy exclaimed, Oh! what dangers there are in the world! I shall be afraid to leave the nest. Why so, my love? said the mother. Every bird does not meet with hawks and cruel children. You have already, as you sat on the nest, seen thousands of the feathered race, of one kind or other, making their airy excursions, full of mirth and gaiety. This orchard constantly resounds with the melody of those who chaunt forth their songs of joy, and I believe there are no beings in the world happier than birds, for we are naturally formed for cheerfulness; and I flatter myself, a prudent precaution will preserve both your father and myself from any future accident. Our parents were young and inexperienced themselves, and could not give us good advice; but we know the dangers of the world, and I hope shall be able to point out to you such rules of conduct, as may, if followed, counteract the usual accidents to which birds are exposed.

Instead of indulging your fears, Flapsy, said the father, summon up all your courage, for to-morrow you shall, with your brothers and sister, begin to see the world. Dicky expressed great delight at this declaration, and Robin boasted that he had not the least remains of fear. Flapsy, though still apprehensive of monsters, yet longed to see the gaieties of life, and Pecksy wished to comply with every desire of her dear parents. The approach of evening now reminded them that it was time to take repose; and turning their heads under their wings, each bird soon resigned itself to the gentle power of sleep.

CHAPTER VIII

AFTER MASTER and Miss Benson had been gratified with the sight of the Robin's nest, they were returning to the house, conducted by their friend Joe, when they were met in the garden by their papa and mamma, accompanied by Miss Lucy Jenkins and her brother Edward. The former was a fine girl about ten years old, the latter a robust rude boy, turned of eleven. We were coming to seek you, my dears, said Mrs. Benson to her children, for I was fearful that the business you went upon would make you forget your young visitors.

I cannot answer for Frederick, replied Miss Benson, but indeed, mamma, I would not on any account have slighted my friends. How do you do, my dear Miss Jenkins? said she, I am happy to see you. Will you go with me into the play-room? I have got some very pretty new books. Frederick, have you nothing to shew Master Jenkins? O yes, said Frederick, I have got a new ball, a new top, a new organ, and twenty pretty things; but I had rather go back and shew him the Robins.

The Robins! said Master Jenkins, what Robins?

Why our Robins, that have built in the ivy-wall. You never saw any thing so pretty in your life as the little ones.

Oh, I can see birds enow at home, said Master Jenkins; but why did you not take the nest? It would have been nice diversion to you to toss the young birds about. I have had a great many nests this year, and do believe I have an hundred eggs.

An hundred eggs! and how do you propose to hatch them? said Miss Harriet, who turned her back on hearing him talk in this manner.

Hatch them, Miss Benson, said he; who ever thinks of hatching birds' eggs?

Oh, then you eat them, said Frederick, or perhaps let your cook make puddings of them?

No, indeed, replied Master Jenkins, I blow out the inside, and then run a thread through them, and give them to Lucy to hang up amongst her curiosities, and very pretty they look, I assure you.

And so, said Miss Harriet, you had rather see a parcel of empty egg-shells, than hear a sweet concert of birds singing in the trees? I admire your taste truly!

Why, is there any harm in taking birds' eggs? said Miss Jenkins; I never before heard that there was.

My dear mamma, replied Miss Benson, has taught me to think, there is harm in every action which gives causeless pain to any living creature; and I own I have a very particular affection for birds.

Well, said Miss Jenkins, I have no notion of such affections, for my part. Sometimes, indeed, I try to rear those which Edward brings home, but they are teasing, troublesome things, and I am not lucky; to tell the truth, I do not concern myself much about them; if they *live*, they *live*, and if they *die*, they *die*. He has brought me three nests this day to plague me; I thought to have fed the birds before I came out, but being in a hurry to come to see you, I quite forgot it. Did you feed them, Edward? Not I, said he, I thought you would do it; 'tis enough for me to find the nests.

And have you actually left three nests of young birds at home without victuals! exclaimed Miss Harriet.

I did not think of them, but will feed them when I return, said Miss Jenkins.

O, cried Miss Benson, I cannot bear the thoughts of what the poor little creatures must suffer.

Well, said Master Jenkins, since you feel so much for them, I think, Miss Harriet, you will make the best nurse. What say you, Lucy, will you give the nests to Miss Benson? With all my heart, replied his sister, and pray do not plague me with any more of them.

I do not know that my mamma will let me accept them, said Miss Benson, but if she will, I shall be glad to do so.

Frederick inquired what birds they were, and Master Jenkins informed him, there was a nest of Linnets, a nest of Sparrows, and another of Blackbirds. Frederick was all impatience to see them, and Miss Harriet longed to have the little creatures in her possession, that she might rescue them from their deplorable condition, and lessen the evils of captivity, which they now suffered in the extreme.

Her mamma had left her with her young companions, that they might indulge themselves in innocent amusements without restraint, but the tender-hearted Harriet could not engage in any diversion, till she had made intercession in behalf of the poor birds; she therefore begged Miss Jenkins would accompany her to her mamma, in order to solicit permission to have the birds' nests. She accordingly went, and made her request known to Mrs. Benson, who readily consented; observing that though she had a very great objection to her children's having birds' nests, yet she could not deny her daughter on the present occasion. Harriet, from an unwillingness to expose her friend, had said but little on the subject, but Mrs. Benson, having great discernment, concluded that she made the request from a merciful motive, and knowing that Miss Jenkins had no kind mamma to give her instruction, she thus addressed her.

I perceive, my young friend, that Harriet is apprehensive the birds will not meet with the same kind treatment from you, which she is disposed to give them. I cannot think you have any cruelty in your nature, but perhaps you have only accustomed yourself to consider birds as play-things, without sense or feeling; to me, who am a great admirer of the beautiful little creatures, they appear in a very different light; and I have been an attentive observer of them, I assure you.

Though they cannot speak our language, each kind has one of its own, which is perfectly understood by those of its own species; and so far intelligible to us, as to convince us they are susceptible of joy, grief, fear, anger, and resentment; and we may easily discover, that they delight in associating with those of their own class, and pursue with alacrity the employments allotted them; from whence we may justly infer, that it is cruel to rob them of their young, deprive them of their liberty, separate them from their respective societies, or place them in situations where they are excluded from the blessings suited to their natures, for which it is impossible for us to give them an equivalent.

Besides, these creatures, insignificant as they appear in your estimation, were made by GOD as well as you. Have you not read in your Testament, my dear, that our Saviour said, *Blessed are the merciful, for they shall obtain mercy.* How can you expect that GOD

will send his blessing upon you, if you, instead of endeavouring to imitate him in being merciful to the *utmost of your power*, are wantonly cruel to innocent creatures which he *designed* for happiness?

This admonition from Mrs. Benson, which Miss Jenkins did not expect, made her look very serious, and brought tears into her eyes; on which the good Lady took her by the hand and kindly said, I wish not to distress you, my dear, but merely to awaken the natural sentiments of your heart: reflect at your leisure on what I have taken the liberty of saying to you, and I am sure you will think me your friend. I knew your dear mamma, and can assure you, she was remarkable for the tenderness of her disposition. But let me not detain you from your amusements; go to your own apartment, Harriet, and use your best endeavours to make your visitors happy. You cannot this evening fetch the birds, because, when Miss Jenkins goes, it will be too late for you to take so long a walk, as you must come back afterwards; and I make no doubt, but that to oblige you, she will feed them to-night.

Miss Harriet and Miss Jenkins returned, and found Frederick diverting himself with the hand organ, which had lately been presented by his god-papa; but Master Jenkins had laid hold of Miss Harriet's dog, and was searching his own pocket for a piece of string, that he might tie him and the cat together, to see, as he said, how nicely they would fight: and so fully was he bent on this cruel purpose, that it was with difficulty he could be prevailed on to relinquish it.

Dear me, said he, if ever I came into such a house in my life, there is no *fun* here. What would you have said to Harry Pritchard and me, the other day, when we made the cats fly?

Made cats fly! said Frederick, how was that?

Why, replied he, *we tied bladders to each side of their necks, and then flung them from the top of the house.* There was an end of their purring and mewing for some time, I assure you, for they lay a long while struggling and gasping for breath; and if they had not had nine lives, I think they must have died; but at last up they jumped, and away they ran scampering. Then out came little Jemmy, crying as if he had flown down himself, because we hurt the poor cats; he had a dog running after him, who, I suppose, meant to call us to task, with his *bow, wow;* but we soon stopped his tongue, for we caught the gentleman, and drove him before us into a narrow lane, and then ran hooting after him into the village; a number of boys joined us, and cried out as we did, *a mad dog! a mad dog!* On this several people pursued him with cudgels and broomsticks, and at last he was shot by a man, but not dead, so others came and knocked him about the head till he expired.

For shame! Master Jenkins, said Miss Harriet, how can you talk in that rhodomontade manner? I cannot believe any young gentleman could bring his heart to such barbarities.

Barbarities, indeed! why have we not a *right* to do as we please to dogs and cats, or do you think they *feel* as we do? Fiddle faddle of your nonsense, say I; come, you must hear the end of my story. When the dog was dead, we carried him home to little Jemmy, who was ready to break his heart for the loss of him; so we did not like to stand hearing his whining, therefore left him and got a Cock, whose legs we tied, and flung at him till he died. Then we set two others to fighting, and fine sport we had; for one was pecked till his breast was laid open, and the other was blinded; so we left them to make up their quarrel as they could. After this we picked all the feathers off a live chicken, and you never saw such a ridiculous little animal in your life. Then we got some puppies, and drowned them while the mother stood by. Oh! how she howled and cried, whilst they struggled on the surface of the water; and there was no quieting her for several days.

Stop! stop! exclaimed Miss Harriet; for pity's sake, stop! I can hear no more of your horrid narrations; nor would I commit even *one* of those barbarities which you boast of for the world! Poor innocent creatures! what had they done to you to deserve such usage?

I beg, Edward, said his sister, that you will find some other way to entertain us, or I shall really tell Mrs. Benson of you.

What! you are growing tender-hearted all at once! cried he.

I will tell you what I think when I go home, replied Miss Jenkins. As for poor Frederick, he could not restrain his tears; and Harriet's flowed in a copious stream, with the bare idea of the sufferings of the poor animals, particularly for the live chicken, and the poor creature, whose puppies were drowned in her sight: but Master Jenkins was so accustomed to be guilty of these things without reflection, that there was no making any impression of tenderness upon his mind; and he only laughed at their concern, and wanted to tell a long story about an ox that had been driven by a cruel drover till he went mad; but Miss Benson and his sister stopped their ears. As soon as they left off doing so, he began another about Bat-fowling which is a treacherous custom of going with a lantern by night to the hedges, where birds roost, and frightening them into a net placed for the purpose. In short, it appeared from his discourse, that he was acquainted with the whole art of tormenting animals.

At last little Frederick went crying to his mamma, and the young Ladies retired to another apartment, so Master Jenkins amused himself with catching flies in the window, pulling the legs off from some, and the wings from others, delighted with their contortions, which were occasioned by the agonies they endured. Mrs. Benson had some visitors, which prevented her talking to this cruel boy, as she otherwise would have done, on hearing Frederick's account of him, but she determined to tell his papa; which she accordingly did some time after, when he returned home: but this gentleman, so far from reproving his son, applauded him as a lad of life and spirit, and said he would be fit to go through the world.

Master Jenkins was now disturbed from his barbarous sport by being called to tea; and soon after that was over, the servant came to fetch him and his sister. Miss Harriet earnestly entreated her friend Lucy to feed the birds properly, till she should be allowed to fetch them, who promised to do so; for she was greatly affected with Mrs. Benson's discourse, and then entreated her brother to take leave, that she might return home; with this he readily complied, as there were no further opportunities for cruelty.

CHAPTER IX

AFTER HER little visitors were departed, Miss Harriet went into the drawing-room, and having paid her compliments, sat herself down that she might improve her mind by the conversation of the company. Her mamma perceived that she had been in tears, of which Frederick had before explained the cause. I do not wonder, my love, said she, that you should have been so affected with the relation of such horrid barbarities, as that thoughtless boy has, by degrees, brought himself to practise, not only without remorse, but by way of amusement. However, do not suffer your mind to dwell on them, as the creatures on which he inflicted them are no longer objects of pity. It is wrong to grieve for the death of animals as we do for the loss of our friends, because they certainly are not of so much consequence to our happiness; and we are taught to think their sufferings end with their lives, as they are not religious beings; and therefore the killing them, even in the cruelest manner, is not like murdering a human creature, who is perhaps unprepared to give an account of himself at the tribunal of Heaven. I have, said a Lady who was present, been for a long time accustomed to consider animals as mere machines, actuated by the unerring hand of Providence, to do those things which are necessary for the preservation of themselves and their offspring; but the sight of the learned Pig, which has lately been shewn in London, has deranged these ideas, and I know not what to think.

If we puzzle our minds for ever, on the subject, Madam, replied a Gentleman who accompanied her, we shall never be able fully to comprehend the capacities and feelings of creatures so different from ourselves. That they have not reasonable souls, like the human race, is evident; but at the same time I think we may plainly discover, that they have some portion of intellect, which is even capable of improvement to a certain degree: this is particularly exemplified in the instance which Mrs. Franks has just mentioned of the learned Pig. Mere instinct, I think, would never lead that creature to distinguish one letter from another, or, which amounts to the same thing, to comprehend the various signs by which they are pointed out to him by his keeper. To what a pitch may Dogs and Horses be improved; nay, every kind of animal that I have had an opportunity of observing, seems to acquire sagacity, by a familiar intercourse with rational creatures; yet, after all, they fall short of human reason beyond comparison.

For my part, replied Mrs. Benson, I find the subject so much above my comprehension, that whenever my mind is disposed to expatiate on it, I check the inclination, from an opinion that it is of no consequence to me, whether animals have intellects or not, and that it is amongst those things which the Almighty has intentionally concealed from our penetration. That they are in the power of man, and subservient to his use and pleasure, gives them a sufficient claim to our compassion and kindness; and while I am partly fed and clothed at the expense of the animal creation, I could not bring myself to inflict wanton cruelties upon them. On the other hand, as Providence has placed them so much beneath us in the scale of beings, I should think it equally wrong to elevate them from their proper rank in life, and suffer them to occupy that share of attention and love, which is due to our own species only.

You are certainly right, Madam, answered the Gentleman; there are objects enow for the employment of human reason, without our endeavouring to penetrate into those things which must for ever remain hidden, unless the inferior creatures were endued with speech. We can form but very imperfect ideas even of our own intellectual powers, still less of those of other men; and the farther any creature is removed from us, the less capable are we of comprehending its nature, as we can only judge in these matters, by what passes in ourselves.

Neither you, Sir, nor Mrs. Benson, said Mrs. Franks, mean, I apprehend, to discourage the study of the natural history of animals. By no means, replied the latter; for as far as it is open to our view, it is replete with amusement and instruction. It leads the mind to contemplate the perfections of the Supreme Being, and also furnishes a variety of useful hints for the conduct of human affairs. Many important arts have, in all probability, been derived from them; and the exact regularity with which they discharge the offices of tenderness and economy, afford examples of real utility to those amongst us, who are disposed to neglect the duties of humanity. An idle person, for instance, may be admonished by an Ant or Bee, a thoughtless mother by a Hen, an unfaithful servant by a Dog, and so on, as one of our poets has elegantly pointed out in his Fable.* I only mean that we should confine our speculations within due bounds, and not caress animals to the neglect of the human species.

Then you would condemn a Lady of my acquaintance, said the Gentleman, who has a little Lap-dog on which her happiness totally depends, and to use a vulgar expression, her very life seems to be wrapped up in his. I am sure it is quite provoking to see a reasonable creature make herself so ridiculous. It is more than ridiculous, replied Mrs. Benson; it is really sinful. At this instant the arrival of Mrs. Franks's coach was announced, and she with the Gentleman took leave.

As soon as they were gone, Pray mamma, said Harriet, what does the learned Pig do? I had a great desire to ask Mrs. Franks, but was fearful she would think me impertinent.

I commend your modesty, my dear, replied Mrs. Benson, but would not have it lead you into such a degree of restraint, as to prevent your gratifying that laudable curiosity, without which young persons must remain ignorant of many things very proper for them to be acquainted with. Mrs. Franks would, I am sure, have been far from thinking you impertinent: Those inquiries only are thought troublesome, by which children interrupt conversation, and endeavour to attract attention to their own insignificant prattle; but all people of good sense and good nature delight in giving them useful information.

---

* Gay's Fable of the Shepherd and Philosopher.

In respect to the learned Pig, I have heard things which are quite astonishing in a species of animals generally regarded as very stupid. The creature was shewn for a sight in a room provided for the purpose, where a number of people assembled to view his performances. Two alphabets of large letters on card paper were placed on the floor; one of the company was then desired to propose a word which he wished the Pig to spell. This his keeper repeated to him, and the Pig picked out every letter successively with his snout, and collected them together till the word was completed. He was then desired to tell the hour of the day, and one of the company held a watch to him; this he seemed with his little cunning eyes to examine very attentively; and having done so, picked out figures for the hour and minutes of the day. He shewed a number of tricks, of the same nature, to the great diversion of the spectators.

For my own part, though I was in London at the time he was exhibited, and heard continually of this wonderful Pig from persons of my acquaintance, I never went to see him; for I am fully persuaded, that great cruelty must have been exercised in teaching him things so foreign to his nature, and therefore would not give any encouragement to such a scheme.

And do you think, mamma, said Harriet, that the Pig knows the letters, and can really spell words?

I think it possible, my dear, for the Pig to be taught to know the letters one from the other, and that his keeper has some private sign, by which he directs him to each that is wanted; but that he has an idea of *spelling*, I can never believe, nor are animals capable of attaining human sciences, because, for these, human faculties are requisite; and no art of men can *change* the nature of any thing, though he may be able to improve that nature to a certain degree, or at least to call forth to view, powers which would be hidden from us, because they would only be exerted in the intercourse of animals with each other. As far as this can be done by familiarizing them, and shewing them such a degree of kindness as is consistent with our higher obligations, it may be an agreeable amusement, but will never answer any important purpose to mankind; and I would advise you Harriet, never to give countenance to those people who shew what they call *learned* animals; as you may assure yourself they exercise great barbarities upon them, of which starving them almost to death is most likely among the number; and you may with the money such a sight would cost you procure for yourself a rational amusement, or even relieve some wretched creature from extreme distress. But, my dear, it is now time for you to retire to rest; I will therefore bid you good night.

CHAPTER X

Early in the morning the hen Redbreast awakened her young brood. Come, my little ones, said she, shake off your drowsiness; remember this is the day fixed for your entrance into the world. I desire that each of you will dress your feathers before you go out; for a slovenly bird is my aversion, and neatness is a great advantage to the appearance of every one.

The father was upon the wing betimes, that he might give each of his young ones a breakfast before they attempted to leave the nest. When he had fed them, he desired his mate to accompany him as usual to Mr. Benson's, where he found the parlour window open, and his young friends sitting with their mamma. Crumbs had been, according to custom, strewed before the window, which the other birds had nearly devoured; but the Redbreasts took their usual post on the tea-table, and the cock bird sung his morning lay; after which they returned with all possible speed to the nest, for having so important an affair to manage, they could not be long absent. Neither could their young benefactors pay so much attention to them as usual, for they were impatient to fetch the birds' nests from Miss Jenkins's; therefore as soon as breakfast was ended, they set out on their expedition. Harriet carried a basket large enough to hold two nests, and Frederick a smaller one for the other; thus equipped, with a servant attending them, they set off.

Mr. Jenkins's house was about a mile from Mr. Benson's; it was delightfully situated: there was a beautiful lawn and canal before it, and a charming garden behind; on one side were corn-fields, and on the other a wood. In such a delightful retreat as this, it was natural to expect to find a great many birds; but, to Miss Harriet's surprise, they saw only a few straggling ones here and there, who fled with the utmost precipitation as soon as she and her brother appeared; on which she observed to Frederick, that she supposed Master Jenkins's practise of taking birds' nests had made them so shy, and entreated him never to commit so barbarous an action. She said a great deal to him about the cruelties that naughty boy had boasted of the evening before, which Frederick promised to remember.

As soon as they arrived at the house, Miss Jenkins ran out to receive them, but her brother was gone to school. We are come, my dear Lucy, said Miss Benson, to claim the performance of Master Jenkins's promise; how are your little prisoners?

O! I know not what to say to you, my dear, said Miss Jenkins, I have very bad news to tell you, and I fear you will blame me exceedingly, though not more than I blame myself. I heartily wish I had returned home immediately after the kind lecture your mamma favoured me with yesterday, which shewed me the cruelty of my behaviour, though I was then ashamed to own my conviction.

I walked as fast as I could all the way from your house, and determined to give each of the little creatures a good supper; for which purpose I had an egg boiled, and nicely chopped; I mixed up some bread and water very smooth, and put a little seed with the chopped egg amongst it, and then carried it to the room where I left the nests. But what was my concern, when I found that my care was too late, for the greatest part of them! Every Sparrow lay dead and bloody; they seemed to have killed each other. Urged I suppose by extreme hunger, each spent on his unhappy associates those pecks and blows which were my proper desert.

In the nest of Linnets, which were very young, I found one dead, two just expiring, and the other almost exhausted, but still able to swallow; to him, therefore, I immediately dispensed some of the food I had prepared, which greatly revived him; and as I thought he would suffer with cold in the nest by himself, I covered him over with wool, and had this morning the pleasure of finding him quite recovered.

What, all the Sparrows and three Linnets dead! said Frederick, whose little eyes swam with tears at the melancholy tale: and pray, Miss Jenkins, have you starved all the Blackbirds too?

Not all, my little friend, answered Miss Jenkins, but I must confess that some of them have fallen victims to my barbarous neglect; however, there are two fine ones alive,

which I shall, with the surviving Linnet, cheerfully resign to the care of my dear Harriet, whose tenderness will, I hope, be rewarded by the pleasure of hearing them sing when they are old enough. But I beg you will stay and rest yourselves after your walk.

Let me see the birds first, said Frederick.

That you shall do, answered Miss Jenkins; and taking him by the hand, conducted him to the room in which she kept them, accompanied by Miss Benson. She then fed the birds, and gave particular instructions for making their food, and declared that she would never be a receiver of birds'-nests any more, but expressed her apprehensions that it would be difficult to wean Edward from his propensity for taking them; however, said she, he is going as a boarder to a private academy soon, where I think he will have better employment for his leisure hours.

Miss Jenkins then took her young friends into the parlour to her Governess (for her mamma was dead), who received them very kindly, and gave each of them a piece of cake and some fruit; after which, Miss Jenkins led them again into the room where the birds were, and very carefully put the nest, with the poor solitary Linnet, into one basket, and that with the two Blackbirds into the other. Frederick was very urgent to carry the latter, which his sister consented to; and then bidding adieu to their friend, they set off on their return home, attended by the maid, as before.

Well, Frederick, said Miss Harriet, as they walked along, what think you of bird-nesting now? Should you like to occasion the death of so many little harmless creatures? No, indeed, said Frederick; and I think Miss Jenkins a very naughty girl for starving them.

She was to blame, but is now sorry for her fault, my dear, therefore you must not speak unkindly of her; besides, you know, she has no good mamma, as we have, to teach her what is proper; and her papa is obliged to be absent from home very often, and leave her to the care of a Governess, who perhaps was never instructed herself to be tender of animals.

With this kind of conversation they amused themselves as they walked, *every now and then peeping into their baskets to see their little birds,* which were very lively and well. They entreated the maid to take them through the orchard, which had a gate that opened into a meadow that lay in their way, having no doubt of obtaining admittance, as it was the usual hour for their friend Joe to work there. They accordingly knocked at the gate, which was immediately opened to them, and Frederick requested Joe to shew him the Robins' nest. But before we proceed to this part of our History, we must return to the Redbreasts, whom we left on the wing, flying back to the ivy-wall, in order to take their young ones abroad.

CHAPTER XI

As the father entered the nest, he cried out, with a cheerful voice, Well, my nestlings, are you all ready? Yes, they replied. The mother then advanced, and desired that each of them would get upon the edge of the nest. Robin and Pecksy sprang up in an instant, but Dicky and Flapsy being timorous, were not so expeditious.

The hearts of the parents felt a rapturous delight at the advantageous view they now had of their young family, who appeared to be strong, vigorous, and lively; and, in a word, endued with every gift of nature requisite to their success in the world.

Now, said the father, stretch your wings, Robin, and flutter them a little, in this manner (shewing him the way), and be sure to observe my directions exactly. Very well, said he; do not attempt to fly yet, for here is neither air nor space enough for that purpose. Walk gently after me to the wall; now hop and perch upon this branch, and as soon as you see me fly away, spread your wings, and exert all the strength you have to follow me.

Robin acquitted himself to admiration, and alighted very safely on the ground.

Now stand still, said the father, till the rest join us: Then going back, he called upon Dicky to do the same as his brother had done: but Dicky was very fearful of fluttering his wings, for he had a great deal of cowardice in his disposition, and expressed many apprehensions that he should not reach the ground without falling, as they were such a great height from it. His father, who was a very courageous bird, was quite angry with him.

Why you foolish little thing, said he, do you mean to stay in the nest by yourself and starve? I shall leave off bringing you food, I assure you. Do you think your wings were given you to be always folded by your sides, and that the whole employment of your life is to dress your feathers, and make yourself look pretty? Without exercise you cannot long enjoy health; besides, you will soon have your livelihood to earn, and therefore idleness would in you be the height of folly; get up this instant.

Dicky, intimidated by his father's displeasure, got up, and advanced as far as the branch from which he was to descend; but here his fears returned, and instead of making an effort to fly, he stood flapping his wings in a most irresolute manner, and suffered his father to lead the way twice without following him. This good parent, finding that he would not venture to fly, took a circuit unperceived by Dicky, and watching the opportunity when his wings were a little spread, came suddenly behind him, and pushed him off from the branch. Dicky, finding himself in actual danger of falling, now gladly stretched his pinions, and, upborne by the air, gently descended to the ground, so near the spot where

Robin stood, that the latter easily reached him by hopping.

The mother now undertook to conduct Flapsy and Pecksy, whilst the father staid to take care of the two already landed. Flapsy made a thousand difficulties, but at length yielded to her mother's persuasions, and flew safely down. Pecksy, without the least hesitation, accompanied her, and by exactly following the directions given, found the task much easier than she expected.

As soon as they had a little recovered from the fatigue and fright of their first essay at flying, they began to look around them with astonishment. Every object on which they turned their eyes excited their curiosity and wonder. They were no longer confined to a little nest, built in a small hole, but were now at full liberty in the open air. The orchard itself appeared to them a world. For some time each remained silent, gazing around, first at one thing, then at another; at length Flapsy cried out, What a charming place the world is! I had no conception that it was half so big!

And do you suppose then, my dear, replied the mother, that you now behold the whole of the world? I have seen but a small part of it myself, and yet have flown over so large a space, that what is at present within our view appears to me a little inconsiderable spot; and I have conversed with several foreign birds, who informed me, that the country they came from was so distant, that they were many days on their journey hither, though they flew the nearest way, and scarcely allowed themselves any resting-time.

Come, said the father, let us proceed to business, we did not leave the nest merely to look about us. You are now, my young ones, safely landed on the ground, let me instruct you what you are to do on it. Every living creature that comes into the world, has something allotted him to perform, and therefore should not stand an idle spectator of what others are doing. We small birds have a very easy task, in comparison of many animals I have had an opportunity of observing, being only required to seek food for ourselves, build nests, and provide for our young ones, till they are able to procure their own livelihood.

We have indeed enemies to dread; Hawks and other birds of prey will catch us up, if we are not upon our guard; but the worst foes we have, are those of the human race; though even among them the Redbreasts have a better chance than many other birds, on account of a charitable action which a pair of our species are said to have performed toward a little boy and girl* who were lost in a wood, where they were starved to death. *The Redbreasts I mention, saw the affectionate pair hand-in-hand, stretched on the cold ground,* and would have fed them, had they been capable of receiving nourishment; but finding them quite dead, and being unable to bury them, resolved to cover them with leaves. This was an arduous task, but many a Redbreast has since shared the reward of it; and I believe, that those who do good to others, always meet with a recompense some way or other. But I declare I am doing the very thing I was reproving you for—chattering away when I should be minding business. Come, hop after me, and we shall soon find something worth having. Fear nothing, for you are now in a place of security; there is no Hawk near, and I have never seen any of the human race enter this orchard, but the monsters who paid you visits in the nest, and others equally inoffensive.

The father then hopped away, followed by Robin and Dicky, whilst his mate conducted the female part of the family. The parents instructed their young ones in what manner to

---

* Alluding to the Ballad of the Children in the Wood.

seek for food, and they proved very successful, for there were a number of insects just at hand.

Dicky had the good fortune to find four little worms together, but instead of calling his brother and sisters to partake of them, he devoured them all himself.

Are you not ashamed, you little greedy creature? cried his father, who observed his selfish disposition. What would you think of your brother and sisters, were they to serve you so? In a family, every individual ought to consult the welfare of the whole, instead of his own private satisfaction. It is his own truest interest to do so. A day may come, when he who has now sufficient to supply the wants of his relations, may stand in need of assistance from them. But setting aside *selfish* considerations, which are the last that ever find place in a generous breast, how great is the pleasure of doing good, and contributing to the happiness of others!

Dicky was quite confounded, and immediately hopped away, to find, if possible, something for his brother and sisters, that he might regain their good opinion.

In the meanwhile, Robin found a caterpillar, which he intended to take for Pecksy; but just as he was going to pick it up, a Linnet, who had a nest in the orchard, snatched it from him and flew away with it.

Inflamed with the most furious rage, Robin advanced to his father, and entreated that he would fly after the Linnet and tear his heart out.

That would be taking violent revenge indeed, said his father. No, [Robin,] the Linnet has as great a right to the caterpillar as you or I; and in all probability, has many little gaping mouths at home ready to receive it. But, however this may be, I had, for my own part, rather sustain an injury than take revenge. You must expect to have many a scramble of this kind in your life; but if you give way to a resentful temper, you will do yourself more harm than all the enemies in the world can do you; for you will be in perpetual agitation from an idea, that every one who does not act in direct conformity to your wishes, has a design against you. Therefore, restrain your anger that you may be happy; for believe me, peace and tranquillity are the most valuable things you can possess.

At this instant, Pecksy came up with a fine fat spider in her mouth, which she laid down at her mother's feet, and thus addressed her. Accept, my dear parent, the first tribute of gratitude which I have ever been able to offer you. How have I formerly longed to ease those toils which you and my dear father endured for our sakes; and gladly would I now release you from farther fatigue on my account, but I am still a poor inexperienced creature, and must continue to take shelter under your wing. All my power to assist you shall however be exerted, and I will hop as long as I am able to procure provisions for the family. The eyes of the mother sparkled with delight; and knowing that Pecksy's love would be disappointed by a refusal, she ate the spider, which the dutiful nestling had so affectionately brought her; and then said—How happy would families be, if every one, like you, my dear Pecksy, consulted the welfare of the rest, instead of turning their whole attention to their own interest.

Dicky was not present at this speech, which he might have considered as a reflection on his own conduct; but he arrived as it was ended, and presented Pecksy with a worm, like those he had himself so greedily eaten. She received it with thanks, and declared it was doubly welcome from his beak.

Certainly, said the mother, fraternal love stamps a value on the most trifling presents. Dicky felt himself happy in having regained the good opinion of his mother, and obliged his sister, and resolved for the future to be generous.

The young Redbreasts soon after all collected together, near the gate which led into the meadow, when they were suddenly alarmed with a repetition of the same noises which had formerly so terrified them in the nest; and Robin, who was foremost, beheld, to his very great amazement, Master and Miss Benson, the maid who attended them, and Joe the gardener, who, having opened the gate, was, at the request of his young Master and Mistress, conducting them to the ivy-wall.

Robin, with all his courage, and indeed he was not deficient in this qualification, was seized with a great tremor; for if the view he had of the faces of these persons had appeared so dreadful to him when he sat in the nest, what must it now be, to behold their full size, and see them advancing with, as he thought, gigantic strides, towards him! He expected nothing less than to be crushed to death with the foot of one of them; and not having yet attained his full strength, and never having raised himself in the air, he knew not how to escape; therefore chirped so loudly, as not only to surprise his brother and sisters, and bring his father and mother to inquire the meaning of his cry, but also to attract the attention of Master and Miss Benson.

What chirping is that? cried the latter.—It was, said the maid, the cry of a young bird; was it not one of those in the baskets? No, said Frederick, the noise came that way, pointing to some currant trees.—My birds are very well—And so is my Linnet, replied Harriet.—Frederick then set down his charge very carefully, and began looking about in the place from whence he supposed the sound proceeded, when to his great joy he soon discovered the Redbreasts and their little family. He called eagerly to his sister, who was equally pleased with the sight. Frederick then stooped down to take a nearer view of them, by which means he directly fronted Robin, who, as soon as the young gentleman's face was on a level with his own eyes, recollected him, and calling to his brother and sisters, told them they need not be afraid.

Miss Benson followed her brother's example, and delighted the little flock with the sight of her benign countenance. She heartily lamented having nothing with which to regale her old favourites and their family, when Frederick produced from his pocket a piece of biscuit which they crumbled and scattered. Miss Benson recollecting that her mamma would expect her at home, and that the birds in the basket would be hungry, persuaded her brother to take up his little load and return; they therefore left the Redbreasts enjoying the fruits of their bounty.

CHAPTER XII

WHEN THE HAPPY birds had shared amongst them the acceptable present made by their young benefactors, the mother reminded her mate that it would be proper to think of returning to the nest. If the little ones fatigue themselves too much with hopping about, said she, their strength will be exhausted, and they will not be able to fly back.

True, my love, replied her mate, gather them under your wings a little, as there is no reason to apprehend danger here, and then we will see what they can do. She complied with his desire, and when they were sufficiently rested, got up, on which the whole brood instantly raised themselves on their feet.

Now Robin, cried the father, let us see your dexterity at flying upwards; come, I will shew you how to raise yourself.

O! you need not take that trouble, said the conceited bird, as I flew down I warrant I know how to fly up: then spreading his wings, he attempted to rise, but in so unskilful a manner, that he only shuffled along upon the ground.

That will not do, however, cried the father—shall I shew you now? Robin persisted in it that he stood in no need of instruction, and tried again; he managed to raise himself a little way, but soon tumbled headlong. His mother then began reproving him for his obstinacy, and advised him to accept his father's kind offer of teaching him.

You may depend upon it, Robin, said she, that he is in every respect wiser than you; and as he has had so much practice, he must of course be expert in the art of flying; and if you persist in making your own foolish experiments, you will only commit a number of errors, and make yourself ridiculous; I should commend your courage, provided you would add prudence to it; but blundering on in this ignorant manner, is only rashness.

Let him alone, let him alone, said the father; if he is above being taught, he may find his own way to the nest, I will teach his brother. Come, said he, Dicky, let us see what you can do at flying *upwards*, you cut a noble figure this morning when you flew *down*.

Dicky with reluctance advanced; he said he did not see what occasion they had to go back to the nest at all; he should suppose they might easily find some snug corner to creep into, till they were strong enough to roost on trees, as other birds did.

Why you, said the father, are as ridiculous with your timidity, as Robin with his conceitedness. Those who give way to groundless fears, generally expose themselves to real dangers; if you rest on the earth all night, you will suffer a great deal from cold and damp, and may very likely be devoured whilst you sleep, by rats and other creatures that go out in the night to seek for food; whereas, if you determine to go back to the nest, you have but one effort to make; for which, I will venture to say, you have a sufficient degree of strength, and then you will lie warm, safe, and quiet: however, do as you will.

Dicky began to think that it was his interest to obey his father, and said he would endeavour to fly up, but was still fearful he should not be able to effect it.

Never despair, replied his father, of doing what others have done before you. Turn your eyes upwards, and behold what numbers of birds are at this instant soaring in the air. They were once all nestlings like yourself. See there that new-fledged Wren, with what courage he skims along; let it not be said, that a Redbreast lies groveling on the earth, while a Wren soars above him!

Dicky was now ashamed of himself, and inspired with emulation; therefore, without delay, spread his wings and his tail; his father with pleasure placed himself in a proper attitude before him, then rising from the ground led the way, and Dicky, by carefully following his example, safely arrived at the nest, which he found a most comfortable resting-place after the fatigue of the morning, and rejoiced that he had a good father to teach him what was most conducive to his welfare.

The father having seen him safe home, returned to his mate, who during his short absence, had been endeavouring to convince Robin of his fault, but to no purpose; he did not like to be taught, what he still persuaded himself he could do by his own exertions; she therefore applied herself to Flapsy.

Come, my dear, said she, get ready to follow me when your father returns, for the sun casts a great heat here, and the nest will be quite comfortable to you. Flapsy dreaded the experiment; however as she could not but blame both Robin's and Dicky's conduct, she resolved to do her best; but entreated her mother to inform her very particularly how to proceed. Well, then, said the tender parent, observe me. First bend your legs, then spring from the ground as quick as you can, stretching your wings as you rise, straight out on each side of your body; shake them with a quick motion, as you will see me do, and the air will yield to you, and at the same time support your weight; which ever way you want to turn, strike the air with the wing on the contrary side, and that will bring you about. She then rose from the ground, and having practised two or three times repeatedly, what she had been teaching, Flapsy at length ventured to follow her, but with a palpitating heart; and was soon happily seated in the nest by the side of Dicky, who rejoiced that his favourite sister was safely arrived.

The mother bird now went back to Pecksy, who was waiting with her father till she returned; for the good parent chose to leave the female part of his family to the particular management of their mother.

Pecksy was fully prepared for her flight, for she had attentively observed the instruction given to the others, and also their errors; she therefore kept the happy medium betwixt self-conceit and timidity, indulging that moderated emulation which ought to possess every young heart; and resolving that neither her inferiors nor equals should soar above her, she sprang from the ground, and with a steadiness and agility, wonderful for her first essay, followed her mother to the nest, who instead of stopping to rest herself there, flew to a neighbouring tree, that she might be at hand to assist Robin should he repent of his folly; but Robin disappointed her hopes, for he sat sulky; though convinced that he had been in the wrong, he would not humble himself to his father; who therefore resolved to leave him a little while and return to the nest. As soon as Robin found himself deserted, instead of being sorry, he gave way to anger and resentment:— Why, cried he, am I to be treated in this manner, who am the eldest of the family, while all the little darlings are fondled and caressed? But I don't care, I can get to the nest yet, I make no doubt: he then attempted to fly, and after a great many trials, at length got up in the air, but knew not which way to direct his course; and sometimes turned to the right, and sometimes to the left; now he advanced forward a little, and now, fearing he was wrong, came back again: at length quite spent with fatigue, he fell to the ground and bruised himself a good deal; stunned with the fall, he lay for some minutes without sense or motion, but soon revived; and finding himself alone in this dismal condition, the horrors of his situation filled him with dreadful apprehensions, and the bitterest remorse.

Oh! cried he, that I had but followed the advice and example of my tender parents, then had I been safe in the nest, blest with their kind caresses, and enjoying the company of my dear brother and sisters! but now I am, of all birds the most wretched! never shall I be able to fly, for every joint of me has received a shock which I doubt it will not recover. Where shall I find shelter from the scorching sun, whose piercing rays already render the ground I lie on intolerably hot? What kind beak will supply me with food to assuage the pangs of hunger which I shall soon feel? By what means shall I procure even a drop of water to quench that thirst which so frequently returns? Who will protect me from the various tribes of barbarous animals which I have been told make a prey of birds? Oh my dear, my tender mother, if the sound of my voice can reach your ear, pity me, and fly to my succour.

The kind parent waited not for farther solicitation, but darting from the branch on which she had been a painful eyewitness of Robin's fall, she instantly stood before him.

I have listened, said she, to your lamentations; and since you seem convinced of your error, will not add to your suffering by my reproaches; my heart relents towards you, and gladly would I afford you all the aid in my power: but alas! I can do little for your relief; however, let me persuade you, to exert all the strength you have, and use every effort for your own preservation; I will endeavour to procure you some refreshment, and at the same time contrive means of fixing you in a place of more security and comfort than that in which you at present lie. So saying, she flew to a little stream which flowed in an adjacent meadow, and fetched from the brink of it, a worm which she had observed an angler to drop as she perched on the tree; with this she immediately returned to the penitent Robin, who received the welcome gift with gratitude.

Refreshed with this delicious morsel, and comforted by his mother's kindness, he was able to stand up, and on shaking his wings, found that he was not so greatly hurt as he apprehended; his head, indeed, was bruised, so that one eye was almost closed, and he had injured the joint of one wing, so that he could not possibly fly: however, he could manage to hop, and the parent bird observing that Joe the gardener was cutting a hawthorn hedge, which was near the spot, desired Robin to follow her; this he did, though with great pain. Now, said she, look carefully about and you will soon find insects of one kind or another for your sustenance during the remainder of the day, and before evening I will return to you again. Summon all your courage, for I make no doubt you will be safe while our friend continues his work, as none of those creatures which are enemies to birds, will venture to come near him. Robin took a sorrowful farewell, and the mother flew to the nest.

You have been absent a long time, my love, said her mate, but I perceived that you were indulging your tenderness towards that disobedient nestling, who has rendered himself unworthy of it; however, I do not condemn you for giving him assistance, for had not you undertaken the task, I would myself have flown to him, instead of returning home: how is he, likely to live and reward your kindness? Yes, said she, he will, I flatter myself, soon perfectly recover, for his hurt is not very considerable; and I have the pleasure to tell you, he is extremely sensible of his late folly, and I dare say will endeavour to repair his fault with future good behaviour. This is pleasing news indeed, said he.

The little nestlings, delighted to hear their dear brother was safe, and convinced of his error, expressed great joy and satisfaction, and entreated their father to let them descend again and keep him company; to this he would by no means consent, because, as he told them, the fatigue would be too great; and it was proper that Robin should feel a little longer the consequences of his presumption: To-morrow, said he, you shall pay him a visit, but to-day he must be by himself: on this they dropped their request, knowing their parent was the best judge what was proper to be done; and not doubting but that his affection would lead him to every thing that was conducive to the real happiness of his family: but yet they could not tell how to be happy without Robin, and were continually perking up their little heads, fancying they heard his cries; both the father and mother frequently took a peep at him, and had the satisfaction of seeing him very safe by their friend Joe the gardener. But it is time to inquire after Master and Miss Benson.

CHAPTER XIII

THIS HAPPY PAIR arrived at the house soon after they left the Redbreasts, and communicated every circumstance of their expedition to their kind mamma; who hearing their little prisoners in the basket chirp very loudly, desired they would immediately go and feed them; which they gladly did, and then took a short lesson. Mrs. Benson told Miss Harriet that she was going to make a visit in the afternoon, and should take her with her, therefore desired she would keep herself quite still, that she might not be fatigued after the walk she had had in the morning; for though she meant to go in the coach, it was her intention to return on foot, as the weather was so remarkably fine. The young lady took great care of the birds, and Frederick engaged, with the assistance of the maid, to feed them during her absence. Miss Benson was then dressed to attend her mamma.

Mrs. Addis, to whose house they were going, was a widow lady; she had two children, Master Charles a boy of twelve years old at school, and Miss Augusta about seven, at home. But these children were quite strangers to Miss Benson.

On entering the hall, the young lady took notice of a very disagreeable smell, and was surprised with the appearance of a parrot, a paroquet, and a macaw, all in most elegant cages. In the next room she came to, were a squirrel and a monkey, which had each a little house neatly ornamented.

On being introduced into the drawing-room, she observed in one corner a lap-dog lying on a splendid cushion; and in a beautiful little cradle, which she supposed to contain a large wax doll, lay in great state, a cat with a litter of kittens. In vain did Miss Harriet look for Mrs. Addis's children, for neither of them appeared.

After the usual compliments of salutation were over, I have, said Mrs. Benson, taken the liberty of bringing my daughter with me, madam, in hopes of inducing you to favor us in return, with the company of Master and Miss Addis.

You are very obliging, madam, replied the lady; but indeed, I never take *my* children with me, they are so *rude;* on the contrary, I am obliged to keep the boy almost continually at school, for he is so cruel to my *dear little precious creatures,* that there is no bearing him *at home;* and as for Augusta, it will be time enough some years hence for her to go a visiting.

I am sorry to hear you say this, madam, said Mrs. Benson, but hope my daughter will at least be indulged with seeing Miss Addis to-day, or I shall think you are displeased at my bringing Harriet here. This in reality was the case, and Mrs. Benson perceived it, for the lady looked very cross; however, she could not refuse having her daughter come into the drawing-room, as her guest so particularly desired it.

Miss Harriet was very curious to examine the various animals which were collected together by this extraordinary lady; but as her mamma never suffered her to run about when she accompanied her to other people's houses, she sat down and kept quite still, only glancing her eye first to one part of the room, and then to the other, as her attention was successively attracted.

Mrs. Addis rang the bell, and ordered that Augusta might come to her. The footman, who had never before received such a command (for Mrs. Addis only saw the child in the nursery), stared with astonishment, and thought he had mistaken it. However, on his Mistress's repeating, "that the little girl was to be brought down," he went to tell the nursery-maid to take her. What new fancy is this? said she. Who would ever have thought of *her* wanting the *child in the drawing-room?* I have no stockings clean for her, nor a frock to put on, but what is all to pieces; I wish she would spend less on her *cats,* and *dogs,* and *monkeys,* and then her *child* might appear as she ought to do. I won't go up stairs, Nanny, said the child, mamma is so cross to me. But you *must,* said Nanny; besides there is a pretty young lady come to see you; and if you will go like a good girl, you shall have a piece of sugar'd bread and butter for your supper; and you shall carry the new doll which your god-mamma gave you to shew your little visitor.

These bribes had the desired effect, and Miss Augusta went into the drawing-room; but instead of entering it like a young lady, with a genteel curtsey, she stopped at the door, hung down her head, and looked like a little simpleton. Miss Benson was so surprised at her awkwardness, that she did not know what to do, and looked at her mamma; who said, Harriet my love, can't you take the little lady by the hand and lead her to me? I believe she is afraid of strangers. On this Miss Harriet arose to do so; but Augusta, apprehensive that she would snatch her doll away, was going to run out, only she was not able to open the door.

Mrs. Benson was quite shocked to see how sickly, dirty, and ragged this child was, and what a very vulgar figure she made, for want of instruction; but Mrs. Addis was so taken up at that instant with the old lap-dog, which had, as she thought, fallen into a fit, that she did not mind her entrance; and before she perceived it, the child went up to the cradle in order to put her doll into it; and seized one of the kittens by the neck, the squeaking of which provoked the old cat to scratch her, and this made her cry and drop the kitten on the floor. Mrs. Addis seeing this, flew to the little beast, endeavoured to sooth it with caresses, and was going to beat Augusta for touching it, but Mrs. Benson interceded for her; though she could scarcely gain attention, Mrs. Addis being so greatly agitated.

Tea was now ordered, and Miss Augusta being urgent to go to her maid, Mrs. Benson thought it best she should be indulged; and therefore said, she was sure Harriet would not desire to detain her against her inclinations; and Augusta was dismissed by her mamma without so much as one tender kiss or kind expression!

The tea things being set, the footman came in with the urn, which employing both his hands, he left the door open; and was, to the great terror of Miss Harriet, and even of her mamma too, followed by the monkey they saw in the hall, who having broke his chain, came to make a visit to his lady: she, far from being disconcerted, seemed highly pleased with his cleverness. O my sweet dear Pug, said she, are you come to see us? Pray shew how like a gentleman you can behave: just as she had said this, *he leaped upon the tea-table, and took cup after cup, and threw them on the ground,* till he broke half the set; then jumped on the back of his mistress's chair, and tore the cover of it: in short, as soon as he had finished one piece of mischief, he began another, till Mrs. Addis, though vastly diverted with his wit, was obliged to have him caught and confined; after which she began making tea, and quietness was for a short time restored. But Mrs. Benson, though capable of conversing on most subjects, could not engage Mrs. Addis in any discourse, but upon the perfections of her birds and beasts; and a variety of uninteresting particulars were related concerning their wit or misfortunes.

On hearing the clock strike seven, she begged Mrs. Benson's excuse; but said she made it a constant rule, to see all her dear darlings fed at that hour, and entreated that she and the young lady would take a turn in the garden in the mean while. This was very unpolite, but Mrs. Benson desired she would use no ceremonies with her, and was really glad of the respite it gave her from company so irksome; and Miss Harriet was happy to be alone with her mamma: she, however, forbore to make any remarks on Mrs. Addis, because she had been taught, that it did not become young persons to censure the behaviour of those who were older than themselves.

The garden was spacious, but overurn with weeds; the gravel walks were so rough for want of rolling, that it was quite painful to tread on them; and the grass on the lawn so long, that there was no walking with any comfort, for the gardener was almost continually going on some errand or other for Mrs. Addis's darlings; so Mrs. Benson and her daughter sat down on a garden seat, with an intention of waiting there till Mrs. Addis should summon them. Miss Harriet could not refrain from expressing a wish that it was time to go home; to which Mrs. Benson replied, that she did not wonder at her desire to

return, But, said she, my dear, as the world was not made merely for us, we must endeavour to be patient under every disagreeable circumstance we meet with. I know what
opinion you have formed of Mrs. Addis, and should not have brought you to be a spectator of her follies, had I not hoped that an hour or two passed in her company, would
afford you a lesson which might be useful to you through life. I have before told you
that our affections towards the inferior parts of the creation should be properly regulated; you have, in your friend Miss Jenkins and her brother, seen instances of cruelty to
them, which I am sure you will never be inclined to imitate; but I was apprehensive you
might fall into the contrary extreme, which is equally blameable. Mrs. Addis, you see, has
absolutely transferred the affection she ought to feel for her child, to creatures who would
really be much happier without it. As for puss, who lies in the cradle in all her splendour,
I will engage to say, she would pass her time pleasanter in a basket of clean straw, placed
in a situation where she could occasionally amuse herself with catching mice. The lap-dog
is, I am sure, a miserable object, full of diseases, the consequences of luxurious living.
How enviable is the lot of a spaniel that is at liberty to be the companion of his master's
walks, when compared with his! Mr. Pug, I am certain, would enjoy himself much more
in his native wood. And I am greatly mistaken, if the parrots, &c. have not cause to
wish themselves in their respective countries, or at least divided into separate families,
where they would be better attended; for Mrs. Addis, by having such a number of
creatures, has put it out of her power to see properly with her own eyes to all. But come,
let us go back into the house, the time for our going home draws near, and I wish not to
prolong my visit. Saying this, she arose, and with her daughter went into the drawing-
room, which opened into the garden; the other door which led to the adjoining apartments
was not shut, and gave them an opportunity of hearing what really distressed Mrs. Benson,
and perfectly terrified the gentle Harriet.

"Begone, wretch," says Mrs. Addis, "begone this instant, you shall not stay a moment
longer in this house." "I hope, madam, you will have the goodness to give me a character;
indeed and indeed, I fed Poll, but I believe he got cold when you let him stand out of
doors the other day." "I will give you no character I tell you, so depart this instant. Oh my
poor, dear, dear, creature! I fear you will never recover; John, Thomas, here run this
instant to Perkins the bird-catcher, perhaps he can tell me what to give him;" then bursting into a flood of tears, she sat down and forgot her guests.

Mrs. Benson thought it necessary to remind her, that she was in the house, and stepped
to the door to ask what was the matter. Mrs. Addis recollected herself sufficiently, to beg
pardon for neglecting to pay attention to her, but declared that the dreadful misfortune
that had befallen her, had made her insensible to every thing else.

What can be the matter, said Mrs. Benson? Have you heard of the death of a dear
friend—has your child met with an accident? Oh! no, said she, but poor Poll is taken suddenly ill; my dear Poll, which I have had these seven years, and I fear he never will
recover.

If this is all, Madam, said Mrs. Benson, I really cannot pity you, nor excuse your behaviour to me; for it is an instance of disrespect, which I believe no other person but yourself
would shew me, and I shall take my leave of your house for ever: but before I go, permit
me to say, that you act in a very wrong manner, and will certainly feel the ill effects of
your injustice to your fellow-creatures, in thus robbing them of the love you owe them, to
lavish it away on those who are really sufferers by your kindness.

At this instant the footman entered to inform Mrs. Benson that her servant was come, on which, accompanied by Miss Harriet, she, without further ceremony, left Mrs. Addis to compose herself as she could.

As they walked along, both Mrs. Benson and her daughter continued silent, for the former was greatly agitated, and the latter quite in consternation at what had lately passed; *but their attention was soon awakened by the supplication of a poor woman,* who entreated them to give her some relief, as she had a sick husband and seven children in a starving condition; of which, she said, they might be eye-witnesses, if they would have the goodness to step into a barn that was very near.

The invitation of wretchedness never was given in vain to Mrs. Benson; her heart was constantly awake to the tender feelings of humanity; and taking her daughter by the hand, and desiring the servant to stop for her, she followed the woman, who conducted her to the abode of real woe, where she beheld a father, surrounded with his helpless family, whom he could no longer supply with sustenance; and he himself, though his disease was subdued, was almost on the point of expiring, for want of some reviving cordial.

How came you to be in this condition, good woman? said Mrs. Benson to his wife; surely you might have obtained relief before your husband was reduced to such extremity?

Oh! my good lady, said the woman, we have not been used to beg, but to earn an honest livelihood by our industry; and never till this sad day, have I known what it was to ask charity: the first time I could bring myself to it, I made application at the only great house in this village, where I made no doubt there was abundance. I told my dismal tale to a servant, and begged she would make it known to her mistress; but she assured me it was in vain to come there, for her Lady had such a family of cats, dogs, monkeys, and all manner of creatures, that she had nothing to spare for poor people; at the same instant I saw the poulterer bring a rabbit and a fowl, which I found were for the favourite cat and dog. This discouraged me from begging; and I had determined to die before I would ask again; but the sight of my dear husband and children in this condition, drives me to it.

Well, comfort yourself, said Mrs. Benson.—Come to my house to-morrow morning, and we will see what we can do; in the mean time here is something for a present supply. Mrs.

Benson then departed, as she was fearful of walking late.

Miss Harriet was greatly affected with this scene, and could no longer help exclaiming against Mrs. Addis.

She is deserving of great blame, indeed, said Mrs. Benson; but I have the pleasure to say, such characters as hers are very uncommon, I mean in the *extreme,* though there are numbers of people who fall into the same fault in some degree, and make themselves truly ridiculous with their unnatural affections. I wish you, while your mind is young, to guard it against such a blameable weakness.

Miss Harriet assured her mamma, that she should never forget either Mrs. Addis, or the lesson she had received on the subject, and then expressed her satisfaction that they had met the poor woman. I rejoice sincerely, said Mrs. Benson, at having been fortunate enough to come in time to assist this poor wretched family, and hope, my love, you will, out of your own little purse, contribute something to-morrow towards their relief. Most willingly, said Harriet, they shall be welcome to my whole store.

They kept talking on this subject till they arrived at home. Little Frederick, who sat up an hour beyond his time, came out to meet them, and assured his sister, that the birds were well and fast asleep. I think, said she, it is time for you and I to follow their example; for my part, with my morning and evening walk together, I am really tired, so shall beg leave to wish you a good night, my dear mamma; papa, I suppose, will not be at home this week? No, my dear, nor the next, said Mrs. Benson, for he has many affairs to settle in the west. I am rather fatigued also, and shall soon retire to rest.

CHAPTER XIV

We will now return to Robin, whom we left under the protection of Joe the gardener, though the honest fellow did not know of his own guardianship, and continued his work without perceiving the little cripple, who hopped and shuffled about, pecking here and there whatever he could meet with.

When he had been for some time by himself, his mother made him another visit, and told him she had interceded with his father, whose anger was abated, and he would come to him before he went to rest. Robin rejoiced to hear that there was a chance of his being reconciled to his father, yet he dreaded the first interview: however, as it must be, he wished to have it over as soon as possible; and every wing he heard beat the air, he fancied to be that of his offended parent. In this state of anxious expectation, he continued almost to the time of sun-setting, when, of a sudden, he heard the well-known voice to which he used to listen with joy, but which now caused his whole frame to tremble; but observing a beam of benignity in that eye, in which he looked for anger and reproach, he cast himself in the most supplicating posture at the feet of his father, who could no longer resist the desire he felt to receive him into favour.

Your present humility, Robin, said he, disarms my resentment; I gladly pronounce your pardon, and am persuaded you will never again incur my displeasure! we will therefore say no more on a subject which gives so much pain to both of us.

Yes, my dear, my too-indulgent father, cried Robin, permit me to make my grateful acknowledgments for your kindness, and to assure you of my future obedience. The delighted parent accepted his submission, and the reconciliation was completed. Robin now felt himself greatly relieved; but on his father's asking him what he intended to do with himself at night, his spirits sunk again, and he answered, he did not know. Well, said the father, I have thought of an expedient to secure you from cold at least.

In a part of the orchard, a very little way from hence, there is a place belonging to our friend the gardener; there I have sheltered myself from several storms, and am sure it will afford you a comfortable lodging; so follow me, before it is too late. The old bird then led the way, and his son followed him; when they arrived, they found the door of the tool-house open, and as the threshold was low, Robin managed to get over it. His father looked carefully about, and at last found in a corner, a parcel of shreds, kept for the purpose of nailing up trees. Here, Robin, said he, is a charming bed for you, let me see you in it, and call your mother to have a peep, and then I must bid you good night; so saying, away he flew, and brought his mate, who was perfectly satisfied with the lodging provided for her late undutiful, but now repentant son; but reminded by her mate, that if they staid longer, they might be shut in, they took leave, telling Robin they would visit him early in the morning.

Though this habitation was much better than Robin expected, and he was ready enough to own, better than he deserved, yet he deeply regretted his absence from the nest, and longed to see again his brother and sisters: however, though part of the night was spent in bitter reflections, fatigue at length prevailed over anxiety, and he fell asleep. The nestlings were greatly pleased to find that Robin was likely to escape the dangers of the night, and even the anxious mother at length resigned herself to repose.

Before the sun shewed his glorious face in the east, every individual of this affectionate family were awake; the father with impatience waited for the gardener's opening the tool-house; the mother prepared her little ones for a new excursion.

You will be able to descend with more ease, my dears, to-day, than you did yesterday, shall you not? O yes, mother, said Dicky; I shall not be at all afraid. Nor I, said Flapsy. Say you so? then let us see which of you will be down first. Come I will shew you the way.

On this, with gradual flight, the mother bent her course to a spot near the place where Robin lay concealed; they all instantly followed her, and surprised their father, who having seen Joe, was every instant expecting he would open the door; at length, to the joy of the whole party, the gardener appeared, and they soon saw him fetch his shears and leave the tool-house open: on this the mother proposed that they should all go together and call Robin. There they found him in his snug little bed; but who can describe the happy meeting; who can find words to express the raptures which filled every little bosom?

When the first transports subsided, I think, said the father, it will be best to retire from hence: if our friend returns, he may take us for a set of thieves, and suppose that we came to eat his seeds, and I should be sorry he should have an ill opinion of us. Well, I am ready, said his mate, and we, cried the whole brood; they accordingly left the tool-house, and hopped about among the currant-bushes. I think, said the father, that you who have the full use of your limbs, could manage to get up those low trees, but Robin must content himself upon the ground a little longer. This was very mortifying, but he had no one to blame excepting himself; so he forebore to complain, and assumed as much cheerfulness as he could; his brother and sisters begged they might stay with him all day, as they could do very well without going up to the nest; to this the parents consented.

At the usual hour of visiting Mrs. Benson's tea-table, the affectionate pair took their morning's flight, and found the young Gentleman and Lady with their mamma. They had

been up a long time, for Frederick had made in his bed-chamber a lodging for the birds, who had awakened both him and his sister at a very early hour, and they rose with great readiness to perform the kind office they had imposed upon themselves.

The two Blackbirds were perfectly well, but the Linnet looked rather drooping, and they began to be apprehensive they should not raise him, especially when they found he was not inclined to eat. As for the Blackbirds, they were very hungry indeed; and their young benefactors, not considering that when fed by their parents young birds wait some time between every morsel, supplied them too fast, and filled their crops so full, that they looked as if they had great wens on their necks; and Harriet perceived one of them gasping for breath. Stop, Frederick, said she, as he was carrying the quill to its mouth, the bird is so full he can hold no more; but she spoke too late; the little creature gave his eyes a ghastly roll, and fell on one side suffocated with abundance. *Oh! he is dead! he is dead! cried Frederick.* He is indeed, said Miss Benson, but I am sure we did not design to kill him; and it is some satisfaction to think that we did not take the nest.

This consideration was not sufficient to comfort Frederick, who began to cry most bitterly. His mamma hearing him, was apprehensive he had hurt himself, for he seldom cried unless he was in great pain; she therefore hastily entered the room, to inquire what was the matter, on which Miss Harriet related the disaster that had happened. Mrs. Benson then sat down, and taking Frederick in her lap, wiped his eyes, and giving him a kiss, said, I am sorry, my love, for your disappointment, but do not afflict yourself, the poor little thing is out of his pain now, and I fancy suffered but for a short time. If you keep on crying so, you will forget to feed your *flock* of birds, which I fancy, by the chirping I heard from my window, are beginning to assemble. Come, let me take the object of your distress out of your sight, it must be buried; then carrying the dead bird in one hand, and leading Frederick with the other, she went down stairs.

While she was speaking, Miss Harriet had been watching the other Blackbird, which she had soon the pleasure to see perfectly at his ease.

She then attempted to feed the Linnet, but he would not eat. I fancy, Miss, said the Maid, he wants air. That may be the case indeed, replied Miss Benson; for you know,

Betty, this room, which has been shut up all night, must be much closer than the places birds build in. Saying this she opened the window, and placed the Linnet near it, waiting to see the effect of the experiment, which answered her wishes; and she was delighted to behold how the little creature gradually smoothed his feathers, and his eyes resumed their native lustre; she once more offered him food, which he took, and quite recovered. Having done all in her power for her little orphans, she went to share with her brother the task of feeding the daily pensioners; which being ended, she seated herself at the breakfast-table by her mamma.

I wonder, said Frederick, who had dried up his tears, that the Robins are not come. Consider, replied his sister, that they have a great deal of. business to do, now their young ones begin to leave the nest; they will be here by-and-bye, I make no doubt.

While she was speaking the servant entered, and informed them that a poor woman was at the gate, who was ordered to attend in the morning. Mrs. Benson desired she might come up. Well, good woman, said the benevolent Lady, how does your husband do this morning? Thanks to your goodness, Madam, and the blessing of God, quite cheery.

I am happy, said the Lady, to find you in better spirits than you were last night, and do not doubt you will do very well. I will order some meat and bread to be sent you every day this week, and will also assist you in clothing the children. Harriet's eyes glistened with benevolence at seeing the woman, whose distress had so greatly affected her, thus comforted; and slipping her purse, which contained seven shillings, into her mamma's hand, begged she would take it for the woman. You shall, my dear, said Mrs. Benson, have the pleasure of relieving her yourself; give this half-crown to her. Miss Harriet, with a delight which none but the compassionate can know, extended the hand of charity. The woman received her benefaction with grateful acknowledgments; and praying that the Almighty might shower down his choicest blessings on this worthy family, respectfully took leave and returned to her husband, who, by means of the nourishment Mrs. Benson supplied him with, gathered strength hourly.

She was scarcely gone out of the room when the Redbreasts entered, as I before related. The sight of them perfectly restored Frederick's cheerfulness; and after they were departed, he requested his mamma, that he and Harriet might go again to the orchard, in hopes of seeing the young Robins. That you shall do, Frederick, said she, upon condition that you continue a very good boy; but as yester-day was rather an idle day with you, you must apply a little closer to-day; and Harriet has a great deal of business to do; therefore you must wait till evening, and then perhaps I may go with you. Frederick was satisfied with this promise, and took great pains to learn to read and spell. He repeated by heart one of Mrs. Barbauld's Hymns, and some other little things which he had been taught; and Miss Benson applied herself to a variety of different lessons with great assiduity, and performed her task of work entirely to her mamma's satisfaction.

CHAPTER XV

As soon as the old Redbreasts left their little family, in order to go to Mr. Benson's, Pecksy, with great solicitude, began to ask Robin where he had hurt himself, and how he did? Oh! said he, I am much better; but it is a wonder I am now alive, for you cannot think what a dreadful fall I had. With turning about as I did in the air, I became quite giddy, so could not make the least exertion for saving myself as I was falling, and came with great force to the ground; you see how much my eye is still swelled, and it was much more so at first. My wing is the worst, and still gives me a good deal of pain; observe how it drags on the ground: but as it is not broke, my father says it will soon be well; and I hope it will soon be so, for I long to be flying, and shall be glad to receive any instructions for the future. I cannot think how I could be so foolishly conceited, as to suppose I knew how to conduct myself without my father's guidance.

Why, young creatures like us, said Pecksy, certainly stand in need of instruction, and ought to think ourselves happy in having parents who are willing to take the trouble of teaching us what is necessary for us to know. I dread the day, when I must quit the nest and take care of myself. Flapsy said, she made no doubt they should know how to fly, and peck, and do every thing before that time: and for her part, she longed to see the world, and to know how the higher ranks of birds behaved themselves, and what pleasures they enjoyed; and Dicky declared he had formed the same wishes, though he must confess he had great dread of birds of prey: Oh, said Flapsy, they will never seize such a pretty creature as you, Dicky, I am sure. Why if beauty can prevail against cruelty, you will also be secure, my sweet sister, replied he, for your delicate engaging shape must plead in your behalf.

Just as he had finished his speech, a Hawk appeared in sight, on which the whole party was seized with a most uncommon sensation, and involuntarily threw themselves on their backs, screaming with all their might; and at the same instant the cries of numbers of little birds besides, echoed through the orchard. The Redbreasts soon recovered, and rising on their feet, looked about to see what was become of the cause of their consternation; when they beheld him high in the air, bearing off some unhappy victim, a few of whose feathers fell near the young family, who on examining them found they belonged to a goldfinch; on which Pecksy observed, that it was evident these savages paid no attention to personal beauty. Dicky was so terrified he knew not what to do, and had thoughts of flying back to the nest; but after Robin's misfortunes, was fearful of offending his father; he therefore got up into a currant-bush, and hid himself in the thickest part of the leaves. Flapsy followed him, but Robin being obliged to keep on the ground, Pecksy kindly resolved to bear him company.

In a few minutes their parents returned from Mr. Benson's, and found the two latter pretty near where they had left them; but missing the others, the mother with great anxiety inquired what was become of them? Robin then related how they had been frightened with a Hawk; and while he was so doing, they returned to him again.

I am surprised, said the father, that a Hawk should venture so near the spot where the gardener was at work. Pecksy informed him that they had not seen him since he left them: then I dare say he is gone to breakfast, replied the mother; and this was the case, for they at this instant saw him return with his shears in his hand, and soon pursue his work. Now you will be safe, cried the father; I shall therefore stay and teach you to fly in different directions, and then your mother and I will make some little excursions, and leave you to practise by yourselves; but first of all let me shew you where to get water, for I fear you must be very thirsty. No, said they, we have had several wet worms and juicy caterpillars, which have served us both for victuals and drink; Robin is very quick at finding them. There is nothing like necessity to teach birds how to live, said the father; I am glad Robin's misfortunes have been so beneficial to him. What would have become of you,

Robin, if you had not exerted yourself as I directed? said his mother; you would soon have died, had you continued to lie on the scorching ground. Remember from this instance, as long as you live, that it is better to use means for your own relief, than to spend time in fruitless lamentations.

In respect to Hawks, said the father, they are frightful creatures to be sure; but there are very few of them in comparison of most other birds, and they can take but one at a time, therefore it is a very great chance whether any of you is that one; your best way will be to keep as near to houses as you can, and make yourselves familiar with mankind, and then I think you will be in little danger. By the way, let me observe, how greatly indebted you are to this good gardener, whom I hope you no longer call a *monster*. Oh no! said Flapsy, he is a dear good creature. But I was going to say, cried the father, that at any rate, it would be wrong to make your life unhappy with apprehensions; you cannot keep Hawks away by fearing them; and it is possible, you may never see another; besides, what thousands escape, in comparison of the few they devour! But come along, Dicky, Flapsy, and Pecksy, there is water so near, that Robin can hop as far: he then conducted them to a pump, from whence Joe watered the garden, and under its spout they found an ample supply of that delightful element, more acceptable to them than the most costly wine.

Here they staid some time, and were greatly amused; still so near the gardener, that they regarded themselves as under his protection. The parents flew up into a tree, and there the father entertained his beloved mate and family with his cheerful music; and sometimes they made various airy excursions for examples to their little ones, who all longed to be able to imitate them. In this manner the day passed happily away, and early in the evening, Flapsy, Pecksy, and Dicky, were conducted to the nest; they mounted in the air with much more ease than the preceding day, and the parents instructed them how to fly to the branches of some trees, which stood near to the ivy wall.

In the mean time they had left Robin by himself, thinking he would be safe, while the gardener was mowing some grass; but what was the grief of both father and mother when they returned, and could neither see nor hear him! The gardener too was gone, they therefore apprehended that a cat or a rat had taken him away and killed him, yet none of his feathers were to be seen: with the most anxious search, they explored every recess in which they thought it possible for him to be, and strained their little voices till they were hoarse with calling him, but all in vain; the tool-house was locked; but had he been there, he would have answered: at length quite in despair of finding him, with heavy hearts they returned to the nest; a general lamentation ensued, and this lately happy abode, was now the region of sorrow. The father endeavoured to comfort his mate and surviving nestlings, and so far succeeded, that they resolved to bear their loss with patience.

After a mournful night, the mother left the nest early in the morning, unwilling to relinquish the hope which still remained, of finding Robin again; but, having spent an hour in this manner, she returned to her mate, who was comforting his little ones.

Come, said he, let us take a flight, if we sit lamenting here for ever it will be to no purpose: the evils which befal us must be borne, and the more quietly we submit to them the lighter they will be. If poor Robin is dead, he will suffer no more; and if he is not, so much as we fly about, it is a chance but we get tidings of him; suppose these little ones attempt to fly with us to our benefactors? If we set out early and let them rest frequently by the way, I think they may accomplish it. This was very pleasing to every one of the little ones, for they longed to go thither; and accordingly it was determined that they should immediately set out, and they accomplished the journey by easy stages; at length they all arrived in the court, just after the daily pensioners were gone. Now, said the father, stop a little, and let me advise you Dicky, Flapsy, and Pecksy, to behave yourselves properly; hop only where you see your mother and me hop, and do not meddle with any thing, but what is scattered on purpose. Stay, father, said Dicky, my feathers are sadly rumpled—And so are mine, said Flapsy. Well, smooth them then, but don't stand finicking for an hour. Pecksy was ready in an instant, but the others were very tedious, so their father and mother would wait for them no longer, and flew into the window; the others directly followed them, and, to the inexpressible satisfaction of master Benson, alighted on the tea-table, where they met with a very unexpected pleasure; for who should they find there, as a guest, but the poor lost Robin!

The meeting was, you may be sure, a happy one for all parties; and the transports it occasioned, may be easier conceived than described. The father poured forth a loud song of gratitude; the mother chirped, she bowed her head, clapped her wings, basked on the tea-table, joined her beak to Robin's, then touched the hand of master Frederick. As for the young ones, they twittered a thousand questions to Robin; but as he was unwilling to disturb his father's song, he desired them to suspend their curiosity to another opportunity. But it is now time to satisfy yours, my young readers, and therefore I shall inform you by what means Robin was placed in this happy situation.

CHAPTER XVI

Y OU MAY REMEMBER, that master Frederick obtained from his mamma a promise, that when the business of daily instruction was finished, he and his sister should go into the orchard in search of the Robins; as soon, therefore, as the air was sufficiently cool, she took them with her, and arrived just after the parent birds had taken their young ones back to the nest. Robin was then left by himself, and kept hopping about, and fearing no danger, got into the middle of the walk. Frederick descried him at a distance, and eagerly called out, There's one of them, I declare: and before his mamma observed him, *he ran to the place and clapped his little hand over it, exulting that he had caught it.* The pressure of his hand hurt Robin's wing, who sent forth piteous cries: on which Frederick let him go, and said, I wont hurt you.

Miss Harriet, who saw him catch the bird, ran as fast as possible to prevent his detaining it; and perceived, that as Robin hopped away he was lame, on which she concluded that her brother had hurt him; but on Frederick's assuring her, that his wing hung down when he first saw him, Mrs. Benson said it was most likely he was lamed by some accident, which had prevented his going with the others to the nest; and if that is the case, said she, it will be charitable to take care of him.

Frederick was delighted to hear her say so, and asked whether he might carry it home? Yes, said his mamma, provided you can take him safely. Shall I carry him, Madam? said Joe, he can lie nicely in my hat. This was an excellent scheme, and all parties approved of it; so Frederick took some of the soft grass which was mowed down to put at the bottom, and poor Robin was safely deposited in his vehicle, which served him for a litter; and perceiving into what hands he was fallen, he inwardly rejoiced, knowing that he had an excellent chance of being provided for, as well as of seeing his dear relations again. I need

not say that great care was taken of him, and you will easily suppose he passed a comfortable night.

When Master and Miss Benson arose the next morning, one of their first cares was to feed the birds, and they had the pleasure to see all their nestlings in a very thriving condition; both the Linnet and the Blackbird now hopped out of their nests to be fed, to the great diversion of Master Frederick: but this pleasure was soon damped by an unlucky accident: for the Blackbird being placed in a window which was open, hopped too near the edge, and fell to the ground, where he was snapped up by a dog, and torn to pieces in an instant. Frederick began to lament as before; but on his sister's reminding him, that the creature was past the sense of pain, he restrained himself, and turned his attention to the Linnet, which he put into a cage, that he might not meet the same fate. He then went to feed the flock, and to inquire after Robin, whom Mrs. Benson had taken into her own room, lest Frederick should handle and hurt him; to his great joy he found him much better, for he could begin to use his injured wing. Frederick was therefore trusted to carry him into the breakfast parlour.

For some time the young Redbreasts behaved very well; but at length Dicky, familiarized by the kind treatment he met with, forgot his father's injunctions, and began to hop about in a very rude manner; he even jumped into the plate of bread and butter; and having a mind to taste the tea, hopped on the edge of a cup, but dipping his foot in the hot liquor, he was glad to make a hasty retreat, to the great diversion of Master Frederick. Flapsy took the freedom of pecking at the sugar, but found it too hard for her tender beak. For these liberties their mother reproved them, saying, she would never bring them with her again, if they were guilty of such rudeness, as to take what was not offered them.

As their longer stay would have broke in on a plan which Mrs. Benson had concerted, she rung her bell, and the footman came to remove the tea things; on which the old birds, having taken leave of Robin, and promised to come again the next day, flew out at the window, followed by Dicky, Flapsy, and Pecksy. Robin was safely deposited in a cage, and passed a happy day, being often allowed to hop out in order to be fed.

The parent birds alighted in the court, and conducted their little ones to the water which was set out for them, after which they all returned to the nest; here the young ones rested till the afternoon, and then their parents took them out in order to shew them the orchard.

CHAPTER XVII

Y OU HAVE NOT YET, said the father, seen the whole extent of this place, and I wish to introduce you to our neighbours.

He then led the way to a pear-tree, in which a Linnet had built her nest. The old Linnets seemed much pleased to see their friends the Redbreasts, who with great pride introduced their little family to them. My own nestlings are just ready to fly, said the hen Linnet, and I hope will make acquaintance with them; for birds so well instructed as, I make no doubt, your offspring are, must be very desirable companions. The little Redbreasts were quite delighted with the hopes of having some agreeable friends; and the old ones replied, that they had themselves received so much pleasure from social friendship, that they wished their young ones to cultivate the same.

They then flew on to a cherry-tree, in which were a pair of Chaffinches in great agitation, endeavouring to part one of their own brood and a young Sparrow, who were engaged in a furious battle; but in vain, neither of the combatants would desist, till the Chaffinch dropped dead to the ground. His parents were greatly shocked at this accident, on which the cock Redbreast attempted to comfort them with his strains; but finding them deaf to his music, he begged to know the cause of the quarrel, which had so fatal a conclusion?

O! answered the hen Chaffinch, my nestling is lost through his own folly. I cautioned him repeatedly not to make acquaintance with Sparrows, knowing they would lead him into mischief; but no remonstrances would prevail. As soon as he began to peck about, he formed a friendship with one of that voracious breed, who undertook to teach him to fly and provide for himself; so he left his parents and continually followed the Sparrow, who taught him to steal corn, and other things, and to quarrel with every bird he met; I expected to see him killed continually. At length his companion grew tired of him, and picked a quarrel, which ended as you have seen. However, this is better than if he had been caught by men, and hung up for a spectacle, to deter others from stealing.

Let me advise you, my young friends, said she, addressing herself to the little Redbreasts, to follow your parents' direction in every respect, and avoid bad company. She then, accompanied by her mate, flew back to her nest, in order to acquaint the rest of her family with this dreadful catastrophe, and the Redbreasts took another flight.

They alighted on the ground, and began pecking about, when all of a sudden they heard a strange noise, which rather alarmed the young ones. Their father desired them to have no fears, but follow him; he led them to the top of a high tree, in which was a nest of Magpies. They had, the day before, made an excursion round the orchard, and were conversing on what they had seen, but in such a confused manner, that there was no such thing as understanding them; one chattered of one thing, and one of another. In short, all were eager to speak, and none inclined to hear.

What a set of foolish ill-bred little creatures are these, said the cock Redbreast; if they would talk one at a time, what each says might afford entertainment to the rest; but by chattering altogether in this manner, they are quite disagreeable. Take example from them, my nestlings, and avoid the fault which renders them so ridiculous.

So saying, he flew on, and they soon saw a Cuckow, surrounded by a number of birds, who had been pecking at her till she had scarce a feather left upon her breast, whilst she kept repeating her own dull note, *Cuckow! Cuckow!* incessantly. Get back again to your own country, said a Thrush; what business have you in ours, sucking the eggs, and taking the nest of any bird you meet with? Surely it would be sufficient, could you have the privilege of building for yourself, as we do who are natives; but you have no right to seize upon our labours, and devour our offspring. The Cuckow deserves his fate, said the hen Redbreast. Though I am far from bearing enmity to foreign birds in general, I detest such characters as his. I wonder mankind do not drive Cuckows away; but I suppose it is on account of their being the harbingers of summer.

How different is the character of the Swallow; he comes here to enjoy the mildness of the climate, and confers a benefit on the land by destroying many noxious insects. I rejoice to see that race sporting in the air, and have had high pleasure in conversing with them; for as they are great travellers, they have much to relate. But come, let us go on.

They soon came to a hollow tree: Peep into this hole, said the cock bird to his young ones; they did so, and beheld a nest of young Owls. What a set of ugly creatures, said Dicky; surely you do not intend to shew your frightful faces in the world! Did ever any one see such dull eyes, such a frightful muffle of feathers?

Whoever you are that reproach us with the want of beauty, you do not shew your own good sense, replied one of the little Owls. Perhaps we may have qualities which render us as amiable as yourselves. You do not appear to know that we are *night,* and not *day* birds. The quantity of feathers in which we are muffled up, is very comfortable to us when we are out in the cold; and I can shew you a pair of eyes, which, if you are *little* birds, will frighten you out of your wits; and if I could fly, I would let you see what else I could do. He then drew back the film which was given him, that the strong light of the day might not injure his sight, and stared full at Dicky, who was struck with astonishment.

At this instant the parent Owl returned, and seeing a parcel of strangers looking into her nest, she set up a screeching, which made the whole party take wing. As soon as they stopped to rest, the cock Redbreast, who was really frightened as well as his mate and family, recollected himself, and said, Well, Dicky, how did you like the owl's eyes? I fancy they proved brighter than you expected; but had they even been as ugly as you supposed, it was very rude and silly in you to notice it. You ought never to censure any bird for natural deformities, since no one contracts them by choice; and what appears disagreeable to you, may be pleasing in the eyes of another. Besides, you should be particularly careful not to insult strangers, because you cannot know their deserts, nor what power they may have of revenging themselves. You may think yourself happy if you never meet one of these Owls by night, for I assure you they often feed upon little birds like us; and you have no reason to think they will spare you, after the affront you have given them. But come, let us fly on.

They soon alighted on a tree, in which was a Mock-bird*, who, instead of singing any note of his own, kept successively imitating those of every bird that inhabited the orchard, and this with a view of making them ridiculous. If any one had any natural imperfection in his singing, he was sure to mimic it; or if any was particularly attentive to the duties of

---

* The Mock-Bird is properly a native of America, but it is introduced here for the sake of the moral.

his station, he ridiculed him as grave and formal. The young Redbreasts were excessively diverted with this droll creature; but their father desired them to consider, whether they should like to hear him mimic them? Every one agreed, that they should be very angry to be ridiculed in that manner. Then, replied the father, neither encourage nor imitate him. The Mock-Bird hearing him, took up his notes, *"Neither encourage nor imitate him,"* said he. The cock Redbreast on this flew at him with fury, plucked some feathers from his breast, and sent him screaming from the place. I have made you sing a *natural note* at last, said he, and hope you will take care how you practise *mimicry* again. His mate was sorry to see him disturb his temper, and ruffle his feathers, for such an insignificant creature; but he told her it was particularly necessary as an example to his nestlings, as *mimicry* was a fault to which young birds were too apt to incline; and he wished to shew them the danger they exposed themselves to in the practice of it.

The whole Redbreast family rested themselves for some time; and whilst they sat still, observed a Chaffinch flying from tree to tree, chattering to every bird he had any knowledge of; and his discourse seemed to affect his hearers greatly, for they perceived some birds flying off in great haste, and others meeting them; many battles and disputes ensued. The little Redbreasts wondered at these circumstances; at length Pecksy inquired the meaning of the bustle. This Chaffinch, replied the father, is a *tell-tale;* it is inconceivable the mischief he makes. Not that he has so much malice in his nature, but he loves to hear himself chatter; and therefore, every anecdote he can collect, he tells to all he meets, by which means he often raises quarrels and animosities; neither does he stop here, for he frequently invents the tales he relates.

As the Redbreast was speaking, the Chaffinch alighted on the same tree. O, my old friend, said he, are you got abroad in the world again? I heard the Linnet in the pear-tree say, you were caught stealing corn, and hung up as a spectacle, but I thought this could not be true; besides, the Blackbird in the cherry-tree told me, that the reason we did not see you as usual was, that you were rearing a family, to whom, he said, you were so severe, that the poor little creatures had no comfort of their lives.

Whatever you may have heard, or whatever you may say, is matter of indifference to me, replied the Redbreast; but as a neighbour, I cannot help advising you to restrain your tongue a little, and consider, before you communicate your intelligence, whether what you are going to say, has not a tendency to disturb the peace of society.

Whilst he was thus advising him, a flock of birds assembled about the tree; it consisted of those to whom the Chaffinch had been chattering, who having come to an explanation with each other, had detected his falsities, and determined to expel him the orchard; which they did, with every mark of contempt and ignominy: all the Redbreasts joined in the pursuit, for even the little ones saw his character in a detestable light, and formed a determination to avoid his fault. When the tell-tale was gone, the party which pursued him alighted all together in the same walk, and amongst them the Redbreasts discovered many of their old friends, with whom they now renewed their acquaintance, knowing they should soon be released from family cares: and the young ones passed a happy day in this cheerful assembly: but at length the hour of repose approached, when each individual fled to his resting-place; and the Redbreasts, after so fatiguing a day, fell asleep.

Let us leave them to enjoy the comfort of the nest, and inquire after their young benefactors.

CHAPTER XVIII

As soon as the breakfast things were removed at Mrs. Benson's, she informed her son and daughter, that she intended to take them with her to Farmer Wilson's, where she made no doubt they would pass a happy day; and desired them to go and get equipped for the journey, while she dressed herself. The young folks obeyed without hesitation, and having given their maid very strict injunctions to feed Robin and the Linnet, they attended their mamma to the coach; *and after a delightful ride arrived at the farm-house,* where they were received with the utmost respect by Mrs. Wilson.

Farmer Wilson was a very worthy man, possessed of a great share of natural good sense and benevolence of heart. He had, by his industry, acquired sufficient to purchase the farm he lived on, and had a fair prospect of making a comfortable provision for a numerous family, whom he brought up with the greatest care, and taught them all to be merciful to the cattle employed in his business.

His wife was a most amiable woman, and had received a good education from her father, who was formerly curate of the parish. This good man had strongly implanted in his daughter's mind the Christian doctrine of UNIVERSAL CHARITY, which she exercised, not only towards the human species, but also extended it to poultry, and every living creature which it was her province to manage.

Mrs. Benson knew that her children would here have an opportunity of seeing many different animals treated with *propriety;* and it was on this account that she took them with her, though she herself complied with an invitation she had received the day before, and visited these good people from a motive of sincere respect.

As soon as they were seated, Mrs. Wilson regaled her young guests with a piece of nice cake, made by her daughter Betsy, a little girl of twelve years old, who sat by, enjoying with a secret delight, the honour which the little Lady and Gentleman did to her performance. It happened fortunately to be a cool day, and Mrs. Benson expressed a desire to walk about and see the farm.

In the first place, Mrs. Wilson shewed her the house, which was in every respect perfectly neat, and in complete order. She then took her guests into her dairy, which was well stored with milk and cream, butter and cheese. From thence they went to visit the poultry-yard, where the little Bensons were excessively delighted indeed; for there were a number of cocks and hens, and many broods of young chickens, besides turkeys and Guinea-hens.

All the fowls expressed the greatest joy, at the sight of Mrs. Wilson and her daughter Betsy; the cocks celebrated their arrival by loud and cheerful crowings; the hens gave notice of their approach by cackling, and assembled their infant train to partake of their bounty; the turkeys and Guinea-fowls ran to meet them; a number of pigeons also alighted from a pigeon-house. Betsy scattered amongst them the grain which she carried in her lap for the purpose, and seemed to have great pleasure in distributing it.

When their young visitors were satisfied with seeing the poultry fed, Mrs. Wilson shewed them the hen-house and other conveniences provided for them, which were excellently calculated to make their lives comfortable; and then opened a little door, which led to a meadow, where the fowls were often indulged to ramble and refresh themselves. On seeing her approach this place the whole party collected, and ran into it like a troop of school-boys into their play-ground.

You, Mrs. Wilson, and your daughter, must have great amusement with these pretty creatures, said Mrs. Benson. We have indeed, Madam, and they furnish us with eggs and chickens, not only for our own use, but for the market also. And can you prevail on yourself to kill these sweet creatures? said Miss Benson. Indeed, Miss, I cannot, said Mrs. Wilson, and never did kill a chicken in my life; but it is an easy matter to find people capable of doing it; and there is an absolute necessity for some of them to die, for they breed so fast, that in a short time we should have more than we could possibly feed: but I make it a rule to render their lives as happy as possible, never shut them up to fatten, any longer than I can help, use no cruel methods of cramming them, nor confine them in a situation where they can see other fowls at liberty; neither do I take the chickens from the hen till she herself deserts them, nor set hens upon ducks' eggs.

I often regret, said Mrs. Benson, that so many lives should be sacrificed to preserve ours; but we must eat animals or they would at length eat us, at least all that would otherwise support us.

Whilst this conversation passed, Master Frederick had followed the fowls into the meadow, where the turkey-cock, taking him for an enemy, had attacked him, and frightened him so much, that he at first cried out for help, but soon recollected that this was cowardly, so pulled off his hat and drove the creature away before Betsy Wilson arrived, who was running to his assistance.

The farmer's wife next proposed (but with many apologies for offering to take them to such a place) to shew them her pig-sties. The name of a pig-sty generally conveys an idea of nastiness, but whoever had seen those of Farmer Wilson's, would have had a very different one. They were neatly paved, and washed down every day; the troughs in which they fed were frequently scoured, and the water they drank was always sweet and wholesome. The pigs themselves had an appearance of neatness, which no one could have expected in such kind of animals; and though they had not the ingenuity which the *learned pig* appears to have, there was really something intelligent in their gruntings, and a very droll arch expression in the eyes of some of them. They knew their benefactors, and found means of testifying their joy at seeing them; which was increased when a boy, whom Mrs. Wilson had ordered to bring some bean-shells, emptied his basket before them. Now a contest ensued who should have the largest share, and each began pushing the other aside, and stuffing as fast as he could, lest they should have more than himself.

Miss Benson said she could not bear to see such greediness. It is indeed, replied Mrs. Benson, very disagreeable; even in such creatures as these, but how much more so in the human species; and yet how frequent is this fault amongst children in particular? Pray look at these pigs, Frederick, and tell me, if you never remember to have met with a little boy who eat strawberries as these pigs do bean-shells? Frederick's cheeks at this question were covered with conscious blushes; on which his mamma kindly kissed him, and said, she hoped he had seen enough of greediness to-day, to serve him for a lesson as long as he lived.

In a separate sty was a sow with a litter of young pigs. This was a very pleasing sight indeed to Master Frederick, who longed to have one of them to play with; but Mrs. Wilson told him it would make the sow very angry, and her gruntings would terrify him more than the turkey-cock had done; on which he dropped his request, but said he should like to keep such a little creature.

If it would always continue little, Frederick, said Mrs. Benson, it would do very well; but it will perhaps grow as large as its mother, and what shall we do then? Familiarized by the kind treatment which I am sure you would give it, we should have it following you into the parlour, and perhaps run grunting after you into your bed-chamber. I myself knew an instance of a person who nursed up a sick pig, which actually ran after her to church, and became the most troublesome thing you can conceive.

I suppose your hogs are very profitable as well as your poultry, Mrs. Wilson? said Mrs. Benson. Yes, Madam, replied she, we cure a good deal of bacon, and pickle a quantity of pork; we sell a great many sucking pigs, so that we are well paid for keeping them; and I never suffer them to be neglected in any particular, and have the pleasure of thinking few pigs are happier than mine. But I fear, Ladies, you will be tired with staying here; will it be agreeable to you to take a walk in the garden? With all my heart, said Mrs. Benson.

Mrs. Wilson then conducted her guests into a garden, which abounded with all kinds of vegetables for the table, quantities of fruit, and a variety of flowers. Master Frederick longed to taste some of the delicacies which presented themselves to his eye, but he had been taught never to gather fruit or flowers without leave, nor ask for any: however, Mrs. Wilson, with his mamma's permission, treated him and his sister with some fine apples and pears, which Betsy gathered and presented in cabbage leaves, and then took them to a shady arbour, where they sat and enjoyed their feast. After which they went to see the bees, who were at work in glass-hives.

CHAPTER XIX

THE SIGHT OF THE BEES was a great entertainment, not only to the children, but to Mrs. Benson also, who was excessively pleased with the ingenuity and industry with which these insects collected their honey and wax, formed their cells, and deposited their store. She had, by books, acquired a knowledge of the natural history of bees, which enabled her to examine their work with much greater satisfaction, than she would have received from the sight of them, had she been only taught to consider them as little stinging creatures, whom it was dangerous to approach. This is quite a treat to me indeed, said she, for I never before had an opportunity of seeing bees work in glass-hives.

Madam, said the good woman, few will be at the expense of them; and indeed, my neighbours laugh at me, and call me very whimsical and extravagant for indulging myself with them; but I find my account in keeping bees thus, even upon a principle of economy; for as I do not destroy them, I have greater numbers to work for me, and more honey every year than the last, notwithstanding I feed my bees in the winter. I have made acquaintance with the queen of every hive, who will come to me whenever I call, and you shall see one of their majesties if you please.

On this she called, in a manner which the inhabitants of the hive they were looking at, were accustomed to, and a large bee soon settled on her hand; in an instant after she was covered, from head to foot, with bees.

Miss Benson was fearful lest they should sting, and Frederick was running away; but Mrs. Wilson assured them the little creatures would not do any mischief, if no one attempted to catch them. Bees are, in their natural disposition, very harmless creatures, I assure you, Master Benson, said she; though I own they will certainly sting little boys who endeavour to catch them in order to suck their bag of honey, or take out their sting: but you see, that though I have hundreds about me, and even on my face and arms, not one offers to do me an injury; and I believe wasps seldom sting but in their own defence. She then threw up her hand, which the queen-bee regarded as a signal of dismission, and flew away in great state, surrounded by her guards, and followed by the rest of her subjects, each ready to lose his own life in the defence of her's.

There is something very wonderful, said Mrs. Benson, in the strong attachment these little creatures have to their sovereign, and very instructive too. I wish our good King could see all his subjects so closely united in his interest! What say you, Frederick, would you fight for your King? Yes, mamma, if papa would.—That I assure you, my dear, he certainly would do, if there were occasion, as loyally as the best bee in the world; and I beg you will remember what I now tell you, as long as you live: That it is your duty to love your King, for he is to be considered as the father of his country.

But mamma, said Frederick, it is the Queen that the bees love, and we have a queen too. Yes, my dear, we have so; and I believe her majesty is as much honoured by her subjects as a queen bee in her hive, though she has not so full a command over them; for it is a king that governs England, as your papa governs his family, and the queen is to be considered as the mother of the country.

But before we take our leave of the bees, let me observe to you, my dears, that several instructive lessons may be taken from their example.

If such little insects as these perform their daily tasks with so much alacrity, surely it must be a shame for children to be idle, and to fret, because they are put to learn things which will be of the utmost consequence to them in the end: and which would indeed conduce to their present happiness, would they but apply to them with a willing mind.

Science of various kinds presents itself to the human race, as the different flowers offer themselves to bees; and nothing is wanting to extract the sweets, but an application of those faculties of which they are by nature possessed. As the industrious bee flies successively to every fragrant plant within his reach, so do you, my dear children, go from one branch of knowledge to another: but observe, the bee does not fly giddily from flower to flower, merely to take a transient view of its beauties; he *rests* on each, till he has obtained all that will answer his purpose: imitate him in this particular also, and be not hurried on, by vain curiosity, from book to book, so as to gain only a superficial knowledge in the different branches of education; but remember, that the bee applies the materials he collects, to purposes valuable to himself, and to the community to which he belongs.

But come, Mrs. Wilson, we must, if you please, think of retiring from this place; for if we stay here much longer, we shall not have time to enjoy the pleasures you have in reserve for us. On this, Mrs. Wilson said, she was ready to wait on them.

As they walked along, Miss Benson took notice of a variety of beautiful insects, and Frederick so far forgot himself, as to run after a moth and catch it; but his mamma obliged him to let it go immediately. Don't you think, Mrs. Wilson, said she, that it is very wrong to let children catch butterflies and moths? Indeed I do, madam, replied the good woman. Poor little creatures, what injury can they do us by *flying about?* In that state at least they are harmless to us. Caterpillars and snails, it is true, we are obliged frequently to destroy, on account of their devouring fruit and vegetables; but unless they abound so as to be likely to do a real injury, I never let them be meddled with. I often think of my good father's maxim, which was, "Never to take away the life of any creature, unless it was necessary for the benefit of mankind." "While there is food and room enough in the world for them and us, let them live and enjoy the blessings they were formed for," he would say.

When I was a little girl, said Mrs. Benson, I had a great propensity to catch flies and other insects, but my father had an excellent microscope, in which he shewed me a number of different objects; by this means I learnt, that even the minutest creatures might be as susceptible of pain as myself; and I declare I cannot put any thing to death without fancying I hear its bones crack, and that I see its blood gushing from its veins and arteries; and so far from having a pleasure in killing even the disagreeable insects which are troublesome in houses, I assure you, I cannot do it myself, nor see it done without pain; yet they certainly may be considered as enemies, and as such we have a right to destroy them.

To be sure, Madam, said Mrs. Wilson, for without cleanliness we could not enjoy health. It goes against me to demolish a fine spider's web, and yet they make a house look very dirty; but I seldom have any in mine, for I took care, when I first came to live in it, to destroy the nests, and the old spiders, finding there was no security for their young ones here, have forsaken the house; and I am inclined to think, that the same vigilance in respect to other disagreeable insects, would have the same effect.

Doubtless, said Mrs. Benson; but pray tell me, do you destroy the webs of garden spiders also? Not unless there are so many as to be troublesome and disagreeable, replied Mrs. Wilson. I should not myself like to have the fruits of my industry demolished, nor my little ones taken out of my arms, or from their warm beds, and crushed to death. I am of opinion, said Mrs. Benson, that it would be a good way to accustom one's self, before one kills any thing, to change situations with it in imagination.

For instance, if I accidentally disturb an ant's nest, instead of crushing the little creatures with thoughtless inhumanity, as a set of insignificant atoms, I can fancy them appearing to me of the same magnitude a microscope would shew them, and one of them addressing me in this manner:—"Step aside, I entreat you, and let me and my associates pass in safety, that we may repair the mischief you have done to our city. The magazine of corn is fallen in, and I fear my dear parents are buried in the ruins; I hear the lamentations of my mate for the danger of our little ones; and behold two of my dear friends, whom you have trod upon, in the agonies of death. Why do you treat with such barbarity a set of innocent beings, who have never wilfully done you the least injury? Do we ever sting the human race but in our own defence? Do you really want the fruit we eat? And can the small quantity of corn we hoard up, be missed from your plentiful stores? Is it not misfortune enough for us that we are the prey of birds, but must mankind, to whom thousands of us would not afford even a single meal, destroy us for sport? Oh! rather ye, whose hearts are alive to the sentiments of humanity, plead our cause to the thoughtless part of your own species; and, as lords of the creation, drive away from us those natural enemies, which you may see darting down to devour us! If you love your own offspring, think of ours, if you would be prosperous in your own occupations, protect those who afford a lesson of industry, which the wisest of mankind has recommended to your serious consideration."

Indeed, Madam, said Mrs. Wilson, I have often wished that poor dumb creatures had somebody to speak for them; many an innocent life would then be saved which is now destroyed to no end.

Well, said Harriet, I am sure I shall never kill any thing without first magnifying it in my mind, and thinking what it would say for itself if able to speak. Then, my dear, I will engage for you, replied her mamma, that you will put but very few creatures to death: but in order to have a proper notion of their form, you must study Natural History; from whence you will learn, how wonderful their construction is; how carefully and tenderly the inferior creatures provide for their young; how ingenious their various employments are; how far they are from harbouring malice against the human species; and how excellently they are informed and instructed by their great Creator, for the enjoyment of happiness in their different classes of existence, which happiness we have certainly no right wantonly to disturb.

Besides, it is really a meanness to destroy any creature merely because it is *little;* and in *children,* particularly absurd to do so; for, upon this principle, they must themselves expect to be constantly ill-treated; though no animal stands more in need of tenderness than they do for many years, from the time of their coming into the world: and even men and women might expect to be *annihilated,* by the power of the great CREATOR.

Neither do I know how we can *precisely* call any thing *great* or *little,* since it is only so by comparing it with others. An ant or fly may appear to one of its own species, whose eyes are formed to see those parts which *we* cannot discover without *glasses,* as considerable as men and women do to each other: and to creatures of the dimensions of a mite, one the size of an ant doubtless looks formidable and gigantic. I therefore think it but justice to view insects with *microscopic* eyes, before we commit cruel devastations upon them.

During this conversation Master Frederick kept running about, making choice of flowers, which Betsy Wilson gathered and formed into nosegays for his mamma, his sister and himself.

CHAPTER XX

THE NEXT PLACE Mrs. Wilson took her guests to was a barn-yard, in which was a large horse-pond. Here her young visitors were delighted with the appearance of a number of geese and ducks; some were swimming in the water, some diving, others routing in the mud to see what fish or worms they could find.

It appears very strange to me, said Miss Benson, that any creatures can take delight in making themselves so dirty: And yet, replied Mrs. Benson, how many *children* do the same, without having any excuse for it? The ducks and geese grub about so in search of the necessaries of life; but I have seen boys do it merely for diversion, and sometimes at the hazard of their lives.

Very true, Madam, said Mrs. Wilson; my little Neddy had like to have been drowned so no longer ago than last Monday. He is a little venturesome rogue, and runs through thick and thin when pleasure is in view; but I fancy he will not hunt ducks about any more: for my part, I do not like any of my children should make sport of teasing animals. I wish every creature I keep to enjoy happiness to the day of its death, and when it must be killed, to have it dispatched by the quickest means possible.

Have you any fish here? said Frederick. I believe none of any consequence, Sir; the ducks and the geese would take care that none should grow to any considerable size; but there are plenty in a pond which you will see in the next field, and I hope to have the pleasure of seeing you at dinner, eat of some perch which were caught there. Sometimes we catch fine carp and tench, but only with nets; for neither my good man nor I can bear the cruel diversion of angling; nor do we allow our children to follow it, from a notion that it hardens the heart and leads to idleness.

Pray, mamma, said Miss Harriet, is it right to catch fish? I should think as they live in water, and we upon land, we have no business with them. You would wish every one then, my dear, to keep to their own element? Your sentiment is a good one in many respects, but it must not be extended so far as to forbid the catching of fish. Man has dominion over the fish, as well as over beasts and fowls, and many of them are excellent food for mankind; and the astonishing increase of them shews that they are designed to be so; for were all that are spawned to grow to full size, there would soon be more than our ponds, or even than the sea itself would hold, and they would be starved; therefore there are the same reasons for our feeding on them as on poultry, but we should be very careful to dispatch them as quickly as possible.

Some people are cruel enough to roast lobsters alive, whose cries I have been told are dreadful to hear; and others will flay eels alive, then put them without their skins into a pail of cold water, and afterwards cut them in pieces, and throw them into a frying-pan of boiling fat, where sometimes every separate piece will writhe about in agony. Thus each poor fish suffers as many deaths as it is divided into pieces. Now, Harriet, this cannot be right, however authorized by custom; therefore I hope you never will suffer such things to be done in your kitchen when you keep house, but always give orders that your lobsters be put into boiling water, which kills them soon, and that your eels are killed before they are skinned, which may soon be done by laying hold of their heads and tails and giving them a sudden pull, which separates the vertebræ of the back.

This is dreadful enough, though little in comparison of what they suffer by the other methods.

Oh, mamma! said Harriet, you make me even shudder; I do not believe I shall ever desire to eat eels; I shall be ready to make speeches for every piece as it lies in a dish before me. But pray tell me, is it cruel to kill frogs and toads? Ask Mrs. Wilson, my dear, she has more to do with such reptiles than I have. Why Miss, replied Mrs. Wilson, I am very singular in regard to such kind of creatures; and though I by no means like to have them in my house, do not make an outcry, and condemn every one to a violent death which is accidentally found in my cellars, or other places; on the contrary, I generally see it thrown into a ditch at some distance to take its chance. There are many birds and water-fowl that feed on young frogs and toads, which will in general keep them from multiplying, so as to be nuisances to us; and it is time enough for us to take arms against them, if there happen to be a very extraordinary increase of them. My good man is as particular in respect to moles; if he finds them in his garden, or any other part of his grounds where they can do mischief, he has them killed, but never suffers them to be molested when they are harmless. Neither does he hunt, or permit any one belonging to him to hunt after snakes; for he says, that if they are not disturbed, they will not come from their haunts to annoy us; and to kill, for the sake of killing, is cruel.

Pray Mrs. Wilson, said Frederick, do your sons ever go a bird-nesting? No, Sir, said she, I hope I have not a child amongst my family capable of such barbarity. In the course of the summer they generally have young birds to nurse, who fall out of their nests or lose their parents, but are seldom lucky enough to raise them; and we have only one in a cage which they reared last summer. Yet we have plenty of singing; for the sweet creatures, finding they may enjoy themselves unmolested in the trees, treat us with their harmony from morning to night, of which you had a specimen in the garden. Sparrows, indeed, my husband is under a necessity of destroying, for they are such devourers, they would leave him but little corn to carry to market if he did not shoot them; but he never kills the Crows, because they are very serviceable in picking up grubs, and other things injurious to farmers; we only set a little boy to watch our new sown grain, and he keeps making a noise, which effectually frightens them. O, said Frederick, I nurse young birds too. I have got a Linnet and a Robin Redbreast, and feed an hundred beside.

Mrs. Wilson smiled, and addressing herself to Mrs. Benson said, Now, Madam, we will, if you please, return to the house, for I fancy by this time dinner is nearly ready, and my husband and sons are about coming home.

Mrs. Benson was a little tired with her ramble, and was really impatient to see farmer Wilson and the rest of his amiable family. When she drew near the house she was met by the worthy man, who gave her a most cordial welcome, and said he was proud to see so much good company. Nancy, the eldest daughter, to whom the mother had intrusted the care of inspecting the additional cookery which she had ordered, and who for that reason was not to be seen in the morning, now made her appearance, dressed with the most perfect neatness; health bloomed in her cheeks, and cheerfulness and good-humour sparkled in her eyes. With this engaging countenance she easily prevailed on Master Frederick to let her place him by her at the table, round which the two other visitors, the master and mistress of the house, and the rest of their offspring, consisting of Thomas, a fine youth of eighteen, four young boys, and little Betsy, were soon seated.

The table was covered with plain food, but by the good management of Nancy, who had made an excellent pudding, an apple-pie, and some delicious custards, it made a very good figure; and Mrs. Benson afterwards declared, that she had never enjoyed an entertainment so much. It was considerably heightened by the happy countenances of the whole family.

The farmer, who was a jocose man, said a number of droll things, which diverted his little visitors very much, and soon after dinner he begged leave to depart, as he was sheep-shearing; but said, he thought the young gentlefolks might be diverted with the sight, so invited them to pay him a visit in the field, and left Joe and Neddy to conduct Master Frederick.

CHAPTER XXI

THE YOUNG FARMERS were rather shy at first, being afraid that their guests would laugh at their country talk; but when they observed how politely they behaved to their sisters, they entered into conversation, and told Master Benson a hundred particulars about animals, with which he was before unacquainted; and he in return related all he knew about his Redbreasts and other pensioners. *They then shewed him a pretty cat with kittens,* and also their favourite Daphne, a bitch with two young puppies; the latter were kept in a kennel, and the cat in a stable, where they were well supplied with food.

As Frederick knew that his sister was remarkably fond of cats, he stepped back to call her to look at them, which, with her mamma's permission, she was greatly pleased to do, and longed to have the kittens to nurse. When she returned, she inquired whether the dogs and cats were ever permitted to come into the house?

Not whilst they have young ones, said Mrs. Wilson, for they make a great deal of dirt, and are very troublesome at that time; but when puss has brought up her family, which is designed for the stable, she shall be admitted amongst us again; for she is a very useful creature, and deserves to be well treated, but I do not suffer my children to handle her; I think it looks very ugly for any one to be all over scratches. Daphne is admitted to a greater share of familiarity; she is very faithful, and extremely good-natured; but we never feed her in the house, for there is no doing so without greasing the floors.

I am of opinion, said Mrs. Benson, that a difference should be made between our treatment of cats and dogs. There is something very savage in the nature of the former; and though they certainly are deserving of our kindness on account of their usefulness, yet they cannot make themselves so agreeable as dogs; and there is really something very formidable in their talons and teeth; and when enraged, a cat is no better than a little tigress.

Besides, were there not danger to one's self in nursing cats, there is no doing it without injury to one's linen; for when puss is best pleased, she generally tramples with her talons unsheathed, by which practice many a fine apron has been torn. And even the cleanliness of cats is injurious, for they usually have recourse to corners of chairs, in order to rub the dirt from their talons. Many people have a great dread of this animal, and on that account it should not be used to come into rooms in which a variety of company is received.

As for dogs, they are in general so very social, grateful, and pleasing, that they seem formed to be the humble companions of mankind; and if kept in proper order, may be familiarised with safety; but then they should be well educated, and taught to know their distance. And as there are different species of them, we should make a prudent selection, and not introduce into the house great mastiffs or tall greyhounds: neither must we indulge those we domesticate to too great a degree, for in that case they will become as troublesome as cats.

Mrs. Benson now expressed her desire to see the sheep-shearing; on which Mrs. Wilson and her daughter conducted her and Miss Harriet to the field, where they arrived at the conclusion of the operation; and a very pleasing sight it was to behold the happy creatures, who lately waddled under a heavy, heating load, relieved from their burden, leaping and frisking with delight, whilst the accumulated wool seemed, as it lay, to promise comfortable clothing for many a naked wretch among the human species, who, destitute of such a supply, would be in danger of perishing with cold in the ensuing winter.

Miss Harriet observed the innocent countenances of the sheep and lambs, and said she thought it was a thousand pities to kill them.

It is so, my dear, said her mamma, but we must not indulge our feelings too far in respect to animals which are given us for food; all we have to do is to avoid barbarity. It is happy for them that they have no apprehension of being killed, and therefore enjoy life in peace and security to the very last; and even when the knife is lifted to their throats, are ignorant of its destination: and a few struggles put an end to their pain for ever. But come, Mrs. Wilson, will you favour us with a sight of your cows. With pleasure, Madam, they are by this time driven up to be milked. She then conducted her visitors towards the farm-yard.

Perhaps, Madam, said Mrs. Wilson, as they walked along, the young Lady and Gentleman may be afraid of horned cattle? I believe, replied Mrs. Benson, I may venture to say, that Harriet has no unreasonable fears of any living creature; it has been my endeavour to guard the minds of my children against so distressing a weakness; but whether

Frederick's heart has acquired fortitude enough to enable him to venture near so many cows, I cannot tell. O yes, mamma, cried Frederick, I would sooner get up and ride into the yard on the horns of one of them, than run away. Well, we shall soon put your courage to the proof, said Mrs. Benson; so come along, Sir.

As for my children, said Mrs. Wilson, they are remarkably courageous in respect to animals: all the creatures belonging to us are very harmless and gentle, which is the natural consequence of kind treatment, and no person need be afraid of walking in any part of our grounds: but it is difficult to persuade some people that there is no danger, for they are apt to imagine, that every loose horse they see will gallop over them, and that every creature with horns will gore and toss them.

Very true, replied Mrs. Benson; and I have known many as much afraid of a toad, a frog, or a spider, as if certain death would be the consequence of meeting them; when if these persons would but make use of their reason, they would soon be convinced that such fears are ill-grounded. Frogs and toads are very harmless creatures, and so far from offering an injury to any human being they may chance to meet, hop away with all possible expedition, from a dread of being themselves destroyed; and spiders drop suddenly down, with a view to their own preservation only: and therefore it is highly ridiculous to be afraid of them.

Horses and oxen are much more formidable creatures; they certainly could do us a great deal of mischief, if they were conscious of their superior strength; but Providence has wisely ordained that they should not be so; and having given mankind dominion over them, has implanted in their natures an awe and dread of the human species, which occasion them to yield subjection to the Lords of the creation, when they exert their authority in a proper manner.

It is really a very wonderful thing, said Mrs. Wilson, to see a fine lively horse submitting to the bit and harness, or a drove of oxen quietly marching under the direction of one man!

Pray, mamma, said Harriet, what do you mean by saying, that *man* is lord *of the creation?* Are *all* brute creatures subject to *every* man? I cannot comprehend how this can be.

I will endeavour to explain it to you, my dear, said Mrs. Benson, the next time we read the Bible together: at present, I have only time to inform you, that the dread of mankind, which prevails so generally amongst the inferior creatures, does not exist in so high a degree, as to render every *individual animal* afraid of every *individual man:* but the human *species,* that is to say, *all mankind together,* have an undoubted superiority and dominion: and there is no *species* of *animals,* which, if collected together, *mankind* could not subdue; for though inferior to many of them in strength, men vastly exceed them in number, and having the use of *reason,* can employ a variety of means to conquer them: and I make no doubt, that, was the experiment possible, to assemble each individual *species,* in opposition to the *whole race of mankind* which exist at one time on the earth, or even an equal number of them, the *dread* and *fear* which is instinctive in their natures, would operate so powerfully on the hearts of the most ferocious of them, as to prevent their attempting any contest.

It is observable, and shews at once the goodness and wisdom of our great Creator, that those creatures, which are the most useful to us, are the easiest tamed; and yield, not only singly, but in flocks, to mankind, nay, even to boys.

From what I have said, you must perceive, that it is a great weakness for a *human being* to be *afraid* of *animals*.

By this time the party were advanced pretty near to the barn-yard, and Frederick espied one of the cows peeping over the gate: on which, with a countenance expressive of fear, he ran hastily to his mamma and asked her, whether cows could toss people over gates and hedges? I will not answer so silly a question, Frederick, said she; pray look again, and you will perceive that it is impossible for such large heavy creatures to do so; and these inclosures are made on purpose to confine them within proper bounds. But did not you boast just now, that you could ride on the horns of one of them? That I shall not require you to do, for it would very likely make the creature angry, because cows are not accustomed to carry any load upon their heads; neither would I allow you to run after them with a stick, or to make any attempt to frighten them; but if you approach as a friend, I make no doubt you will be received as such; so summon your courage, and attend us; the cows will not hurt you, I can assure you.

Neddy Wilson then began laughing, from the idea that a boy should be afraid of a cow! which made Frederick ashamed of himself; and quitting his mamma's gown, by which he had held fast while she was speaking, he laid hold of Neddy's hand, and declared his resolution to go as near the cows as he would. I will not take upon me to say, that his little heart was perfectly free from palpitation; but that lay in his own bosom, where none could discover its feelings but himself; so let us give him credit for as much courage as we can, and acknowledge him to have been a noble little fellow, in thus trusting himself amongst a number of horned cattle.

CHAPTER XXII

T<small>HE WHOLE PARTY</small> now entered the farm-yard, where they saw eight fine cows, fat, sleek, and beautifully clean, who yielded several pails of rich milk, the steam of which, added to the breath of the cows, cast a delightful fragrance around. Mrs. Wilson then entreated her company to return to the house, where tea was provided, and a delicious syllabub.

The farmer now came back, and refreshed himself with a cup of ale, which was very comfortable after the fatigues of the day.

I have had, said Mrs. Benson, great pleasure in viewing your farm, Mr. Wilson, which appears to me to afford all the desirable comforts and conveniences of life, and I most sincerely wish a continuance of your prosperity. If it is not an impertinent question, pray tell me, did you inherit it from your father, or was it purchased with the fruits of your own industry? Neither my wife nor I have led an idle life, I assure you, Madam, replied the farmer; but, next to the blessing of heaven, I think myself in a great degree indebted to my cattle for my good success. My father left me master of a little farm, with a few acres of land well cropped, three horses, two cows, ten sheep, a sow and pigs, a jack-ass, and a few poultry; these have gradually multiplied to what you now see me possess, besides numbers that I have sold; and I have had fine crops of hay and corn; so that every year I laid by a little money, till I was able to purchase this farm, which has proved a very good one to me.

There is something so uncommon in hearing a farmer attribute a part of his success in life to his cattle, that I should be obliged to you, Mr. Wilson, said the Lady, if you would account to me for this circumstance. Most readily, Madam, said he.

When I was a very young man, I heard a fine sermon from the pulpit, preached by my dear wife's father, on the subject of shewing mercy to brutes, which made a great impression on my mind; and I have ever since acted towards all dumb creatures, as I would to mankind, upon the principle of doing as I would be done by.

I always considered every beast that works for me as my servant, and entitled to wages; but as they cannot use money, I pay them in things of more value to them; and make it a rule, unless in case of great necessity (when corn or hay, for instance, are likely to be spoiled), to let them enjoy rest on the Sabbath-day.

I am very cautious in not letting any beast work beyond its strength, and always give them their food in due season; nor do I ever suffer them to be beat or cruelly used. Besides giving them what I call their daily wages, I indulge them with all the comforts I can afford them.

In summer, when the business of the day is over; my horses enjoy themselves in a good pasture; and in winter, they are sheltered from the inclemencies of the weather in a warm stable. If they get old, I contrive some easy task for them; and when they can work no longer, let them live on the common without it, till age and infirmities make their lives burthensome to themselves, when I have them put to as easy a death as possible.

Though my cows and sheep do not work for me, I think them entitled to a recompense for the profit I receive from their milk and wool, and endeavour to re-pay them with the kindest usage: and even my jack-ass finds mercy from me; for I could not bear to see so useful a creature ill-treated; and as for my dogs, I set great store by them on account of their fidelity.

These are very excellent rules indeed, Mr. Wilson, and I wish they were generally followed, said Mrs. Benson; for I believe many poor beasts suffer a great deal from the ill-treatment inflicted on them, the horses in post-chaises and hackney-coaches in London particularly. Yes, Madam, said the farmer, I have heard so, and could tell you such stories of cruelties exercised on brutes in the country, as would quite shock you; and have seen in my own family such an instance of the ill-effects of neglecting them, as has confirmed me in the notions I learnt from the good sermon I told you of.

I have a brother, whom I at present maintain; my father gave him an equal portion with myself, but neither he nor his wife were industrious, nor had they any feeling for dumb creatures. He trusted the care of his horses to careless carters, who used to let them go without water, and frequently neglect both to feed and clean them; and, indeed he himself grudged them victuals: so they grew leaner and leaner, and at last were really killed with hard work and hard living.

His cows were kept so badly in the winter, that they soon lost their milk; and the calves they had, for want of proper management, died; as did the cows themselves in a short time afterwards. The sheep got a distemper, which soon put an end to them.

His pigs being kept in the most dirty way in the world, and sometimes left without food for two days together, got hide-bound and full of vermin; and his poultry dropped off with the roup and other disorders, till he had none left.

The jack-ass used to be put to hard drudgery in his own service, or let out to draw a sand-cart; this excessive labour, with scarcely time allowed him to seek a scanty living amongst the thistles and hedges, soon put an end to him. These losses my brother had no means to repair, for without cattle he could not cultivate his farm, and was soon reduced to poverty; and were I not to maintain him, he must be a beggar; for through want of air and exercise he lost his health, and is now incapable of working. His wife died some years before of an illness, which was the consequence of indolence and inactivity. I am much obliged to you for your story, Mr. Wilson, said Mrs. Benson, and hope my children will never forget it; for it certainly is a duty to extend our clemency to beasts and other animals. Nay, we are strictly commanded in the Scriptures to shew compassion to the beasts of others, even to those of our enemies; surely, then, those which are our own property, and work for us, have a peculiar claim to it. There is one custom which shocks me very much, and that is, pounding of cattle; I fancy, Mr. Wilson, you do not practise that much.

Madam, replied he, I should much rather pound the owners of them, through whose neglect or dishonesty it generally happens that horses trespass on other people's land. If any beast accidentally gets into my grounds, I send it home to its owner, for it certainly is no wilful fault in the creature to seek the best pasture it can find; but if I have reason to suppose his owner turned him in, I then think myself obliged to do what the law directs in that respect: but though it is a secret I am obliged to keep from my neighbours, I may safely confess to you, Madam, that I have not the heart to let a poor beast *starve*, in a pound. As there are no Courts of Justice in which they can seek redress, I erect one for them in my own breast, where humanity pleads their cause.

I wish they had such an advocate in every breast, Mr. Wilson, said the Lady; but my watch reminds me we must now take our leave, which I do with many thanks to you and Mrs. Wilson, for your kind entertainment and good cheer, and shall be happy to return your civilities at my own house, and pray bring your whole family with you.

She then desired her son and daughter to prepare for their departure. Frederick was grown so intimate with little Neddy, that he could scarcely be prevailed on to leave him, till he recollected Robin and the Linnet.

As they returned in the coach, Mrs. Benson remarked, that farmer Wilson's story was enough to make every one who heard it careful of their live stock, for their own sakes: but, said she, the pleasure and advantage will be greatly increased, if it is done from a principle of humanity as well as interest. Miss Benson answered, that she hoped she should neither treat animals ill, nor place her affections on them too strongly. That, my dear, replied her good mamma, is the proper medium to be observed. The speech you made for the ant, mamma, said Harriet, has scarcely ever been out of my head since: I should like to hear what you could say for every live creature we see. I had need have strong lungs, my dear, to perform such a task as that, replied Mrs. Benson. I shall, on all proper occasions, be ready to lend my tongue to the dumb, and to speak for those who cannot utter their own sorrows and injuries.

In a short time they arrived at home. The maid, to whose care the birds had been intrusted, gave a good account of her charge; and Miss Harriet and Master Frederick went to bed in peace, after a day spent with so much pleasure and improvement.

CHAPTER XXIII

THE NEXT MORNING the Redbreasts attended as usual, and Robin was still better, but his father began to fear he would never perfectly recover from his accident; however he kept his apprehensions to himself, and suffered the little ones to entertain their lame brother with a relation of what they had seen the day before in the orchard. Frederick and Harriet were so diverted with the chattering and chirping of the little things, that they did not miss the parent's song.

When the young ones had staid as long as she thought right, the hen Redbreast summoned them away, and all took leave of Robin, who longed to go with them, but was not able. The father reminded him, that he had great reason to rejoice in his present situation, considering all things; on which he resumed his cheerfulness, and giving a sprightly twitter, hopped into Master Frederick's hand, which was spread open to receive him. The rest then flew away, and Miss Harriet and her brother prepared for their morning tasks.

The Redbreasts alighted as usual to drink in the court-yard, and were preparing to return to the orchard, when Flapsy expressed a desire to look a little about the world; for she said it would be very mopish to be always confined to the orchard; and Dicky seconded her request. Pecksy replied, that however her curiosity might be excited, she had known so much happiness in the nest, that she was strongly attached to the paternal spot, and could gladly pass her life there. The parents both commended her contented disposition; but her father said, that as there was nothing blameable in the inclination Dicky and Flapsy discovered for seeing the world, provided it was kept within due bounds, he would readily gratify it: then asking if they were sufficiently refreshed, took wing, and led the way to a neighbouring grove, where he placed his little tribe amongst the branches of a venerable oak.

Here their ears were charmed with a most enchanting concert of music. On one tree a Blackbird and a Thrush poured forth their strong melodious notes; on another a number of Linnets joined their sweet voices: exalted in the air a Skylark modulated his delightful pipe: whilst a brother of the wood, seated on a cool-refreshing turf, made the grove re-echo with his melody; to these the Nightingale joined his enchanting lay. In short, not a note was wanting to complete the harmony.

The little Redbreasts were so exceedingly charmed, that for a while they continued listening with silent rapture; at length, Dicky exclaimed, How happy should I be to join the cheerful band, and live for ever in this charming place!

It is, replied his mother, a very pleasant situation, to be sure; but could you be sensible of the superior advantages, which, as a Redbreast, you may enjoy by taking up your abode in the orchard, you would never wish to change it: for my own part, I find myself so happy in that calm retreat, that nothing but necessity shall ever drive me from it.

Pecksy declared, that though she was much delighted with the novelty of the scene, and charmed with the music, she now felt an ardent desire to return home; but Flapsy wished to see a little more first. Well, said the father, your desire shall be gratified; let us take a circuit in this grove, for I wish you to see every thing worth observation in every place you go to; and not to fly about the world, as many giddy birds do, without the least improvement from their travels. On this he spread his wings as the signal of departure, which his family obeyed.

Observing a parcel of boys creeping silently along, Stop, said he, let us perch on this tree, and see what these little *monsters* are about. Scarcely were they seated, when one of the boys mounted an adjacent tree, and took a nest of half-fledged Linnets, which he brought in triumph to his companions.

At this instant, a family of Thrushes unfortunately chirped, which directed another boy to the place of their habitation; on which he climbed, and eagerly seized the unfortunate little creatures. Having met with so much success, they left the grove to exult, at their own homes, over their wretched captives, for ever separated from their tender parents; who soon came back, laden with the gain of their labour, which they had kindly destined for the sustenance of their infant broods.

The little Redbreasts were now spectators of those parental agonies which had been formerly described to them; and Pecksy cried out, Who would desire to live in this grove, who had once experienced the comforts of the orchard? Dicky and Flapsy were desirous to depart, being alarmed for their own safety. No, said the father, let us stay a little longer—now we will go on.

They accordingly took another flight, and saw a man scattering seed upon the ground. See there, said Dicky, what fine food that man throws down; I dare say he is some good creature who is a friend to the feathered race; shall we alight and partake of his bounty?

Do not form too hasty an opinion, Dicky, said the father; watch here with me a little while, and then do as you think proper. All the little ones stretched their necks, and kept a curious eye fixed on the man. In a few minutes a number of Sparrows, Chaffinches, and Linnets, descended, and began to regale themselves; but in the midst of their feast, a net was suddenly cast over them, and they were all taken captive. The man, who was a bird-catcher by profession, called to his assistant, who brought a cage, divided into a number of small partitions, in which the Linnets and Chaffinches were separately deposited. In this dismal prison, where they had scarcely room to flutter, were those little creatures confined, who lately poured forth their songs of joy, fearless of danger. As for the Sparrows, their necks were wrung, and they were put in a bag together. The little Redbreasts trembled for themselves, and were in great haste to take wing. Stay, said the father, Dicky has not yet made acquaintance with this friend of the feathered race. No, said Dicky, nor do I desire it; defend me, and all who are dear to me, from such friends as these! Well, said the father, learn from this instance, never to form an hasty judgment, nor to put yourself into the power of strangers, who offer you favours you have no right to expect from their hands.

Indeed, my love, said the mother bird, I am very anxious to get home; I have not lately been used to be long absent from it, and every excursion I make endears it to me. O, the day is not half spent, replied her mate; and I hope, that for the gratification of the little ones, you will consent to complete the ramble. Come, let us visit another part of the grove; I am acquainted with its inmost recesses. His mate acquiesced, and they proceeded on their journey.

At length the father hastily called out, Turn this way! turn this way! The whole party obeyed the word of command, and found the good effects of their obedience; for in an instant they saw a flash of fire, a thick smoke followed it, and immediately they heard a dreadful sound, and saw a young Redstart fall bleeding to the ground, on which he struggled just long enough to cry, Oh! my dear father! why did I not listen to your kind admonitions, which I now find, too late, were the dictates of tenderness! and then expired.

The little Redbreasts were struck with consternation at this dreadful accident; and Pecksy, who recovered the soonest, begged her father would inform her by what means the Redstart was killed. He was shot to death, said he; and had you not followed my directions, it might have been the fate of every one of you: therefore, let it be a lesson to you, to follow every injunction of your parents with the same readiness for the future.

You may depend on it, our experience teaches us to foresee many dangers, which such young creatures as you have no notion of; and when we desire you to do, or to forbear any thing, it is for the sake of your safety or advantage: therefore, Dicky, never more stand, as you sometimes have done, asking *why* we tell you to do so and so? for had that been the case now, you who were in a direct line with the gunner, would have been inevitably shot.

They all said they would observe implicit obedience. Do so, said he; but in order to this, you must also remember to practise, in our absence, what we enjoin you when present. For instance, some kinds of food are very prejudicial to your health, which we would not, on any account, let you taste when we are by; these you must not indulge in when away from us, whatever any other bird may say in recommendation of them. Neither must you engage in any dangerous enterprise, which others, who have natural strength or acquired agility, go through with safety; nor should you go to any places which we have pointed out as dangerous, nor join any company which we have forbid you to make acquaintance with.

This poor Redstart might have avoided his fate; for I heard his father, when I was last in the grove, advise him not to fly about by himself, till he had shewn him the dangers of the world.

Pecksy answered, that she knew the value of parental instruction so well, that she should certainly treasure up in her heart every maxim of it; and the others promised to do the same: but, said Flapsy, I cannot understand the nature of the accident which occasioned the death of the Redstart.

Neither can I explain it to you, my dear, replied the father; I only know, that it is a very common practice with some men to carry instruments, from which they discharge what proves fatal to many a bird; but I have, by attentive observation, learnt how to evade the mischief. Whenever I go from the orchard I always get upon a high tree, and look all around me; if I see any gunners I take a different course (the thickness of the underwood prevented my discovering him who shot the Redstart). I also carefully avoid associating with those birds, who do mischief to the property of mankind; for those that join with thieves and ravagers deserve, and must justly expect to share, their fate: therefore be particularly careful to keep proper company, and gain an honest character, as it will ensure you the good opinion of others.

But come, let us descend, and refresh ourselves a little, as we may do it with safety, and then we will see if we cannot find a place where you can have amusement, without being exposed to such dangers as attend the inhabitants of woods.

Are you sufficiently rested to take a pretty long flight? O yes, cried Dicky, who was quite eager to leave the spot, in which, a short time before, he had longed to pass his life: the rest joined in the same wish, and every wing was instantly expanded.

CHAPTER XXIV

THE FATHER LED the way, and in a very short space of time he and his family arrived at the estate of a gentleman, who, having a plentiful fortune, endeavoured to collect all that was curious in art and nature, for the amusement of his own mind, and the gratification of others. He had a house like a palace, furnished with every expensive rarity; his gardens, to which the Redbreasts took their flight, were laid out in such a manner as to afford the most delightful variety to the eye.

Amongst other articles of taste were an aviary and menagerie. The former was built like a temple, enclosed with brass wire; the frame-work was painted green, and ornamented with carving gilt: in the middle a fountain continually threw up fresh water, which fell into a bason whose brink was enamelled with flowers; at one end were partitions for birds' nests, and troughs containing various kinds of seed, and materials for building nests: this part was carefully sheltered from every inclemency of the weather, and numbers of perches were placed in different parts of the aviary, and it was surrounded by a most beautiful shrubbery.

A habitation like this, in which all the conveniences of life seemed to be collected, where abundance was supplied without toil, where each gay songster might sing himself to repose in the midst of ease and plenty, safe from the dangers of the woods, appeared to our young travellers desirable beyond all the situations in the world, and Dicky expressed an earnest wish to be admitted into it. Well, said the father, let us not determine hastily, it will be adviseable first to inquire whether its inhabitants are really happy, before you make interest to become one of the number; place yourselves by me on this shrub, and whilst we rest, we shall have an opportunity of observing what passes.

The first bird that attracted their notice was a Dove, who sat cooing by himself in a corner, in accents so gentle and sweet, that a stranger to his language would have listened to them with delight; but the Redbreasts, who understood their import, heard them with sympathetic concern. "Oh, my dear, my beloved mate," said he, "am I then divided from you for ever? What avails it, that I am furnished here with all the elegancies and luxuries of life? Deprived of your company, I have no enjoyment of them? the humblest morsel, though gained with toil and danger, would be infinitely preferable to me if shared with you. Here am I shut up for the remainder of my days, in society for which I have no relish, whilst she, who has hitherto been the beloved partner of all my joys, is for ever separated from me! In vain will you, with painful wing, pursue your anxious search in quest of me; never, never more, shall I bring you the welcome refreshment; never shall I hear your soothing voice, and delight the soft murmurs of the infant pair, which you hatched with such care, and nursed with such tenderness! No, my beloved nestlings, never will your wretched father be at liberty to guide your flight, and instruct you in your duty." Here his voice faltered, and he resigned himself a prey to silent sorrow.

This Dove is not happy, however, said the hen Redbreast to her mate, and no wonder: but let us attend to the notes of that Lark. His eyes were turned up towards the sky, he fluttered his wings, he strained his throat, and would, to a human eye, have appeared in raptures of joy; but the Redbreasts perceived that he was inflamed with rage. "And am I to be constantly confined in this horrid place?" sang he. "Is my upward flight to be impeded by bars and wires? Must I no longer soar towards that bright luminary, and make the arch of heaven resound with my singing? Shall I cease to be the herald of the morn, or must I be so in this contracted sphere? No, ye partners of my captivity, henceforth sleep on and take ignoble rest; and may you lose in slumber the remembrance of past pleasures! O cruel and unjust man! was it not enough that I proclaimed the approach of day, that I soothed your sultry hours, that I heightened the delights of evening, but must I, to gratify your unfeeling wantonness, be secluded from every joy my heart holds dear, and condemned to a situation I detest? Take your delicious dainties, reserve your flowing stream for those who can relish them, but give me liberty! But why do I address myself to you who are heedless of my misery?" Here casting an indignant look around, he stopped his song.

What think you now, Dicky, said the Redbreast, have you as high an idea of the happiness of this place, as you conceived at the first view of it? I cannot help thinking still, replied Dicky, that it is a charming retreat, and that it must be very comfortable to have every thing provided for one's use. Well, said the father, let us move, and observe those Linnets who are building their nest. Accordingly they flew to a tree, whose branches formed a part of the shelter of the aviary, where they easily heard, without being themselves observed, all that passed in it.

"Come," said one of the Linnets, "let us go on with our work, and finish the nest, though it will be rather a melancholy task to hatch a set of little prisoners. How different was the case when we could anticipate the pleasure of rearing a family to all the joys of liberty! Men, it is true, now, with officious care, supply us with the necessary materials, and we may make a very good nest; but I had much rather be at the trouble of seeking them. What pleasure have we experienced in plucking a bit of wool from a sheep's back, in searching for moss, in selecting the best feather where numbers were left to our choice, in stopping to rest on the top of a tree, which commanded an extensive prospect, in joining a choir of songsters whom we accidentally met!—But now our days pass with repeated sameness; variety, so necessary to give a relish to all enjoyment, is wanting. Instead of the songs of joy we formerly heard from every spray, our ears are constantly annoyed with the sound of mournful lamentations, transports of rage, or murmurs of discontent. Could we reconcile ourselves to the loss of liberty, it is impossible to be happy here."

"True," said his mate; "yet I am resolved to try what patience, resignation, and employment will effect; and hope, as our young ones will never know what liberty is, they will not pine as we do for it." Saying this she picked up a straw, her mate followed the example, and they pursued their work.

At this instant a hen Goldfinch brought forth her brood, who were full fledged. Come, said she, my nestlings, use your wings: I have taught you to fly in all directions. So saying, the little ones divided: one flew upwards; but emulous to outdo a little Sparrow which was flying in the air above the aviary, he hit himself against the wires of the dome, and would have fallen to the bottom, but that he was stopped by one of the perches.

As soon as he recovered, "Why cannot I soar as I see other birds do?" said he. "Alas!" cried the mother, "we are in a place of confinement, we are shut up and can never get out; but here is food in abundance, and every other necessary." "Never get out?" exclaimed the whole brood, "then adieu to happiness!" She attempted to sooth them, but in vain.

The little Redbreasts rejoiced in their liberty, and Dicky gave up the desire of living in the aviary, and wished to be gone. "Stop," said his father, "let us first hear what those Canaries are saying."

The Canaries had almost completed their nest. "How fortunate is our lot," said the hen bird, "in being placed in this aviary! How preferable is it to the small cage we built in last year." "Yes," replied her mate; "yet how comfortable was that, in comparison with the still smaller ones in which we were once separately confined. For my part I have no wish to fly abroad, for I should neither know what to do, nor where to go; and it shall be my endeavour to inspire my young ones with the same sentiments I feel. Indeed, we owe the highest gratitude to those who make such kind provision for a set of foreigners, who have no resources but their bounty; and my best lays shall be devoted to them. Nothing is wanted to complete the happiness of this place, but to have other kinds of birds excluded. Poor creatures! it must be very mortifying to them to be shut up here, and see others of their kind enjoying full freedom. No wonder they are perpetually quarrelling; for my part, I sincerely pity them, and am ready to submit to the occasional insults and affronts I meet with, out of compassion."

You now perceive, Dicky, said the cock Redbreast, that this place is not, as you supposed, the region of perfect happiness; you may also observe, that it is not the abode of universal wretchedness.

It is by no means desirable to be shut up for life, let the place of confinement be ever so splendid; but should it at any time be your lot to be caught and imprisoned, which may possibly be the case, adopt the sentiments of the Linnet and the Canary Bird: employment will pass away many an hour, that would have been a heavy load if spent in grief and anxiety; and reflections on the blessings and comforts that are still in your power, will lessen your regret for those which are lost. But come, pick up some of the seeds which are scattered on the outside of the aviary, for that is no robbery, and then I will shew you another scene.

As soon as they had regaled themselves with the superfluities of the feathered captives, they took their flight to another part of the garden, in which was a menagerie.

The menagerie consisted of a number of pens, built round a grass-plat; in each was a pan of water, a sort of box containing a bed or nest, a trough for food, and a perch. In every pen was confined a pair of birds, and every pair was either of a different species, or distinguished for some beautiful variety either of form or plumage. The wooden bars which were put in the front, were painted partly green and partly white, which dazzled the sight at the first glance, and so attracted the eyes, that there was no seeing what was behind without going close up to the pens.

The little Redbreasts knew not what sight to expect, and begged their parent to gratify their curiosity. Well, follow me, said the father; but I believe you must alight upon the cross bars, or you will not be able to examine the beauties of these fowls. They did so, and in the first pen was a pair of Partridges.

The size of these birds, so greatly exceeding their own, astonished them all; but notwithstanding this, the amiable Pecksy was quite interested with their modest gentle appearance, and said, she thought no one could ever wish to injure them.

True, Pecksy, replied the father, they have, from the harmlessness of their dispositions a natural claim to tenderness and compassion; and yet I believe there are few birds who meet with less: for I have observed, that numbers share the same fate as the Redstart, which you saw die in the grove. I have myself seen many put to death in that manner.

For a long time I was excessively puzzled to account for this fatality, and resolved if possible to gratify my curiosity. *At length I saw a man kill two and take them away.* This very man had shewn me great kindness in feeding me when I first left my father's nest; so I had no apprehension of his doing me an injury, and resolved to follow him.

When he arrived at his own house I saw him deliver the victims of his cruelty to another person, who hung them up together by the legs, in a place which had a variety of other dead things in it, the sight of which shocked me exceedingly, and I could stay

no longer. I therefore flew back to the field in which I had seen the murder committed; and in searching about, found the nest belonging to the poor creatures, in which were several young ones just hatched, who in a short time were starved to death! how dreadful is the fate of young animals, who lose their parents before they are able to shift for themselves! and how dutiful ought those to be to whom the blessing of parental instruction and assistance is continued!

When the next morning arrived I went again to see after the dead Partridges, and found them hanging as before; and this was the case the day after; but the following morning, I saw a boy stripping all their feathers off. As soon as he had completed this horrid operation, a woman took them, whom I ventured to follow, as the window of the place she entered stood open; where, to my astonishment, I beheld her twist their wings about, and fasten them to their sides, then cross their legs upon their breasts, and run something quite through their bodies. After this she put them before a place which glowed with a brightness something resembling the setting sun, which on the woman's retiring, I approached, and found intolerably hot; I therefore made a hasty retreat; but resolving to know the end of the Partridges, kept hovering about the house; and at last, looking in at a window, I saw them, smoking hot, set before the man who murdered them, who was accompanied by several others; all of whom eyed them with as much delight as I have seen any of you discover at the sight of the finest worm or insect that could be procured. In an instant after this the poor Partridges were divided limb from limb, and each one of the party present had his share till every bone was picked.

There were some other things devoured in the same manner; from which I learnt, that men feed on birds and other animals, as we do on those little creatures which are destined for our sustenance, only they do not eat them alive. Pray, father, said Dicky, do they eat Redbreasts? I believe not, said he; but I have reason to suppose they make many a meal on Sparrows, for I have beheld vast numbers of them killed.

At this instant their attention was attracted by one of the Partridges in the pen, who thus addressed his mate.

"Well, my love, as there is no chance for our being set at liberty, I think we may as well prepare our nest, that you may deposit your eggs in it. The employment of hatching and raising your little ones will, at least, mitigate the wearisomeness of confinement, and I promise myself many happy days yet; for as we are so well fed and attended, I think we may form hopes that our offspring will also be provided for; and though they will not be at liberty to range about as we formerly did, they will avoid many of those terrors to which our race are exposed at one season of the year in particular."

"I am very ready to follow your advice (said the hen-Partridge), and the business will soon be completed, for the nest is in a manner made for us, it only wants a little adjusting: I will therefore set about it immediately, and will no longer waste the hours in fruitless lamentations, since I am convinced, that *content* will render every situation easy in which we can enjoy the company of our dearest friends, and obtain the necessaries of life." So saying, she retired into the place provided for the purpose on which she was now intent, and her mate followed, in order to lend her all the assistance in his power.

I am very glad, said the hen Redbreast, that my young ones have had the opportunity of seeing such an example as this. You now understand what benefit it is of to have a temper of resignation; more than half the evils of life, I am well convinced, arise from fretfulness and discontent: and would every one, like these Partridges, try to make the best of their condition, we should seldom hear complaints; for there are much fewer *real* than *imaginary* misfortunes. But come, let us take a peep into the next pen.

Here they beheld a pair of fine Pheasants, who were quietly picking up some grain that was scattered for them; from which might be inferred, that they had, like the Partridges, reconciled themselves to their lot. The little Redbreasts were much pleased with the beauty of the cock bird; but as there was no conversation to be heard here, their parents desired them to fly on; as pleasures by which the eye only was amused, were not deserving of long attention.

They accordingly hopped to the next partition in which were confined a pair of penciled Pheasants. Flapsy was quite delighted with the elegance of their form, and the beauty of their plumage, and could have staid the whole day looking at them; but as these birds were also tame and contented, nothing more could be learnt here, than a confirmation of what the Partridges had taught. Our travellers therefore proceeded still farther, and found a pair of gold Pheasants. Their splendid appearance struck the young Redbreasts with astonishment, and raised such sentiments of respect, that they were even fearful of approaching birds which they esteemed as so much superior to themselves: but their father desiring they would never form a judgment of birds from a glittering outside, placed his family where they had an opportunity of observing, that this splendid pair had but little intrinsic merit.

They were proud of their fine plumage, and their chief employment was walking backwards and forwards to display it; sometimes they endeavoured to push through the bars of their prison, that they might get abroad to shew their rich plumage to the world, and exult over those who were, in this respect, inferior to them. How hard, said one of them, it is to be shut up here where there are no other birds to admire us, and where we have no little ugly creatures to ridicule.

If such are your desires, said the hen Redbreast, I am sure you are happier here than at liberty; for you would by your proud affected airs, excite the contempt of every bird who has right sentiments, and consequently meet with continual mortification, to which even the ugliest might contribute.

Pecksy desired to know if all fine birds were proud and affected? By no means, replied her mother; you observed the other two pair of Pheasants, who were, in my opinion, nearly equal to these for beauty and elegance. How easy and unassuming were they, and how much were their charms improved by the graces of humility! I often wonder that any bird should indulge itself in pride. What have such little creatures as we to boast of? The largest species amongst us is very inferior to many animals we see in the world; and man is lord over the greatest and strongest even of these. Nay, man himself has no cause to be *proud;* for he is subject to death as well as the meanest creature, as I have had opportunities of observing. But come, let us view the other parts of this enclosure.

On this, the father conducted his family to a variety of pens, in which were different sorts of foreign birds, of whom he could give but little account; and would not suffer his young ones to stand gazing at them long, lest they should imbibe injurious notions of them: especially when he heard Dicky cry out, as he left the last pen, I dare say that bird is a very cruel voracious creature; I make no doubt but he would eat us all one after the other if he could get at us.

Take care, Dicky, said the father, how you form an ill opinion of any one on slight grounds. You cannot possibly tell what the character of this Stork is, merely from his appearance; you are a stranger to his language, and cannot see the disposition of his heart. If you give way to a suspicious temper, your own little breast will be in a state of constant perturbation; you will absolutely exclude yourself from the blessings of society, and will be shunned and despised by every bird of every kind. This Stork, whom you thus censure, is far from deserving your ill opinion. He would do you no harm, and is remarkable for his filial affection.

I saw him taken prisoner. He was carrying his aged father on his back, whom he had for a long time fed and comforted: the weight of this precious burden impeded his flight; and being at length wearied with it, he descended to the ground to rest himself, when a cruel man, who was out on the business of bird-catching, threw a net over them, and then seized him by the neck. His poor father, who was before worn out with age and infirmities, unable to bear this calamity, fell from his back and instantly expired. This Stork, after casting a look of anguish on his dear parent, which I shall never forget, turned with fury on his persecutor, whom he beat with his wings with all the strength he had; but in spite of all his exertions, he was conveyed to this place.

But come, let us pick up a little refreshment, and then return to the orchard. Saying this, he alighted on the ground, as did his mate and her family, where they met with a plentiful repast in the provisions which had been accidentally scattered by the person whose employment it was to bring food for the inhabitants of the menagerie. When they had regaled themselves, all parties gladly returned to the nest, and every heart rejoiced in the possession of liberty and peace.

CHAPTER XXV

FOR THREE SUCCESSIVE days nothing remarkably happened, either at Mr. Benson's or the Redbreasts' nest. The little family came daily to the breakfast-table, and Robin recovered daily from his accident, though not sufficiently to fly well; but Dicky, Flapsy, and Pecksy continued so healthy, and improved so fast, that they required no further care; and the third morning after their tour to the grove, &c., they did not commit the least error. When they retired from the parlour into the court-yard, to which Robin accompanied them, the father expressed great delight that they were at length able to shift for themselves.

And now a wonderful change took place in his own heart. That ardent affection for his young, which had hitherto made him, for their sakes, patient of toil, and fearless of danger, was on a sudden quenched; but from the goodness of his disposition, he still felt a kind of solicitude for their future welfare; and calling them around him, he thus addressed them.

"You must be sensible, my dear young ones, that from the time you left the egg-shell, till the present instant, both your mother and I have nourished you with the tenderest love. We have taught you all the arts of life which are necessary to procure you subsistence, and preserve you from danger. We have shewn you a variety of characters in the different classes of birds: and pointed out those which are to be shunned. You must now shift for yourselves; but before we part, let me repeat my admonition, to use industry, avoid contention, cultivate peace, and be contented with your condition. Let none of your own species excel you in any amiable quality, for want of your endeavours to equal the best; and do your duty in every relation of life, as we have done ours by you. To the gay scenes of levity and dissipation, prefer a calm retirement, for there is the greatest degree of happiness to be found. You, Robin, I would advise, on account of your infirmity, to attach yourself to the family, where you have been so kindly cherished."

Whilst he thus spake, his mate stood by, who finding the same change beginning to take place in her own breast, she viewed her young ones with tender regret; and when he ceased, cried out: "Adieu, ye dear objects of my late cares and solicitude! may ye never more stand in need of a mother's assistance! Though nature now dismisses me from the arduous task which I have long daily performed, I rejoice not, but would gladly continue my toil, for the sake of its attendant pleasures. O! delightful sentiments of maternal love, how can I part with you? Let me, my nestlings, give you a last embrace." Then spreading her wings, she folded them successively to her bosom, and instantly recovered her tranquillity.

Each young one expressed its grateful thanks to both father and mother, and with these acknowledgments filial affection expired in their breasts; instead of which, a respectful friendship succeeded. Thus was that tender tie dissolved, which had hitherto bound this little family together; for the parents had performed their duty, and the young ones had no need of farther assistance.

The old Redbreasts having now only themselves to provide for, resolved to be no longer burthensome to their benefactors; and after pouring forth their gratitude in the most lively strains, they took their flight together resolving never to separate. Every care now vanished, and their little hearts felt no sentiments but those of cheerfulness and joy. They ranged the fields and gardens, sipped at the coolest springs, and indulged themselves in the pleasures of society, joining their cheerful notes with those of other gay choristers, who animate and heighten the delightful scenes of rural life.

The first morning that the old Redbreasts were missing from Mrs. Benson's breakfast-table, Frederick and his sister were greatly alarmed for their safety; but their mamma said, she was of opinion, that they had left their nestlings; as it was the nature of animals in general to dismiss their young, as soon as they were able to provide for themselves. That is very strange, replied Miss Harriet; I wonder what would become of my brother and me, were you and papa to serve us so?

And is a boy of six, or a girl of eleven years old, capable of shifting for themselves? said her mamma. No, my dear child, you have need of a much longer continuance of our care than birds and other animals; and therefore GOD has ordained that parental affection, when once awakened, should always remain in the human breast, unless extinguished by the undutiful behaviour of a child.

And shall we see the old Redbreasts no more? cried Frederick. I do not know that you will, replied Mrs. Benson, though it is not unlikely that they may visit us again in the winter; but let not their absence grieve you, my love, for I dare say they are safe and happy.

At that instant the young ones arrived, and met with a very joyful reception. The amusement they afforded to Master Benson, reconciled him to the loss of their parents; but Harriet declared, she could not help being sorry that they were gone. I shall, for the future, mamma, said she, take a great deal of notice of animals; for I have had much entertainment in observing the ways of these Robins. I highly approve your resolution, my dear, said Mrs. Benson, and hope the occasional instruction I have at different times given you, has furnished you with general ideas respecting the proper treatment of animals. I will now inform you, upon what principles the rules of conduct I prescribe to myself on this subject, are founded.

I consider, that the same almighty and good GOD, who created mankind, made all other living creatures likewise; and appointed them their different ranks in the creation, that they might receive and confer reciprocal benefits.

There is no doubt, that the Almighty designed all beings for happiness, proportionable to the faculties he endued them with; and whoever wantonly destroys that happiness, acts contrary to the will of his Maker.

The world we live in, seems to have been principally designed for the use and comfort of mankind, who, by the divine appointment, have dominion over the inferior creatures; in the exercise of which, it is certainly their duty to imitate the *supreme Lord of the Universe*, by being merciful to the utmost of their power. They are endued with reason, which enables them to discover the different natures of brutes, the faculties they possess, and how they may be made serviceable in the world; and, as beasts cannot apply these faculties to their own use in so extensive a way, and numbers of them (being unable to provide for their own sustenance) are indebted to men for many of the necessaries of life, men have an undoubted right to their labour in return.

Several other kinds of animals, which are sustained at the expense of mankind, cannot labour for them; from such they have a natural claim to whatever they can supply towards the food and raiment of their benefactors; and therefore, when we take the wool and milk of the flocks and herds, we take no more than our due, and what they can very well spare; as they seem to have an over-abundance given them, that they may be able to return their obligations to us.

Some creatures have nothing to give us but their own bodies; these have been expressly destined, by the *supreme Governor*, as food for mankind, and he has appointed an extraordinary increase of them for this very purpose; such an increase as would be very injurious to us if all were suffered to live. These we have an undoubted right to kill;

but should make their short lives as comfortable as possible.

Other creatures seem to be of no particular use to mankind, but as they serve to furnish our minds with contemplations on the widom, power, and goodness of GOD, and to exhilarate our spirits by their cheerfulness. These should not be wantonly killed, nor treated with the least degree of cruelty, but should be at full liberty to enjoy the blessings assigned them, unless they abound to such a degree, as to become injurious, by devouring the food which is designed for man, or for animals more immediately beneficial to him, whom it is his duty to protect.

Some animals, such as wild beasts, serpents, &c. are in their natures ferocious, noxious, or venomous, and capable even of destroying the lives of men, and other creatures of a higher rank than themselves: these, if they leave their secret abodes, certainly may be killed.

In a word, my dear, we should endeavour to regulate our regards according to the utility and necessities of every living creature with which we are any ways connected; and consequently should prefer the happiness of *mankind* to that of any *animal* whatever. Next to these (who being partakers of the same nature with ourselves, are more properly our *fellow-creatures*) we should consider our cattle and domestic animals, and take care to supply every creature that is dependent on us, with proper food, and keep it in its proper place: after their wants are supplied, we should extend our benevolence and compassion as far as possible to the inferior ranks of beings; and if nothing farther is in our power, should at least refrain from exercising cruelties on them. For my own part, I never willingly put to death, or cause to be put to death, any creature but when there is a real necessity for it; and have my food dressed in a plain manner, that no more lives may be sacrificed for me, than nature requires for my subsistence in that way which GOD has allotted me.

While Mrs. Benson was giving these instructions to her daughter, Frederick diverted himself with the young Robins, who having no kind parents now to admonish them, made a longer visit than usual; so that Mrs. Benson would have been obliged to drive them away, had not Pecksy, on seeing her move from her seat, recollected that she and her brother and sister had been guilty of an impropriety; she therefore reminded them that they should no longer intrude, and led the way out at the window; the others followed her, and Mrs. Benson gave permission to her children to take their morning's walk before they began their lessons.

CHAPTER XXVI

As the old robins, who were the Hero and Heroine of my tale, are made happy, it is time for me to put an end to it: but my young readers will doubtless wish to know the sequel of the history.

Miss Harriet followed her mamma's example, and grew up an *universal benefactress* to all people, and all creatures, with whom she was any ways connected.

Frederick was educated upon the same plan, and was never known to be cruel to animals, or to treat them with an improper degree of fondness: he was so remarkable for his benevolence, as to deserve and obtain the character of a GOOD MAN.

Miss Lucy Jenkins was quite reformed by Mrs. Benson's lecture, and her friend's example; but her brother continued his practice of exercising barbarities on a variety of unfortunate animals, till he went to school; where having no opportunity of doing so, he gratified his malignant disposition on his school-fellows, and made it his diversion to pull the hair, pinch and teaze the younger boys; and by the time he became a man, had so hardened his heart, that no kind of distress affected him, nor did he care for any person but himself; consequently, he was despised by all with whom he had any intercourse. In this manner he lived for some years; at length, as he was inhumanly beating and spurring a fine horse, merely because it did not go a faster pace than it was able to do, the poor creature, in its efforts to evade his blows, threw his barbarous rider, who was killed on the spot.

Farmer Wilson's prosperity increased with every succeeding year, and he acquired a plentiful fortune, with which he gave portions to each of his children, as opportunities offered, for settling them in the world; and he and his wife lived to a good old age, beloved and respected.

Mrs. Addis lost her parrot, by the disorder with which it was attacked while Mrs. Benson was visiting at the house; and before she had recovered the shock of this *misfortune,* as she called it, her grief was renewed by the death of the old lap-dog. About a year afterwards her monkey escaped to the top of the house, from whence he fell and broke his neck. The favourite cat went mad, and was obliged to be killed. In short, by a series of calamities, all her *dear darlings* were successively destroyed. She supplied their places with new favourites, who gave her a great deal of fatigue and trouble.

In the mean while her children grew up, and having experienced no tenderness from her, they scarcely knew they had a mamma; nor did those who had the care of their education inculcate, that *her* want of affection *did not cancel their duty;* they therefore treated her with the utmost neglect, and she had no friend left. In her old age, when she was no longer capable of amusing herself with cats, dogs, parrots, and monkies, she became sensible of her errors, and wished for the comforts which other parents enjoyed; but it was now too late, and she ended her days in sorrow and regret.

This unfortunate Lady had tenderness enough in her disposition for all the purposes of humanity: and had she placed it on proper objects, agreeably to Mrs. Benson's rule, might have been, like her, a good wife, mother, friend, and mistress, consequently, respectable and happy. But when a child, Mrs. Addis was (under an idea of making her *tender hearted*) permitted to lavish *immoderate fondness* on animals, the care of which engrossed her whole attention, and greatly interrupted her education.

Her children fell into faults of a different nature. Miss Addis being, as I observed in a former part of this history, left to the care of servants, grew up with very contracted notions. Amongst other prejudices, she imbibed that of being afraid of spiders, frogs, and other harmless things; and having been bit by the monkey when it escaped, as I before related, and terrified by the cat, when it went mad, she extended her fears to every kind of creature, and could not take a walk in the fields, or even in the street, without a thousand apprehensions. At last, her constitution, which, from bad nursing, had become delicate, was still more weakened by her continual apprehensions; and a rat happening to run across the path, as she was walking, she fell into fits, which afflicted her, at intervals, during the remainder of her life.

Master Addis, as soon as he became sensible of his mother's foible, conceived an inveterate hatred to animals in general, whom he regarded as his enemies; and thought he was avenging his own cause when he treated any with barbarity. Cats and dogs, in particular, he singled out as the objects of his revenge, because he considered them as his mother's greatest favourites; and many a one fell an innocent victim to his mistaken ideas.

The parent Redbreasts visited their kind benefactors the next winter; but as they were flying along one day, they saw some crumbs of bread, which had been scattered by Miss Lucy Jenkins, who (as I observed before) had adopted the sentiments of her friend, in respect to compassion to animals, and resolved to imitate her in every excellence. The Redbreasts gratefully picked up the crumbs, and, encouraged by the gentle invitation of her looks, determined to repeat their visits; which they accordingly did, and found such an ample supply, that they thought it more adviseable to go to her with their next brood, than to be burdensome to their old benefactors, who had a great number of pensioners to support: but Master and Miss Benson had frequently the pleasure of seeing them, and knew them from all their species by several particularities, which so long an acquaintance had given them the opportunity of observing.

Robin, in pursuance of his father's advice, and agreeably to his own inclinations, attached himself to Mr. Benson's family, where he was an exceeding great favourite. He had before, under the conduct of his parents, made frequent excursions into the garden, and was, by their direction, enabled to get up into trees, but his wing never recovered sufficiently to enable him to take long flights: however, he found himself at liberty to do as he pleased, and during the summer months, commonly passed most of his time abroad, and roosted in trees, but visited the tea-table every morning; and there he usually met his sister Pecksy, who took up her abode in the orchard, where she enjoyed the friendship of her father and mother. Dicky and Flapsy, who thought their company too grave, flew giddily about together. In a short time they were both caught in a trap-cage, and put into the aviary, which Dicky once longed to inhabit. Here they were at first very miserable; but after a while, recollecting their good parent's advice, and the example of the Linnets and Pheasants, they reconciled themselves to their lot, and each met with a mate, with whom they lived tolerably happy.

From the foregoing examples, I hope my young readers will select the best for their own imitation, and take warning by the rest; otherwise my histories have been written in vain.

Happy would it be for the animal creation, if every human being, like good Mrs. Benson, consulted the welfare of inferior creatures, and neither spoiled them by indulgence, nor injured them by tyranny! Happy would mankind be, if every one, like her, acted in conformity to the will of their Maker; by cultivating in their own minds, and those of their children, the *divine principle* of UNIVERSAL BENEVOLENCE!

THE END.

Original Stories from Real Life

By MARY WOLLSTONECRAFT

ORIGINAL STORIES

FROM

REAL LIFE;

WITH

CONVERSATIONS,

CALCULATED TO

REGULATE THE AFFECTIONS,

AND

FORM THE MIND

TO

TRUTH AND GOODNESS.

BY MARY WOLLSTONECRAFT.

LONDON:

PRINTED FOR J. JOHNSON, NO. 72, ST.
PAUL'S CHURCH-YARD.

1791.

MARY WOLLSTONECRAFT GODWIN *(1759–1797), in a letter to her publisher, claimed that no children's books, not even her own, could rival chats between parent and child: "If parents attended to their children I would not have written the stories; for what are books, compared to conversations which affection enforces." Despite Wollstonecraft's disclaimer,* Original Stories *(1788) was published and had six editions by 1835, plus three in Dublin, and a German translation as well. E. V. Lucas reprinted it in 1906 along with the treasured Blake illustrations. The only other work for children by Wollstonecraft was* Das Moralische Elementarbuch *by C. G. Salzmann, which she translated and adapted as* Elements of Morality *(2 vols., 1790).*

Today Wollstonecraft is best known for Thoughts on the Education of Daughters *(1780) and* A Vindication of the Rights of Women *(1792), in which she challenged Rousseau's depiction of women as creatures of sensibility rather than reason. In* Original Stories, *there is more evidence of Rousseau, whose* Émile *she read in 1788. While the tutor Mrs. Mason has been criticized for her stoicism, she is presented as an example of true sensibility. The children turn away from a bird's "exquisite pain," unlike Mrs. Mason: "I must put him out of pain; to leave him in his present state would be cruel. . . . Saying so, she put her foot on the bird's head, turning her own another way." Duty is not pleasant.*

Mary Wollstonecraft was a symbol that the times were changing. Hannah More, on learning that Mary had penned A Vindication of the Rights of Women, *exclaimed: "Rights of Women! We will be hearing of the Rights of Children next!" The eighteenth century, for all its interest in the child and his education, was not ready to hear about children's rights. But the romantic cult of the child was just around the corner, and today* A Vindication of the Rights of Women *has been reprinted as a treasured document in the library of women's liberation.*

Original Stories *is reprinted here from a London 1791 second edition (the first edition to have the Blake illustrations) from the Rare Book Room of the University of Illinois Library, Urbana, Illinois.*

PREFACE

THESE CONVERSATIONS and tales are accommodated to the present state of society; which obliges the author to attempt to cure those faults by reason, which ought never to have taken root in the infant mind. Good habits, imperceptibly fixed, are far preferable to the precepts of reason; but, as this task requires more judgment than generally falls to the lot of parents, substitutes must be sought for, and medicines given, when regimen would have answered the purpose much better. I believe those who examine their own minds, will readily agree with me, that reason, with difficulty, conquers settled habits, even when it is arrived at some degree of maturity: why then do we suffer children to be bound with fetters, which their half-formed faculties cannot break.

In writing the following work, I aim at perspicuity and simplicity of style; and try to avoid those unmeaning compliments, which slip from the tongue, but have not the least connexion with the affections that should warm the heart, and animate the conduct. By this false politeness, sincerity is sacrificed, and truth violated; and thus artificial manners are necessarily taught. For true politeness is a polish, not a varnish; and should rather be acquired by observation than admonition. And we may remark, by way of illustration, that men do not attempt to polish precious stones, till age and air have given them that degree of solidity, which will enable them to bear the necessary friction, without destroying the main substance.

The way to render instruction most useful cannot always be adopted; knowledge should be gradually imparted, and flow more from example than teaching: example directly addresses the senses, the first inlets to the heart; and the improvement of those instruments of the understanding is the object education should have constantly in view, and over which we have most power. But to wish that parents would, themselves, mould the ductile passions, is a chimerical wish, for the present generation have their own passions to combat with, and fastidious pleasures to pursue, neglecting those pointed out by nature: we must therefore pour premature knowledge into the succeeding one; and, teaching virtue, explain the nature of vice. Cruel necessity!

The Conversations are intended to assist the teacher as well as the pupil; and this will obviate an objection which some may start, that the sentiments are not quite on a level with the capacity of a child. Every child requires a different mode of treatment; but a writer can only choose one, and it must be modified by those who are actually engaged with young people in their studies.

The tendency of the reasoning obviously tends to fix principles of truth and humanity on a solid and simple foundation; and to make religion an active, invigorating director of the affections, and not a mere attention to forms. Systems of Theology may be complicated, but when the character of the Supreme Being is displayed, and He is recognised as the Universal Father, the Author and Centre of Good, a child may be led to comprehend that dignity and happiness must arise from imitating Him; and this conviction should be twisted into—and be the foundation of every inculcated duty.

At any rate, the Tales, which were written to illustrate the moral, may recall it, when the mind has gained sufficient strength to discuss the argument from which it was deduced.

INTRODUCTION

MARY AND CAROLINE, though the children of wealthy parents were, in their infancy, left entirely to the management of servants, or people equally ignorant. Their mother died suddenly, and their father, who found them very troublesome at home, placed them under the tuition of a woman of tenderness and discernment, a near relation, who was induced to take on herself the important charge through motives of compassion.

They were shamefully ignorant, considering that Mary had been fourteen, and Caroline twelve years in the world. If they had been merely ignorant, the task would not have appeared so arduous; but they had caught every prejudice that the vulgar casually instill. In order to eradicate these prejudices, and substitute good habits instead of those they had carelessly contracted, Mrs. Mason never suffered them to be out of her sight. They were allowed to ask questions on all occasions, a method she would not have adopted, had she educated them from the first, according to the suggestions of her own reason, to which experience had given its sanction.

They had tolerable capacities; but Mary had a turn for ridicule, and Caroline was vain of her person. She was, indeed, very handsome, and the inconsiderate encomiums that had, in her presence, been lavished on her beauty made her, even at that early age, affected.

Moral Conversations and Stories

CHAPTER I

The treatment of animals—The ant—The bee— Goodness—The lark's nest—The asses.

ONE FINE MORNING in spring, some time after Mary and Caroline were settled in their new abode, Mrs. Mason proposed a walk before breakfast, a custom she wished to teach imperceptibly, by rendering it amusing.

The sun had scarcely dispelled the dew that hung on every blade of grass, and filled the half-shut flowers; every prospect smiled, and the freshness of the air conveyed the most pleasing sensations to Mrs. Mason's mind; but the children were regardless of the surrounding beauties, and ran eagerly after some insects to destroy them. Mrs. Mason silently observed their cruel sports, without appearing to do it; but stepping suddenly out of the foot-path into the long grass, her buckle was caught in it, and striving to disentangle herself, she wet her feet; which the children knew she wished to avoid, as she had been lately sick. This circumstance roused their attention; and they forgot their amusement to enquire *why* she had left the path; and Mary could hardly restrain a laugh, when she was informed that it was to avoid treading on some snails that were creeping across the narrow footway. Surely, said Mary, you do not think there is any harm in killing a snail, or any of those nasty creatures that crawl on the ground? I hate them, and should scream if one was to find its way from my clothes to my neck! With great gravity, Mrs. Mason asked how she dared to kill any thing, unless it were to prevent its hurting her? Then, resuming a smiling face, she said, Your education has been neglected, my child; as we walk along attend to what I say, and make the best answers you can; and do you, Caroline, join in the conversation.

You have already heard that God created the world, and every inhabitant of it. He is then called the Father of all creatures; and all are made to be happy, whom a good and wise God has created. He made those snails you despise, and caterpillars, and spiders; and when he made them, did not leave them to perish, but placed them where the food that is most proper to nourish them is easily found. They do not live long, but He who is their Father, as well as your's, directs them to deposit their eggs on the plants that are fit to support their young, when they are not able to get food for themselves.—And when such a great and wise Being has taken care to provide every thing necessary for the meanest creature, would you dare to kill it, merely because it appears to you ugly? Mary began to be attentive, and quickly followed Mrs. Mason's example, who allowed a caterpillar and a spider to creep on her hand. You find them, she rejoined, very harmless; but a great number would destroy our vegetables and fruit; so birds are permitted to eat them, as we feed on animals; and in spring there are always more than at any other season of the year, to furnish food for the young broods.—Half-convinced, Mary said, but worms are of little consequence in the world. Yet, replied Mrs. Mason, God cares for them, and gives them every thing that is necessary to render their existence comfortable. You are often troublesome—I am stronger than you—yet I do not kill you.

Observe those ants; they have a little habitation in yonder hillock; they carry food to it for their young, and sleep very snug in it during the cold weather. The bees also have comfortable towns, and lay up a store of honey to support them when the flowers die, and snow covers the ground: and this forecast is as much the gift of God, as any quality you possess.

Do you know the meaning of the word Goodness? I see you are unwilling to answer. I will tell you. It is, first, to avoid hurting any thing; and then, to contrive to give as much pleasure as you can. If some insects are to be destroyed, to preserve my garden from desolation, I have it done in the quickest way. The domestic animals that I keep, I provide the best food for, and never suffer them to be tormented; and this caution arises from two motives:—I wish to make them happy; and, as I love my fellow-creatures still better than the brute creation, I would not allow those that I have any influence over, to grow habitually thoughtless and cruel, till they were unable to relish the greatest pleasure life affords,— that of resembling God, by doing good.

A lark now began to sing, as it soared aloft. The children watched its motions, listening to the artless melody. They wondered what it was thinking of—of its young family, they soon concluded; for it flew over the hedge, and drawing near, they heard the young ones chirp. Very soon both the old birds took their flight together, to look for food to satisfy the craving of the almost fledged young. An idle boy, who had borrowed a gun, fired at them—they fell; and before he could take up the wounded pair, he perceived Mrs. Mason; and expecting a very severe reprimand, ran away. She and the little girls drew near, and found that one was not much hurt; but that the other, the cock, had one leg broken, and both its wings shattered; and its little eyes seemed starting out of their sockets, it was in such exquisite pain. The children turned away their eyes. Look at it, said Mrs. Mason; do you not see that it suffers as much, and more than you did when you had the small-pox, when you were so tenderly nursed. Take up the hen; I will bind her wing together; perhaps it may heal. As to the cock, though I hate to kill any thing, I must put him out of pain; to leave him in his present state would be cruel; and avoiding an unpleasant sensation myself, I should allow the poor bird to die by inches, and call this treatment tenderness, when it would be selfishness or weakness. Saying so, she put her foot on the bird's head, turning her own another way.

They walked on; when Caroline remarked, that the nestlings, deprived of their parents, would now perish; and the mother began to flutter in her hand as they drew near the hedge, though the poor creature could not fly, yet she tried to do it. The girls, with one voice, begged Mrs. Mason to let them take the nest, and provide food in a cage, and see if the mother could not contrive to hop about to feed them. The nest and the old mother were instantly in Mary's handkerchief. A little opening was left to admit the air; and Caroline peeped into it every moment to see how they looked. I give you leave, said Mrs. Mason, to take those birds, because an accident has rendered them helpless; if that had not been the case, they should not have been confined.

They had scarcely reached the next field, when they met another boy with a nest in his hand, and on a tree near him saw the mother, who, forgetting her natural timidity, followed the spoiler; and her intelligible tones of anguish reached the ears of the children, whose hearts now first felt the emotions of humanity. Caroline called him, and taking sixpence out of her little purse, offered to give it to him for the nest, if he would shew her where he had taken it from. The boy consented, and away ran Caroline to replace it,—

Look what a fine morning it is. — Insects,
Birds, & Animals, are all enjoying existence

crying all the way, how delighted the old bird will be to find her brood again. The pleasure that the parent-bird would feel was talked of till they came to a large common, and heard some young asses, at the door of an hovel, making a most dreadful noise. Mrs. Mason had ordered the old ones to be confined, lest the young should suck before the necessary quantity had been saved for some sick people in her neighbourhood. But after they had given the usual quantity of milk, the thoughtless boy had left them still in confinement, and the young in vain implored the food nature designed for their particular support. Open the hatch, said Mrs. Mason, the mothers have still enough left to satisfy their young. It was opened, and they saw them suck.

Now, said she, we will return to breakfast; give me your hands, my little girls, you have done good this morning, you have acted like rational creatures. Look, what a fine morning it is. Insects, birds, and animals, are all enjoying this sweet day. Thank God for permitting you to see it, and for giving you an understanding which teaches you that you ought, by doing good, to imitate Him. Other creatures only think of supporting themselves; but man is allowed to ennoble his nature, by cultivating his mind and enlarging his heart. He feels disinterested love; every part of the creation affords an exercise for virtue, and virtue is ever the truest source of pleasure.

CHAPTER II

The treatment of animals—The difference between them and man—Parental affection of a dog—Brutality punished.

AFTER BREAKFAST, Mrs. Mason gave the children *Mrs. Trimmer's Fabulous Histories;* and the subject still turned on animals, and the wanton cruelty of those who treated them improperly. The little girls were eager to express their detestation, and requested that in future they might be allowed to feed the chickens. Mrs. Mason complied with their request; only one condition was annexed to the permission, that they did it regularly. When you wait for your food, you learn patience, she added, and you can mention your wants; but those helpless creatures cannot complain. The country people frequently say,—How can you treat a poor dumb beast ill; and a stress is very properly laid on the word dumb;—for dumb they appear to those who do not observe their looks and gestures; but God, who takes care of every thing, understands their language; and so did Caroline this morning, when she ran with such eagerness to re-place the nest which the thoughtless boy had stolen, heedless of the mother's agonizing cries!

Mary interrupted her, to ask, if insects and animals were not inferior to men; Certainly, answered Mrs. Mason; and men are inferior to angels; yet we have reason to believe, that those exalted beings delight to do us good. You have heard in a book, which I seldom permit you to read, because you are not of an age to understand it, that angels, when they sang glory to God on high, wished for peace on earth, as a proof of the good will they felt towards men. And all the glad tidings that have been sent to men, angels have proclaimed: indeed, the word angel signifies a messenger. In order to please God, and our happiness depends upon pleasing him, we must do good. What we call virtue, may be thus explained:—we exercise every benevolent affection to enjoy comfort here, and to fit ourselves to be angels hereafter. And when we have acquired human virtues, we shall have a nobler employment in our Father's kingdom. But between angels and men a much greater resemblance subsists, than between men and the brute creation; because the two former seem capable of improvement.

The birds you saw to-day do not improve—or their improvement only tends to self-preservation; the first nest they make and the last are exactly the same; though in their flights they must see many others more beautiful if not more convenient, and, had they reason, they would probably shew something like individual taste in the form of their dwellings; but this is not the case. You saw the hen tear the down from her breast to make a nest for her eggs; you saw her beat the grain with her bill, and not swallow a bit, till the young were satisfied; and afterwards she covered them with her wings, and seemed perfectly happy, while she watched over her charge; if any one approached, she was ready to defend them, at the hazard of her life: yet, a fortnight hence, you will see the same hen drive the fledged chickens from the corn, and forget the fondness that seemed to be stronger than the first impulse of nature.

Animals have not the affections which arise from reason, nor can they do good, or acquire virtue. Every affection, and impulse, which I have observed in them, are like our inferior emotions, which do not depend entirely on our will, but are involuntary; they seem to have been implanted to preserve the species, and make the individual grateful for actual kindness. If you caress and feed them, they will love you, as children do, without knowing why; but we neither see imagination nor wisdom in them; and, what principally exalts man, friendship and devotion, they seem incapable of forming the least idea of. Friendship is founded on knowledge and virtue, and these are human acquirements; and devotion is a preparation for eternity; because when we pray to God, we offer an affront to him, if we do not strive to imitate the perfections He displays every where for our imitation, that we may grow better and happier.

The children eagerly enquired in what manner they were to behave, to prove that they were superior to animals? The answer was short,—be tender-hearted; and let your superior endowments ward off the evils which they cannot foresee. It is only to animals that children *can* do good, men are their superiors. When I was a child, added their tender friend, I always made it my study and delight, to feed all the dumb family that surrounded our house; and when I could be of use to any one of them I was happy. This employment humanized my heart, while, like wax, it took every impression; and Providence has since made me an instrument of good—I have been useful to my fellow-creatures. I, who never wantonly trod on an insect, or disregarded the plaint of the speechless beast, can now give bread to the hungry, physic to the sick, comfort to the afflicted, and, above all, am preparing you, who are to live for ever, to be fit for the society of angels, and good men made perfect. This world, I told you, was a road to a better—a preparation for it; if we suffer, we grow humbler and wiser: but animals have not this advantage, and man should not prevent their enjoying all the happiness of which they are capable.

A she-cat or dog have such strong parental affection, that if you take away their young, it almost kills them; some have actually died of grief when all have been taken away; though they do not seem to miss the greatest part.

A bitch had once all her litter stolen from her, and drowned in a neighbouring brook: she sought them out, and brought them one by one, laid them at the feet of her cruel master;—and looking wistfully at them for some time, in dumb anguish, turning her eyes on the destroyer, she expired!

I myself knew a man who had hardened his heart to such a degree, that he found pleasure in tormenting every creature whom he had any power over. I saw him let two guinea-pigs roll down sloping tiles, to see if the fall would kill them. And were they killed? cried Caroline. Certainly; and it is well they were, or he would have found some other mode of torment. When he became a father, he not only neglected to educate his children, and set them a good example, but he taught them to be cruel while he tormented them: the consequence was, that they neglected him when he was old and feeble; and he died in a ditch.

You may now go and feed your birds, and tie some of the straggling flowers round the garden sticks. After dinner, if the weather continues fine, we will walk to the wood, and I will shew you the hole in the lime-stone mountain (a mountain whose bowels, as we call them, are lime-stones) in which poor crazy Robin and his dog lived.

CHAPTER III

The treatment of animals—The story of crazy Robin— The man confined in the Bastille.

IN THE AFTERNOON the children bounded over the short grass of the common, and walked under the shadow of the mountain till they came to a craggy part; where a stream broke out, and ran down the declivity, struggling with the huge stones which impeded its progress, and occasioned a noise that did not unpleasantly interrupt the solemn silence of the place. The brook was soon lost in a neighbouring wood, and the children turned their eyes to the broken side of the mountain, over which ivy grew in great profusion. Mrs. Mason pointed out a little cave, and desired them to sit down on some stumps of trees, whilst she related the promised story.

In yonder cave once lived a poor man, who generally went by the name of crazy Robin. In his youth he was very industrious, and married my father's dairy-maid; a girl deserving of such a good husband. For some time they continued to live very comfortably; their daily labour procured their daily bread; but Robin, finding it was likely he should have a large family, borrowed a trifle, to add to the small pittance which they had saved in service, and took a little farm in a neighbouring county. I was then a child.

Ten or twelve years after, I heard that a crazy man, who appeared very harmless, had piled by the side of the brook a great number of stones; he would wade into the river for them, followed by a cur dog, whom he would frequently call his Jacky, and even his Nancy; and then mumble to himself,—thou wilt not leave me—we will dwell with the owls in the ivy.—A number of owls had taken shelter in it. The stones which he waded for he carried to the mouth of the hole, and only just left room enough to creep in. Some of the neighbours at last recollected his face; and I sent to enquire what misfortune had reduced him to such a deplorable state.

The information I received from different persons, I will communicate to you in as few words as I can.

Several of his children died in their infancy; and, two years before he came to his native place, one misfortune had followed another till he had sunk under their accumulated weight. Through various accidents he was long in arrears to his landlord; who, seeing that he was an honest man, who endeavoured to bring up his family, did not distress him; but when his wife was lying-in of her last child, the landlord dying, his heir sent and seized the stock for the rent; and the person from whom he had borrowed some money, exasperated to see all gone, arresting him immediately, he was hurried to gaol, without being able to leave any money for his family. The poor woman could not see them starve, and trying to support her children before she had gained sufficient strength, she caught cold; and through neglect, and her want of proper nourishment, her illness turned to a putrid fever; which two of the children caught from her, and died with her. The two who were left, Jacky and Nancy, went to their father, and took with them a cur dog, that had long shared their frugal meals.

The children begged in the day, and at night slept with their wretched father. Poverty and dirt soon robbed their cheeks of the roses which the country air made bloom with a peculiar freshness; so that they soon caught a jail fever,—and died. The poor father, who was now bereft of all his children, hung over their bed in speechless anguish; not a groan or a tear escaped from him, whilst he stood, two or three hours, in the same attitude, looking at the dead bodies of his little darlings. The dog licked his hands, and strove to attract his attention; but for awhile he seemed not to observe his caresses; when he did, he said, mournfully, thou wilt not leave me—and then he began to laugh. The bodies were removed; and he remained in an unsettled state, often frantic; at length the phrenzy subsided, and he grew melancholy and harmless. He was not then so closely watched; and one day he contrived to make his escape, the dog followed him, and came directly to his native village.

After I had received this account, I determined he should live in the place he had chosen, undisturbed. I sent some conveniences, all of which he rejected, except a mat; on which he sometimes slept—the dog always did. I tried to induce him to eat, but he constantly gave the dog whatever I sent him, and lived on haws and blackberries, and every kind of trash. I used to call frequently on him; and he sometimes followed me to the house I now live in, and in winter he would come of his own accord, and take a crust of bread. He gathered water-cresses out of the pool, and would bring them to me, with nosegays of wild thyme, which he plucked from the sides of the mountain. I mentioned before, that the dog was a cur. It had, indeed, the bad trick of a cur, and would run barking after horses heels. One day, when his master was gathering water-cresses, the dog running after a young gentleman's horse, made it start, and almost threw the rider; who grew so angry, that though he knew it was the poor madman's dog, he levelled his gun at his head—shot him,—and instantly rode off. Robin ran to his dog,—he looked at his wounds, and not sensible that he was dead, called to him to follow him; but when he found that he could not, he took him to the pool, and washed off the blood before it began to clot, and then brought him home, and laid him on the mat.

I observed that I had not seen him pacing up the hills as usual, and sent to enquire about him. He was found sitting by the dog, and no entreaties could prevail on him to quit the body, or receive any refreshment. I instantly set off for this place, hoping, as I had always been a favourite, that I should be able to persuade him to eat something. But when I came to him, I found the hand of death was upon him. He was still melan-

The Dog strove to attract his attention. —
He said, Thou wilt not leave me !

choly; yet there was not such a mixture of wildness in it as formerly. I pressed him to take some food; but, instead of answering me, or turning away, he burst into tears,—a thing I had never seen him do before, and, sobbing, he said, Will any one be kind to me!—you will kill me!—I saw not my wife die—No!—they dragged me from her—but I saw Jacky and Nancy die—and who pitied me?—but my dog! He turned his eyes to the body—I wept with him. He would then have taken some nourishment, but nature was exhausted—and he expired.—

Was that the cave? said Mary. They ran to it. Poor Robin! Did you ever hear of any thing so cruel? Yes, answered Mrs. Mason; and as we walk home I will relate an instance of still greater barbarity.

I told you, that Robin was confined in a jail. In France they have a dreadful one, called the Bastille. The poor wretches who are confined in it live entirely alone; have not the pleasure of seeing men or animals; nor are they allowed books.—They live in comfortless solitude. Some have amused themselves by making figures on the wall; and others have laid straws in rows. One miserable captive found a spider; he nourished it for two or three years; it grew tame, and partook of his lonely meal. The keeper observed it, and mentioned the circumstance to a superiour, who ordered him to crush it. In vain did the man beg to have his spider spared. You find, Mary, that the nasty creature which you despised was a comfort in solitude. The keeper obeyed the cruel command; and the unhappy wretch felt more pain when he heard the crush, than he had ever experienced during his long confinement. He looked round a dreary apartment, and the small portion of light which the grated bars admitted, only served to shew him, that he breathed where nothing else drew breath.

CHAPTER IV

Anger.—History of Jane Fretful.

A FEW DAYS AFTER these walks and conversations, Mrs. Mason heard a great noise in the play-room. She ran hastily to enquire the cause, and found the children crying, and near them, one of the young birds lying on the floor dead. With great eagerness each of them tried, the moment she entered, to exculpate herself, and prove that the other had killed the bird. Mrs. Mason commanded them to be silent; and, at the same time, called an orphan whom she had educated, and desired her to take care of the nest.

The cause of the dispute was easily gathered from what they both let fall. They had contested which had the best right to feed the birds. Mary insisted that she had a right, because she was the eldest; and Caroline, because she took the nest. Snatching it from one side of the room to the other, the bird fell, and was trodden on before they were aware.

When they were a little composed, Mrs. Mason calmly thus addressed them:—I perceive that you are ashamed of your behaviour, and sorry for the consequence; I will not therefore severely reprove you, nor add bitterness to the self-reproach you must both feel, —because I pity you. You are now inferiour to the animals that graze on the common; reason only serves to render your folly more conspicuous and inexcusable. Anger, is a little despicable vice: its selfish emotions banish compassion, and undermine every virtue.

It is easy to conquer another; but noble to subdue oneself. Had you, Mary, given way to your sister's humour, you would have proved that you were not only older, but wiser than her. And you, Caroline, would have saved your charge, if you had, for the time, waved your right.

It is always a proof of superior sense to bear with slight inconveniences, and even trifling injuries, without complaining or contesting about them. The soul reserves its firmness for great occasions, and then it acts a decided part. It is just the contrary mode of thinking, and the conduct produced by it, which occasions all those trivial disputes that slowly corrode domestic peace, and insensibly destroy what great misfortunes could not sweep away.

I will tell you a story, that will take stronger hold on your memory than mere remarks.

Jane Fretful was an only child. Her fond weak mother would not allow her to be contradicted on any occasion. The child had some tenderness of heart; but so accustomed was she to see every thing give way to her humour, that she imagined the world was only made for her. If any of her playfellows had toys, that struck her capricious sickly fancy, she would cry for them; and substitutes were in vain offered to quiet her, she must have the identical ones, or fly into the most violent passion. When she was an infant, if she fell down, her nurse made her beat the floor. She continued the practice afterwards, and when she was angry would kick the chairs and tables, or any senseless piece of furniture, if they came in her way. I have seen her throw her cap into the fire, because some of her acquaintance had a prettier.

Continual passions weakened her constitution; beside, she would not eat the common wholesome food that children, who are subject to the small-pox and worms, ought to eat, and which is necessary when they grow so fast, to make them strong and handsome. Instead of being a comfort to her tender, though mistaken, mother, she was her greatest torment. The servants all disliked her; she loved no one but herself; and the consequence was, she never inspired love; even the pity good-natured people felt, was nearly allied to contempt.

A lady, who visited her mother, brought with her one day a pretty little dog. Jane was delighted with it; and the lady, with great reluctance, parted with it to oblige her friend. For some time she fondled, and really felt something like an affection for it: but, one day, it happened to snatch a cake she was going to eat, and though there were twenty within reach, she flew into a violent passion, and threw a stool at the poor creature, who was big with pup. It fell down; I can scarcely tell the rest; it received so severe a blow, that all the young were killed, and the poor wretch languished two days, suffering the most excruciating torture.

Jane Fretful, who was now angry with herself, sat all the time holding it, and every look the miserable animal gave her, stung her to the heart. After its death she was very unhappy; but did not try to conquer her temper. All the blessings of life were thrown away on her; and, without any real misfortune, she was continually miserable.

If she had planned a party of pleasure, and the weather proved unfavourable, the whole day was spent in fruitless repining, or venting her ill-humour on those who depended on her. If no disappointment of that kind occurred, she could not enjoy the promised pleasure; something always disconcerted her; the horses went too fast, or, too slow; the dinner was ill-dressed, or, some of the company contradicted her.

She was, when a child, very beautiful; but anger soon distorted her regular features, and gave a forbidding fierceness to her eyes. But if for a moment she looked pleased, she still resembled a heap of combustible matter, to which an accidental spark might set fire; of course quiet people were afraid to converse with her. And if she ever did a good, or a humane action, her ridiculous anger soon rendered it an intolerable burden, if it did not entirely cancel it.

At last she broke her mother's heart, or hastened her death, by her want of duty, and her many other faults: all proceeding from violent, unrestrained anger.

The death of her mother, which affected her very much, left her without a friend. She would sometimes say, Ah! my poor mother, if you were now alive, I would not teaze you—I would give the world to let you know that I am sorry for what I have done: you died, thinking me ungrateful; and lamenting that I did not die when you gave me suck. I shall never—oh! never see you more.

This thought, and her peevish temper, preyed on her impaired constitution. She had not, by doing good, prepared her soul for another state, or cherished any hopes that could disarm death of its terrors, or render that last sleep sweet—its approach was dreadful!—and she hastened her end, scolding the physician for not curing her. Her lifeless countenance displayed the marks of convulsive anger; and she left an ample fortune behind her to those who did not regret her loss. They followed her to the grave, on which no one shed a tear. She was soon forgotten; and I only remember her, to warn you to shun her errors.

CHAPTER V

Lying—Honor—Truth—Small Duties—History of
Lady Sly, and Mrs. Trueman.

THE LITTLE GIRLS were very assiduous to gain Mrs. Mason's good opinion; and, by the mildness of their behaviour, to prove to her that they were ashamed of themselves. It was one of Mrs. Mason's rules, when they offended her, that is, behaved improperly, to treat them civilly; but to avoid giving them those marks of affection which they were particularly delighted to receive.

Yesterday, said she to them, I only mentioned to you one fault, though I observed two. You very readily guess I mean the lie that you both told. Nay, look up, for I wish to see you blush; and the confusion which I perceive in your faces gives me pleasure; because it convinces me that it is not a confirmed habit: and, indeed, my children, I should be sorry that such a mean one had taken deep root in your infant minds.

When I speak of falsehood, I mean every kind; whatever tends to deceive, though not said in direct terms. Tones of voice, motions of the hand or head, if they make another believe what they ought not to believe, are lies, and of the worst kind; because the contrivance aggravates the guilt. I would much sooner forgive a lie told directly, when perhaps fear entirely occupied the thoughts, and the presence of God was not felt: for it is His sacred Majesty that you affront by telling an untruth.

How so? enquired Mary.

Because you hope to conceal your falsehood from every human creature: but, if you consider a moment, you must recollect, that the Searcher of hearts reads your very thoughts; that nothing is hid from him.

You would blush if I were to discover that you told a lie; yet wantonly forfeit the favour of Him, from whom you have received life and all its blessings, to screen yourselves from correction or reproof, or, what is still worse, to purchase some trifling gratification, the pleasure of which would last but a moment.

You heard the gentleman who visited me this morning, very frequently use the word Honour. Honour consists in respecting yourself; in doing as you would be done by; and the foundation of honour is Truth.

When I can depend on the veracity of people, that is to say, am convinced that they adhere to truth, I rely on them; am certain they have courage, because I know they will bear any inconvenience rather than despise themselves, for telling a lie. Besides, it is not necessary to consider what you intend to say, when you have done right. Always determine, on every occasion, to speak the truth, and you will never be at a loss for words. If your character for this scrupulous attention is once fixed, your acquaintance will be courted; and those who are not particularly pleased with you, will, at least, respect your honourable principles.

It is impossible to form a friendship without making truth the basis; it is indeed the essence of devotion, the employment of the understanding, and the support of every duty.

I govern my servants, and you, by attending strictly to truth, and this observance keeping my head clear and my heart pure, I am ever ready to pray to the Author of good, the Fountain of truth.

While I am discussing the subject, let me point out to you another branch of this virtue; Sincerity.—And remember that I every day set you an example; for I never, to please for the moment, pay unmeaning compliments, or permit any words to drop from my tongue, that my heart does not dictate. And when I relate any matter of fact, I carefully avoid embellishing it, in order to render it a more entertaining story; not that I think such a practice absolutely criminal; but as it contributes insensibly to wear away a respect for truth, I guard against the vain impulse, lest I should lose the chief strength, and even ornament, of my mind, and become like a wave of the sea, drifted about by every gust of passion.

You must in life observe the most apparently insignificant duties—the great ones are the pillars of virtue; but the constant concurrence of trifling things, makes it necessary that reason and conscience should always preside, to keep the heart steady. Many people make promises, and appointments, which they scruple not to break, if a more inviting pleasure occurs, not remembering that the slightest duty should be performed before a mere amusement is pursued—for any neglect of this kind embitters play. Nothing, believe me, can long be pleasant, that is not innocent.

As I usually endeavour to recollect some persons of my acquaintance, who have suffered by the faults, or follies, I wish you to avoid; I will describe two characters, that will, if I mistake not, very strongly enforce what I have been saying.

Last week you saw Lady Sly, who came to pay me a morning visit. Did you ever see such a fine carriage, or such beautiful horses? How they pawed the ground, and displayed their rich harnesses! Her servants wore elegant liveries, and her own clothes suited the equipage. Her house is equal to her carriage; the rooms are lofty, and hung with silk; noble glasses and pictures adorn them: and the pleasure-grounds are large and well laid out; beside the trees and shrubs, they contain a variety of summer-houses and temples, as they are called.—Yet my young friends, this is *state*, not *dignity*.

This woman has a little soul, she never attended to truth, and obtaining great part of her fortune by falsehood, it has blighted all her enjoyments. She inhabits that superb house, wears the gayest clothes, and rides in that beautiful carriage, without feeling pleasure. Suspicion, and the cares it has given birth to, have wrinkled her countenance, and banished every trace of beauty, which paint in vain endeavours to repair. Her suspicious temper arises from a knowledge of her own heart, and the want of rational employments.

She imagines that every person she converses with means to deceive her; and when she leaves a company, supposes all the ill they may say of her, because she recollects her own practice. She listens about her house, expecting to discover the designs of her servants, none of whom she can trust; and in consequence of this anxiety her sleep is unsound, and her food tasteless. She walks in her paradise of a garden, and smells not the flowers, nor do the birds inspire her with cheerfulness.—These pleasures are true and simple, they lead to the love of God, and all the creatures whom He hath made—and cannot warm a heart which a malicious story can please.

She cannot pray to God;—He hates a liar! She is neglected by her husband, whose only motive for marrying her was to clear an incumbered estate. Her son, her only child, is undutiful; the poor never have cause to bless her; nor does she contribute to the happiness of any human being.

To kill time, and drive away the pangs of remorse, she goes from one house to another, collecting and propagating scandalous tales, to bring others on a level with herself. Even those who resemble her are afraid of her; she lives alone in the world, its good things are poisoned by her vices, and neither inspire joy nor gratitude.

Before I tell you how she acquired these vicious habits, and enlarged her fortune by disregarding truth, I must desire you to think of Mrs. Trueman, the curate's wife, who lives in yonder white house, close to the church; it is a small one, yet the woodbines and jessamins that twine about the windows give it a pretty appearance. Her voice is sweet, her manners not only easy, but elegant; and her simple dress makes her person appear to the greatest advantage.

She walks to visit me, and her little ones hang on her hands, and cling to her clothes, they are so fond of her. If any thing terrifies them, they run under her apron, and she looks like the hen taking care of her young brood. The domestic animals play with the children, finding her a mild attentive mistress; and out of her scanty fortune she contrives to feed and clothe many a hungry shivering wretch; who bless her as she passes along.

Though she has not any outward decorations, she appears superior to her neighbours, who call her the *Gentlewoman*; indeed every gesture shews an accomplished and dignified mind, that relies on itself; when deprived of the fortune which contributed to polish and give it consequence.

Drawings, the amusement of her youth, ornament her neat parlour; some musical instruments stand in one corner; for she plays with taste, and sings sweetly.

All the furniture, not forgetting a book-case, full of well-chosen books, speak the refinement of the owner, and the pleasures a cultivated mind has within its own grasp, independent of prosperity.

Her husband, a man of taste and learning, reads to her, while she makes clothes for her children, whom she teaches in the tenderest, and most persuasive manner, important truths and elegant accomplishments.

When you have behaved well for some time you shall visit her, and ramble in her little garden; there are several pretty seats in it, and the nightingales warble their sweetest songs, undisturbed, in the shade.

I have now given you an account of the present situation of both, and of their characters; listen to me whilst I relate in what manner these characters were formed, and the consequence of each adhering to a different mode of conduct.

Lady Sly, when she was a child, used to say pert things, which the injudicious people about her laughed at, and called very witty. Finding that her prattle pleased, she talked incessantly, and invented stories, when adding to those that had some foundation, was not sufficient to entertain the company. If she stole sweetmeats, or broke any thing, the cat, or the dog, was blamed, and the poor animals were corrected for her faults; nay, sometimes the servants lost their places in consequence of her assertions. Her parents died and left her a large fortune, and an aunt, who had a still larger, adopted her.

Mrs. Trueman, her cousin, was, some years after, adopted by the same lady; but her parents could not leave their estate to her, as it descended to the male heir. She had received the most liberal education, and was in every respect the reverse of her cousin; who envied her merit, and could not bear to think of her dividing the fortune which she had long expected to inherit entirely herself. She therefore practised every mean art to prejudice her aunt against her, and succeeded.

A faithful old servant endeavoured to open her mistress's eyes; but the cunning niece contrived to invent the most infamous story of the old domestic, who was in consequence of it dismissed. Mrs. Trueman supported her, when she could not succeed in vindicating her, and suffered for her generosity; for her aunt dying soon after, left only five hundred pounds to this amiable woman, and fifty thousand to Lady Sly.

They both of them married shortly after. One, the profligate Lord Sly, and the other a respectable clergyman, who had been disappointed in his hopes of preferment. This last couple, in spite of their mutual disappointments, are contented with their lot; and are preparing themselves and children for another world, where truth, virtue and happiness dwell together.

For believe me, whatever happiness we attain in this life, must faintly resemble what God Himself enjoys, whose truth and goodness produce a sublime degree, such as we cannot conceive, it is so far above our limited capacities.

I did not intend to detain you so long, said Mrs. Mason; have you finished *Mrs. Trimmer's Fabulous Histories?* Indeed we have, answered Caroline, mournfully, and I was very sorry to come to the end. I never read such a pretty book; may I read it over again to Mrs. Trueman's little Fanny? Certainly, said Mrs. Mason, if you can make her understand that birds never talk. Go and run about the garden, and remember the next lie I detect, I shall punish; because lying is a vice;—and I ought to punish you if you are guilty of it, to prevent your feeling Lady Sly's misery.

CHAPTER VI

Anger—Folly produces Self-contempt, and the Neglect of others.

MRS. MASON had a number of visitors one afternoon, who conversed in the usual thoughtless manner which people often fall into who do not consider before they speak;

they talked of Caroline's beauty, and she gave herself many affected airs to make it appear to the best advantage. But Mary, who had not a face to be proud of, was observing some peculiarities in the dress or manners of the guests; and one very respectable old lady, who had lost her teeth, afforded her more diversion than any of the rest.

The children went to bed without being reproved, though Mrs. Mason, when she dismissed them, said gravely, I give you to-night a kiss of peace, an affectionate one you have not deserved. They therefore discovered by her behaviour that they had done wrong, and waited for an explanation to regain her favour.

She was never in a passion, but her quiet steady displeasure made them feel so little in their own eyes, they wished her to smile that they might be something; for all their consequence seemed to arise from her approbation. I declare, said Caroline, I do not know what I have done, and yet I am sure I never knew Mrs. Mason find fault without convincing me that I had done wrong. Did you, Mary, ever see her in a passion? No, said Mary, I do believe that she was never angry in her life; when John threw down all the china, and stood trembling, she was the first to say that the carpet made him stumble. Yes, now I do remember, when we first came to her house, John forgot to bring the cow and her young calf into the cow-house; I heard her bid him do it directly, and the poor calf was almost frozen to death—she spoke then in a hurry, and seemed angry. Now you mention it, I do recollect, replied Caroline, that she was angry, when Betty did not carry the poor sick woman the broth she ordered her to take to her. But this is not like the passion I used to see nurse in, when any thing vexed her. She would scold us, and beat the girl who waited on her. Poor little Jenny, many a time was she beaten, when we vexed nurse; I would tell her she was to blame now if I saw her—and I would not tease her any more.

I declare I cannot go to sleep, said Mary, I am afraid of Mrs. Mason's eyes—would you think, Caroline, that she who looks so very good-natured sometimes, could frighten one so? I wish I were as wise and as good as she is. The poor woman with the six children, whom we met on the common, said she was an angel, and that she had saved her's and her children's lives. My heart is in my mouth, indeed, replied Caroline, when I think of to-morrow morning, and yet I am much happier than I was when we were at home. I cried, I cannot now tell for what, all day; I never wished to be good—nobody told me what it was to be good. I wish to be a woman, said Mary, and to be like Mrs. Mason, or Mrs. Trueman,—we are to go to see her if we behave well.

Sleep soon over-powered them, and they forgot their apprehensions. In the morning they awoke refreshed, and took care to learn their lessons, and feed the chickens, before Mrs. Mason left her chamber.

CHAPTER VII

Virtue the Soul of Beauty—The Tulip and the Rose— The Nightingale—External Ornaments—Characters.

THE NEXT MORNING Mrs. Mason met them first in the garden; and she desired Caroline to look at a bed of tulips, that were then in their highest state of perfection. I, added she, choose to have every kind of flower in my garden, as the succession enables me to vary my daily prospect, and gives it the charm of variety; yet these tulips afford me less pleasure than most of the other sort which I cultivate—and I will tell you why—they are only beautiful. Listen to my distinction;—good features, and a fine complexion, I term *bodily* beauty. Like the streaks in the tulip, they please the eye for a moment; but this uniformity soon tires, and the active mind flies off to something else. The soul of beauty, my dear children, consists in the body gracefully exhibiting the emotions and variations of the informing mind. If truth, humanity, and knowledge inhabit the breast, the eyes will beam with a mild lustre, modesty will suffuse the cheeks, and smiles of innocent joy play over all the features. At first sight, regularity and colour will attract, and have the advantage, because the hidden springs are not directly set in motion; but when internal goodness is reflected, every other kind of beauty, the shadow of it, withers away before it—as the sun obscures a lamp.

You are certainly handsome, Caroline; I mean, have good features; but you must improve your mind to give them a pleasing expression, or they will only serve to lead your understanding astray. I have seen some foolish people take great pains to decorate the outside of their houses, to attract the notice of strangers, who gazed, and passed on; whilst the inside, where they received their friends, was dark and inconvenient. Apply this observation to mere personal attractions. They may, it is true, for a few years, charm the superficial part of your acquaintance, whose notions of beauty are not built on any principle of utility. Such persons might look at you, as they would glance their eye over these tulips, and feel for a moment the same pleasure that a view of the variegated rays of light would convey to an uninformed mind. The lower class of mankind, and children, are fond of finery; gaudy, dazzling appearances catch their attention; but the discriminating judgment of a person of sense requires, besides colour, order, proportion, grace and usefulness, to render the idea of beauty complete.

Observe that rose, it has all the perfections I speak of; colour, grace, and sweetness—and even when the fine tints fade, the smell is grateful to those who have before contemplated its beauties. I have only one bed of tulips, though my garden is large, but, in every part of it, roses attract the eye.

You have seen Mrs. Trueman, and think her a very fine woman; yet her skin and complexion have only the clearness that temperance gives; and her features, strictly speaking, are not regular: Betty, the house-maid, has, in both these respects, much the superiority over her. But, though it is not easy to define in what her beauty consists, the eye follows her whenever she moves; and every person of taste listens for the modulated sounds which proceed out of her mouth, to be improved and pleased. It is conscious worth, *truth*, that gives dignity to her walk, and simple elegance to her conversation. She has, indeed, a most excellent understanding, and a feeling heart: sagacity and tenderness, the result of both, are happily blended in her countenance; and taste is the polish, which makes them appear to the best advantage. She is more than beautiful; and you see her varied excellencies again and again, with increasing pleasure. They are not obtruded on you, for knowledge has taught her true humility: she is not like the flaunting tulip, that forces itself forward into notice; but resembles the modest rose, you see yonder, retiring under its elegant foliage.

I have mentioned flowers—the same order is observed in the higher departments of nature. Think of the birds; those that sing best have not the finest plumage; indeed just the contrary; God divides His gifts, and amongst the feathered race the nightingale (sweetest of warblers, who pours forth her varied strain when sober eve comes on) you would seek in vain in the morning, if you expected that beautiful feathers should point out the songstress: many who incessantly twitter, and are only tolerable in the general concert, would surpass her, and attract your attention.

I knew, some time before you were born, a very fine, a very handsome girl; I saw she had abilities, and I saw with pain that she attended to the most obvious, but least valuable gift of heaven. Her ingenuity slept, whilst she tried to render her person more alluring. At last she caught the small-pox—her beauty vanished, and she was for a time miserable; but the natural vivacity of youth overcame her unpleasant feelings. In consequence of the disorder, her eyes became so weak that she was obliged to sit in a dark room. To beguile the tedious day she applied to music, and made a surprising proficiency. She even began to think, in her retirement, and when she recovered her sight grew fond of reading.

Large companies did not now amuse her, she was no longer the object of admiration, or if she was taken notice of, it was to be pitied, to hear her former self praised, and to hear them lament the depredation that dreadful disease had made in a fine face. Not expecting or wishing to be observed, she lost her affected airs, and attended to the conversation, in which she was soon able to bear a part. In short, the desire of pleasing took a different turn, and as she improved her mind, she discovered that virtue, internal beauty, was valuable on its own account, and not like that of the person, which resembles a toy, that pleases the observer, but does not render the possessor happy.

She found, that in acquiring knowledge, her mind grew tranquil, and the noble desire of acting conformably to the will of God succeeded, and drove out the immoderate vanity which before actuated her, when her equals were the objects she thought most of, and whose approbation she sought with such eagerness. And what had she sought? To be stared at and called handsome. Her beauty, the mere sight of it, did not make others good, or comfort the afflicted; but after she had lost it, she was comfortable herself, and set her friends the most useful example.

The money that she had formerly appropriated to ornament her person, now clothed the naked; yet she really appeared better dressed, as she had acquired the habit of employing her time to the best advantage, and could make many things herself. Besides, she did not implicitly follow the reigning fashion, for she had learned to distinguish, and in the most trivial matters acted according to the dictates of good sense.

The children made some comments on this story, but the entrance of a visitor interrupted the conversation, and they ran about the garden, comparing the roses and tulips.

CHAPTER VIII

Summer Evening's Amusement.—The Arrival of a Family of Haymakers.—Ridicule of personal Defects censured.—A Storm.— The Fear of Death.—The Cottage of honest Jack, the ship-wrecked Sailor.—The History of Jack, and his faithful Dog Pompey.

THE EVENING WAS PLEASANT; Mrs. Mason and the children walked out; and many rustic noises struck their ears. Some bells in a neighbouring village, softened by the distance, sounded pleasingly; the beetles hummed, and the children pursued them, not to destroy them; but to observe their form, and ask questions concerning their mode of living. Sheep were bleating and cattle lowing, the rivulet near them babbled along, while the sound of the distant ocean died away on the ear—or they forgot it, listening to the whistling of the hay-makers, who were returning from the field. They met a whole family who came every year from another county where they could not find constant employment, and Mrs. Mason allowed them to sleep in her barn. The little ones knew their benefactress, and tried to catch a smile; and she was ever ready to smile on those whom she obliged; for she loved all her fellow creatures, and love lightens obligations. Besides, she thought that the poor who are willing to work, had a right to the comforts of life.

A few moments after, they met a deformed woman; the children stared her almost out of countenance; but Mrs. Mason turned her head another way, and when the poor object was out of hearing, said to Mary, I intended to reprove you this morning for a fault which I have frequently seen you commit; and this moment and the other evening it was particularly conspicuous. When that deformed woman passed us, I involuntarily looked at something else, and would not let her perceive that she was a disgusting figure, and attracted notice on that account. I say I did it involuntarily, for I have accustomed myself to think of others, and what they will suffer on all occasions: and this lothness to offend, or even to hurt the feelings of another, is an instantaneous spring which actuates my conduct, and makes me kindly affected to every thing that breathes. If I then am so careful not to wound a stranger, what shall I think of your behaviour, Mary? when you laughed at a respectable old woman, who beside her virtues and her age, had been particularly civil to you. I have always seen persons of the weakest understandings, and whose hearts benevolence seldom touched, ridicule bodily infirmities, and accidental defects. They could only relish the inferiour kind of beauty, which I described this morning, and a silly joy has elated their empty souls, on finding, by comparison, that they were superiour to others in that respect, though the conclusion was erroneous, for merit, mental acquirements, can only give a just claim to superiority. Had you possessed the smallest portion of discernment, you would soon have forgotten the tones, loss of teeth made drawling, in listening to the chearful good sense which that worthy woman's words conveyed. You laughed, because you were ignorant, and I now excuse you; but some years hence, if I were to see you in company, with such a propensity, I should still think you a child, an overgrown one, whose mind did not expand as the body grew.

The sky began to thicken, and the lowing of the cattle to have a melancholy cadence; the nightingale forgot her song, and fled to her nest; and the sea roared and lashed the rocks. During the calm which portended an approaching storm, every creature was running for shelter.—We must, if possible, said Mrs. Mason, reach yon cottage on the cliff, for we shall soon have a violent thunder-storm. They quickened their pace, but the hurricane overtook them. The hail-stones fell, the clouds seemed to open and disclose the lightning, while loud peals of thunder shook the ground; the wind also in violent gusts rushed among the trees, tore off the slender branches and loosened the roots.

The children were terrified; but Mrs. Mason gave them each a hand, and chatted with them to dispel their fears. She informed them that storms were necessary to dissipate noxious vapours, and to answer many other purposes, which were not, perhaps, obvious to our weak understandings. But are you not afraid? cried the trembling Caroline. No, certainly, I am not afraid.—I walk with the same security as when the sun enlivened the prospect—God is still present, and we are safe. Should the flash that passes by us, strike me dead, it cannot hurt me, I fear not death!—I only fear that Being who can render death terrible, on whose providence I calmly rest; and my confidence earthly sorrows cannot destroy. A mind is never truly great, till the love of virtue overcomes the fear of death.

By this time they had mounted the cliff, and saw the tumultuous deep. The angry billows rose, and dashed against the shore; and the loud noise of the raging sea resounded from rock to rock.

They ran into the cottage; the poor woman who lived in it, sent her children for wood, and soon made a good fire to dry them.

The father of the family soon after came in, leaning on crutches; and over one eye there was a large patch. I am glad to see you honest Jack, said Mrs. Mason, come and take your seat by the fire, and tell the children the story of your shipwreck.

He instantly complied. I was very young, my dear ladies, said Jack, when I went to sea, and endured many hardships,—however I made a shift to weather them all; and whether the wind was fair or foul, I ran up the shrouds and sung at the helm. I had always a good heart, no lad fore or aft had a better; when we were at sea, I never was the first to flinch; and on shore I was as merry as the best of them. I married she you see yonder, (lifting his crutch to point to his wife) and her work and my wages did together, till I was shipwrecked on these rocks. Oh! it was a dreadful night; this is nothing to it; but I am getting to the end of my story before I begin it.

During the war, I went once or twice to New York. The last was a good voyage, and we were all returning with joy to dear England, when the storm rose; the vessel was like a bird, it flew up and down, and several of our best hands were washed clean overboard— My poor captain! a better never plowed the ocean, he fell overboard too, and it was some time before we missed him; for it was quite dark, except that flashes of lightning, now and then, gave us light. I was at the helm, lashing it to the side of the ship—a dreadful flash came across me, and I lost one of my precious eyes.—But thank God I have one left.

The weather cleared up next day, and, though we had been finely mauled, I began to hope, for I hate to be faint-hearted, and certainly we should have got into the channel very soon, if we had not fell in with a French man of war, which took us; for we could not make any resistance.

I had a dog, poor Pompey! with me. Pompey would not leave me, he was as fond of me as if he had been a christian. I had lost one eye by the lightning, the other had been sore, so that I could hardly call it a peep-hole. Somehow I fell down the hatchway, and bruised one of my legs; but I did not mind it, do ye see, till we arrived at Brest, and were thrown into a French Prison.

There I was worse off than ever; the room we were all stowed in, was full of vermin, and our food very bad; mouldy biscuits, and salt fish. The prison was choke full, and many a morning did we find some honest fellow with his chops fallen—he was not to be waked any more!—he was gone to the other country, do ye see.

Yet the French have not such hard hearts as people say they have! Several women brought us broth, and wine; and one gave me some rags to wrap round my leg, it was very painful, I could not clean it, nor had I any plaister. One day I was looking sorrowfully at it, thinking for certain I should lose my precious limb; when, would you

Indeed we are very happy !——

believe it? Pompey saw what I was thinking about, and began to lick it.—And, I never knew such a surprizing thing, it grew better and better every day, and at last was healed without any plaister.

After that I was very sick, and the same tender-hearted creature who gave me the rags, took me to her house; and fresh air soon recovered me. I for certain ought to speak well of the French; but for their kindness I should have been in another port by this time. Mayhap I might have gone with a fair wind, yet I should have been sorry to have left my poor wife and her children. But I am letting all my line run out! Well, by-and-by, there was an exchange of prisoners, and we were once more in an English vessel, and I made sure of seeing my family again; but the weather was still foul. Three days and nights we were in the greatest distress; and the fourth the ship was dashed against these rocks. Oh! if you had heard the crash! The water rushed in—the men screamed, Lord have mercy on us! There was a woman in the ship, and, as I could swim, I tried to save her, and Pompey followed me; but I lost him—poor fellow! I declare I cried like a child when I saw his dead body. However I brought the woman to shore; and assisted some more of my mess-mates; but, standing in the water so long, I lost the use of my limbs—yet Heaven was good to me; Madam, there, sent a cart for us all, and took care of us; but I never recovered the use of my limbs. So she asked me all about my misfortunes, and sent for wife, who came directly, and we have lived here ever since. We catch fish for Madam, and I watch for a storm, hoping some time or other to be as kind to a poor perishing soul as she has been to me. Indeed we are very happy—I might now have been begging about the streets, but for Madam, God bless her.

A tear strayed down Mrs. Mason's cheek, while a smile of benevolence lighted up her countenance—the little girls caught each hand—They were all silent a few minutes when she, willing to turn the discourse, enquired whether they had any fish in the house? Some were produced, they were quickly dressed, and they all eat together. They had a chearful meal, and honest Jack sung some of his seafaring songs, and did all he could to divert them and express his gratitude. Getting up to reach the brown loaf, he limped very awkwardly, Mary was just beginning to laugh, when she restrained herself; for she recollected that his awkwardness made him truly respectable, because he had lost the use of his limbs when he was doing good, saving the lives of his fellow-creatures.

The weather cleared up, and they returned home. The children conversed gaily with each other all the way home, talking of the poor sailor, and his faithful dog.

CHAPTER IX

The Inconveniences of immoderate Indulgence.

THE CHILDREN were allowed to help themselves to fruit, when it made a part of their meal; and Caroline always took care to pick out the best, or swallow what she took in a hurry, lest she should not get as much as she wished for. Indeed she generally eat more than her share. She had several times eaten more than a person ought to eat at one time, without feeling any ill effects; but one afternoon she complained of a pain in her stomach in consequence of it, and her pale face, and languid eyes, plainly shewed her indisposition. Mrs. Mason gave her an emetic, and after the operation she was obliged to go to bed, though she had promised herself a pleasant walk that evening. She was left alone, for Mary was not permitted to stay at home with her, as she offered to do. Had her sickness been accidental, we would both have tried to amuse her, said Mrs. Mason; but her greediness now receiving its natural and just punishment, she must endure it without the alleviation which pity affords; only tell her from me, that the pleasure was but momentary, while the pain and confinement it produced, has already lasted some hours.

The next morning, though scarcely recovered, she got up, as usual, to have a walk before breakfast. During these walks, Mrs. Mason told them stories, pointed out the wisdom of God in the creation, and took them to visit her poor tenants. These visits not only enabled her to form a judgment of their wants, but made them very industrious; for they were all anxious that she might find their houses and persons clean. And returning through the farm-yard, Mrs. Mason stopped according to custom, to see whether the poor animals were taken care of—this she called earning her breakfast. The servant was just feeding the pigs, and though she poured a great quantity into the trough, the greedy creatures tried to gobble it up from one another. Caroline blushed, she saw this sight was meant for her, and she felt ashamed of her gluttony. But Mrs. Mason, willing to impress her still more strongly, thus addressed her.

Providence, my child, has given us passions and appetites for various purposes—two are generally obvious, I will point them out to you. First to render our present life more comfortable, and then to prepare us for another, by making us sociable beings; as in society virtue is acquired, and self-denial practiced. A moderate quantity of proper food recruits our exhausted spirits, and invigorates the animal functions; but, if we exceed moderation, the mind will be oppressed, and soon become the slave of the body, or both grow listless and inactive. Employed various ways, families meet at meals, and there giving up to each other, learn in the most easy, pleasant way to govern their appetites. Pigs, you see, devour what they can get; but men, if they have any affections, love their fellow-creatures, and wish for a return; nor will they, for the sake of a brutish gratification, lose the esteem of those they value. Besides, no one can be reckoned virtuous who has not learned to bear poverty: yet those who think much of gratifying their appetites, will at last act meanly in order to indulge them. But when any employment of the understanding, or strong affection occupies the mind, eating is seldom thought a matter of greater importance than it ought to be. Let the idle *think* of their meals; but do you employ the intermediate time in a different manner, and only enjoy them when you join the social circle. I like to see children, and even men, eat chearfully, and gratefully receive the blessings sent by Heaven; yet I would not have them abuse those blessings, or ever let the care necessary to support the body, injure the immortal spirit: many think of the sustenance the former craves, and entirely neglect the latter.

I remarked to you before, that in the most apparently trivial concerns, we are to do as we would be done by. This duty must be practised constantly; at meals there are frequent opportunities, and I hope, Caroline, I shall never again see you eager to secure dainties for yourself. If such a disposition were to grow up with you, you ought to live alone, for no one should enjoy the advantages and pleasures which arise from social intercourse, who is unwilling to give way to the inclinations of others, and allow each their share of the good things of this life.

You experienced yesterday, that pain follows immoderate indulgence; it is always the case, though sometimes not felt so immediately; but the constitution is insensibly destroyed, and old age will come on, loaded with infirmities. You also lost a very pleasant walk, and some fine fruit. We visited Mrs. Goodwin's garden, and as Mary had before convinced me that she could regulate her appetites, I gave her leave to pluck as much fruit as she wished; and she did not abuse my indulgence. On the contrary, she spent most part of the time in gathering some for me, and her attention made it taste sweeter.

Coming home I called her my friend, and she deserved the name, for she was no longer a child; a reasonable affection had conquered an appetite; her understanding took the lead, and she had practised a virtue.

The subject was now dropped; but, Caroline determined to copy in future her sister's temperance and self-denial.

CHAPTER X

The Danger of Delay—Description of a Mansion-house in Ruins— The History of Charles Townley.

MRS. MASON who always regulated her own time, and never loitered her hours irresolutely away, had very frequently to wait for the children, when she wished to walk, though she had desired them to be ready at a precise time. Mary in particular had a trick of putting every thing off till the last moment, and then she did but half do it, or left it undone. This indolent way of delaying made her miss many opportunities of obliging and doing good; and whole hours were lost in thoughtless idleness, which she afterwards wished had been better employed.

This was the case one day, when she had a letter to write to her father; and though it was mentioned to her early in the morning, the finest part of the evening slipped away whilst she was finishing it; and her haste made her forget the principal thing which she intended to have said.

Out of breath she joined them; and after they had crossed several fields, Mrs. Mason turning down a long avenue, bade them look at a large old mansion-house. It was now in ruins. Ivy grew over the substantial walls, that still resisted the depredations of time, and almost concealed a noble arch, on which maimed lions couched; and vultures and eagles, who had lost their wings, seemed to rest for ever there. Near it was a rookery, and the rooks lived safe in the high trees, whose trunks were all covered with ivy or moss, and a number of fungusses grew about their large roots. The grass was long, and remaining undisturbed, save when the wind swept across it, was of course pathless. Here the mower never whet his scythe, nor did the haymakers mix their songs with the hoarse croaking of the rooks. A spacious basin, on the margin of which water plants grew with wild luxuriance, was overspread with slime; and afforded a shelter for toads and adders. In many places were heaped the ruins of ornamental buildings, whilst sun-dials rested in the shade;—and pedestals that had crushed the figures they before supported. Making their way through the grass, they would frequently stumble over a headless statue, or the head would impede their progress. When they spoke, the sound seemed to return again, as if unable to penetrate the thick stagnated air. The sun could not dart its purifying rays through the thick gloom, and the fallen leaves contributed to choke up the way, and render the air more noxious.

I brought you to this place on purpose this evening, said Mrs. Mason to the children, who clung about her, to tell you the history of the last inhabitant; but, as this part is unwholesome, we will sit on the broken stones of the drawbridge.

Charles Townley was a boy of uncommon abilities, and strong feelings; but he ever permitted those feelings to direct his conduct, without submitting to the direction of reason; I mean, the present emotion governed him.—He had not any strength or consistency of character; one moment he enjoyed a pleasure, and the next felt the pangs of remorse, on account of some duty which he had neglected. He always indeed intended to act right in every particular *to-morrow*; but *to-day* he followed the prevailing whim.

He heard by chance of a man in great distress, he determined to relieve him, and left his house in order to follow the humane impulse; but meeting an acquaintance, he was persuaded to go to the play, and *to-morrow*, he thought, he would do the act of charity. The next morning some company came to breakfast with him, and took him with them to view some fine pictures. In the evening he went to a concert; the day following he was tired, and laid in bed till noon; then read a pathetic story, well wrought up, *wept* over it—fell asleep—and forgot to *act* humanely. An accident reminded him of his intention, he sent to the man, and found that he had too long delayed—the relief was useless.

In this thoughtless manner he spent his time and fortune; never applying to any profession, though formed to shine in any one he should have chosen. His friends were offended, and at last allowed him to languish in a gaol; and as there appeared no probability of reforming or fixing him, they left him to struggle with adversity.

Severely did he reproach himself—He was almost lost in despair, when a friend visited him. This friend loved the latent sparks of virtue which he imagined would some time or other light up, and animate his conduct. He paid his debts, and gave him a sum of money sufficient to enable him to prepare for a voyage to the East Indies, where Charles wished to go, to try to regain his lost fortune. Through the intercession of this kind, considerate friend, his relations were reconciled to him, and his spirits raised.

He sailed with a fair wind, and fortune favouring his most romantic wishes, in the space of fifteen years, he acquired a much larger fortune than he had even hoped for, and thought of visiting, nay, settling in his native country for the remainder of his life.

Though impressed by the most lively sense of gratitude, he had dropped his friend's correspondence; yet, as he knew that he had a daughter, his first determination was to reserve for her the greater part of his property, as the most substantial proof which he could give of his gratitude.—The thought pleased him, and that was sufficient to divert him for some months; but accidentally hearing that his friend had been very unsuccessful in trade, this information made him wish to hasten his return to his native country. Still a procrastinating spirit possessed him, and he delayed from time to time the arduous task of settling his affairs, previous to his departure: he wrote, however, to England, and transmitted a considerable sum to a correspondent, desiring that this house might be prepared for him, and the mortgage cleared.

I can scarcely enumerate the various delays that prevented his embarking; and when he arrived in England, he came here, and was so childishly eager to have his house fitted up with taste, that he actually trifled away a month, before he went to seek for his friend.

But his negligence was now severely punished. He learned that he had been reduced to great distress, and thrown into the very gaol, out of which he took Townley, who, hastening to it, only found his dead body there; for he died the day before. On the table was lying, amidst some other scraps of paper, a letter, directed in an unsteady hand to Charles Townley. He tore it open. Few were the scarcely legible lines; but they smote his heart. He read as follows:

"I have been reduced by unforeseen misfortunes; yet when I heard of your arrival, a gleam of joy cheered my heart—*I thought I knew your's*, and that my latter days might still have been made comfortable in your society, for I loved you; I even expected pleasure; but I was mistaken; death is my only friend."

He read it over and over again; and cried out, Gracious God, had I arrived but one day sooner I should have seen him, and he would not have died thinking me the most ungrateful wretch that ever burdened the earth! He then knocked his clinched fist against his forehead, looked wildly round the dreary apartment, and exclaimed in a choked, though impatient tone, You sat here yesterday, thinking of my ingratitude— Where are you now! Oh! that I had seen you! Oh! that my repenting sighs could reach you!—

He ordered the body to be interred, and returned home a prey to grief and despond- ency. Indulging it to excess, he neglected to enquire after his friend's daughter; he intended to provide amply for her, but now he could only grieve.

Some time elapsed, then he sent, and the intelligence which he procured aggravated his distress, and gave it a severe additional sting.

The poor gentle girl had, during her father's life, been engaged to a worthy young man; but, some time after his death, the relations of her lover had sent him to sea to prevent the match taking place. She was helpless, and had not sufficient courage to com- bat with poverty; to escape from it, she married an old rake whom she detested. He was ill-humoured, and his vicious habits rendered him a most dreadful companion. She tried in vain to please him, and banish the sorrow that bent her down, and made wealth and all the pleasures it could procure tasteless. Her tender father was dead—she had lost her lover—without a friend or confident, silent grief consumed her. I have told you friendship is only to be found amongst the virtuous; her husband was vicious.

Ah! why did she marry, said Mary?

Because she was timid; but I have not told you all; the grief that did not break her heart, disturbed her reason; and her husband confined her in a mad-house.

Charles heard of this last circumstance; he visited her. Fanny, said he, do you recollect your old friend? Fanny looked at him, and reason for a moment resumed her seat, and informed her countenance to trace anguish on it—the trembling light soon disappeared— wild fancy flushed in her eyes, and animated her incessant rant. She sung several verses of different songs, talked of her husband's ill-usage—enquired if he had lately been to sea? And frequently addressed her father as if he were behind her chair, or sitting by her.

Charles could not bear this scene—If I could lose like her a sense of woe, he cried, this intolerable anguish would not tear my heart! The fortune which he had intended for her could not restore her reason; but, had he sent for her soon after her father's death, he might have saved her and comforted himself.

The last stroke was worse than the first; he retired to this abode; melancholy creeping

Be calm, my child, remember that you must do all the good you can the present day.

on him, he let his beard grow, and the garden run wild. One room in the house the poor lunatic inhabited; and he had a proper person to attend her, and guard her from the dangers she wished to encounter. Every day he visited her, the sight of her would almost have unhinged a sound mind—How could he bear it, when his conscience reproached him, and whispered that he had neglected to do good, to live to any rational purpose— The sweets of friendship were denied, and he every day contemplated the saddest of all sights—the wreck of a human understanding.

He died without a will. The estate was litigated, and as the title to this part could not be proved, the house was let fall into its present state.

But the night will overtake us, we must make haste home—Give me your hand, Mary, you tremble; surely I need not desire you to remember this story—Be calm, my child, and remember that you must attend to trifles; do all the good you can the present day, nay hour, if you would keep your conscience clear. This circumspection may not produce dazzling actions, nor will your silent virtue be supported by human applause; but your Father, who seeth in secret, will reward you.

CHAPTER XI

Dress.—A Character.—Remarks on Mrs. Trueman's Manner of dressing. —Trifling Omissions undermine Affection.

MARY'S PROCRASTINATING TEMPER produced many other ill consequences; she would lie in bed till the last moment, and then appear without washing her face or cleaning her teeth. Mrs. Mason had often observed it, and hinted her dislike; but, unwilling to burden her with precepts, she waited for a glaring example. One was soon accidentally thrown in her way, and she determined that it should not pass unobserved.

A lady, who was remarkable for her negligence in this respect, spent a week with them; and, during that time, very frequently disconcerted the œconomy of the family. She was seldom fit to be seen, and if any company came by chance to dinner, she would make them wait till it was quite cold, whilst she huddled on some ill-chosen finery. In the same style, if a little party of pleasure was proposed, she had to dress herself, and the hurry discomposed her, and tired those, who did not like to lose time in anticipating a trifling amusement.

A few hours after she had left them, Mrs. Mason enquired of Mary, what effect this week's experience had had on her mind? You are fond of ridicule, child, but seldom in the right place; real cause for it you let slip, and heed not the silent reproof that points at your own faults: do not mistake me, I would not have you laugh at—yet I wish you to feel, what is ridiculous, and learn to distinguish folly. Mrs. Dowdy's negligence arises from indolence; her mind is not employed about matters of importance; and, if it were, it would not be a sufficient excuse for her habitually neglecting an essential part of a man's as well as a woman's duty. I said habitually; grief will often make those careless, who, at other times, pay a proper attention to their person; and this neglect is a sure indication that the canker-worm is at work; and we ought to pity, rather than blame the unfortunate. Indeed when painful activity of mind occasions this inattention, it will not last long; the soul struggles to free itself, and return to its usual tone and old habits.

The lady we have been speaking of, ever appears a sloven, though she is sometimes a disgusting figure, and, at others, a very taudry flirt.

I continually caution Caroline not to spend much time in adorning her person; but I never desired you to neglect yours. Wisdom consists in avoiding extremes—immoderate fondness for dress, I term vanity; but a proper attention to avoid singularity does not deserve that name. Never waste much time about trifles; but the time that is necessary, employ properly. Exercise your understanding, taste flows from it, and will in a moment direct you, if you are not too solicitous to conform to the changing fashions; and loiter away in laborious idleness the precious moments when the imagination is most lively, and should be allowed to fix virtuous affections in the tender youthful heart.

Of all the women whom I have ever met with, Mrs. Trueman seems the freest from vanity, and those frivolous views which degrade the female character. Her virtues claim respect, and the practice of them engrosses her thoughts; yet her clothes are apparently well chosen, and you always see her in the same attire. Not like many women who are eager to set off their persons to the best advantage, when they are only going to take a walk, and are careless, nay slovenly, when forced to stay at home. Mrs. Trueman's conduct is just the reverse, she tries to avoid singularity, for she does not wish to disgust the generality; but it is her family, her friends, whom she studies to please.

In dress it is not little minute things, but the *whole* that should be attended to, and that every day; and this attention gives an ease to the person because the clothes appear unstudily graceful. Never, continued Mrs. Mason, desire to excel in trifles, if you do—there is an end to virtuous emulation, the mind cannot attend to both; for when the main pursuit is trivial, the character will of course become insignificant. Habitual neatness is laudable; but, if you wish to be reckoned a well, an elegantly dressed girl; and feel that praise on account of it gives you pleasure, you are vain; and a laudable ambition cannot dwell with vanity.

Servants, and those women whose minds have had a very limited range, place all their happiness in ornaments, and frequently neglect the only essential part in dress,—neatness.

I have not the least objection to your dressing according to your age; I rather encourage it, by allowing you to wear the gayest colours; yet I insist on some degree of uniformity: and think you treat me disrespectfully when you appear before me, and have forgotten to do, what should never be neglected, and what you could have done in less than a quarter of an hour.

I always dress myself before breakfast, and expect you to follow my example, if there is not a sufficient, and obvious excuse. You, Mary, missed a pleasant airing yesterday; for if you had not forgotten the respect which is due to me, and hurried down to breakfast in a slovenly manner, I should have taken you out with me; but I did not choose to wait till you were ready, as your not being so was entirely your own fault.

Fathers, and men in general, complain of this inattention; they have always to wait for females. Learn to avoid this fault, however insignificant it may appear in your eyes, for that habit cannot be of little consequence that sometimes weakens esteem. When we frequently make allowance for another in trifling matters, notions of inferiority take root in the mind, and too often produce contempt. Respect for the understanding must be the basis of constancy; the tenderness which flows from pity is liable to perish insensibly, to consume itself—even the virtues of the heart, when they degenerate into weakness, sink a character in our estimation. Besides, a kind of gross familiarity, takes place of decent affection; and the respect which alone can render domestic intimacy a lasting comfort is lost before we are aware of it.

CHAPTER XII

Behaviour to Servants.—True Dignity of Character.

THE CHILDREN not coming down to breakfast one morning at the usual time, Mrs. Mason went herself to enquire the reason; and as she entered the apartment, heard Mary say to the maid who assisted her, I wonder at your impertinence, to talk thus to me—do you know who you are speaking to?—she was going on; but Mrs. Mason interrupted her, and answered the question—to a little girl, who is only assisted because she is weak. Mary shrunk back abashed, and Mrs. Mason continued, as you have treated Betty, who is ten years older than yourself improperly, you must now do every thing for yourself; and, as you will be some time about it, Caroline and I will eat our breakfast, and visit Mrs. Trueman. By the time we return, you may perhaps have recollected that children are inferior to servants—who act from the dictates of reason, and whose understandings are arrived at some degree of maturity, while children must be governed and directed till *their's* gains strength to work by itself: for it is the proper exercise of our reason that makes us in any degree independent.

When Mrs. Mason returned, she mildly addressed Mary. I have often told you that every dispensation of Providence tended to our improvement, if we do not perversely act contrary to our interest. One being is made dependent on another, that love and forbearance may soften the human heart, and that linked together by necessity, and the exercise of the social affections, the whole family on earth might have a fellow feeling for each other. By these means we improve one another; but there is no real inferiority.

You have read the fable of the head supposing itself superior to the rest of the members, though all are equally necessary to the support of life. If I behave improperly to servants, I am really their inferior, as I abuse a trust, and imitate not the Being, whose servant I am, without a shadow of equality. Children are helpless. I order my servants to wait on you, because you are so; but I have not as much respect for you as for them; you may possibly become a virtuous character.—Many of my servants are really so already; they have done their duty, filled an humble station, as they ought to fill it, conscientiously. And do you dare to despise those whom your Creator approves?

Before the greatest earthly beings I should not be awed, they are my fellow servants; and, though superior in rank, which, like personal beauty, only dazzles the vulgar; yet I may possess more knowledge and virtue. The same feeling actuates me when I am in company with the poor; we are creatures of the same nature, and I may be their inferiour in those graces which should adorn my soul, and render me truly great.

How often must I repeat to you, that a child is inferiour to a man; because reason is in its infancy, and it is reason which exalts a man above a brute; and the cultivation of it raises the wise man above the ignorant; for wisdom is only another name for virtue.

This morning, when I entered your apartment, I heard you insult a worthy servant. You had just said your prayers; but they must have been only the gabble of the tongue; your heart was not engaged in the sacred employment, or you could not so soon have forgotten that you were a weak, dependent being, and that you were to receive mercy and kindness only on the condition of your practising the same.

I advise you to ask Betty to pardon your impertinence; till you do so, she shall not assist you; you would find yourself very helpless without the assistance of men and women—unable to cook your meat, bake your bread, wash your clothes, or even put them on—such a helpless creature is a child—I know what you are, you perceive.

Mary submitted—and in future after she said her prayers, remembered that she was to endeavour to curb her temper.

CHAPTER XIII

Employment—Idleness produces Misery—
The Cultivation of the Fancy raises us above the Vulgar,
extends our Happiness, and leads to Virtue.

ONE AFTERNOON, Mrs. Mason gave the children leave to amuse themselves; but a kind of listlessness hung over them, and at a loss what to do, they seemed fatigued with doing nothing. They eat cakes though they had just dined, and did many foolish things merely because they were idle. Their friend seeing that they were irresolute, and could not fix on any employment, requested Caroline to assist her to make some clothes, that a poor woman was in want of, and while we are at work, she added, Mary will read us an entertaining tale, which I will point out.

The tale interested the children, who chearfully attended, and after it was finished, Mrs. Mason told them, that as she had some letters to write, she could not take her accustomed walk; but that she would allow them to represent her, and act for once like women. They received their commission, it was to take the clothes to the poor woman, whom they were intended for; learn her present wants; exercise their own judgment with respect to the immediate relief she stood in need of, and act accordingly.

They returned home delighted, eager to tell what they had done, and how thankful, and happy they had left the poor woman.

Observe now, said Mrs. Mason, the advantages arising from employment; three hours ago, you were uncomfortable, without being sensible of the cause, and knew not what to do with yourselves. Nay, you actually committed a sin; for you devoured cakes without feeling hunger, merely to kill time, whilst many poor people have not the means of satisfying their natural wants. When I desired you to read to me you were amused; and now you have been useful you are delighted. Recollect this in future when you are at a loss what to do with yourselves—and remember that idleness must always be intolerable, because it is only an irksome consciousness of existence.

Every gift of Heaven is lent to us for our improvement; fancy is one of the first of the inferiour ones; in cultivating it, we acquire what is called taste, or a relish for particular employments, which occupy our leisure hours, and raise us above the vulgar in our conversation. Those who have not any taste talk always of their own affairs or of their neighbours; every trivial matter that occurs within their knowledge they canvass and conjecture about—not so much out of ill-nature as idleness: just as you eat the cakes without the impulse of hunger. In the same style people talk of eating and dress, and long for their meals merely to divide the day, because the intermediate time is not employed in a more interesting manner. Every new branch of taste that we cultivate, affords us a refuge from idleness, a fortress in which we may resist the assaults of vice; and the more noble our employments, the more exalted will our minds become.

Music, drawing, works of usefulness and fancy, all amuse and refine the mind, sharpen the ingenuity; and form, insensibly, the dawning judgment.—As the judgment gains strength, so do the passions also; we have actions to weigh, and need that taste in conduct, that delicate sense of propriety, which gives grace to virtue. The highest branch of solitary amusement is reading; but even in the choice of books the fancy is first employed; for in reading, the heart is touched, till its feelings are examined by the understanding, and the ripenings of reason regulate the imagination. This is the work of years, and the most important of all employments. When life advances, if the heart has been capable of receiving early impressions, and the head of reasoning and retaining the conclusions which were drawn from them; we have acquired a stock of knowledge, a gold mine which we can occasionally recur to, independent of outward circumstances.

The supreme Being has every thing in himself; we proceed from Him, and our knowledge and affections must return to Him for employment suited to them. And those who most resemble Him ought, next to Him, to be the objects of our love; and the beings whom we should try to associate with, that we may receive an inferiour degree of satisfaction from their society.—But be assured our chief comfort must ever arise from the mind's reviewing its own operations—and the whispers of an approving conscience, to convince us that life has not slipped away unemployed.

CHAPTER XIV

Innocent Amusements.—Description of a Welsh Castle.— History of a Welsh Harper.— A tyrannical Landlord.—Family Pride.

As it was now harvest time, the new scene, and the fine weather delighted the children, who ran continually out to view the reapers. Indeed every thing seemed to wear a face of festivity, and the ripe corn bent under its own weight, or, more erect, shewed the laughing appearance of plenty.

Mrs. Mason always allowing the gleaners to have a sufficient quantity, a great number of poor came to gather a little harvest; and she was pleased to see the feeble hands of childhood and age, collecting the scattered ears.

Honest Jack came with his family; and when the labours of the day were over, would play on a fiddle, that frequently had but three strings. But it served to set the feet in motion, and the lads and lasses dancing on the green sod, suffered every care to sleep.

An old Welsh harper generally came to the house about this time of the year, and staid a month or more; for Mrs. Mason was particularly fond of this instrument, and interested in the fate of the player; as is almost always the case, when we have rescued a person out of any distress.

She informed the children, that once travelling through Wales, her carriage was overturned near the ruins of an old castle. And as she had escaped unhurt, she determined to wander amongst them, whilst the driver took care of his horses, and her servant hastened to the neighbouring village for assistance.

It was almost dark, and the lights began to twinkle in the scattered cottages. The scene pleased me, continued Mrs. Mason, I thought of the various customs which the lapse of time unfolds; and dwelt on the state of the Welsh, when this castle, now so desolate, was the hospitable abode of the chief of a noble family. These reflections entirely engrossed my mind, when the sound of a harp reached my ears. Never was any thing more opportune, the national music seemed to give reality to the pictures which my imagination had been drawing. I listened awhile, and then trying to trace the pleasing sound, discovered, after a short search, a little hut, rudely built. The walls of an old tower supported part of the thatch, which scarcely kept out the rain, and the two other sides were stones cemented, or rather plaistered together, by mud and clay.

I entered, and beheld an old man, sitting by a few loose sticks, which blazed on the hearth; and a young woman, with one child at her breast, sucking, and another on her knee: near them stood a cow and her calf. The man had been playing on the harp, he rose when he saw me, and offered his chair, the only one in the room, and sat down on a large chest in the chimney-corner. When the door was shut, all the light that was admitted came through the hole, called a chimney, and did not much enliven the dwelling. I mentioned my accident to account for my intrusion, and requested the harper again to touch the instrument that had attracted me. A partition of twigs and dried leaves divided this apartment from another, in which I perceived a light; I enquired about it, and the woman, in an artless manner, informed me, that she had let it to a young gentlewoman lately married, who was related to a very good family, and would not lodge any where, or with any body. This intelligence made me smile, to think that family pride should be a solace in such extreme poverty.

I sat there some time, and then the harper accompanied me to see whether the carriage was repaired; I found it waiting for me; and as the inn I was to sleep at was only about two miles further, the harper offered to come and play to me whilst I was eating my supper. This was just what I wished for, his appearance had roused my compassion as well as my curiosity, and I took him and his harp in the chaise.

After supper he informed me, that he had once a very good farm; but he had been so unfortunate as to displease the justice, who never forgave him, nor rested till he had ruined him. This tyrant always expected his tenants to assist him to bring in his harvest before they had got in their own. The poor harper was once in the midst of his, when an order was sent to him to bring his carts and servants, the next day, to the fields of this petty king. He foolishly refused; and this refusal was the foundation of that settled hatred which produced such fatal consequences. Ah, Madam, said the sufferer, your heart would ache, if you heard of all his cruelties to me, and the rest of his poor tenants. He employs many labourers, and will not give them as much wages as they could get from the common farmers, yet they dare not go any-where else to work when he sends for them. The fish that they catch they must bring first to him, or they would not be allowed to walk over his grounds to catch them; and he will give just what he pleases for the most valuable part of their pannier.

But there would be no end to my story were I to tell you of all his oppressions. I was obliged to leave my farm; and my daughter, whom you saw this evening, having married an industrious young man, I came to live with them. When,—would you believe it? this

*Trying to trace the sound, I discovered
a little hut, rudely built.*

same man threw my son into jail, on account of his killing a hare, which all the country folks do when they can catch them in their grounds. We were again in great distress, and my daughter and I built the hut you saw in the waste, that the poor babes might have a shelter. I maintain them by playing on the harp,—the master of this inn allows me to play to the gentry who travel this way; so that I pick up a few pence, just enough to keep life and soul together, and to enable me to send a little bread to my poor son John Thomas.

He then began one of the most dismal of his Welsh ditties, and, in the midst of it cried out, he is an upstart, a mere mushroom!—His grandfather was cow-boy to mine!—So I told him once, and he never forgot it.—

The old man then informed me that the castle in which he now was sheltered formerly belonged to his family—such are the changes and chances of this mortal life—said he, and hastily struck up a lively tune.—

While he was striking the strings, I thought too of the changes in life which an age had produced. The descendant of those who had made the hall ring with social mirth now mourned in its ruins, and hung his harp on the mouldering battlements. Such is the fate of buildings and of families!

After I had dismissed my guest, I sent for the landlord, to make some farther enquiries; and found that I had not been deceived; I then determined to assist him, and thought my accident providential. I knew a man of consequence in the neighbourhood, I visited him, and exerted myself to procure the enlargement of the young man. I succeeded; and not only restored him to his family; but prevailed on my friend to let him rent a small farm on his estate, and I gave him money to buy stock for it, and the implements of husbandry.

The old harper's gratitude was unbounded; the summer after he walked to visit me; and ever since he has contrived to come every year to enliven our harvest-home.—This evening it is to be celebrated.

The evening came; the joyous party footed it away merrily, and the sound of their shoes was heard on the barn-floor. It was not the light fantastic toe, that fashion taught to move, but honest heart-felt mirth, and the loud laugh, if it spoke the vacant head, said audibly that the heart was guileless.

Mrs. Mason always gave them some trifling presents at this time, to render the approach of winter more comfortable. To the men, she generally presented warm clothing, and to the women flax and worsted for knitting and spinning; and those who were the most industrious received a reward when the new year commenced. The children had books given to them, and little ornaments.—All were anxious for the day; and received their old acquaintance, the harper, with the most cordial smiles.

CHAPTER XV

Prayer.—A Moon-light Scene.—Resignation.

THE HARPER would frequently sit under a large elm, a few paces from the house, and play some of the most plaintive Welsh tunes. While the people were eating their supper, Mrs. Mason desired him to play her some favourite airs; and she and the children walked round the tree under which he sat, on the stump of another.

The moon rose in cloudless majesty, and a number of stars twinkled near her. The softened landscape inspired tranquillity, while the strain of rustic melody gave a pleasing melancholy to the whole—and made the tear start, whose source could scarcely be traced. The pleasure the sight of harmless mirth gave rise to in Mrs. Mason's bosom, roused every tender feeling—set in motion her spirits.—She laughed with the poor whom she had made happy, and wept when she recollected her own sorrows; the illusions of youth—the gay expectations that had formerly clipped the wings of time.—She turned to the girls—I have been very unfortunate, my young friends; but my griefs are now of a placid kind. Heavy misfortunes have obscured the sun I gazed at when first I entered life—early attachments have been broken—the death of friends I loved has so clouded my days; that neither the beams of prosperity, nor even those of benevolence, can dissipate the gloom; but I am not lost in a thick fog.—My state of mind rather resembles the scene before you, it is quiet—I am weaned from the world, but not disgusted—for I can still do good—and in futurity a sun will rise to cheer my heart.—Beyond the night of death, I hail the dawn of an eternal day! I mention my state of mind to you, that I may tell you what supports me.

The festivity within, and the placidity without, led my thoughts naturally to the source from whence my comfort springs—to the Great Bestower of every blessing. Prayer, my children, is the dearest privilege of man, and the support of a feeling heart. Mine has too often been wounded by ingratitude; my fellow-creatures, whom I have fondly loved, have neglected me—I have heard their last sigh, and thrown my eyes round an empty world; but then more particularly feeling the presence of my Creator, I poured out my soul before Him—and was no longer alone!—I now daily contemplate His wonderful goodness; and, though at an awful distance, try to imitate Him. This view of things is a spur to activity, and a consolation in disappointment.

There is in fact a constant intercourse kept up with the Creator, when we learn to consider Him, as the fountain of truth, which our understanding naturally thirsts after. But His goodness brings Him still more on a level with our bounded capacities—for we trace it in every work of mercy, and feel, in sorrow particularly, His fatherly care. Every blessing is doubled when we suppose it comes from Him, and afflictions almost lose their name when we believe they are sent to correct, not crush us.—Whilst we are alive to gratitude and admiration, we must adore God.

The human soul is so framed, that goodness and truth must fill it with ineffable pleasure, and the nearer it approaches to perfection, the more earnestly will it pursue those virtues, discerning more clearly their beauty.

The Supreme Being dwells in the universe. He is as essentially present to the wicked as to the good; but the latter delight in His presence, and try to please Him, whilst the former shrink from a Judge, who is of too pure a nature to behold iniquity.—The wicked wish for the rocks to cover them, mountains, or the angry sea, which we the other day surveyed, to hide them from the presence of that Being—in whose presence only they could find joy. You feel emotions that incite you to do good; and painful ones disturb you, when you have resisted the faithful internal monitor. The wiser, and the better you grow, the more visible, if I may use the expression, will God become—For wisdom consists in searching Him out—and goodness in endeavouring to copy his attributes.

To attain any thing great, a model must be held up to exercise our understanding, and engage our affections. A view of the disinterested goodness of God is therefore calculated to touch us more than can be conceived by a depraved mind. When the love of God is shed abroad in our hearts; true courage will animate our conduct, for nothing can hurt those who trust in Him. If the desire of acting right is ever present with us, if admiration of goodness fills our souls; we may be said to pray constantly. And if we try to do justice to all our fellow-creatures, and even to the brute creation; and assist them as far as we can, we prove whose servants we are, and whose laws we transcribe in our lives.

Never be very anxious, when you pray, what *words* to use; regulate your *thoughts;* and recollect that virtue calms the passions, gives clearness to the understanding, and opens it to pleasures that the thoughtless and vicious have not a glimpse of. You must, believe me, be acquainted with God to find peace, to rise superior to worldly temptations. Habitual devotion is of the utmost consequence to our happiness, as what oftenest occupies the thoughts will influence our actions. But, observe what I say,—*that* devotion is mockery and selfishness, which does not improve our moral character.

Men, of old, prayed to the devil, sacrificed their children to him; and committed every kind of barbarity and impurity. But we who serve a long-suffering God should pity the weakness of our fellow-creatures; we must not beg for mercy and not shew it;—we must not acknowledge that we have offended, without trying to avoid doing so in future. We are to deal with our fellow-creatures as we expect to be dealt with. This is practical pray-er!—Those who practise it feel frequently sublime pleasures, and lively hopes animate them in this vale of tears; that seem a foretaste of the felicity they will enjoy, when the understanding is more enlightened, and the affections properly regulated.

To-morrow I will take you to visit the school-mistress of the village, and relate her story, to enforce what I have been saying.

Now you may go and dance one or two dances; and I will join you after I have taken a walk, which I wish to enjoy alone.

CHAPTER XVI

The Benefits arising from Devotion.—
The History of the Village School-mistress.—
Fatal Effects of Inattention to Expences, in the History of Mr. Lofty.

T HE next morning Mrs. Mason desired the children to get their work, and draw near the table whilst she related the promised history; and in the afternoon, if the weather be fine, they were to visit the village school-mistress.

Her father, the honourable Mr. Lofty, was the youngest son of a noble family; his education had been liberal, though his fortune was small. His relations, however, seemed determined to push him forward in life, before he disobliged them by marrying the daughter of a country clergyman, an accomplished, sensible woman.

Some time after the birth of his daughter Anna, his elder brother, the Earl of Caer-marthen, was reconciled to him; but this reconciliation only led him into expences, which his limited fortune could not bear. Mr. Lofty had a high sense of honour, and rather a profuse turn; he was, beside, a very humane man, and gave away much more than he could afford to give, when his compassion was excited. He never did a mean action; but sometimes an ostentatious pride tarnished the lustre of very splendid ones, made them appear to judicious eyes, more like tinsel, than gold. I will account for it. His first impulse arose from sensibility, and the second from an immoderate desire of human applause: for he seemed not to be alive to devotional feelings, or to have that rock to rest on, which will support a frail being, and give true dignity to a character, though all nature combined to crush it.

Mrs. Lofty was not a shining character—but I will read you a part of a letter, which her daughter, the lady we are to visit, wrote to me.

"This being the anniversary of the day on which an ever loved, and much revered parent was released from the bondage of mortality, I observe it with particular seriousness, and with gratitude; for her sorrows were great, her trials severe—but her conduct was blameless: yet the world admired her not; her silent, modest virtues, were not formed to attract the notice of the injudicious crowd, and her understanding was not brilliant enough to excite admiration. But she was regardless of the opinion of the world; she sought her reward in the source from whence her virtue was derived—and she found it.—He, who, for wise and merciful purposes, suffered her to be afflicted, supported her under her trials; thereby calling forth the exercise of those virtues with which He had adorned her gentle soul; and imparting to her a degree of heart-felt comfort, which no earthly blessing could afford."

This amiable parent died when Anna was near eighteen, and left her to the care of her father, whose high spirit she had imbibed. However, the religious principles which her mother had instilled regulated her notions of honour, and so elevated her character, that her heart was regulated by her understanding.

Her father who had insensibly involved himself in debt, after her mother's death, tried many different schemes of life, all of which, at first wore a promising aspect; but wanting that suppleness of temper, that enables people to rise in the world, his struggles, instead of extricating, sunk him still deeper. Wanting also the support of religion, he became sour, easily irritated, and almost hated a world whose applause he had once eagerly courted. His affairs were at last in such a desperate state, that he was obliged, reluctantly, to accept of an invitation from his brother, who with his wife, a weak fine lady, intended to spend some time on the continent; his daughter was, of course, to be of the party.

The restraint of obligations did not suit his temper, and feeling himself dependent, he imagined every one meant to insult him.

Some sarcasms were thrown out one day by a gentleman, in a large company; they were not personal, yet he took fire. His sore mind was easily hurt, he resented them; and heated by wine, they both said more than their cool reason would have suggested. Mr. Lofty imagined his honour was wounded, and the next morning sent him a challenge—They met—and he killed his antagonist, who, dying, pardoned him, and declared that the sentiments which had given him so much offence, fell from him by accident, and were not levelled at any person.

The dying man lamented, that the thread of a thoughtless life had been so suddenly snapped—the name of his wife and children he could not articulate, when something like a prayer for them escaped his livid lips, and shook his exhausted frame—The blood flowed in a copious stream—vainly did Mr. Lofty endeavour to staunch it—the heart lost its vital nourishment—and the soul escaped as he pressed the hand of his destroyer.—Who, when he found him breathless, ran home, and rushed in a hurry into his own chamber. The dead man's image haunted his imagination—he started—imagined that he was at his elbow—and shook the hand that had received the dying grasp—yet still it was pressed, and the pressure entered into his very soul—On the table lay two pistols, he caught up one,—and shot himself.—The report alarmed the family—the servants and his daughter, for his brother was not at home, broke open the door,—and she saw the dreadful sight! As there was still some appearance of life, a trembling ray—she supported the body, and sent for assistance. But he soon died in her arms without speaking, before the servant returned with a surgeon.

Horror seized her, another pistol lay charged on the table, she caught it up, but religion held her hand—she knelt down by a dead father, and prayed to a superior one. Her mind grew calmer—yet still she passionately wished she had but heard him speak, or that she had conveyed comfort to his departing spirit—where, where would it find comfort? again she was obliged to have recourse to prayer.

After the death of her father, her aunt treated her as if she were a mere dependent on her bounty; and expected her to be an humble companion in every sense of the word. The visitors took the tone from her ladyship, and numberless were the mortifications she had to bear.

The entrance of a person about business interrupted the narration; but Mrs. Mason promised to resume it after dinner.

CHAPTER XVII

The Benefits arising from Devotion—
The History of the Village School-mistress concluded.

As SOON AS THE CLOTH was removed, Mrs. Mason concluded the narration; and the girls forgot their fruit whilst they were listening to the sequel.

Anna endured this treatment some years, and had an opportunity of acquiring a knowledge of the world and her own heart. She visited her mother's father, and would have remained with him; but she determined not to lessen the small pittance which he had anxiously saved out of a scanty income for two other grand-children. She thought continually of her situation, and found, on examining her understanding, that the fashionable circle in which she moved, could not at any rate have afforded her much satisfaction, or even amusement; though the neglect and contempt that she met with rendered her very uncomfortable. She had her father's spirit of independence, and determined to shake of[f] the galling yoke which she had long struggled with, and try to earn her own subsistence. Her acquaintance expostulated with her, and represented the miseries of poverty, and the mortifications and difficulties that she would have to encounter. Let it be so, she replied, it is much preferable to swelling the train of the proud or vicious great, and despising myself for bearing their impertinence, for eating their bitter bread;—better, indeed, is a dinner of herbs with contentment. My wants are few. When I am my own mistress, the crust I earn will be sweet, and the water that moistens it will not be mingled with tears of sorrow or indignation.

To shorten my story; she came to me, after she had attempted several plans, and requested my advice. She would not accept of any considerable favour, and declared that the greatest would be, to put her in a way of supporting herself, without forfeiting her highly valued independence. I knew not what to advise; but whilst I was debating the matter with myself, I happened to mention, that we were in want of a school-mistress. She eagerly adopted the plan, and persevering in it these last ten years, I find her a most valuable acquisition to our society.

She was formed to shine in the most brilliant circle—yet she relinquished it, and patiently labours to improve the children consigned to her management, and tranquilize her own mind. She succeeds in both.

She lives indeed alone, and has all day only the society of children; yet she enjoys many true pleasures; dependence on God is her support, and devotion her comfort. Her lively affections are therefore changed into a love of virtue and truth: and these exalted speculations have given an uncommon dignity to her manners; for she seems above the world, and its trifling commotions. At her meals, gratitude to Heaven supplies the place of society. She has a tender, social heart, and, as she cannot sweeten her solitary draught, by expressing her good wishes to her fellow creatures, an ejaculation to Heaven for the welfare of her friends is the substitute. This circumstance I heard her mention to her grandfather, who sometimes visits her.

I will now make some alteration in my dress, for when I visit those who have been reduced from their original place in society by misfortunes, I always attend a little to ceremony; lest too much familiarity should appear like disrespect.

CHAPTER XVIII

Visit to the School-mistress.—True and false Pride.

THEIR DRESS was soon adjusted, and the girls plucked flowers to adorn themselves, and a nosegay to present to the school-mistress, whose garden was but small.

They met the children just released from confinement; the swarm came humming round Mrs. Mason, endeavouring to catch her eye, and obtain the notice they were so proud of. The girls made their best courtesies, blushing; and the boys hung down their heads, and kicked up the dust, in scraping a bow of respect.

They found their mistress preparing to drink tea, to refresh herself after the toils of the day; and, with the ease peculiar to well-bred people, she quickly enabled them to partake of it, by giving the tea-board a more sociable appearance.

The harvest-home was soon the subject of conversation, and the harper was mentioned. The family pride of the Welsh, said Anna, has often diverted me; I have frequently heard the inhabitants of a little hut, that could scarcely be distinguished from the pig-sty, which stood in the front of it, boast of their ancestors and despise trade. They have informed me, that one branch of their family built the middle aisle of the church; that another beautified the chancel, and gave the ten commandments, which blaze there in letters of gold. Some rejoice that their forefathers sleep in the most conspicuous tombs—and that their ashes have an inscription to point out where they are returning to their mother earth. And those graves, which only a little stone at the head gives consequence to, are adorned every Sunday with flowers, or ever-greens. We perceive, in all the various customs of men, a desire to live in the past and in the future, if I may be allowed the expression.

Mrs. Mason then observed, that of all the species of pride which carry a man out of himself, family pride was the most beneficial to society. Pride of wealth produces vanity and ostentation; but that of blood seems to inspire high notions of honour, and to banish meanness. Yet it is productive of many ill consequences, the most obvious is, that it renders individuals respectable to the generality, whose merit is only reflected: and sometimes the want of this accidental advantage throws the most shining personal virtues and abilities into obscurity. In weak minds this pride degenerates into the most despicable folly; and the wise will not condescend to accept of fame at second-hand, replied Anna. We ought to be proud of our original, but we should trace it to our Heavenly Father, who breathed into us the breath of life.—We are his children when we try to resemble Him, when we are convinced that truth and goodness must constitute the very essence of the soul; and that the pursuit of them will produce happiness, when the vain distinctions of mortals will fade away, and their pompous escutcheons moulder with more vulgar dust! But remember, my young friends, virtue is immortal; and goodness arises from a quick perception of truth, and actions conformable to the conviction.

Different subjects beguiled the time, till the closing evening admonished them to return home; and they departed reluctantly, filled with respect.

CHAPTER XIX

Charity.—The History of Peggy
and her Family.—The Sailor's Widow.

I HAVE OFTEN REMARKED to you, said Mrs. Mason, one morning, to her pupils, that we are all dependent on each other; and this dependence is wisely ordered by our Heavenly Father, to call forth many virtues, to exercise the best affections of the human heart, and fix them into habits. While we impart pleasure we receive it, and feel the grandeur of our immortal soul, as it is constantly struggling to spread itself into futurity.

Perhaps the greatest pleasure I have ever received, has arisen from the habitual exercise of charity, in its various branches: the view of a distressed object has made me now think of conversing about one branch of it, that of giving alms.

You know Peggy, the young girl whom I wish to have most about my person; I mean, I wish it for her own sake, that I may have an opportunity of improving her mind, and cultivating a good capacity. As to attendance, I never give much trouble to any fellow-creature; for I choose to be independent of caprice and artificial wants; unless indeed, when I am sick; then, I thankfully receive the assistance I would willingly give to others in the same situation. I believe I have not in the world a more faithful friend than Peggy; and her earnest desire to please me gratifies my benevolence, for I always observe with delight the workings of a grateful heart.

I lost a darling child, said Mrs. Mason, smothering a sigh, in the depth of winter—death had before deprived me of her father, and when I lost my child—he died again.

The wintery prospects suiting the temper of my soul, I have sat looking at a wide waste of tractless snow for hours; and the heavy sullen fog, that the feeble rays of the sun could not pierce, gave me back an image of my mind. I was unhappy, and the sight of dead nature accorded with my feelings—for all was dead to me.

As the snow began to melt, I took a walk, and observed the birds hopping about with drooping wings, or mute on the leafless boughs. The mountain, whose sides had lost the snow, looked black; yet still some remained on the summit, and formed a contrast to diversify the dreary prospect.

I walked thoughtfully along, when the appearance of a poor man, who did not beg, struck me very forcibly. His shivering limbs were scarcely sheltered from the cold by the tattered garments that covered him; and he had a sharp, famished look. I stretched out my hand with some relief in it, I would not enquire into the particulars of such obvious distress. The poor wretch caught my hand, and hastily dropping on his knees, thanked me in an extacy, as if he had almost lost sight of hope, and was overcome by the sudden relief. His attitude, for I cannot bear to see a fellow-creature kneel, and eager thanks, oppressed my weak spirits, so that I could not for a moment ask him any more questions; but as soon as I recollected myself, I learned from him the misfortunes that had reduced him to such extreme distress, and he hinted, that I could not easily guess the good I had done. I imagined from this hint that he was meditating his own destruction when I saw him, to spare himself the misery of seeing his infant perish,—starved to death, in every sense of the word.

I will now hasten to the sequel of the account. His wife had lately had a child, she was very ill at the time, and want of proper food, and a defence against the inclemency of the weather, hurried her out of the world. The poor child, Peggy, had sucked in disease and nourishment together, and now even that wretched source had failed—the breast was cold that had afforded the scanty support; and the little innocent smiled, unconscious of its misery. I sent for her, added Mrs. Mason, and her father dying a few years after, she has ever been a favourite charge of mine, and nursing of her, in some measure, dispelled the gloom in which I had been almost lost.—Ah! my children, you know not how many, "houseless heads bide the pitiless storm!"

I received soon after a lesson of resignation from a poor woman, who was a practical philosopher.

She had lost her husband, a sailor, and lost his wages also, as she could not prove his death. She came to me to beg some pieces of silk, to make some pin-cushions for the boarders of a neighbouring school. Her lower weeds were patched with different coloured rags; but they spoke not variety of wretchedness, on the contrary, they shewed a mind so content, that want, and bodily pain, did not prevent her thinking of the opinion of casual observers. This woman lost a husband and a child suddenly, and her daily bread was precarious.—I cheered the widow's heart, and my own was not quite solitary.

But I am growing melancholy, whilst I am only desirous of pointing out to you how very beneficial charity is—because it enables us to find comfort when all our worldly comforts are blighted: besides, when our bowels yearn to our fellow-creatures, we feel that the love of God dwelleth in us—and then we cannot always go on our way sorrowing.

CHAPTER XX

Visit to Mrs. Trueman.—The Use of Accomplishments.—
Virtue the Soul of all.

IN THE AFTERNOON they visited Mrs. Trueman unexpectedly, and found her sitting in the garden playing to her children, who danced on the green sod. She approached to receive them, and laid aside her guitar; but, after some conversation, Mrs. Mason desired her to take it up again, and the girls joined in the request. While she was singing Mary whispered Mrs. Mason, that she would give the world to be able to sing as well. The whisper was not so low but a part of it reached Mrs. Trueman's ears, who said to her, smiling, my young friend, you value accomplishments much too highly—they may give grace to virtue—but are nothing without solid worth.—Indeed, I may say more, for any thing like perfection in the arts cannot be attained, where a relish; nay, a delight in what is true and noble is wanting. A superficial observer may be pleased with a picture in which fine colours predominate; and quick movements in music may tickle the ear, though they never reach the heart: but it is the simple strain which affection animates, that we listen to with interest and delight. Mr. Trueman has a taste for the fine arts; and I wish in every thing to be his companion. His conversation has improved my judgment, and the affection an intimate knowledge of his virtues has inspired, increases the love which I feel for the whole human race. He lives retired from the world; to amuse him after the business of the day is over, and my babes asleep, I sing to him. A desire to please, and the pleasure I read in his eyes, give to my music energy and tenderness. When he is ruffled by worldly cares, I try to smooth his wrinkled brow, and think mine a voice of melody, when it has had that effect.

Very true, replied Mrs. Mason, accomplishments should be cultivated to render us pleasing to our domestic friends; virtue is necessary; it must ever be the foundation of our peace and usefulness; but when we are capable of affection, we wish to have something peculiar to ourselves. We study the taste of our friends, and endeavour to conform to it; but, in doing so, we ought rather to improve our own abilities than servilely to copy theirs. Observe, my dear girls, Mrs. Trueman's distinction, her accomplishments are for her friends, her virtues for the world in general.

I should think myself vain, and my soul little, answered Mrs. Trueman, if the applause of the whole world, on the score of abilities, which did not add any real lustre to my character, could afford me matter of exultation. The approbation of my own heart, the humble hope of pleasing the Most High, elevates my soul; and I feel, that in a future state, I may enjoy an unspeakable degree of happiness, though I now only experience a faint foretaste. Next to these sublime emotions, which I cannot describe, and the joy resulting from doing good; I am happy when I can amuse those I love; it is not then vanity, but tenderness, that spurs me on, and my songs, my drawings, my every action, has something of my heart in it. When I can add to the innocent enjoyments of my children, and improve them at the same time, are not my accomplishments of use? In the same style, when I vary the pleasures of my fire-side, I make my husband forget that it is a lonely one; and he returns to look for elegance at home, elegance that he himself gave the polish to; and which is only affected, when it does not flow from virtuous affections.

I beg your pardon, I expatiate too long on my favorite topic; my desire to rectify your notions must plead my excuse.

Mr. Trueman now joined them, and brought with him some of his finest fruit. After tea Mrs. Trueman shewed them some of her drawings; and, to comply with their repeated request, played on the harpsichord, and Mr. Trueman took his violin to accompany her. Then the children were indulged with a dance, each had her favourite tune played in turn.

As they returned home, the girls were eagerly lavishing praises on Mrs. Trueman; and Mary said, I cannot tell why, but I feel so glad when she takes notice of me. I never saw any one look so good-natured, cried Caroline. Mrs. Mason joined in the conversation. You justly remarked that she is good-natured; you remember her history, she loves truth, and she is ever exercising benevolence and love—from the insect, that she avoids treading on, her affection may be traced to that Being who lives for ever.—And it is from her goodness her agreeable qualities spring.

CHAPTER XXI

The Benefit of bodily Pain.—Fortitude the Basis of Virtue.— The Folly of Irresolution.

T HE CHILDREN had been playing in the garden for some time, whilst Mrs. Mason was reading alone. But she was suddenly alarmed by the cries of Caroline, who ran into the room in great distress. Mary quickly followed, and explaining the matter said, that her sister had accidently disturbed some wasps, who were terrified, and of course stung her. Remedies were applied to assuage the pain; yet all the time she uttered the loudest and most silly complaints, regardless of the uneasiness she gave those who were exerting themselves to relieve her.

In a short time the smart abated, and then her friend thus addressed her, with more than usual gravity. I am sorry to see a girl of your age weep on account of bodily pain; it is a proof of a weak mind—a proof that you cannot employ yourself about things of consequence. How often must I tell you that the Most High is educating us for eternity?

> "The term virtue, comes from a word signifying strength. Fortitude of mind is, therefore, the basis of every virtue, and virtue belongs to a being, that is weak in its nature, and strong only in will and resolution."

Children early feel bodily pain, to habituate them to bear the conflicts of the soul, when they become reasonable creatures. This, I say, is the first trial, and I like to see that proper pride which strives to conceal its sufferings. Those who, when young, weep if the least trifle annoys them, will never, I fear, have sufficient strength of mind, to encounter all the miseries that can afflict the body, rather than act meanly to avoid them. Indeed, this seems to be the essential difference between a great and a little mind: the former knows how to endure—whilst the latter suffers an immortal soul to be depressed, lost in its abode; suffers the inconveniences which attack the one to overwhelm the other. The soul would always support the body, if its superiority was felt, and invigorated by exercise. The Almighty, who never afflicts but to produce some good end, first sends diseases to children to teach them patience and fortitude; and when by degrees they have learned to bear them, they have acquired some virtue.

In the same manner, cold or hunger, when accidentally encountered, are not evils; they make *us feel what wretches feel,* and teach us to be tender-hearted. Many of your fellow-creatures daily bear what you cannot for a moment endure without complaint. Besides, another advantage arises from it, after you have felt hunger, you will not be very anxious to choose the particular kind of food that is to satisfy it. You will then be freed from a frivolous care.

When it is necessary to take a nauseous draught, swallow it at once, and do not make others sick whilst you are hesitating, though you know that you ought to take it. If a tooth is to be drawn, or any other disagreeable operation to be performed, determine resolutely that it shall be done immediately; and debate not, when you clearly see the step that you ought to take. If I see a child act in this way, I am ready to embrace it, my soul yearns for it—I perceive the dawning of a character that will be useful to society, as it prepares its soul for a nobler field of action.

Believe me, it is the patient endurance of pain, that will enable you to resist your passions; after you have borne bodily pain, you will have firmness enough to sustain the still more excruciating agonies of the mind. You will not, to banish momentary cares, plunge into dissipation, nor to escape a present inconvenience, forget that you should hold fast virtue as the only substantial good.

I should not value the affection of a person who would not bear pain and hunger to serve me; nor is that benevolence warm, which shrinks from encountering difficulties, when it is necessary, in order to be useful to any fellow creature.

There is a just pride, a noble ambition in some minds, that I greatly admire. I have seen a little of it in Mary! for whilst she pities others, she imagines that she could bear their inconveniences herself; and she seems to feel more uneasiness, when she observes the sufferings of others, than I could ever trace on her countenance under the immediate pressure of pain.

Remember you are to bear patiently the infirmities of the weakest of your fellow-creatures; but to yourselves you are not to be equally indulgent.

CHAPTER XXII

Journey to London.

THE GIRLS were visibly improved; an air of intelligence began to animate Caroline's fine features; and benevolence gave her eyes the humid sparkle which is so beautiful and engaging. The interest that we take in the fate of others, attaches them to ourselves;—thus Caroline's goodness inspired more affection than her beauty.

Mary's judgment grew every day clearer; or, more properly speaking, she acquired experience; and her lively feelings fixed the conclusions of reason in her mind. Whilst Mrs. Mason was rejoicing in their apparent improvement, she received a letter from their father, requesting her to allow his daughters to spend the winter in town, as he wished to procure them the best masters, an advantage that the country did not afford. With reluctance she consented, determining to remain with them a short time; and preparations were quickly made for the journey.

The wished for morning arrived, and they set off in a tumult of spirits; sorry to leave the country, yet delighted with the prospect of visiting the metropolis. This hope soon dried the tears which had bedewed their cheeks; for the parting with Mrs. Mason was not anticipated. The autumnal views were new to them; they saw the hedges exhibit various colours, and the trees stripped of their leaves; but they were not disposed to moralize.

For some time after their arrival, every thing they saw excited wonder and admiration; and not till they were a little familiarized with the new objects, did they ask reasonable questions.

Several presents recruited their purses; and they requested Mrs. Mason to allow them to buy some trifles they were in want of. The request was modest, and she complied.

CHAPTER XXIII

Charity.—Shopping.—The distressed Stationer.—
Mischievous Consequences of delaying Payment.

As THEY WALKED in search of a shop, they both determined to purchase pocket-books; but their friend desired them not to spend all their money at once, as they would meet many objects of charity in the numerous streets of the metropolis. I do not wish you, she continued, to relieve every beggar that you casually meet; yet should any one attract your attention, obey the impulse of your heart, which will lead you to pay them for exercising your compassion, and do not suffer the whispers of selfishness, that they may be imposters, to deter you. However, I would have you give but a trifle when you are not certain the distress is real, and reckon it given for pleasure. I for my part would rather be deceived five hundred times, than doubt once without reason.

They stopped at a small shop, Mrs. Mason always sought out such; for, said she, I may help those who perhaps want assistance; bargains I never seek, for I wish every one to receive the just value for their goods.

In the shop which they chanced to enter, they did not find the kind of pocket-book that they had previously fixed on, and therefore wished precipitately to leave it; but were detained by their more considerate friend. While they had been turning over the trinkets, the countenance of the woman, who served them, caught her eye, and she observed her eager manner of recommending the books. You have given much unnecessary trouble, said she, to the mistress of the shop; the books are better, and more expensive than you intended to purchase, but I will make up the deficiency. A beam of pleasure enlivened the woman's swollen eyes; and Mrs. Mason, in the mild accents of compassion, said, if it is not an impertinent question, will you tell me from what cause your visible distress arises? perhaps I may have it in my power to relieve you.—The woman burst into tears.—Indeed, Madam, you have already relieved me; for the money you have laid out will enable me to procure some food for my poor little grandchildren, and to send a meal to their poor father, who is now confined for debt, though a more honest man never breathed. Ah! Madam, I little thought I should come to this—Yesterday his wife died, poor soul! I really believe things going so cross broke her heart. He has been in jail these five months; I could not manage the shop, or buy what was proper to keep up the credit of it, so business has been continually falling off; yet, if his debts were paid, he would now be here, and we should have money in our pockets. And what renders it more provoking, the people who owe us most are very rich. It is true, they live in such a very high style, and keep such a number of horses and servants, that they are often in want of money, and when they have it, they mostly have some freak in their heads, and do not think of paying poor trades-people. At first we were afraid to ask for payment lest we should lose their custom, and so it proved; when we did venture, forced by necessity, they sent to other shops, without discharging our demand.

And, my dear Madam, this is not all my grief; my son, before his misfortunes, was one of the most sober, industrious young men in London; but now he is not like the same man. He had nothing to do in the jail, and to drive away care he learned to drink; he said it was a comfort to forget himself, and he would add an oath—I never heard him swear till then. I took pains when he was a child to teach him his prayers, and he rewarded me by being a dutiful son. The case is quite altered now—he seems to have lost all natural affection—he heeds not his mother's tears.—Her sobs almost suffocated her, as she strove to go on—He will bring my grey hairs with sorrow to the grave—and yet I pity my poor boy, he is shut up with such a number of profligate wretches, who laugh at what is right. Every farthing I send him he spends in liquor, and used to make his poor wife pawn her clothes to buy him drink—she was happy to die, it was well for her not to live to hear the babe she gave suck to despise her!

A passion of tears relieved the sufferer, and she called her grandchildren; these innocent babes, said she, I shall not be able to keep them, they must go to the workhouse. If the quality did but know what they make us poor industrious people suffer—surely they would be more considerate.

Mrs. Mason gave her something to supply her present wants, and promised to call on her again before she left town.

They walked silently down two or three streets; I hope you have learned to think, my dear girls, said Mrs. Mason, and that your hearts have felt the emotions of compassion; need I make any comments on the situation of the poor woman we have just left. You perceive that those who neglect to pay their debts, do more harm than they imagine; perhaps, indeed, some of these very people do, what is called, a noble action, give away a large sum, and are termed generous; nay, very probably, weep at a tragedy, or when reading an affecting tale. They then boast of their sensibility—when, alas! neglecting the foundation of all virtue, *justice,* they have occasioned exquisite distress;—led a poor wretch into vice; heaped misery on helpless infancy, and drawn tears from the aged widow.

CHAPTER XXIV

Visit to a poor Family in London.—Idleness the Parent of Vice.—
Prodigality and Generosity incompatible.—
The Pleasures of Benevolence.—True and false Motives for saving.

AFTER THE IMPRESSION which the story, and the sight of the family had made, was a little worn off; Caroline begged leave to buy one toy, and then another, till her money was quite gone. When Mrs. Mason found it was all expended, she looked round for an object in distress; a poor woman soon presented herself, and her meagre countenance gave weight to her tale.—A babe, as meagre, hung at her breast, which did not seem to contain sufficient moisture to wet its parched lips.

On enquiry they found that she lodged in a neighbouring garret. Her husband had been out of employment a long time, and was now sick. The master who had formerly given him work, lost gradually great part of his business; for his best customers were grown so fond of foreign articles, that his goods grew old in the warehouse. Consequently a number of hands were dismissed, who not immediately finding employment elsewhere, were reduced to the most extreme distress. The truth of this account a reputable shopkeeper attested; and he added that many of the unhappy creatures, who die unpitied at the gallows, were first led into vice by accident[al] idleness.

They ascended the dark stairs, scarcely able to bear the bad smells that flew from every part of a small house, that contained in each room a family, occupied in such an anxious manner to obtain the necessaries of life, that its comforts never engaged their thoughts. The precarious meal was snatched, and the stomach did not turn, though the cloth, on which it was laid, was died in dirt. When to-morrow's bread is uncertain, who thinks of cleanliness? Thus does despair encrease the misery, and consequent disease aggravate the horrors of poverty!

They followed the woman into a low garret, that was never visited by the chearful rays of the sun.—A man, with a sallow complexion, and long beard, sat shivering over a few cinders in the bottom of a broken grate, and two more children were on the ground, half naked, near him, breathing the same noxious air. The gaiety natural to their age, did not animate their eyes, half sunk in their sockets; and, instead of smiles, premature wrinkles had found a place in their lengthened visages. Life was nipped in the bud; shut up just as it began to unfold itself. "A frost, a killing frost," had destroyed the parent's hopes: they seemed to come into the world only to crawl half formed,—to suffer, and to die.

Mrs. Mason desired the girls to relieve the family; Caroline hung down her head abashed—wishing the paltry ornaments which she had thoughtlessly bought, in the bottom of the sea. Mary, meanwhile, proud of the new privilege, emptied her purse; and Caroline, in a supplicating tone entreated Mrs. Mason to allow her to give her neck-handkerchief to the little infant.

Mrs. Mason desired the woman to call on her the next day; and they left the family cheered by their bounty.

Caroline expected the reproof that soon proceeded from the mouth of her true friend. I am glad that this accident has occured, to prove to you that prodigality and generosity are incompatible. Æconomy and self-denial are necessary in every station, to enable us to be generous, and to act conformably to the rules of justice.

Mary may this night enjoy peaceful slumbers; idle fancies, foolishly indulged, will not float in her brain; she may, before she closes her eyes, thank God, for allowing her to be His instrument of mercy. Will the trifles that you have purchased, afford you such heartfelt delight, Caroline?

Selfish people save to gratify their own caprices and appetites; the benevolent curb both, to give scope to the nobler feelings of the human heart. When we squander money idly, we defraud the poor, and deprive our own souls of their most exalted food. If you wish to be useful, govern your desires, and wait not till distress obtrudes itself—search it out. In the country it is not always attended with such shocking circumstances as at present; but in large cities, many garrets contain families, similar to those we have seen this afternoon. The money spent in indulging the vain wishes of idleness, and a childish fondness for pretty things not regulated by reason, would relieve the misery that my soul shrinks back from contemplating.

CHAPTER XXV

Mrs. Mason's farewell Advice to her young Friends.

THE DAY BEFORE Mrs. Mason was to leave her pupils, she took a hand of each, and

Œconomy & Self-denial are necessary, in
every station, to enable us to be genero—

pressing them tenderly in her own, tears started into her eyes—I tremble for you, my dear girls, for you must now practise by yourselves some of the virtues which I have been endeavouring to inculcate: and I shall anxiously wait for the summer, to see what progress you have made by yourselves.

We have conversed on several very important subjects; pray do not forget the conclusions I have drawn.

I now, as my last present, give you a book, in which I have written the subjects that we have discussed. Recur frequently to it, for the stories illustrating the instruction it contains, you will not feel in such a great degree the want of my personal advice. Some of the reasoning you may not thoroughly comprehend, but, as your understandings ripen, you will feel its full force.

Avoid anger; exercise compassion; and love truth. Recollect, that from religion your chief comfort must spring, and never neglect the duty of prayer. Learn from experience the comfort that arises from making known your wants and sorrows to the wisest and best of Beings, in whose hands are the issues, not only of this life, but of that which is to come.

Your father will allow you a certain stipend; you have already *felt* the pleasure of doing good; ever recollect that the wild pursuits of fancy must be conquered, to enable you to gratify benevolent wishes, and that you must practise œconomy in trifles to have it in your power to be generous on great occasions. And the good you intend to do, do quickly;—for know that a trifling duty neglected, is a great fault, and the present time only is at your command.

You are now candidates for my friendship, and on your advancement in virtue my regard will in future depend. Write often to me, I will punctually answer your letters; but let me have the genuine sentiments of your hearts. In expressions of affection and respect, do not deviate from truth to gain what you wish for, or to turn a period prettily.

Adieu! when you think of your friend, observe her precepts; and let the recollection of my affection, give additional weight to the truths which I have endeavoured to instill; and, to reward my care, let me hear that you love and practice virtue.

FINIS.

The Fairy Spectator;
or, The Invisible Monitor

By ELLENOR FENN

THE VISION.

THE

FAIRY SPECTATOR;

OR, THE

Invisible Monitor.

BY

Mrs. *TEACHWELL*

AND

Her FAMILY.

London.

PRINTED BY AND FOR JOHN MARSHALL, NO. 4,
A DERMARY CHURCH-YARD, BOW-LANE;
AND NO. 17, QUEEN-STREET, CHEAPSIDE.

ELLENOR FRERE *(1743–1813) became Mrs. John Fenn in 1766 and Lady Fenn in 1787 when her husband was knighted. She was also known as Mrs. Lovechild, Mrs. Teachwell, and even Solomon Lovechild, pseudonyms used in at least a dozen and a half books she wrote initially for her own nieces and nephews. The homemade books which she bound herself for her relatives were eventually published by John Marshall in undated editions. In short titles they include* Fables in Monosyllables *(1783),* Rational Sports *(1783?),* Cobwebs to Catch Flies *(ca. 1783), and* The Juvenile Tatler *(1789). In the last-mentioned title, Mrs. Teachwell presents an urn to her young lady students in which they place their compositions. "The Innocent Romp" is especially lively: Miss Briskly, full of tricks, dresses a cat in baby clothes and takes it to the curate to be christened.* The Juvenile Tatler *and* The Female Guardian *(1784), also by Lady Fenn, show the influence of the adult journal on the juvenile book.*

The Invisible Monitor, *the subtitle to* The Fairy Spectator, *is a better signpost for those who expect fairy tales from an author who vowed "there is no need of invention; the world is full of wonders"* (The Rational Dame, *ca. 1785). Note that the first words of the fairy are: "I am your guardian, to watch over your mind." Enchanted mirrors are used merely to show the child as she is and as she might be.*

Interest in science, as opposed to fantasy, prevails in Lady Fenn's books for children. In Cobwebs to Catch Flies *she suggests that children study gnats on windows, flies on sugar, and then get out their microscopes. She blames nurses for tainting girls with a "groundless fear of insects, and innocent reptiles." Boys, she complains, often show "want of tenderness to the same creatures." The interest in natural science and attention to Rousseau make Fenn's books typical of the many works suddenly appearing for the children of the 1780s and 1790s. Fenn's publisher, John Marshall, was already advertising "seventy sorts of books" for children in the mid 1780s, and Elizabeth Newbery, the wife of Francis Newbery (John Newbery's nephew), put out over three hundred juvenile books from 1788 to 1802.*

For a facsimile reprint of another Fenn book see Fables in Monosyllables with Morals to a Set of Fables *(New York: Johnson Reprint Corp., 1970).* The Fairy Spectator *is reprinted here from an undated copy of what probably is the first edition from the Rare Book Room of the University of Illinois Library, Urbana, Illinois.*

To MISS M— — — —. My Dear, I dedicate this little book to you as a token of affection.

Were I a Fairy I should devote much of my attention to you. Had I the Bonnet which Miss *Child* prudently declined accepting, I should be frequently at your elbow: but if I were in possession of the wonderful Ring which was offered to her, I should, probably, sometimes conceal myself from your sight, for the friendly purpose of remarking your conduct when you suppose yourself to be unobserved: and I hope that I should have the pleasure to see you act always, as if you were in the presence of your dear Mamma; or, to speak in still higher terms, as if you remembered that *there is an Eye which sees us wherever we are.*

These are *my* thoughts: now I will tell you *yours.*

You think, that if you had such a pair of Looking-glasses as those which were placed in Miss *Child*'s closet, you would consult them on every occasion; and always be careful to act in a becoming manner.

You think, that any little girl, who had Miss *Playful*'s Rose, would be most exceedingly circumspect in her behaviour.

You think, that with Miss *Child*'s Locket, you should surely never be guilty of a fault.

Let us strive to improve these thoughts, by doing what is in our power.—I will endeavour to improve you by admonition, though I cannot drop from the bell of a Lilly to attend you. Do you make the best use of the opportunities of improvement you enjoy; which, (though not supernatural) are great; for though no Fairy watches over you, you are blest with one of the best of mothers! That her care for you, and the rest of her children, may be blessed with success, is the sincere wish of,

My dear, Your affectionate friend,
E — — — — — — F — — —.

THE DREAM.

ONE MORNING Miss *Sprightly,* in stead of rising the moment she was called, burst into tears, and complained that she was awakened from the most pleasing dream which she ever had in her life.

Mrs. *Teachwell* inquired whether she was sick, that she was so slow in rising?

Madam, said she, I beg your pardon, but I cannot banish the thought of my dream. Idle girl! replied Mrs. *Teachwell,* make haste!

When the young ladies were running and playing in the garden, Miss *Sprightly* was found in a corner of a room in tears.

Mrs. *Teachwell* accosted her with great good-humour, saying,

My dear, what ails you?

Miss replied,

Madam, I am sorry and ashamed; I thought so much of my dream that I could not attend as I ought to do to my prayers.

Mrs. *Teachwell* answered,

My dear! I hope that your sorrow will produce amendment; you must lay aside all other thoughts when you pray.

Madam, said Miss *Sprightly,* I strive to do so, but I never can forget this dream.

Silly child! exclaimed the Governess, go and play; among your companions you will soon lose the thought of such folly.

Miss *Sprightly* courtesied, and was going out of the room, in obedience to Mrs. *Teachwell's* commands, but her air was so pensive, that the good lady called her back; and tapping her shoulder, asked what this dream was, which dwelt so long upon her thoughts? then bidding her sit down, indulged her wish to relate what had passed in her mind, which she did in the following words:

'I had been reading in *Gay's Fables;* and as the evening was very bright, I took the book into my chamber; after I was in bed I read *The Mother, Nurse,* and *Fairy;* and I believe that I dropped asleep with the book in my hand.'

But your dream? interrupted Mrs. *Teachwell.*

Madam, said Miss *Sprightly,* you shall hear. I thought that I was sitting alone in that pretty summer-house where I once drank tea with you, as a reward, because I came of my own accord to tell you that I chanced to break the looking-glass which hung in our chamber; and as I was amusing myself in observing a very fine dragon-fly, I was surprized with the sound of the softest, sweetest music that I had ever heard; at the same time the most delicate perfume seemed to proceed from the wings of the fly: I was all wonder; yet how did my surprize increase, to see the wings of the insect spread into a loose robe; and the little creature itself change to a woman no bigger than the smallest wax doll. O dear! she was so very pretty, that I could have looked at her all day: at last she spoke.

I am, said she, a Fairy. I am your guardian, to watch over your mind; although you never saw me before, yet I have always seen you. I have known every action, every word, nay, every thought.

I smiled and was going to speak, when she interrupted me; and, pulled out of her pocket two of the prettiest looking-glasses that ever were seen, she extended her hand; I reached to take them, and that moment I awoke. Miss *Friendly* was at my bedside, calling me to rise, else I should have tried to fall asleep again, in hope—I see you smile, Madam; but indeed I would have given my week's allowance to have recovered my dream.

THE CONVERSATION.

Mrs. TEACHWELL, who is indulgent to every innocent wish, which can be directed to any good purpose, told Miss *Sprightly,* that she would continue her dream, that is, said she, I will write you a dialogue, in which the Fairy shall converse; and I will give you a moral for your dream.—You know that stories of Fairies are all fabulous?

MISS SPRIGHTLY.

Oh yes! Madam.

MRS. TEACHWELL.

Do you wish for such a Fairy-guardian?

MISS SPRIGHTLY.

Very much, Madam.

MRS. TEACHWELL.

Why, my dear?

MISS SPRIGHTLY.

Because she would teach me to be good; for I should be ashamed to have even a naughty thought.

MRS. TEACHWELL.

I love you for your earnest wish to be good—but tell me, is not every action, word, and thought known?

MISS SPRIGHTLY.

To whom, Madam?

MRS. TEACHWELL.

Consider!

MISS SPRIGHTLY.

I know whom you mean, Madam.

MRS. TEACHWELL.

Well, my dear, are you not afraid to indulge a naughty thought?

MISS SPRIGHTLY.

I did not consider this before; for we are apt to forget what we do not see.

MRS. TEACHWELL.

Remember, that He, who sees all you do; who knows all you say, or think, will either reward you if you be good, or punish you if you be wicked.

'God, who seeth in secret, himself shall reward thee openly.'

Company coming in put an end to Mrs. *Teachwell*'s stay in the room, and Miss *Sprightly*, retiring to her own chamber, wrote as follows in her memorandum book.

May I always consider that God is every-where present; that He knows all which we do, say, or even think; and oh! may I always strive to please Him!

In the afternoon Mrs. *Teachwell* called Miss *Sprightly* to her: she ran with beating heart, hoping that her good Governess had written the dialogue, but it was only to give her some directions respecting her work. The little girl was rather disappointed, but she said to herself; my dear Mrs. *Teachwell* is very kind to promise me so much pleasure; and I ought not to trouble her with impatience, but wait her leisure, rather than teize her with inquiries when she will gratify my curiosity.

The next day Miss *Sprightly* was called to read the following story:

THE MIRRORS.

Shewing What we are, and What we ought to be.
Story of Miss Child.
WRITTEN AT THE REQUEST OF MISS SPRIGHTLY,
BY HER FRIEND, E. TEACHWELL.

STORY.

MISS CHILD had the misfortune to lose her mamma when she was but five years of age. She was put immediately under the direction of a governess: this lady was genteel in her appearance, and pleasing in her manner; had a fashionable address, and appeared to be at least *not* unaccomplished; these external advantages misled the judgment of some of her acquaintance, who overlooked her deficiency in more material points, and recommended her to Sir *Thomas Child,* as a person well qualified for the important office of educating his daughter.

It is easy to suppose that the attention of such a governess would be engrossed by outward accomplishments. Miss *Child's* person and dress appeared to great advantage, and her father being either too indolent, or too busy to inquire further, flattered himself that she improved very fast, and applauded the choice to which his friends had directed him.

But alas! the poor girl's mind and temper were neglected; so that she grew proud, selfish, peevish, and vain.

Miss had a closet which Lady *Child* had taken delight in fitting up for her, in a manner suited to her age. There were toys to amuse her, and such books as she was capable of understanding. There were *The Good Child's Delight; Little Stories for Little Folk; The History of Little Boys and Girls;* and many other entertaining and instructive little books, such as were suited to her tender age.*

These little books had cuts in them, which drew the young lady's attention at first; but they were soon laid aside, and the useful lessons which they contained forgotten.

Her ladyship's intention was, as her daughter advanced in years, to have removed the childish toys, and those first books, and to have filled the shelves with such volumes as were adapted to the more improved state of her mind.

Happy in the idea of seeing her daughter's progress, she had provided a *series* of books for her use, to be produced as she should have occasion for them; but her death put a stop to the improvement which she had planned; and the closet remained as childish a place as when the owner was really a baby.

Miss had an allowance for her pocket expenses; she kept no account, neither was any inquiry made how the money was expended, nor advice given how she ought to dispose of it.

The Governess carried her pupil constantly to the dancing-school, where she met a great many genteel children. Exceeding pains were taken that her coat should be made in the most fashionable manner; her cap be as smart as that of the first young lady there; but this care stopped at appearances.

A stranger would often say; 'Miss *Child* is a fine girl!'—but no body replied to that stranger, 'she is an amiable girl!'—Nay, some could not refrain from shaking their heads, and saying, 'it is a pity that her mind is not as agreeable as her person.'

THE CLOSET.

The Story of Miss Child continued.

O NE DAY MISS CHILD was sitting in her closet; she was engaged in looking over a box of feathers and artificial flowers, in order to make choice of such as should be most becoming to her complexion.

As she waved her head to admire herself in the glass, she saw the reflection of a very beautiful female looking over her shoulder: she started, and turning about, called out peevishly,—Who are you?

---

*Since the writing of this, many very pleasing books have appeared, which would have made a most agreeable addition to Lady *Child's* Library for her daughter on the projected plan.

FAIRY.

Your guardian.

MISS CHILD.

One governess is enough for me.

FAIRY.

I am the guardian of your mind; I know all your thoughts.

MISS CHILD.

What do I think now?

FAIRY.

That you neither desire nor need such a director.

MISS CHILD.

Bless me! it is true. What was I thinking when you came in?

FAIRY.

That you will buy a larger looking-glass to hang in your closet; now I have brought— *(producing something.)*

MISS CHILD.

Oh dear! what are they?

FAIRY.

Two mirrors.

MISS CHILD.

For me?

FAIRY.

If you please——take this.

MISS CHILD.

(looking in the glass, exclaims as she throws it down.)

Frightful!

FAIRY.

(picking it up, holds it to Miss Child, *who, seeing her own image again reflected, exclaims, with emotion.)*

Worse! I look uglier than I did before.

FAIRY.

This is because you are in an ill-humour; you are angry at having your faults observed.

MISS CHILD.

Certainly I am! Who is not?

FAIRY.

Now look in the other glass.

(holding it up.)

MISS CHILD.

Charming! oh, give *this* to me.

FAIRY.

I will give you both.

MISS CHILD.

I will not have *that*——take it away; it made me appear so hideous!

FAIRY.

You *shall* have both; if it be not your own fault you will appear agreeable in each. These are ENCHANTED GLASSES: *one* shows you as you *are,* the *other* as you *might* and *should be;* but they are best explained by examples, which I will give you; first making known to you the character of the persons who have had them in possession. I shall begin with Miss *Pettish.*

PEEVISHNESS AND PRODIGALITY.
Peevishness.
FAIRY.

M ISS PETTISH was so ill-tempered that every person hated her; till by the use of this pair of glasses, she reformed her disposition.

You are to observe, that I insist that my pupils shall write an account of what passes, as they find it in the mirrors; this is to be done journal-wise, in two opposite pages of the same book.

The first day that Miss *Pettish* had the mirrors, this was the account, by which you will find that the reflection of your image in *one* glass shows your disposition; in the *other,* teaches you how you ought to behave.

This then is Miss *Pettish*'s account from her appearance in the *First Glass*, which shows things *as they are.*

"My new cap, made by Miss *Modish,* was awry; I found fault with it, and though Mrs. *Fancy,* my Mamma's woman, said in excuse, that she had just received a letter, acquainting her that her sister was dangerously ill; and that her distress at this melancholy intelligence occasioned the mistake; yet I pouted, complained, and would have it altered immediately.

SECOND GLASS.
Showing things as they ought to be.

"I SHOULD HAVE merely observed civilly that there was a little mistake in the cap; and when I had heard the circumstance which occasioned it, I should have considered how concerned poor Mrs. *Fancy* must be at the melancholy account of her sister, that it was exceedingly obliging in her to attend at all to my dress in such a situation; and I ought to have begged of her to think no more of such trifles on my account: nay, I should have told her, that I would request leave of my Mamma for her to visit her sister."

PRODIGALITY.

M ISS LAVISH spent all the money which she received as soon as she had it; she fancied herself *generous,* because it sometimes happened by chance that an object fell in her way, just as some person had given her money; and in that case she parted from it without thought, and went to her Papa an hour after for more. She likewise thought that she was *charitable,* because she was willing to give away whatever halfpence she might happen to receive, to the first poor child whom she met.

But she never would sacrifice the slightest whim of her own, to enable her to relieve the actual wants of another.

She never parted from any thing to gratify a little friend, unless when she was tired of it herself.

She kept no account of her expenses; but when she was asked how she had spent the last money, used to reply, 'indeed I do not know, it is gone!'

Nay, sometimes, if she wanted money in her Papa's absence, she would borrow, and often forget to pay.

In her own opinion, and that of a few silly inconsiderate people, Miss *Lavish* was, as I have said, of a noble disposition, *generous* and *charitable*.

You find that she was not *just;* but that never entered her mind.

How would she have startled to be told that she was *mean, selfish, covetous;* perhaps she might not have blushed at being called *extravagant;* which she was with respect to herself, but niggardly to others.

CAPRICE;
OR, THE
CAPRICIOUS GIRL.
Miss Lavish's account of her expenditure of money on reflection.

MY PAPA made me a present of money to expend as I liked on my birth-day.

I bought a suit of the new spangled ribbons and a fan; these cost all my guinea, except half a crown, and that was not quite enough to buy the pocket glass for which I wished, so I asked for some more money. He gave me half a guinea. As I went out to get the glass, for which I was very impatient, a poor woman came to the door; I wished that I had had something for her, as she seemed to be almost starved, and I asked both the servants whether they had any money; but they could not lend me any. Away we drove—As I passed through *Holborn* I saw a man who sold birds; I then changed my mind, determined to wait for the glass, and purchase a bird. For this I gave five shillings. I then drove to the next street to get a cage. I was obliged to give half a guinea for one, which was gilt, fit to hang in my dressing-room; this was half a crown more than I had; but the man civilly offered to trust me for that.

Miss Lavish's conscious recollection of what she ought to have done.

I should have gone to the poor widow, whose husband was killed last week in the gravel-pit, and have given her something to enable her to buy bread for her five small children.

I should not have turned away in a huff when *Betty Broom* said to me, 'Miss! the price of one yard of that ribbon would keep poor *Mary Need* from starving;'—but have thanked her for reminding me of my duty.

I should not have asked my Papa for more money, unless it had been for a much better purpose; and I should have given him an account how I had expended his bounty.

I should have inquired who the poor woman was, whom I met at the door: I should have informed myself how she was circumstanced, and have applied a part of my half guinea in the relief of her family.

I should on no account have contracted a debt.

I should have been contented with a plain cage—the price of that which I bought would have clothed a poor child.

Now, said the Fairy, to Miss *Child*, you understand how these glasses may improve you—make a proper use of them.

Look in *this*—nay, never start; you must first see your faults, before you can mend them. To me you appear just as deformed without the glass, whenever you are ill-disposed, or act unworthily.

I will hang the glasses here. Promise me that you will consult them every evening; they will bring to your recollection the transactions of the day; they will instruct you how to judge of your actions. Record in this book the report of the glasses; on one leaf *what you are;* on the opposite, *what you should be*. Adieu!

> *So saying, the Fairy vanished.*

REFORMATION.

As soon as the glasses were placed, and the Fairy gone, Miss *Child* surveyed her closet, in order to observe how the mirrors appeared as a part of the furniture.

As she cast her eye upon the first glass she remarked that her little prints and toys, with the number of looking glasses, had a very pretty appearance, and she herself seemed like a great wax doll in a baby-house.

Well, said she, I look very smart! and my dolls and all my play-things look very pretty in the glass; this is like having two sets of toys.

Turning her head to survey the closet, she caught a glimpse of the second glass, which showed *what ought to be*.

In that she saw a girl like herself, dressed with great neatness, yet in a plain and modest manner. This phantom took down all the childish toys, and distributed them among a number of little people, who stood around, smiling and thanking her for making them so happy.

She stood looking very earnestly, and soon after she saw this figure take all the little books off the shelves, and give them to the children; afterwards the looking-glasses, and lastly, the little coloured prints.

Miss *Child* then saw her likeness fill the shelves with another set of books. She could discern, *Birth-day Present; Sunday Improvements; Course of Lectures for Sunday Evenings;* and several other little volumes—then Mrs. *Chapone*, Miss *Talbot*, and many more authors of whom she had never before heard the names.

A standish and paper next appeared upon the table, which was before strewed with rags of gause and snips of ribbon. There stood too a work-basket, with scissars, thimble, needle-book, and thread-papers. The young lady seated herself, and took out a piece of fine old cloth, cut out a little shirt, and began to work.

Bless me! said Miss *Child*, I dare say that the linen is for some poor little babe—I have seen many who were almost naked: oh! that I had made so good a use of my time!

Just as she spoke, her friend the Fairy appeared.

Miss courtesied, and returned thanks for the glasses; but alas! said she, they make me miserable; because they convince me, that I am very different from what I ought to be.

Shame for past faults, said the Fairy, is the first step towards amendment.

I feel shame enough for my folly, exclaimed Miss *Child;* alas! I am only a great over-grown baby; my person and limbs have so got the start of my mind, that I blush at myself.

Your regret, said the Fairy, at your want of improvement, must be a spur to your future diligence; since you are conscious of ignorance, and desirous of knowledge, application will soon repair your lost time.

But my disposition is as uncultivated as my understanding; I have no command of my temper; no regular mode of action; caprice and passion govern me.

My dear, said the Fairy, I am charmed to find that you have the discernment to see your faults, and the humility to own them. I will assist you in the necessary work of refor-mation.

THE LOCKET.

Miss CHILD was so diffident of herself, that she perpetually summoned her friend the Fairy to afford her an opportunity of conversing with her on the subject of her conduct.

One day, when the amiable girl had discovered an unusual degree of modesty, the good Fairy produced a small casket, took from thence a Locket, set with pale rubies, and pre-sented it to Miss *Child.*

Madam! I thank you, said the young lady; but I had rather be excused from excepting your present; had it been a book which would instruct me in your absence!—but an ornament to wear!—no, Madam! I am too vain already: pardon me.

This, replied the Fairy, is not such a trinket as will increase your vanity: wear it constantly about your neck. You see that it is of a delicate pink colour; the hue will vary as your disposition changes.

If you feel envious, one of those rubies will turn to a dirty yellow. If you be angry that stone will glow like fire; if you be foolishly timid, that lower stone will become white; should you be niggardly, these points will have a dull blackish hue, and jealousy will turn the whole locket to a colour like that of a common pebble in a gravel-pit.

Thus explained, said Miss *Child,* I shall rejoice to wear the ornament, and accept it with exceeding thankfulness.

By degrees this young lady acquired every good quality with which her friends could wish to see her endowed.

The last virtue which she gained, was that active benevolence which seeks to discover the wishes of another in order to gratify them.

I mentioned the toys and little books being removed from her closet, but did not say what became of them—they were thrown promiscuously into a chest, and laid by dis-regarded and unthought of. One day it occurred to Miss *Child,* what pleasure they would afford little people to whom they were suitable.

Immediately she sent for several of her young friends and acquaintance, whom she introduced into her chamber. She received them with so much condescension and kindness, that they were quite charmed with her; she regaled them with a treat, composed of fruits and cakes; talked with them of their improvement, and, in short, showed every mark of attention and civility that she could think of.

Before they left her room, she presented each with a small token of affection, suited to their respective ages, from among the toys and little books with which her closet had been filled.

The children were all delighted, and jumped and danced round her with joy and thankfulness.

Now, said she, these little treasures give me more real satisfaction than they ever did formerly, even when they were suited to my years. How much better continued she, is this, than to hoard up what was of no use to me, and proves so agreeable to my little friends! I never saw any object so pleasing as this little group of happy beings smiling upon me! So saying, she cast her eye upon the Locket, which hung in her bosom, and was surprised to see it glow and sparkle like coals when they are blown; reflecting at the same time, all sorts of faint and beautiful colours, like a fine diamond.

Bless me! exclaimed she, this is an appearance which I was not taught to expect; I wish I could see the charming Fairy—surely nothing is amiss!

She then dismissed her little visiters with civility and gentleness; they could not cease to talk of the change in Miss *Child*.

'How gentle she is! how obliging! how generous! said the little people as they retired.'

THE GIFTS.

As soon as MISS CHILD was left alone, she went into her closet to consult the mirrors; and to her unspeakable satisfaction she found, that her image appeared the same in both; for she was now become *what she ought to be*.

The Fairy entered, and expressed her satisfaction at what had passed. You were surprised, said she, at the glowing appearance of your Locket; you had not been apprised of that, nor could you have conceived an idea of the complacency attending a consciousness of doing well—of obliging and pleasing by acts of beneficence, till you had experienced it.

Miss *Child* returned abundance of thanks to the good Fairy, and entreated that she would never forsake, but continue to watch over her. I am now, said she, sensible how unfit I am to guide myself. The Fairy assured the charming girl of her protection, and grew more familiar and frequent than ever in her visits.

Miss *Child* became so perfectly amiable, that she was the darling of her guardian Fairy; who one day made her an offer of the following gifts, out of which she might choose one.

A *Purse*, which she should always find full of money.

A *Bonnet*, that would convey her to any place of which she should think as she put it on.

A *Ring* which would make her invisible.

Miss *Child* acknowledged her obligation to the Fairy for her offer; but said, that she was fearful to accept such gifts.

If, added she, I had a Purse which would always be full of money, I might not make a proper use of it; or, even if I did not spend it in an improper manner, yet I should at least lose all merit in giving to my friends or the poor; since I could be neither *generous* nor *charitable*, if I had not myself the *less* for what I gave.

Had I the Bonnet which would convey me instantly to any place where I might wish to be; though it appears to me that I should be very happy in the power of flying to assist my friends, or relieve any person in distress; yet I will not presume too much; I should probably sometimes convey myself for purposes less important, and less amiable, from a place where I might have been employed in doing kind offices, which my duty required.

For the Ring—I dare not accept that on any account. Should curiosity ever tempt me to listen to a conversation which was not designed for me to hear, I should be very culpable, and, perhaps, gain no satisfaction; for even if what I heard were agreeable, my heart would reproach me with the crime of prying into the secrets of another person; and so deprive me of that pleasure which I now enjoy, if I hear myself praised; when I hear *fairly* what passes.

The Fairy embraced her, and said, Now, my dear, I am convinced of your prudence. I made this trial of you with trembling; for though we know the present thoughts of our wards, yet we cannot be certain what they will be on occasions which may arise. You have withstood such a temptation as I should not have ventured to place before you, but that I had a high opinion of your discretion; yet I could not with propriety have given you the reward which I proposed, without making this trial; from this time you shall be my companion; no longer called Miss *Child,* but *Amiable,* and your employment shall be such as I know will be very agreeable to you—I appoint you guardian to the little people in Mrs. *Teachwell's* family; to form their dispositions, and regulate their conduct—For this purpose I will endow you with the power of assuming what shape you please, a privilege which I am confident you will only exert for excellent purposes.

THE DOLL.

ONE MORNING, when the school-bell rang for breakfast, Miss *Playful* not appearing, Miss *Friendly* sought for her throughout the house and play-ground, and, at last, found her sitting alone in an arbour, in the most remote part of the garden. She had in her hand a doll; and was so busily engaged in dressing it, that she neither saw Miss *Friendly* enter, nor heard her speak, but kept prattling to the wax baby in her lap.

Hey day! said Miss *Friendly,* are you there? what brought you so far from the house.

I will tell you, said Miss *Playful:* this is my new doll, which Lady *Lovewell* sent me: and I took it into this close walk, because I had a mind to dress it alone, lest any of the young ladies should interrupt me; for really, when one has any thing new or pretty, they throng about one so that there is no comfort in playing with it.

And was not this very selfish in you? said Miss *Friendly;* would you have liked that *Mary Freewill* should have served you thus, when her new toys came? or do you think she would have done so? you may recollect that the dear little girl, when her baby-house came, did not give herself time to unpack her whole set of furniture till she had called you?—'*Polly,* said she, will like to see the things as they are taken out.'

The little girl blushed, and made no reply—but was very attentive whilst Miss *Friendly* continued speaking. I am very sorry, my dear, you should so far forget yourself, as to neglect this opportunity of obliging your friends; what satisfaction could you have in hiding yourself in a corner? and what joy would it have been to a good-natured girl, to assemble those young ladies with whom she was intimate, and make them sharers in her pleasure! How differently would *Amiable* [the Fairy] have counselled Miss *Child* to behave.

Indeed, said Miss *Playful,* I am ashamed; but I have no Fairy to advise me: as she said these words, they reached the door of the breakfast-room. Miss *Friendly* observed the behaviour of the little girl at her entrance: much surprise was expressed at the absence of *Polly;* a thousand encomiums bestowed on the doll; the beauty of her face, and the elegance of her dress delighted the little people in general; and several of them expressed a wish to play with it a little while, and assist in undressing it.

Miss *Friendly* thought this a favourable opportunity for conveying a lesson in an agreeable manner: she remarked all that passed on this occasion, and others which arose in the course of the day; and the next morning presented Miss *Playful* with a paper, containing a narrative of the morning transaction, and a conversation *supposed* to have passed in the arbour between herself and the Fairy *Amiable,* whom she is feigned to have seen in a vision.

THE VISION.

A LITTLE GIRL, whose name was *Playful,* had a present made her; it was a nice wax doll: the morning after she received this treasure, she rose very early, stole slily to her drawers, and packed the doll, and all her cloaths into a small work-trunk: thus prepared, she waited with impatience till the time for the young ladies taking their morning walk, and seized the first opportunity of running unperceived along a close walk which led to an arbour, where she thought she could amuse herself with the doll, unobserved by her school-fellows.

With beating heart she unlocked the trunk which contained the object of her joy; seated herself on a bench, and placing the doll by her side, felt in her pocket for a pin-cushion.

A bird flew into the arbour; alighted upon a branch of jasmine close at her elbow, and hopped about, singing all the while. She forgot her doll, and sat silent with pleasure.

Presently the bird flew away; she then turned about to look at the doll, and saw her arm move: surprised, she exclaimed, 'Are you alive?'—I am[,] said the doll, but be not frightened. No, indeed, said the little girl, I am not afraid; for I have done no harm, nor do I mean to do any; but this is strange!—she said no more; when

Thus spoke the doll!

'My name is *Amiable;* the good Fairy, who, as you have heard, watched over my conduct, when I was a girl like yourself, has bestowed upon me some privileges annexed to fairy-hood. One of these privileges is the power of assuming any shape which we please, with this restriction; that we cannot injure those who are *good* in *thought, word,* and *deed;* nor can we even frighten them.—Now, you were not perfectly free from suspicion of a slight fault, since your coming *alone* into this corner, with your new doll appeared selfish: I thought that this fault might make you liable to a slight punishment, and was fearful that your surprise at my sudden appearance might become your punishment; though I did not wish to inflict any.'

'No indeed,' replied the little girl, 'I say my prayers constantly; in them I ask to be freed from *fear* as well as *danger,* and I feel confident of safety.'

'You charm me, my dear: did you observe the bird which flew into the arbour?'

'Yes, it was a sweet little creature!'

'I was the bird: had you spoken to me, I should have conversed with you in that disguise—as you did not, I took this shape, as being familiar to your eye, and agreeable to your fancy; but now I will appear in my splendor.'

Down dropped the doll.

Soft harmony breathed through the fluttering leaves—gales of perfume were wafted all around; the flowers seemed to glow with livelier tints: Miss *Playful* sat in silent expectation, when, from the bell of a white lilly, descended a human figure, majestic, though so small, and graceful beyond any mere mortal being; cloathed in a loose flowing mantle, ample, and falling in elegant folds, she appeared stately like the queen of Fairies on a court day; yet her garment, though it seemed so full, did not conceal the beauty of her figure, which was so delicately formed, that description can give little idea of it. Upon her head she wore a coronet of diamonds, emeralds, and rubies.

Miss *Playful* gazed and smiled; but said not a word: when, behold, this little creature vanished, and in her place appeared a female of still more exquisite beauty: her robe was light as air; if I were to compare it to any thing terrestial, I should say that it resembled purple gauze, and silver gauze, folded together; and purple brilliant gauze; and it fluttered like the garment of an air-nymph. Her lovely hair was bound with a wreath of the most delicate flowers.

Smiling, she said, "You see here a specimen of my power; I can vary my appearance at pleasure; but I came on an errand of importance: See here!"

"I have brought you a Rose; place it in your bosom; it will adorn and delight you; but it has a Thorn, which you will feel whenever you do amiss."

"I must now haste away. I see you part from me with regret; but I will soon return. Whenever you are desirous of seeing me, rub the green leaf of your Rose (*thus*) gently with your finger. Adieu!"

THE ROSE.

_____ __ __ *"a pigmy spright*
"Popt through the key-hole, swift as light."—GAY.

MISS *Playful* took an early opportunity of summoning her friend the Fairy, who inquired how she liked the flower?

MISS PLAYFUL.

I like the Rose, but not the Thorn.

FAIRY.

I told you that it had a Thorn:—I hope—

MISS PLAYFUL.

It has never wounded me much; yet often makes me start without reason. If it were only to prick me when I am really naughty I should not complain; but it stings me when I am not to blame.

FAIRY.

Tell me an instance of this.

MISS PLAYFUL.

Soon after you left me I ran in to eat my breakfast, and I felt the Thorn as I entered the room.

FAIRY.

Your little heart exulted with pride.

MISS PLAYFUL.

The young ladies asked me a great many questions about my doll; I took pleasure in answering them; and all this time I smelt a delicious perfume from my Rose.

FAIRY.

Very well.

MISS PLAYFUL.

But when Miss *Pert* told me that I was too big to play with a doll, and that it was babyish in me to carry it about, I felt the Thorn; yet I said not a syllable.

FAIRY.

But you felt angry?

MISS PLAYFUL.

I did indeed think she was rude.

FAIRY.

You have not told me all now—your Rose reproved you for a little envy, when Miss *Trifle* produced her new buckles; and for some vanity in showing your fan.

MISS PLAYFUL.

I am sorry to find, that I am not so free from naughty passions as I thought I was.

FAIRY.

My dear, self-knowledge is hard to attain: if you make a proper use of my flower it will render you a most amiable girl.

I know you, and will show you to yourself without flattery. You discovered some wisdom in being willing to submit to the hints of the Rose: and, by the accusation which you urge against it, (that the Thorn pricked you without just cause) you only prove the need you have of such a monitor.

MISS PLAYFUL.

Pride, envy, and vanity!—Who would have thought that I had such evil dispositions!— I am quite unhappy to have been so mistaken in my opinion of myself—I thought that I was free.

FAIRY.

Be not discouraged: the wisest persons may err in judging of themselves. Do you patiently submit to endure the rebukes of your bosom friend: turn them to your advantage, by striving to correct the beginnings of every evil passion, and you will be delighted with the beauty and fragrance of my Rose: for if you be as good as you can be, the flower will look fresh and beautiful, and smell deliciously; but it will abate in delicacy of hue and scent whenever you transgress; and you know from experience, that every time that you swerve from your duty, even in thought, you will feel pain in consequence of your fault; but I must further tell you, that in proportion as you were to blame, the Thorn would wound you—will you venture to wear it?

MISS PLAYFUL.

Certainly, I will.

FAIRY.

Were you to transgress materially, the Rose would fade proportionably to the greatness and frequency of your faults: and if you were to be incorrigible (which heaven avert!) the flower would wither, and seem to die; it is, however, really immortal, and would in time revive to torment you.—Do you persist in saying you will accept my gift?

MISS PLAYFUL.

Gladly! I wish I had more for my friends.

FAIRY.

You would not think how often my offers of this kind are rejected: people love not to be reminded of their faults; because they are too proud to confess, and too indolent to correct them.

THE END